Fifth Canadian Edition

Becoming a Teacher

Forrest W. Parkay
Washington State University

John P. Vaillancourt
Acadia University

Heather C. Stephens
Acadia University

James Robert Harris
Harris Educational Consulting

Janette Hughes
University of Ontario Institute of Technology

George Gadanidis
Western University

Diana Petrarca
University of Ontario Institute of Technology

Editorial Director: Claudine O'Donnell
Acquisitions Editor: Kimberley Veevers
Marketing Manager: Michelle Bish
Program Manager: John Polanszky
Project Manager: Jessica Mifsud
Developmental Editor: Daniella Balabuk
Production Services: iEnergizer Aptara®, Ltd.
Permissions Project Manager: Shruti Jamadagni
Photo Permissions Research: Integra Publishing Services

Text Permissions Research: Integra Publishing Services
Interior Designer: Anthony Leung
Cover Designer: iEnergizer Aptara®, Ltd.
Cover Image: Rawpixel/Fotolia
Cover Art: Hero Images Inc./Alamy Stock Photo
Vice-President, Cross Media and Publishing Services: Gary Bennett

---

Pearson Canada Inc., 26 Prince Andrew Place, Don Mills, Ontario M3C 2T8.

Library and Archives Canada Cataloguing in Publication

Parkay, Forrest W., author
      Becoming a teacher/Forrest W. Parkay, Washington
State University, John P. Vaillancourt, Acadia University, Heather C. Stephens,
Acadia University, James Robert Harris, Harris Educational Consulting,
Janette Hughes, University of Ontario Institute of Technology,
George Gadanidis, Western University, Diana Petrarca,
University of Ontario Institute of Technology.–Fifth Canadian edition.

Includes bibliographical references and index.
ISBN 978-0-13-308158-9 (paperback)

      1. Teaching–Vocational guidance–Canada. 2. Education–
Study and teaching–Canada. 3. Teachers–Canada–Attitudes.
I. Title.

LB1775.P37 2016   371.10023'71   C2016-905460-8

2 17

ISBN-10:   0-13-308158-3
ISBN-13: 978-0-13-308158-9

Dedication

This book is dedicated to our students—their spirit continually renews us and inspires confidence in the future of teaching.

Contents

PART FOUR Your Teaching Future

10 Teachers as Educational Leaders 260

11 Your First Teaching Position 282

12 Education Issues for the Twenty-First Century 306

Preface

We hope you share our belief that teaching is the world's most important profession. We also hope you recognize the service Pearson Education Canada has provided to preserve Canadian teachers through the publication of this revised guide to the Canadian educational landscape. The demand for a Canadian book of this type was evident for many years. However, until Pearson Canada made the decision to produce this text, instructors at Canadian universities and colleges were faced with a bleak choice: use an American text without any Canadian flavour, use a host of smaller Canadian texts and booklets that touch on selected topics while ignoring many others, or overwhelm their students with a flood of photocopied handouts. The broad range of topics covered in this fifth Canadian edition of *Becoming a Teacher* helps to overcome these problems. Additionally, the 12 chapters mesh easily with the standard academic term. Canadian examples, historical data, and statistics are included throughout, and because of its breadth of topics, *Becoming a Teacher* can be customized for use in a variety of courses.

We highlight teacher leadership throughout the book, since today's teachers must assume diverse leadership roles beyond the classroom. For instance, in "Teachers as Educational Leaders" (Chapter 10), readers learn about the exciting new leadership roles that await teachers. In "The Role of Technology in Education" (Chapter 9), which has been extensively updated for this edition, students are given an overview of how educational technologies are influencing schools and the teaching profession.

ORGANIZATION OF THE BOOK

To allow for comprehensive coverage of critical trends and issues in education, we organized the book into four parts: "Part One: The Teaching Profession," "Part Two: Foundations of Teaching," "Part Three: The Art of Teaching," and "Part Four: Your Teaching Future."

Chapters 1 and 2, which make up Part One, focus on the theme of teachers and teaching. After reading these chapters, readers will be better able to determine whether teaching is a good career choice for them. Among the topics we address are why people choose to teach, the challenges and realities of teaching, the knowledge and skills needed to become a teacher, the various roles of a teacher, and how to establish mentoring relationships.

In Chapters 3 to 5 of Part Two, we consider the foundations of education, which every professional teacher needs to know. These foundational areas include the philosophical, historical, social, cultural, political, financial, and legal dimensions of Canadian education. Philosophical and historical foundations are addressed in "Ideas and Events That Have Shaped Education in Canada" (Chapter 3).

Chapters 6 to 9, which make up Part Three, examine student characteristics and the worlds of the classroom and the school. Here, readers learn about characteristics of students at different stages of development, about students as learners, about the dynamics of classroom life, about the curricula that are taught in schools, and about teaching with technology. A thoroughly revised technology chapter explains how teachers can integrate technology into teaching and learning in order to engage today's tech-savvy students fully and to adjust to the reality that technology has transformed how, when, and where students can learn.

Finally, in Part Four, Chapters 10 to 12, we discuss issues and trends that will impact each reader's quest to become an effective teacher—especially the expanding leadership role of teachers, planning for a successful first year of teaching, international education in a changing world, and the teacher's role in shaping the future of education.

FEATURES AND LEARNING AIDS

Included in *Becoming a Teacher* are many features we believe will help to prepare readers for rewarding futures as professional teachers. To guide study, "Focus Questions" at the beginning of each chapter reflect the questions addressed in that chapter. The fifth Canadian edition offers the voices of those who care deeply about teaching—novices just starting out as well as expert teachers and other professionals—in new sections called "Readers' Voices" and "Voices from the Field." These features include comments that will help readers feel confident about joining the wider community of those preparing to teach.

"Case to Consider" features include new classroom case studies that present problem-solving and decision-making situations that allow readers to apply practical solutions to various challenges. These cases are based on interviews with teachers across the country and illustrate how teachers apply chapter content to actual classroom situations by providing readers with first-hand insights into real-world challenges.

The new "Focus on Research" boxes reflect the importance of using evidence-based research to improve education standards and the quality of teaching. All teachers should integrate current educational research into their classroom instruction. The Canadian educational research that is highlighted in these sections focuses on cutting-edge contributions that are influencing the shape of education across the country.

This edition of *Becoming a Teacher* offers the rich and engaging end-of-chapter "Applications and Activities" feature, which will enable preservice teachers to document their growth and accomplishments over time, explore and reflect on specific issues and topics in further depth, and collaborate with others in the field to learn more about classroom and school-based practices.

As a further study aid, key terms and concepts are boldfaced in the text and defined in the margins. A glossary at the end of the book helps readers to quickly locate the definitions of key terms and concepts and the text pages on which they appear.

Other end-of-chapter learning aids in this edition include a concise summary and suggested applications and activities, including journal-writing opportunities, which can be written in the space provided. These short, optional journal-writing activities are based on the "writing to learn" and "writing across the curriculum" concepts.

NEW TO THIS EDITION

- This edition includes a fully revised chapter on Technology in Education that focuses on the latest trends in the use of technology for teaching and learning, which will help readers become proficient users, critics, and producers of digital tools.

- "Focus on Research" feature highlights the findings of Canadian educational researchers and describes exciting curricular approaches that take a student-centred approach and directly involve learners.

- "Readers' Voices" feature at the beginning of each chapter provides comments by preservice teacher education candidates about the importance of chapter content and helps guide reading.

- "Voices from the Field" features the voices of experienced teachers in order to focus on important issues such as how they interact with students, particularly those with exceptionalities.

- A new focus on cultural diversity permeates this edition, addressing equity and inclusive education for all students, regardless of race, gender, sexual orientation, or socioeconomic status.

- Updated information, figures, and statistics provide the reader with a current understanding of the social, cultural, ethical, and legal realities confronting today's schools, including new information on issues like bullying and cyberbullying.

- Current curricular trends are identified in all subject areas, such as the integration of STEM subjects, a new focus on mental health and sex education, Indigenous education, and technology education.

- New information about working with students with exceptionalities is provided, including an introduction to Universal Design for Learning, Differentiated Instruction, and the use of assistive technology for students who deal with learning challenges.

- An emphasis on inquiry-based learning provides readers with an introduction to project- and problem-based learning pedagogies, which place students at the forefront when teachers are preparing lessons and units.

- Comprehensive national coverage ensures that students and teachers from all over Canada see themselves mirrored in the content.

SUPPLEMENTS

The following supplements are available to instructors on Pearson Canada's password-protected online catalogue (**http://catalogue.pearsoned.ca**):

The **Instructor's Manual** provides, for each chapter of the text, a "Chapter Overview" and a "Chapter-at-a-Glance" organizer that correlates chapter outlines, learning objectives, and teaching supplements; an "Annotated Lecture Outline" with examples, discussion questions, and student activities; and suggestions for additional readings and media to extend chapter learning.

The **Testbank**, available in Word, includes more than 1000 questions, including multiple-choice and true–false items, essay questions, case studies, and authentic assessments plus text-page references and answer feedback.

A set of **PowerPoint Presentations** is also provided with this edition. Each chapter is outlined in a series of slides that include key points, figures, and tables.

Acknowledgments

Many members of the Pearson Canada team provided expert guidance and support during the preparation of this fifth Canadian edition of *Becoming a Teacher*. Daniella Balabuk, our developmental editor, heads the list. From suggestions for revision to feedback on draft manuscripts and skilful coordination of the revision process from beginning to end, Daniella's ongoing support, professionalism, patience, and keen organizational skills are deeply appreciated. The authors also extend a very special thanks to all the other members of the Pearson Canada team for their steadfast support throughout the prepublication period.

We also owe thanks to educators working in schools, teacher professional organizations, and departments of education throughout Canada with whom we consulted during the preparation of *Becoming a Teacher*. Invariably, they were courteous and helpful. A common reaction among them was delight that someone was going to make use of their material.

We are also very grateful to the authors of the U.S. edition of *Becoming a Teacher* (10th ed.) for the superb foundation they provided for this Canadian edition. We felt a great responsibility to honour these other writers' material. We tried to be consistent in writing style and true to their overall intent—judiciously cutting here, modifying something there, and inserting appropriate Canadian material whenever it was available.

Janette Hughes, George Gadanidis, and Diana Petrarca thank the many individuals who provided inspiration and assistance in the preparation of this book. Janette and Diana, at the University of Ontario Institute of Technology, and George Gadanidis, at Western University, particularly appreciate the contributions made by their preservice teacher candidates and graduate students who continually teach them about the art and craft of teaching.

Janette Hughes
George Gadanidis
Diana Petrarca

Chapter 1

Teaching: Your Chosen Profession

Corbis

FOCUS QUESTIONS

1. Why do you want to teach?
2. What are the benefits of teaching?
3. What are the challenges of teaching?
4. How will you become a good teacher?

*The best part of teaching is being a "learning catalyst." I love it when
I can introduce my students to a project or concept and then "take the ball
and run with it." My goal is accomplished when they go beyond what
I know and I start learning from them.*

—Sonya Vanderhoeden-Bracken
Teacher of Senior Mathematics
Laurentian Regional High School
Lachute, Quebec

Congratulations on deciding to become a teacher! Teaching is exciting, rewarding, and uplifting. Teachers receive great satisfaction from knowing that they really do make a difference in their students' lives. We hope you share our belief that teaching

I want to teach because I was taught. Throughout my childhood and into my adult life, I have had important teachers who inspired me to accomplish my dreams. These wonderful people in my life inspired me to become a teacher.

—DENISEA, teacher education program, first year

I originally didn't start out wanting to be a teacher, but, eventually, I realized that teaching is the profession for me. I get a sense of accomplishment from helping people learn.

—ALAN, teacher education program, first year

Children are the leaders of tomorrow. I want to encourage my future students to be the best they can be. I want to be the person that motivates them to aim high in life.

—JA'NAE, teacher education program, first year

is the world's most important profession. We also hope your commitment to teaching will become deeper and stronger as you move through your teacher education program.

This book will orient you to the world of teaching and help you answer your own questions about the career you have chosen. What is teaching really like on a day-to-day basis? What rewards do teachers experience? What are the trends and issues in the profession? What problems can you expect to encounter in the classroom? What will you need to know and be able to do to become a highly qualified teacher?

We believe that successful teachers know why they want to teach. They examine their motives carefully, and they understand why, at first, they might have been uncertain about choosing teaching as a profession. The first chapter of this book, then, addresses the four focus questions listed above, which will help you decide if teaching is the right profession for you.

The focus questions in each chapter will address your future as a teacher. Answers to these questions will provide you with a realistic view of the world of teachers, students, classrooms, and schools and their surrounding communities. After reading this book, you will have a broad understanding of one of the most exciting, satisfying, and honourable professions the world has ever known. And you will know if teaching is the right profession for you.

WHY DO YOU WANT TO TEACH?

You may want to teach for many reasons. Your desire to teach may be the result of positive experiences with teachers when you were a child. You may want to improve on the teaching that you experienced in school. You may see teaching as a way of making a significant contribution to the world and experiencing the joy of helping others grow and develop. Or you may be attracted to teaching because the life of a teacher is exciting, varied, and stimulating.

Desire to Work with Children and Young People

Though the conditions under which teachers work may be challenging, their salaries modest, and education reform a point of contention in the political arena, most teach simply because they care about students.

Effective teachers derive their greatest satisfaction when they are successful in promoting students' learning—when they "make a difference" in students' lives. As a teacher, your day-to-day interactions with students will build strong bonds between you and them. Daily contact will enable you to become familiar with your students' personal and academic needs. Concern for their welfare will help you cope with the difficulties and frustrations of teaching. As the following quotations from highly accomplished individuals illustrate, the teacher's potential to make a difference in students' lives can be profound:

> *The dream begins, most of the time, with a teacher who believes in you, who tugs and pushes and leads you on to the next plateau, sometimes poking you with a sharp stick called truth.*
>
> —Dan Rather, national news commentator

> *Compassionate teachers fill a void left by working parents who aren't able to devote enough attention to their children. Teachers don't just teach; they can be vital personalities who help young people to mature, to understand the world and to understand themselves.*
>
> —Charles Platt, science fiction novelist

> *One looks back with appreciation to the brilliant teachers who touched our human feelings. The curriculum is so much necessary raw material, but warmth is the vital element for the growing plant and for the soul of the child.*
>
> —Carl Jung, world-renowned psychoanalyst

Like most teachers, you may appreciate the unique qualities of youth. You enjoy the liveliness, curiosity, freshness, openness, and trust of young children, or the abilities, wit, spirit, independence, and idealism of adolescents. As one teacher puts it, you want to "truly make a difference in the lives of children who [do] not always come 'ready to learn' [and to] be a part of helping students see themselves as literate and able to solve problems" (Ferris, 2008, p. 16). Students are our future, and teachers play a crucial role in their development.

Teachers also derive significant rewards from meeting the needs of diverse learners. While Canadian students come from increasingly diverse racial and ethnic backgrounds and those with special needs are increasing in number, effective teachers recognize that their classrooms are enriched by the varied backgrounds of students. To enable you to experience the satisfaction of helping all students learn, significant portions of this book are devoted to **student variability** (differences among students in regard to their developmental needs, interests, abilities, and disabilities) and **student diversity** (differences among students in regard to gender, race, ethnicity, culture, and socioeconomic status). An appreciation for such diversity will help you to experience the rewards that come from enabling each student to make his or her unique contribution to classroom life.

Student variability: differences among students in regard to their developmental needs, interests, abilities, and disabilities.

Student diversity: differences among students in regard to gender, race, ethnicity, culture, and socioeconomic status.

Like the following two teachers, a likely reason you have been drawn to teaching is the privilege of working with children and youth, regardless of their stages of development or their life circumstances:

Where else can you regularly get smeared with fingerpaints, receive handmade cards, wipe tears, share smiles, wiggle loose teeth, share awful cafeteria food, read silly stories, and know that you are changing the world?

The rewards are great, when you see a child suddenly grasp a concept or write that poem that he/she thought [he/she] couldn't, these are the moments that let me know that I am in the right profession! (Harris Interactive, Inc., 2001, p. 118)

The opportunity to work with young people, whatever their stage of development and whatever their life circumstances, is a key reason people are drawn to teaching and remain in the profession.

A Passion for Teaching

Why do teachers find teaching so satisfying? What does it mean to *love* teaching?

A Passion for the Subject   Teachers who express a love of teaching may mean that they love teaching in their discipline. The opportunity to continually learn more in one's profession and to share that knowledge with students is a definite attraction. In a journal article from *Educational Leadership* (pp. 44–46) titled "The Satisfactions of Teaching," Eliot Eisner points out that "teaching provides the occasion to share with others your deep affection for what you teach. When your eyes twinkle with delight at the prospect of introducing students to what you love, you create a sense of contagion and convey your love of what you teach. Your passion for your subject is the sincerest and most powerful invitation you can extend" (Eisner, 2006, p. 45). Whitacker (2012, p. 7) notes, "[I]f a school has great teachers, it is a great school. Teachers are a school's keystone of greatness."

A Passion for the Teaching Life   For those teachers who always enjoyed school, it is often the life of a teacher that has appeal—to be in an environment that encourages a high regard for education and for the life of the mind, and to have daily opportunities to see students become excited about learning. Albert Einstein, for example, regretted that he did not devote his career to the teaching life:

> Believe it or not, one of my deepest regrets [is that I didn't teach]. I regret this because I would have liked to have had more contact with children. There has always been something about the innocence and freshness of young children that appeals to me and brings me great enjoyment to be with them. And they are so open to knowledge. I have never really found it difficult to explain basic laws of nature to children. When you reach them at their level, you can read in their eyes their genuine interest and appreciation. (quoted in Bucky, 1992, p. 99)

A Passion for the Teaching–Learning Process   You may be passionate about teaching because you are excited about helping students learn. The prospect of thinking "on your feet" and capitalizing on teachable moments is appealing. Perhaps you have had "expert" teachers who made you realize that "teaching well requires improvisation without constraints" and that "teaching is a custom job" (Eisner, 2006, p. 45).

"Canada's Top 20 Jobs" reported on an online survey of nearly 8000 Canadians that asked participants to evaluate their jobs based on 11 factors, including salary, corporate culture, creativity, and stress level. The survey revealed, "While corporate executives report the greatest job satisfaction in Canada, a new study shows that teachers—whose average salary is almost $70 000 less than their business counterparts—are the second most content." For teachers, the ability to be creative proved the most rewarding aspect of their profession, and a lack of high salaries the main detriment (*Ottawa Citizen*, March 30, 2007). Also, polls consistently show that teachers are ranked among the most trusted professionals.

A poll of 1000 Ontario teachers released by the Ontario College of Teachers in 2006 revealed that teachers love their jobs, but suffer stress brought on by time constraints, parent complaints, performance reviews, and school politics. Eighty-one percent said they would recommend teaching as a career—a marked jump from the 67 percent who said the same three years before (Jamieson, 2006). In a Canada-wide study (Karsenti & Colin, 2013) titled "Why Are New Teachers Leaving the Profession?," it was reported that 50 percent of teachers who leave the profession do so in the first two years, indicating that the early development of a support structure, including mentoring, may help with teacher retention. Despite constraints and challenges, teachers generally feel an important sense of freedom in their classrooms to be creative and to plan programs that best meet the needs of their students.

In a single school day, teachers have numerous interactions with students and make many pedagogical decisions. Most decisions are easy and come naturally, but some require critical thinking. Thinking on their feet for teachers becomes easier with experience, as the following example of Ms. Robinson, a grade 7 English Language Arts teacher, demonstrates:

> I was circulating among the Literature Circle groups in my grade 7 English Language Arts class to check on their progress and trouble shoot any problems they were having. At the beginning of class, several groups had individual questions but I asked them to go to their groups to get started and told them I would be around soon to see them. My thinking was that if I stopped to address individual questions, the rest of the class would have to wait to get their directions for the class and things could have gotten out of hand and precious class time would be wasted.
>
> I asked each group to go to their designated places in the room, take out their novels and role sheets, and begin their discussions. I explained that three groups would be evaluated according to a pre-established rubric; I was, however, not going to tell them which groups would be assessed that day. Students had been involved in developing how their participation would be evaluated, including cooperation. My rationale for this was that all groups would be more likely to adhere to the rubric requirements if they knew they would be accountable for their participation and behaviour.
>
> The groups quickly settled down and began to engage in discussions of their reading and the role sheets they had prepared for the class. Students in each Literature Circle had previously decided as a group how much reading would be completed for that day's class along with who would assume what role in the day's discussion. This approach appeared to be working well and, overall, the students were taking responsibility for their learning.
>
> One group started complaining about a group member being absent and I helped them to resolve this by encouraging them to problem solve on ways to help the missing student get the work completed.
>
> As I was talking with that group I began to sense something amiss with one of the other groups. The five students in that group appeared to be arguing so I headed over to see if I needed to intervene. Four of the five students in the group seemed upset and were berating the fifth group member. I was able to discern that the problem had stemmed from one student who had not completed the role sheet that the group had agreed upon for homework. The student was offering some weak excuses for his failure to complete the work and voices were becoming loud. All eyes were on the group and on me. I quietly asked the four students who had completed the assignment to share their work and the student who had not would come in at lunch hour and do his work. Although the student started to protest, I did not argue with him, but rather indicated calmly but firmly that this was nonnegotiable. On the following day, that student would be expected to share his work with the others at the beginning of class.

Influence of Teachers

The journey toward becoming a teacher often begins early in life. While few people are "born teachers," their early life experiences often encourage them to become teachers. With the exception of parents or guardians, the adults who have the greatest influence on children are often their teachers. Perhaps a positive relationship with a teacher was the catalyst for your decision to become one.

Similar to most people who become teachers, you may have been more influenced by your teachers in their roles as fellow human beings rather than as subject-matter experts. Perhaps you had a teacher similar to Salina Gray, who made the following self-reflective observation during her first year of teaching: "I have evaluated my beliefs as a teacher, asking what education should be, what it means, and what I actually show my students. Do my actions show my values to my students? So, I have become a kinder, more honest Ms. Gray. My students have noticed" (Oakes & Lipton, 2007, p. 490). The inspirational memories you have of teachers from earlier in your life may have led you to the teaching profession.

Desire to Serve

Many choose to teach because they want to serve others; they want the results of their labour to extend beyond themselves and their families. Some decide to select another program or to leave teaching in order to earn more money elsewhere, only to return to teaching, confiding that they found the other program or work lacking in meaning or significance. Being involved in a service profession is their draw to the field.

For many, the decision to serve through teaching was influenced by their experiences as volunteers. During admission interviews, teacher education program applicants often cite their volunteer work in Boy Scouts, Girl Guides, summer camps, church activities, and other child and youth organizations as influential in their decision to enter the profession.

Explore more deeply your reasons for becoming a teacher. The following Professional Reflection feature focuses on several characteristics that may indicate your probable satisfaction with teaching as a career.

⟫ Assessing Your Reasons for Choosing to Teach

For each of the following characteristics, indicate on a scale from 1 to 5 the extent to which it applies to you. Which factors are most applicable for you? What is your strongest reason for becoming a teacher?

	Very applicable			Not at all applicable	
1. A passion for learning	1	2	3	4	5
2. Success as a student	1	2	3	4	5
3. Good sense of humour	1	2	3	4	5
4. Positive attitudes toward students	1	2	3	4	5
5. Tolerance toward others	1	2	3	4	5
6. Patience	1	2	3	4	5
7. Good verbal and writing skills	1	2	3	4	5
8. Love for a subject area	1	2	3	4	5
9. Experiences working with children (camp, church, tutoring, etc.)	1	2	3	4	5
10. Other teachers in family	1	2	3	4	5
11. Encouragement from family to enter teaching	1	2	3	4	5
12. Desire to serve students and the community	1	2	3	4	5

As you read beginning teacher Kelly McCall's story on the next page, notice how she reveals her passion for teaching, desire to work with youth, and the influence of former teachers as reasons for her selection of teaching as her chosen profession.

Practical Benefits of Teaching

Perhaps you are drawn to teaching by its practical benefits. Teachers' hours and vacations are widely recognized as benefits. Though the number of hours most teachers devote to their work goes far beyond the number of hours they actually spend at school, their schedules do afford them a measure of flexibility not found in other professions. For example, teachers with school-age children can often be at home during the summer when their children are not in school, and nearly all teachers, regardless of their years of experience, receive the same generous vacation time: holiday breaks and a long summer vacation. For Canadian teachers, the official classroom day usually runs from 8:30 or 9:00 a.m. to 3:30 or 4:00 p.m. Weekends and statutory holidays are not required teaching days, and vacations usually include a Christmas and a spring break of a week or more each, and eight weeks of time off from the classroom during the summer.

Salaries and Benefits   Although intangible rewards represent a significant attraction to teaching, teachers are now demanding that the public acknowledge the value and professional standing of teaching by supporting higher salaries. Though there is still a general consensus that teachers are underpaid, teacher salaries are becoming more competitive with other occupations; in fact, salaries are becoming one of the main draws of the profession.

According to the Canadian Teachers' Federation (CTF), in Canada, the basic salary scale and benefit package offered to a newly hired teacher is established through negotiations between the teachers' association and representatives of the provincial or

---

▶▶▶ CASE TO CONSIDER | Differentiated Instruction

With the current focus on differentiation, I am concerned about being able to effectively accommodate every kind of learner. We need to find ways to reach each and every one of the students we encounter; in reality, this can seem like a daunting task. Is it really possible to forge connections with all of our learners when they each bring different emotional, physical, socioeconomic, and intellectual needs?

Tools for Learning

I look forward to challenging my future students by providing them with authentic learning opportunities that will help them meet the challenges of the twenty-first century. This includes helping them become competent problem-solvers in the face of the changes they are likely to encounter.

I am becoming more aware of student needs as well as the resources that are available to make learning more accessible and effective. Learning resources can range from a specific strategy that is used to teach a lesson in a classroom to technology such as computer programs to assist in a content area such as literacy or mathematics. These resources can even be used in a more general area such as organization. As teachers we need to be able to make decisions about how we use technology as a tool and to determine

the possibilities it affords. However, we need to remember the power of the human connections we make with our students.

I realize that my own positive learning experiences will serve as a foundation for me to tackle and overcome challenges in teaching that may arise in the coming years. One of my passionate beliefs is that disengaged learners can be shown how to love learning. We know our students do not always show up with an enthusiastic approach to learning. However, it starts with hopeful teachers who believe they can transform challenges into opportunities. This is what I want to do for my learners and this is what makes teaching seem like the best job in the world!

Ontario resident Kelly McCall is a teacher who graduated with a Bachelor of Education degree in May 2010 from Acadia University's School of Education in Nova Scotia.

1. How could you use a "student interest survey" to help differentiate your instruction?

2. How could you add visual, tactile, auditory, and kinesthetic elements to your classroom teaching?

3. How could you incorporate "student choice" in your lessons to help differentiate your instruction?

territorial government. Generally, teacher salary schedules are determined by a combination of years of post-secondary education and years of teaching experience. Additional allowances are paid to teachers whose position will include additional administrative responsibilities.

Teacher salary varies depending on the jurisdiction. For example, in Alberta, B.C., and Ontario in 2014, the entry level salary ranged from $47 000 to $49 410 annually, while the salary in the tenth year of experience ranged from $81 500 to $99 300 annually (Global News, 2014). Teachers with advanced and graduate training can expect salaries that are higher than the maximum level.

Benefit packages can vary from jurisdiction to jurisdiction but will include a combination of the following:

Benefit packages: various negotiated nonsalary compensation provided to teachers in addition to their negotiated salaries.

- Dental insurance
- Life insurance
- Maternity leave
- Compassionate leave
- Cumulative sick leave
- Sabbatical and study leave
- Supplementary medical insurance
- Long-term disability insurance
- Retirement gratuities (CTF, 2006)

Canadian Teacher Supply and Demand   Research from the Nova Scotia Department of Education reflects the teacher supply and demand projections and the predicted trends in the rest of Canada.

In Nova Scotia, the new supply of teachers is estimated to average 930 per year through 2017–2018. However, the ratio of number of students per teacher is also expected to decrease due to a projected 15.8 percent decrease in enrolment. Although there is not an aggregated shortage of teachers, some rural regions and other geographical areas across the province may experience difficulty in attracting teachers, especially in certain content areas and specialties. Rural and smaller school boards in particular have reported difficulty finding substitute teachers at the middle school and senior high levels. Overall demand by subject and specialty between now and 2017–2018 is projected to be highest at the elementary, administration, and resource levels. The market is also likely to be tight in the areas of physical education, fine arts, physics, and family studies, and there may be shortages in technology education and French (Nova Scotia Department of Education, 2012).

Job Opportunities for Teachers from Diverse Groups   During this first part of the twenty-first century, changing Canadian demographics will be increasingly reflected in the student population. For a society to understand cultural and ethnic diversity, teachers need to reflect that diversity. Clearly, students from diverse racial, ethnic, and cultural backgrounds and students with disabilities benefit from having role models with whom they can easily identify. In addition, teachers from diverse groups and teachers with disabilities may have, in some instances, an enhanced understanding of student diversity and student variability that they can share with other teachers.

Research compiled by the CTF reveals that teachers are underrepresented relative to the under-15 school-aged population for North American Indian, Chinese, and East Indian ethnic origin groups. Aboriginal representation within the Canadian education system is also of equal concern. By province, teacher underrepresentation was highest in Manitoba and Saskatchewan. This is a particular cause for concern given Statistics Canada's recent projection that in 2017, Aboriginal children aged 0 to 14 years in Saskatchewan could account for 37 percent of this age group, while in Manitoba, 31 percent of children 0 to 14 years could be Aboriginal (CTF, 2006).

WHAT CHALLENGES DOES TEACHING PRESENT?

Like all professions, teaching has undesirable or difficult aspects. Frank McCourt, a teacher at four New York City high schools over a 30-year period and a noted author after his retirement from teaching, has said that a teacher needs to be "a drill sergeant, a rabbi, a disciplinarian, a low-level scholar, a clerk, a referee, a clown, a counselor, and [a] therapist" (McCourt, 2005, p. 19).

As a prospective teacher, you should consider the challenges as well as the satisfactions you are likely to encounter. You can make the most of your teacher education program if you are informed. Awareness of the realities of teaching will enable you to develop your personal philosophy of education, build a repertoire of teaching strategies, strengthen your leadership skills, and acquire a knowledge base of research and theory to guide your actions. In this manner, you can become a true professional—free to enjoy the many satisfactions of teaching and confident of your ability to deal with its challenges.

Long Working Hours

The length of a teacher's workday may appear attractive, but teachers' actual working hours are another matter. Teachers' contracts do not include additional hours for lesson planning and evaluating students' work, nor do they include noninstructional assignments found at all levels of teaching—from recess duty to club sponsorship and coaching.

The need to keep accurate, detailed records of students' academic progress, absences, and lateness, as well as other forms of paperwork, is one of the teacher's most time-consuming tasks. Other nonteaching tasks include supervising students on the playground, at extracurricular events, and in the hallways, study halls, and lunchrooms; and attending faculty meetings, parent conferences, and open houses. Nonteaching responsibilities are often enjoyable and provide opportunities to interact informally with students; however, they can lessen the amount of time and energy teachers have available for teaching-related tasks.

Classroom Management and Increasing Violence

Not surprisingly, lack of discipline and increased crime and violence among youth are strong concerns for teacher education students, especially in secondary school settings. Before teachers can teach, they must manage their classrooms effectively. Even when parents and the school community are supportive and problems are relatively minor, dealing with discipline issues can be a disturbing, emotionally draining aspect of teaching.

Teacher–student ratios: a ratio that expresses the number of students taught by a teacher.

Student-mobility rates: the proportion of students within a school or district who move during an academic year.

Cyberbullying: the use of digital technology devices such as cell phones and the Internet to harass, threaten, or intimidate others.

Taber, Alberta, in 2004 and Toronto, Ontario, in 2007 were thrust into the national spotlight as a result of fatal school shootings carried out by students. Though acts of violence of this magnitude in schools are rare in Canada, the possibility of experiencing such events can cause additional job-related stress for teachers. Students, too, can experience stress regarding their safety at school.

In addition, many schools have high **teacher–student ratios**, which can make classroom management more difficult. Feeling the pressure of overcrowding and valiantly resisting the realization that they cannot meet the needs of all their students, teachers may try to work faster and longer to give their students the best possible education. In facing such challenges, teachers may learn to put off, overlook, or otherwise attend inadequately to many students each day.

The problem of high teacher–student ratios becomes even more acute when complicated by the high **student-mobility rates** in some schools, especially in socioeconomically depressed areas. In such situations, teachers have trouble not only in meeting students' needs, but also in recognizing students and remembering their names! As you will see, developing a leadership plan, a learning environment, and communication skills will help you face the challenges of classroom management.

Of particular concern in recent years have been problems associated with the pervasiveness of social media in students' lives. For example, **cyberbullying**, a digital form of bullying, presents new challenges for schools and communities in general. The 2008 National Issues in Education Poll, commissioned by the CTF, revealed that Canadian teachers ranked cyberbullying as an issue of highest concern—89 percent said bullying and violence are serious problems in our public schools. A 2010 study by Faye Mishna of 33 Toronto junior high and high schools reported that almost 50 percent of students surveyed had been bullied online.

According to the CTF policy proposal, cyberbullying is the use of information and communication technologies to bully, embarrass, threaten, or harass another. It also includes the use of these technologies to engage in conduct or behaviour that is derogatory, defamatory, degrading, illegal, or abusive.

Other key findings of the CTF poll that should be of particular concern for educators:

> Nine in 10 Canadians believe that an effective measure to prevent cyberbullying by students is for parents to become more knowledgeable and more responsible in monitoring their child's activities with the Internet and electronic communication devices; 86% believe that an effective measure to prevent cyberbullying by students is to have teachers trained to respond to cyberbullying when it impacts them or their students; 96% believe that school boards should develop and enforce policies that hold their students accountable when they are identified as cyberbullies. About 7 in 10 Canadians think that school boards should hold students accountable when the cyberbullying originates outside the school, such as from the student's home. (CTF, 2008)

Sexting, the sharing of sexually explicit images and videos via text messages, is an issue of increasing importance and is often associated with cyberbullying. The suicide of Rehtaeh Parsons in Nova Scotia in 2013 highlights the possible tragic consequences of sexting and cyberbullying. Although teens polled report that they see the sharing of sexual images as an issue of consent, in Canada the sharing of such images of minors is covered by child pornography laws and can be considered a criminal act regardless of consent.

Educating students about cyberbullying and sexting and the safe use of social media is of increasing importance in schools.

Social Problems That Impact Students

Many social problems affect the lives and learning of many children and youth. For example, substance abuse, teen pregnancy, homelessness, poverty, family distress, child abuse and neglect, violence and crime, suicide, and health problems such as human immunodeficiency virus (HIV), acquired immune deficiency syndrome (AIDS), and fetal alcohol syndrome all affect students in the classroom. The social problems that place students at risk of school failure are not always easy to detect. Students' low productivity, learning difficulties, and attitude problems demand teacher attention, yet teachers may be unaware of the source of those difficulties. Even when teachers do recognize the source of a problem, they may lack the resources or expertise to offer help. Teachers often feel frustrated by the wasted potential they observe in their students. In addition, when the public calls for schools to curb or correct social problems, that expectation can increase the stress that teachers experience.

Canada's Rural and Urban Challenges

Teacher education programs are being designed to better prepare education students for the challenges they will face in rural and urban schools. Schools in inner-city areas must have teachers who care about children living in poverty and who are willing to make the extra efforts to meet their diverse needs. Many teachers and administrators leave these schools after a year or two because of the immense pressure of the social and educational environment. Beginning teachers need to become familiar with the literature on the literacy levels of children in poverty. In addition, teacher education programs need to emphasize the importance of developing school–family–community partnerships for student success.

Canada's large land mass provides challenges in terms of furnishing equitable educational services to small and isolated communities, especially those in the north. Northern and geographically isolated school boards have difficulty attracting and maintaining staff, and providing appropriate educational experiences is costly. The education systems of these regions must be developed to meet the needs of the students in the context of their communities. The culture of the local communities must be valued and should shape the curriculum. Teachers need to be prepared to meet the special challenges of these regions. In addition, initiatives that encourage young people to become teachers and to remain in their home communities are important.

In recent years, technology has had a positive effect on the ability of rural schools to reach out and communicate with other areas of the country. Continuing technology advances and expansion of online social networks will no doubt help schools in isolated areas to make important connections.

Diverse Populations

Canada is becoming increasingly diverse in its population, and such diversity enriches the school systems, while providing challenges. Large urban areas, such as Vancouver and Toronto, have significant populations of immigrants from Asia, Africa, and Latin America who have joined the more established populations with European roots, as well as Aboriginal people.

Canadian public schools have a duty to respond to the social and academic needs of immigrant and First Nations students through the enactment of inclusive practices. These include forging strong connections with other social agencies to offer an array of services to support families.

Need for Family and Community Support

Support from parents and the community can make a significant difference in the teacher's effectiveness in the classroom. Increasingly, there has been a realization that school, parents, and community must work together so that children and youth develop to their maximum potential academically, socially, emotionally, and physically. Parents who talk with their children, help with homework, read to them, monitor their use of technology, and attend meetings of their Parent Council and school open houses can enhance their children's ability to succeed in school. Similarly, communities can support schools by providing essential social, vocational, recreational, and health support services to students and their families.

Today's Tech-Savvy Students

Understanding how technology affects students and schools and integrating technology into teaching come easily for some teachers; for other teachers, however, it can be a challenge. Students in your classroom will have grown up in "a techno-drenched atmosphere that has trained them to absorb and process information in fundamentally different ways" (McHugh, 2005, p. 1). For example, students in grades 6–12 spend an average of 7.8 hours each day on sedentary screen-based devices (Leatherdale & Ahmed, 2011). Homework, however, receives much less attention. In 2010, 31 percent of students aged 8–18 surveyed said that they were watching TV, texting, or listening to music while they were doing homework (Rideout, Foehr, & Roberts, 2010).

For these students, using computers and mobile devices is an everyday part of their lives. How can teachers remain up to date regarding the role that technology plays in their students' lives?

Generally speaking, schools have not kept up with the rapid changes in technology. "For this digital generation, electronic media is increasingly seductive, influential, and pervasive, yet most schools treat the written word as the only means of communication worthy of study" (George Lucas Educational Foundation, February 9, 2008).

For these students, using advanced technology is an everyday part of their lives. How can teachers remain up to date regarding the role that technology plays in their students' lives?

Vlue/Shutterstock

Used by permission of George Gadanidis

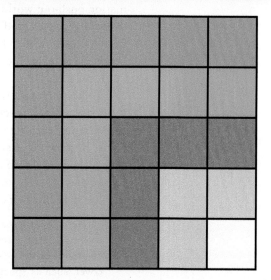

What Did You Do in Math Today?

George Gadanidis is Professor of Mathematics Education at Western University. Through his research, he spends 50–60 days each year in elementary school classrooms, collaborating with teachers to develop better ways of engaging young children with mathematics. The guiding question for lesson planning is "What did you do in math today?" The goal is to design lessons that prepare children to share learning stories that capture the imagination and offer the pleasure of mathematical surprise and insight. For example, in studying growing patterns, grade 2 students notice that odd numbers hide in squares (see the figure). Where do even numbers hide?

And, in studying area representations of fractions, grade 3 students learn that it is possible to hold infinity in their hands. Can you see that the infinite set of fractions 1/2, 1/4, 1/8, 1/16, and so on depicted in the figure all fit inside a single square?

You can see classroom documentaries of Gadanidis's work at www.researchideas.ca.

It's the Real Thing

HOLD IT IN YOUR HAND

Infinity

www.ResearchIdeas.ca

Think of a topic you have to teach. Can you design a learning experience that will offer your students conceptual surprise and insight?

Today's students have iPods, cell phones, laptops, and digital cameras. Social media tools like Facebook, Twitter, and MySpace are changing the way students communicate, socialize, and network. Sites like YouTube and iTunes bring media to students seamlessly, whether at home, at school, or on the move. Media content comes into schools through cell phones, the Internet, email, text messages, and general entertainment (for example, music, video, and blogs). "[W]e no longer live in an information push-out world where we passively receive information that is broadcast out to us by large, centralized entities. Instead, we now live within multidirectional conversation spaces in which 15-year-olds can reach audiences at scales that previously were reserved for major media companies, large corporations, and governments" (McLeod, 2011, p. 1).

To keep up with the media and technology environment today's students inhabit outside school, teachers must integrate technology into their teaching. Moodle, a free virtual learning environment, can be used to manage class-related conversations, homework assignments, and quizzes. Students can be encouraged to keep blogs (short for "web log"), and school-related activity can be viewed by the teacher in one place.

See the following example of how wikis are used in a grade 10 social studies class:

> Maria Valquez has asked her grade 10 social studies students to track and report on national election activities. She has organized her four social studies classes into 28 groups of three students each. Each group is assigned an aspect of the election to cover, such as specific political parties, an individual candidate, hot topic issues, media campaign messages, and so on. Maria wants students to be able to share the information they find among the four classes, with the rest of the school, and even with the community. In addition to researching election activities, she hopes that students will strive to find common ground and form a consensus on controversial issues. To facilitate this communication and sharing of information, Maria needs a technology tool that is not controlled by a single group or individual. She needs a tool that allows all students in her social studies classes to have an equal say. She decides to use a wiki.

Coming out of the social web movement, wikis follow the logic that many voices are better than one. A wiki is a website that allows collaborative work by various authors. A wiki website allows anyone or designated members of a group to create, delete, or edit its content. Several free wiki services are available to educators. A simple Google search yields promising results. One powerful example of how a wiki can be used for collaboration and knowledge creation is Wikipedia, the free online encyclopedia written in a collaborative way by people who use it.

Effective teachers recognize that technology can be a powerful tool for enhancing students' inquiry, reflection, and problem solving. They also realize that technology cannot be grafted onto existing teaching strategies; it must be integrated into those strategies. Chapter 9 of this book is designed to help you become a tech-savvy teacher.

WHAT IS THE WORK OF TEACHERS?

At first, this question may appear easy to answer. Based on your own experiences as a student, you know that teachers assign learning tasks. Teachers ask questions and evaluate students' responses; they lecture and, on occasion, demonstrate what students are to do. Teachers assign chapters to read in the text and then conduct recitations or give quizzes on that material. They praise some students for right answers or good work, and they prod, chastise, and at times embarrass others in the hope that their work will improve. And, near the end of the term or semester, teachers decide who has passed and who has failed. However, the role of today's teachers includes responsibilities that go beyond actual teaching in the classroom.

Teaching is more than the sum of the behaviours you observed in your own teachers. As you move ahead in your journey toward becoming a teacher, you will discover that teaching involves more than performing certain behaviours in front of a group of students. A significant portion of a teacher's work is mentally based and involves problem solving in response to unforeseen events that emerge in the classroom (Martinez, 2006). Teaching is a creative act in which teachers continually shape and reshape lessons, events, and the experiences of their students.

Although your teachers reflected different personalities and methods, your experiences as a student are similar to the experiences of other students. Our recollections about teachers who had a good or bad influence, were easy or hard on us, and were interesting or dull educators are drawn from a commonly shared set of experiences. The universality of these experiences leads us to conclude that we know "the way teaching is" and what teachers do.

The following sections examine three dimensions of teaching that illustrate how, on the one hand, teaching involves "enduring puzzlements, persistent dilemmas, complex conundrums, [and] enigmatic paradoxes" (Eisner, 2006, p. 44), while on the other it offers opportunities for "saving lives, rescuing a child from despair, restoring a sense of hope, soothing discomfort" (p. 46). Effective teachers understand that they are role models for students, spontaneous problem-solvers, and reflective thinkers. "Teachers are the filters for the day-to-day reality of the school. Whether we are aware of it or not, our behavior sets the tone" (Whitacker, 2012, p. 58).

Teacher as a Role Model for Students

Clearly, teachers are role models for their students. In the elementary grades, teachers are idolized by their young pupils. At the high school level, teachers have the potential to inspire students' admiration if they model positive attitudes and behaviours. Actually, teachers teach "not only by what [they] say but also by what [they] do" (Ormrod, 2003, p. 342). Teachers are "active agents whose words and deeds change lives and mold futures, for better or worse. Teachers can and do exert a great deal of power and influence in the lives of their students" (Nieto, 2003, p. 19).

Teachers also model attitudes toward the subjects they teach and show students through their example that learning is an ongoing, life-enriching process that does not end with diplomas and graduations. The need for teachers to function as role models for students confirms the timeless message of Sir Rabindranath Tagore that is inscribed above the doorway of a public building in India: "A teacher can never truly teach unless he is still learning himself. A lamp can never light another lamp unless it continues to burn its own flame."

On the next page is a letter of advice from a seasoned teacher to a former student who is entering the teaching profession. Reflect on how the teacher highlights important characteristics of "good teaching."

Teacher as a Spontaneous Problem-Solver

In the classroom, teachers must respond to unpredictable events that are rapidly changing, multidimensional, and fragmented. Furthermore, teachers are the only professionals who practise their craft almost exclusively under the direct, continuous gaze of up to 30 or 40 clients.

When teachers are preparing to teach or reflecting on previous teaching, they can afford to be consistently deliberate and rational. Planning for lessons, grading papers, reflecting on the misbehaviour of a student—such activities are usually done alone

Dear David:

Congratulations! I hear you are about to graduate and soon will have your first assignment as a new teacher. I am sending you a little gift—nothing much, just some words of wisdom that have inspired me in my teaching. It is this quotation from William Butler Yeats. "Education is not the filling of a pail, but the lighting of a fire."

This captures the essence of good teaching in very few words. If you keep them in mind, you may find that teaching will not become any easier, but will certainly become more interesting and more satisfying.

"Education is not the filling of a pail" means that you are teaching human beings. If you learn to know your students as individuals, you will treat them with more consideration and respect. They have deep feelings. Do not, intentionally, do or say anything to embarrass or humiliate a student in front of his or her peers. If you have to discipline a student, speak to him or her privately if possible. Try to be fair with your students—do not play favourites. When it comes to "teacher's pet," all or none is the best rule.

Another thing is implied in those first few words. It is that learning is not a passive process, but an active one. Students need to be doing something with their new skills or information in order to make the lesson stick. Think of as many different activities as you can to reinforce new learning.

"Not the filling of a pail" also means that you don't have to teach them everything. You do not have to know it all. You should be knowledgeable in your subject area, yet it is not possible to know everything. Admit it when you don't know an answer—it can lead to a good discussion. You should know where to find the answer, however. Invite an expert to class to answer the question, or get the student who came up with the $64 000 question to e-mail it to an expert.

The last part of the quote touches on the artistry of teaching. This is something beyond expert subject knowledge or command of pedagogical technique. The "lighting of a fire" refers to inspiring a student with a lifelong love of learning. There are no lesson plans for this, but if there were, they might include some of these things:

Believe in yourself. Set goals. Be reflective. Keep a journal. Create a welcoming space where students are free from contempt, indifference, and "putdowns." Do not allow students to "put themselves down" or engage in negative self-talk (e.g., "I'm stupid. I can't . . ."). Believe in your students. Maintain high expectations. Believe that every student has at least one gift, one thing they can do like no other. Help them to find their gift(s). Create opportunities for them to develop their gift(s).

No doubt, you heard a lot about motivation in your studies. Here is another tidbit of advice:

> A teacher who is attempting to teach without inspiring the pupil with a desire to learn is hammering on a cold iron.
> —Horace Mann (1796–1859)

I mention this because I believe motivation is not well understood. I may be wrong, but I see it in this way. Most of us have what I call a Personal Relevance Filter (PRF). This operates to screen incoming sensory experience and allows us to separate our experiences into two piles—things that are important to us, and things that are not. This natural process prevents our brains from being overloaded by the sheer abundance of sensory impressions. Your goal, as a teacher, is to try to get your lessons placed in the "important" pile. A way to do this is to frame your lessons and activities in a "real world" or authentic context. Another way is to use theatrical techniques, particularly humour or suspense. I am sure you will think of more ways to create personal relevance for your students. Knowing what "makes them tick" is a good place to start.

Best of luck from your former teacher,

Warren Dobson

Interactive teaching: teaching characterized by face-to-face interactions between teachers and students; in contrast to preactive teaching.

and lack the immediacy and sense of urgency that characterize **interactive teaching**. While working face-to-face with students, however, you must be able to think on your feet and to respond appropriately to complex, ever-changing situations. You must be flexible and ready to deal with the unexpected. During a discussion, for example, you must operate on at least two levels. On one level, you respond appropriately to students' comments, monitor other students for signs of confusion or comprehension, formulate the next comment or question, and remain alert for signs of misbehaviour. On another level, you ensure that participation is evenly distributed among students, evaluate the content and quality of students' contributions, keep the discussion focused and moving ahead, and emphasize major content areas. During interactive teaching, the awareness that you are responsible for the forward movement of the group never lets up.

Teacher as a Reflective Thinker

Teaching involves a unique mode of being between teacher and student—a mode of being that can be experienced but not fully defined or described. On your journey to becoming a teacher, you will gradually develop your capacity to listen to students and to convey an authentic sense of concern for their learning. Unfortunately, there is no precise, easy-to-follow formula for demonstrating this. You will have to take into account your personality and special gifts to discover your own best way for showing this concern.

One reason it is difficult to describe teaching is that an important domain of teaching, teachers' thought processes (including professional reflection), cannot be observed directly. Figure 1.1 shows how the unobservable domain of the teacher's "interior reflective thinking" interacts with and is influenced by the observable domain of the teacher's "exterior reflective action." Teachers' thought processes include their theories and beliefs about students and how they learn, their plans for teaching, and the

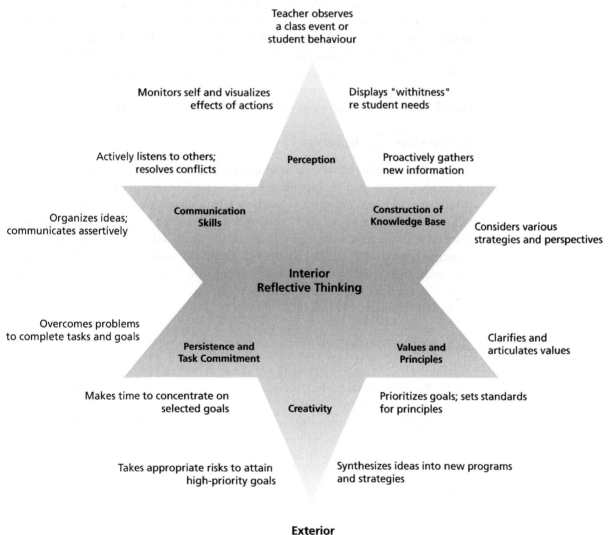

Figure 1.1 A model of reflective action in teaching

Source: Eby, Judy W., *Reflective Planning, Teaching, and Evaluation for The Elementary School,* 2nd ed., © 1997, p. 14. Reprinted and Electronically reproduced by permission of Pearson Education, inc., New York. NY.

decisions they make while teaching. Thought processes and actions can be constrained by the physical setting of the classroom or by external factors such as the curriculum, the principal, or the community. On the other hand, teachers' thought processes and actions may be influenced by unique opportunities, such as the chance to engage in curriculum reform or school governance. The model also illustrates a further complexity of teaching—namely, that the relationships among teacher behaviour, student behaviour, and student achievement are reciprocal. What teachers do is influenced not only by their thought processes before, during, and after teaching, but also by student behaviour and student achievement. This complexity contributes to the uniqueness of the teaching experience.

HOW DO ACCOMPLISHED TEACHERS VIEW THEIR WORK?

Accomplished teachers derive greatest satisfaction when they are effective in promoting students' learning—when they "make a difference" in students' lives. When you recall your most effective teachers, you probably think of particular individuals, not idealizations of the teacher's many roles. What good teachers do can be described in terms of five **modes of teaching**, which are more general and significant than a discussion of roles. You may recognize these modes in your observations of teachers and in the writings of gifted teachers when they reflect on their work. You may even acknowledge these modes of teaching as deeper reasons for becoming a teacher.

Modes of teaching: different aspects of the teaching function—for example, teaching as a way of being, as a creative endeavour, as a live performance, and so on.

A Creative Endeavour

Teaching is a creative endeavour in which teachers are continually shaping and reshaping lessons, events, and the experiences of their students. With careful attention to the details of classroom life, effective teachers artistically develop educative relationships with their students; they "read" the myriad events that emerge while teaching and respond appropriately. One high school teacher identified as highly successful by her principal reported: "I have to grab the kids that don't want to do math at all and somehow make them want to do this work. I'm not sure how I do it, but kids just want to do well in my class. For some mysterious reason, and I don't care why, they really want to do well" (Hansen, 1995, p. 13).

A Live Performance

Teaching is a live performance, with each class period and each day involving responding to the unpredictable. Further, teachers are engaged in live dialogues with their classes and individual students. The experience of teaching is thus an intense, attention-demanding endeavour—an interactive one that provides minute-to-minute challenges. Some teachers embrace the live performance aspect of teaching more than others, believing that within it lies true learning.

A Form of Empowerment

Power is the dimension of teaching most immediately evident to the new teacher. It is recognized in the first-grader's awed question "Teacher, is this good?" on through the high school senior's query "How much will this paper count?"

Even in the most democratic classrooms, teachers have more influence than students because they are responsible for what happens when students are with them, for establishing the goals, for selecting the methods, for setting the pace, for evaluating the

Knowledge of how to integrate technology into teaching is essential for today's teachers. What steps can you take to remain technologically up to date?

progress, and for deciding whether students should pass or fail. How you use this power is critical. As you know, students at any level can be humiliated by teachers who misuse their power or convey negative expectations to students.

An Opportunity to Serve

To become a teacher is to serve others. Most who come to teaching do so for altruistic reasons. The altruistic dimension of teaching is at the heart of the motivation to teach. The paycheque, the public regard, and the vacations have little holding power compared to the opportunity to serve. Whatever form the altruistic rewards of teaching takes, they ennoble the profession and remind teachers of the significance of their work.

Teaching for Excellence

Many of our country's most talented beginning teachers and most dedicated veteran teachers retain the desire to teach. In part, the desire endures because teachers have been positively influenced by one or more teachers of their own, who enriched, redirected, or significantly changed their lives. The desire also endures because teachers recognize the many joys and rewards the profession offers.

Reflecting on dedicated teachers and their contributions to our lives, we are guided to teaching for the benefit it brings to others. Every year, the Prime Minister's Awards for Teaching Excellence recognize the efforts of outstanding teachers in all disciplines. Go to www.ic.gc.ca/eic/site/pmate-ppmee.nsf/eng/home to view the most recent awards.

SUMMARY

Why Do You Want to Teach?

- An important reason for becoming a teacher is a desire to work with children and young people.

- Practical benefits of teaching include on-the-job hours at school, vacations, increasing salaries and benefits, job security, and a feeling of respect in society.

What Challenges Does Teaching Present?

- Working conditions for teachers can be difficult and stressful; however, for most teachers, satisfactions outweigh dissatisfactions.

- Though problems in schools vary according to size of community, location, and other factors, teachers in most schools face challenges: classroom management, social problems that impact students, rural and urban populations, diverse ethnicities, need for family and community support, and today's tech-savvy students.

What Is the Work of Teachers?

- Teaching is more than the sum of observable behaviours; much of the work of teachers involves responding to unforeseeable events in the classroom.

- With the role of teacher comes the power to influence others by example.

- Teachers must be spontaneous problem-solvers as they respond to unpredictable events.

How Do Accomplished Teachers View Their Work?

- Helping students to learn and making a difference in students' lives provide teachers with their greatest satisfaction.

APPLICATIONS AND ACTIVITIES

1. Consider your reasons for deciding to become a teacher. How do they compare with those described in this chapter?

2. Describe a former teacher who has had a positive influence on your decision to teach. In what ways would you like to become like that teacher?

3. Individual Task: Interview a *beginning teacher* (one with five years or less experience in the profession) and a *seasoned teacher* (one with 10 or more years in the profession) by asking the following guiding questions:

   a. What are the greatest challenges in your daily practice?

   b. What brings you the most satisfaction as a teacher?

   c. If you could change one thing about today's education system, what would it be?

   d. "If I knew then what I know now . . ." What is the best single piece of advice you could give to a person who is considering the teaching profession as a career?

Write a short, reflective paper on what you learned from the exercise, identifying what surprised you the most.

4. Make a list of recent portrayals of teachers in movies, television, and other media. Analyze the portrayals in terms of the type of teacher image they present—positive, neutral, or negative. Some classic movies to consider include:

   a. *Dangerous Minds*: portrays someone who dares to teach the "unteachables"

   b. *Stand and Deliver*: presents the message that teachers should never believe that students are unable to learn

   c. *Lean on Me*: features a principal whose goal is to reform a troubled New York high school

d. *Mr. Holland's Opus*: speaks to the impact a teacher can have on the lives of his students

e. *Dead Poets Society*: portrays an unconventional teacher who motivates his students in a conservative private boys' school

5. On the Web, use your favourite search engine and search for information by key words on topics such as teacher burnout, accountability, diverse learners, cyberbullying, sexting, and teacher–student ratios.

6. Arrange to observe a teacher's class. During your observation, note how the teacher must make decisions on a moment-by-moment basis, as discussed in this chapter.

7. Ask your instructor to arrange group interviews between students in your class and students at local elementary, middle, junior, and senior high schools. At each interview session, ask the students what characterizes accomplished and nonaccomplished teachers. Also ask the students what advice they would give to beginning teachers.

Chapter 2
Learning to Teach

FOCUS QUESTIONS

1. What essential knowledge do you need to teach?

2. How are Canadian teachers educated and certified?

3. How can you gain practical experience for becoming a teacher?

4. What opportunities for continuing professional development will you have?

Education is not preparation for life; education is life itself.

—John Dewey

When I began seriously listening to my life, my teaching life, I also began to listen to my students' lives at a different level . . . I became more tolerant of those who were different from me. . . . I became a more patient teacher. I more often saw the students and their parents as people.

—Excerpt from Karen Hale Hankins (1998), "Cacophony to Symphony: Memoirs in Teacher Research," *Harvard Educational Review,* 68(1), pp. 80–95. Copyright © 1998 by the President and Fellow of Harvard College. All rights reserved.

Today's teachers want to be a part of a child's life. They want to better a child's life in some way, big or small.

—LACI, teacher education program, first year

Today's teachers are people much like me—they have a passion for teaching and want to make sure that today's children have a better and brighter future.

—MATTHEW, teacher education program, first year

Today's teachers are the students of yesterday. They come from many different backgrounds and have many different life experiences. They teach because they had teachers who greatly influenced their lives and inspired them to do well.

—RYAN, teacher education program, first year

WHAT ESSENTIAL KNOWLEDGE AND SKILLS DO YOU NEED TO BE A TEACHER?

Just as people hold different expectations for schools and for teachers, there are different views of the knowledge and skills teachers need in order to teach well. In addition to being knowledgeable about the subjects they teach, teachers must have the ability to communicate, to inspire trust and confidence, and to motivate students, as well as to understand their students' educational and emotional needs. Teachers must be able to recognize and respond to individual and cultural differences and to employ different teaching methods that will result in higher student achievement. They should be organized, dependable, patient, creative, and able to present their lessons in an interesting manner that leads to the enhancement of student learning. Teachers must also be able to work cooperatively and communicate effectively with other teachers, support staff, parents, and members of the community.

To respond effectively to the complexities of teaching, you must have four kinds of knowledge: knowledge of yourself and your students, knowledge of subject, knowledge of educational theory and research, and knowledge of how to integrate technology into teaching. The following sections examine these four forms of essential knowledge.

Self-Knowledge

Effective teachers understand themselves and are sensitive to students' needs. "They recognize that the child's personality is a fragile work in progress" (Erickson, 2008, p. 225). Naturally, you should understand your students as much as possible. What is the connection, however, between self-knowledge and the ability to promote student learning? If you understand your own needs (and can satisfy those needs), you are in a better position to help students learn. A teacher's self-understanding and self-acceptance help students to know and to accept themselves.

Your self-evaluations as a teacher are influenced by the feelings you may experience while teaching—feelings that may range from great joy and satisfaction to anxiety or loneliness. Anxiety is a common feeling experienced by teachers who are embarking on a new or more complex teaching strategy.

As a teacher, you will likely experience feelings of happiness, excitement, and wonder as a result of the time you spend with students. You may also experience occasional loneliness or isolation because most of your time will be spent with children and youth rather than with adults. Though teachers are in their classrooms most of the day, today's teachers have the opportunity to collaborate with their colleagues, whether it be serving on a school improvement committee, developing new curricula, or mentoring new teachers.

Knowledge of Students

Without doubt, knowing your students is important. Knowledge of student characteristics such as aptitudes, talents, learning styles, stages of development, and readiness to learn new material is essential. The importance of this knowledge is evident in comments made by an intern at a middle school: "To teach a kid well you have to know a kid well. . . . Teaching middle school takes a special breed of teachers who understand the unique abilities and inabilities . . . [of] those undergoing their own metamorphosis into teenagers" (Henry, Huntley, McKamey, & Harper, 1995, pp. 124–125). In Chapter 5, you will learn about the diverse groups of students who comprise today's school population, and in Chapter 6, you will learn about learners' individual needs. In addition, after you

---

▶▶▶ CASE TO CONSIDER | Dealing with the Unexpected

Teacher education programs do what they can to prepare students for careers in teaching, but in the end, if graduates have not developed good problem-solving skills, their teaching lives will be lacking in success. When dealing with classroom problems, there are some situations in which time for thoughtful consideration exists; in others, the response time can be as short as a few seconds. The examples that follow posed problems for four student teachers during their practicum (field experience) teaching. After reading each problem, give thought to what you might have done if placed in a similar situation.

Problem 1: Bert is one of the few males who elected to become an elementary teacher. His supervising teacher, Mrs. Swenson, is a veteran teacher within a few years of a well-earned retirement. As they enter the classroom after completing recess playground supervision, they notice a mixed group of their grade 3 students giggling and laughing as they leaf through a book open before them. Approaching the group, Bert and Mrs. Swenson discover that the students are examining a sex manual with some very explicit pictures. Mrs. Swenson turns to Bert and simply says, "Deal with it."

Problem 2: Nadia is teaching a class of grade 5 students in a small rural school. She notices that one of her male students, who gives the impression of being both sad and fearful, remains in the classroom during recess and spends most of his noon hours in the library, which is supervised by a teacher aide. Careful inquiries of other students convince her that the student is being bullied, but no one will say by whom. Attempting to be helpful, Nadia and her supervising teacher speak with the student regarding the suspicion, but he denies that that is the case. With her supervising teacher's permission, Nadia contacts the boy's single parent regarding the situation. The parent's response is that her son "has to learn to stick up for himself."

Problem 3: Isaac is teaching mathematics to a class of grade 9 students. Molly, who is seated at the back of the room, is whispering to her best friend, Carol, who sits directly in front of her. Isaac politely asks her to stop talking.

She stops but appears distracted and keeps her head down except for furtive, upward glances toward Isaac. After a short period, Molly is again whispering to her friend. Again, she is asked to cease talking and pay attention. After several repeats of this situation, Isaac walks toward Molly and notices her texting on her cell phone. Molly has apparently been texting to Carol. Although the school has a bring your own device (BYOD) policy permitting students to bring cell phones and other mobile devices to school, their use is limited to educational purposes. Isaac says confidently, "Molly, you've been texting. Please give me your phone. I will give it back to you at the end of class." Molly replies that she was not texting and refuses to hand over her phone.

Problem 4: Amy is an attractive individual who looks younger than her actual age of 23. As part of her field experience assignment, she is teaching Canadian history to a class of academic-stream grade 12 students. One of her students is particularly enthusiastic in his response to her teaching and often lingers after class to discuss various points from her lessons. Two weeks into her practicum, she receives a telephone call from the student asking for advice regarding a project required for another course he is taking. Quite unsuspecting, and rather flattered that a student had asked for her assistance, Amy agrees to help and says she will meet with the student after school the following day. During the meeting, the student volunteers that he is "very attracted" to her and asks her out on a date. He also mentions that everyone in the class is aware of his affection for her.

1. In Problem 1, how could Bert respond to the situation with his supervising teacher?

2. In Problem 2, how could Nadia follow up on her suspicion that a student is being bullied?

3. In Problem 3, how could Isaac deal with the texting situation?

4. In Problem 4, how could Amy respond to the student comment of being "very attracted" to her?

become a teacher, you will expand your knowledge of students through further study, observation, and interactions with them.

Knowledge of Subject

Teachers are assumed to have extensive knowledge. People who are not teachers expect a teacher to have knowledge far beyond their own. Without doubt, teachers who have extensive knowledge of their subjects are better equipped to help students learn.

However, extensive knowledge of subject matter entails more than being able to recite dates, multiplication tables, or rules of grammar. Accomplished teachers possess what is sometimes referred to as **pedagogical content knowledge**. Such understanding is the joint product of wisdom about teaching, learning, and students and a deep, conceptual understanding of content. It includes knowledge of the most appropriate ways to present the subject matter to students through analogies, metaphors, experiments, demonstrations, and illustrations. The blend of good pedagogy and good content allows teachers to present ideas in ways that are conceptually rich yet accessible and engaging. For example, starting a science unit on density and buoyancy in grade 8, a teacher might pose this problem: "I am going to pick up the tiniest pebble I can find and toss it into a pond. Will it sink or will it float? Now I am going to pick up a heavy log and toss it into the same pond. Will it sink or will it float?" After students respond, the teacher adds: "Now that's puzzling. How can a tiny pebble that weighs so very little sink, while a heavy log can float?"

Pedagogical content knowledge: the knowledge accomplished teachers possess regarding how to present subject matter to students through the use of analogies, metaphors, experiments, demonstrations, illustrations, and other instructional strategies.

Knowledge of Methods for Applying Educational Theory and Research

Theories about learners and learning will guide your decision making as a teacher. Not only will you know that a certain strategy works, but you will also know why it works. Because you realize the importance of theories, you will have a greater range of available options for problem solving than teachers who do not have such a repertoire. Your ultimate goal as a professional is to learn how to apply theoretical knowledge to the practical problems of teaching.

Research on students' learning does not set forth, in cookbook fashion, exactly what you should do to increase it. Instead, it may be helpful to think of educational research as providing you with "rules of thumb" to guide your practice, and to recall a comment by noted educational psychologist Lee Cronbach (quoted in Eisner, 1998, p. 112): "Educational [research] is to help practitioners use their heads."

Educational researchers are still learning what good teachers know and how they use that knowledge. As a result, many people believe that a **knowledge base** for teaching should consist of not only what educational researchers have learned about teaching, but also what teachers themselves know about teaching. Clandinin (2013) suggests that the knowledge that teachers possess is not simply theoretical (such as knowing theories of education) or practical (such as knowing children), but rather a personal combination of the two, "blended by the personal background and characteristics of the teacher" (p. 67).

Knowledge base: the body of knowledge that represents what teachers need to know and be able to do.

Knowledge of How to Integrate Technology into Teaching

As a teacher, you will be expected to know how to integrate technology into your teaching. And throughout your teaching career, you will be expected to be familiar with newly emerging technologies and how they can be used in the classroom.

Using technology to enhance students' learning requires more than knowing how to use the latest hardware and software. Conducting classroom demonstrations

AVAVA/Shutterstock

augmented with multimedia, using presentation graphics to address students' varied learning styles, and designing lessons that require students to use technology as a tool for inquiry should be second nature for teachers.

Knowledge of how to integrate technology into teaching is essential for today's teachers. Consider taking the following steps to remain technologically up to date. Learn all you can about:

■ Software, online courses, social networking tools, mobile devices, and other technology-based digital learning solutions tools, which are used to broaden and strengthen learning and teaching through authenticity, real-world problem solving, critical thinking, communication, production for students, and support through online communities

■ Real-time information that can assist you in making sound instructional decisions

Reflection and Problem Solving

The preceding discussion of essential knowledge and skills for teaching highlights the fact that teaching is complex and demanding. As you use your knowledge and skills to meet the challenges of teaching, you will be guided by reflection and an orientation toward problem solving. As Figure 2.1 shows, reflection and problem solving will enable you to determine how to use knowledge of self and students (including cultural differences), knowledge of subject matter, knowledge of educational theory and research, and knowledge of how to integrate technology into teaching to create optimum conditions for student learning. The figure also shows that you can use reflection and problem solving to decide which essential skills to use and how to use them.

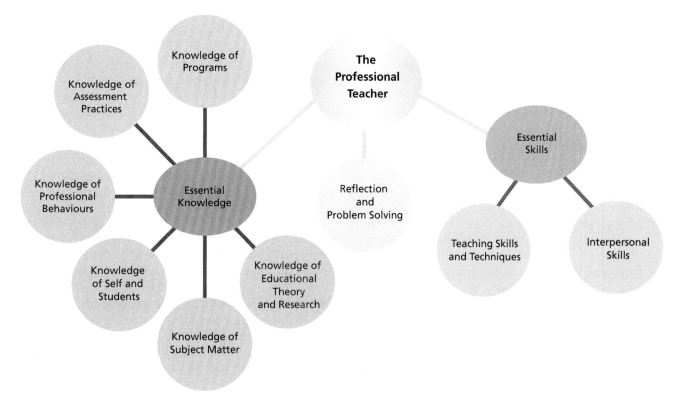

Figure 2.1 Essential knowledge and skills for the professional teacher

| Technology in Education: Problems, Potentials, Unknown Possibilities

Canadian Researcher: Dr. Gregory MacKinnon
University: Acadia University, School of Education
Teaching Specialties: Science and Technology

Technology is often defined as "a way of adapting"—a problem-solving process that presumes that humans want to better their lives by using more efficient tools to serve their daily needs. In turn, because improved "life conditions" are central to human existence, technological improvements have become increasingly pervasive throughout society. Everywhere we look we see new technologies that assist in solving both new and old problems. Interestingly, Dr. David Suzuki has often said that as humans we prefer not to reverse technology. In other words, we would rather fix, or adapt, older technologies to respond to new problems than step backward and abandon them entirely.

Technology has an almost insidious way of inserting itself into our lives, a situation that makes it crucial for educators to be critical of, and to teach the critical assessment of, new technologies when they may impact the educational process. To achieve both these goals is a challenging task. Today's students are technologically savvy; they are the "net generation" (Koh, 2015) that has arisen with the multitude of technologies that have changed the very social fabric of their culture. While communications technologies have arguably had the greatest influence (consider the preponderance of smartphones), others, such as tablets, laptops, apps, and social media networks like Facebook and Twitter, have also exerted their influence—and newer technologies emerge almost daily. Some researchers are beginning to argue that with the host of co-existing technologies available, students have developed new learning capacities.

There are suggestions that present public school curricula do not respond sufficiently to the needs of the net generation. Collins and Halverson (2009) astutely present a challenge to educators that schools should now offer "just-in-case learning," while letting technology foster "just-in-time learning" (p. 48). Much of what we presently teach students has the end purpose of preparing them for the next level of education, whereas what technology potentially affords is the access to, and application of, knowledge of real and current problems. Consider, for instance, the exponential increase in the knowledge available to students through information technologies. It is obvious that computers and handheld devices have given the nontraditional student access to education as never before. The number of online courses and degree programs available continues to grow as education becomes—unfortunately, some might say—increasingly commodified. Access technologies have moved the classroom from learning "communities of place to communities of interest" (Collins & Halverson, 2009, p. 11). However, beyond simple access issues, the real question becomes: How is the nature of learning changing with technological advancements?

Progress with Second-Order Technology Applications

Jonassen (2000) introduced the concept of using computer technologies as educational mindtools—unique, and sometimes subversive, strategies that represent a second-order use of technologies (Maddux & Johnson, 2006). First-order use of technologies promotes an instrumental use, while second-order use offers opportunities and scaffolds for engaging students in investigation, conjecturing, and sense making.

In many cases, while communication technologies may be useful for their intended first-order interactions between students, the nature of this communication within a more complex classroom framework may promote new skills and understandings. Consider a classroom where multiple types of communications are happening between teacher and students via presentation software, connected mobile devices, social networks, Internet searches, and other online resources. The potential for unique types of learning is enormous.

Knowledge building in virtual communities has been the life work of Canadian researchers Scardamalia and Bereiter (1994, 2003), who have promoted the interaction of diverse and distance learners within the framework of productive constructivist learning. Scardamalia and Bereiter (2015) note: "Education now functions in an open informational world in which there are essentially no boundaries constraining the information that may be brought to bear on any topic, question, or activity."

Most recently, there has been a resurgent focus on coding (computer programming) for children of all ages. In England, for example, the 2014 curriculum "replaces the old ICT programme of study, which focused on computer literacy, with more up-to-date content teaching children how to code, create programmes and understand how a computer works" (UK Government News Release, February 4, 2014). In Canada, schools and curriculum developers are looking into ways of using coding to enhance learning in curriculum areas, using easy-to-learn block-based programming languages such as Scratch (www.scratch.mit.edu). As well, the development of "digital tangibles" using programmable circuits and wearable electronics, and robots that can be programmed by children, adds a new dimension to learning with technology.

Teachers are faced with new technology tools of great potential everyday. It is incumbent upon educators to explore such tools as cell phones, tablets, and digital tangibles in an effort to find unique ways to empower education so that today's children use today's technology to extend both teaching and learning potential.

WHAT ARE SIX WAYS OF VIEWING THE TEACHER KNOWLEDGE BASE?

Just as people hold different expectations for schools and teachers, there are different views on the knowledge and abilities teachers need in order to teach well. The complexities of teaching make it difficult to describe in exact detail the knowledge base on which teaching as a profession rests. This difficulty results, in part, because there is no universally accepted definition of what good teaching is. Educational researchers are still learning what good teachers know and how they use that knowledge.

A Personal Development View

One view of what teachers need to know and be able to do places primary emphasis on who the teacher is as a person. According to this view, teachers should be concerned with developing themselves as people so that they may learn to use their insights more effectively. The importance of personal development is described as follows by the authors of *On Being a Teacher*: "[t]eachers who appear in charge of their own lives, who radiate power, tranquility, and grace in their actions, are going to command attention and respect. People will follow them anywhere. . . . What we are saying is that you have not only the option, but also the imperative, to develop the personal dimensions of your functioning, as well as your professional skills" (Kottler & Zehm, 1993, p. 15).

What this approach requires, then, is that teachers continually develop their powers of observation and reflection so that they can most effectively respond to the needs of students. Teaching becomes an authentic, growth-oriented encounter between teacher and students. An important dimension of this **personal development view** is the teacher's need for self-knowledge, particularly in regard to the self as a learner.

Personal development view: the belief that teachers become more effective by increasing their self-knowledge and developing themselves as persons.

Research-Based Competencies

Since the late 1980s, most provinces, or the school districts within them, have developed their own lists of **research-based competencies** that beginning teachers must demonstrate. These competencies are derived from educational research that has identified what effective teachers do. Typically, many provinces have behavioural indicators for each competency, which trained observers use to determine to what extent teachers actually exhibit target behaviours in the classroom. Teachers are required to demonstrate effective pedagogical behaviours in a number of domains: planning and preparation, effective classroom management, control of student conduct, instructional organization and development, presentation of subject matter, verbal and non-verbal communication, and testing (student preparation, administration, and feedback).

Research-based competencies: specific behaviours that educational research has identified as characteristic of effective teachers.

Provincial Standards

In addition to sets of research-based competencies for evaluating practising teachers, some provinces have developed performance-based standards for what new teachers should know and should be able to do. Known as **outcome-based** or **performance-based teacher education**, the new approach is based on several assumptions:

- Outcomes are demonstrations of learning rather than a list of teaching specializations, college courses completed, or concepts studied.

- Outcomes are performances that reflect the richness and complexity of the teacher's role in today's classrooms—not discrete, single behaviours.

- Demonstrations of learning must occur in authentic settings—that is, settings similar to those within which the teacher will teach.

- Outcomes are culminating demonstrations of what beginning teachers do in real classrooms.

Typically, outcome-based standards are developed with input from teachers, teacher educators, provincial departments of education personnel, and various professional associations. However, outcome-based standards are not without their critics. Sharp criticism of the Atlantic Provinces Education Foundation (APEF) outcomes-based curriculum (see Teacher's Resource 2.3 at www.MyEducationLab.com) is articulated

Outcome-based: an educational reform that focuses on developing students' ability to demonstrate mastery of certain desired outcomes or performances.

Performance-based teacher education: an approach to teacher education emphasizing performance (what teachers should be able to do, think, and feel) rather than the courses they should take.

by Dr. David MacKinnon, author of *A Wolf in Sheep's Clothing: The Erosion of Democracy in Education* (Portelli & Solomon, 2001, p. 136):

> [A]n outcomes-based approach to education provides an inadequate foundation for public education. Behavioral outcomes, by definition, are confined to that which is observable and measurable . . . [P]rojects like the APEF initiative are necessarily incomplete and, perhaps, unwittingly misguided . . . [T]he APEF initiative is a reductionist and anti-democratic exercise at increasing system accountability.

A Subject Matter Expert View

Almost three decades ago, Shulman (1987) suggested that teacher development had "a blind spot with respect to content" and that the emphasis was solely "on how teachers manage classrooms, organize activities, allocate time and turns, structure assignments, ascribe praise and blame, formulate the levels of their questions, plan lessons, and judge general student understanding" (p. 8). However, developing as a teacher is not simply a matter of knowing content but rather of knowing content in ways that can be effectively communicated to students. One way to judge how well you understand the subject matter you teach is to imagine sharing the key idea or concept in your lesson in a way that engages, surprises, and offers conceptual insight to a nonexpert. If you can do this, then you can design learning experiences to prepare your students to know your subject matter in similar ways. Gadanidis and Hughes (2011), working in the area of elementary school mathematics education, note:

> We believe that good math stories and good math experiences go hand-in-hand. In our work in elementary school classrooms, we ask ourselves: are the activities we are planning for students going to prepare them to share good math stories with their peers and with the wider community? If the answer is "no", then we take the time to rethink the mathematics learning experiences we are offering to our students. (p. 495)

A Job-Analysis Approach

Another view of what teachers need to know and be able to do is based on the job analyses conducted by some school districts. Typically, a **job analysis** begins with a review of existing job descriptions and then proceeds to interviews with those currently assigned to the job and their supervisors regarding the activities and responsibilities associated with the job. These data are then analyzed to identify the dimensions of the job. Finally, interview questions based on those dimensions are developed and used by district personnel responsible for hiring.

The following excerpt from a study by the Urban Network to Improve Teacher Education (UNITE), an organization comprising both Canadian and American universities, illustrates the knowledge, skills, and attitudes needed by successful urban teachers.

> Twenty-two teachers and five administrators were involved in focus group interviews conducted during the study. Over half of the 27 participants have been working in the field of education for less than five years, although four have been teaching in their present school for over 15 years. On average, the participants graduated from a faculty of education 11 years ago. The teachers interviewed represented all grade levels, from Kindergarten to senior secondary, and represented a variety of subject areas and roles within a school community (e.g., physical education, visual arts, resource teacher, special education teacher). All but one of the participants received their preservice education in the province of Ontario.
>
> **Characteristics of a Successful Urban Teacher**
>
> Eight characteristics were identified in all focus group interviews as being important for teachers to possess in order to be successful in an urban school. These eight characteristics are discussed in order of the degree of emphasis placed on them by the focus group participants.

Empathy—Because most teachers never experience many of the traumas and issues that their students deal with on a daily basis, they strongly believed that teachers in urban schools need to be empathetic. They mentioned the importance of "not placing your morals, judgments and values on the students and parents," and "making greater attempts at trying to understand the different cultures and religions."

Respect for the students—Teachers need to respect students and to operate on the belief that all students have the right to learn, and to achieve success. Participants stated that teachers in urban schools should not compromise expectations and that they should "believe that all students have a future."

Flexibility—Teachers in urban schools need to be flexible. Teachers reported that this flexibility was necessary when dealing with such things as curriculum guidelines, programming, evaluation, classroom disruptions, and student behaviour. One teacher stated, "You set up a wonderful day, and then it isn't working, and you have to step back and reassess. It's constant."

Self-care—In order to be a successful teacher in an urban school, participants stressed the need for caring for their personal needs. Since urban schools "really challenge you, you have to make sure you take care of the whole you, emotionally, physically, personally, and manage your stress. You have to find the balance."

Patience—Teachers in urban schools need to be patient. Dealing with the diverse population of students, and all of the other challenges previously mentioned, the need for "infinite patience" was believed to be necessary in order to be successful as a teacher in an urban school.

Sense of humour—Participants in the focus group interviews strongly believed that in order to be a successful teacher in an urban school one must possess a sense of humour. One teacher described this need in connection with self-care, stating, "If you don't have the ability to laugh, you run the risk of becoming emotionally drained."

Collegiality—Another important characteristic for teachers in urban schools is collegiality and peer support. Participants described the need, in urban schools, for staff to work together, to "share their ups and downs," to share their resources, and to be there to support one another.

High energy level—In order to deal with the plethora of daily challenges facing urban school teachers, interview participants stated that these teachers need to have high energy levels. A number of participants extended this characteristic to include a willingness "to make the commitment of time, energy and effort it takes to work in a school like this."

Source: The Canadian Journal of Educational Administration and Policy. "Characteristics of a Successful Urban Teacher" Issue #6, March 25, 1996. Used with permission.

Professional Views

While there are differing opinions regarding what teachers should be able to do, it seems evident that becoming a teacher is complex and demanding. Most Canadian school districts have policies that detail the essential skills and responsibilities of the teachers they employ (see Figure 2.2). While details vary from one jurisdiction to another, the following topics are common to most:

- A well-organized learning environment with appropriate learning resources for students
- Interesting and effective teaching skills appropriate to the age and abilities of students
- Effective classroom management and discipline skills
- Positive interactions with teachers, other school personnel, parents, and members of the greater school community

Directions: *As you observe, note the ways that students are motivated intrinsically (from within) and extrinsically (from factors outside themselves).*

Intrinsic Motivation	Extrinsic Motivation
What things seem to interest students at this age?	How do teachers show their approval to students?
Which activities and assignments seem to give them a sense of pride?	What phrases do teachers use in their praise?
When do they seem to be confused? Bored? Frustrated?	What types of rewards do teachers give (e.g., grades, points, tangible rewards)?
What topics do they talk about with enthusiasm?	What reward programs do you notice (e.g., points accumulated toward free time)?
In class discussions, when are they most alert and participating most actively?	What warnings do teachers give?
What seems to please, amuse, entertain, or excite them?	What punishments are given to students?
What do they joke about? What do they find humorous?	How do teachers arouse concern in their students?
What do they report as being their favourite subjects? Favourite assignments?	How do students motivate other students?
What do they report as being their least favourite subjects and assignments?	What forms of peer pressure do you observe?
How do they respond to personalized lessons (e.g., using their names in exercises)?	How do teachers promote enthusiasm for an assignment?
How do they respond to activity-oriented lessons (e.g., fieldwork, project periods)?	How do teachers promote class spirit?
How do they respond to assignments calling for presentations to groups outside the classroom (e.g., parents, another class, the chamber of commerce)?	How do teachers catch their students' interest in the first few minutes of a lesson?
How do they respond to being given a choice in assignments?	Which type of question draws more answers—recall or open-ended?
	How do teachers involve quiet students in class discussions?
	How do teachers involve inactive students in their work?
	In what ways do teachers give recognition to students' accomplishments?

Figure 2.2   Guiding questions for observing motivation

- Fair and effective assessment practices
- Strict adherence to local board policies and provincial or territorial curriculum guidelines

For a list of best teaching practices, you might visit the EduGAINS website: www.edugains.ca/newsite/HOME/index.html. "Sites That Help Classroom Teachers," at www.internet4classrooms.com/teacher.htm, is another excellent resource.

HOW ARE CANADIAN TEACHERS EDUCATED AND CERTIFIED?

Because education is a provincial rather than a federal responsibility, each province is free to elect its preferred method for educating those intent on pursuing careers as professional teachers. The result is a patchwork quilt of Bachelor of Education programs, each with its own specific admission requirements, and each with its own particular curriculum.

Additionally, while the academic body bestows the Bachelor of Education degree on its graduates, each province and territory has a teacher certification body that establishes the requirements that must be met before a teaching licence will be awarded. In some provinces, such as Newfoundland and Labrador and Nova Scotia, the certifying agency is each province's department of education. However, in other jurisdictions, such as British Columbia and Ontario, independent agencies such as the British Columbia College of Teachers and the Ontario College of Teachers are responsible for teacher certification.

In Manitoba, Alberta, and Ontario, teacher associations negotiate their contracts at the regional or local level. In all other provinces and territories, the negotiations are conducted between the teachers' associations and departments of education personnel. Salary scales are quite variable. Canadian teacher salaries are determined by two major factors: years of post-secondary education and years of teaching experience. Depending on the exact combination, and the province or territory in which one is teaching, teacher annual salaries can range from $45 000 to $95 000. Administrators, such as department heads and school principals, receive further allowances in addition to their basic teacher salaries. The highest rates of teacher pay are offered by the Yukon, Nunavut, and the Northwest Territories.

Canadian Schools of Education: A Variety of Models

Concurrent Program   Students enrol in a Bachelor degree and take regular academic courses and education courses at the same time. Most such programs are four years in duration and provide their graduates with the least expensive route to a teaching degree. However, the majority of students in concurrent programs must decide at a very early stage in their lives that teaching is their chosen profession.

Eight-Month Post-Degree Program   This has been by far the most common model. Applicants for admission to a school of education first obtain a three- or four-year undergraduate degree that contains the appropriate academic prerequisites as established by the university or department of education. Successful applicants then take a specified number of courses designed to assist them with their teaching practice. As part of their program, they also spend a designated amount of time—usually five to eight weeks—working with associate teachers in the field. Critics of eight-month programs argue that this format does not provide sufficient time for student teachers to learn all the things necessary for them to be truly effective educators. In addition, provinces with more comprehensive Bachelor of Education programs will sometimes decline to grant teaching licences to those who have graduated from such programs.

Twelve-Month Post-Degree Program   There are relatively few 12-month Bachelor of Education programs available in Canada. Twelve-month programs have more coursework for students to complete and provide more time for fieldwork in classrooms. They are also more expensive for students, but as they are completed within an extended academic year, graduates can be employed as teachers in September of the year in which they graduate.

Two-Year Post-Degree Program   At present, Ontario, Nova Scotia, and Prince Edward Island have two-year post-degree Bachelor of Education programs. Applicants to these programs first obtain a three-year or four-year undergraduate degree, and then complete two academic years of educational studies in combination with 20 or more weeks of field experience. Some colleges and universities also offer two or more of the models described above. Some universities offer the two-year degree as a Master's degree (such as the University of Toronto) rather than a Bachelor of Education degree or offer Bachelor of Education course credits toward a Master's degree (such as Western University).

WHAT CAN YOU LEARN FROM OBSERVING IN CLASSROOMS?

Classroom observations are a vital element of many **field experiences**. Students report that these experiences aid them greatly in making a final decision about entering the teaching field. Most become more enthusiastic about teaching and more motivated to learn the needed skills, although a few decide that teaching is not for them. Recognizing the value of observations, many teacher education programs are increasing the amount of field experience required and scheduling such fieldwork earlier in students' programs.

Focused Observations

Observations are more meaningful when they are focused and conducted with clear purpose. Observers may focus on the students, on the teacher, on the interactions between the two, on the structure of the lesson, or on the setting. More specifically, for example, observers may note differences between the ways boys and girls or members of different ethnic groups communicate and behave in the classroom. They may note student interests and ability levels, study student responses to a particular teaching strategy, or analyze the question and response patterns in a class discussion.

Observations may also be guided by sets of questions related to specific areas. For instance, since beginning teachers are frequently frustrated by their lack of success in interesting their students in learning, asking questions specifically related to motivation can make an observation more meaningful and instructive. Similar questions can be generated for other focus areas such as classroom management, student involvement, questioning skills, evaluation, and teacher–student rapport.

Observation Instruments

A wide range of methods can be used to conduct classroom observations, ranging from informal, qualitative descriptions to formal, quantitative checklists. With reform efforts to improve education in Canada has come the development of instruments to facilitate the evaluation of teacher performance, a task now widely required of school administrators. Students preparing to teach can benefit by using these evaluative instruments in their observations.

All teachers, including student teachers, are subject to both formal and informal observations and evaluations. To give you some idea about how you may come to be evaluated for your instructional skills, an actual evaluation of a first-term student teacher's very first formative (preliminary) evaluation is included in Teacher's Resource 2.4 at www. MyEducationLab.com. When reading this report, ask yourself if you might commit any of the errors noted by the associate teacher.

HOW CAN YOU GAIN PRACTICAL EXPERIENCE FOR BECOMING A TEACHER?

A primary aim of teacher education programs is to give students opportunities to experience, to the extent possible, the real world of the teacher. Through field experiences and carefully structured experiential activities, preservice teachers are given limited exposure to various aspects of teaching. Observing, tutoring, instructing small groups, analyzing video cases, operating instructional media, performing student teaching, and completing various noninstructional tasks are among the most common experiential activities.

Classroom Experiences

Because of the need to provide opportunities to put theory into practice before student teaching, many teacher education programs enable students to participate in microteaching, teaching simulations, analyses of video cases, field-based practica and clinical experiences, and classroom aide programs.

Microteaching   Introduced in the 1960s, **microteaching** was received enthusiastically and remains a popular practice. The process calls for students to teach brief, single-concept lessons to a small group (5 to 10 students) while concurrently practising a specific teaching skill, such as positive reinforcement. Often the microteaching is recorded for later study.

As originally developed, microteaching includes the following six steps:

1. Identify a specific teaching skill to learn about and practise.
2. Read about the skill in one of several pamphlets.
3. Observe a master teacher demonstrate the skill in a short movie or on video.
4. Prepare a three- to five-minute lesson to demonstrate the skill.
5. Teach the lesson, which is recorded, to a small group of peers.
6. Critique, along with the instructor and student peers, the recorded lesson.

> **Microteaching:** a brief, single-concept lesson taught by a teacher education student to a small group of students; usually designed to give the education student an opportunity to practise a specific teaching skill.

Simulations   As an element of teacher training, **teaching simulations** provide opportunities for vicarious practice of a wide range of teaching skills. In simulations, students analyze teaching situations that are presented in writing, on audio recordings, in short films, or on video. Typically, students are given background information about a hypothetical school or classroom and the pupils they must prepare to teach. After this orientation, students role-play the student teacher or the teacher who is confronted with the problem situation. Following the simulation, participants discuss the appropriateness of solutions and work to increase their problem-solving skills and their understanding of the teacher's multifaceted role as a decision maker. Additionally, recent technological advances now make computer-based simulations available for use in faculty of education programs.

> **Teaching simulations:** an activity in which teacher education students participate in role plays designed to create situations comparable to those actually encountered by teachers.

Video Cases   Teacher education students who view, analyze, and then write about video cases have an additional opportunity to appreciate the ambiguities and complexities of real-life classrooms, to learn that "there are no clear-cut, simple answers to the complex issues teachers face" (Wasserman, 1994, p. 606). Viewing authentic video cases enables students to see how "teaching tradeoffs and dilemmas emerge in the video 'text' as do the strategies teachers use, the frustrations they experience, the brilliant and less-brilliant decisions they make" (Grant, Richard, & Parkay, 1996, p. 5). With the prevalence of online learning, many video cases are now offered online. For example, the Ontario Ministry of Education provides online classroom videos along with lesson plans and activity sheets for K–6 literacy and numeracy at www.eworkshop.on.ca.

Practica   A **practicum** is a short-term field-based experience (usually about two weeks long) that allows teacher education students to spend time observing and assisting in classrooms. Though practica vary in length and purpose, students are often able to begin instructional work with individuals or small groups. For example, a cooperating teacher may allow a practicum student to tutor a small group of students, read a story to the whole class, conduct a spelling lesson, monitor recess, help students with their homework, or teach students a song or game.

> **Practicum:** a short field-based experience during which teacher education students spend time observing and assisting in classrooms.

Classroom Assistants   Serving as a teacher assistant is another popular means of providing field experience before student teaching. A teacher assistant's role depends primarily on the unique needs of the school and its students. Generally, assistants work under the supervision of a certified teacher and perform duties that support the teacher's instruction. Assisting teachers in classrooms familiarizes teacher education students with class schedules, record-keeping procedures, and students' performance levels, and provides ample opportunity for observation. In exchange, the classroom teacher receives much-needed assistance.

Student Teaching

The most extensive and memorable field experience in teacher preparation programs is the period of student teaching. As *The Student Teacher's Handbook* points out, student teaching "is the only time in a teaching career that one is an apprentice under the close guidance of an experienced mentor" (Schwebel, Coslett, Bradt, & Friedman, 1996, p. 4). Depending on the province, Bachelor of Education students may be required to have as few as five weeks of student teaching or, as in Nova Scotia, as many as 15 weeks before being certified as teachers. The nature of student teaching varies considerably among teacher education programs. Typically, a student is assigned to a cooperating (or master) teacher in the school, and a university supervisor makes periodic visits to observe the student teacher. Some programs even pay student teachers during the student teaching experience. All schools of education recognize the importance of preparing their students for life as a professional teacher.

Student teaching is a time of responsibility. As one student teacher puts it, "I don't want to mess up [my students'] education!" It is also an opportunity for growth and a chance to master critical skills. Time is devoted to observing, participating in classroom activities, and actively teaching. The amount of time one actually spends teaching, however, is not as important as one's willingness to reflect carefully on the student teaching experience. Two excellent ways to promote reflection during student teaching are journal writing and maintaining a reflective teaching log.

Preservice Teacher Journal Writing Many supervisors require student teachers to keep a journal of their classroom experiences so that they can engage in reflective teaching and can begin the process of criticizing and guiding themselves. The following

What strategies can you use to make your student teaching experience truly valuable? In what sense will you remain a student teacher throughout your career?

two entries—the first written by a student teacher in a grade 4 classroom, the second by a student teacher in a high school English class—illustrate how journal writing can help student teachers develop strategies for dealing with the realities of teaching.

> Today I taught a geography lesson and the kids seemed so bored. I called on individuals to read the social studies text, and then I explained it. Some of them really struggled with the text. Mr. H. said I was spoon-feeding them too much. So tomorrow I am going to put them into groups and let them answer questions together rather than give them the answers. This ought to involve the students in the learning a bit more and enable some of the better readers to help out those who have difficulty, without the whole class watching. I feel bad when I see those glazed looks on their faces. I need to learn how to be more interesting. (Pitton, 1998, p. 120)

> I had good feedback on small groups in their responses to questions on *Of Mice and Men*. They were to find a paragraph that might indicate theme and find two examples of foreshadowing. We found five!

> The short story unit was awful during fourth hour. The kids just didn't respond. I quickly revamped my approach for the next hour. Fifth hour did seem to go better. (Mostly though, I think it was just that I was more prepared, having had one class to try things out.) I can see how experience really helps. Now that I've tried the story "The Tiger or the Lady," I would use the same material, but I would know HOW to use it more effectively! (Pitton, 1998, p. 143)

Relatively unstructured, open-ended journals, such as the ones from which these entries were selected, provide student teachers with a medium for subjectively exploring the student teaching experience.

Reflective Teaching Logs   To promote the practice of reflecting more analytically, some supervisors ask their student teachers to use a more directed and structured form of journal keeping, the **reflective teaching log**. In this form, a student lists and briefly describes the daily sequence of activities, selects a single episode to expand on, analyzes the reason for selecting it and what was learned from it, and considers the possible future application of that knowledge.

Reflective teaching log: a journal of classroom observations in which the teacher education student systematically analyzes specific episodes of teaching.

Though student teaching will be the capstone experience of your teacher education program, the experience should be regarded as an initial rather than a terminal learning opportunity—your first chance to engage in reflection and self-evaluation for a prolonged period.

To illustrate a reflective teaching log, a partial entry for one episode follows. The entry shows how a college student can disagree with a supervising teacher's response to a classroom situation.

Log for December 1—Erin Tompkins

Sequence of Events

1. Arrival—end of eighth period
2. Ninth period—helped Sharad study science
3. After-school program—worked on science with Ricki, P.K., and Tom
4. Late bus duty with Ms. Soto
5. Departure

Episode: I was helping Ricki and P.K. fill out a table about the location and function of the different cell parts. P.K. asked me a question and two other students laughed at him. I began to answer his question when Ms. Soto came over to the table where we were working and yelled at P.K. She said, "P.K. I don't need you distracting other students who are trying to get their work done." He started to tell her what he asked me and she said, "I don't care. You can leave the room if you don't knock it off. Just do your work and be quiet or you're out!" She then apologized to me and went back to helping another student.

Analysis: I was very frustrated after this episode. This is the first time I've seen Ms. Soto raise her voice with a student and accuse him of causing problems when he was getting his work done and other students were being disruptive. P.K. had asked me a legitimate question; the other students who laughed at him were the problem. I was frustrated because Ricki and P.K. were working hard and asking me good questions. I was annoyed that P.K. was being reprimanded for asking a question that was relevant to the topic we were working on. I also felt helpless because I wanted to tell Ms. Soto that it wasn't P.K. who was the problem. I didn't feel it was my place to correct her in front of her students and kept quiet. I decided that my saying something would only make things worse because it would encourage P.K. to continue arguing with Ms. Soto and he would be in more trouble. (Posner, 2003, p. 122)

Source: Posner, George J., Field Experience: A Guide to Reflective Teaching, 6th ed., © 2005. Reprinted and Electronically reproduced by permission of Pearson Education, Inc., New York, NY.

Gaining Experience in Multicultural Settings

Canadian schools will enrol increasing numbers of students from diverse cultural backgrounds during the twenty-first century. As this trend continues, it is vitally important that those entering the teaching profession achieve an understanding of children's differing backgrounds. As a result, many teacher education programs now have courses that deal with equity issues to help prepare student teachers for the diversity that exists in almost every classroom.

As a teacher you can be assured that you will teach students from backgrounds that differ from your own—including students from the more than 100 racial and ethnic groups in Canada, and students who are poor, are gifted, or have disabilities. You will have the challenge of reaching out to all students and teaching them that they are persons of worth and that they can learn. You will also be confronted with the difficult challenge of being sensitive to differences among students, while at the same time treating all equally and fairly. To prepare for these realities of teaching, you should make every effort to gain experiences in multicultural settings.

Supply Teaching

On completion of a teacher education program and prior to securing a full-time teaching assignment, many students choose to gain additional practical experience in classrooms by **supply or daily occasional teaching** or **substitute teaching**. Others, unable to locate full-time positions, decide to supply, knowing that many districts prefer to hire from their pool of supply teachers when full-time positions become available. Supply teachers replace regular teachers who are absent due to illness, family responsibilities, personal reasons, or professional workshops and conferences.

Each day, thousands of supply teachers are employed in schools across Canada. For example, during one school year at the 15 high schools in a large urban district, the total number of absences for 1200 regular teachers equalled 14 229 days. Multiplying this figure by five (the number of classes per day for most high school teachers) yields 71 145 class periods taught by supply teachers in one school year.

Qualifications for supply teachers vary from province to province. An area with a critical need for supply teachers will often relax its requirements to provide classroom coverage. In many districts, it is possible to supply without regular certification if no fully certified teacher can be located. Some districts have less stringent qualifications for short-term, day-to-day supply teachers and more stringent ones for long-term, full-time assignments. In many districts, the application process for supply teachers is the

Supply or daily occasional teaching: temporary teachers who replace regular teachers absent due to illness, family responsibilities, personal reasons, or professional workshops and conferences.

Substitute teaching: temporary teachers who replace regular teachers absent due to illness, family responsibilities, personal reasons, or professional workshops and conferences.

Advantages and Disadvantages of Supply Teaching

Advantages
- Gain experience without all the nightly work and preparation
- Compare and contrast different schools and their environments
- Be better prepared for interviews by meeting administrators and teachers
- Teach and learn a variety of material
- Get to know people—network
- See job postings and hear about possible vacancies
- Gain confidence in your abilities to teach
- Practice classroom management techniques
- Learn about school and district politics—get the "inside scoop"
- Choose which days to work—flexible schedule

Disadvantages
- Pay is not as good as full-time teaching
- No benefits such as medical coverage, retirement plans, or sick days
- Lack of organized representation to improve wages or working conditions
- May receive a cool reception in some schools
- Must adapt quickly to different school philosophies
- Lack of continuity—may be teaching whole language one day; phonetics the next

Figure 2.3 Advantages and disadvantages of supplying

Source: John F. Snyder, "The Alternative of Substitute Teaching." In *1999 Job Search Handbook for Educators.* Evanston, IL: American Association for Employment in Education, 1999, p. 38.

same as that for full-time applicants; in others, the process may be somewhat briefer. Often, supply teachers are not limited to working in their area of certification; however, schools try to avoid making out-of-field assignments. If you decide to supply teach, contact the schools in your area to learn about the qualifications and procedures for hiring supply teachers.

In spite of the significant role supply teachers play in the day-to-day operation of schools, "research tells us that they receive very little support, no specialized training, and are rarely evaluated. . . . In short, the substitute will be expected to show up to each class on time, maintain order, take roll, carry out the lesson, and leave a note for the regular teacher about the classes and events of the day without support, encouragement, or acknowledgement" (St. Michel, 1995, pp. 6–7). While working conditions such as these are certainly challenging, supplying can be a rewarding, professionally fulfilling experience. Figure 2.3 presents several advantages and disadvantages of supplying.

HOW CAN YOU DEVELOP YOUR TEACHING PORTFOLIO?

Now that you have begun your journey toward becoming a teacher, you should acquire the habit of assessing your growth in knowledge, skills, and attitudes. Toward this end, you may wish to collect the results of your reflections and self-assessment in a **professional portfolio**. A professional portfolio is a collection of work that documents an individual's accomplishments in an area of professional practice. An artist's portfolio, for example, might consist of a résumé, sketches, paintings, slides and

Professional portfolio: a collection of various kinds of evidence (e.g., projects, written work, and video demonstrations of skills) documenting the achievement and performance of individuals in an area of professional practice.

photographs of exhibits, critiques of the artist's work, awards, and other documentation of achievement. Recently, new approaches to teacher evaluation have included a professional portfolio. Teacher education programs at several universities now use portfolios as one means of assessing the competencies of candidates for teacher certification.

Portfolio Contents

What will your portfolio contain? Written materials might include the following: lesson plans and curriculum materials, reflections on your development as a teacher, journal entries, writing assignments given by your instructor, sample tests you have prepared, critiques of textbooks, evaluations of students' work at the level for which you are preparing to teach, sample letters to parents, and a résumé. Non-print materials might include video and audio recordings featuring you in simulated teaching and role-playing activities, audiovisual materials (transparencies, charts, or other teaching aids), photographs of bulletin boards, charts depicting room arrangements for cooperative learning or other instructional strategies, sample grade book, certificates of membership in professional organizations, and awards.

Your portfolio should represent your best work and give you an opportunity to become an advocate of who you are as a teacher. Because a primary purpose of the professional portfolio is to stimulate reflection and dialogue, you may wish to discuss what entries to make in your portfolio with your instructor or other teacher education students. In addition, the following questions from *How to Develop a Professional Portfolio: A Manual for Teachers* (Campbell, Melenyzer, Nettles, & Wyman, 2003, p. 5) can help you select appropriate portfolio contents:

> Would I be proud to have my future employer and peer group see this? Is this an example of what my future professional work might look like? Does this represent what I stand for as a professional educator? If not, what can I revise or rearrange so that it represents my best efforts?

What questions might you ask a mentor teacher that might help you develop as a professional?

Using a Portfolio

In addition to providing teacher education programs with a way to assess their effectiveness, portfolios can be used by students for a variety of purposes. A portfolio can be used as:

1. A way to establish a record of quantitative and qualitative performance and growth over time

2. A tool for reflection and goal setting as well as a way to present evidence of your ability to solve problems and to achieve goals

3. A way to synthesize many separate experiences; in other words, a way to get the "big picture"

4. A vehicle for you to collaborate with professors and advisors in individualizing instruction

5. A vehicle for demonstrating knowledge and skills gained through out-of-class experiences, such as volunteering

6. A way to share control and responsibility for your own learning

7. An alternative assessment measure within the professional education program

8. A potential preparation for national, regional, and state accreditation

9. An interview tool in the professional hiring process

10. An expanded résumé to be used as an introduction during the student teaching experience

HOW CAN YOU BENEFIT FROM MENTORING RELATIONSHIPS?

Mentoring opportunities can occur at various stages of a teacher's career:

> As a preservice teacher working with an associate teacher, as a teacher developing with the guidance and support of a principal, as an associate teacher working to develop rich practicum experiences for preservice teachers, as an administration protégé working with a principal mentor, and so forth. (Hughes, 2007)

As a developing teacher, a mentoring relationship will offer you guidance and support. When asked, "What would have been most helpful in preparing you to be a teacher?" one first-year suburban high school teacher responded: "I wish I had one [a mentor] here. . . . There are days that go by and I don't think I learn anything about my teaching, and that's too bad. I wish I had someone" (Dollase, 1992, p. 138). Research on the impact of induction and mentoring programs has found that teachers "performed better at various aspects of teaching, such as keeping students on task, developing workable lesson plans, using effective student questioning practices, adjusting classroom activities to meet students' interests, maintaining a positive classroom atmosphere, and demonstrating successful classroom management" (Ingersol & Strong, 2012, p. 201).

An urban middle school intern's description of how his mentor helped him develop effective classroom management techniques exemplifies "learning the ropes": "'You've got to develop your own sense of personal power,' [my mentor] kept saying. 'It's not something I can teach you. I can show you what to do. I can model it. But I don't know, it's just something that's got to come from within you'" (Henry, Huntley, McKamey, & Harper, 1995, p. 114).

Those who have become highly accomplished teachers frequently point out the importance of mentors in their preparation for teaching. A mentor can provide moral support, guidance, and feedback to students at various stages of professional preparation. In addition, a mentor can model for the protégé an analytical approach to solving problems in the classroom.

WHAT OPPORTUNITIES FOR CONTINUING PROFESSIONAL DEVELOPMENT WILL YOU HAVE?

Professional development is a lifelong process; any teacher, at any stage of development, has room for improvement. Many school systems and universities have programs in place for the continuing professional development of teachers. Indeed, teachers are members of a profession that provides them with a "continuous opportunity to grow, learn, and become more expert in their work" (Lieberman, 1990, p. viii).

Self-Assessment for Professional Growth

Self-assessment: the process of measuring one's growth in regard to the knowledge, skills, and attitudes possessed by professional teachers.

Reflection: the process of thinking carefully and deliberately about the outcomes of one's teaching.

Self-assessment, or **reflection**, is a necessary first step in pursuing opportunities for professional growth. The simplest level of reflection occurs when, after a particular lesson has been taught, a teacher asks such questions as: How did that lesson go? What might have been done to improve it? What were the good lesson elements that should be retained when I teach it again? A deeper level of reflection might include such questions as: How has that lesson contributed to my students' overall educational growth? Is society as a whole in any way better off as a consequence of what my students just learned?

Several questions can help you make appropriate choices as a teacher: In which areas am I already competent? In which areas do I need further development? How will I acquire the knowledge and skills I need? How will I apply new knowledge and practise new skills? Answers to such questions will lead you to a variety of sources for professional growth: teacher workshops, teacher centres, professional development schools, the opportunity to supervise and mentor student teachers, and graduate programs. Figure 2.4 illustrates the relationship of these professional development experiences to your teacher education program.

Teacher Workshops

In-service workshops: on-site professional development programs in which teachers meet to learn new techniques, develop curricular materials, share ideas, or solve problems.

The quality of **in-service workshops** is uneven, varying with the size of school district budgets and with the imagination and knowledge of the administrators and teachers who arrange them. It is significant that the most effective in-service programs tend to be the ones that teachers request—and often design and conduct.

Some workshops focus on topics that all teachers (regardless of subject or level) can benefit from: classroom management, writing across the curriculum, multicultural education, and strategies for teaching students with learning disabilities in the general education classroom, for example. Other workshops have a sharper focus and are intended for teachers of a subject at a certain level—for example, whole language techniques for middle school students, discovery learning for high school science students, and student-centred approaches to teaching literature in the high school classroom.

Teacher Centres

Teacher centres: centres where teachers provide other teachers with instructional materials and new methods, and where teachers can exchange ideas.

Teacher centres provide opportunities for teachers to take the lead in the decision making and implementation of staff development programs based on the needs of teachers. Within limits, they provide opportunities for teachers to have a level of

Figure 2.4 Professional development: From teacher education student to practitioner

control over their own professional development. In contrast to in-service programs, the initiatives undertaken are more clearly directed by teachers. Some centres cooperate with a local or neighbouring college of education and include members of the faculty on their planning committees.

Many teachers find teacher centres stimulating because they offer opportunities for collegial interaction in a quiet, professionally oriented setting. Teachers often find that the busy, hectic pace of life in many schools provides little time for professional dialogue with peers. Furthermore, in a teacher centre, teachers are often more willing to openly discuss areas of weakness in their performance. As one teacher puts it:

> At the teacher centre, I can ask for help. I won't be judged. The teachers who have helped me the most have had the same problems. I respect them, and I'm willing to learn from them. They have credibility with me.

Supervision and Mentoring of Student Teachers

After several years in the classroom, teachers may be ready to stretch themselves further by supervising student teachers. Some of the less obvious benefits of doing so are that teachers must rethink what they are doing so that they might explain, and sometimes justify, their behaviours to someone else, learning about themselves in the process. Furthermore, because they become a model for their student teachers, they continually strive to offer the best example. In exchange, they gain an assistant in the classroom—another pair of eyes, an aid with record keeping—and, more than occasionally, fresh ideas and a spirit of enthusiasm.

Graduate Study

A more traditional form of professional development is to undertake graduate study. With the recent reforms, many provinces now require teachers to take some graduate courses to keep their certifications and knowledge up to date. Some teachers take only courses that are of immediate use to them; others use their graduate study to prepare for new teaching or administrative positions; and still others pursue doctoral work in order to teach prospective teachers or others in their discipline at the college or university level.

Study on the Internet

Using the Internet, you can find many possibilities for continuing professional development. Teachers use the Internet to exchange ideas and experiences and to acquire additional expertise in teaching or to share their expertise with others. You will find an abundance of learning resources (videos, lesson plans, courses, etc.) through an online search specific to your needs. You will also find such resources at the websites of ministries of education and teacher organizations. Increasingly, you will also find MOOCs (Massive Online Open Courses) offered by various universities that are freely available.

SUMMARY

What Essential Knowledge Do You Need to Be a Teacher?

- Teachers must know their students' aptitudes, talents, learning styles, stage of development, and readiness to learn new material.

- Teachers must understand their subjects deeply so that they can modify instructional strategies based on students' perception of content.

- Knowledge of educational theory enables professional teachers to know why certain strategies work.

What Are Six Ways of Viewing the Teacher Knowledge Base?

- There is no universally accepted definition of "good" teaching.

- Many provinces have developed standards for outcome-based or performance-based teacher education. Outcomes are based on what beginning teachers do in real classrooms.

- Effective teachers are guided by reflection and a problem-solving orientation.

How Are Canadian Teachers Educated and Certified?

- Both provincial departments of education and independent professional organizations set criteria for the certification of teachers.

What Can You Learn from Observing in Classrooms?

■ The opportunity to observe in classrooms helps some students make a final decision about becoming a teacher.

■ Observations can focus on a particular aspect of classroom life or be guided by a set of questions related to a specific area, such as how the teacher motivates students.

■ Observation instruments range from informal, qualitative descriptions to formal, quantitative checklists.

How Can You Gain Practical Experience for Becoming a Teacher?

■ Teacher education students can gain practical experience through focused classroom observations, microteaching, teaching simulations, analyses of video cases, field-based practica and clinical experiences, and classroom assistant programs.

■ Journal writing and reflective teaching logs increase the benefits of the student teaching experience.

■ Supply teaching provides additional practical experience after completing a teacher education program.

How Can You Develop Your Teaching Portfolio?

■ A portfolio documents professional growth and development over time.

■ Portfolio contents should represent one's best work.

■ Professional portfolios can be used in teacher evaluation, self-evaluation, and hiring.

How Can You Benefit from Mentoring Relationships?

■ Ask for advice from teachers you admire.

■ Mentoring can be a source of professional growth for experienced teachers.

■ Mentoring can occur at various stages of a teacher's career.

What Opportunities for Continuing Professional Development Will You Have?

■ Self-assessment is necessary to select appropriate professional development experiences.

■ Opportunities for professional development include teacher workshops, teacher centres, professional development schools, supervision and mentoring of student teachers, graduate study, and the Internet.

APPLICATIONS AND ACTIVITIES

1. As a teacher, you will encounter challenges related to student variability (differences in developmental needs, interests, abilities, and disabilities) and student diversity (differences in gender, race, ethnicity, culture, and socioeconomic status). To begin thinking about how you will acquire and use knowledge about your students, write a brief profile of yourself as a student in elementary school, in middle school or junior high school, and in high school.

2. On the basis of your field experiences to date and the information in Chapters 1 and 2, ask yourself these questions and respond in your journal or blog: Do I have the aptitude to become a good teacher? Am I willing to acquire the essential knowledge and skills teachers need? Do I really want to become a teacher?

3. Find out more about the use of technology to enhance teaching and learning. Join one of the online teacher discussion groups that deal with the educational use of information technology.

4. Arrange to interview a school administrator about the knowledge, skills, and aptitude he or she thinks teachers must have. Which of the knowledge and skills discussed in this chapter does the administrator mention? Does he or she mention knowledge and skills not discussed in this chapter?

5. Observe a teacher in the classroom for the purpose of identifying examples that help to answer the following questions: How does the teacher demonstrate or use knowledge of self and students? Knowledge of subject matter? Knowledge of educational theory and research?

6. Create a plan for developing your portfolio. What specific outcomes or standards will you use to organize your portfolio entries? What artifacts will you use to demonstrate your professional growth and development?

PART ONE   THE TEACHING PROFESSION

Now that you have read and have had a chance to think about the teaching profession, take the time to record your reasons for wanting to become a teacher and the steps you will take during your first year as a teacher to increase your teaching knowledge and skills.

Chapter 3

Ideas and Events That Have Shaped Education in Canada

Slavoljub Pantelic/Shutterstock

FOCUS QUESTIONS

1. What determines your educational philosophy?

2. What philosophical orientations are central to teaching?

3. What psychological orientations have influenced teaching philosophies?

4. What historical and cultural traditions have led to the development of the Canadian educational landscape?

5. What is the history of schooling for First Nations peoples?

6. What are the major characteristics of today's system of education in Canada?

7. What are some current trends in Canadian education?

8. What are some alternative types of Canadian schools?

Educational philosophy is a way not only of looking at ideas, but also of learning how to use ideas in better ways.

—Howard A. Ozmon and Samuel M. Craver
Philosophical Foundations of Education, 6th ed., 1999

Philosophy gives teachers a foundation from which to work. It provides universal guidelines for what is expected of teachers and what they should strive for when teaching students. Philosophy provides a basic understanding of what teaching is, why it is important, and how it affects not only students, but society as well.

—LACI, teacher education program, first year

Philosophy deals with how children should be educated, what they should be educated in, and what the ultimate purpose of education should be for society. In other words, philosophy is the foundation of education. A carefully developed philosophy of education allows a teacher to make better decisions in the classroom.

—PRECIOUS, teacher education program, first year

Philosophy clarifies the important role of beliefs and ethics in the classroom. From the first day of class, teachers communicate their educational philosophies to students. While these philosophies may differ, they have the same ultimate goal—learning for everyone.

—MONICA, teacher education program, first year

Instead of relying uncritically on custom, convention, or prepackaged scripts, educators can draw upon their educational philosophy to devise creative, fruitful responses to issues and problems that are tailored to their specific circumstances.

—David T. Hansen, *Ethical Visions of Education: Philosophies in Practice*, 2007, p. 7

You may wonder about the value of studying the philosophy and history of Canadian education. Will such knowledge help you become a better teacher? Yes. Knowledge of the ideas and events that have influenced our schools will help you more effectively evaluate current proposals for change. You will be in a better position to evaluate these changes if you understand how schools developed and how current proposals might relate to previous change efforts. In addition, awareness of ideas and events that have influenced teaching is an important facet of professionalism in education.

The first half of this chapter presents several basic philosophical concepts that will help you answer five important questions teachers should consider in the development of an educational philosophy:

1. What should the purposes of education be?
2. What is the nature of knowledge?
3. What values should students adopt?
4. What knowledge is of most worth?
5. How should learning be evaluated?

We cannot understand schools today without a look at what they were yesterday. The current system of public and private education in Canada is an ongoing reflection of its philosophical and historical foundations and of the aspirations and values brought to this country by its founders and by generations of settlers. Developing an appreciation for the ideas and events that have shaped the school system in Canada is an important part of your education as a professional.

The second half of the chapter presents brief overviews of how education developed in Canada's major geographical regions. We will discuss the philosophical concepts, social forces, and events that have had the greatest impact on education in our country.

You are having an animated conversation in the teachers' lounge with four colleagues—Manjit, Yuliya, Kim, and Claude—about educational reform and the changes being made throughout Canada's schools. The discussion was sparked by a television special that had aired the night before about new approaches to teaching and assessing students' learning.

"I was really glad to see teachers portrayed in a professional light," you say. "The message seemed to be 'Let's get behind teachers and give them the support and resources they need to implement new ideas and technologies. Effective schools are important to our nation's well-being.'"

"I think it's just a case of schools trying to jump on the bandwagon," Claude says. "All this talk about restructuring schools, developing partnerships with the community, and using technology—they're supposed to be the silver bullets that transform education. These ideas just take time away from what we should be doing, and that's teaching kids how to read, write, and compute. If we don't get back to what really matters, our country is going to fall apart." He paused. "But that's my educational philosophy."

"But times have changed—the world is a different place," Manjit replies. "Look at how the Internet has changed things in just a few years. We can't return to the 'good old days.' Students need to learn how to learn. They need to learn how to solve problems we can't even imagine today."

"Just a minute," Yuliya interjects. "I don't think the 'good old days' ever were. That's a nostalgia trap. What kids need is to see how education is the key to understanding themselves and others. If we can't get along as human beings on this planet, we're in trouble. Look at the ethnic cleansing in Kosovo, the killing in Rwanda, Angola, Northern Ireland . . . Sure, we've got the Internet and all this technology, but, as a species, we haven't evolved at all."

"Of course we can't return to the past," Kim says, "but we can learn a lot from it. That's one of the main purposes of education—to see how the great ideas can help us improve things. As I tell my students, there isn't one problem today that Shakespeare didn't have tremendous insight into 400 years ago—racism, poverty, war . . ."

"Well, all I know is that, when I started teaching 30 years ago, we taught the basics," Claude says. "It was as simple as that. We were there to teach, and the kids, believe it or not, were there to learn. Nowadays, we have to solve all of society's problems—eliminate poverty, racism, crime, or whatever."

Claude pauses a moment then turns his attention to you. "What do you think? What's your educational philosophy?"

1. What are three key components of your educational philosophy?

2. How would you respond to Claude's comment about "trying to jump on the bandwagon"?

3. How would you respond to Claude's comment about "we taught the basics"?

WHAT DETERMINES YOUR EDUCATIONAL PHILOSOPHY?

In simple terms, your **educational philosophy** comprises what you believe about education—the set of principles that guides your professional action (see Figure 3.1). Every teacher, whether he or she recognizes it, has a philosophy of education—a set of beliefs about how human beings learn and grow and what one should learn in order to follow a successful path. Teachers differ, of course, in regard to the amount of effort they devote to the development of their personal philosophy or educational platform. Some feel that philosophical reflections have nothing to contribute to the actual act of teaching. (This belief is itself a philosophy of education.) Other teachers recognize that teaching, because it is concerned with what ought to be, is an essentially philosophical enterprise. Becoming aware of your personal philosophy of education is a first step to growing as a teacher, and starting toward the path of developing a robust teaching philosophy that will guide your classroom practice.

Your behaviour as a teacher is strongly connected to your personal values and your beliefs about teaching and learning, students, knowledge, and what is worth knowing. Regardless of where you stand in regard to the five dimensions of teaching, you should be aware of the need to continually reflect on what you believe and why you believe it.

Educational philosophy: a set of ideas and beliefs about education that guides the professional behaviour of educators.

For each pair of statements about the teacher's role, circle the response that most closely reflects where you stand regarding the two perspectives. Remember, there are no correct responses, and neither perspective is better than the other.

Constructivist Perspective		Transmission Perspective
"I mainly see my role as a facilitator. I try to provide opportunities and resources for my students to discover or construct concepts for themselves."	**VS.**	"That's all nice, but students really won't learn the subject unless you go over the material in a structured way. It's my job to explain, to show students how to do the work, and to assign specific practice."

Definitely Prefer	Tend to Prefer	Cannot Decide	Tend to Prefer	Definitely Prefer

"It is a good idea to have all sorts of activities going on in the classroom. Some students might produce a scene from a play they read. Others might create a miniature version of the set. It's hard to get the logistics right, but the successes are so much more important than the failures."	**VS.**	"It's more practical to give the whole class the same assignment, one that has clear directions, and one that can be done in short intervals that match students' attention spans and the daily class schedule."

Definitely Prefer	Tend to Prefer	Cannot Decide	Tend to Prefer	Definitely Prefer

"The most important part of instruction is that it encourage 'sense-making' or thinking among students. Content is secondary."	**VS.**	"The most important part of instruction is the content of the curriculum. That content is the community's judgment about what children need to be able to know and do."

Definitely Prefer	Tend to Prefer	Cannot Decide	Tend to Prefer	Definitely Prefer

"It is critical for students to become interested in doing academic work—interest and effort are more important than the particular subject matter they are working on."	**VS.**	"While student motivation is certainly useful, it should not drive what students study. It is more important that students learn the history, science, math, and language skills in their textbooks."

Definitely Prefer	Tend to Prefer	Cannot Decide	Tend to Prefer	Definitely Prefer

Figure 3.1 Philosophical assessment

Source: Adapted from Jason L. Ravitz, Henry Jay Becker, and Yan Tien Wong. *Constructivist-Compatible Beliefs and Practices Among U.S. Teachers*. Center for Research on Information Technology and Organizations, University of California, Irvine; and University of Minnesota, July 2000.

Beliefs about Teaching and Learning

One of the most important components of your educational philosophy is how you view teaching and learning. In other words, what is a teacher's primary role? Is the teacher a subject-matter expert who can efficiently and effectively impart knowledge to students? Is he or she a helpful adult who establishes caring relationships with students and nurtures their growth in needed areas? Or is the teacher a skilled technician who can manage the learning of many students at once?

Some teachers emphasize individual student experiences and cognitions. Others stress students' behaviour. Learning, according to the first viewpoint, is seen as the changes in thoughts or actions that result from personal experience; that is, learning is largely the result of internal forces within the individual. In contrast, the other view defines learning as the associations between various stimuli and responses. Here, learning results from forces that are external to the individual.

Beliefs about Students

Your beliefs about students will have a great influence on how you teach. Every teacher formulates an image in her or his mind of what students are like—their dispositions, skills, motivation levels, and expectations. What you believe students are like is based on your unique life experiences, particularly your observations of young people and your knowledge of human growth and development.

As a teacher, you should guard against negative attitudes toward individual students or groups of students. While you cannot eliminate the prejudice, inter-group hostility, and racism that are found in society at large, you will have an obligation to see that your actions in the classroom do not convey negative attitudes about students on the basis of factors such as gender, race, ethnicity, religion, sexual orientation, family lifestyle, manner of dress, language, or socioeconomic status.

Negative views of students may promote teacher–student relationships based on fear and coercion rather than on trust and helpfulness. A teacher with extremely positive views may risk not providing students with sufficient structure and direction and not communicating sufficiently high expectations. In the final analysis, the truly professional teacher—the one who has a carefully thought-out educational philosophy—recognizes that, although children differ in their predispositions to learning and growing, they all can learn.

Beliefs about Knowledge

How a teacher views knowledge is directly related to how she or he goes about teaching. If teachers view knowledge as the sum total of small pieces of subject matter or discrete facts, their students will most likely spend a great deal of time learning that information in a straightforward, rote manner.

Other teachers view knowledge more conceptually—that is, as consisting of big ideas that enable us to understand and influence our environment. Such teachers would want students to be able to explain how legislative decisions are made in provincial capitals, how an understanding of the eight parts of speech can empower the writer and vitalize one's writing, and how chemical elements are grouped according to their atomic numbers.

Finally, teachers differ in their beliefs as to whether students' increased understanding of their own experiences is a legitimate form of knowledge. Knowledge of self and of one's experiences in the world is not the same as knowledge about a particular subject; yet personal knowledge is essential for a full, satisfying life.

Beliefs about What Is Worth Knowing

Teachers have different ideas about what should be taught. Some believe it is most important that students learn the basic skills of reading, writing, and computation. These teachers believe that such skills are needed in order for students to be successful in their chosen occupations, and that it is the school's responsibility to prepare students for the world of work. Other teachers, however, believe that the most worthwhile content is to be found in the classics or the "great books." Through mastering noteworthy ideas in the sciences, in mathematics, in literature, and in history, such teachers believe that students will be well prepared to deal with the future. Still others are most concerned with students learning how to reason, how to communicate effectively, and how to solve problems. Students who master these cognitive processes will have learned how to learn—and this is the most realistic preparation for an unknown future. And, finally, some teachers are deeply concerned with developing the whole child and teaching students to become self-actualizing. Thus, the curriculum should be meaningful and contribute to the student's efforts to become a mature, self-possessed individual.

WHAT ARE THE BRANCHES OF PHILOSOPHY?

To provide you with further tools to formulate and clarify your educational philosophy, this section presents brief overviews of six areas of philosophy that are of central concern to teachers: metaphysics, epistemology, axiology, ethics, aesthetics, and logic. Each area focuses on some of the questions that have concerned the world's greatest philosophers for centuries: What is the nature of reality? What is the nature of knowledge? Is truth ever attainable? What values should one follow? What is good and what is evil? What is the nature of beauty and excellence? What processes of reasoning will yield consistently valid results?

Metaphysics

Metaphysics: a branch of philosophy concerned with the nature of reality.

Metaphysics is concerned with explaining, as rationally and as comprehensively as possible, the nature of reality (in contrast to how reality appears). What is reality? What is the world made of? These are metaphysical questions. Metaphysics is also concerned with the nature of being and explores questions such as: What does it mean to exist? What is humankind's place in the scheme of things? Metaphysical questions such as these are at the very heart of educational philosophy. As two educational philosophers put it, "Our ultimate preoccupation in educational theory is with the most primary of all philosophic problems: metaphysics, the study of ultimate reality" (Morris & Pai, 1994, p. 28).

Metaphysics has important implications for education because school curricula are based on what we know about reality. And what we know about reality is driven by the kinds of questions we ask about the world. In fact, any position regarding what schools should teach has behind it a particular view of reality—and a particular set of responses to metaphysical questions.

Epistemology

Epistemology: a branch of philosophy concerned with the nature of knowledge and what it means to know something.

The next major set of philosophical questions that concerns teachers can be classified as **epistemology**. These questions focus on knowledge: What knowledge is true? How does knowing take place? How do we know that we know? How do we decide between opposing views of knowledge? Is truth constant, or does it change from situation to situation? What knowledge is of most worth? How you answer the epistemological questions that confront all teachers will have significant implications for your teaching. First, you will need to determine what is true about the content you will teach; then you must decide on the most appropriate means of conveying this content to students. Even a casual consideration of epistemological questions reveals that there are many ways of knowing about the world, at least five of which are of interest to teachers:

1. *Knowing Based on Authority*—for example, knowledge from the sage, the poet, the expert, the ruler, the textbook, or the teacher

2. *Knowing Based on Divine Revelation*—for example, knowledge in the form of supernatural revelations from the sun god of early peoples, the many gods of the ancient Greeks, or the Judeo/Christian/Muslim god

3. *Knowing Based on Empiricism (Experience)*—for example, knowledge acquired through the senses, the informally gathered empirical data that direct most of our daily behaviour

4. *Knowing Based on Reason and Logical Analysis*—for example, knowledge inferred from the process of thinking logically

5. *Knowing Based on Intuition*—for example, knowledge arrived at without the use of rational thought

Axiology

The next set of philosophical problems concerns values. Teachers are concerned with values because "school is not a neutral activity. The very idea of schooling expresses a set of values. [We] educate and we are educated for some purpose we consider good. We teach what we think is a valuable set of ideas. How else could we construct education?" (Nelson, Carlson, & Palonsky, 2000, p. 304).

Among the axiological questions teachers must answer are: What values should teachers encourage students to adopt? What values raise us to our highest expression of humanity? What values are held by a truly educated person?

Axiology highlights the idea that the teacher has an interest not only in the quantity of knowledge that students acquire, but also in the quality of life that becomes possible because of that knowledge. Extensive knowledge may not benefit the individual if he or she is unable to put that knowledge to good use. This point raises additional questions: How do we define quality of life? What curricular experiences contribute most to quality of life? All teachers must deal with the issues raised by these questions.

Axiology: the study of values, including the identification of criteria for determining what is valuable.

Ethics   While axiology addresses the question "What is valuable?," **ethics** focuses on "What is good and evil, right and wrong, just and unjust?"

Knowledge of ethics can help a teacher solve many of the dilemmas that arise in the classroom. Frequently, teachers must take action in situations where they are unable to gather all the relevant facts and where no single course of action is totally right or wrong. For example, say a student whose previous work was above average plagiarizes a term paper: Should the teacher fail the student for the course if the example of swift, decisive punishment will likely prevent other students from plagiarizing? Or should the teacher, following her hunches about what would be in the student's long-term interest, have the student redo the term paper and risk the possibility that other students might get the mistaken notion that plagiarism has no negative consequences? Another ethical dilemma: Is an elementary mathematics teacher justified in trying to increase achievement for the whole class by separating two disruptive girls and placing one in a mathematics group beneath her level of ability?

Ethics: a branch of philosophy concerned with principles of conduct and determining what is good and evil, and right and wrong, in human behaviour.

Aesthetics   The branch of axiology known as **aesthetics** is concerned with values related to beauty and art. Although we expect that teachers of music, art, drama, literature, and writing regularly have students make judgments about the quality of art, we can easily overlook the role that aesthetics ought to play in all areas of the curriculum.

Aesthetics can also help a teacher increase his or her effectiveness. Teaching, because it may be viewed as a form of artistic expression, can be judged according to artistic standards of beauty and quality. In this regard, the teacher is an artist whose medium of expression is the spontaneous, unrehearsed, and creative encounter between teacher and student.

Aesthetics: the branch of axiology concerned with values related to beauty and art.

From an examination of this famous statue by Rodin, what might art teachers want their students to learn about aesthetics? How were aesthetic values reflected in the K–12 curricula you experienced?

Logic: a branch of philosophy concerned with the processes of reasoning and the identification of rules that will enable thinkers to reach valid conclusions.

Perennialism: a philosophical orientation that emphasizes the ideas contained in the great books and maintains that the true purpose of education is the discovery of the universal, or perennial, truths of life.

Logic **Logic** is the area of philosophy that deals with the process of reasoning and identifies rules that will enable the thinker to reach valid conclusions. The two kinds of logical thinking processes that teachers most frequently have students master are deductive and inductive thinking. The deductive approach requires the thinker to move from a general principle or proposition to a specific conclusion that is valid. By contrast, inductive reasoning moves from the specific to the general. Here, the student begins by examining particular examples that eventually lead to the acceptance of a general proposition. Inductive teaching is often referred to as discovery teaching—students discover, or create, their own knowledge of a topic.

Perhaps the best-known teacher to use the inductive approach to teaching was the Greek philosopher Socrates (ca. 470–399 BCE). His method of teaching, known today as the Socratic method, consisted of holding philosophical conversations (dialectics) with his pupils. The legacy of Socrates lives in all teachers who use his questioning strategies to encourage students to think for themselves.

WHAT ARE FIVE MODERN PHILOSOPHICAL ORIENTATIONS TO TEACHING?

Five major philosophical orientations to teaching have been developed in response to the branches of philosophy we have just examined. These orientations, or schools of thought, are perennialism, essentialism, progressivism, existentialism, and social reconstructionism. The following sections present a brief description of each of these orientations, beginning with those that are teacher-centred and ending with those that are student-centred (see Figure 3.2).

Perennialism

Perennialism, as the term implies, views truth as constant, or perennial. The aim of education, according to perennialist thinking, is to ensure that students acquire

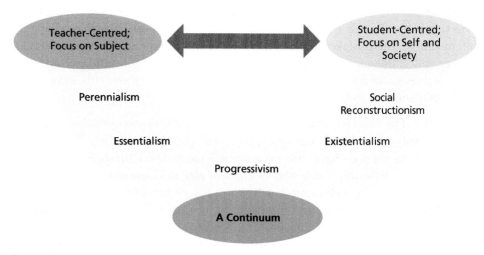

Figure 3.2 Five philosophical orientations to teaching

knowledge of unchanging principles or great ideas. Perennialists believe that the great ideas continue to have the most potential for solving the problems of any era.

Curricula, according to perennialists, should stress students' intellectual growth in the arts and sciences. To become "culturally literate," students should encounter in these areas the best, most significant works ever created. Thus a high school English teacher would require students to read Melville's *Moby-Dick* or any of Shakespeare's plays rather than a novel on the current bestseller list.

Similarly, science students would learn about the three laws of motion or the three laws of thermodynamics rather than build a model of the space shuttle.

Perennialist Educational Philosophers   Two of the best known advocates of the perennialist philosophy have been Robert Maynard Hutchins (1899–1977) and, more recently, Mortimer Adler, who together developed an undergraduate curriculum based on study of the great books and discussions of these classics in small seminars. Adler and Hutchins were instrumental in organizing the Great Books of the Western World curriculum. Through focusing study on over 100 enduring classics, from Plato to Einstein, the great books approach aims at the major perennialist goal of teaching students to become independent and critical thinkers. It is a demanding curriculum that focuses on the enduring disciplines of knowledge rather than on current events or student interests.

Essentialism

Essentialism, which has some similarities to perennialism, is a conservative philosophy of education. It was originally formulated by William C. Bagley (1874–1946), an American professor of education, as a criticism of progressive trends in schools. Essentialists believe that human culture has a core of common knowledge that schools are obligated to transmit to students in a systematic, disciplined manner. Unlike perennialists, who emphasize a set of external truths, essentialists stress what they believe to be the essential knowledge and skills (often termed "the basics") that productive members of our society need to know.

According to essentialist philosophy, schooling should be practical and provide children with sound instruction that prepares them to live life; schools should not try to influence or set social policies. Critics of essentialism, however, charge that such a tradition-bound orientation to schooling will indoctrinate students and rule out the possibility of change. Essentialists respond that, without an essentialist approach, students will be indoctrinated in humanistic and behavioural curricula that run counter to society's accepted standards and need for order.

Essentialism: formulated in part as a response to progressivism, this philosophical orientation holds that a core of common knowledge about the real world should be transmitted to students in a systematic, disciplined way.

Progressivism

Progressivism is based on the belief that education should be child-centred rather than teacher- or content-centred. The writing of John Dewey (1859–1952) in the 1920s and 1930s contributed a great deal to the spread of progressive ideas. Briefly, Deweyan progressivism is based on the following three central assumptions:

1. The content of the curriculum ought to be derived from students' interests rather than from the academic disciplines.

2. Effective teaching takes into account the whole child and his or her interests and needs in relation to cognitive, affective, and psychomotor areas.

3. Learning is essentially active rather than passive.

Progressivism: a philosophical orientation based on the belief that life is evolving in a positive direction, that people may be trusted to act in their own best interests, and that education should focus on the needs and interests of students.

Progressive Strategies   The progressive philosophy also contends that knowledge that is true in the present may not be true in the future. Hence, the best way to prepare students for an unknown future is to equip them with problem-solving strategies that will enable them to discover meaningful knowledge at various stages of their lives.

Educators with a progressive orientation give students a considerable amount of freedom in determining their school experiences. Contrary to the perceptions of many, though, progressive education does not mean that teachers do not provide structure or that students are free to do whatever they wish. Progressive teachers begin where students are and, through the daily give-and-take of the classroom, lead students to see that the subject to be learned can enhance their lives.

In a progressively oriented classroom, the teacher serves as a guide or resource person whose primary responsibility is to facilitate student learning. The teacher helps students learn what is important to them rather than passing on a set of so-called enduring truths. Students have many opportunities to work cooperatively in groups, often solving problems that the group, not the teacher, has identified as important.

Existentialism

Existential philosophy is unique in that it focuses on the experiences of the individual. Other philosophies are concerned with developing systems of thought for identifying and understanding what is common to all reality, human existence, and values. **Existentialism**, on the other hand, offers the individual a way of thinking about his or her own life, what has meaning for him or her, and what is true for him or her. In general, existentialism emphasizes creative choice, the subjectivity of human experiences, and concrete acts of human existence over any rational scheme for human nature or reality.

Life, according to existential thought, has no meaning, and the universe is indifferent to the situation humankind finds itself in. Moreover, "existentialists [believe] that too many people wrongly emphasize the optimistic, the good, and the beautiful—all of which create a false impression of existence" (Ozmon & Craver, 1999, p. 253). With the freedom we have, however, each individual must commit him- or herself to assign meaning to his or her own life. As Maxine Greene, an eminent philosopher of education whose work is based on existentialism, states, "We have to know about our lives, clarify our situations, if we are to understand the world from our shared standpoints . . ." (1995, p. 21). The human enterprise that can be most helpful in promoting this personal quest for meaning is the educative process. Teachers, therefore, must allow students freedom of choice and provide them with experiences that will help them find the meaning of their lives. This approach, contrary to the belief of many, does not mean that students may do whatever they please; logic indicates that freedom has rules, and respect for the freedom of others is essential.

Existentialists judge the curriculum according to whether it contributes to the individual's quest for meaning and results in a high level of personal awareness. The ideal curriculum is one that provides students with extensive individual freedom and requires them to ask their own questions, to conduct their own inquiries, and to draw their own conclusions.

Social Reconstructionism

As the name implies, **social reconstructionism** holds that schools should take the lead in changing or reconstructing society. Theodore Brameld (1904–1987) acknowledged as the founder of social reconstructionism, based his philosophy on two fundamental premises about the post–World War II era: (1) We live in a period of great crisis, most evident in the fact that humans now have the capability of destroying civilization overnight; and (2) humankind also has the intellectual, technological, and moral potential to create a world civilization of "abundance, health, and humane capacity" (Brameld, 1959, p. 19). In this time of great need, then, social reconstructionists like Yuliya,

Existentialism: a philosophical orientation that emphasizes the individual's experiences and maintains that each individual must determine his or her own meaning of existence.

Social reconstructionism: a philosophical orientation based on the belief that social problems can be solved by changing, or *reconstructing,* society.

whom we met in this chapter's opening scenario, believe that schools should become the primary agent for planning and directing social change. Schools should not only transmit knowledge about the existing social order; they should seek to reconstruct it as well.

Social Reconstructionism and Progressivism   Social reconstructionism has clear ties to progressive educational philosophy. Both provide opportunities for extensive interactions between teacher and students and among students themselves. Furthermore, both place a premium on bringing the community, if not the entire world, into the classroom. Student experiences often include field trips, community-based projects of various sorts, and opportunities to interact with people beyond the four walls of the classroom.

According to Brameld and social reconstructionists such as George Counts, who wrote *Dare the School Build a New Social Order?* (1932), the educative process should provide students with methods for dealing with the significant crises that confront the world: war, economic depression, international terrorism, hunger, inflation, and ever-accelerating technological advances. The logical outcome of such education would be the eventual realization of a worldwide democracy (Brameld, 1956). Unless we actively seek to create this kind of world through the intelligent application of present knowledge, we run the risk that the destructive forces of the world will determine the conditions under which humans will live in the future.

Another of the important contributors to the reconstructivist viewpoint is Paulo Freire, founder of the **critical pedagogy** school of educational philosophy. Freire strongly recommended a teaching approach that assists students in questioning and challenging commonly accepted beliefs and practices. He was very concerned with **praxis**—informed action based on specific values—and believed that students would eventually reach a point of revelation where, recognizing their society as oppressive and deeply problematic, they would work toward bringing about positive change. Freire also believed that true education requires a mutually respectful dialogue among individuals and that people work positively with one another. Too much teaching, he argued, was like a form of banking with the educator making deposits in the heads of students (Freire, 2007).

Critical pedagogy: educational theory and teaching and learning practices designed to raise students' critical awareness regarding oppressive social conditions.

Praxis: practical application or exercise of an art, science, skill, or branch of learning.

WHAT PSYCHOLOGICAL ORIENTATIONS HAVE INFLUENCED TEACHING PHILOSOPHIES?

In addition to these five philosophical orientations to teaching, several schools of psychological thought have also formed the basis for teaching philosophies. These psychological theories are comprehensive world views that serve as the basis for the way many teachers approach teaching practice. Psychological orientations to teaching are concerned primarily with understanding the conditions that are associated with effective learning. In other words, what motivates students to learn? What environments are most conducive to learning? Chief among the psychological orientations that have influenced teaching philosophies are humanistic psychology, behaviourism, and constructivism.

Humanistic Psychology

Humanistic psychology emphasizes personal freedom, choice, awareness, and personal responsibility. As the term implies, it also focuses on the achievements, motivations, feelings, actions, and needs of human beings. The goal of education, according to this orientation, is individual self-actualization.

Humanistic psychology: an orientation to human behaviour that emphasizes personal freedom, choice, awareness, and personal responsibility.

Humanism: a philosophy based on the belief that individuals control their own destinies through the application of their intelligence and learning.

Humanistic psychology is derived from the philosophy of **humanism**, which developed during the European Renaissance and Protestant Reformation and is based on the belief that individuals control their own destinies through the application of their intelligence and learning. People "make themselves." The term *secular humanism* refers to the closely related belief that the conditions of human existence relate to human nature and human actions rather than to predestination or divine intervention.

In the 1950s and 1960s, humanistic psychology became the basis of educational reforms that sought to enhance students' achievement of their full potential through self-actualization (Maslow, 1954, 1962; Rogers, 1961). According to this psychological orientation, teachers should not force students to learn; instead, they should create a climate of trust and respect that allows students to decide what and how they learn, to question authority, and to take initiative in "making themselves." Teachers should be what noted psychologist Carl Rogers called "facilitators," and the classroom should be a place "in which curiosity and the natural desire to learn can be nourished and enhanced" (1982, p. 31). Through their nonjudgmental understanding of students, humanistic teachers encourage students to learn and grow.

Behaviourism

Behaviourism: a philosophical orientation based on behaviouristic psychology that maintains that environmental factors shape people's behaviour.

Behaviourism is based on the principle that desirable human behaviour can be the product of design rather than accident. According to behaviourists, it is an illusion that humans have a free will. Although we may act as if we are free, our behaviour is really determined by forces in the environment that shape our behaviour. "We are what we are and we do what we do, not because of any mysterious power of human volition, but because outside forces over which we lack any semblance of control have us caught in an inflexible web. Whatever else we may be, we are not the captains of our fate or the masters of our soul" (Power, 1982, p. 168).

Founders of Behaviouristic Psychology   John B. Watson (1878–1958) was the principal originator of behaviouristic psychology, and B. F. Skinner (1904–1990) its best-known promoter. Watson first claimed that human behaviour consisted of specific stimuli that resulted in certain responses. In part, he based this new conception of learning on the classic experiment conducted by Russian psychologist Ivan Pavlov (1849–1936). Pavlov had noticed that a dog he was working with would salivate when it was about to be given food. By introducing the sound of a bell when food was offered and repeating this several times, Pavlov discovered that the sound of the bell alone (a conditioned stimulus) would make the dog salivate (a conditioned response). Watson came to believe that all learning conformed to this basic stimulus–response model (now termed classical or type S conditioning).

Skinner went beyond Watson's basic stimulus–response model and developed a more comprehensive view of conditioning known as operant (or type R) conditioning. Operant conditioning is based on the idea that satisfying responses are conditioned and unsatisfying ones are not. In other words, "The things we call pleasant have an energizing or strengthening effect on our behaviour" (Skinner, 1972, p. 74). Thus, the teacher can create learners who exhibit desired behaviours by following four steps:

1. Identify desired behaviours in concrete (observable and measurable) terms.

2. Establish a procedure for recording specific behaviours and counting their frequencies.

3. For each behaviour, identify an appropriate reinforcer.

4. Ensure that students receive the reinforcer as soon as possible after displaying a desired behaviour.

Constructivism

In contrast to behaviourism, **constructivism** focuses on processes of learning rather than on learning behaviour. According to constructivism, students use cognitive processes to construct understanding of the material to be learned—in contrast to the view that they receive information transmitted by the teacher. Constructivist approaches support student-centred rather than teacher-centred curricula and instructions. The student is the key to learning.

Unlike behaviourists who concentrate directly on observable behaviour, constructivists focus on the mental processes and strategies that students use to learn. Our understanding of learning has been extended as a result of advances in **cognitive science**—the study of the mental processes students use in thinking and remembering. By drawing from research in linguistics, psychology, anthropology, neurophysiology, and computer science, cognitive scientists are developing new models for how people think and learn.

Teachers who base classroom activities on constructivism know that learning is an active, meaning-making process, and that learners are not passive recipients of information. In fact, students are continually involved in making sense out of activities around them. Thus the teacher must understand students' understanding and realize that students' learning is influenced by prior knowledge, experience, attitudes, and social interactions.

Constructivism: a psychological orientation that views learning as an active process in which learners *construct* understanding of the material they learn—in contrast to the view that teachers transmit academic content to students in small segments.

Cognitive science: the study of the learning process that focuses on how individuals manipulate symbols and process information.

HOW CAN YOU DEVELOP YOUR EDUCATIONAL PHILOSOPHY?

As you read the preceding brief descriptions of five educational philosophies and three psychological orientations to teaching, perhaps you felt that no single philosophy fit perfectly with your image of the kind of teacher you want to become. Or there may have been some element of each approach that seemed compatible with your own emerging philosophy of education. In either case, don't feel that you need to identify a single educational philosophy around which you will build your teaching career. In reality, few teachers follow only one philosophical stance. Rather, most have an eclectic position based on strands taken from the various branches of educational philosophy.

These children are active learners in a real or relevant context, and they are constructing their own meanings through direct experience. How might this lesson be seen as an eclectic blend of progressive, existential, and constructivist ideals?

Hurst Photo/Shutterstock

Creative studio/sfu

Kieran Egan is interested in engaging children's and teachers' imaginations to make what is taught and learned

"vivid and meaningful." Toward this end, he has developed the Learning in Depth program:

> "Learning in Depth" is a simple though radical innovation in curriculum and instruction designed to ensure that all students become experts about something during their school years. Each child is given a particular topic to learn about through her or his whole school career, in addition to the usual curriculum, and builds a personal portfolio on the topic. To the surprise of many, children usually take to the program with great enthusiasm, and within a few months LiD begins to transform their experience as learners. The program usually takes about an hour a week, with the students working outside school time increasingly. (Retrieved from http://ierg.ca/LID)

Vincent Van Gogh once said:

> If one is master of one thing and understands one thing well, one has, at the same time, insight into and understanding of many things.

As you study to become a teacher, select an education topic of personal interest to study in depth. The skills, knowledge, and attitudes that you will develop as you immerse yourself deeply in learning will serve you well in your professional development. The experience may also serve as a model for creating similar experiences for your students.

An important part of the process of developing your educational philosophy is putting it into practice, and critically reflecting on the dialectic relationship between your beliefs and your practice. Your practice will improve over time, and move closer to your beliefs. At the same time, your practice will challenge and change some of your beliefs.

The self-knowledge you glean from the philosophical constructs presented in the first half of this chapter will provide a useful framework for studying the six periods in the historical development of schools that follow. For example, you will be able to see how philosophical orientations to education waxed and waned during each period—whether it was the perennialism and essentialism that characterized colonial schools, the progressivism of the 1920s and 1930s, the essentialism of the 1950s and 1980s, the humanism and social reconstructionism of the 1960s, or the constructivism of the past two decades.

WHAT CULTURAL TRADITIONS HAVE LED TO THE DEVELOPMENT OF THE CANADIAN EDUCATIONAL LANDSCAPE?

The Canadian educational landscape has roots that can be traced to four cultural traditions. The earliest schools of New France were, quite naturally, modelled after the educational practices common in France. Later, after the fall of Quebec and the rise to governmental supremacy of the British, practices common to English schools were introduced. Later still, after the American Revolution of 1776 and the resultant emigration of the Loyalists to Canada, educational practices based on the American model were given support. And finally, during the period 1760–1840, thousands of Scots immigrated to Canada, bringing with them their strong regard for schools based on democracy and merit. In areas of the country where only one cultural tradition was common, as in New Brunswick, where the Loyalists initially had the field to themselves, development of a coherent education system was accomplished with ease. However, in Nova Scotia, where the Scottish, English, and American traditions were all represented, several systems vied for supremacy, with the consequence that factionalism, tumult, and discord enriched the level of educational discourse.

The French Tradition

During the period 1650–1700, most adult citizens of New France—an area that extended from Cape Breton to the Great Lakes—had received their education in France. In the **French tradition**, the dominant educational philosophy was based on the traditions of the Roman Catholic Church. Elementary **parochial schools**, known as *petites écoles*, were relatively common in most areas of France. While there was a general belief among the upper classes that the children of the lower classes should be educated, their education was to deal with only the most rudimentary facts. Girls and boys attended **separate schools**, with the boys' education tending to be of a better quality. Instruction in the curriculum (catechism, singing, arithmetic, reading, writing, and grammar) was delivered by the parish priests or their assistants.

Funding for the support of the *petites écoles* was provided by the church and those parents who could afford to make contributions. Teacher colleges, also known as **normal schools**, were starting to appear, and several religious orders, most notably the Jesuits priests and the Ursuline nuns, were becoming involved in the education process. Secondary schools, while not common, did exist and were almost exclusively the responsibility of specific religious orders.

French tradition: based on church-controlled schools with classes often taught by members of the clergy.

Parochial schools: schools founded on religious beliefs.

Petites écoles: early schools within the French tradition that provided a rudimentary education.

Separate schools: publicly funded schools based on religion or language.

Normal schools: schools that focused on the preparation of teachers.

The English Tradition

During the period 1760–1840, the English school system emerged. The **English tradition** reflected the beliefs and attitudes of the upper classes and had two salient characteristics. First, education was primarily a responsibility of the church rather than the state; second, education was a function of class rather than merit. Education for the lower classes was primarily provided by the Church of England, although other organizations did have some modest involvement. While charitable groups sometimes provided schooling for the poor, some children attended **dame-schools** run by widows and housewives, who taught within their own homes and collected small fees from their students' parents. At the other end of the educational spectrum were the "public" schools reserved for the privileged and the wealthy.

There were various religious groups who wanted to improve the quality of education given to the lower classes—most notably the Puritans, who eventually decamped to the American colonies. The group with the most outstanding success, however, was the Society for the Propagation of the Gospel in Foreign Parts (SPG). While its main goal was the teaching of the Bible for the benefit of overseas British settlers, the SPG soon involved itself with the development of schools in Canada and other parts of the British Empire.

English tradition: a model of education based on church control, class, and separate schools for boys and girls.

Dame-schools: colonial schools, usually held in the homes of widows or housewives, for teaching children basic reading, writing, and mathematical skills.

The American Tradition

The United States' education system, the **American tradition**, had its primary roots in English culture. The settlers initially tried to develop a system of schooling that

American tradition: an approach to education that the frontier experience of the United States modified to make it more practical than the British model upon which it was originally based.

paralleled the British two-track system. If students from the lower classes attended school at all, it was at the elementary level for the purpose of studying an essentialist curriculum of reading, writing, and computation and receiving religious instruction. Students from the upper classes had the opportunity to attend Latin grammar schools, where they were given a college-preparatory education that focused on subjects such as Latin and Greek classics. Above all, the American colonial curriculum stressed religious objectives. Generally, no distinction was made between secular and religious life in the colonies. The religious motives that impelled the Puritans to endure the hardships of settling in a new land were reflected in the schools' curricula. The primary objective of elementary schooling was to learn to read so that one might read the Bible and religious catechisms and thereby achieve salvation.

In the period immediately following the American Revolution of 1776, thousands of Loyalists fled to Canada. However, because they had a strong distrust of all things Republican, and because they were staunchly loyal to Britain, the Loyalists tended to reinforce the provincial elites, who were predominantly Anglicans in control of government counsels. In reality, the American influence on early Canadian education was essentially a modified, somewhat more practical, version of the English influence. During the many nineteenth-century battles fought for control of Canadian schools, the Loyalists usually supported the entrenched "family compacts" that favoured the English educational tradition. It was a struggle they were destined to lose.

The Scottish Tradition

Scottish tradition: offered both elementary and secondary education to boys and girls in combined classes regardless of their social class.

At the time of the great Scottish migration (1760–1840), the **Scottish tradition** of education, based on a combination of parish and burgh (town) schools, had several characteristics that led to its easy transference to the New World. The first of these characteristics was of primary importance; it resulted in the Scots having an educational impact that far outweighed their actual numbers as a percentage of the Canadian population. In Scotland, almost every child attended a school, which frequently had students from all ranks of society. The class-based system of education found in England was absent. In addition, both male and female students often attended the same school, and had done so for hundreds of years. The practice of having separate schools for boys and girls, a dominant characteristic of the French educational tradition, was absent. Additionally, many Scottish schools provided education at both the elementary and secondary levels. There was no great divide between the two. Rather than placing a strong emphasis on the classics as the foundation of the curriculum, subjects such as science and art were also taught. In combination with its strong democratic tradition, the characteristics of the Scottish education system would flourish in Canada's frontier environment.

WHAT WERE TEACHING AND SCHOOLS LIKE IN CANADA PRIOR TO 1875?

Canada can be roughly divided into five geographic regions: Atlantic Canada, Quebec, Ontario, the West, and the North. As each region was settled at a different time by immigrants from a variety of cultural, linguistic, and religious backgrounds, it is not surprising that the school systems that evolved had their own individual characteristics. In the early years, almost all schooling was controlled by religious authorities. However, as Canada's population increased in size, and as economic development became more important to the life of the citizenry, the state began to take a greater interest in educational matters. This increased interest led to the two great educational questions of the eighteenth and nineteenth centuries: Who would control the schools? Who would pay for their maintenance and operation? These questions were largely answered by 1875—but how they were answered differed from one geographic region to another.

Quebec

1608–1760 The earliest Quebec schools were modelled exactly after the *petites écoles* of the mother country. There were separate schools for girls and boys with instruction usually provided by members of religious orders. However, lay teachers who met the moral and competency requirements of the clergy were present in small numbers. Student attendance (by those who had access to a school) varied, and most students left soon after learning the rudiments of reading, writing, and arithmetic. Financial support for the *petites écoles* was provided by the church, by the students' parents, and, in some cases, by the king of France. If an educational issue required resolution, an appeal was made to the bishop of Quebec. It was not until after 1760 that any civil laws concerning the schools came into existence.

From its earliest days until 1760, the pattern of education in New France underwent little change. The various religious societies continued to provide a modest degree of schooling to those children who lived in or near urban communities; children in rural areas had very limited access to schools and many received no education of any kind. However, the ecclesiastical school system established by the religious orders formed the basis for the system that would evolve after the start of British rule.

1760–1875 During the first 30 years of British rule, Protestant immigrants from England, Scotland, Ireland, and other British colonies settled in the urban areas of Quebec. During this period, a few Anglo-Protestant schools were established through the initiative of interested clergy and lay persons. Nothing resembling a coherent school system for either the English-speaking or French-speaking citizens was evident. Education was still an essentially private or church-sponsored enterprise.

The first tentative steps toward the establishment of a centralized school system took place in the last 10 years of the eighteenth century, when citizens of all religious groups recognized that economic and social development required a sound education system. But there were some immediate problems. Should the schools be English or French, Protestant or Roman Catholic? Should the state or the church control the schools? And, most importantly, who should pay for the maintenance and operation of the education system that would be established? It would take an additional 75 years of acrimonious political and social debate before these questions were answered.

By 1875, all the elements of a systematic school system were in place. In actuality, there were two distinct and totally separate school systems: one for Protestants and one for Roman Catholics. While religious groups would continue to operate their schools, it would be the state, via a centralized bureaucracy, that would establish teaching standards, set curriculum, and, through taxation based on local assessment, pay for school maintenance and teacher salaries. The state would also provide grants for the establishment of normal schools for the training of teachers. By the late 1850s, three such schools had been successfully established. While this separate system of schools was a political solution acceptable to both religious groups, it created a divide between them that lasted well into the twentieth century.

Atlantic Canada

Despite their geographical proximity, the school systems that developed in the four Atlantic provinces were the result of significantly different influences. During the formative years of its education system, Nova Scotia had a population that was predominantly Scottish in origin, whereas New Brunswick was composed primarily of

Jean-Baptiste Meilleur, first superintendent of education in Lower Canada (1842–1855)

Sir John William Dawson, first superintendent of education in Nova Scotia (1850–1853) and later president of McGill University (1855–1893)

Loyalists. Both Prince Edward Island and Newfoundland had populations that were much more varied. The degree of difficulty each province would experience in its drive to establish a comprehensive school system became a function of the cultural traditions within each, and of how these cultural traditions interacted.

Nova Scotia

After the expulsion of the Acadians in 1755, 8000 New England citizens (traditionally referred to as the Planters) moved to Nova Scotia to take over the vacant farm lands. Prior to the Planters' arrival, most of the schools in existence were administered by the Church of England's Society for the Propagation of the Bible (SPG). In an effort to keep the Planters from establishing their own schools, the SPG had the House of Assembly pass *An Act Concerning Schools and Schoolmasters* in 1766. This act, designed to protect the Church of England's monopoly over education, ironically marked the first official recognition that education was actually the responsibility of the state.

In the 10 years following the 1776 American War of Independence, the Loyalists formed a second, larger wave of American immigrants to Nova Scotia. At approximately the same time, an even larger group of Scottish settlers started their migration to the province. The Scots arrived in such numbers that they quickly became the largest, and eventually most influential, faction within the colony.

By 1800, there was recognition that an effective school system was needed for the ever-expanding population. The questions that needed to be answered were somewhat simple in nature: Should the state or the Church of England control the schools? Who should pay for the maintenance and operation of the education system? The numerical strength of the Scots provided the answers. By 1875, after the usual series of acrimonious debates in the legislature, there was agreement that the state would be responsible for the governance and maintenance of schools, and that financial support would be provided through taxation based on local assessment.

New Brunswick

Prior to 1783, New Brunswick was sparsely settled. There were pockets of Acadians who had fled there as a result of their expulsion from Nova Scotia, and a few New England Planters were also present in small numbers. Therefore, when large numbers of Loyalists arrived in the 1775–1785 period, they quickly became the dominant group within the colony. The school system envisaged by the Loyalists, most of whom were Anglican, was one in which church and state would work together in support of the aristocratic English tradition. Initially, this is what took place. The SPG had the full support of the Executive Council of the legislature, and grammar schools and other institutions of higher learning had their enrolments limited to members of the Anglican Church.

Unfortunately for the Loyalists, settlers from other areas of the world began to arrive in large numbers during the period 1815–1825. In particular, there was a great influx of immigrants from Ireland. Scots, business people from other parts of the British Empire, and settlers from non-Anglican denominations were also becoming increasingly common. After years of confused and rancorous debate among the various factions, the situation began to improve. In 1871, the *Common School Act* made provision for free, nonsectarian schools supported by taxation based on local assessment.

Prince Edward Island

The early history of education in Prince Edward Island is one of unrelenting sectarian strife. Acadians missed by the expulsion formed a small part of the population, but there were also Loyalists, Irish, Roman Catholic and Protestant Scots, and English immigrants. In the early part of the 1800s, a small number of private schools were in existence. In general, they were operated by itinerant schoolmasters who made their services available to the residents of PEI's ethnic communities.

In 1800, there were fewer than 5000 people in the colony; that number had grown to 70 000 by 1855. Roman Catholics comprised approximately 40 percent of the population, whereas various Protestant denominations formed the remainder. It was this approximate balance between the two religious groups that was at the heart of the sectarian warfare and dominated discussion in the provincial legislature. The fundamental issue upon which the two groups could not agree concerned authorization of the Bible for use in PEI public schools. Both groups recognized the need for establishing a comprehensive system of education, but the "Bible Question" hindered progress until the *Public School Act* was passed in 1873. This act established the office of Superintendent of Education; decreed that taxation based on local assessment would support free, nondenominational schools; and created an improved Board of Education for administration of the new system of schooling.

Newfoundland and Labrador   While Prince Edward Island experienced a great deal of sectarian strife during its journey toward a system of publicly funded, nonsectarian schools, the situation in Newfoundland was more protracted and bitter, by several orders of magnitude. The roots of Newfoundland's education system are similar to the roots of other systems in Canada. The first schools were established and operated by the SPG. Roman Catholics, Methodists, and other Protestant groups established schools in various communities, and private schools also sprang up. However, for reasons deeply locked in Newfoundland's cultural history, the state's battle for free, nondenominational schools was lost. In 1874, the legislature gave its formal approval to fund all the parochial schools that had been founded. Separate schools for everyone became part of the established educational order. Of all the British North American colonies, Newfoundland was the only one to develop such a unique educational model. It wasn't until 1998 that the system of parochial schools was discontinued.

Labrador, with its harsh climate and very scattered and nomadic Inuit population, also had a church-based system of schooling. In the second half of the 1700s, the

⫸ The Little Red Schoolhouse

During the early days of Canadian education, any available room in a church, tavern, or public meeting house was pressed into service as a school. If a community did go to the trouble and expense of building a school, the structure was usually made of five-metre long, rough-cut logs. In very few instances was it painted red. The ceiling was relatively low and a simple fireplace was the only source of heat. Students were required to supply the firewood. During the winter months, those who sat farthest from the fireplace were often uncomfortably cold.

The older students sat on simple benches arranged around three of the walls. In some cases, these benches were accompanied by crude desks. Arranged around the centre of the room were more deskless, backless benches for the younger children. Other than a desk for the teacher, the room was almost completely empty. There were no blackboards, no maps, no reference books, and no teaching aids. Quill pens were common, however, and students would practise their writing skills for as long as two hours each day. In cases where paper was scarce, birch bark was used. Writing slates, which the students would often "erase" by spitting and wiping, became relatively common after 1825.

Textbooks were in very short supply, and the modern concept of a "class set" was unknown. Students would bring to school any textbook they might have been able to buy or borrow. Those who could not supply a textbook shared with students who could. The few textbooks that were available were often of American origin, much to the annoyance of the Loyalist faction.

The teaching strategies were simple. Students were often required to memorize and then recite material assigned to them by the teacher. Instruction of groups within the school was rare. Most often, the teacher dealt with individual students.

The strap was freely used to maintain discipline, and, depending on the seriousness of the offence, a specific number of lashes was administered to the offender. Arriving at school with dirty hands might result in two lashes, and fighting might result in five; swearing or playing cards at school would engender even more.

The teacher was usually an unmarried young woman who, if she married and became pregnant, would be expected to resign her position. The administration of the school was usually in the hands of three male trustees—some of whom might be illiterate.

Church of the United Brethren (also known as the Moravian Church) took an interest in converting and educating the indigenous Inuit population. The Moravians carried out their work with skill and energy and helped to make their Inuit students literate in their own language. Unlike Newfoundland, where numerous religious groups vied for the souls and minds of the citizens, the Moravians carried out their work without competition from any other church.

Ontario

Prior to the arrival of approximately 6000 Loyalists in 1884–1886, Upper Canada (Ontario) had very few settlers. While most of the new Loyalist settlers were farmers, among them were small numbers of well-educated individuals with a high regard for good schooling. These Loyalists wanted their children to have access to American grammar (secondary) schools in addition to the locally supported nondenominational schools. Their educational concerns received support from a second wave of American settlers who, enticed by offers of free land grants, arrived in large numbers during the 20 years preceding the War of 1812. However, although these two groups of American settlers constituted a majority of the population, the government was primarily in the hands of British officials, who believed that the state should control education while leaving its administration to Church of England officials. As most of the population had religious affiliations that were non-Anglican, it is not surprising that a struggle between the English and American traditions developed.

In 1816, the passage of the *Common School Act* suggested that free schools might come into existence with a minimum of difficulty. This act, which permitted any community with sufficient resources to establish a public school, toward which the government would make an annual grant for a teacher's salary, was undermined by the 1820 *Common School Act*, which reduced the government grant. It effectively neutralized the act of 1816 and established a pattern that would last for another 25 years, where acts regarding schools would be passed and later rescinded or rendered irrelevant by later acts. While Upper Canada would not be spared the legislative struggles that had dogged the other Canadian provinces, it did continue to make incremental steps toward a comprehensive education system. By the early 1840s, progress toward a centralized bureaucracy had been made, and provisions for a normal school had been put in place. Local assessment in support of schools was effectively introduced in

The District School in Cornwall, Ontario, ca. 1810

1846, and, with the passing of the *School Act* in 1843, members of religious groups were permitted to operate their own schools. Interestingly, the impetus for separate schools came not from Roman Catholics but from adherents of the Church of England and other Protestant groups. Leading the fight to keep schools under church influence was Right Rev. Dr. John Strachan, a staunch supporter of the British monarchy and the Church of England. One of his major objectives, in an effort to avoid what he considered to be the tainted influence of American settlers, was to keep the schools under the control of the Church of England. Opposing him was Egerton Ryerson, an individual who was dismayed at the dismal shape of Upper Canadian schooling. Promoted to the office of Chief Superintendent of Schools in 1846, Ryerson soon persuaded the government to undertake responsibility for education. The result was common schools publicly supported by government grants whenever 20 students could be gathered together. Other advances soon followed, and, by the early 1870s, the major features common to Ontario's present system of schooling had been established.

The West of Canada

The Prairies   Until 1869, western Canada was under the control of the Hudson Bay Company, which had the fur trade as its exclusive interest. Prior to 1810, most of those living in what would eventually become Manitoba, Saskatchewan, and Alberta were either First Nations peoples or French-speaking Catholic Métis. However, in 1811, Thomas Douglas, the fifth Earl of Selkirk, made the first concerted effort to colonize this area. He wanted to provide relief to distressed Scottish farmers while also providing the Hudson Bay Company with a source of food and labour. To this end, he established the agriculturally based Red River Settlement near present-day Winnipeg. Early attempts to provide the settlers with a school were unsuccessful, and it would be almost 40 years before a Presbyterian school was established. In the interim, schools that did exist for the French-speaking population were run by Roman Catholic priests or their French-Canadian lay recruits. By 1820, Roman Catholics had access to three schools, while Protestants had access to none.

Between 1820 and 1870, the population of the Prairies experienced a slow but steady growth and a concurrent increase in the number of schools (see Figure 3.3). In general, the schools that were established during this period were of a sectarian nature. By 1840, the Roman Catholics and Methodists were active in what is presently northern Alberta. By the late 1860s, Saskatchewan also had a small number of Protestant schools. While both Saskatchewan and Alberta recognized separate schools based on religious affiliation, Manitoba followed a separate path.

With the completion of the Canadian National Railway in 1885, access to settlement areas in western Canada became much easier. In the period from 1886 to 1914, over 750 000 immigrants entered Canada from the United States, Sweden, Germany, Norway, Iceland, Hungary, and Ukraine. Because many of the new immigrants spoke little or no English, attempts to assimilate them were concentrated on their second-generation children, who were expected to have their schooling conducted only in English. Objections to this practice were raised by many of the newcomers—in particular the Ukrainians who settled in Manitoba, who wished to preserve their language and culture. These objections led in turn to the Rutharian issue, also known as the "Manitoba School Question." In 1897, a compromise that satisfied neither side was reached. Officially termed the Laurier-Greenway Agreement, a uniform, nondenominational school system with English as the formal language of instruction was to be imposed. However, if the parents of 10 students at a school requested that their children be instructed in

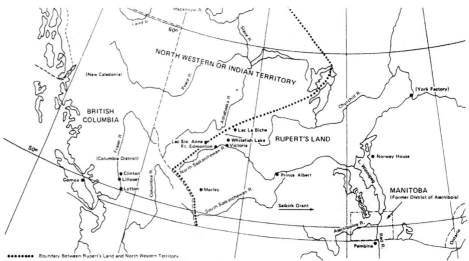

●●●●●●● Boundary Between Rupert's Land and North Western Territory
Centres Where Schools Were Established in Western Canada Before 1873

Figure 3.3 Centres where Western schools were established prior to 1873

Source: G. F. Stanley, *The Birth of Western Canada: The Riel Rebellions.* Reprinted with permission from the University of Toronto Press.

a language other than English, the school was to make the necessary accommodations. In effect, Manitoba developed Canada's only multilingual education system.

British Columbia   Like the Prairies, British Columbia was initially under the control of the Hudson Bay Company. Prior to 1858, the nonindigenous population was less than 1000. As a result, the first British Columbia school was not established until 1849. Nine years later, the gold rush of 1858 brought about dramatic changes. Thousands of gold seekers from all parts of the world descended on the territory and brought an end to the influence of the Hudson Bay Company. The new arrivals, who were of numerous cultural and ethnic backgrounds, immediately began to agitate for schools that were both nondenominational and free. Unlike other areas of Canada, where protracted battles for control of the schools had been waged by primarily sectarian interests, the conflict in B.C. was remarkably brief. The *Common School Act* of 1865, supplemented by the common School Ordinance of 1869, decreed that B.C. schools would be both free and nonsectarian. The state was now firmly in control of the education system.

The Canadian North

Canada's northern educational history began in the nineteenth century with the missionary activities of both Protestant and Roman Catholic churches. The *North-West Territories Act* of 1875 and the *Yukon Act* of 1898 granted the territories authority over the education of non–First Nations school-age children. However, the reality was that not until 1950 did the territories have sufficient resources to support anything but the most rudimentary of school systems. What little financial assistance the territories could provide came in the form of variably sized grants based upon the number of students enrolled in a school.

The federal government, under the provisions of the *British North America Act* and the *Indian Act*, became responsible for the education of First Peoples. This division of educational responsibilities was to have serious consequences for First Nations children. The federal government of the early twentieth century had no real interest in educating First Nations children and simply passed its educational responsibilities over to the churches. The result was the most horrific episode in Canadian educational history: the establishment by the churches of the now infamous residential schools.

Confederation and the *British North America Act* of 1867

As Canada's colonial period came to an end, political figures from all parts of England's remaining North American provinces discussed a confederation that would bind them together as one nation. The **British North America Act (BNA Act)** of 1867 was the legal instrument used to set out the federal and provincial responsibilities of those provinces that wished to become part of this new country. Under Article 93 of the agreement, education was to be a provincial responsibility. Careful reading of Article 93 clearly indicates that the diverse school systems established in the various geographical areas of the country would not be threatened by the newly established federal government. Indeed, any separate school rights acquired by a minority group prior to 1867 were constitutionally guaranteed by the *BNA Act*. The act also placed Canada in a unique category: Today, it is one of the few developed countries in which there is no national system of education.

British North America Act (BNA Act): the act that established Canada as a nation and laid the framework for public institutions such as schools.

WHAT PATTERNS DEVELOPED IN CANADIAN EDUCATION FROM 1875 TO 1918?

In 1875, Canada's population was primarily rural. Most schools were relatively small, with most accurately representing the concept of the little red schoolhouse. The curriculum was simple and concentrated on the three R's (Reading, Writing, and Arithmetic). However, as Canada approached the twentieth century, the number of immigrants increased significantly, while industrialization and urbanization also began to place additional strains on every province's education system. The basic education provided by existing schools was becoming inadequate for the needs of a society that was slowly but certainly changing from a rural focus to an urban one. A result of this evolving demographic was a philosophical debate over the basic goals of education. Was the purpose of schools to help individuals read the Bible, do simple mathematical calculations, and write simple communications, or was the purpose to provide skilled workers who could meet the demands of commerce and industry?

While the roots of science and technical education can be traced back to the work of educators such as Sir John William Dawson, president of McGill University from 1855 to 1893, by the early twentieth century, science had become a significant component of provincial curricula. Technical education had also made significant inroads, and by 1918, it was available in most urban centres. However, while urban area schools were successfully making the transition to a more scientifically and technologically based curriculum, rural areas were experiencing serious educational distress. The Federal Census of 1871 indicated that almost 88 percent of Canada's population resided in rural areas, but the Census of 1911 indicated that rural populations had decreased to only 54 percent. Additionally, urban areas paid teachers salaries that were often twice as high as those available in rural communities. This led to most of the best qualified teachers moving to and remaining in urban centres. Rural groups, composed mainly of farmers, began to make demands for a more relevant curriculum, better teachers, and better educational opportunities for their children.

By the early 1900s, the demand for teachers had grown dramatically. An increasing number of women entered the teaching field at this time, beginning a trend often referred to as the "feminization of teaching." Female teachers were given less respect from the community than their male predecessors, though they were still more highly regarded than women who worked in factories or in the domestic sphere. In addition, they were expected to be of high moral character. They were subjected to a level of public scrutiny hard to imagine today.

Attempts by education officials to meet the demands of their rural citizens encountered varying degrees of success. Perhaps the most successful of these efforts was the consolidation of small rural school districts into larger ones, a process that, to some degree, is still taking place as Canada's rural population continues to shrink. Because of their larger student bodies, consolidated schools could provide greater opportunities for curriculum diversity. However, rural education still faced many challenges. The Prairie provinces, for example, had experienced a large influx of settlers from eastern and central Europe. Some of these settlers wanted their children to be at home working the land rather than at school. Others wanted their children educated in their native tongue; but as there were few teachers with the linguistic knowledge to provide such a service, English became the language of instruction.

At the conclusion of World War I in 1918, the Canadian education system was taking on the basic elements of its present form. All provinces had developed centralized educational bureaucracies. Curricular issues around the preparation of students for an industrial, urban-focused life were being discussed and implemented; secondary schools were becoming more prevalent; normal schools for the preparation of teachers were becoming more common; and, while some provinces had separate schools, these schools were publicly funded.

WHAT IS THE HISTORY OF SCHOOLING FOR FIRST NATIONS PEOPLES?

From the beginning, settlers' efforts to indoctrinate First Nations children with European values through education was a shameful exercise, undertaken to exterminate First Nations peoples by assimilation. The settlers and the clerics—first Roman Catholic, and later also Protestant—shared a common belief that the First Nations way of life was inferior in every way to their own.

However, as Barman, McCaskill, and Hebert point out in *Indian Education in Canada, Volume 1: The Legacy* (1986, pp. 2–4), there was much that was admirable about the education provided by First Nations for their children. They taught about the unity of all life, honourable conduct, family responsibilities, individual responsibility, the importance of sharing, self-reliance, and survival skills. Their history was transmitted through stories, myths, and legends.

Unfortunately for First Nations peoples, the colonial clerical and other designated educators were primarily interested in "civilizing" First Nations peoples by converting them to Christianity. Because First Nations languages, culture, and political structures were different and non-Christian, they were deemed barbaric, and thus worthy of eradication. This belief in First Nations inferiority was institutionalized in the Treaty of Utrecht (which transferred Acadia from France to Britain) and was incorporated into the *British North America Act* in 1867.

The *British North America Act*, Section 91:24, placed the responsibility for "Indians and Indian Lands" firmly in the hands of the federal government. The later *Indian Act* of 1876 was enacted by Canada's Parliament to manage that responsibility, with the goal being the complete assimilation of First Nations peoples—following exactly the British example.

The *Indian Act* of 1876 included paternalistic provisions for how the government would manage band membership, education, First Nations estates, and practically every social service. First Nations governments were made subservient to the federal government. Residential schools for First Nations children were first established in the 1840s. Like First Nations day schools, residential schools were created to assimilate First Nations peoples. Children were forcibly taken from their families, locked up, forbidden to speak their own languages, and often subjected to harsh or even criminal acts. The stories of mental, physical, and sexual abuse to which they were subjected are deeply disturbing. In 1922 Dr. Peter Bryce, former medical inspector for the Department of Indian Affairs (DIA), published *The Story of a National Crime: An Appeal for Justice to the Indians of Canada*. On this tract's cover page, Bryce revealed his discovery that a death rate of almost 50 percent was evident among First Nations children enrolled in residential schools, a fact actively suppressed by the Canadian government and the involved churches. Fortunately, the National Indian Brotherhood's (NIB) 1972 call for greater First Nations control of education was eventually heeded.

One example of what the future may hold is Piqqusilirivvik, "a place that has those things important to us," a school so radically different from a conventional educational institution that government officials claim it should not even be called a school. Located in Nunavut, students don't need to show grades to gain entry, tuition and living expenses are paid by the territory, and classrooms are called "learning studios."

While the funding for First Nations schools is provided by the federal government, some control of education, primarily through federal–provincial agreements, is now in the hands of various bands. There are still difficulties, however. High dropout rates are an ongoing problem, and they perpetuate the shortage of First Nations teachers and other professionals. School funding and equipment shortages also continue to exist.

On the positive side, educational challenges faced by First Nations children are now well-recognized, and First Nations leaders are working toward the creation of a fairer and more effective system of schools. Thus, the wrongs of the past are unlikely to be repeated. The rest of Canadian society watches with supportive hope as Canada's First Nations attempt the recreation of the first-class education system that was taken from them over the past 350 years.

Note: This section was collaboratively written by one of the authors and Mr. Daniel Paul, a First Nations author and former district chief for the Shubenacadie Mi'kmaq Bands.

WHAT EDUCATIONAL ADVANCEMENTS TOOK PLACE BETWEEN THE GREAT WARS (1918–1939)?

World War I made government officials recognize the need for technical and industrial education. War was becoming more automated and scientific. Soldiers with technical experience were becoming a necessity of modern warfare. As a consequence, through the *Technical Education Act* of 1919, the federal government made funds available to the provinces for the development of technical/vocational schools and programs. While all areas of the country participated to a greater or lesser degree in the establishment of vocational programs, the exact nature of what was developed varied. Some added programs to existing schools, some established schools devoted exclusively to technical and vocational training, and others set up correspondence courses or summer schools.

The problems associated with the decline of rural populations continued throughout this period. Studies of these problems were conducted in provinces such as Ontario, New Brunswick, and Alberta. However, other than through the continued amalgamation of rural school districts into ever larger consolidated ones, little could be done to alleviate the rural school issue.

The period between the wars also saw a dramatic increase in the number of students who went on to post-elementary education. A partial explanation for this may lie with the Great Depression, which started in 1929. Students who might have wanted to enter the labour force could not do so as there were no jobs. However, other factors were likely involved. Schools were becoming more appealing places, and there was a growing recognition that a good education was often the prerequisite for a good job. An additional factor almost certainly relates to the school-leaving age requirements that were beginning to be introduced. For example, in 1922, Ontario had a law that every child must attend school; it also required children to attend until they were 16 years of age.

Curriculum and student discipline were subjects of great concern and much discussion during this period. What should be taught? Should the emphasis be placed on traditional academic courses, such as English and mathematics? Should there be technical and vocational courses? Should some courses be required for all students to take, while others could be electives? Should junior high schools be established, thus changing the model of eight years of elementary education followed by three or four years of secondary school? What types of disciplinary procedures should be established? Opinions on these and related topics varied from province to province. There was little agreement, and definitive answers would not be determined until after 1945.

Other newer ideas and issues also made their appearance during this period. The theories of psychologists such as Edward Lee Thorndike started to receive attention, as did the concepts of progressive education espoused by John Dewey. Universities began to take an interest in teacher education, and, as early as 1923, the University of British Columbia established a school of education for university graduates. Other universities followed this lead, and within the next 50 years, most of the traditional normal schools would cease to exist.

The period from 1918 to 1939 did not result in a great number of truly significant changes to the Canadian education system. The ideas and forces that were to give our present-day system its final characteristics were now in place. The extended period of peace and prosperity that followed World War II would provide the ideal environment for the final evolution of Canada's present system of education.

WHAT ARE THE MAJOR CHARACTERISTICS OF TODAY'S SYSTEM OF EDUCATION IN CANADA?

At the end of World War II, Canadian education continued its evolution into the system we know today. The trend evident by 1945 would, for the most part, become well-established by the end of the twentieth century. While each of the 10 provinces and 4 territories has its own distinctive features, there are many commonalities.

Elementary

Education is compulsory for all children between the ages of 6 and 16, although most provinces and territories have kindergarten (called Primary in some jurisdictions) for students who are five years of age. The length of the elementary program varies from five years in Saskatchewan to eight years in Ontario and Manitoba. Depending on the length of their elementary program, students next proceed to middle school (normally grades 6–8), junior high (grades 7–9), or secondary school (in many areas, grades 9–12).

Secondary

Secondary schools (high schools) offer a variety of courses, both academic and vocational. High school students have compulsory courses in areas such as mathematics, languages, social studies, and the sciences. Elective courses, such as music, drama, and geology, also form part of the high school curriculum. Most schools have programs that prepare students for admission to university or to community college. In Quebec, the model is somewhat different. At the end of grade 11, students can attend a *collège d'enseignement général et professional* (**CEGEP**) for either two years of preparatory study toward admission to university or three years of study in a technical/vocational program.

CEGEP: collège d'enseignement général et professional, a Quebec junior college that students can attend for one or two years of study.

School Year

The lengths of both the **school year** and the school day are set by each province or territory's department of education. The Canadian average is 188 student days, with seven additional professional development days for teachers. However, Alberta, Saskatchewan, and Quebec have set the school year at 200 days. An additional factor in determining what constitutes a school year is the length of the school day. On average, this constitutes 300 minutes of teacher–student contact time per day, but there are variations.

School year: the required number of days required for students to attend school.

All Alberta students receive 950 hours of instruction per year, while secondary students in Ontario receive 925 hours and elementary students only 850. By way of comparison with other countries, Canada's school year is in the middle. China has 251 days in its school year, Taiwan has 222 days, and the United Sates has 178 days. At 172 days, the school years of Portugal and Ireland are the shortest.

Separate Schools

Canada's publicly funded separate schools reflect the country's religious and linguistic diversity. Alberta, Saskatchewan, Ontario, Quebec, New Brunswick, and Newfoundland all have separate school systems based on religious affiliation or language. While Nova Scotia does not have a separate school system, it does have schools whose students are almost exclusively French Acadians.

HOW ARE CANADIAN SCHOOLS FUNDED?

In 2011, Canada spent approximately 5.3 percent of its GDP (over $50 billion a year) to finance the education of 5 million elementary and secondary students, who attend any of the country's 15 000 public and separate schools. Teacher salaries consume an estimated 80 percent of the school budget, while the remainder goes for maintenance, student transportation, school supplies, and new construction. On average, in 2011 it cost approximately $11 000 to educate one student for one year.

Figure 3.4 compares Canada's per-student level of educational spending to that of other industrialized countries. The actual money required for the operation of schools is raised through taxation at the territorial or provincial and municipal levels.

School Funding Formulas

School funding formulas are used to determine how much money is allocated to the operation of schools within a particular school district. While these formulas vary from one jurisdiction to another, the following constitutes a representative example.

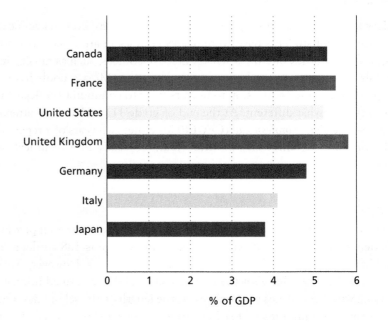

Figure 3.4 International comparison of direct public spending on education

Source: The World Bank, Government expenditures in education, 2011.

Operating Formula for the Basic Costs of School Operation

- For every student in a school district, the government gives the board a specified amount of money.

- A student is defined as someone who is under 21 years of age and listed on a class register as of September 30. (Some provinces give schools half their funding for students enrolled on September 30, and the remainder for students enrolled as of May 30.)

- Rural school districts receive a special allocation to cover the costs of student transportation.

- Some students are more expensive than others to educate. For example, a student who is deaf or blind might cost as much to educate as 2.2 students without special needs.

Maintenance Formula for the Upkeep and Repair of a School

- Very similar to operating formulas but pertaining to buildings and equipment.

- Boards are given a grant for each instruction area (classroom = 1.0) with adjustments made for laboratories (2.1 classroom units) and gymnasiums (4.5).

- Telephone costs, paper costs, janitorial services, and other similar expenses are covered by this formula.

Capital Funding for Major Repairs or New Construction

- A school board submits to its department of education a proposal for construction of a new school or major repairs to an existing school.

- Department of education officials then review the proposal, compare it to other similar requests, and make a decision to accept or reject each on a case-by-case basis.

Local Funding

■ A municipality must pay a specified percentage of its board's operating expenses. Typically, this percentage can range from a low of 1 percent to as much as 20 percent. The municipality can, however, elect to allocate funds above the required percentage should it wish to do so.

■ Municipalities raise their required funding through the taxation of local property.

WHAT ARE SOME CURRENT TRENDS IN CANADIAN EDUCATION?

Several educational trends have developed during recent years. Some have had a very positive impact and reflect the vibrant nature of our collective public and separate school systems. Many of these topics will receive greater attention in later chapters.

Evaluation and Assessment

Most Canadians have a great interest in educational matters and are quick to express their concerns about curriculum issues and issues related to the quality of instruction their children receive. As a direct consequence of the criticism levelled at schools in these areas, there has been an increased emphasis on the evaluation and assessment of the curriculum and the teachers who deliver it. The Council of Ministers of Education, Canada (CMEC), which meets regularly for the discussion of issues of common interest, established the Pan-Canadian Assessment Program (PCAP) as one method for determining the effectiveness of provincial and territorial education programs. PCAP, which came into effect in 2007, initially assesses student performance in mathematics, reading and writing, and science, and will evaluate other subjects if the need arises. In Ontario, students are assessed annually in literacy and in mathematics, in each of grades 3, 6, and 9. These assessments help influence the direction of professional and curriculum development at the school, school district, and provincial levels. Additionally, many school districts have created their own evaluation instruments to determine how well their schools are performing. While PCAP, national teacher conferences, and other groups with an interest in education now share their practices regarding evaluation and assessment, they also deal with other topics. This mutual sharing of ideas has become one of the most valuable trends in Canadian education.

Students with Special Needs

The inclusive school movement has made significant gains in making schools more responsive to the needs of children with learning difficulties or physical disabilities. (Chapter 6 will deal with the complexities related to this topic.) The needs of groups such as children of recent immigrants, members of our First Nations communities, and African-Canadian students are also being addressed (see Chapter 5). Indeed, many school districts now have departments or officials designated with the responsibility of meeting the needs of minorities.

Mental Health

The mental health of children and youth in Canada is a current focus in education. Emotional difficulties such as anxiety, lack of self-confidence and self-esteem, and depression (often leading to suicide) are on the rise. One in five students in the average classroom suffers from some type of mental disorder. (See Chapter 5 for a more breakdown of the statistics.) As the onset of mental health problems typically occurs prior to the age of 18, it is incumbent on school districts to put appropriate programs in place and to ensure that their teachers/administrators know how to deal with these issues by pointing students to the appropriate support networks.

Bullying/Cyberbullying

School should be a safe harbour for students; however, children and youth experience bullying at all levels across North America. Whether it is teasing, name calling, or physical assaults, bullying can adversely impact students both mentally and emotionally. With the advent of the Internet, cyberbullying is also becoming a prevalent problem. Many provinces have created anti-bullying legislation, and school districts are developing anti-bullying policies and campaigns in schools to deter this abusive behaviour.

Ancillary Services

Canadian schools are responding to requests for additional services. Daycare facilities, for example, are now available in some secondary schools, as are programs in anger management, peer mediation, peer drug-education, and respect for differences. The educational role of schools is becoming increasingly intermixed with providing guidance traditionally thought to be the responsibility of the family.

Technology

The advent of the Internet, the pervasiveness of personal mobile devices such as tablets and smartphones, and the need to prepare students for the proliferation of technology have led to increased funding for computers, tablets, data projectors, printers (including 3D printers), scanners, and other related pieces of hardware and software. Most recently, there has been an increased focus on teaching children coding (computer programming) at all levels. Teachers now require increased professional development to deal with new teaching and learning methodologies that rely on technology. Persuading them to give up some of their more traditional teaching strategies is one of the many challenges facing the leaders of today's technology-enriched schools.

Curriculum Development

All departments of education now provide teachers with curriculum guides that contain specific learning outcomes. There is increased emphasis on language development and use, mathematical skills and concepts, thinking skills, and the sciences. Teachers no longer have to develop curricula based on some general guidelines for a particular subject at a specific grade level. The trend is now to provide a very specific curriculum to deliver along with concrete suggestions as to how it might be delivered effectively. On the one hand, this constitutes a reduction in teacher autonomy; on the other, it is a response to the criticisms of those who believe that teachers require more guidance to carry out their classroom responsibilities.

Second Language Acquisition

Canada is a leader in the area of second language instruction. French as a second language is taught in most Canadian school districts, and French immersion (FI) programs are common in many areas. However, the shortage of qualified FI teachers is generating concerns. While most FI programs start at some point in the lower elementary grades, the true difficulties arise at the secondary level where subjects such as physics, mathematics, and chemistry need to be taught in French. Finding a qualified English-speaking teacher for these subjects is already very difficult. Finding someone who can teach them in French is more challenging still.

A particular difficulty for many schools, especially those in large urban centres such as Montreal, Toronto, and Vancouver, is the large number of immigrant children who, upon enrolment, speak little or no English. **English as a second language (ESL)** classes are an absolute requirement, but the number of teachers qualified to instruct such classes is still rather limited.

There can be no doubt that Canadian schools are still in an evolutionary process. However, the independence of each province or territory, which makes our education system quite different from those of other countries, provides Canadians with a great advantage. The provinces and territories are uniquely free to experiment with new educational practices without having to seek permission from a centralized federal bureaucracy. If a new practice is successful, the high degree of collaboration among the various Canadian units ensures that it may be instituted in other areas of the country. The cultural divisiveness and sectarian wrangling that characterized much of Canada's educational history has actually been a valuable gift. Rather than having a centralized bureaucracy within which a single bureaucrat might have the authority to stifle a good idea, Canada has 14 independent departments of education. As a consequence, the possibilities for a novel educational practice to receive a valid field test are much higher here than in many other countries.

English as a second language (ESL): English language training for individuals whose first language is not English.

WHAT ARE SOME ALTERNATIVE TYPES OF CANADIAN SCHOOLS?

While the large majority of Canadian students attend government-funded public or separate schools, there are several other options available to parents who are unhappy with the education provided by these schools. While it is not possible to list all of these options, the following examples provide a representative sample.

Independent Schools

Independent schools have existed from the earliest days of Canadian education. Often referred to as private schools (a term not embraced in such schools because of its elitist connotation), these schools charge tuition that can range from as low as $2000 per year to as high as over $50 000 annually. Most are religious in nature, or at least in origin, and often have a boarding school component. Parents who elect to send their children to independent schools do so for a variety of reasons. Some want the religious and/or social values of the home reinforced by the school, some believe the quality of the education delivered is better than in public schools, and others believe that the characteristically small class sizes foster an environment in which their children are more likely to thrive.

Independent schools: also known as private schools, which charge a tuition fee.

In some provinces, such as Quebec and the Western provinces, limited public funding is available under certain conditions. In all other areas, independent schools must provide their own funding. Overall, perhaps 5 to 6 percent of Canadian students attend independent schools.

Montessori Schools

Maria Montessori (1870–1952), an Italian physician who was influenced by Rousseau, believed that children's mental, physical, and spiritual development could be enhanced by providing them with developmentally appropriate educational activities.

At Montessori's school for poor preschool-age children in Rome, teachers created learning environments based on students' levels of development and readiness to learn new material. According to the **Montessori method**, prescribed sets of materials and physical exercises are used to develop students' knowledge and skills, and students are allowed to use or not use the materials as they see fit. The materials arouse students' interest, and the interest motivates them to learn. Through highly individualized instruction, students develop self-discipline and self-confidence. Montessori's ideas spread throughout the world. While most Canadian Montessori schools are located in Ontario and British Columbia, there are a few in other provinces (Webb, Metha, & Jordan, 1999). Today, Montessorian materials and activities are a standard part of the early childhood and elementary curricula in public schools throughout Canada.

Montessori method: a method of teaching, developed by Maria Montessori, based on a prescribed set of materials and physical exercises to develop children's knowledge and skills.

Home-Schooling

While there are laws requiring that all children be educated, there is no legal requirement that parents send their children to a publicly or privately funded institution. It is perfectly valid for children to be educated at home. Fifteen years ago, there were fewer than 2000 Canadian children who were being home-schooled. The situation has since changed, and there are now over 40 000 children being taught at home by one or both parents. The **home-schooling** movement is growing at such a rate that provincial and territorial departments of education are developing new rules, regulations, and procedures for parents who wish to home-school their children. While there is little formal research that compares the later academic success of home-schooled children with that of children who had a more traditional educational experience, initial indications suggest that home-schooled children do as well on standardized achievement tests as those who attend publicly or privately funded schools. When one home-schooled child was asked what she did not like about the practice, her only complaint was: "We don't get storm days off like the other kids."

Home-schooling: the practice of parents taking on the role of teacher and educating their children at home.

Virtual Schools

New **virtual schools** are becoming popular in Canada. Virtual schools vary in significant ways from traditional schools. The courses are taken electronically via the Internet rather than in person in a regular classroom, and while some courses are scheduled for a particular time, most may be taken at the convenience of the student. In the model that has specifically scheduled class times, all students taking a particular class are expected to be online at the same time. They can take part in discussions, listen to a lecture, and send or receive information. In the model without scheduled online time, the student takes the course as she or he decides. The discussion is asynchronous, and communication with the instructor is via email or through the online learning management system.

Virtual schools: public schools that offer programs over the Internet.

SUMMARY

What Determines Your Educational Philosophy?

■ A teacher's educational philosophy is made up of personal beliefs about teaching and learning, students, knowledge, and what is worth knowing.

What Are the Branches of Philosophy?

■ The branches of philosophy and the questions they address are (1) metaphysics (What is the nature of reality?), (2) epistemology (What is the nature of knowledge, and is truth attainable?), (3) axiology (What values should one live by?), (4) ethics (What is good and evil, right and wrong?), (5) aesthetics (What is beautiful?), and (6) logic (What reasoning processes yield valid conclusions?).

What Are Five Modern Philosophical Orientations to Teaching?

■ The five modern philosophical orientations to teaching are progressivism (based on the needs and interests of students), perennialism (based on enduring great ideas), essentialism (based on "essential" knowledge and skills), social reconstructionism (based on creating a new social order), and existentialism (based on assigning meaning to life).

What Psychological Orientations Have Influenced Teaching Philosophies?

■ Three psychological orientations have influenced teaching philosophies: humanism (focus on individual needs, personal freedom, and self-actualization), behaviourism (careful control of the educational environment and reinforcement techniques), and constructivism (learning is an active process in which learners construct meaning).

What Historical and Cultural Traditions Have Led to the Development of the Canadian Education Landscape?

■ Early Canadian education was founded on the cultural traditions of France, England, Scotland, and the United States.

■ The primary purpose of each tradition was the promotion of religion.

■ During the formative period of Canada's educational history (prior to 1875), the school systems that evolved were a reflection of the cultural traditions of Quebec, Atlantic Canada, Ontario, and the Northwest. In all areas, the struggle for state-supported schools was the cause of rancorous debate.

■ The *British North America Act* of 1867 established that education was to be a purely provincial responsibility.

■ In 1875, Canada's population was primarily rural; by 1918, it had become increasingly urban.

■ All areas of the country developed centralized educational bureaucracies.

■ Secondary schools became common; normal schools for the training of teachers became prevalent.

■ Between the Great Wars (1918–1939), vocationally based education became common.

■ Larger numbers of students went on to post-elementary education.

■ Discussions about curricular and student discipline issues became common.

■ The writings of educational psychologists and philosophers began to have an impact on Canadian schools.

What Is the History of Schooling for First Nations Peoples?

■ First Nations peoples used myths and legends to teach their children about the unity of all life, honourable conduct, individual and family responsibilities, and survival skills.

■ Colonial clerical educators initially attempted to assimilate First Nations peoples by converting them to Christianity.

- Residential schools, established in the 1840s, were created to assimilate First Nations peoples into European culture. Children at these schools were forbidden to speak their native language and were often abused.
- Since the 1970s, control of education has been in the hands of various First Nations bands.

What Are the Major Characteristics of Today's System of Education in Canada?

- Education is compulsory for all children.
- The average school year in most provinces and territories is 188 days.
- Some jurisdictions have separate schools based upon either religion or language; others do not.

How Are Canadian Schools Funded?

- The costs of operating all of Canada's schools for one year is over $50 billion.
- The operating, maintenance, and capital funding needs of school boards are met according to funding formulas, which differ from one province or territory to the next.

What Are Some Current Trends in Canadian Education?

- Evaluation and assessment are receiving increased attention.
- The inclusive school movement has led to students with special needs receiving increased attention and funding.
- Many Canadian schools now provide a variety of ancillary services, such as day-care and respect-for-differences programs.
- Information technology is now widely available in schools.
- Curriculum guides with specific recommendations for teachers are available in all school districts.
- French immersion programs are available in all provinces and territories.

What Are Some Alternative Types of Canadian Schools?

- Independent schools, also known as private schools, charge tuition for the educational services they provide. Many of these schools have a religious affiliation. Some provide boarding facilities; others do not.
- Montessori schools, which base their curriculum upon the Montessori method, are most commonly found in Ontario and British Columbia.
- The home-schooling movement is becoming more popular. Departments of education are developing regulations and procedures for parents who wish to teach their children at home.
- Virtual schools have become more prevalent. Students "attend" class electronically via the Internet.

APPLICATIONS AND ACTIVITIES

1. Recall one of your favourite teachers in grades K–12. Which of the educational philosophies or psychological orientations to teaching described in this chapter best captures that teacher's approach to teaching? Write a descriptive sketch of that teacher in action.

2. Based on what you have read in this chapter, identify several broad or long-term trends in the development of Canadian education that continue today. How were those trends reflected in educational policies and practices throughout the past decade? How is this trend evident at different points in the past and now? How might it manifest in the future?

3. Explore encyclopedias, bibliographies, periodicals, news sources, and online reference works to research in greater detail the contributions of a pioneer in education or a historical development described in this chapter.

4. Interview a teacher for the purpose of understanding his or her educational philosophy. Formulate your interview questions in light of the philosophical concepts discussed in this chapter. Discuss your findings with classmates.

5. Observe the class of a teacher at the level at which you plan to teach. Which of the five philosophies or three psychological orientations to teaching discussed in this chapter most characterizes this teacher?

6. Visit a school and interview the principal about the school's educational philosophy. Ask him or her to comment on what is expected of teachers in regard to achieving the goals contained in the statement of philosophy.

7. Prepare a written (or videotaped) statement in which you describe a key element of your educational philosophy. To organize your thoughts, focus on one of the following dimensions of educational philosophy:

- Beliefs about teaching and learning
- Beliefs about students
- Beliefs about knowledge
- Beliefs about what is worth knowing
- Personal beliefs about the six branches of philosophy

Develop your statement of philosophy throughout the course, covering all dimensions. On completion of your teacher education program, review your portfolio entry and make any appropriate revisions. Being able to articulate your philosophy of education and your teaching philosophy will be an important part of finding your first job as a teacher.

Chapter 4
Canadian School Governance and Law

FOCUS QUESTIONS

1. Who is involved in Canadian school governance?

2. What is the historical basis for the governance of Canadian schools?

3. What is the role of the federal government in Canadian education?

4. What is the role of provincial governments in Canadian education?

5. What is the role of local district school boards?

6. Why do you need a professional code of ethics?

7. How does the law affect teaching?

8. What are your legal rights as a teacher?

9. What are your legal responsibilities as a teacher?

Constitutionally, education in Canada is the responsibility of the provinces and territories. There are at present a few national or pan-Canadian groups concerned with education, such as the Council of Ministers of Education, Canada, the Canadian Education Association, the Canadian Association of School Administrators, the Canadian Teachers' Federation, and the Canadian

*Association of Principals, among others. While not wishing to interfere with
the prerogatives of these groups, deans, directors, and chairs of education
nevertheless feel the need to speak with a pan-Canadian voice to achieve,
maintain, and advocate for commonly held professional goals across
institutions. The General Accord provides the means to do so.*

—Association of Canadian Deans of Education,
as quoted in the General Accord (2006), an agreement that
outlines shared commitments and values relative to
education (ACDE General Accord, 2006, p. 3)

After reading the brief scenarios mentioned below, what questions do you have about each situation? How would you go about learning more so that if you experienced this situation, you would respond in an appropriate manner? After reading the rest of the chapter, revisit these scenarios. Do you now have different questions? Where will you go to locate information to help you address the scenarios?

■ A colleague notices that a teacher within her department is using an outdated version of the Science and Technology Curriculum document.

■ A teacher returns from lunch only to realize that he forgot his phone in the staff room. The students are just getting organized, and his classroom is just three doors down from the staff room. Should he just run down the corridor to retrieve his phone?

■ The provincial test scores are released and your school did not fare so well. The School Advisory Council is setting up an emergency meeting demanding answers as to why the scores dropped from last year.

⟫⟫ READERS' VOICES — Why Is Studying School Governance Important?

As future teachers, most of us have been students in public education systems ourselves, so going into the profession of teaching we all have this preconceived notion of the role of a teacher. However, what we often don't think about is all the governance that encompasses teaching as we typically don't experience that aspect as students. It is for this reason that teacher candidates need to learn about education law, governance, and the roles of all associated parties in education.

TAYLOR, teacher education program, first year

In my opinion, the question really needs to shift from "Why do I need to learn about school governance, educational law, and the government's role in education?" to "Thank goodness I'm learning this information!" As professionals, regardless of the field of work, we want the best and the brightest in the field and it is important to be knowledgeable about the many aspects of education. When tricky situations come up, you can then hopefully make informed decisions to help yourself, colleagues, parents, and students.

KAITLIN, teacher education program, first year

As a new teacher candidate, I think learning about governance structures in education and educational law is extremely important because as a teacher we need to understand the rights and responsibilities of all parties involved. I need to ensure that my students are safe, and knowing the laws and policies that govern teachers' work is part of what I need to know. Going forward, I know that policies and governance structures could change, and I will strive to continue to be current in this field.

AERIC, teacher education program, first year

- A vice-principal received a phone call from an angry parent complaining about the lack of consistency between the chemistry teachers at the school. His child happens to be in a class where the teacher does not typically co-plan with the other two chemistry teachers.

- You walk into a rant session in the staff room where a group of teachers with considerable experience are complaining about how little control they have over their profession. They feel that politicians are uninformed about what really happens in schools, claiming to make the education system more accountable just for re-election purposes.

- The school principal is looking for volunteers from various school departments to sit on a committee to explore technology purchases for the school.

- Two teachers were in the prep room and speaking negatively about their principal, who they felt was too hard on teachers who missed their hall duty. The discussion then turned to gossip about the principal's personal life and clothing choices.

WHO IS INVOLVED IN CANADIAN SCHOOL GOVERNANCE?

Understanding how power is shared in the governance of schools and being aware of the rights and responsibilities of today's educators are important and somewhat confusing matters for beginning teachers. Policy issues can be complex as a result of the different levels of jurisdiction involved in policy-making, including provincial ministries or departments of education, local school boards, teachers unions, local parent councils, and individual schools.

A number of forces influence the governance of Canadian schools. For example, various stakeholders such as parents, students, teachers, administrators, researchers, and other special interest groups have competing and shared interests in what happens in Canadian schools, at times shaping school policies.

The following sections examine the governance of Canadian schools and the degree to which they are influenced by various political forces.

WHAT IS THE HISTORICAL BASIS FOR THE GOVERNANCE OF CANADIAN SCHOOLS?

British North America Act: the act that established Canada as a nation and laid the framework for public institutions such as schools.

Constitution Act, 1982: historic act amending Canada's Constitution, most notably by setting out the *Charter of Rights and Freedoms* and by providing methods to further amend the Constitution without the British Parliament.

The defining moment in the governance of Canadian schools was the confederation of Canada in 1867 with the passage of the **British North America Act**, later renamed the **Constitution Act, 1982**. The *British North America Act* established the nation and laid out a framework for public institutions. Section 93 of the Act granted authority for education to the provinces in the following terms:

In and for each Province, the Legislature may exclusively make laws in relation to Education, subject, and according to the following Provisions:

(1) Nothing in any law shall prejudicially affect any Right or Privilege with respect to Denominational Schools which any Class of Persons have by Law in the Province at the Union

Under Section 4 of the *Constitution Act, 1871*, all constitutional power in extra-provincial territories (the Northwest Territories, Nunavut, and Yukon) was vested in the Parliament of Canada. However, most of this power has been delegated to the territorial legislatures. All three territories have departments of education that resemble their legislative counterparts, and they perform similar functions (Bezeau, 2007).

Apart from the limitations of the Constitution with respect to denominational and minority language education rights, the provinces have the authority to enact legislation dealing with education and have assumed full legal responsibility for it. The systems that have been implemented are partly centralized and partly decentralized. Centralized functions were placed under the administration of provincial departments of education, while decentralized functions became the responsibility of locally appointed or elected school boards.

WHAT IS THE ROLE OF THE FEDERAL GOVERNMENT IN CANADIAN EDUCATION?

The granting of authority over education to the provinces meant there would be no national or federal education office to direct or coordinate educational activities. This influenced the shape and direction of school governance in Canada today. The nature and extent of federal involvement in education has been debated for decades. Federal involvement in elementary and secondary education in Canada ranks among the lowest of the industrialized world. Canada is one of the few countries without a federal office, department, or ministry of education. Although there have been calls for more federal input, strong opposition from many groups and provinces exists (Bezeau, 2007).

Although there is no federal department of education in Canada, the federal government still plays a role in education in various contexts. At the national level, a number of federal departments also interact with provincial education ministries. For example, Statistics Canada provides data and analysis about all aspects of education while the Social Sciences and Humanities Research Council (SSHRC) and the Canadian Institute for Health Research (CIHR) fund educational research.

Educational programs such as literacy or skills training initiatives are either operated by the federal government or done so in conjunction with other provinces (Young, Levin, & Wallin, 2014). The federal government is also responsible for the education of personnel in the armed forces and the coast guard, and inmates in federal correctional facilities (CMEC, n.d.).

The federal government also has responsibilities relating to the elementary and secondary education of registered First Nations children attending First Nations–administered or federal schools on reserves, or provincially administered schools off reserves, and provides financial assistance to these students at the post-secondary level. The federal government's Truth and Reconciliation Commission (TRC) has made several recommendations that directly influence public education and Canadian teachers. The following section provides a brief overview of the TRC and the historical context that led to its landmark report.

The Truth and Reconciliation Commission

The TRC was created in response to Canada's largest class action by former residential school students. **Residential schools** were church-run schools within a wide-ranging school system funded by the Canadian federal government to educate and assimilate Canada's Indigenous peoples. Beginning in the 1880s, children were removed from their families to enter a school system where they would be forced to learn English or French and to adopt Christianity, and prohibited from speaking their languages and acknowledging their culture and heritage, or severe punishment would ensue (First Nations Studies Program at UBC, 2009).

The **Indian Residential Schools Settlement Agreement** is the largest class-action settlement in Canadian history, in response to former residential school students initiating a lawsuit against the churches and federal government. The agreement not only provided compensation to former students but also mandated the establishment of the Truth and Reconciliation Commission of Canada. The TRC's mandate

Residential schools: government-funded, church-run schools established to eliminate parental involvement in the intellectual, cultural, and spiritual development of Aboriginal children, dating back to the 1870s. The last of the over 130 residential schools closed in 1996.

Indian Residential Schools Settlement Agreement: the largest class-action settlement in Canadian history as a result of a lawsuit put forth by former residential school students against the federal government and churches; resulting in compensation and the mandated establishment of the Truth and Reconciliation Commission of Canada (TRC).

Residential schools for **Indigenous people** in Canada date back to the 1870s. Over 130 residential schools were located across the country, and the last school closed in 1996. These government-funded, church-run schools were set up to eliminate parental involvement in the intellectual, cultural, and spiritual development of Indigenous children.

During this era, more than 150,000 **First Nations, Métis, and Inuit** children were placed in these schools, often against their parents' wishes. Many were forbidden to speak their language and practise their own culture. While there are an estimated 80 000 former students living today, the ongoing impact of residential schools has been felt throughout generations and has contributed to social problems that continue to exist.

On June 11, 2008, the prime minister, on behalf of the Government of Canada, delivered a formal apology in the House of Commons to former students, their families, and communities for Canada's role in the operation of the residential schools.

(Truth and Reconciliation Commission of Canada, 2015)

Indigenous people: peoples (First Nations, Métis, and Inuit) who were the first inhabitants of Canada.

First Nations, Métis, and Inuit: three unique groups of Aboriginal peoples recognized by the Canadian Constitution.

was to document the truth about what happened in residential schools and to inform Canadians of this tragic history as beginning steps to promote healing and reconciliation.

The TRC's mandate focuses on both truth and reconciliation. The TRC spent six years addressing "truth" through conducting research, collecting testimonies from over 6000 witnesses of residential school survivors, documenting the abuse and deaths they endured and witnessed, and public education. The TRC acknowledged that "getting to the truth was hard, but getting to reconciliation will be harder," noting that reconciliation is an ongoing process and will take time to repair and establish the relationship between Indigenous people and the rest of Canada.

The overall objective of reconciliation will be achieved through public education and engagement, commemoration, and recommendations. The TRC recognizes the key role of education for reconciliation, and as a beginning teacher you have a critical role in this process.

> Much of the current state of troubled relations between Indigenous and non-Indigenous Canadians is attributable to educational institutions and what they have taught, or failed to teach, over many generations. Despite that history, or, perhaps more correctly, because of its potential, the Commission believes that education is also the key to reconciliation. Educating Canadians for reconciliation involves not only schools and post-secondary institutions, but also dialogue forums and public history institutions such as museums and archives. Education must remedy the gaps in historical knowledge that perpetuate ignorance and racism. (Truth and Reconciliation Commission of Canada, 2015, p. 234)

The TRC's 2012 Interim Report recommended that all provincial and territorial governments review school curricula for inclusion of residential school history and that the provinces and territories work closely with the TRC to develop age-appropriate educational materials addressing residential schools. Another recommendation included a public education campaign to inform the Canadian public about the history and impact of residential schools (Truth and Reconciliation Commission of Canada, 2012).

Prior to the recommendations, however, some jurisdictions were already working to develop more responsive, inclusive, and culturally affirming First Nations education, as well as joint initiatives and increased sharing of responsibility, with First Nations and Métis peoples actively participating in decision making in the field of education. For example, the 2003 Saskatchewan document *Building Partnerships: First Nations and Métis Peoples and the Provincial Education System* outlined a policy framework for Saskatchewan's pre-kindergarten to grade 12 education system that encourages more collaborative working relationships between the provincial government and First Nations and Métis communities.

Moving forward, it is essential for Canadian district school boards and educators to support and commit to education initiatives in Indigenous education.

National Organizations

From a national perspective, there are also several Canadian organizations that provide coordination and exchange of information amongst various stakeholders; these include the Canadian Education Association (CEA), the Canadian Association of Teacher Educators (CATE), the Canadian Teachers' Federation, and the **Canadian School Boards Association (CSBA)**, to name a few.

The **Council of Ministers of Education, Canada** (CMEC) is an intergovernmental body formed in 1967 to act as the national voice of education in Canada. The CMEC provides a forum for all the provincial and territorial ministers to meet and discuss matters of mutual interest. This organization is also the body that represents provincial and territorial interests in working with national education organizations, the federal government, foreign governments, and international organizations.

The CMEC's *Learn Canada 2020* framework identifies four overarching goals for education: (1) early childhood learning and development; (2) elementary and secondary schooling; (3) post-secondary education; and (4) adult learning and skills development. The ministers of education have also focused on several key activity areas such as Indigenous education, literacy and numeracy, and international relations (CMEC, n.d.). A full description of initiatives and key activities is available at www.cmec.ca/8/Programs-and-Initiatives/index.html.

Canadian School Boards Association (CSBA): national voice of school boards in Canada comprising 10 provincial school board associations.

Council of Ministers of Education, Canada: established in 1967, acts as a forum for provincial and territorial ministers of education to meet and discuss matters of mutual interest.

WHAT IS THE ROLE OF THE PROVINCIAL GOVERNMENT IN CANADIAN EDUCATION?

With the exception of areas identified in the previous section, the 10 provinces and 3 territories in Canada are responsible for elementary, secondary, technical, vocational, and post-secondary education (CMEC, n.d.). Some jurisdictions combine the responsibilities into one department or ministry, while others have one department or ministry dedicated to elementary and secondary education, and another dedicated to post-secondary and skills training (CMEC, n.d.).

Provincial and territorial legislatures pass statutes that provide for educational management and funding. Most provinces and territories have one primary statute, called an **education act** or public schools act. Other statutes that relate directly to education include such matters as the creation of the **ministry or department of education**, private schools, teacher organizations, collective bargaining by teachers, and pension funds.

In most provinces, education at the elementary and secondary levels is the formal responsibility of a **minister of education**, who has authority over the ministry or department of education and its staff. A **deputy minister of education**, an appointed civil servant, reports directly to the minister and manages the department on a day-to-day basis (Bezeau, 2007).

Although there are similarities among Canada's provinces and territories, each is affected by the diversity of its own regional culture, history, and geography. These differences are also reflected in the provincial and territorial education systems to ensure that the needs of the various populations are served (CMEC, 2008). "The comprehensive, diversified, and widely accessible nature of the education systems in Canada reflects the societal belief in the importance of education" (CMEC, 2008, p. 1).

Provincial and territorial ministries or departments of education use legislation on education and related regulations to exercise jurisdiction in areas such as the following:

- Curriculum development
- School funding
- Establishing requirements for student certificates or diplomas

Education act: provincial statute that creates an education system and provides for its management and funding.

Ministry or department of education: the provincial or territorial government ministry responsible for all aspects of education.

Minister of education: elected cabinet minister with the formal responsibility for the provincial department of education and its staff.

Deputy minister of education: appointed civil servant whose position is directly below the minister of education; responsible for the day-to-day management of the department of education.

- Establishing policies for school board officials
- Constitutions of school boards
- Choice and approval of authorized materials
- Determination of school district boundaries

As seen in Figure 4.1, in most provinces, the public education system begins with primary or kindergarten (sometimes preceded by pre-K or pre-P programs), followed by elementary school for five to eight years. Education is compulsory from ages 5, 6, or 7 to age 16. Secondary schools usually then continue to grade 12. Many provinces include a junior high or middle school between the elementary and secondary levels; these usually run from two to four years.

Three publicly funded separate school systems (Catholic schools and a small number of separate Protestant schools) exist in three Canadian jurisdictions. Approximately 93 percent of all Canadian students attend publicly funded (public and separate) schools (CMEC, 2008). Private schools do not receive provincial funding; however, they may still be regulated by the department or ministry. The Council of Ministers of Education, Canada (2008) reports that "six jurisdictions provide partial funding for private schools if certain criteria, which vary among jurisdictions, are met" (CMEC, n.d.).

Canada is a bilingual country where French and English are the two official languages. The Canadian Charter of Rights and Freedoms protects the minority language rights of both English and French speaking students, depending on jurisdiction. Each

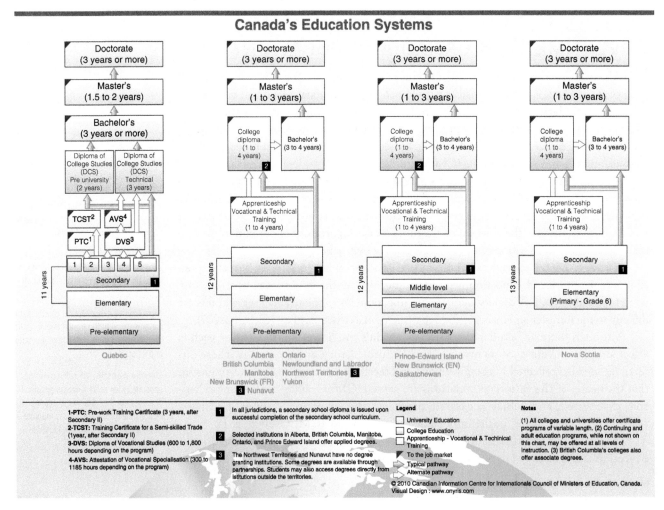

Figure 4.1 Canada's education systems, from CMEC (2008)

Source: © Council of Ministers of Education, Canada. Used with permission.

jurisdiction has French and English language school boards so that students who speak the minority language can attend a publicly funded school (CMEC, n.d.).

WHAT IS THE ROLE OF LOCAL DISTRICT SCHOOL BOARDS?

Local school districts vary greatly in regard to demographics, such as numbers of school-age children; educational, occupational, and income levels of parents; operating budgets; numbers of teachers; economic resources; and numbers of school buildings.

At the local level, public education comes under the jurisdiction of the various district **school boards**. The powers and duties of school boards are defined in provincial or territorial statutes, and school board members are generally elected to office in public elections (CMEC, n.d.). The statutes that define school boards and prescribe how they are created, dissolved, funded, and elected are of considerable importance. The powers of school boards are spelled out in detail and are the only powers the boards can wield. All provinces have a system of grants to school boards administered by the ministry or department of education. These grants supplement money raised from local property taxes in some provinces and provide virtually all of the funding for boards in others. Provincial grants are often accompanied by prescribed accounting and budgeting procedures and expenditure controls (Bezeau, 2007).

School boards: the primary governing body of a local school district.

The responsibilities of the district school boards typically centre on the daily operation and administration of the local schools guided by the legislative and regulatory constraints of the province or territory (Young, Levin, & Wallin, 2014). Examples include the implementation of curriculum, budgeting, personnel, student enrolment, dealing with issues specific to the local community, and proposing the establishment or closures of schools (Young, Levin, & Wallin, 2014).

The CSBA (cdnsba.org) outlines the following common functions of school boards:

- Hiring the district superintendent or director of education, who in turn hires school district staff on behalf of the board
- Serving as a check to provincial powers
- Ensuring that provincial education legislation and regulations are implemented at the local level
- Managing and controlling school property
- Setting annual budgets; hiring administrators and teachers
- Making policy
- Operating schools
- Developing district education plans

School boards are corporations, and, as such, are legal entities that can enter into contracts, sue, and be sued. School boards benefit from limited liability. Taxpayers and board members acting in good faith are not liable for the obligations of the board (Bezeau, 2007). Many school board meetings are open to the public; in fact, many communities even provide radio and television coverage. Open meetings allow parents and interested citizens the opportunity to express their concerns and to get more information about problems in the district.

School boards have historically existed as a reflection of society's deep-rooted belief that educational governance should reflect community and regional values and priorities. (Galway, Sheppard, Brown, & Wiens, 2013, p. 6)

The following excerpt from the 2014 Good Governance Guide lists the responsibilities of a school board:

- operating schools according to provincial legislation;

- having a vision statement that reflects the board's philosophy and local needs and priorities;

- setting the board's budget within the provincial grants and accompanying regulations;

- implementing curriculum according to ministry curriculum policy;

- developing and delivering other programs that reflect provincial policies and local priorities;

- providing for the hiring of teachers and other staff required in their schools;

- maintaining school buildings and property with regard to student safety and in accordance with provincial legislation; and

- monitoring the policies of the schools and the achievement of students and, through the director of education, holding the entire system accountable for meeting provincial and board standards. (http://cge.ontarioschooltrustees.org/files/en_good-governance.pdf)

Restructuring of School Districts

Since the early 1990s, many Canadian provinces have been involved in areas of school reform and have examined issues of educational governance. Efficiency, accountability, financial equity, parental and community involvement, and educational improvement were all reasons cited for governance restructuring (Saskatchewan School Trustees Association, 1997). During the 1990s, many provinces reduced their number of school boards and enlarged their size, reducing the number of school boards in Canada from 815 to 397 (CEA, 2007). The consolidation and restructuring of school boards resulted in changes in the roles and responsibilities of school boards, ministries and departments of education, parents, teachers, and administrators. There has been a move away from locally elected school board powers toward centralization at the provincial level.

Superintendent of Schools

School board organization varies, but most boards have a chief executive officer, its highest-ranking employee, who reports directly to the elected school board members. In most Canadian provinces, this person is the superintendent of schools, or **superintendent or director of education**. Though school boards operate very differently, the superintendent is invariably the key figure in determining a district's educational policy. The superintendent is the chief administrator of the school district, the person charged with the responsibility of seeing that schools operate in accordance with provincial guidelines as well as policies set by the local school board. Though the school board delegates broad powers to the superintendent or director of education, his or her policies require board approval.

Depending on the school board, supervisory officers—also referred to as superintendents—report to the director of education and are responsible for the implementation, operation, and supervision of educational programs. A recent study by Galway, Sheppard, Brown, and Wiens (2013) revealed that the provincial governments' new accountabilities have shaped and continue to shape the roles and responsibilities of district school boards. At times, the political and ideological interests of the government may "run counter to the democratic mandates of school boards" (p. 27).

Superintendent or director of education: the chief administrator of a school district.

Dr. Shirley Van Nuland

Dr. Shirley Van Nuland is Associate Professor at the University of Ontario Institute of Technology. Dr. Van Nuland came to academia with experience in teaching and administration at elementary, secondary, and tertiary levels of education and experience from Ontario's Ministry of Education. Her areas of research include codes of conduct, implications of Supreme Court of Canada judgments for schools, school boards, teachers, and students, and standards of practice and ethical standards for the teaching profession.

Each day thousands of teachers in Canada teach and encourage millions of children in "the pursuit of learning" to question ideas and to think critically. Parents entrust teachers and the school districts with their children so that they are provided "the opportunity to acquire knowledge and skills, fair and equitable discipline and a safe learning environment" (Brown & Zuker, 2007, p. 99) to ensure their growth and well-being. Within this environment, teachers and students build teacher–student trust, a trust that society recognizes, whereby teachers are "guardians and purveyors of knowledge, truth, and virtue" (Dickinson, 2001, p. 15).

To support teacher–student trust, student growth, and student development, a range of laws, policies, and rules exist that come from the various levels of governmental and nongovernmental organizations, teachers' professional associations, and school boards in the form of governance. Governance does not equal government but rather a system in which responsibility and decision-making powers are distributed among the organization(s) through legislation and policy that people make come alive.

Unlike many other countries, Canada does not have a federal department of education or an integrated national education system but rather a federal system of shared powers (so very Canadian of us) where, under our *Constitution Act*, provinces and territories have exclusive jurisdiction over education,

subject to certain safeguards. The provinces delegate responsibility for elementary and secondary school education to school boards/school authorities to develop policy and services. The federal government does not interfere in provincial educational matters but does exercise authority over education of Indigenous peoples. One filter through which legislation must pass is the *Canadian Charter of Rights and Freedoms*; decisions and directives must comply with the *Charter*.

While the provincial departments of education provide educational services with policy and legislative frameworks, school boards through elected boards of trustees implement these directives by developing their legal policies and procedures. Teachers and school staffs, principals, and superintendents, along with the school district director, put these policies and procedures into place by providing curriculum and curricular activities, local guidelines, and an environment where students can learn. Each of the above has a specific and different role for successful student learning, but through their actions and decisions they continue to engage with each other. The duties that each undertakes are spelled out in the education or school acts and regulations.

Teachers belong to provincial teachers' federations, which represent the interests of their members in dealing with many education organizations, including provincial governments and school boards. The federations may also function as trade unions that negotiate collective agreements ("teacher contracts") that set salaries, benefits, and working conditions for teachers employed in school boards. They also help members handle myriad issues related to teachers' professional development, maternity and parental leave, transfers, employment insurance, long-term disability, professional ethics, pension and retirement planning, etc. Each provincial federation has local units that coincide with the same geographical regions as district school boards. A requirement of teachers' unions or associations is the "duty of fair representation," meaning that the union represents its members in a fair way that is not arbitrary or discriminatory.

When teacher candidates receive their teacher certification, they are licensed and qualified to teach. In Ontario and Saskatchewan, teacher certification and discipline is the responsibility of the Ontario College of Teachers (OCT) and the Saskatchewan Professional Teachers Regulatory Board (SPTRB), respectively. In other jurisdictions, provincial governments, specifically ministries of education (sometimes in accord with the provincial teachers' federations), oversee teacher certification and discipline.

At a distance from direct contact with teachers, various agencies at both the provincial and federal levels influence teachers and school boards. The Information Privacy Commissions oversee the application of statutes (rules) governing access to information and the protection of privacy in the public sector, including school boards. The Human

Rights Commissions supervise the regulation of human rights codes that pertain to equal rights and opportunities without discrimination in specific social areas (e.g., housing, services, facilities, contracts). Child protection is addressed through legislation such as the *Child, Youth, and Family Services Act* (Newfoundland and Labrador) where children's aid societies ensure the safety and well-being of children and youth by protecting them from harm and preventing child abuse and neglect. In addition, each provincial and territorial ministry of education has its own agencies, boards, and commissions (e.g., Nova Scotia's Council on African-Canadian Education, Ontario's Education Quality and Accountability Office, Manitoba's Board of Reference) that provide advice and support on specific local issues for the improvement of education, in the long run benefiting teachers and children.

—Dr. Shirley Van Nuland

The Role of Parents

Parents play an important role in education. One characteristic of successful schools is that they have developed close working relationships with parents. Additionally, children whose parents or guardians support and encourage school activities have a definite advantage in school. Most jurisdictions in Canada have attempted to enhance the parental voice within the education system through required **school advisory councils**, typically composed of community (including parents) and school representatives. These councils or committees are referred to in a variety of ways, including but not limited to parent advisory councils/committees, school advisory councils, or school councils.

School advisory councils: councils mandated at school levels to allow and encourage parents and community members to become involved in school-level decision making; also referred to as parent advisory councils or committees.

Through these groups, parents can become involved in the life of the school in a variety of ways—from making recommendations regarding school policies to providing much-needed volunteer services and initiating school-improvement activities such as fundraising drives. Many parents influence the character of education through involvement in the growing number of private schools in Canada. In addition, many parents are activists in promoting school choice and the home-schooling movement. The following are two examples of parent involvement influencing public education.

The first example of a national parent organization that has influenced programs in public schools is **Canadian Parents for French (CPF)**, a nationwide voluntary organization with its head office in Ottawa. Established in 1977, the CPF promotes the teaching of French in Canadian schools. It is primarily anglophone and is devoted to the teaching of French as a second language. CPF has a research and publishing program that provides information to parents interested in French instruction, particularly French immersion. It lobbies at the federal, provincial, and school board levels (Bezeau, 2007).

Canadian Parents for French: nationwide volunteer organization to promote the teaching of French in schools, especially French immersion programs.

The second example of parent involvement to improve education is Ontario's **Parent Involvement Committee (PIC)**. All school boards in Ontario are required to have a PIC, which is typically made up of the director of education, a trustee, parents, community members, and potentially a principal, teacher, and staff members. The chair or co-chair must be a parent, and the majority of the PIC members must be parents. A PIC serves as an advisory body to the local district school board by directly connecting parents to the school board. In Ontario, school councils work at the local and community levels, but the PIC participates at the board level (Ministry of Education, 2015). PICs typically advise boards on issues of parent engagement and communication as well as communicating and supporting school community council work within the district school board.

Parent Involvement Committee (PIC): an advisory body for Ontario school boards that provides advice, information, and support to help schools increase parental involvement in their child(ren)'s education.

School-Based Management

School-based management refers to the decentralization of decision making regarding school operations at the school level. The decision making is carried out within a centralized framework of goals, policies, curriculum, standards, and accountability. The manner in which school-based management is defined and implemented varies greatly; however, a common element is the increased school-level authority and responsibility within the centrally based framework (Caldwell, 2005).

Decision making could be delegated to teachers, principals, parents, community members, and students at local schools. For example, teachers can become directly involved in making decisions about curricula, textbooks, standards for student behaviour, staff development, promotion and retention policies, teacher evaluation, school budgets, and the selection of teachers and administrators.

⟫ School Board Budgeting Simulation

In the following simulation, consider a rural school board faced with budget cuts. As you read through the exercise, reflect on the chapter issues surrounding the topic of school governance.

School Board Budgeting Simulation

A rural school board is faced with the following situation:

1. The board is in the third year of a "period of restraint" and is faced with an overall 3 percent reduction in the operating budget.
2. The previous two years of restraint, each of which reduced revenues by 3 percent, have done away with any "fat" in the system. The board is running a barebones operation with large class sizes and overworked teachers and administrators. The board has also had to postpone many needed routine renovations to schools and equipment that hadn't yet exceeded safety standards.
3. While teachers' salaries have been frozen, the costs of fuel, electricity, paper, and other supplies have continued to increase at an average annual rate of 4 percent. An early retirement package for teachers has been vetoed by the teachers' union. Unless the board can find some method for reducing costs even further, it will have to start cutting programs.

Here are the basic facts with which the board must deal:

1. The number of students in the district is 9000, distributed among 15 elementary schools and 2 secondary schools. All schools are within 10 to 15 kilometres of the next nearest school. There are 6430 elementary school students distributed evenly among all grade levels. These elementary school students typically feed into the two secondary schools. There are 2572 secondary school students distributed evenly among the two secondary schools.

The organization of the district includes two secondary schools and their elementary feeder schools, as follows:

Secondary School #1:

- 1286 students
- Four feeder schools composed of 286 students, 500 students, 300 students, and 200 students, respectively

Seondary School #2:

- 1286 students
- Six feeder schools composed of 225 students, 300 students, 125 students, 250 students, 200 students, and 186 students, respectively

Provincial funding generates the following distribution of teachers:

- JK/SK: 1 teacher per 30 students
- Grades 1 to 3: 1 teacher per 20 students
- Grades 4 to 8: 1 teacher per 24.5 students
- Teacher Release: .2 teacher per teacher above
- Grades 9–12: 1 teacher per 22 students
- Specialty Teachers/Teacher Librarian: 1 teacher per 655 students
- Specialty Teachers/Special Education: 1 teacher per 500 students
- Specialty Teachers/Secondary School Guidance: 1 teacher per 500 students
- Vice-Principal: 1 VP per 500 students
- Principal: 1 principal per school
- School Secretary: 1 school secretary per school
- Custodian: 1 custodian per school

2. The number of teachers in the school district is 505; of this number, 10 are probationary teachers who can be released without difficulty in reverse order of seniority, at an annual savings. Teachers with "permanent contracts" can be released in reverse order of seniority. All of the probationary

teachers, and almost all of those with limited seniority, are the "bright lights" in the system. Some believe that the release of these teachers will leave the system with an aging, tired staff, most with no time or energy for extracurricular activities. In addition, many of the most recently hired educators teach science, math, and information technology at the secondary level. If they leave, there is no one to replace them and, while someone will have to take on their courses, the quality of instruction is certain to suffer. Release of any teacher will save approximately $100 000, whereas release of non-teaching staff will save approximately $50 000 per position. Release of a principal and vice-principal will save approximately $150 000 and $125 000, respectively. It is important to note that the aforementioned salaries also include benefits, so the total is not indicative of the take-home salary.

3. The total budget last year was $72.5 million.

4. The total budget this year is $70.4 million.

5. Salaries and benefits are $56.3 million.

6. All central office staff make up 20 percent of the salaries and benefits expenditures.

7. Transportation, fuel, maintenance, administration, paper, telephone, and other services consume $6 million a year, but all the reductions possible in these areas have already been made. Further cuts would mean that the heat would be turned off, the few remaining secretaries would be laid off, and the teaching staff would perform custodial duties in addition to their teaching duties.

8. Transportation considerations include:

- Two-thirds of all students in this rural community are bused, based on a 1.6 km walking distance (elementary students) and 3.2 km walking distance (secondary students); increasing the distance by .1 km would remove the need for one bus for the district.

- Each bus carries approximately 50 students (120 buses are needed).

- Each bus costs approximately $37 000 a year to operate.

What are some potential options for the school board to reduce expenses by $1.2 million? Brainstorm all areas for consideration for reduction. Use the financial information above to approximate the savings for your proposed ideas. As you work through the reductions, here are some questions to consider:

1. How might the number of teachers be optimized?

2. What might happen to class sizes if numbers of teachers are reduced?

3. What program areas might be eliminated, reduced, or combined? Why? What are the implications for students? Teachers? Community?

4. How might the number of non-teaching staff, including school administration, be optimized? What are the implications?

5. What are the pros and cons for each area of reduction on your list?

(Next year, you have to find another $1.2 million—but that's another story.)

Instructions for Individual to Large Group Role Play

Individual Activity:

1. Put yourself in the role of an elected school board member. Each board member has been asked to individually review the budget problems as they have been outlined and to make a list of cuts from each of the areas listed. Consider all social, economic, political, and educational aspects. Reflect on the advantages and disadvantages associated with making cuts in each of the areas listed. Make a list of the cuts you eventually decide to make, giving the rationale that underlies each decision.

Small Group Activity:

2. Present your list to a "school board meeting." In groups of six to eight, role-play a meeting where you share your individual lists. During the "meeting" you must, as a "board," reach a consensus.

Large Group Activity:

3. Each "school board" group should present its list to the whole class and compare and contrast their decisions with the other groups. Vote on a final list of cuts that will be released to the "public."

4. The final part of this exercise* will involve the role-play of a large town meeting, where people have an opportunity to react to the final list of cuts. Twelve people will act as the "school board"; these board members must defend the choices that have been made against the criticism of the citizens. The rest of the class will assume different perspectives and will express their reaction to the cuts. Suggestions for the different perspectives include:

- Elementary, middle, and secondary teachers and administrators

- Parents of special needs students

- Parents of gifted students

- Parents of students involved in athletics, drama, music, and other extracurricular activities

- Taxpayers with school-age children

- Taxpayers with no school-age children

- Business representatives

* Special thanks to former Durham District School Board Superintendent Mark Joel for his professional expertise for this exercise.

Ethical and Legal Questions

Closely related to issues of school governance are ethical and legal considerations. In this section of the chapter, we examine significant ethical and legal issues that affect the rights and responsibilities of teachers, administrators, students, and parents. Teachers must act in accordance with a wide range of federal and provincial legislations and court decisions. As a teacher, you may need to deal with such legal issues as the teacher's responsibility for accidents, freedom of speech, and student rights. Without knowledge of the legal dimensions of such issues, you will be ill-equipped to protect your rights and the rights of your students.

WHY DO YOU NEED A PROFESSIONAL CODE OF ETHICS?

The actions of professional teachers are determined not only by what is legally required of them, but also by what they know they *ought* to do. They do what is legally right, and they do the right thing. A specific set of values guides them. A deep and lasting commitment to professional practice characterizes their work. They have adopted a high standard of professional ethics, and they model behaviours that are in accordance with that code of ethics.

At present, the teaching profession does not have a universal **code of ethics** similar to the Hippocratic oath that all doctors are legally required to take when they begin practice. However, many provincial bodies have developed codes of ethics for educators.

Code of ethics: a set of guidelines that defines appropriate behaviour for professionals.

Ethical Teaching Attitudes and Practices

Teaching is an ethical enterprise—that is, a teacher has an obligation to act ethically, to follow what he or she knows to be the most appropriate professional action. The best interests of students, not the teacher, guide ethical decisions. Behaving ethically is more than a matter of following the rules or not breaking the law—it means acting in a way that promotes the learning and growth of students and helps them realize their potential.

What are the values and principles that teachers stand by as professionals and that the public expects?

The Ontario College of Teachers (OCT) was established in 1997 to regulate the teaching profession in the public interest. The College accredits teacher education programs, sets the certification requirements for entry into the profession, investigates complaints, and establishes the ethical standards and standards of practice for the teaching profession. Every teacher working in a publicly funded school or school system in the province must be a member of the College.

The OCT's CEO and Registrar, Dr. Michael Salvatori, has the following to say about ethics in teaching:

Dr. Michael Salvatori, OCT CEO and Registrar
Source: Courtesy of Michael Salvatori. Used with permission.

> The ethical standards and standards of practice are a collective articulation of what it means to be a teacher in Ontario. They describe the professional aspirations, values, and ethical responsibilities central to the profession of teaching and inform our professional practice. College members use these standards to guide their teaching and leadership, their interactions with students and colleagues, and how they communicate with parents and the public.
>
> The four ethical standards—Care, Respect, Trust, and Integrity—establish the core ethics of teaching and are implicit in the standards of practice for the teaching

profession. The ethical standards are the principles that inspire confidence in members of the profession.

Care: encourages us to be compassionate, accepting, empathic, committed to our students' well-being, and dedicated to learning.

Respect: asks us to be fair-minded and respectful of spiritual and cultural values, social justice, confidentiality, freedom, democracy, and the environment.

Trust: invites us to be fair, open, and honest with students, parents, guardians, and our colleagues.

Integrity: reminds us to be reliable, honest, and true to our professional commitments and responsibilities.

Although the Ontario College of Teachers is responsible for establishing these standards, we do so in collaboration with our members. These words, concepts, and everyday examples come from members of the profession themselves.

Developing students' potential, supporting their well-being, modelling fairness, openness, and honesty, honouring human dignity, emotional wellness, and cognitive development, embracing social justice, freedom, and democracy, respecting the environment, acting honestly, reliably, morally, and professionally—these are the hallmarks of teaching in Ontario.

Parents and members of the public want to know that their trust in our profession is well placed. Classroom teachers, school leaders, and administrators advance that trust and garner the respect of their students, parents, and the public every day.

Teachers and educational leaders' professional judgment is enhanced when the ethical standards and standards of practice are embodied in daily professional practice. Open and honest communication builds trust and demonstrates accountability. As we model care and respect in the classroom, students learn and adopt these values as contributing members of our civil society.

This is the importance of teaching in the public interest in accordance with our ethical standards. As members model these standards in our daily practice, students will develop the mindset and skills they need to achieve their potential, exceed their dreams, and become the next generation of caring and engaged citizens.

Provincial Codes of Ethics for Teachers   The following websites provide information on specific provincial codes of ethics for teachers. Review these codes of ethics before you read "Case to Consider." Think about whether there are specific links between the codes and the problems posed in the case study *Open for Debate*.

Association des enseignantes et des enseignants franco-ontariens
www.aefo.on.ca

Alberta Teachers' Association
www.teachers.ab.ca/About%20the%20ATA/UpholdingProfessionalStandards/
ProfessionalConduct/Pages/CodeofProfessionalConduct.aspx

BC Teachers' Federation
http://bctf.ca/ProfessionalResponsibility.aspx?id=4292

Manitoba Teachers' Society
www.mbteach.org/inside-mts/professionalcode.html

New Brunswick Teachers' Association
www.nbta.ca/resources/code_of_ethics/Code_of_Professional_Conduct.pdf

Newfoundland and Labrador Teachers' Association

http://files.nlta.nl.ca/wp-content/uploads/public/documents/abcbook.pdf

Northwest Territories Teachers' Association

www.ece.gov.nt.ca/files/Early-Childhood/handbook/Section%201%20documents/
NWTTA%20Code%20of%20Ethics%202012.pdf

Nova Scotia Teachers Union

www.nstu.ca/the-nstu/about-us/about-nstu/code-of-ethics/

Nunavut Teachers' Association

www.ntanu.ca/nta-documents/code-of-ethics/

Ontario College of Teachers

www.oct.ca/public/professional-standards

⟫⟫ CASE TO CONSIDER | Open for Debate

What kinds of ethical issues might confront a teacher candidate?

Shoshonna Hegman is enjoying a successful student teaching block in the North Hills Consolidated High School. Thanks to her strong background in drama and English language arts, Shoshonna was told by the Department Chair that the grade 11 English teacher will be retiring in a few years and Shoshonna would be an excellent fit. She sets high standards for her students, and engages her classes in challenging and active learning activities. It is obvious that Shoshonna spends a great deal of time on lesson planning and that she is willing to go the extra mile by becoming involved in the extracurricular life of the school. This term, she not only helped to direct the school musical, she also helped her associate teacher, Ms. Carmen, to coach the debate club—an established group that always attracts proud, capable students.

Debating is a well-respected, prestigious activity at the school, and every year the team spends hours practising and honing their skills. Shoshonna, a debater in university, is a keen competitor and stayed after school several evenings each week to help prepare the team. Parents and the school administration have complimented Shoshonna on the team's strong showing at the district level this term. In fact, for the first time in North Hills's history, the team earned the district title. After winning the regional championship last weekend, the team is preparing to head to the provincials this Friday at noon. The whole school is behind the team and its coaches, and Shoshonna is excited to be part of this history-making trip. If the team wins at the provincial level, the team and the coaches will have a shot at a national title.

At lunchtime on Thursday, Shoshonna receives a phone call from the school that hosted last weekend's regional competition; she takes the call in the main office,

since her associate teacher is off on a professional development day. The debate coach from that school is calling to let Shoshonna and Ms. Carmen know that North Hills's star debater has been accused of using a racial slur against one of the opposing team members over lunch during the regional competition. The coach, Mr. Mallory, is extremely upset and wants North Hills to cooperate in investigating whether the allegation levelled against its debater is true. Further, he suggests that the individual in question should not be allowed to represent North Hills until a thorough investigation has been carried out. Shoshonna promises to look into the matter and assures the coach that she will do so promptly.

Shoshonna leaves the office dumbfounded; she cannot believe that the student against whom the accusations were made could be guilty. The young man is an honours student involved in many extracurricular activities, and is the student council vice-president. His father's business sponsors the team, and his parents plan to drive team members to the provincials this weekend.

There are less than 24 hours before the team is scheduled to leave, and a pep rally is planned for the end of the day to wish the team luck in their pursuit of the provincial title. Shoshonna leaves the main office in turmoil.

1. There are many problems inherent in this case for a teacher candidate. Put yourself in Shoshonna's situation, and identify as many issues as you can that would impact her and influence her response to the complaint she received.
2. What are the ethical issues involved in the case?
3. What is the most prudent action for Shoshonna to take?
4. Is there anything wrong with Shoshonna choosing to do nothing until after the provincial competition?

PEI Teachers' Federation
http://peitf.com/members_only/987647T787T/resources/handbook/VII/VII_1.pdf

Quebec Association of Educators
www.garthgoodwin.info/QAE.htm

Saskatchewan Teachers' Federation
www.stf.sk.ca/portal.jsp?Sy3uQUnbK9L2RmSZs02CjVy0w7ZkI/ks6g2u00gzAtsk=
F#https://www.stf.sk.ca/portal.jsp?Sy3uQUnbK9L2RmSZs02CjV/
Lfyjbyjsxs6KkgNMMYRKI=F

Yukon Teachers' Association
www.yta.yk.ca/documents/pdfs/yta_code_of_ethics.pdf

Ethical Dilemmas in the Classroom and School

Teachers routinely encounter **ethical dilemmas** in the classroom. They often have to take action in situations in which all the facts are not known or for which no single course of action can be called right or wrong. At these times, it can be quite difficult to decide what an ethical response might be. Dealing satisfactorily with ethical dilemmas in teaching often requires the ability to see beyond short-range consequences to consider long-range effects.

Consider, for example, the following three questions based on actual case studies. On the basis of the information given, how would you respond to each situation?

1. Should the sponsor of the high school literary magazine refuse to print a well-written story by a budding writer if the piece appears to satirize a teacher and a student?

2. Is an English teacher justified in trying to increase achievement for an entire class by separating two disruptive students and placing one in a reading group beneath his reading level?

3. Should a chemistry teacher discipline a student (on the basis of circumstantial, inconclusive evidence) for a laboratory explosion if decisive, swift consequences will likely prevent the recurrence of a similar event and thereby ensure the safety of all students?

As you can see, as a teacher candidate, it is important that you begin your practicum or field experience with knowledge of the legal aspects of teaching and a clear idea of your rights and responsibilities.

HOW DOES THE LAW AFFECT TEACHING?

As a teacher candidate in Canada, it is important that you are aware of how teaching is shaped and affected by the law in a variety of ways. The following summary from Young, Levin, and Wallin (2014) presents a broad overview of how Canadian law affects teaching.

WHAT ARE YOUR LEGAL RIGHTS AS A TEACHER?

The necessary balance between rights and responsibilities is perhaps more critical to teaching than to any other profession. While schools have limited power over teachers, teachers' rights to **due process** cannot be violated. Teachers, like all

Ethical dilemmas: problem situations in which an ethical response is difficult to determine; that is, no single response can be called "right" or "wrong."

Due process: a set of specific guidelines that must be followed to protect individuals from arbitrary, capricious treatment by those in authority.

The Basic Structure of the Educational System

- provincial or territorial responsibility for education;
- existence of denominational and linguistic minority schools and school systems;
- existence and powers of provincial ministries or departments of education; and
- existence and powers of school boards

All of the following issues are outlined in Canadian law.

Conditions of Teaching

- who can teach (certification);
- duties and powers of teachers;
- conditions of employment;
- grounds for dismissal;
- labour laws; and
- collective bargaining

Many aspects of teaching are regulated directly in law, or are subject to the provisions of collective bargaining, which is itself regulated by law.

Physical Safety of Students

- negligence and liability of teachers;
- trespass and site safety; and
- child abuse

The requirement to protect students from harm has an important effect on many aspects of teaching, and creates tensions between the responsibility of teachers for their students' safety and their sense of what experiences might most facilitate students' learning.

School Attendance

- compulsory attendance and exemptions from it

The fact that education is compulsory has an enormous impact on teaching in that it means that students must attend whether or not they want to do so.

Maintaining Order

- discipline;
- suspension and expulsion; and
- corporal punishment and the use of force with students

If the requirement for discipline is at least partly due to the compulsory nature of education, the ability of administrators and teachers to maintain order, and the way in which they do so, is shaped by legal decisions governing disciplinary practice.

Student Rights and Democratic Practice in Schools

Freedom of speech, assembly, belief, and participation in governance by teachers and students are hallmarks of democratic society but have a particular meaning in schools.

Teaching Practices

Many aspects of teaching, such as the subjects to be taught, the content within each subject (the curriculum), the length of the school year, the treatment of children with exceptionalities, and copyright control over teaching materials are controlled by statute or regulation.

---

citizens, are protected from arbitrary treatment by those in authority. A principal who disagrees with a teacher's methods cannot suddenly fire that teacher. A school board cannot ask a teacher to resign merely by claiming that the teacher's political activities outside of school are "disruptive" of the education process. A teacher cannot be dismissed for "poor" performance without ample documentation and without being given sufficient time to meet clearly stated performance evaluation criteria.

Because board of education policies and regulations vary, you should carefully read any available teacher handbook or school policy handbook in your province (see Figure 4.1).

Most provinces have **collective bargaining** laws that require them to negotiate contracts with teacher organizations. An important part of most collective bargaining agreements is the right of a teacher to file a **grievance**—a formal complaint against his or her employer. A teacher may not be dismissed for filing a grievance, and he or she is entitled to have the grievance heard by a neutral third party. Often, the teachers' union or professional association that negotiated the collective bargaining agreement will provide free legal counsel to a teacher who has filed a grievance.

Collective bargaining: a process followed by employers and employees in negotiating salaries, hours, and working conditions; in most provinces, school boards must negotiate contracts with teacher organizations.

Grievance: a formal complaint filed by an employee against his or her employer or supervisor.

WHAT ARE YOUR LEGAL RESPONSIBILITIES AS A TEACHER?

Teachers are legally responsible for the safety and well-being of students assigned to them. Although it is not expected that a teacher be able to completely control the behaviour of students, he or she can be held liable for any injury to a student if it is shown that the teacher's negligence contributed to the injury.

Since it is the duty of teachers and school administrators to maintain a safe and orderly learning environment, it is important for you to have an understanding of the legal and regulatory frameworks that govern schools. These frameworks confer duties and place constraints on the exercise of power within the context of a school.

> At the most basic level, teachers need to be concerned about the safety of their students, and teachers can be sued or prosecuted, possibly leading to loss of their right to teach, if they neglect their responsibilities. More importantly, law is one of the primary forces that has shaped, and continues to shape, Canadian education. (Young, Levin, & Wallin, 2014)

Legal Frameworks

The legal authority of schools in Canada is derived from the following areas of law:

- Constitutional law
- Federal and provincial statutes
- Common law

Constitutional Law

> *In 1982, the Canadian Charter of Rights and Freedoms was signed into law and became an integral part of the Canadian Constitution. The Charter outlines the fundamental rights and freedoms guaranteed to individuals and groups in Canada, and it provides protection against government actions and laws that may infringe on those rights.*
>
> —www.thecharterrules.ca

With the proclamation of the *Canadian Charter of Rights and Freedoms* in 1982, Canadian courts gained expanded authority to review provincial and federal legislation for consistency with constitutional principles. Since public schools are created under provincial statutory authority, the actions of school-based personnel exercising authority are subject to Charter scrutiny.

The Charter applies to all federal, provincial, and territorial government matters, including ministries and departments of education. This means that school boards and schools must ensure that any laws, policies, and practices that are related to education must be consistent with the Charter. Beginning teachers should access *The Charter in the Classroom: Students, Teachers and Rights (CC: STAR)* (www.thecharterrules.ca) to learn more about how the Charter applies to education via interviews, case re-enactments, activities, and resource links.

The Influences of the *Canadian Charter of Rights and Freedoms* The Charter has increased awareness of issues of rights when considering the manner in which schools are structured and function (Young, Levin, & Wallin, 2014). For example, school policies reflect an increased awareness of principles of natural justice, as well as increased attention to parent, teacher, and student considerations (Young, Levin, & Wallin, 2014). In a later section, you will also see how the Charter influences your role as a teacher.

Federal and Provincial Statutes In Canadian provinces, the various education or school acts provide the legal basis for how education is delivered to students who are enrolled in the publicly funded school systems. In addition to the education acts, more general laws such as those related to labour, safety, and occupational health also have an impact on education (MacKay, Sutherland, & Pochini, 2013).

Although provincial laws have the most direct application to public education in Canada, there are federal statutes that influence responses to cases of serious student misconduct. One of most important of these is the **Youth Criminal Justice Act** (2003), a federal criminal statute applying to persons who are at least 12 years of age and under 18 years of age. Certain actions committed by students may not only violate school rules, but may also be considered criminal offences.

Youth Criminal Justice Act: act replacing the *Young Offenders' Act* to ensure criminal justice for youth; emphasizes rehabilitation and reintegration of youth.

Common Law The interpretation of provincial and federal laws is the responsibility of the courts and judges, whose decisions are recorded and published for use in successive cases. This creates a body of jurisprudence known as **case law** or **common law**.

For centuries, a key legal principle derived from common law has provided the foundation of teachers' disciplinary authority over their students. This principle holds that teachers stand *in loco parentis* ("in the place of parents") with respect to their students, and may thus exercise discipline consistent with that of a parent. The teacher–student relationship established under common law can be assumed to regulate teachers' disciplinary authority over students except where expressly altered by statute or policy. This being said, the notion that the authority of a teacher based solely on the traditional and common law–based principle of *in loco parentis* is now supplemented and supplanted by statutes where teachers act as educational agents of the state under provincial education legislation and regulations (MacKay, Sutherland, & Pochini, 2013).

Common or case law: law developed by courts and judges based on the interpretation of provincial and federal laws, and then recorded and published for use in successive cases.

School and School District Policies School employees are also subject to policies established by schools and school boards according to their statutory authority. This means they are legally bound by policies set out by their school boards, directors of education or superintendents, and school principals. District policies may, for example, regulate the procedures to be followed before suspending a student. These policies may be more restrictive than the statutory provisions (Brien, 2002).

Legal Role and Status of Teachers

As previously mentioned, the teacher's legal status is no longer solely defined by *in loco parentis*; however, it is still deeply entrenched in school environments and is the starting point for the standard of care in schools (MacKay, Sutherland, & Pochini, 2013).

MacKay, Sutherland, and Pochini (2013) provide a clear framework from which to examine the legal roles and responsibilities of educators. Their framework is used to introduce two of these major roles, "teachers as parents" and "teachers as state agents," in the following sections.

Teachers as Parents: Negligence, Liability, Corporal Punishment Negligence in the school setting is of importance to teachers who may worry about under what circumstances they can be sued. Negligence cases follow a four-step analysis:

Negligence: failure to exercise reasonable, prudent care in providing for the safety of others.

Duty of care: special obligation of teachers to prevent reasonably foreseeable harm to those under their supervision. Duties are often clarified through regulations, school board bylaws, policy statements, and job descriptions.

1. What was the **duty of care** owed to the injured person?
   - Teachers must take reasonable steps to minimize the risk of injury.
   - Teachers are entrusted with large numbers of students, and their duties of care extend inside and outside the classroom.

- Teachers must take care to ensure that students are not exposed to any unnecessary risk of harm.

2. What is the **standard of care** required by the person?
   - Standard of care may vary depending on circumstance.
   - Courts attempt to establish what a "reasonable person" would do in similar circumstances; the question is one of good judgment.
   - Courts have determined that a teacher's standard of care is that of a "careful parent."
   - Some factors that are considered in determining appropriate conduct in a particular situation: age of student(s), nature of activity, amount of instruction given to student(s), school policies, foreseeable risk of danger, previous accidents in similar circumstances.

3. Was this standard of care breached?
   - The law expects teachers to act reasonably to minimize the occurrence of accidents.
   - Courts must consider whether students contributed to their own misfortune.

4. What damages, if any, did the injured person suffer that were caused by the breach of the standard of care?
   - What damages, if any, were suffered by the injured person?
   - The plaintiff must have suffered some ascertainable damage as recognized by law.

Standard of care: level of care expected of school personnel; level of care to be that of careful or prudent parents in the care of their own children.

Negligence in School Settings: Tort Liability   A tort is a civil wrong done by one person to another. According to **tort liability** law, an individual who is negligent and at fault in the exercise of his or her legal duty may be required to pay monetary damages to the injured party. Teachers are held to a higher standard than ordinary citizens, and certain teachers (physical education and chemistry teachers, for example) are held to an even higher standard because of the increased risk of injury involved in the classes they teach.

Tort liability: conditions that would permit the filing of legal charges against a professional for breach of duty and/or behaving in a negligent manner.

A grade 8 science teacher in Louisiana left her class for a few moments to go to the school office to pick up some forms. While she was gone, her students continued to do some laboratory work that involved the use of alcohol-burning devices. Unfortunately, one girl was injured when she tried to relight a defective burner. Could the teacher be held liable for the girl's injuries?

This event actually occurred in 1974 *(Station v. Travelers Insurance Co.)*. The court that heard the case determined that the teacher had failed to provide adequate supervision

Should the teacher supervising this activity have any concerns about tort liability? How might this teacher reduce the risk of liability?

Hill Street Studios/Blend Images/Getty Images

while the students were exposed to dangerous conditions. Considerable care is required, the court observed, when students handle inherently dangerous objects, and the need for this care is magnified when students are exposed to dangers they don't appreciate.

Specific Areas of Responsibility   (MacKay, Sutherland, & Pochini, 2013)

The Classroom

- Teachers have a duty to supervise students in their classrooms.
- Reasons for absence, its duration, the type of accident, and the nature of the class are factors that are considered in determining negligence.

Playgrounds and Outside

- Injuries outside schools are examined to determine if an adequate system of supervision was in place and if teachers sufficiently performed their tasks.
- Playground equipment should be monitored for safety (loose boards, nails, broken glass, etc.).

Before and after School

- It is advisable for schools to establish clear hours of supervision before and after school hours and to communicate this information to parents.
- In the area of after-school supervision, teachers have the responsibility to abide by parents' instructions and to be mindful of special circumstances such as early dismissal or emergencies and inclement weather.

Special Classrooms and Labs

- Classrooms in which there are increased dangers, such as special equipment, dangerous tools, open flames, or chemicals, require a greater degree of supervision by school personnel, proper protection and adequate instruction, and precise warnings to students.
- Specialist teachers in industrial arts shops, science labs, gymnasiums, and family studies (home economics) classes are held to a higher standard of care than regular classroom teachers.

Emergencies

- Teachers who take students on field trips or are in charge of high-risk activities such as physical education classes may be directly confronted with emergency situations.
- Teachers are expected to take reasonable measures to cope with emergency situations.
- Basic first aid, life-saving techniques such as CPR, and proper training in emergency procedures are recommended for such teachers.
- Children who have severe anaphylactic reactions due to allergies from foods (peanuts or peanut butter, for example) or bee stings, or who suffer from diabetes, seizures, or other serious medical conditions, need special protection and monitoring. Teachers should make every effort to obtain medical information from parents at the beginning of the school year. A plan for management should be devised with the parents; this may include the storing and administration of medication such as epinephrine.

Sports

- Injuries in school sports activities are common, and may occur in the absence of negligence given the physical nature of athletic activities; however, teachers must still take steps to ensure the safety of all students under their supervision.

- Teachers and schools are typically considered negligent if the injured student was exposed to unreasonable risk.

Bullying

- If bullying is a foreseeable risk, schools must take steps to reduce the risk of victims; failing to reduce the risk may be considered negligent and schools may be liable.

- Student bullying of another student resulting in legal action against a teacher is rare in Canada. With the growing body of work documenting the increasing negative effects on students, increased legal action may result.

School Violence and Risk Assessment

- Violence in schools has increased in recent years, and school boards are advised to provide preventive and response-based training opportunities for school staff.

Off School Property—Field Trips

- Protecting against legal liability is a must for field trips. Proper risk management can reduce the possibility of a lawsuit resulting from accidents.

- Teachers should be aware of the need for waivers and parental permission forms, proper insurance, and safe practices.

Check with your school, school board, or professional association, union, or federation for specific guidelines regarding other areas of responsibilities. For example, in Alberta, *The Safety Guidelines for Physical Activity in Alberta Schools* is a very useful resource that provides recommendations for safe conduct in a variety of activities and provides information about supervision, instruction, and equipment. A copy of the extensive document is found at https://education.alberta.ca/media/1109586/sg_physicalactivity.pdf.

In Ontario, the Council of the Ontario College of Teachers has approved several professional advisories to inform professional judgment and practice on various topics including safety in learning environments, use of electronic communications and social media, and professional misconduct related to sexual abuse and sexual misconduct. The full list of the OCT professional advisories can be found at www.oct.ca/resources/categories/professional-advisories.

Liability for Corporal Punishment in Schools

Corporal punishment: physical punishment applied to a student by a school employee as a disciplinary measure.

Corporal punishment refers to the intentional use of physical force for an alleged offence or misbehaviour.

- Touching without consent is a technical assault; in real terms, legal action is likely only when the touching results in some physical or emotional damage to the victim.

- Corporal punishment (the use of the strap, for example) in schools has been largely abolished by school board policies.

- Criminal Code protections that allow teachers to use force as a means of correction remain in Section 43:

  Every schoolteacher, parent or person standing in the place of a parent is justified in using force by way of correction toward a pupil or child, as the case may be, who is under his care, if the force does not exceed what is reasonable under the circumstances. (Department of Justice Canada, http://laws-lois.justice.gc.ca/PDF/C-46.pdf)

- In spite of Section 43, it is not recommended practice for teachers to resort to physical violence as a means of correction (MacKay, Sutherland, & Pochini, 2013).

As an employer, the school board is generally held liable for the acts of its employees. If teachers are negligent, a ruling of **liability** is usually found against the relevant school board under what is known as **vicarious liability**.

To protect students from harm and themselves from litigation, teachers should be vigilant about potentially harmful or dangerous situations. They are, for example, encouraged to be vigilant about seeking permission from a school administrator or the school board for trips off school property and should also ensure that they have adequate personal insurance coverage if it is permissible for teachers to transport students in their own vehicles.

Liability: responsibility for damages or harm.

Vicarious liability: responsibility of an employer for damage caused by an employee, even though the employer may not have done anything wrong.

Teachers as Educational State Agents

One of the key roles of today's teachers is to deliver public education in a manner that is in accordance with the established laws and regulations. MacKay, Sutherland, and Pochini (2013) explain that Section 32 of the *Canadian Charter of Rights and Freedoms* articulates the Charter's application to government action and government actors, and that this includes education legislation of each province. They stress that teachers are employees of the state and not solely the representatives of parents. The following sections of the Charter also directly affect how teachers, as state agents, deal with and relate to students:

Section 2: Fundamental Freedoms

Section 7: Rights of Fundamental Justice

Section 8: The Right to Be Secure

Section 9: The Right Not to Be Arbitrarily Detained

Section 12: The Right Not to Be Subjected to Cruel or Unusual Punishment

Section 15: Equality before the Law

Section 23: Language of Instruction

The full Charter can be accessed at http://laws.justice.gc.ca/en/charter, and to learn more about how the Charter applies to education, visit www.thecharterrules.ca.

Reporting Child Abuse

Virtually every school board in Canada has policies, regulations, and guidelines for protecting students from abuse. Teachers, who are *required* by law to report any suspected **child abuse**, are in a position to monitor and prevent physical, emotional, and sexual abuse and the neglect and exploitation of children. Teachers' professional journals and information from local, provincial, and federal child welfare agencies encourage teachers to be more observant of children's appearance and behaviour in order to detect symptoms of abuse. Such sources often provide lists of physical and behavioural indicators of potential child abuse, similar to that shown in Table 4.1. Many communities, through their police departments or other public and private agencies, provide programs to educate children about their rights in child-abuse situations and about how to ask for help.

Child abuse: any kind of harm that causes injury to a child, including physical, sexual, and emotional abuse, and neglect.

Physical and Behavioural Indicators of Child Abuse and Neglect

If you are concerned for a student's well-being, the indicators listed in Table 4.1 may help guide your thought process. It's possible that many of these symptoms or signs could be the result of things other than abuse or neglect. Generally, though, these indicators suggest that a child's safety may be at risk and, at the very least, the situation should be assessed by a professional.

TABLE 4.1 Types of Child Abuse

Neglect: Failure to give due attention or care to a child resulting in serious emotional or physical harm.

Behavioural Indicators

- pale, listless, unkept
- frequent absence from school
- inappropriate clothing for the weather
- dirty clothes
- inappropriate acts or delinquent behaviour
- abuse of alcohol/drugs
- begging /stealing food
- frequently tired
- seeks inappropriate affection
- mature for their age
- reports their is no caretaker

Physical Indicators

- poor hygiene
- unattended physical or medical needs
- consistent lack of supervision
- underweight, poor growth, failure to thrive
- constant hunger
- under nourished

Emotional Abuse: Verbal attacks or demeaning actions that impact on a childs self esteem and self worth.

Behavioural Indicators

- depression
- withdrawal or aggressive behaviour
- overly compliant
- too neat and clean
- habit disorders (sucking, biting, rocking, etc.)
- learning disorders
- sleep disorders
- unusual fearfulness
- obsessive compulsive behaviour
- phobias
- extreme behaviour
- suicide attempts
- developmental delays

Physical Indicators

- bed-wetting
- headaches
- nausea
- speech disorders
- lags in physical development
- disruptive behaviour

Physical Abuse: the intentional use of force against a child resulting in injury or causing bodily harm.

Behavioural Indicators

- inconsistent explanation for injuries or cannot remember
- wary of adults

TABLE 4.1 Types of Child Abuse (*continued*)

- flinch if touched unexpectedly
- extremely aggressive or extremely withdrawn
- feels deserving of punishment
- apprehensive when others cry
- frightened of parents
- afraid to go home

Physical Indicators

- injuries not consistent with explanation
- numerous injuries in varying stages of recovery or healing
- presence of injuries over an extended period of time
- facial injuries
- injuries inconsistent with the child's age and developmental phase

Sexual Abuse: any form of sexual conduct (touching, exploitation, intercourse) directed at a child.

Behavioural Indicators

- sexual knowledge or play inappropriate to age
- sophisticated or unusual sexual knowledge
- prostitution
- poor peer relationships
- delinquent or runaway
- reports sexual assault by caretaker
- change in performance in school
- sleeping disorders
- aggressive behaviour
- self-abusive behaviours
- self mutilation

Physical Indicators

- unusual or excessive itching in the genital or anal area
- stained or bloody underwear
- pregnancy
- injuries to the vaginal or anal areas
- venereal disease
- difficult in walking or sitting
- pain when urinating
- vaginal/penile discharge
- excessive masturbation
- urinary tract infections

Source: Excerpt from Royal Canadian Mounted Police (2008). Retrieved from http://www.rcmp-grc.gc.ca/pubs/ccaps-spcca/chi-enf-eng.htm.

In dealing with suspected abuse cases, schools usually have a specific process involving the principal and a counsellor as well as the reporting teacher. Because a child's physical welfare may be further endangered if abuse is reported, caution and sensitivity are required. Teachers are in a unique position to help abused students, both because they have daily contact with them and because children learn to trust them.

Four Cases: You Be the Judge!

The following four cases illustrate some of the principles discussed in this chapter. Judge the cases, and then read the decisions of the courts provided after each case description.

Legal Cases

Plumb Case

The plaintiff, a 15-year-old from British Columbia, was injured when struck by a ball thrown during a game of catch. The plaintiff had forgotten his glove that day and was not participating in the game. Instead, he was lying on the grass to one side of the game. He was injured by a wild throw, which was missed by the intended catcher, bounced once on the grass, and struck the plaintiff. The supervising teacher had seen the game but did not believe it posed any special risks. The school board and the child who had thrown the ball were named as defendants.

Guiding Question: Were the school board and the child who threw the ball liable in this case? Was the supervising teacher negligent?

Cropp Case

In this Saskatchewan case, the 14-year-old plaintiff was wearing cowboy boots with five-centimetre heels when he slipped, fell, and injured himself on a temporary walkway on school grounds. He was required to take two classes in adjacent buildings and was moving between buildings one morning when the accident happened. This walkway was made of coarse crushed rock held in place by board sidewalls supported by stakes.

Guiding Question: Was the school negligent in this case?

Simard Case

In a Quebec case, an eight-year-old child was injured in a fall while climbing down from closing a classroom window. The teacher had asked her to close the window, which required that she step onto a chair, then onto a radiator, and then onto a small table on the windowsill in order to reach. After closing the window, the child fell, striking the chair.

Guiding Question: Was the teacher liable in this incident?

Road Pizza Case

In *Strong v. Moon*, the mother of an elementary school child suffered minor, though painful, injuries in an automobile accident that occurred just after she had dropped her daughter off at school. While the mother was lying on the road awaiting an ambulance, a school bus passed by, carrying children to the same school. Some children recognized the accident victim and later described the scene to her daughter, referring to the mother as "road pizza." Although the mother quickly recovered, the daughter suffered continuing psychological disturbances and was eventually forced to repeat her year. The plaintiff child and her mother sued the driver who had caused the mother's injuries for the suffering of the child.

Guiding Question: Was the driver liable in this case?

Judicial Decisions The following verdicts on the cases just described illustrate a range of decisions. The first involves a failure or alleged failure of supervision, and the second and third concern only occupiers' liability. The fourth case has elements of both, but was decided on the basis of supervision. This case, although not, strictly speaking, a school case, has important implications for teachers.

Plumb Decision

The judge found no negligence on the part of any defendants. The level of supervision was adequate, and the game of catch was not inherently dangerous. There had been no recklessness or intent to injure. The injury resulted from a purely accidental misthrow, which could not have been anticipated. A careful and prudent parent would reasonably allow teenaged children to play catch.

Cropp Decision

The school board was found to be negligent in failing to provide a safe walkway. The vice-chairman of the board admitted during the cross-examination that he believed the walkway to be unstable and below the standard of safety that a school board should provide for its students. The student was not found to be contributorily negligent.

Simard Decision

The teacher was found to be negligent and fully responsible in asking the child to close the window. She had not acted as diligently as a conscientious parent. Because of the age of the child and the request of the teacher that the child close the window, the Quebec Superior Court found neither voluntary assumption of risk nor contributory negligence on the part of the child.

Road Pizza Decision

In the *Strong v. Moon* case, school officials had done everything they could to console and help the child and were not named as defendants. The driver responsible for the mother's injuries was not liable on grounds of excessive remoteness. The court held that the child's problems were not reasonably foreseeable by the offending driver. This case poses an obvious question for teachers: Can they prevent the type of behaviour that caused the child's distress? If so, how?

Source: © Lawrence M. Bezeau, 2007.

SUMMARY

Who Is Involved in Canadian School Governance?

- Parents, students, teachers, administrators, taxpayers, politicians, educational researchers, and special interest groups are among the groups that exert influence on school policies in Canada.

- Schools reflect the society they serve and are thus influenced by a variety of issues.

What Is the Historical Basis for the Governance of Canadian Schools?

- The *British North America Act* of 1867 established the nation of Canada and laid out the framework for public institutions such as schools.

- Section 93 of the *British North America Act* granted authority for education to the provinces.

- Provinces have the authority to enact legislation dealing with education and have full legal responsibility for education.

What Is the Role of the Federal Government in Canadian Education?

- There is no national or federal department of education in Canada; however, the federal government supports to varying degrees some literacy or skills training initiatives, and education of armed forces and coast guard personnel and inmates in federal correctional facilities.

- The federal government has responsibilities for education of registered First Nations children attending First Nations–administered or federal schools on reserves, or provincially administered schools off reserves, and provides financial assistance to these students at the post-secondary level.

- The Truth and Reconciliation Committee recognizes the key role of education for reconciliation, and school curricula must be reviewed and developed to include and address Canada's residential school history.

- At the national level, a number of federal departments and national organizations intersect with education.

What Is the Role of the Provincial Government in Canadian Education?

- Canadian systems of education begin at the provincial level with the passing of statutes that create the education system and provide for its management and funding.

- Most Canadian provinces have an education act or public school act and an elected minister of education who is responsible for education at the elementary and secondary levels, and an appointed deputy minister who manages the day-to-day operations of the department.

What Is the Role of Local District School Boards?

- At the local level, public education comes under the jurisdiction of school boards, and school boards exist as a result of provincial legislation.

- Local school districts, which vary greatly in size, setting, organizational structure, demographics, and wealth, are responsible for the management and operation of schools.

- Among the functions of school boards are the implementation of provincial education legislation and regulations at the local level, the operation of schools, the setting of policy, the determination of annual budgets, and the hiring of administrators and teachers.

- The superintendent or director of education is the chief administrator of a local school district, and reports directly to the elected school board members.

- Provinces fund school boards through a system of grants that, in some provinces, supplement money raised from local property taxes, and in others provide virtually all of the funding.

- Parents play an important role in education both informally and formally. Most jurisdictions in Canada have parent or school advisory councils where parent membership allows for parents to participate in school life.

- Local school boards, whose members are usually elected, set educational policies for a district; however, many people believe that boards should be more responsive to individual school needs.

- As part of restructuring in Canada, the number of school boards in most provinces has been reduced in recent years.

Why Do You Need a Professional Code of Ethics?

- Teaching requires ethical behaviour, and many provincial teachers' associations have developed codes of ethics to guide their members.

- A professional code of ethics guides teachers' actions and enables them to build relationships with students based on trust and respect.

- A code of ethics helps teachers see beyond the short-range consequences of their actions to long-range outcomes, and helps them respond appropriately to ethical dilemmas in the classroom.

How Does the Law Affect Teaching?

■ The law affects teaching in a variety of ways, including legislation that grants provincial or territorial responsibility for education, conditions of teaching, physical safety of students, maintaining order, student rights, democratic practices, and teaching practices.

What Are Your Legal Rights as a Teacher?

■ The right to due process protects teachers from arbitrary treatment by school districts and education officials regarding certification, nondiscrimination, contracts, tenure, dismissal, and academic freedom.

■ Most provinces have collective bargaining laws that require the negotiation of contracts with teacher organizations and allow for teachers to file grievances or formal complaints against employers.

What Are Your Legal Responsibilities as a Teacher?

■ Teachers are responsible for meeting the terms of their teaching contracts, including providing for their students' safety and well-being.

■ Teacher candidates should be aware of their potential liability and should clarify their rights and responsibilities prior to beginning student teaching.

■ Legal authority of schools in Canada is derived from constitutional law, federal and provincial statute law, and case or common law.

■ Legal roles and responsibilities of teachers still include teacher as parent; however, it is now supplemented and supplanted by statutes where teachers act as educational state agents.

■ The *Canadian Charter of Rights and Freedoms* directly affects how teachers deal with, and relate to, students.

■ Among the legal responsibilities that concern teachers are avoiding tort liability (specifically negligence), recognizing the physical and behavioural indicators of child abuse and reporting suspected instances, and observing.

APPLICATIONS AND ACTIVITIES

1. Read the code of ethics for teachers in your province. Consider an ethical dilemma that you may have experienced as a teacher candidate within the context of the code of ethics for teachers in your province. How did you respond to the dilemma? How might you respond today? Why? In general, what steps should a person take to ensure that his or her response to an ethical dilemma is the "best" course of action?

2. In a Canadian province, a grade 12 student who had been suspended for almost a full school year for assaulting a fellow student and causing him serious injury in the hallway at lunchtime returned to school the following September. He was passing all his courses, but had borderline results in English, a subject required for graduation. Then, near the end of the school year, he wrote a short story for an English assignment that counted heavily toward the term mark. The story was filled with guns and violence and depicted fellow students getting shot. It was also well written. The teacher gave a mark of 25 percent for "expression" and 0 percent for "content" on the assignment and insisted that the student rewrite the violent scenes—or risk failing the course and not graduating. How should teachers respond to student work, including essays, creative writing, videos, and art, that has violent content? (Refer to the Teachers as Educational State Agents section of this chapter.)

3. Most school districts have a Race Relations, Cross-Cultural Understanding, and Human Rights Policy (RCH) in place. Locate such a policy for the school district in which you will

be teaching, and review its intent, recommendations, and guiding principles. What value is there for teacher candidates to be familiar with such a policy? Would such a policy inform how Shoshonna (in the *Open for Debate* scenario) should handle the incident with the star debater?

4. How much do you know about Canada's history with respect to the residential schools where more than 150 000 First Nations, Métis, and Inuit children were forced to attend? What prior assumptions do you have about Canada's Indigenous peoples? How will you address your assumptions? Spend some time exploring the following resources, and consider your own education regarding the relationship between Indigenous and non-Indigenous peoples.

   - Truth and Reconciliation of Canada
     - www.trc.ca
   - Indigenous Foundations
     - http://indigenousfoundations.arts.ubc.ca
   - Indigenous and Northern Affairs
     - www.aadnc-aandc.gc.ca

5. How might you use social media to continue to keep up to date on the issues discussed in this chapter? Brainstorm potential national, provincial, and local organizations that you could follow on Twitter to continue learning. Here are a few to help you get started:

   - Your province's ministry or department of education
   - Your teachers' federation, association, or union
   - Your local district school board
   - Your school's parent advisory group
   - Canadian Human Rights Commission @CdnHumanRights @DroitPersonneCa
   - Canadian Journal of Education @CJE_RCE
   - Council of Ministers of Education in Canada @CCMEC
   - Canadian Teachers' Federation @CanTeachersFed @EnseigneCanada
   - Department of Justice Canada @JusticeCanadaEN @JusticeCanadaFR
   - Truth and Reconciliation Committee @TRC_en

6. Conduct an Internet search on one or more of the topics listed below or on another topic from this chapter. Narrow your search to issues and information relating to school law and the legal rights and responsibilities of school districts and schools, teachers and administrators, and students and parents. Include a search of news sources, such as the *Canadian Journal of Educational Administration and Policy* on the Web, for summaries of recent court rulings pertaining to education and school law.

   Possible topics to search from this chapter:
   - School uniforms
   - Free speech
   - Search and seizure
   - Collective bargaining
   - Professional ethics
   - Any current education/school topic that is creating controversy amongst teachers, parents, the general public

7. Use the Internet to gather information about the structure of education and school funding in your province. How many school boards are in your province? Which is the largest? What are enrolment figures, trends, and projections for your province? What are the figures for household income and the poverty rate? Begin your data search at Statistics Canada and the provincial department of education.

Chapter 5
Social and Cultural Realities Confronting Today's Schools

svinka/Shutterstock

1. What are the aims of education today?

2. How can schools be described?

3. What are schools like as social institutions?

4. How is cultural diversity represented in Canadian schools?

5. What is diversity, equity, and inclusive education?

6. How is gender a dimension of equity, diversity, and inclusive education?

7. What characteristics distinguish successful schools?

8. What social problems affect schools and place students at risk?

9. How are schools addressing societal problems?

The educational system is part of the common life and cannot escape suffering the consequences that flow from the conditions prevailing outside the school building.

—John Dewey, "Introduction," *The Use of Resources in Education*

The role of today's schools is not only to provide children with education needed later in life, but to teach children how to behave properly, to interact with peers and adults, and to manage themselves and their time.

—**LACI, teacher education program, first year**

The role of schools today is vastly different than it was 20 years ago. The pressure is intense for the education system to prepare students for the challenging road ahead. With 65 percent of jobs not even invented yet, today's students need knowledge and skills to survive in an increasingly complex and competitive world.

—**RYAN, teacher education program, first year**

The role of today's schools is continuously evolving. Technology is making it easier for students and parents to pursue alternatives to public schools, making education more accessible in some ways. On the downside, it seems there are more social problems to deal with than ever before, with cyberbullying and a higher incidence of anxiety and mental illness among children.

—**JAMES, teacher education program, first year**

WHAT ARE THE AIMS OF EDUCATION TODAY?

In Canada, there is consensus that the purpose of schools is to educate. Unlike other institutions in society, schools have been developed exclusively to carry out one very important purpose. That we are not necessarily of the same mind about what the **aims of education** should be, however, is illustrated by our disagreement about what it means to be an educated person. Is a person with a college degree educated? Is a person who has overcome extreme hardships in life with dignity and grace educated?

Debate about the aims of education is not new. Fourth-century BCE philosopher Aristotle expressed the dilemma this way: "The existing practice [of education] is perplexing; no one knows on what principle we should proceed—should the useful in life, or should virtue, or should the higher knowledge, be the aim of our training; all three opinions have been entertained" (1941, p. 1306). Definitive answers to Aristotle's questions have not been realized; instead, each generation has developed its own idea of what the aims of education should be.

Aims of education: what a society believes the broad, general purposes of education should be—for example, socialization, achievement, personal growth, and social improvement.

Education for Prosocial Values

Although there is widespread debate about what schools should teach in terms of academic content, there is agreement that **prosocial values** such as honesty, fairness, civility, and respect for the law should be imparted. The well-being of any society requires support of such values; they enable people from diverse backgrounds to live together peacefully. Parents, politicians, business people, and others might include respect for others, industry, perseverance, compassion, integrity, and politeness in the list. Strong support for prosocial values reflects societal beliefs that schools should play a key role in promoting the democratic ideal of equality for all.

Prosocial values: values such as honesty, patriotism, fairness, and civility that promote the well-being of a society.

Education for Socialization

Schools are places where young people are socialized—where they learn to participate intelligently and constructively in Canadian society. In schools, more than in any other institution in our society, persons from diverse cultural backgrounds learn about

Canadian values and customs. Schools also facilitate the learning of English or French for people from diverse backgrounds, teach the nature of the Canadian parliamentary system, and instruct in the basic workings of our economic institutions. In effect, schools reflect or mirror society; they reproduce the knowledge, skills, values, and attitudes that society has identified as essential for participation in a vibrant democracy.

To help students understand that they are members of a larger community to which they are accountable, provinces such as British Columbia and Ontario have implemented service-learning components for secondary school students based on the assumption that service-learning activities (1) prepare students to serve others through volunteerism and (2) prepare students to participate politically. For example, in Ontario, secondary school students are required to complete 40 hours of community service in order to graduate, and in B.C., secondary school students must participate in at least 30 hours of community involvement as part of their "Graduation Transitions Program." **Service learning** provides students with opportunities to deliver service to their communities while engaging in reflection and study on the meaning of those experiences. Service learning brings young people into contact with the elderly, the sick, the poor, and the homeless and acquaints them with neighbourhood and governmental issues.

Service learning: a teaching and learning approach that includes community service and reflection to promote civic responsibility.

Of the various aims of schools, achievement is the most universally agreed upon. For most people, the primary purpose of schools is to impart to students the academic knowledge and skills that will prepare them either for additional schooling or for the world of work. Regardless of political ideology, religious beliefs, and cultural values, people want schools to teach academic content.

Education for Personal Growth and Societal Improvement

Society places great value on the dignity and worth of the individual. Accordingly, one aim of schools is to enable young people to become all that they are capable of. Unlike socialization or achievement, an emphasis on personal growth puts the individual first and society second. According to this view, the desired outcomes of education go beyond achievement to include the development of a positive self-concept and interpersonal skills, or what psychologist Daniel Goleman has termed "**emotional intelligence**." According to Goleman (1997, 1998), schools should emphasize five dimensions of emotional intelligence: self-awareness, the handling of emotions, motivation, empathy, and social skills. Emotional intelligence is essential for achievement in school, job success, healthy relationships, and physical health; it enables students to live independently and to seek out the "good" life according to their own values, needs, and wants. The knowledge and skills students acquire at schools are seen as facilitating the achievement of personal growth and self-actualization.

Emotional intelligence: a level of awareness and understanding of one's emotions that allows the person to achieve personal growth and self-actualization.

More recently, emphasis has been placed on the importance of **self-regulation**, or the ability of a child to remain calmly focused and alert, or self-controlled. York University research professor Stuart Shanker (2013) argues that teachers should enhance their students' self-regulatory skills through the implementation of instructional strategies that enhance their ability to cope with everyday stressors. According to Shanker, doing this will lead to an increased capacity to

Self-regulation: the ability to stay calmly focused and alert.

> attain, maintain, and change one's level of energy to match the demands of a task or situation; monitor, evaluate, and modify one's emotions; sustain and shift one's attention when necessary and ignore distractions; understand both the meaning and variety of social interactions and how to engage in them in a sustained way and connect with and care about what others are thinking and feeling—to empathize and act accordingly. (p. 4)

Schools also provide students with the knowledge and skills to improve their quality of life and to adapt to rapid social change. Naturally, a wide range of opinions exists about how society might be improved. Some teachers believe that one purpose of schooling is to address social problems such as violence, whereas others believe schools should teach academic content and not try to change society. However, as James Banks (1999, p. 4) suggests, "Education within a pluralistic society should affirm and help students understand their home and community cultures. [To] create and maintain a civic community that works for the common good, education in a democratic society should help students acquire the knowledge, attitudes, and skills needed to participate in civic action to make society more equitable and just."

HOW CAN SCHOOLS BE DESCRIBED?

Many models have been proposed for describing the distinguishing characteristics of schools. Schools can be categorized according to the focus of their curricula; for example, high schools might be university preparatory, vocational, or general. Another view is based on age; for example, by divisions—primary (K–3), junior (grades 4–6), intermediate (grades 7–10), or high school (grades 9–12). In Canada, most schools are organized by grade: elementary (K–6 or K–8) and secondary (grades 9–12). Middle schools that house students in grades 6–8 are relatively uncommon in Canada. Most recently, alternative schools are becoming more popular, especially in larger cities like Toronto.

Other models view schools metaphorically; that is, what is a school like? Some schools, for example, have been compared to factories, where students enter as raw material, move through the curriculum in a systematic way, and exit as finished products. Terrence Deal and Kent Peterson (2009, p. 31) suggest that exemplary schools "become like tribes or clans, with deep ties among people and with values and traditions that give meaning to everyday life." Other views see schools as similar to banks, gardens, prisons, mental hospitals, homes, churches, families, or teams. For example, Paulo Freire, in his influential book *Pedagogy of the Oppressed*, referred to traditional schooling using a banking metaphor: students are viewed as empty containers and teachers make deposits of knowledge into them. In the school-as-family metaphor, the effective school is an inclusive, anti-oppressive, caring community of adults who attend to the academic, emotional, social, and physical needs of the children and youth entrusted to their care.

Schools and Social Class

In spite of a consensus that schools should promote social improvement and equal opportunity, some individuals believe that schools "reproduce" the existing society by presenting different curricula and educational experiences to students from different socioeconomic classes. Students at a school in an affluent suburb, for example, may study chemistry in a well-equipped lab and take a field trip to a high-tech firm to see the latest application of chemical research, while students attending a school in another school district may learn chemistry from out-of-date texts, with no adequate lab in which to conduct experiments and limited opportunities for field trips due to limited funding. Schools, in effect, preserve the stratification within society and maintain the differences between the "haves" and the "have-nots." As Joel Spring (2008, p. 75) explains: "[T]he economic level of the family determines educational attainment. Children from low-income families do not attain so high a level of education as children from rich families. From this standpoint the school reinforces social stratification and contributes to intergenerational immobility." Moreover, rich families can afford to live in affluent school districts or send their children to private schools. This, in turn, increases the chances that their children will attend the "best" colleges and universities and, ultimately, maintain or increase the family's social class status.

In addition, children from lower-income families tend to develop "restricted" language patterns with their use of English, while children from more affluent backgrounds tend to develop more "elaborated" language patterns (Bernstein, 1996; Heath, 1983). In many cases, children from lower-income families encounter a mismatch between the language patterns used in the home and those they are expected to use in school. This mismatch can be "a serious stumbling block for working class and nonwhite pupils" (MacLeod, 1995, p. 18). Therefore, it is important for teachers to understand the different types of knowledge students bring with them into the classroom and how this knowledge can conflict with the norms and values of schools and teachers.

WHAT ARE SCHOOLS LIKE AS SOCIAL INSTITUTIONS?

Schools are social institutions. An **institution** is an organization established by society to maintain and improve its way of life. Schools are the institutions our society has established for the purpose of educating the young. During the past 200 years, Canadian schools have developed complex structures, policies, and curricula to accomplish this mission (see Figure 5.1).

Institution: any organization a society establishes to maintain and improve its way of life.

The School as a Reflection of Society

As you might expect, schools mirror the national, provincial or territorial, and surrounding local culture and other special interests. Independent and parochial schools, for example, are often maintained by groups that see the school as a means of perpetuating their preferred way of life. Nevertheless, as Henry (1993, p. 29) points out, "Schools are . . . not simply puppets of the dominant mainstream society. They have their own unique concerns and their own 'poetry' of people and events. Whether public or private, all schools are not the same."

Rural, Suburban, and Urban Schools

Schools also reflect their location. Schools in rural, urban, and suburban settings have significantly different cultures. Rural schools are often the focal point for community life and reflect values and beliefs that tend to be more conservative than those associated with urban and suburban schools. While the small size of a rural school may contribute to the development of a family-like culture, its size may also make it difficult to provide students with an array of curricular experiences equal to that found at larger schools in more populated areas. In contrast, large suburban or urban schools may provide students with more varied learning experiences, but these schools may lack the cohesiveness and community focus of rural schools.

For an interesting look at the variety of resources and programs offered in Canadian school districts, visit the Canadian School Boards Association at cdnsba.org. In addition to school district information, there are important resources about twenty-first century learning, Aboriginal education, student health and wellness, and school governance.

Schools and Community Environments

The effects of a school's local environment are considerable. Urban schools, especially those in less affluent districts, may reflect the social problems of the surrounding area. Middle-class families who can afford to move away from such urban areas or place their children in independent schools often do so. As a result, students in some urban school

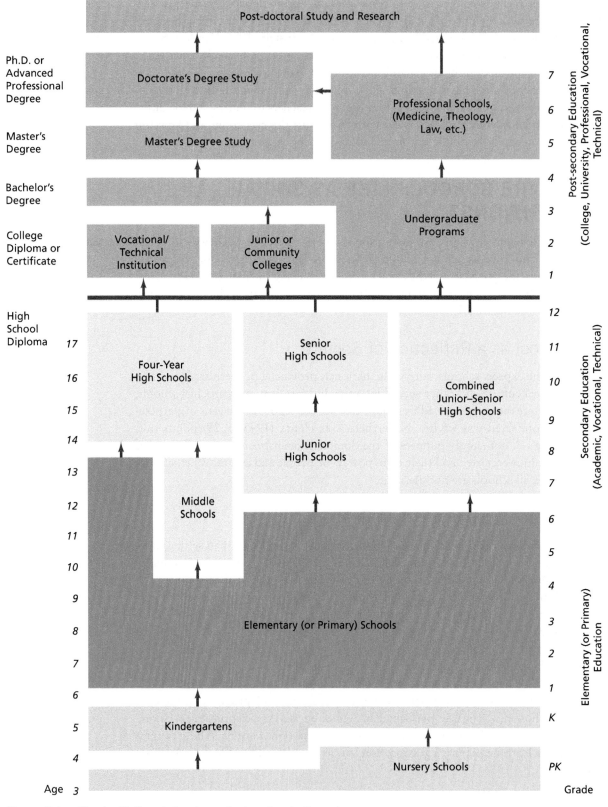

Figure 5.1 The institutional structure of education in Canada

districts are increasingly from low-income backgrounds. Children who experience poverty, especially on a continuous basis, are at higher risk of suffering health problems, developmental delays, and behaviour disorders. According to a 2012 UNICEF report called *Measuring Child Poverty*, Canada is lagging behind the other "economically advanced countries" studied, with 13.3 percent of Canadian children living in poverty. Even more startling, *half* of Indigenous children in Canada live in poverty.

Though some communities may impact their schools in undesirable ways, many teachers at low-income area schools find their work stimulating and rewarding.

In what ways do schools reflect their communities and the wider Canadian society? What influence might the community have on this school? On the students who attend it? On the teachers?

The Culture of the School

Although in general schools share a few universal characteristics, each school is unique. Each has a culture of its own—a network of beliefs, values and traditions, and ways of thinking and behaving that distinguishes it from other schools.

⟫⟫ VOICES FROM THE FIELD | Teaching in a High-Needs School

After teaching in many affluent communities, I chose to enhance my teaching career by moving to a high-needs area. Many of my colleagues questioned my decision, but I knew I was needed, and as much as I would be teaching my students, I knew they would be teaching me too. As in years past, I was anxious about my class and worried about all the stories I'd heard throughout the summer. After the first day, my anxieties were diminished. I had in front of me 24 faces who were looking to me for guidance, care, attention, and an opportunity to shine. It was my job to give them all that they needed.

My students had to learn many different ways to show their emotions (such as Zones of Regulation) to help ease them into a day of learning. There were times when the curriculum had to wait a few minutes while we worked out some issues. Many of the students had difficult situations in their home lives, and soon the classroom became their safe zone. My job was to teach my students, but I also provided them with guidance in difficult situations. At times, they would act out in the classroom because that was the only way they knew how to get the attention they needed. I was always available to sit with my students at lunch or recess to resolve any issues they were dealing with. I had to become someone they could talk to so they could make better choices throughout the day.

There were times when it was exhausting because I questioned how much of the curriculum I was able to teach that day. But then there were times when they would learn more than I expected because I had laid the groundwork for building a safe and secure environment to learn in. When

students know that their teacher believes in them and cares about them, it is amazing how much they will learn for you.

The school community was very different from ones I had taught at in the past. I did not see any bullying amongst the students. Rather, the students worked together to support each other to learn. Within the school, the teachers also worked together to help each other with behavioural issues as well as shared resources. The school became a community where everyone helped each other and students felt safe to learn. The community lacked deep roots because it was very transient. I had many students arriving or leaving throughout the year. Often students would come to my classroom with large gaps in their education because of the many different schools they had already been in. Due to the gaps, their education lacked the deep foundation needed for a child to succeed, and thus frustration and then poor behaviour would result. Building that community within the classroom is essential for this reason.

Many of the parents were anxious to meet with me during the first week of school. This demonstrated their concern and love for their child. Although they could not provide some of the basic needs, they wanted the same thing that every parent wants—the best education for their child. My students and parents have taught me the true meaning of helping and caring for others. Although they do not have a lot to offer in material things, my students have given me more in love and appreciation in my classroom.

Courtesy of Cheryl Carmichael OCT, B.A., B.Ed, Durham District School Board. Used with permission.

Much like a community, a school has a distinctive culture—a collective way of life. Terms that have been used to describe **school culture** include *climate*, *ethos*, *atmosphere*, and *character*. Some schools may be characterized as community-like places with a shared sense of purpose and commitment to providing the best education possible for all students. Other schools lack a unified sense of purpose or direction. Still others are characterized by internal conflict and divisiveness and may even reflect what Deal and Peterson (2009) term a "toxic" school culture that students, teachers, administrators, and parents feel does not sufficiently meet their needs.

The Physical and Virtual Environment

The physical environment of a school both reflects and helps to create the school's overall culture. Displays of student art, trophy cabinets, bulletin boards with a section for "Student of the Week" and newspaper clippings highlighting school activities or accomplishments all play a part in the creation of a school's culture. "Whether school buildings are squeezed between other buildings or located on sprawling campuses, their fenced-in area or other physical separation distinguishes them from the community-at-large" (Ballantine 1997, p. 210). A school's virtual presence can also have an impact on its culture. Schools that have effective websites and that use social media to communicate about school-related events to the broader community are able to promote a spirit of cohesiveness.

Formal Practices of Schools

The formal practices of Canadian schools are evident to past and present students. With few exceptions, students attend school from 4 or 5 years of age through 16, at the least, and usually to age 18. Classes run Monday through Friday, September through June, for 12 or 13 years. For the most part, students are assigned to a grade level on the basis of age rather than ability or interest. Assignment to individual classes or teachers at a given grade level, however, may be made on the basis of ability or interest.

Teachers and students are grouped in several ways at the elementary-school level but follow one dominant pattern in secondary school. In elementary schools, the **self-contained classroom** is the most traditional arrangement. In this type of classroom, one teacher teaches all or nearly all subjects to a group of about 25–30 children, with the teacher and students remaining in the same classroom for the entire day. Music and physical education and other subjects that require special equipment or space are often taught in other parts of the school, so students may leave the classroom for scheduled periods. Specialists often teach some subjects, such as French, music, and art, and these teachers usually travel to the students' classroom for regular instruction. In the intermediate grades (7–8) in elementary schools, the system whereby homeroom teachers provide basic instruction in subjects such as mathematics and language arts and subject specialists teach the rest is known as **rotary instruction**. Individual students may also attend special classes for remediation, English language instruction, or speech therapy. Some school districts offer gifted programs for students who are identified as intellectually gifted through formal testing. In other districts, gifted and talented students are provided with enrichment through special events that occur on a regular basis.

In **open-space schools**, students are free to move among various activities and learning centres. Instead of self-contained classrooms, open-space schools have large instructional areas with movable walls and furniture that can be rearranged easily. Grouping for instruction is much more fluid and varied. Students do much of their work independently, with a number of teachers providing individual guidance as needed.

In middle schools and secondary schools, students frequently study four or five academic subjects taught by teachers who specialize in them. In this organizational arrangement, called **departmentalization**, students move from classroom to classroom for their lessons. Secondary school teachers often share their classrooms with other teachers and use their rooms only during scheduled class periods.

Departmentalization: an organizational arrangement for schools in which students move from classroom to classroom for instruction in different subject areas.

The Culture of the Classroom

Just as schools develop their unique cultures, each classroom develops its own culture or way of life. The culture of a classroom is determined in large measure by the manner in which teachers and students participate in common activities. An additional factor is the diversity of cultural, ethnic, and linguistic groups represented within some classrooms. In Canada's larger urban areas, it is not uncommon for an individual school to have students from as many as 50 different cultural, ethnic, or linguistic groups. In addition, the environment of the classroom and the inhabitants of that environment—students and teachers—are constantly interacting. Each aspect of the classroom affects all others (Woolfolk, 2007). Indeed, as any teacher can attest, the addition or removal of as few as one or two students in a class can positively or negatively affect the classroom's culture.

The quality of teacher–student interactions is influenced by the physical characteristics of the setting (classroom, use of space, materials, resources, etc.) and the social dimensions of the group (norms, rules, expectations, cohesiveness, distribution of power and influence). These elements interact to shape **classroom culture**. Teachers who appreciate the importance of the salient elements of classroom culture are more likely to create environments that they and their students find satisfying and rewarding.

Classroom culture: the "way of life" characteristic of a classroom group; determined by the social dimensions of the group and the physical characteristics of the setting.

HOW IS CULTURAL DIVERSITY REPRESENTED IN CANADIAN SCHOOLS?

The percentage of ethnic minorities in Canadian schools has been growing steadily since the end of World War II. According to Statistics Canada's report on the census of 2006, 18.4 percent of Canada's population was born in other countries, the highest percentage of any country except Australia. Statistics Canada also reports that over 90 percent of new citizens settle in Ontario, British Columbia, Quebec, and Alberta in large urban areas, with Montreal, Toronto, and Vancouver accounting for approximately 75 percent of the total (Statistics Canada, 2011).

In 2012, Canada welcomed a record number of immigrants for its seventh consecutive year, with 257 515 newcomers entering the country. Today, newcomers to Canada represent over 20 percent of the total Canadian population, the highest proportion among G-8 countries. According to the 2011 National Household Survey, over 200 ethnic origins were reported in Canada, with 13 of those surpassing the 1 million population mark (Evans, 2013).

Clearly, the increasing **diversity** of Canadian society has extensive implications for schools. There is, for example, an increased demand for English as a second language (ESL) programs and teachers. All but a few school districts face a critical shortage of minority teachers. As well, there is an imperative to develop curricula and strategies that address the needs and backgrounds of all students—regardless of their social class, gender, sexual orientation, or ethnic, racial, or cultural identity.

Diversity: differences among people in regard to gender, race, ethnicity, culture, and socioeconomic status.

The Meaning of Culture

Culture is *the way of life* common to a group of people. It consists of the values, attitudes, and beliefs that influence their traditions and behaviour. It is also a way of

Culture: the way of life common to a group of people; includes knowledge deemed important, shared meanings, norms, values, attitudes, ideals, and view of the world.

interacting with and looking at the world. Although at one time it was believed that Canada was a "melting pot" in which ethnic cultures would melt into one, ethnic and cultural differences have remained very much a part of life in Canada. A "salad-bowl" analogy more accurately captures the multicultural diversity of Canadian society. That is, the distinguishing characteristics of cultures tend to be preserved and valued rather than blended into a single monoculture. An **ethnic group** is made up of individuals within a larger culture who share a self-defined racial or cultural identity and a set of beliefs, attitudes, and values. Members of an ethnic group distinguish themselves from others in the society both physically and socially. The composition of ethnic groups can change over time, and there is often as much variability within groups as between them. The notion that **race** or **gender** are biological concepts that suggest natural physical variations among humans has been largely refuted by social scientists who argue that race, gender, and even social class are socially constructed. While most individuals have a personal concept of what constitutes race or gender, this issue is complicated and goes far beyond the scope of this text; however, for more information on this topic, see the work of influential cultural theorist Stuart Hall, who believed identity to be an ongoing product of history and culture rather than a finished product.

Ethnic group: individuals within a larger culture who share a racial or cultural identity and a set of beliefs, values, and attitudes and who consider themselves members of a distinct group or subculture.

Race: a concept of human variation used to distinguish people on the basis of biological traits and characteristics.

Gender: the socially constructed roles we enact based on our sex.

Dimensions of Culture

Within Canada, we find cultural groups that differ according to other distinguishing factors, such as religion, politics, economics, and geographic region. The regional culture of Newfoundland, for example, is quite different from that of Alberta. Similarly, British Columbians are culturally different from *les québécois*. However, everyone in Canada shares some common dimensions of culture. James Banks, an authority on multicultural education, has termed this shared culture the "national macro-culture" (Banks, 1999). In addition to belonging to the national macro-culture, people in Canada are often members of specific ethnic groups.

Students in today's classrooms have diverse cultural identities. As a teacher, what steps will you take to integrate all students into the classroom?

Thomas M Perkins/Shutterstock

Cultural Identity

Besides membership in the macro-culture, every Canadian individual participates in an array of subcultures, each with its own customs and beliefs. Collectively, these subcultures determine an individual's **cultural identity**, an overall sense of who one is. Elements that shape a person's cultural identity include age, racial background, language, religion, gender, sexual orientation, and income level. These elements can have varied influence on an individual. For example, cultural identity for some people is most strongly determined by their occupations; for others, by their ethnicity; and for others still, by their religious beliefs.

Remember that your future students will have their own complex cultural identities, which are no less valid than your own. For some, these identities foster a sense of "disconnection" from the attitudes, expectations, and values conveyed by the school. At present, the educational curriculum in Canada has a strong Eurocentric focus. Ghosh and Galczynski (2014) argue such a biased approach is unfair to culturally diverse students, especially new immigrants, as they do not understand the cultural context and often even the language in which they are taught. As well, minority students may feel they are being treated unfairly if they believe they are required to be "representatives" of their culture. Teachers should not require such students to teach the rest of their classmates about their cultures, as singling them out from their Euro-Canadian peers constitutes an insensitive practice.

As a teacher, you will be challenged to understand the subtle differences in cultural identities among your students and to create a learning environment that enables all students to feel comfortable in school and "connected to" their school experiences.

> **Cultural identity:** an overall sense of oneself, derived from the extent of one's participation in various subcultures within the national macro-culture.

Language and Culture

Culture is embedded in language, a fact that has sometimes resulted in conflict between the English- and French-speaking groups in our society. While Canadians generally support the preservation of ethnic cultures, most believe that new immigrants should learn one of the two official languages in order to function effectively within Canadian society. ESL programs vary from one jurisdiction to another (see Figure 5.2).

Four Types of Bilingual Education Programs

Immersion programs: Students learn English and other subjects in classrooms where only English is spoken. Aides who speak the first language of students are sometimes available, or students may also listen to equivalent audiotaped lessons in their first language.

Transition programs: Students receive reading lessons in their first language and lessons in English as a second language (ESL). Once they sufficiently master English, students are placed in classrooms where English is spoken and their first language is discontinued.

Pull-out programs: On a regular basis, students are separated from English-speaking students so that they may receive lessons in English or reading lessons in their first language. These are sometimes called sheltered English programs.

Maintenance programs: To maintain the student's native language and culture, instruction in English and instruction in the native language are provided from kindergarten through grade 12. Students become literate.

Figure 5.2 Four types of bilingual education programs

Supporting English Language Learners

Teachers must meet the needs of English language learners (ELLs) in their classrooms. These needs are best met by teachers who speak their native language as well as English. However, this is often not possible, and monolingual teachers, particularly those in large urban areas, can expect to find increasing numbers of ELLs in their classrooms. All teachers need professional development and support in this area—through additional courses and workshops offered by faculties of education or school districts. There are also many resources available online. One example is a resource created by the Ontario Ministry of Education, called *Many Roots, Many Voices*, which can be accessed at www.edu.gov.on.ca/eng/document/manyroots/manyroots.pdf. Among other strategies, this document offers the following advice to teachers of ELLs:

- Begin with essentials: the language of everyday life.
- Build bridges: use students' prior knowledge as a foundation and welcome first languages.
- Get them talking: the value of oral language cannot be underestimated.
- Teach language everywhere: use a cross-curricular approach.
- Measure success: focus on monitoring and assessment. (p. 14)

WHAT IS DIVERSITY, EQUITY, AND INCLUSIVE EDUCATION?

The concept of diversity acknowledges the existence of a wide range of human attributes and qualities within a group. According to Ontario's Equity and Inclusive Education Strategy document, titled *Realizing the Promise of Diversity*, the dimensions of diversity include, but are not limited to, "ancestry, culture, ethnicity, gender, gender identity, language, physical and intellectual ability, race, religion, sex, sexual orientation, and socio-economic status" (2009, p. 4). It might also include age, political beliefs, or other ideologies. Inclusive education is based on the recognition that each individual is unique and that our individual differences need to be accepted and respected. This is particularly important in schools and classrooms because in order for learning to occur, these spaces need to be positive, safe, and nurturing.

As a teacher, you have an obligation toward all your students to see that your curriculum and instruction are based on the principles of equity and inclusion. Teachers need to be fair, inclusive, and respectful of all students. Providing equal educational opportunity to all students means that teachers and schools promote the full development of students as individuals, without regard for ethnicity, gender, sexual orientation, socioeconomic status, abilities, or disabilities. More specifically, educators fulfil this important mission by continually evaluating the appropriateness of the curricular and instructional experiences they provide. Students need to see themselves reflected in the curricular materials being used as well as in the physical surroundings of the classroom and school environment.

> *Inclusive education is central to the achievement of high-quality education for all learners and the development of more inclusive societies. Inclusion is still thought of in some countries as an approach to serving children with disabilities within general educational settings. Internationally, however, it is increasingly seen more broadly as a reform that supports and welcomes diversity amongst all learners.*
>
> —UNESCO, 2008, p. 5

Multicultural Education

Multicultural education, which was born out of the *Multicultural Act* in 1988 as Bill-C-93, was popular during the 1980s and 1990s. It emphasized the promotion of acceptance, understanding, and respect for cultural diversity in Canada. Going beyond "tolerance" of cultural differences, multicultural education sought to promote equality among ethnocultural groups and recognition that cultural diversity is a positive feature of Canadian society. Preferring the idea of a "cultural mosaic" to the "melting pot" model of the United States, proponents of multicultural education wanted to ensure that all students could participate as valued members of society, regardless of racial, ethnic, religious, or cultural background.

Anti-Racist Education

Although multicultural education provided students with opportunities to explore and appreciate the cultural heritage of their peers, some critics argued that celebrating pride in heritage through multicultural festivals and reading material about other cultures would do little to promote the elimination of the systemic policies and practices that contribute to racism. This kind of attention to surface culture, Bolgatz (2005) argued, results in a "heroes and holidays approach" that is largely superficial and actually promotes stereotypes by portraying ethnic and racial groups in isolated ways. A multicultural approach positions non-white students as "the other" and encourages white students to perceive themselves as the norm.

Proponents of **anti-racist education**, a movement that emerged in the late 1990s, argued that educators need to go beyond promoting harmony and cross-cultural understanding to identifying the root causes of racism at the individual and system levels. This involves exploring the power relationships that exist in society and providing students with opportunities to take individual responsibility for eliminating all forms of racism, including stereotypes, prejudice, and discrimination.

Anti-racist education: a movement that focuses on examining the power imbalances between racialized people and nonracialized/white people.

Critical Multiculturalism

Despite the promise of multicultural and anti-racist education to provide equity for all students, the challenge of marginalization remains for those who are not positioned by society as existing within the norm. Stephen May (1999) proposed the concept of **critical multiculturalism** to address the criticism of multicultural education as being too focused on curricular change rather than on the impact of structural racism in schools. In his book *Critical Multiculturalism: Rethinking Multicultural and Antiracist Education*, May argues that the principal consequence for many minorities has been the loss of their cultural identities, including their language, as the price they pay to enter the "civic realm" (1999, p. 11).

Critical multiculturalism: an approach that focuses on examining the impact of structural racism in schools and encourages educators and students to work toward social change.

Teaching for Diversity, Equity, and Inclusion

More recently, educators and policy-makers have focused on addressing the need to reach all learners. As a teacher, you will teach students who, historically, have not received full educational opportunity—students from the many racial and ethnic minority groups in Canada, students from low-income families or communities, students with exceptional abilities or disabilities, students who are gay or lesbian, and students who are male or female. You will face the challenge of reaching out to all students and teaching them that they are persons of worth who can learn.

In developing a curriculum that promotes equity and diversity, you should be sensitive to how your instructional materials, strategies, and classroom environment can be made more inclusive so that they reflect cultural "voices" that were previously silent or marginalized in discussions about what should be taught in schools and how it should be taught. "Non-dominant groups representing diversity in the school whose voices traditionally have not been heard include those defined by race, language, gender, sexual orientation, alternative family structures, social class, disability, bilingualism, and those with alien or refugee status" (Henry, 1996, p. 108). Effective teachers attend to these previously unheard voices not as an act of tokenism but with a genuine desire to make the curriculum more inclusive. Teachers also need to critically explore their own identities, biases, and values and consider how these may shape the way they plan their daily lessons and interactions with their students. This includes trying to look at different resources and classroom situations from multiple perspectives, thinking about how power relationships shape their decisions, responses, and actions, and reflecting and taking action to correct imbalances of power as needed.

Instructional Materials and Strategies

To create classrooms that are truly inclusive, teachers must select instructional materials that are sensitive, accurately portray the contributions of cultural groups, and reflect diverse points of view. Teachers must also recognize that "[s]ome of the books and other materials on ethnic groups published each year are insensitive, inaccurate, and written from mainstream and insensitive perspectives and points of view" (Banks, 1997, p. 124). Some guidelines for selecting diverse instructional materials are as follows:

- Books and other materials should accurately portray the perspectives, attitudes, and feelings of a wide variety of cultural groups.
- Fictional works should have strong characters that reflect diverse perspectives.
- Books should describe settings and experiences with which all students can identify and yet should accurately reflect different cultures and lifestyles.
- The protagonists in books should face conflicts and problems universal to all cultures and groups.
- The illustrations in books should be accurate, culturally sensitive, and technically good.
- Instructional materials should not contain racist concepts, clichés, phrases, or words.
- Factual materials should be historically accurate.
- Resources and textbooks should discuss major events and documents related to the history of a variety of cultural groups. (Adapted from Banks, 1997, pp. 125–126)

Yvonne Wilson, an Indigenous elementary teacher, points out that a teacher's willingness to learn about other cultures is very important to students and their parents:

> People in the community know if you are trying to understand their culture. Students also see it. Becoming involved—going to a powwow or participating in other cultural events—shows people that here is a teacher who is trying to learn about our culture.

Participating wholeheartedly in cross-cultural experiences will help you grow as a teacher.

HOW IS GENDER A DIMENSION OF EQUITY, DIVERSITY, AND INCLUSIVE EDUCATION?

Sex: the biological makeup of a person's reproductive anatomy.

Gender identity: the way we define how we align (or don't align) with what we see as options for gender.

There is a distinction between **sex** (the biological makeup of a person's reproductive anatomy) and gender (the socially constructed roles we enact based on our sex). **Gender identity** refers to the way we define how we align (or don't align) with what we see as options for gender. **Gender expression** refers to the ways we present our gender through dress, demeanour, and actions and how these are interpreted based on gender norms. In some cases, a person's biological or assigned sex and gender do not align, and this might result in someone identifying as **transgender** or **gender fluid**. When one's biological sex matches one's gender identity and expression, this is referred to as **cisgender**. People who are cisgender have privilege because they do not have to worry on a daily basis about the things that transgender or gender fluid people do. Today's teachers need to be cognizant that transgender or gender fluid students struggle daily with things other students take for granted, such as which restroom to use or whether they will be able to use the change room in the gym without fear or anxiety. For more information, see http://itspronouncedmetrosexual.com/2015/03/the-gender-bread-person-v3.

Gender expression: the ways we present our gender through dress, demeanour, and actions and how these are interpreted based on gender norms.

Transgender: people who identify with or express a gender identity that differs from the one that corresponds to that person's sex at birth.

Gender fluid: a gender that varies over time or includes a mix of both male and female.

Cisgender: when one's biological sex matches one's gender identity and expression.

Gender Differences

Cultural differences between males and females are partially shaped by society's traditional expectations of them. Through **sex role stereotyping**, families, media, schools, and other powerful social forces condition boys and girls to act in certain ways regardless of abilities or interests. As mentioned previously, one of the aims of schools is to socialize students to participate in society. One dimension of the **sex role socialization** process sometimes conveys to students certain expectations about the way boys and girls are "supposed" to act. We used to suggest that girls are supposed to play with dolls, and boys with trucks. It was also believed that girls are supposed to be passive, whereas boys should be active. Girls are supposed to express their feelings and emotions when in pain; boys should repress their feelings and deny pain.

Sex role stereotyping: beliefs that subtly encourage males and females to conform to certain behavioural norms regardless of abilities and interests.

Sex role socialization: socially expected behaviour patterns conveyed to individuals on the basis of gender.

Students may be socialized into particular gender-specific roles as a result of the curriculum materials they use at school. By portraying males in more dominant, assertive ways and portraying females in ways that suggest they are passive and helpless, textbooks can subtly reinforce expectations about the way girls and boys "should" behave. Over the past few decades, though, publishers of curriculum materials have become more vigilant about avoiding these stereotypes.

However, some gender differences in academic skills do appear to exist. In a Canadian Council on Learning report (2011) called *Exploring the "Boy Crisis" in Education*, Dr. Paul Cappon presented and analyzed data that suggest that an achievement gap exists between boys and girls, with boys ranking behind girls in various measures of scholastic achievement, including standardized tests. According to the report, boys trail in reading and writing, with 30 percent of them scoring in the bottom quarter of standardized tests compared with 19 percent of girls. The report also notes that more boys drop out of school and are identified as having behavioural problems. The Canadian media has focused on the so-called "boy crisis" and has called for more male teachers and role models, especially in elementary schools, in addition to advocating for same-sex classes in an attempt to address the issue. However, the roots of the gender gap are much more complex and nuanced than often reported. Many factors can account for the discrepancies between the academic achievement of boys and girls. It is a picture that continues to emerge, and most recently has focused on social norms for boys and girls and the way those standards impact educational success. Wayne Martino (see Focus on Research) suggests that the question we should focus on is which boys and which girls are not achieving. "Teachers are at the centre of such educational reform, one that resists over-simplification of differences in gender and achievement" (2008, p. 3).

Wayne J Martino

rather than adopting "quick-fix" policies such as hiring more male teachers, we need to focus our attention on which boys are underachieving or at risk, because many boys are doing well. Martino argues that focusing on the question of which boys (and which girls) are not achieving "would lead to identifying how other factors (such as race, ethnicity, social class, and sexuality) intersect with gender to impact students' engagement with schooling. The resulting approach would emphasize identifying productive pedagogies, developing an intellectually demanding curriculum, and building safe classroom learning environments" (p. 3).

Martino's book, *Gender, Race, and the Politics of Role Modelling: The Influence of Male Teachers*, co-authored with Goli Rezai-Rashti in 2011, is a response to policy-related concerns and media calls for more male teachers and role models in elementary schools. The book includes the perspectives of minority teachers and students in an attempt to focus attention on the structural inequalities that still exist in the education system.

Martino identifies the following pedagogical approach as good teaching for boys and girls:

Dr. Wayne Martino is Professor in the Faculty of Education, Western University, in London, Ontario. His research and teaching interests include gender issues and reform in urban education; equity and social justice education; adolescent boys' and girls' perspectives on gender; queer, trans, and feminist studies in education; and boys' underachievement in schools. He has written extensively about the so-called "boy crisis" fuelled by Canadian media reports that boys were trailing girls in nearly every measure of scholastic achievement. While various data sources do report an achievement gap, Martino (2008) argues that

- Develop a research-based knowledge of gender reform strategies.
- Connect curriculum and assessment practices to the everyday lives of students while maintaining a focus on developing their higher-order and analytic thinking skills.
- Refuse to treat all boys or all girls as a homogenous group.
- Create a safe learning environment in which gender, sexual, racial, and ethnic diversity is acknowledged and incorporated into the curriculum (Martino, 2008, p. 3).

Gender-Fair Classrooms and Curricula

Gender bias: subtle bias or discrimination on the basis of gender; reduces the likelihood that the target of the bias will develop to the full extent of his or her capabilities.

Gender-fair classroom: education that is free of bias or discrimination on the basis of gender.

Although research and debate about the bias boys and girls encounter in school will no doubt continue, it is clear that teachers must encourage girls and boys to develop to the full extent of their abilities and must provide an education free from **gender bias**—subtle favouritism or discrimination on the basis of gender. Because it is through language that gender fairness is most easily observed, it is important for teachers to be very careful in their selection of words when interacting with students.

Following is a list of basic guidelines for creating a **gender-fair classroom**. Adherence to these guidelines will help teachers address the structural inequities of schools as well as critically examine both what they teach and how they teach it.

- Reduce young children's self-imposed sexism.
- Teach about sexism and sex-role stereotyping.

- Foster an atmosphere of collaboration between girls and boys.
- Provide a wide variety of reading material in the classroom and library.
- Allow students choice in their reading.
- Select books and other instructional resources that reflect students' images of themselves.

Sexual Orientation

In addition to gender bias, some students experience discrimination on the basis of their sexual orientation. According to a 2009 Statistics Canada survey, 2 percent of Canadians aged 18–59 said they are gay, lesbian, or bisexual. To help all students realize their full potential, teachers should acknowledge

Gender-orientation symbols

the special needs of lesbian, gay, bisexual, and transgender (LGBT) students. According to Egale's First National School Climate Survey on Homophobia, Biphobia, and Transphobia in Canadian Schools, 64 percent of LGBT students feel unsafe at school, with 51 percent reporting being verbally harassed and another 21 percent reporting being physically harassed about their sexual orientation. Although some Canadian schools have been slow or reluctant to meet the needs of LGBT students, many now have Gay-Straight Alliances (GSA) to promote safe and inclusive learning environments. In 2012, the Ontario Ministry of Education amended the *Education Act* to ensure that every board would support students who want to establish and lead activities and organizations that promote a safe and inclusive learning environment, including GSAs.

Similarly, in Alberta, the legislative assembly passed Bill 10 in March 2015, mandating GSAs in any of the province's public and Catholic schools where students want them.

WHAT CHARACTERISTICS DISTINGUISH SUCCESSFUL SCHOOLS?

At this point in your professional education, you may, because of the diverse nature of today's school populations, be uncertain of your ability to develop a positive classroom climate. However, many schools in all settings and with all kinds of students are highly successful, including inner-city and isolated rural schools and schools that serve pupils of all socioeconomic, racial, and ethnic backgrounds. What are the characteristics of these schools? Do they have commonalities that account for their success?

Measures of Success

First, we must define what we mean by a **successful school**. One measure of success, naturally, is that students at these schools achieve at a high level and complete requirements for graduation. Whether reflected in scores on standardized tests or other documentation of academic gains, students at these schools are learning. They are achieving literacy in reading, writing, computation, and computer skills. They are learning to solve problems and to think creatively and analytically, and, most importantly, they are learning to learn.

Successful school: schools characterized by a high degree of student learning, results that surpass those expected from comparable schools, and steady improvement rather than decline.

Additionally, successful schools are those that are improving, rather than deteriorating. School improvement is a slow process, and schools that are improving in achievement and student morale can be considered successful.

Research on School Effectiveness

During the 1980s and early 1990s, much research was conducted to identify the characteristics of successful (or effective) schools. These characteristics were defined in different ways in several research projects. The following list, which is a synthesis of these findings, presents the most commonly mentioned characteristics:

- *Strong leadership*—Successful schools have strong leaders—individuals who value education and see themselves as educational leaders, not just as managers or bureaucrats. They monitor the performance of everyone at the school—teachers, staff, students, and themselves. These leaders have a vision of the school as an effective learning environment, and they take decisive steps to bring that about.

- *High expectations*—Teachers at successful schools have high expectations of students. These teachers believe that all students, rich or poor, can learn, and they communicate this through realistic, yet high, expectations.

- *Emphasis on basic skills*—Teachers at successful schools emphasize student achievement in the basic skills of reading, writing, and mathematics.

- *Orderly school environment*—The environments of successful schools are orderly, safe, and conducive to learning. Discipline problems are at a minimum, and teachers are able to devote greater amounts of time to teaching.

- *Frequent, systematic evaluation of student learning*—The learning of students in successful schools is monitored closely. When difficulties are noticed, appropriate remediation is provided quickly.

- *Sense of purpose*—Those who teach and those who learn at successful schools have a strong sense of purpose. From the principal to the students, everyone at the school is guided by a vision of excellence.

- *Collegiality and a sense of community*—Teachers, administrators, and staff at successful schools work well together. They are dedicated to creating an environment that promotes not only student learning, but also their own professional growth and development.

School improvement research: research studies that identify the characteristics of schools that improve over time.

Since the 1990s, researchers have increasingly focused on the characteristics of schools that improve over time. A key finding of **school improvement research** is that teachers must play a significant role in providing leadership for the improvement process. In other words, "If real reform is to occur, classroom teachers must be active in defining its objectives, design, implementation, and assessment. Reform as a product handed down to teachers must be redesigned to be a process in which teachers are vital contributors" (Armstrong, 2008, p. 142).

Schools that are improving are made up of collaborative teams of teachers, school administrators, and other stakeholders who are committed to working together to increase student learning. Teacher leadership teams, parent and community representation on school councils, and open, two-way communication with all stakeholders are examples of shared leadership. In short, the culture of a school that is improving encourages teachers to grow and to develop in the practice of their profession. It encourages them to develop knowledge and skills to respond to social problems such as those described in the following sections.

WHAT SOCIAL PROBLEMS AFFECT SCHOOLS AND PLACE STUDENTS AT RISK?

A complex and varied array of social issues impact schools. These problems often detract from the ability of schools to educate students according to the aims discussed at the beginning of this chapter: educational goals, prosocial values, socialization, achievement, personal growth, social change, and equal opportunity. Furthermore, schools are often charged with the difficult (if not impossible) task of providing a frontline defence against such problems. Nevertheless, effective teachers understand how social issues influence student learning, and they are able to reduce the negative impact of those issues.

For some time, Canadian schools have served to combat social problems by offering a wide array of health, education, and social service programs. Many school districts provide breakfasts, nutritional counselling, diagnostic services related to health and family planning, after-school child care, job placement, sex and drug education, and other services. In the following sections, we examine several societal problems that directly influence schools, teachers, and students.

Identifying Students at Risk

An increasing number of young people live under conditions of extreme stress, chronic poverty, crime, and lack of adult guidance. According to Calder Stegemann and Roberts, students are said to be "at risk" when they "belong to an identifiable group that has a higher-than-average probability of an adverse outcome" such as low academic achievement or school failure (2015, p. 2). Typically, negative environmental, social, and family conditions adversely affect a student's personal development and academic achievement. **Students at risk** of dropping out tend to get low grades, perform below their grade level academically, are older than the average student at their level because of previous retention, and have behavioural problems at school. Fortunately, the drop-out rate in Canada has steadily decreased since 2002, reaching a low of 7.8 percent in 2012.

Many children in Canada live in families that help them grow up healthy, confident, and skilled, but many do not. Instead, their life settings are characterized by problems of alcoholism or other substance abuse, family or gang violence, unemployment, poverty, poor nutrition, teenage parenthood, and a history of school failure. Such children live in communities and families that have many problems and frequently become dysfunctional, unable to provide their children with the support and guidance they need.

It is important to remember that at-risk factors are only an indication of *potential* academic problems. The majority of children and youth who live in environments affected by poverty, crime, and other social problems are academically successful.

> **Students at risk:** students whose living conditions and backgrounds place them at risk for dropping out of school.

Family Stress

The stress placed on families in a complex society is extensive and not easily handled. For some families, such stress can be overwhelming. The structure of families experiencing the effects of financial problems, substance abuse, or violence, for example, can easily begin to crumble. Health challenges in which a family member has developed cancer or another serious disease can also lead to significantly increased levels of stress.

Stress within the family can have a significant negative effect on students and their ability to focus on learning while at school. Such stress is often associated with health and emotional problems, failure to achieve, behavioural problems at school, and dropping out.

With the rise in the divorce rate and women's increased presence in the workforce over the past few decades, family constellations have changed dramatically. No longer is a working father, a mother who stays at home, and two or three children the only kind of family in Canada. The number of single-parent families, same-sex parent families, step-parent families, blended families, and extended families has increased dramatically. In 2005, the **Pan-Canadian Education Indicators Program (PCEIP)**, a joint venture of Statistics Canada and the Council of Ministers of Education, Canada, reported that 25 percent of children in single-parent homes live below the poverty line. A report based on data from the 2012 UNICEF Innocenti Research Centre, *Measuring Child Poverty*, indicated that children who live in poverty (and that is one in five in Canada) were more likely to suffer from lower levels of health and educational achievement and more likely to engage in conduct disorders that involve judicial and social protection systems.

Just as there is diversity in the composition of today's families, so, too, is there diversity in the styles with which children are raised. Because of the large number of homes with lone parents or both parents working, an alarming number of **latchkey children** are unsupervised during much of the day. To meet the needs of these children, some schools now offer before- and after-school programs.

Substance Abuse

One of the most pressing social problems confronting today's schools is the abuse of illegal tobacco, drugs, and alcohol. Although still a major concern for Canadian youth, the overall trend shows a decrease in substance abuse for students in grades 6–12. In a 2012–2013 survey administered by Health Canada, 13 percent of students in grades 6–9 reported trying cigarettes, down from 45 percent in 1994. Alcohol was the substance with the highest prevalence (41 percent), followed by marijuana (19 percent); however, use of both has declined over the past five years. The prevalence of psychoactive pharmaceuticals use to get high was third highest; the abuse of over-the-counter sedatives, stimulants, and pain relievers is a growing concern, with 4 percent of students in grades 7–12 reporting using one or more of these substances to get high. There is a decreasing trend in the prevalence of ecstasy, salvia, and synthetic stimulants related to cathinone (known as "bath salts"), with only 1 percent of the youth surveyed reporting use of these substances.

The abuse of drugs not only poses the risks of addiction and overdose, but is also related to problems such as STDs, teenage pregnancy, depression, suicide, automobile accidents, criminal activity, and dropping out. The 2010 International Youth Survey found that delinquent behaviour was linked to substance use and was higher when young people have little parental supervision. For an alarming number of young people, drugs provide a means of coping with life's problems.

Violence and Crime

Although Canada experienced a decline in serious violent crime during the 1990s, crime rates among Canada's 2 million adolescents have remained relatively constant in recent years. The 2010 International Youth Survey found that 37 percent of youth (predominantly males, at 72 percent) reported having engaged in one or more delinquent behaviours in their lifetime, whether acts of violence, theft, vandalism, or drug offences. However, Canadian concern about school crime and safety has led to increased security measures within schools. It is now commonly required that all visitors to a school sign in, that most school-access doors be locked at all times, and that

Pan-Canadian Education Indicators Program (PCEIP): a joint venture of Statistics Canada and the Council of Ministers of Education.

Latchkey children: children who, because of family circumstances, must spend part of each day unsupervised by a parent or guardian.

all school grounds be supervised whenever students are using them. Because of several shooting incidents at both Canadian schools and schools in other countries, the installation of metal detectors has also been given careful consideration. Additional measures include a **Child Abuse Registry** and **criminal record** checks for anyone working with or supervising students. Many schools have also developed crisis management plans to cope with violent incidents on campus and regularly review their ability to provide students, faculty, and staff with a safe environment for learning. The section entitled How Are Schools Addressing Social Problems? later in this chapter outlines what educators and policy-makers are doing to address these issues.

Child Abuse Registry: record kept of individuals who have abused children.

Criminal record: record kept of individuals convicted of criminal offences.

Bullying and Cyberbullying

The increased incidence of aggression and bullying among young people has school authorities and parents alike worried about the long-term effects of such behaviour on individual students as well as on the climate of schools. How does violence—of all levels—affect the educational environments of schools and their communities? As the Ontario Ministry of Education's 2009 Equity and Inclusive Education strategy indicates, "Research findings about the effects of rejection and bullying on young people are clear and consistent. Rejection, exclusion, and estrangement are associated with behaviour problems in the classroom, lower interest in school, lower student achievement, and higher dropout rates" (Osterman, 2000, pp. 323–367). According to PREVNet, a Canadian organization that conducts research into bullying prevention, 75 percent of people have been affected by bullying. In the tragic wake of several recent bullying-related suicides in Canada, it is apparent that there is an urgent need for a solution. Although politicians are calling for national strategies to deal with bullying and cyberbullying, the best interventions occur at the community level, and educators have an important role to play. School-wide anti-bullying initiatives, though well intentioned, have proven to be only moderately successful in confronting the problem of bullying in schools (Vreeman & Carroll, 2007). In a recent review of the research around anti-bullying initiatives administered as school programs that involve all students across all grades, Swearer, Espelage, Vaillancourt, and Hymel (2010) note, "the research suggests that the majority of school-based bullying prevention programs have had little impact on reducing bullying behaviour" (p. 43). There is research, however, to support the use of young adult literature and other curricular materials with students in an effort to help them understand and deal with issues around bullying both in and outside of school (Henkin, 2012; Morris, Taylor, & Wilson, 2000; Trent & Chisholm, 2012). It is clear that classroom teachers can play a role in the process of dismantling bullying in their students' lives.

With the increased use of technology, specifically social media sites and texting, many children now experience cyberbullying (Hinduja & Patchin, 2009). According to PREVNet, over one-third of Canadian teens have witnessed cyberbullying and one in five teens report being victims of cyberbullying. Like traditional bullying, cyberbullying involves an imbalance of power, aggression, and repetitive, negative actions, but these occur online through instant messaging, email, chat room posts, website posts, and/or digital messages sent to a cell phone. Some researchers have found that up to 30–40 percent of students have experienced or engaged in cyberbullying (Belsey, 2009), and with more students going online these numbers are increasing rapidly.

Although students who are cyberbullied do not have to fear physical harassment, this type of bullying can be even more damaging than traditional forms of bullying (Dehue et al., 2009). The anonymity of the online world may make it easier for bullies to target their victims without adults looking on. This anonymity can even lead students who might not bully in person to engage in cyberbullying (Hinduja & Patchin, 2009).

The increased incidence of aggression and bullying among young people has school authorities and parents worried about the long-term effects of such behaviour on individual students as well as on the climate of schools. How does violence—of all levels—affect the educational environments of schools and their communities?

A traditional bully can sometimes be avoided, but one cannot hide from an anonymous bully. The accessibility of the Internet can open up more times and spaces for bullies to harass their victims, and they can cause more damage because they can expose their victims to much wider audiences by forwarding images and emails via cell phones and computers and posting on social networking sites (Hinduja & Patchin, 2009). For more information about how to prevent and deal with bullying and cyberbullying, see www.prevnet.ca/bullying/facts-and-solutions.

Teen Pregnancy

Each year, thousands of Canadian women (1 in every 20) between the ages of 15 and 19 will become pregnant, and about 85 percent of these pregnancies are unintended. Indeed, most teachers of adolescents today may expect to have at least some students who are, or have been, pregnant. Teenage pregnancy can be a serious problem, since many teen mothers drop out of school, forfeiting their high school diplomas and limiting their access to decent, higher-paying job opportunities. As a consequence, they and their children often tend to remain at the bottom of the economic ladder. However, with the increasing numbers of Canadian high schools now making daycare facilities available, some of the problems arising from teen pregnancies are being addressed.

Suicide among Children and Youths

The increase in individual and multiple suicides is alarming. Among Canadians between the ages of 10 and 24, it is the second leading cause of death. According to the Canadian Mental Health Association, suicide accounts for 24 percent of all deaths in Canada among 15- to 24-year-olds the third highest suicide rate for youth in the industrialized world. Although female students are almost three to four times more likely than male students to attempt suicide, about three times as many male students as females follow through. Lesbian, gay, and bisexual youth are two to three times more

Jeff Banks, a history teacher at Lakeside High School, enters the faculty lunchroom and sees a group of his colleagues at their usual table in the corner. Lakeside, located in a low- to medium-income area of a fairly large city in central Canada, has an enrolment of almost 1400 students. About 70 percent of the student body self-identify as Anglo-European Canadians, with the remaining 30 percent from various ethnic and cultural groups. After English, Italian and several East Indian languages are the most common mother tongues. Lakeside has a reputation for being a "good" school—for the most part, students are respectful of their teachers and many parents are involved in school activities in spite of their heavy work schedules. The consensus among teachers is that most parents recognize that education is key if their children are to "better themselves." Jeff approaches the table and finds his friends discussing the recent tragic suicide by a gay teen at a Canadian high school. According to the media, persistent cyberbullying by his peer group was a factor in the youth's death.

"It's so scary," Sue says to the group. "Who knows, something like that could happen right here at Lakeside. We have no idea what kids have to deal with today. Things were so much simpler before the Internet. Of course there was bullying, but we could catch it more easily."

"Yeah, we have no idea what's going on outside of school for many of these kids, especially when they're so immersed in social networking sites," Bret chimes in. "The kind of bullying that happens online is so much more difficult to deal with because it is relentless and aggressive. It happens 24/7 and they have to deal with it everywhere they are. There's no safe zone or place to hide, and giving up their cell phones wouldn't be an option for most teens."

"What I want to know," Sue says, "is how we can prevent something like this from happening here. I read that lesbian and gay teens are up to three times more likely to commit suicide than straight teens. We should be doing

more to support these kids than just setting up a Gay-Straight Alliance at the school."

"Well, I'm not sure how much we can do about cyberbullying here. Kids can hide behind the technology, making it hard to figure out who's doing it, even if the victim is willing to report it in the first place," says Bret. "We could impose stiffer penalties for kids who engage in cyberbullying if we knew who was doing it, but that's not necessarily the answer. First, we need to decide whether schools are responsible for what kids are doing on their own time, and second, I think the more important question is, Why are they doing it in the first place?"

"Right! And how can we prevent it, especially when we aren't certain who is doing it and whether it's really an issue at this school?" Jeff asks.

"Well, I think we can assume it is," adds Nancy with a sigh, putting down the cell phone she has been using. "I just did a search for cyberbullying in Canada and found out that 38 percent of Canadian girls and 26 percent of boys online reported being cyberbullied. And those stats are a couple of years old!"

"If we're going to change things," says Sue, "we've got to figure out how to identify and help kids who feel so desperate that they would rather die than carry on."

1. What is the role of schools in identifying and dealing with issues such as homophobia, cyberbullying, and teen suicide?

2. Are teachers responsible for addressing these kinds of social problems?

3. Once schools identify a problem like the one in this case, what policies and procedures can the school put in place to prevent future incidents from occurring?

4. What might teachers do to promote respect for diversity and inclusion in their classroom and the halls?

likely to attempt suicide than their heterosexual peers, and in an Ontario-based survey, 77 percent of trans respondents had seriously considered suicide and 45 percent had attempted it. The Aboriginal suicide rate for youth is five to six times higher than the non-Aboriginal rate for Canadian youth.

The following statistics from the Canadian Mental Health Association demonstrate the urgent need to raise awareness about mental health and to create community supports to assist youth in crisis:

- In Canada, only one out of five children who need mental health assistance receives support.

- Ten to 20 percent of Canadian youth are affected by a mental illness or disorder.

- Approximately 5 percent of male youth and 12 percent of female youth (aged 12 to 19) have experienced a major depressive episode.

- The total number of 12- to 19-year-olds in Canada at risk for developing depression is a staggering 3.2 million.
- Mental health support can make a difference for 80 percent of people who are affected.
- Mental disorders in youth account for the highest hospital care expenditure in Canada, next to accidents.

Source: www.cmha.ca/media/fast-facts-about-mental-illness/#.VSBcFbqpd4U

While teachers do not have the training and expertise to act as counsellors, it is clear that they have a role to play in assisting youth in crisis. A 2013 report by Children's Mental Health Ontario, called *Building a Better School Environment for Youth with Mental Health and Addiction Issues*, outlines five important findings and provides helpful recommendations for educators:

1. Build more effective communication and respect between school leaders and students.
2. Combat feelings of isolation for youth by talking more openly in classes to dismantle the stigma associated with mental health issues.
3. Provide better access to resources, including a designated safe space in school for students experiencing difficulty managing mental health symptoms.
4. Incorporate mental health and addiction education across the school curriculum, not just in health class.
5. Seek professional development and training in the area of mental health.

HOW ARE SCHOOLS ADDRESSING SOCIAL PROBLEMS?

Responding to the needs of at-risk students continues to be a crucial challenge for schools, families, and communities. Since most children attend school, it is logical that this pre-existing system be used for reaching large numbers of at-risk children and their families. During the past decade, many school districts have taken innovative steps to address social problems that impact students' lives.

Though programs that address social problems are costly, the public believes that schools should be used for the delivery of health and social services. However, there is some disagreement about the extent to which school facilities should be used for anything but meeting students' educational needs. There is a widespread belief that the primary goal of schools should be the education of children, and that schools should not be expected to solve all of society's ills.

Regardless of where you stand on the issue, it is critical that educators do all they can to achieve a positive school climate and provide a safe environment in which students can learn, grow, and develop. Based on this premise, most provinces have now introduced legislation called Safe Schools or Safe and Caring Schools that mandate a focus on equity, inclusivity, and bullying prevention. For an example, see the report on Ontario's *Safe Schools Act*: www.edu.gov.on.ca/eng/ssareview/report0626.pdf.

Intervention Programs

Under pressure to find solutions to increasing social problems among children and youth, educators have developed an array of intervention programs. In general, the aim of these programs is to address the behavioural, social, and academic adjustment of at-risk children and youth so that they can receive maximum benefit from their school experiences.

In the following sections, we provide a brief overview of two strategies that have proven effective in addressing academic, social, and behavioural problems in different communities. This chapter presents additional information about recent, innovative steps for the *prevention* of the effects of social problems on students.

Peer Counselling

Some schools have initiated student-to-student **peer counselling** programs—usually monitored by a counsellor or another specially trained adult. In peer counselling programs, students can address issues such as low academic achievement, interpersonal problems at home and at school, substance abuse, and career planning. Evidence indicates that both peer counsellors and students experience increased self-esteem and greater ability to deal with problems.

Peer counselling: an arrangement whereby students, monitored by a school counsellor or teacher, counsel one another in such areas as low achievement, interpersonal problems, substance abuse, and career planning.

When peer counselling is combined with cross-age tutoring, younger students can learn about drugs, alcohol, pregnancy, delinquency, dropping out, STDs, suicide, and other relevant issues. Groups are often composed of college- and university-aged students meeting with high school students, or high school students meeting with junior high or middle school students. In these preventive programs, older students sometimes perform dramatic role plays that portray students confronting problems and model strategies for handling the situations presented. It should be noted that peer counsellors, despite the name, do not offer psychological counselling, but rather lead sessions that provide spaces for students to discuss topics of concern. When the need for professional help arises, peer counsellors and their adult supervisor direct students to the appropriate agencies for support.

School-Based Intervention Programs

Some schools work in collaboration with community agencies to provide in-school programs that are student-led and teacher-facilitated but still connected to important community support services. Two examples are Uniting Our Nations and Make a Difference.

Uniting Our Nations: In this program, Aboriginal students, First Nations counselors, educators, and community partners collaborate to create and implement a violence prevention program that reflects and honours Indigenous cultures and ways of knowing. The programs range from one-day conferences to three-day culturally relevant experiences or weekly sessions spaced out over the school year.

⟫⟫⟫ Make a Difference

The Durham District School Board (DDSB), located east of Toronto, is implementing an early-years intervention program called "Make a Difference" in response to data showing that 19.8 percent of children aged 0–12 in Oshawa are living below the low income cut-off (LICO). The DDSB planned a coordinated, integrated multipronged approach to provide a range of programs to support the children and families at 12 of their schools. Included in the services and programs they are implementing are nutrition and breakfast programs; vision, dental, and hearing screening; parent/family literacy centres; parent activities and workshops to support community needs; kindergarten support programs; affordable early years and child care programs; and targeted oral language programs. Members of the planning committee include community partners, school administrators, teachers, parents, and the local university. Decisions about what programs to put into place are data-driven, based primarily on the Early Development Instrument (EDI). Outcomes are measured through a variety of indexes, including student achievement and parent and teacher surveys. There are similar interventions in other school districts across the country, as educators begin to recognize the importance of the correlation between poor academic achievement and poverty. Schools play a crucial role in supporting families with reduced or limited financial means, and the DDSB initiative is one example of how schools and community partners can collaborate to provide a range of programs that can support learners and their families in these circumstances.

Slavoljub Pantelic/Shutterstock

Teachers are increasingly asked to provide students with special-needs assistance that goes beyond the purely academic. How far do you think classroom teachers should be expected to go in responding to this request?

Alternative Schools and Curricula

To meet the needs of at-risk students, many school districts have developed alternative schools and curricula. Usually, an **alternative school** is a small, highly individualized school separate from the regular school; in other cases, the alternative school is organized as a **school-within-a-school**. Alternative school programs serve different purposes. Some provide remedial instruction, some vocational training and individualized counselling. Others cater to specialized areas or groups. In the Toronto District School Board (TDSB), the largest in North America, there is a wide variety of alternative schools, including an Africentric school that focuses on improving success for Black students; schools for elite athletes; schools focused on the arts; and even an elementary school focused on environmental education, community activism, and social justice, where traditional subject areas are taught through the lens of race, class, gender, sexuality, and ability. The first gaycentric secondary school program in Canada was established in Toronto in 2014.

Since they generally offer much smaller class sizes than conventional schools, alternative school teachers can monitor students' progress more closely and, when problems arise, respond more quickly and with greater understanding of student needs. To reach students who are not successful at regular schools, alternative schools offer a program of individualized instruction, small class sizes, and various enrichment programs delivered in what school staff describe as a supportive, noncoercive, nontraditional setting.

Many highly effective conventional school teachers develop alternative curricula to meet the unique learning needs of students at risk. Many teachers, for example, link students' learning to business, civic, cultural, and political segments of their communities. The rationale is that connecting at-risk students to the world beyond their schools will enable them to see the relevance of education.

School-within-a-school: an alternative school (within a regular school) designed to meet the needs of students at risk.

SUMMARY

What Are the Aims of Education Today?

■ Though debate about the aims of education continues, there is general agreement that schools have a responsibility to address problems confronting Canadian society.

■ Agreement exists regarding broad educational aims—education for prosocial values, socialization, achievement, personal growth, social change, and equal opportunity.

How Can Schools Be Described?

- Schools can be categorized according to the focus of their curricula and according to their organizational structures.

- Some people believe that schools reproduce the existing social class structure—that they maintain the differences between the "haves" and "have-nots."

What Are Schools Like as Social Institutions?

- Schools develop their own unique cultures, and the community environment that surrounds a school can impact it positively or negatively.

- Elements of a school's physical environment, such as self-contained classrooms, open-space arrangements, and departmentalization, contribute to a school's character and culture. Similarly, each classroom develops its own culture, which is influenced by the physical setting and the social dimensions of the group.

How Is Diversity Represented in Canadian Schools?

- Culture is defined as the way of life common to a group of people, including beliefs, attitudes, habits, values, and practices.

- Dimensions of diversity include beliefs, attitudes, and values; racial identity; language; religion; gender; sexual orientation; ethnicity; income level; and occupation.

What Is Diversity, Equity, and Inclusive Education?

- A multicultural curriculum addresses the needs and backgrounds of all students—regardless of their cultural identity—and expands students' appreciation for diversity. Effective multicultural materials and instructional strategies include the contributions of ethnic groups that reflect diverse points of view, including "voices" that previously may have been silenced or marginalized in society.

- Anti-racist education focuses on identifying the root causes of racism at the individual and system levels and on exploring the power relationships that exist in society.

- Critical multiculturalism is born out of criticisms of multicultural and anti-racist education. Its focus is on the link between education theory, policy, and practice.

How Is Gender a Dimension of Equity, Diversity, and Inclusive Education?

- Gender includes ways of knowing and modes of conduct, thought, and expression specific to sex.

- Both boys and girls experience inequities in the classroom; teachers, however, can provide an education free of *gender bias* by creating gender-fair classrooms and curricula.

- Teachers should acknowledge the special needs of students who are gay, lesbian, bisexual, or trans and provide them with safe, supportive learning environments.

What Characteristics Distinguish Successful Schools?

- Three aspects of successful schools have been suggested: (1) their students manifest a high level of learning; (2) their results surpass those for comparable schools; (3) they are improving rather than deteriorating.

- Research has identified seven characteristics of effective schools: strong leadership, high expectations, emphasis on basic skills, an orderly school environment, frequent and systematic evaluation of student learning, sense of purpose, and collegiality and a sense of community.

What Social Problems Affect Schools and Place Students at Risk?

- Among the many social problems that impact a school's ability to educate students are poverty, family stress, substance abuse, violence and crime, teen pregnancy, suicide, and mental health issues.

- Children at risk tend to get low grades, to underachieve, to be older than other students at the same grade level, and to have behavioural problems at school.

What Are Schools Doing to Address Social Problems?

- Schools have developed intervention and prevention programs to address social problems.

- Many school districts have developed alternative schools or schools-within-a-school that provide highly individualized instructional and support services for students who have not been successful in regular schools.

APPLICATIONS AND ACTIVITIES

1. Identify and then defend your choice of school improvements that you consider most important for increasing the quality of education in Canada. What aims of education do your choices reflect?

2. During your school years, did you ever experience discrimination as a member of a "different" group? Write about one outstanding incident that you feel affected your performance as a student.

3. As a teacher, what activities and materials might you use in a specific learning context to reduce the prejudices of students toward groups different from theirs?

4. In a small group, read the paragraph below and the instructions that follow.
   The culture of a classroom can be directly affected by the physical ambience of the room and the items within it. Bare walls, external noise from traffic or other sources, poor lighting, crowded seating, and a miscellany of other items can affect student learning. Design your concept of the ideal classroom environment to create inclusion in your elementary or secondary school classroom.

5. Join or start an interactive online discussion on one or more of the following topics discussed in this chapter. You might join a newsgroup already in progress or request discussion partners via email or from one of the message board opportunities offered at many of the websites you have already explored. You might also establish a communication link among your classmates or with students in other schools who are taking a similar course.

teen pregnancies	effective schools
at-risk students	family stress
gender equity	multicultural education
cultural diversity	bullying/cyberbullying
substance abuse	youth suicide
crime and violence in schools	school-based clinics
school improvement	alternative schools
children in poverty	

6. Develop a collaborative project with classmates to investigate and report on issues in at-risk intervention or drug abuse or violence prevention.

7. If possible, visit a school that has an enrolment of students whose cultural or socioeconomic backgrounds differ from your own. What feelings and questions emerge as a result of your observations? How might your feelings affect your teaching effectiveness? How might you go about finding answers to any questions that arise?

8. Develop a case study of a school's culture. Visit a local school, or base your study on a school you have attended. Organize your case in terms of the following categories of information:

- *Environment*—How would you describe the school facility or physical plant and its material and human resources? How is space organized? What is the climate of the school?

- *Formal Practices*—What grades are included at the school? How is the school year organized? How is time structured? How are students and teachers grouped for instruction?

- *Traditions*—What events, activities, and products seem important to students, teachers, and administrators? What are the mission and vision statements developed by the school? What symbols, slogans, and ceremonies identify membership in the school? How do community members view and relate to the school?

Draw conclusions from your case study: What aspects of the school culture seem to support learning and academic achievement? On the basis of your study, draft a position statement on the kind of culture you would like to create or promote in your classroom.

9. Prepare an annotated directory of local resources for teaching students about diversity, for implementing diversity curricula, and for promoting harmony or equity among diverse groups. For each entry, include an annotation—a brief description of the resource materials and their availability.

PART TWO   FOUNDATIONS OF TEACHING

Your teaching philosophy filters how you see students, the subjects you teach, your role as a teacher, and your connection to the wider community. You will refine your teaching philosophy with experience; however, you will base everything you do on this foundation so it is important to reflect on it early and often. When articulating your philosophy, consider the code of ethics for the teaching profession in your province or territory, your own personal code of ethics and the kinds of social problems impacting students today, and how will you try to address these in your role as a teacher.

Chapter 6

Addressing Learners' Individual Needs

Lisa F. Young/Shutterstock

FOCUS QUESTIONS

1. How do the needs of students change as they develop?

2. How do students vary in intelligence?

3. How do students vary in ability and disability?

4. What are special education, mainstreaming, and inclusion?

5. How can you teach all learners in your inclusive classroom?

I was . . . fortunate that I chose theoretical physics, because it is all in the mind. So my disability has not been a serious handicap.

—Stephen W. Hawking
*A Brief History of Time:
From the Big Bang to Black Holes*

> No two students are alike. They don't learn the same, play the same, or speak the same. Teachers should not assume that, if one student understands, all students understand. Effective teachers make accommodations for students' individuality.
>
> **ALAN, teacher education program, first year**
>
> Successful teachers know how to modify their teaching for students who need individual attention. If students know their teacher is willing to "go the extra mile" to help them learn, they will feel equal and not left behind.
>
> **AMANDA, teacher education program, first year**

HOW DO THE NEEDS OF STUDENTS CHANGE AS THEY DEVELOP?

Development refers to the predictable changes that all human beings undergo as they progress through the life span from conception to death. It is important to acknowledge that students develop at different rates. Within a given classroom, for example, some students will be larger and physically more mature than others; some will be socially more sophisticated; and some will be able to think at a higher level of abstraction.

As humans progress through different **stages of development**, they mature and learn to perform the tasks that are a necessary part of daily living. There are several different types of human development. For example, as children develop physically, their bodies undergo numerous changes. As they develop cognitively, their mental capabilities expand to allow the use of language and other symbol systems to solve problems. As they develop socially, they learn to interact effectively with other people—as individuals and in groups. And as they develop morally, their actions come to reflect a greater appreciation of principles such as equity, justice, fairness, and altruism.

Because no two students progress through the stages of cognitive, social, and moral development in quite the same way, teachers need perspectives on the three types of development that are flexible, dynamic, and, above all, useful. By becoming familiar with models of cognitive, social, and moral development, teachers at all levels can better serve their students. Three such models are Piaget's theory of **cognitive development**, Erikson's stages of **psychosocial development**, and Kohlberg's stages of **moral reasoning**.

Piaget's Model of Cognitive Development

Jean Piaget (1896–1980), noted Swiss biologist and epistemologist, made extensive observational studies of children. He concluded that children reason differently from adults and have different perceptions of the world. Piaget surmised that children learn through actively interacting with their environments, much as scientists do, and proposed that a child's thinking progresses through a sequence of four cognitive stages. According to Piaget's theory of cognitive development, the rate of progress through the four stages varies from individual to individual.

During the school years, students move through the **preoperational stage**, the **concrete operations stage**, and the **formal operations stage**; yet because of individual

Stages of development: predictable stages through which individuals pass as they progress through life.

Cognitive development: the process of acquiring the intellectual ability to learn from interaction with one's environment.

Psychosocial development: the progression of an individual through various stages of psychological and social development.

Moral reasoning: the reasoning process people follow to decide what is right or wrong.

Preoperational stage: the stage of cognitive development (two to seven years of age) proposed by Jean Piaget in which the individual begins to use language and symbols to think of objects and people outside the immediate environment.

Concrete operations stage: the stage of cognitive development (seven to 11 years of age) proposed by Jean Piaget in which the individual develops the ability to use logical thought to solve concrete problems.

Formal operations stage: the stage of cognitive development (11 to 15 years of age) proposed by Jean Piaget in which cognitive abilities reach their highest level of development.

interaction with the total environment, each student's perceptions and learning will be unique. According to Piaget:

> The principal goal of education is to create [learners] who are capable of doing new things, not simply repeating what other generations have done—[learners] who are creative, inventive, and discoverers. [We] need pupils who are active, who learn early to find out by themselves, partly by their own spontaneous activity and partly through material we set up for them; who learn early to tell what is verifiable and what is simply the first idea to come to them. (Quoted in Ripple & Rockcastle, 1964, p. 5)

Erikson's Model of Psychosocial Development

Psychosocial crisis: a life crisis at one of eight different stages of growth and development. According to psychologist Erik Erikson, individuals must resolve each crisis to reach the next stage.

Erik Erikson's model of psychosocial development delineates eight stages, from infancy to old age (see Table 6.1). For each stage, a **psychosocial crisis** is central in the individual's emotional and social growth. Erikson expresses these crises in polar terms; for instance, in the first stage (infancy), the psychosocial crisis is trust versus mistrust. Erikson explains that the major psychosocial task for the infant is to develop a sense of trust in the world but not to give up totally a sense of distrust. In the tension between the poles of trust and mistrust, a greater pull toward the more positive pole is considered healthy and is accompanied by a virtue. In this case, if trust prevails, the virtue is hope.

TABLE 6.1 Erikson's Eight Stages of Psychosocial Development

Stage	Approximate Age	Psychosocial "Crisis"	Description	"Basic Strength" (Positive Result if Crisis Is Adequately Resolved)
1. Infancy	Birth to 18 months	Trust versus basic mistrust	Infant needs to be nurtured and loved; if not, he or she becomes insecure and mistrustful.	Drive and hope
2. Early childhood	18 months to 3 years	Autonomy versus shame	Child focuses on developing physical skills—toilet training, walking, talking, feeding self; inadequate resolution of crisis leads to feelings of shame and doubt.	Self-control, courage, and will
3. Play age	3 to 6 years	Initiative versus guilt	Child learns to develop skills through play and cooperation; inadequate resolution of crisis leads to sense of guilt and fearfulness.	Purpose and direction
4. School age	6 to 12 years	Industry versus inferiority	Child acquires new skills, knowledge; develops sense of achievement; inadequate resolution of crisis leaves child feeling inadequate and inferior.	Competence and method
5. Adolescence	12 to 20 years	Identity versus role confusion, identity diffusion	Adolescent focuses on clarifying identity, developing social relationships with peers and others, and grappling with moral issues; inadequate resolution crisis leads to self-doubt and self-consciousness.	Fidelity and devotion
6. Young adulthood	20 to 35 years	Intimacy versus isolation	Young adult seeks companionship and love through relationships with friends and becoming intimate with a "significant other"; inadequate resolution of crisis leads to feelings of isolation and distance from others.	Love and affiliation
7. Middle adulthood	35 to 65	Generativity versus self-absorption or stagnation	Adult focuses on family relationships, parenting, and creative and meaningful work; inadequate resolution of crisis leads to feelings of stagnation and alienation.	Care and production
8. Late adulthood	65 to death	Integrity versus despair	Adult focuses on meaning and purpose in one's life, lifetime accomplishments and contributions, acceptance of oneself and fulfillment; inadequate resolution of crisis leads to feelings of failure, disdain for world, and fear of death.	Wisdom and acceptance

Shortly before his death in 1994 at the age of 91, Erikson postulated a ninth stage in the human life cycle, *gerotranscendence*, during which some people mentally transcend the reality of their deteriorating bodies and faculties. In the final chapter of an extended version of Erikson's *The Life Cycle Completed*, first published in 1982, his wife and lifelong colleague, Joan M. Erikson (1901–1997), described the challenge of the ninth stage:

> Despair, which haunts the eighth stage, is a close companion in the ninth, because it is almost impossible to know what emergencies and losses of physical ability are imminent. As independence and control are challenged, self-esteem and confidence weaken. Hope and trust, which once provided firm support, are no longer the sturdy props of former days. To face down despair with faith and appropriate humility is perhaps the wisest course. (Erikson, 1997, pp. 105–106)

When we examine the issues and concerns of students in childhood and early and late adolescence later in this chapter, we will return to Erikson's model of psychosocial development. For further information on this significant and useful theory, we recommend that you read Erikson's first book, *Childhood and Society* (1963).

Kohlberg's Model of Moral Development

According to Lawrence Kohlberg (1927–1987), the reasoning process people use to decide what is right and wrong evolves through three levels of development. Within each level, Kohlberg has identified two stages. Table 6.2 shows that, at Level I (the preconventional level), the individual decides what is right on the basis of personal needs and rules developed by others. At Level II (the conventional level), moral decisions

---

TABLE 6.2 Kohlberg's Theory of Moral Reasoning

I. Preconventional Level of Moral Reasoning

Child is responsive to cultural rules and labels of good or bad and right or wrong, but interprets these in terms of consequences of action (punishment, reward, exchanges of favours).

Stage 1: Punishment-and-obedience orientation
Physical consequences of action determine its goodness or badness.
Avoidance of punishment and deference to power are valued.

Stage 2: The instrumental-relativist orientation
Right action consists of that which satisfies one's own needs and occasionally the needs of others.
Reciprocity is a matter of "You scratch my back and I'll scratch yours."

II. Conventional Level of Moral Reasoning

Maintaining the expectations of the individual's family, group, or nation is perceived as valuable, regardless of consequences.

Stage 3: The interpersonal concordance or "good boy–nice girl" orientation
Good behaviour is that which pleases or helps others and is approved by them.

Stage 4: The "law and order" orientation
Orientation toward fixed rules and the maintenance of social order. Right behaviour consists of doing one's duty and showing respect for authority.

III. Postconventional, Autonomous, or Principled Level of Moral Reasoning

Effort to define moral principles that have validity and application apart from the authority of groups.

Stage 5: The social-contract, legalistic orientation
Right action defined in terms of rights and standards that have been agreed upon by the whole society.

Stage 6: The universal-ethical-principle orientation
Right is defined by conscience in accord with self-chosen ethical principles appealing to logic and universality.

Source: Adapted from Lawrence Kohlberg, "The Cognitive-Developmental Approach to Moral Education." In *Curriculum Leadership: Readings for Developing Quality Educational Programs*, 9th ed., Forrest W. Parkay, Eric J. Anctil, and Glen Hass (eds.). Boston: Allyn and Bacon, 2010, p. 149. The original version appeared in *Journal of Philosophy, 70*(18), 1973, pp. 631–632.

reflect a desire for the approval of others and a willingness to conform to the expectations of family, community, and country. At Level III (the postconventional level), the individual has developed values and principles that are based on rational, personal choices that can be separated from conventional beliefs.

Kohlberg suggests that "over 50 percent of late adolescents and adults are capable of full formal reasoning [i.e., they can use their intelligence to reason abstractly, form hypotheses, and test these hypotheses against reality], but only 10 percent of these adults display principled (Stages 5 and 6) moral reasoning" (2010, p. 150). In addition, Kohlberg purports that maturity of moral judgment is not highly related to IQ or verbal intelligence.

Some individuals have criticized Kohlberg's model as being too systematic and sequential, limited because it focuses on moral reasoning rather than on actual behaviour, or biased because it tends to look at moral development from a male perspective (Bracey, 1993). Carol Gilligan suggests that male moral reasoning tends to address the rights of the individual, whereas female moral reasoning addresses the individual's responsibility to others. In her book *In a Different Voice: Psychological Theory and Women's Development* (1993), Gilligan refers to women's principal moral voice as the "ethics of care," which emphasizes care of others over the male-oriented "ethics of justice." Thus, when confronted with a moral dilemma, females tend to suggest solutions based more on altruism and self-sacrifice than on rights and rules (Gilligan, 1993).

The question remains: Can moral reasoning be taught? Can teachers help students develop so that they live according to principles of equity, justice, caring, and empathy? Kohlberg (2010, pp. 155–156) suggests that the following three conditions can help children internalize moral principles:

1. Exposure to the next higher stage of reasoning

2. Exposure to situations posing problems and contradictions for the child's current moral structure, leading to dissatisfaction with his [or her] current level

3. An atmosphere of interchange and dialogue combining the first two conditions, in which conflicting moral views are compared in an open manner

Character education: an approach to education that emphasizes the teaching of values, moral reasoning, and the development of "good" character.

One approach to teaching values and moral reasoning is known as **character education**, a movement that stresses the development of students' "good character." Books and resources for Canadian teachers who wish to introduce character education into their classrooms are readily available, and most provincial departments of education have given varying degrees of attention to the topic. For example, the Alberta Ministry of Education created a resource for teachers and administrators, in collaboration with school districts and the Alberta Teachers' Association, called *The Heart of the Matter: Character and Citizenship Education in Alberta Schools* (2005). Similarly, the Ministry of Education in Ontario released its document, *Finding Common Ground: Character Development in Ontario Schools, K–12,* in 2008. The document identifies four essential components of a character development program: learning and academic achievement; respect for diversity; citizenship development; and parent and community partnerships. Even service organizations are becoming involved. The Lions Club of Canada now offers its Lions-Quest life skills program to students and teachers. "Lions-Quest programs teach youth to accept responsibility, communicate effectively, set goals, make healthy decisions, and resist pressure to use alcohol and drugs. Lions clubs, districts and multiple districts support Lions-Quest through funding, coordination of teacher training, and in other ways." Figure 6.1 illustrates 12 strategies teachers can use to create moral classroom communities.

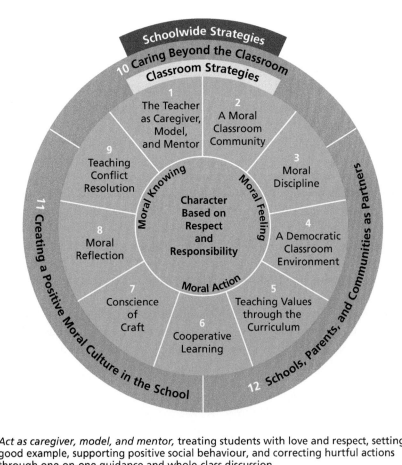

Schoolwide Strategies

10 Caring Beyond the Classroom
Classroom Strategies

1. The Teacher as Caregiver, Model, and Mentor
2. A Moral Classroom Community
9. Teaching Conflict Resolution
3. Moral Discipline
8. Moral Reflection
Character Based on Respect and Responsibility
4. A Democratic Classroom Environment
7. Conscience of Craft
6. Cooperative Learning
5. Teaching Values through the Curriculum

Moral Knowing
Moral Feeling
Moral Action

11 Creating a Positive Moral Culture in the School
12 Schools, Parents, and Communities as Partners

1. *Act as caregiver, model, and mentor,* treating students with love and respect, setting a good example, supporting positive social behaviour, and correcting hurtful actions through one-on-one guidance and whole-class discussion.

2. *Create a moral community,* helping students know one another as persons, respect and care about one another, and feel valued membership in, and responsibility to, the group.

3. *Practise moral discipline,* using the creation and enforcement of rules as opportunities to foster moral reasoning, voluntary compliance with rules, and a respect for others.

4. *Create a democratic classroom environment,* involving students in decision making and the responsibility for making the classroom a good place to be and learn.

5. *Teach values through the curriculum,* using the ethically rich content of academic subjects (such as literature, history, and science) as vehicles for teaching values and examining moral questions.

6. *Use cooperative learning* to develop students' appreciation of others, perspective taking, and the ability to work with others toward common goals.

7. *Develop the "conscience of craft"* by fostering students' appreciation of learning, capacity for hard work, commitment to excellence, and sense of work as affecting the lives of others.

8. *Encourage moral reflection* through reading, research, essay writing, journal keeping, discussion, and debate.

9. *Teach conflict resolution,* so that students acquire the essential moral skills of solving conflicts fairly and without force.

10. *Foster caring beyond the classroom,* using positive role models to inspire altruistic behaviour and providing opportunities at every grade level to perform school and community service.

11. *Create a positive moral culture in the school,* developing a schoolwide ethos that supports and amplifies the values taught in classrooms.

12. *Recruit parents and the community as partners in character education,* letting parents know that the school considers them their child's first and most important moral teacher.

Figure 6.1 A comprehensive approach to values and character education

Maslow's Model of Hierarchy of Needs

Hierarchy of needs: a set of seven needs, from the basic needs for survival and safety to the need for self-actualization, that motivate human behaviour.

Students' developmental levels also vary according to how well their biological and psychological needs have been satisfied. Psychologist Abraham Maslow (1908–1970) formulated a model of a **hierarchy of needs** (see Figure 6.2) that suggests that people are motivated by basic needs for survival and safety first. When these basic needs have been met sufficiently, people naturally seek to satisfy higher needs, the highest of which is self-actualization—the desire to use one's talents, abilities, and potential to the fullest. Students whose needs for safety have been fairly well satisfied will discover strong needs for friendship, affection, and love, for example. If efforts to satisfy the various needs are thwarted, the result can be maladjustment and interruption or delay in the individual's full and healthy development.

The hierarchy of needs model has particular relevance for teachers, because students differ markedly in terms of where they are on the hierarchy. Many families lack the resources to adequately provide for children's basic needs. Children from families that are concerned with day-to-day survival may not receive the support that could help them succeed in school. They come to school tired and hungry and may have trouble paying attention in class. Others may be well fed and clothed but feel unsafe, alien, or unloved; they may seek to protect themselves by withdrawing emotionally from activities around them.

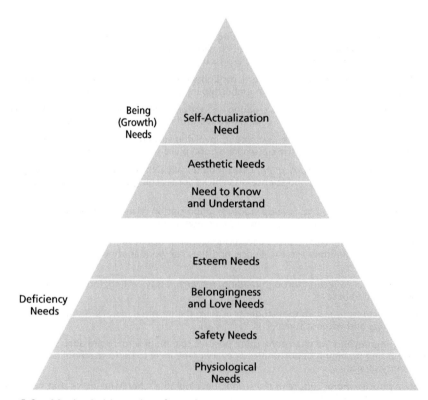

Figure 6.2 Maslow's hierarchy of needs

NOTE: The four lower-level needs are called Deficiency Needs because the motivation to satisfy them decreases when they are met. By contrast, when Being (Growth) Needs are met, motivation to fulfil them increases.

Source: Compiled from Abraham H. Maslow, *Toward a Psychology of Being,* 3rd ed. New York, New York: John Wiley & Sons, 1998; and *Motivation and Personality,* 3rd ed. Addison-Wesley Publishing Company, 1987.

Developmental Stresses and Tasks of Childhood

During Erikson's school-age stage, children strive for a sense of industry and struggle against feelings of inferiority. If successful, they gain the virtue of competence, believing in their abilities to do things. If children find evidence that they are inferior to others, if they experience failure when they try new tasks, and if they struggle without ever gaining a sense of mastery, then they feel incompetent.

Children gain the sense of industry needed at this age by playing seriously, mastering new skills, producing results, and being workers. When they first go to school, they are oriented toward accomplishing new things (some kindergartners expect to learn to read on their first day of school and are disappointed when they don't). For young children, the idea of work is attractive; it means that they are doing something grown-up.

Is childhood a time of carefree play or a period of stress? Certainly, the answer depends on the life circumstances and personality of the individual child. In a study of stressful events in the lives of more than 1700 children in grades 2–9 in six countries, Karou Yamamoto and his associates found that the most stressful events "threaten[ed] one's sense of security and occasion[ed] personal denigration and embarrassment" (Yamamoto et al., 1996, p. 139). Other studies have shown that serious stress is experienced by latchkey children, who are left on their own or in each other's care for part or all of the day.

Developmental Stresses and Tasks of Adolescence

Many psychologists believe that adolescence contains two distinct stages: an early period from the ages of 10 to 12 through the ages of 14 to 16, and a late period from approximately 15 to 16 years old through 19. Although continuity exists in each individual's life, the psychosocial issues of adolescence—coping with change and seeking identity—vary in form and importance as individuals progress through the transition from childhood to adulthood.

In Erikson's eight-state model, identity versus role diffusion is the psychosocial crisis for the adolescent years. Although the quest for identity is a key psychosocial issue for both early and late adolescence, many believe that Erikson's identity-versus-role diffusion stage fits best for early adolescence. During this time, young adolescents, using their new thinking abilities, begin integrating a clearer sense of personal identity. Erikson's role diffusion refers to the variety of roles that adolescents have available to them.

According to Erikson's theory, when adolescents identify with a peer group, with a school, or with a cause, their sense of fidelity—the "virtue" of this stage—is clear and strong. At this stage, adolescents are loyal and committed, sometimes to people or ideas that may dismay or alarm their parents, and sometimes to high ideals and dreams.

In late adolescence, the quest for identity shifts from relying on others to self-reliance. Young people continue to work on strengthening their sense of identity in this period, but as they do so, they draw less on the reactions of their peers and more on their own regard for what matters. Although late adolescents possess an array of interests, talents, and goals in life, they share a desire to achieve independence. More like adults than children, late adolescents are anxious to use newly acquired strengths, skills, and knowledge to achieve their own purposes, whether through marriage, parenthood, full-time employment, education beyond high school, a career, or military service.

The vulnerability of today's adolescents is evident in the results of a survey based on 40 "developmental assets" youth need to become healthy, mature adults. For optimal development, youth should have the following "external" and "internal" assets:

> *External Assets*—Support, Empowerment, Boundaries and Expectations, and Constructive Use of Time; *Internal Assets*—Commitment to Learning, Positive Values, Social Competencies, and Positive Identity. The survey of almost 150,000 6th- to 12th-grade youth in 202 communities revealed that the average young person experiences only 18.6 of the 40 assets. In general, older youth have lower average levels of assets than younger youth. And boys experience fewer assets than girls. While there is no "magic number" of assets young people should have . . . data indicate that 31 is a worthy, though challenging, benchmark for experiencing their positive effects most strongly. Yet . . . only 8 percent of youth have 31 or more assets. More than half have 20 or fewer assets. (Search Institute, 2010)

Moreover, "a solid majority of American adults—two thirds—spontaneously describe adolescents in starkly negative terms: *wild, rude, irresponsible*. Half give those descriptions even to younger children" (Scales, 2001, p. 64). The list of alarming concerns in adolescence includes academic failure and retention, accidents, assaultive behaviour, criminal activity, cultism, depression, discipline problems, dropping out, drug abuse, eating disorders, homicide, incest, prostitution, running away, school absenteeism, suicide, teenage pregnancy, vandalism, and the contraction of sexually transmitted diseases. While there is little data to support a contention that an exactly similar situation exists in Canada, Canadian students do face an alarming number of risks.

What can teachers do to help children and adolescents develop to their full potential? To help prevent the problems that place them at risk, an energetic, creative, and multifaceted approach is necessary. Figure 6.3 presents several strategies for assisting students in developing competence, positive self-concepts, and high esteem, and for intervening to prevent or address problems that place them at risk.

HOW DO STUDENTS VARY IN INTELLIGENCE?

In addition to developmental differences, students differ in terms of their intellectual capacity. Unfortunately, test scores, and sometimes intelligence quotient (IQ) scores,

What needs must be met for these students for healthy development? What stresses do they face? What developmental tasks must they accomplish? What needs, stresses, and developmental tasks will affect them as adolescents? Why is information about development important to teachers?

Marcel Jancovic/Shutterstock

1. **Provide opportunities and encouragement for students to develop competence.**

   - Provide a learning environment in which students can risk making mistakes.
   - Assign work that students can perform successfully and still be challenged.
   - Have realistic but high expectations for students.
   - Express belief in students' ability to succeed.
   - Encourage industry by letting students work on goals or projects of their choosing.
   - Provide opportunities for students to take special responsibility.
   - Assign older students to work with younger ones.
   - Reward industry and competence.

2. **Promote the development of positive self-concept and high self-esteem.**

   - Give praise more than criticism.
   - Take students and their work seriously.
   - Respect students' dignity.
   - Plan individual and group activities that boost morale.
   - Provide opportunities for students to interact and work cooperatively.
   - Teach and model acceptance of human diversity and individuality.
   - Develop systems for the recognition and reward of individual and group achievement.
   - Support students' efforts to achieve and appropriately express independence.

3. **Intervene to prevent or address problems that place students at risk.**

   - Provide a safe and structured learning environment where students feel secure.
   - Practise effective leadership and classroom management.
   - Provide opportunities to discuss preferences, values, morals, goals, and consequences.
   - Teach and model critical thinking, decision making, and problem solving.
   - Teach and model prosocial attitudes and behaviours and conflict resolution strategies.
   - Provide information on subjects of special concern to students and parents.
   - Cultivate family involvement.
   - Collaborate, consult, network, and refer on behalf of students.

Figure 6.3 What teachers can do to help children and adolescents develop

are treated as accurate measurements of students' intellectual ability because of their convenience and long-time use. What is **intelligence**, and how has it been redefined to account for the many ways it can be expressed? Though many definitions have been proposed, the term has yet to be completely explained. One view is that intelligence is the ability to learn. As David Wechsler, the developer of the most widely used intelligence scales for children and adults, said: "Intelligence, operationally defined, is the aggregate or global capacity to act purposefully, to think rationally, and to deal effectively with the environment" (Wechsler, 1958, p. 7). Other perspectives on intelligence include the following:

Intelligence: the ability to learn; the cognitive capacity for thinking.

- It is adaptive. It involves modifying and adjusting one's behaviour to accomplish new tasks successfully.

- It is related to learning ability. Intelligent people learn information more quickly and easily than less intelligent people.

- It involves the use of prior knowledge to analyze and understand new situations effectively.

- It involves the complex interaction and coordination of many different thinking and reasoning processes.

- It is culture-specific. What is "intelligent" behaviour in one culture is not necessarily intelligent behaviour in another culture. (Ormrod, 2006, p. 153)

Intelligence Testing

The intelligence tests now in use can be traced to the 1905 Metrical Scale of Intelligence designed by French psychologists Alfred Binet and Theodore Simon, who were part of a Paris-based commission that wanted a way to identify children who would need special help with their learning. Binet revised the scale in 1908, which was adapted for American children in 1916 by Lewis Terman, a psychologist at Stanford University. Terman's test was, in turn, further adapted, especially by the U.S. Army, which transformed it into a paper-and-pencil test that could be administered to large groups. The use of such intelligence tests has continued throughout the years. Approximately 67 percent of the population have an IQ between 85 and 115—the range of normal intelligence. "Gifted" individuals have an IQ of 130 or more, while those at the genius level have an IQ of 140 or better.

Individual intelligence tests are presently valued by psychologists and those in the field of special education because they can be helpful in diagnosing a student's strengths and weaknesses. However, group intelligence tests given for the purpose of classifying students into like-score groups have received an increasing amount of criticism and have been greatly reduced in scope. The criteria for a gifted identification differ from school district to school district in Canada; however, all school districts use some kind of cognitive abilities screening, typically administered by a Special Education Resource Teacher (SERT) in a group setting, but sometimes parents will opt to test their children privately through a psychologist. Most school districts conduct a routine assessment of all students in grade 3 or 4 to flag students who are gifted or at risk. In addition, testing might be initiated by parents or teachers who notice specific characteristics in children.

The most significant and dramatic criticism of group IQ tests has been that test items and tasks are culturally biased, drawn mostly from white middle-class experience. Thus the tests are more assessments of how informed students are about features in a specific class or culture than of intelligence in general. A number of psychometricians continue to design culture-free intelligence tests.

Multiple Intelligences

Many theorists believe that intelligence is a basic ability that enables one to perform mental operations in the following areas: logical reasoning, spatial reasoning, number ability, and verbal meaning. However, other theorists believe "that conventional notions of intelligence are incomplete and hence inadequate. [One's] ability to achieve success depends on capitalizing on one's strengths and correcting or compensating for one's weaknesses through a balance of analytical, creative, and practical abilities" (Sternberg, 2002, pp. 447–448). Howard Gardner, for example, believes that humans possess at least nine separate forms of intelligence: "[e]ach intelligence reflects the potential to solve problems or to fashion products that are valued in one or more cultural settings. [Each] features its own distinctive form of mental representation" (Gardner, 1999, pp. 71–72). Drawing on the theories of others and research findings on savants, prodigies, and other exceptional individuals, Gardner originally suggested in *Frames of Mind* (1983) that humans have seven intelligences: logical-mathematical, linguistic, musical, spatial, bodily-kinesthetic, interpersonal, and intrapersonal. In the mid-1990s, he identified an eighth intelligence, that of the naturalist. According to Gardner, every person possesses the eight intelligences (see Figure 6.4), yet each person has his or her particular blend of them. And in his most recent book, *The Disciplined Mind*, he suggests that "it is possible that human beings also exhibit a ninth, existential intelligence—the proclivity to pose (and ponder) questions about life, death, and ultimate realities" (Gardner, 1999, p. 72); however, he suggests that there is not yet enough neurological evidence of this existential ability.

Linguistic intelligence allows individuals to communicate and make sense of the world through language. Poets exemplify this intelligence in its mature form. Students who enjoy playing with rhymes, who pun, who always have a story to tell, who quickly acquire other languages—including sign language—all exhibit linguistic intelligence.

Musical intelligence allows people to create, communicate, and understand meanings made out of sound. While composers and instrumentalists clearly exhibit this intelligence, so do the students who seem particularly attracted by the birds singing outside the classroom window or who constantly tap out intricate rhythms on the desk with their pencils.

Logical-mathematical intelligence enables individuals to use and appreciate abstract relations. Scientists, mathematicians, and philosophers all rely on this intelligence. So do the students who "live" baseball statistics or who carefully analyze the components of problems—either personal or school-related—before systematically testing solutions.

Spatial intelligence makes it possible for people to perceive visual or spatial information, to transform this information, and to recreate visual images from memory. Well-developed spatial capacities are needed for the work of architects, sculptors, and engineers. The students who turn first to the graphs, charts, and pictures in their textbooks, who like to "web" their ideas before writing a paper, and who fill the blank space around their notes with intricate patterns are using their spatial intelligence.

Bodily-kinesthetic intelligence allows individuals to use all or part of the body to create products or solve problems. Athletes, surgeons, dancers, choreographers, and craftspeople all use bodily-kinesthetic intelligence. The capacity is also evident in students who relish gym class and school dances, who prefer to carry out class projects by making models rather than writing reports, and who toss crumpled paper with frequency and accuracy into wastebaskets across the room.

Interpersonal intelligence enables individuals to recognize and make distinctions about others' feelings and intentions. Teachers, parents, politicians, psychologists, and salespeople rely on interpersonal intelligence. Students exhibit this intelligence when they thrive on small-group work, when they notice and react to the moods of their friends and classmates, and when they tactfully convince the teacher of their need for extra time to complete the homework assignment.

Intrapersonal intelligence helps individuals to distinguish among their own feelings, to build accurate mental models of themselves, and to draw on these models to make decisions about their lives. Although it is difficult to assess who has this capacity and to what degree, evidence can be sought in students' uses of their other intelligences—how well they seem to be capitalizing on their strengths, how cognizant they are of their weaknesses, and how thoughful they are about the decisions and choices they make.

Naturalist intelligence allows people to distinguish among, classify, and use features of the environment. Farmers, gardeners, botanists, geologists, florists, and archaeologists all exhibit this intelligence, as do students who can name and describe the features of every make of car around them.

Figure 6.4 The eight intelligences

Source: Project SUMIT (Schools Using Multiple Intelligence Theory), "Theory of Multiple Intelligences". Used with permission.

Gardner's theory of **multiple intelligences** is valuable for teachers. As Robert Slavin suggests, "Teachers must avoid thinking about children as smart or not smart because there are many ways to be smart" (Slavin, 2000, p. 130). Some students are talented in terms of their interpersonal relations and exhibit natural leadership abilities. Others seem to have a high degree of what Peter Salovey and David Sluyter (1997)

Multiple intelligences: a perspective on intellectual ability proposed by Howard Gardner suggesting that there are at least seven types of human intelligence.

term *emotional intelligence*—awareness of and ability to manage their feelings. Differences in musical, athletic, and mechanical abilities can be recognized by even the minimally informed observer. Because these intelligences are not tested or highlighted, they may go unnoticed and possibly wasted.

However, keep in mind Gardner's "reflections" 14 years after the publication of *Frames of Mind*:

> MI [multiple intelligences] may be appealing, but it is not for the fainthearted, nor for those in search of a quick fix. After initial experimentation with the ideas and practices of MI, practitioners realize that MI is not an end in itself. To say that one has an MI classroom or an MI school is not meaningful—one has to ask "MI for what?" (1997, p. 20)

Learning Preferences

Students vary greatly in regard to learning preferences, the approaches to learning that work best for them. These differences lead students to interact with their environments in differing ways. Some, for example, might prefer a highly structured approach to learning, while others might have a preference for a learning environment that is less structured and less predictable. The variety of student learning styles strongly suggests that teachers develop a broad range of instructional methodologies as a fundamental part of their educational practice. It is equally important for teachers to recognize their own preferred learning styles and that, if they are not careful, they will have a strong tendency to teach in a manner that reflects how they themselves would prefer to be taught.

HOW DO STUDENTS VARY IN ABILITY AND DISABILITY?

Students also differ according to their special needs and talents. Some enter the world with exceptional abilities or disabilities; others encounter life experiences that change their capabilities significantly; and still others struggle with conditions that medical scientists have yet to understand. Where possible, all children and youth with exceptionalities are given a public education in provincial and territorial schools.

Exceptional Learners

Exceptional learners: students whose growth and development deviate from the norm to the extent that their educational needs can be met more effectively through a modification of regular school programs.

Exceptional learners are students whose growth and development deviate from the norm to the extent that their educational needs can best be met through a modification of their regular school programs. They are taught by special education teachers and by regular teachers into whose classrooms they have been integrated or *included*. Among the many exceptional children teachers may encounter in the classroom are students who have physical, intellectual, or emotional disabilities and students who are gifted or talented. In Ontario, students with exceptionalities are classified within five categories: Behaviour; Communication (includes autism, deaf or hard of hearing, language impairment, speech impairment, learning disability); Intellectual (includes giftedness, mild intellectual disability, developmental disability); Physical (includes blindness, low vision); and Multiple (any student with a combination of the above) (Bennett, 2009).

Special-needs students are often referred to synonymously as *handicapped* or *disabled*. However, it is important for teachers to understand the following distinction between a disability and a handicap:

> Many individuals with disabilities believe that the terms disability and handicap have very different meanings and interpretations. They are convinced that it is because of their disabilities (e.g., conditions and impairments) that society handicaps them (e.g., presents

challenges and barriers). . . . Thus the ways in which people are treated by society and by other individuals are what present the real barriers that influence people's outcomes. Difficult situations occur not because of a condition or disability but, rather, because people with disabilities are denied full participation in society as a consequence of their minority status. (Smith, 2007, pp. 9–10)

For example, Stephen W. Hawking, the gifted physicist who provides the epigraph for this chapter, has amyotrophic lateral sclerosis (also known as Lou Gehrig's disease), which requires him to use a wheelchair for mobility and a speech synthesizer to communicate. If Hawking had to enter a building accessible only by stairs, or if a computer virus infected his speech synthesizer program, his disability would become a handicap.

Teachers should know that current language use emphasizes the concept of "people first." In other words, a disabling condition should not be used as an adjective to describe a person. Thus, one should say "a child with a visual impairment"—not "blind child" or even "visually impaired child."

Teachers should also realize that the definitions for disabilities are generalized, open to change, and significantly influenced by the current cultural perception of normality. During the past half century, the definition of mental retardation has gone through several evolutions to reflect shifting views of people with cognitive disabilities.

Cautions about labelling should also apply to gifted and talented students. Unfortunately, people commonly have a negative view of gifted and talented youngsters. Like many ethnic groups, gifted students are "different" and thus have been the target of many myths and stereotypes. However, a landmark study of 1528 gifted males and females begun by Lewis Terman (Terman, Baldwin, & Bronson, 1925; Terman & Oden, 1947, 1959) in 1926, which continued until 2010, "exploded the myth that high-IQ individuals [are] brainy but physically and socially inept. In fact, Terman found that children with outstanding IQs were larger, stronger, and better coordinated than other children and became better adjusted and more emotionally stable adults" (Slavin, 2003, p. 429).

Students with Disabilities

Determining what to consider a disability is an exceptionally difficult problem. The following data must therefore be regarded as approximations of the **students with disabilities** situation in Canada.

Students with disabilities: students who need special education services because they possess one or more of the following disabilities: learning disabilities, speech or language impairments, mental retardation, serious emotional disturbance, hearing impairments, orthopedic impairments, visual impairments, or other health impairments.

1. The Canadian Council on Learning (CCL) and Statistics Canada published a joint report in 2010 related to access and barriers to educational services for children with disabilities in Canada (Dafna, 2010). They found that the majority of children with disabilities in Canada attend regular school (64 percent), with "one quarter attending a regular school that offers special education classes (26%), and only a small minority (6%) attending special education schools" (p. 2).

2. According to the Learning Disabilities Association of Canada, 1 in 10 Canadians has a learning disability.

3. Mental Health Canada reports that between 3 and 5 percent of children have ADHD, at least one in every classroom of 25 to 30 students.

4. In Ontario, in 2009, just under 300 000 students were identified as exceptional through Identification Placement and Review Committees (IPRCs) and given Individualized Educational Plans (IEPs). Just over 80 percent of these students spent more than half their day within a regular classroom setting (Bennett, 2009, p. 1).

5. A reasonable estimate regarding the number of students with a special need that requires some form of intervention by educators would be 10 to 15 percent. Table 6.3 gives a brief definitional overview of the various types of disabilities students may experience.

TABLE 6.3 Types of Disability

1. Specific learning disabilities (LD)—Learning is significantly hindered by difficulty in listening, speaking, reading, writing, reasoning, or computing
2. Speech or language impairments—Significant difficulty in communicating with others as a result of speech or language disorders
3. Intellectual impairments —Significant limitations in cognitive ability
4. Serious emotional disturbance (SED)—Social and/or emotional maladjustment that significantly reduces the ability to learn
5. Hearing impairments—Permanent or fluctuating mild to profound hearing loss in one or both ears
6. Orthopedic impairments—Physically disabling conditions that affect locomotion or motor functions
7. Other health impairments—Limited strength, vitality, or alertness caused by chronic or acute health problems
8. Visual impairments—Vision loss that significantly inhibits learning
9. Multiple disabilities—Two or more interrelated disabilities
10. Deaf-blindness—Vision and hearing disability that severely limits communication
11. Autism and other—Significantly impaired communication, learning, and reciprocal social interactions

Learning disability (LD): a limitation in one's ability to take in, organize, remember, and express information.

Since the term **learning disability (LD)** was first introduced in the early 1960s, there has been no universally accepted definition. However, the following statement, adopted by the Learning Disabilities Association of Canada on January 30, 2002, and re-endorsed on March 2, 2015, provides an excellent overview of how broadly defined this specialized area has become.

"Learning Disabilities" refer to a number of disorders which may affect the acquisition, organization, retention, understanding or use of verbal or nonverbal information. These disorders affect learning in individuals who otherwise demonstrate at least average abilities essential for thinking and/or reasoning. As such, learning disabilities are distinct from global intellectual deficiency.

Learning disabilities result from impairments in one or more processes related to perceiving, thinking, remembering or learning. These include, but are not limited to: language processing; phonological processing; visual spatial processing; processing speed; memory and attention; and executive functions (e.g., planning and decision-making).

Learning disabilities range in severity and may interfere with the acquisition and use of one or more of the following:

■ Oral language (e.g., listening, speaking, understanding)

■ Reading (e.g., decoding, phonetic knowledge, word recognition, comprehension)

■ Written language (e.g., spelling and written expression); and

■ Mathematics (e.g., computation, problem solving)

Learning disabilities may also involve difficulties with organizational skills, social perception, social interaction and perspective taking.

Learning disabilities are lifelong. The way in which they are expressed may vary over an individual's lifetime, depending on the interaction between the demands of the environment and the individual's strengths and needs. Learning disabilities are suggested by unexpected academic under-achievement or achievement which is maintained only by unusually high levels of effort and support.

Learning disabilities are due to genetic and/or neurobiological factors or injury that alters brain functioning in a manner which affects one or more processes related to learning. These disorders are not due primarily to hearing and/or vision problems, socio-economic factors, cultural or linguistic differences, lack of motivation or ineffective teaching, although these factors may further complicate the challenges faced by individuals with learning disabilities. Learning disabilities may co-exist with various conditions including attentional, behavioural and emotional disorders, sensory impairments or other medical conditions.

For success, individuals with learning disabilities require early identification and timely specialized assessments and interventions involving home, school, community and workplace settings. The interventions need to be appropriate for each individual's learning disability subtype and, at a minimum, include the provision of: specific skill instruction; accommodations; compensatory strategies; and self-advocacy skills.

Source: Official Definition of Learning Disabilities. (2002, January). Reprinted by permission of the Learning Disabilities Association of Canada. Retrieved April 26, 2015, from www.ldac-acta. ca/learn-more/ld-defined/official-definition-of-learning-disabilities.

Imagine you are concerned about two of your new students—Mary and Beomjoon. Mary has an adequate vocabulary and doesn't hesitate to express herself, but her achievement in reading and mathematics doesn't add up to what you believe she can do. Often, when you give the class instructions, Mary seems to get confused about what to do. In working with her one-on-one, you've noticed that she often reverses letters and numbers the way much younger children do—she sees a *b* for a *d* or a 6 for a 9. Mary may have a learning disability, causing problems in taking in, organizing, remembering, and expressing information. Like Mary, students with learning disabilities often show a significant difference between their estimated intelligence and their actual achievement in the classroom.

Beomjoon presents you with a different set of challenges. He is obviously bright, but he frequently seems to be "out of sync" with classroom activities. He gets frustrated when he has to wait for his turn. He sometimes blurts out answers before you've even asked a question. He can't seem to stop wiggling his toes and tapping his pencil, and he often comes to school without his backpack and homework. Beomjoon may have **attention deficit hyperactivity disorder (ADHD)**, one of the most commonly diagnosed disabilities among children. ADHD is a "neurobiological condition that affects between 5 and 12 per cent of children worldwide with impairing levels of inattentive or hyperactive/impulsive behaviour" (Tannock, 2007). Students with ADHD have difficulty remaining still so that they can concentrate. Students with an **attention deficit disorder (ADD)** have difficulty focusing their attention long enough to learn well.

Treatment for students with ADD or ADHD includes various types of psychotherapy; education and training for teachers, parents, and students; social skills training; and multimodal approaches and medication (Tannock, 2007). Since the early 1980s, Ritalin has become the most commonly prescribed drug for ADD and ADHD, and thousands of Canadian children are currently prescribed Ritalin or Adderall to increase their impulse control and attention span.

By being alert for students who exhibit several of the following characteristics, teachers can help in the early identification of learning disabilities so that these students can receive the instructional adaptations or special education services they need.

- Significant discrepancy between potential and achievement
- Inability to problem-solve
- Substantial delay in academic achievement
- Lack of engagement with learning tasks
- Poor language and/or cognitive development
- Lack of basic reading and decoding skills

Attention deficit hyperactivity disorder (ADHD): a learning disability characterized by difficulty in remaining still so that one can concentrate on learning.

Attention deficit disorder (ADD): a learning disability characterized by difficulty in concentrating on learning.

- Lack of attention during lectures or class discussion
- Excessive movement, hyperactivity
- Impulsivity
- Poor motor coordination and spatial relation skills
- Poor motivation

Students Who Are Gifted and Talented

You are concerned about the poor performance of Paul, a student in your eighth-period high school class. Paul is undeniably bright. When he was 10, he had an IQ of 145 on the Stanford-Binet Intelligence Scale. Last year, when he was 16, he scored 142. Paul's father is a physician, and his mother is a professor. Both parents clearly value learning and are willing to give Paul any needed encouragement and help.

Throughout elementary school, Paul had an outstanding record. His teachers reported that he was brilliant and very meticulous in completing his assignments. He entered high school amid expectations by his parents and teachers that he would continue his exceptional performance. Throughout his first two years of high school, Paul never seemed to live up to his promise. Now, halfway through grade 11, Paul is failing English and geometry. He seems to be well adjusted to the social side of school. He has a lot of friends and says he likes school. Paul explains his steadily declining grades by claiming an aversion to studying.

Paul may be gifted. **Gifted and talented** students—those who have demonstrated a high level of attainment in intellectual ability, academic achievement, creativity, or visual and performing arts—are evenly distributed across all ethnic and cultural groups and socioeconomic classes. Although you might think it is easy to meet the needs of gifted and talented students, you will find that this is not always the case. "Students with special gifts or talents often challenge the system of school, and they can be verbally caustic. Their superior abilities and unusual or advanced interests demand teachers who are highly intelligent, creative, and motivated" (Hallahan & Kauffman, 2000, p. 497). The ability of such students to challenge the system is reflected in a recent U.S. Department of Education study that found that gifted and talented elementary school-children master 35 to 50 percent of the grade curriculum in five basic subject areas *before* starting the school year. The situation in Canada is likely similar.

Giftedness can take many forms. Joseph S. Renzulli (1998, p. 310), director of the National Research Center on the Gifted and Talented at the University of Connecticut, for example, suggests two kinds of giftedness: "schoolhouse giftedness [which] might also be called test-taking or lesson-learning giftedness" and "creative-productive giftedness." The trend of the past few decades has been to broaden our view of what characterizes giftedness. Depending on the criteria, estimates of the number of gifted and talented students range from 3 to 5 percent of the total population.

Among the characteristics of gifted students are the following:

- Precocity—verbal precocity
- Perceptual sensitivity—good at detecting critically relevant, salient cues; notices what others fail to notice
- Persistent concentration—ability to attend to a task intensively, without being distracted by noise in the environment
- Superior memory—may be restricted to domain(s) of excellence
- Efficient coordination—ability to coordinate two or more tasks
- Curtailed learning and reasoning—ability to "intuit" solutions without following step-by-step procedures; solves problems by making "intuitive leaps"

Gifted and talented: exceptional learners who demonstrate high intelligence, high creativity, high achievement, or special talent(s).

- Flexible thinking—knowing when to call upon inner resources and deciding which resources to apply for the best result
- Metacognitive awareness—awareness of one's own thinking; keeping track of one's understanding of a problem
- Speedy processing—ability to process information quickly
- Philosophical thinking—concern with "larger questions" that focus on, for example, the future of humankind or the cosmos (Hoh, 2008, pp. 57–83)

Effective teachers of the gifted and talented have many of the same characteristics as their students. "Characteristics that reoccur across the studies of exemplary teachers of the gifted include: intellectualism, subject matter expertise, a personal rapport with high-ability learners, and enjoyment in teaching them" (Robinson, 2008, p. 676). Three innovative approaches for meeting the educational needs of gifted students are acceleration, self-directed or independent study, and individualized educational programs.

- *Acceleration*—Accelerated programs for intellectually precocious students have proven successful. For example, in a review of hundreds of research findings in education, Kulik was "not able to find any educational treatment that consistently yielded higher effect size (i.e., positive results) than [acceleration]" (2004, p. 20). The following acceleration options have proven to be the most beneficial at different grade levels:
  - Elementary school—early entrance, grade skipping, nongraded classes, and curriculum compacting (modifying the curriculum to present it at a faster pace)
  - Junior high school—grade skipping, grade telescoping (shortening the amount of time to complete a grade level), concurrent enrolment in a high school or college/university, subject acceleration, and curriculum compacting
  - Senior high school—concurrent enrolment, subject acceleration, advanced placement (AP) classes, mentorships, credit by examination, and early admission to college/university
- *Self-directed or independent study*—For some time, self-directed or independent study has been recognized as an appropriate way for teachers to maintain the

Gifted and talented students benefit from accelerated and enriched learning experiences. What are some forms of acceleration and enrichment that you will offer your students?

Apollofoto/Shutterstock

interest of gifted students. Gifted students usually have the academic backgrounds and motivation to do well without constant supervision and the threat or reward of grades.

■ *Individual education programs*—Because all Canadian provinces and territories have some version of IEPs for special education students, IEPs have been promoted as an appropriate means of educating gifted students. Most IEPs for gifted students involve various enrichment experiences, self-directed study, and special, concentrated instruction. There are generally two programming models for gifted students. They can remain in the regular class placement at the home-school with accommodations provided by the classroom teacher or be placed in a self-contained class with other identified gifted students.

WHAT ARE SPECIAL EDUCATION, MAINSTREAMING, AND INCLUSION?

Prior to the twentieth century, children with disabilities were usually segregated from regular classrooms and taught by teachers in provincially or privately operated schools. Today, an array of programs and services in both general and special education classrooms is aimed at developing the potential of exceptional students. Two critical concepts to promote their growth, talents, and productivity are special education and inclusion.

Special education: a teaching specialty for meeting the special educational needs of exceptional learners.

Special education refers to "services and supports that teachers provide to meet the needs of students who are identified with disabilities" (McLeskey, Rosenberg, & Westling, 2010, p. 9). Teachers trained in special education become familiar with special materials, techniques, and equipment and facilities for students with disabilities. For example, children with visual impairment may require reading materials in large print or Braille; students with hearing impairment may require hearing aids or instruction in sign language; those with physical disabilities may need special equipment; children with emotional disturbances may need small and highly structured classes; and students with special gifts or talents may require access to working professionals. "[R]elated services may include parent counseling and training, physical therapy, occupational therapy, school health services, or special transportation" (Mastropieri & Scruggs, 2010, p. 19).

Special Education Laws

Prior to 1980, the needs of students with disabilities were primarily met through self-contained special education classes within regular schools. However, over the past 35 years, this situation changed dramatically. The self-contained special education class has disappeared from most school districts, and a more inclusive educational philosophy, based on an increased concern for human rights, has taken hold. Students who would previously have been placed in segregated classrooms are now integrated into regular classrooms. All provinces and territories now have laws, regulations, or policies that support this practice. For example, in 2005, the Ontario Ministry of Education released *Education for All: The Report of the Expert Panel on Literacy and Numeracy Instruction for Students with Special Education Needs, Kindergarten to Grade 6*. This document promotes the use of Universal Design for Learning and Differentiated Instruction to create learning environments that enable all students to get the support they need to learn in the regular classroom setting. While the exact nature of how inclusion is accomplished varies from one jurisdiction to another, as does the degree to which the various laws, policies, and regulations are enforced, the advocates of children with special needs have achieved a remarkable degree of success. Of particular assistance to these advocates has been the **Canadian Charter of Rights and Freedoms**. Because only Quebec and Saskatchewan have human rights codes that guarantee every citizen the right to an education, the Charter has been increasingly used to support the rights of students with special needs, as illustrated in the ruling in Figure 6.5.

Individualized education plan—A student with a disability of sufficient severity is given a written **individualized educational program (IEP)** or individualized program plan that meets the child's needs and specifies educational goals, methods for achieving those goals, and the number and quality of special educational services to be provided. The IEP is regularly reviewed by five parties: (1) a parent or guardian; (2) the child; (3) a teacher; (4) a professional who has recently evaluated the child; and (5) others, usually the principal or a special-education resource person from the school district. When appropriate, IEPs sometimes have related agreements to ensure that students with disabilities receive any necessary services such as special transportation arrangements or other supportive services as may be required. Sample IEPs and blank templates for Ontario can be accessed at https://specialeducationontario.wikispaces.com/IEP.

Confidentiality of records—Protocols ensure that records on a child are kept confidential. In some provinces, parental permission is required before any official examines a child's records. Moreover, parents can amend a child's records if they feel that information in them is misleading, inaccurate, or violates the child's rights.

Due process—Parents have the right to disagree with an IEP or an evaluation of their child's abilities. If a disagreement arises, in most boards it is settled through an impartial hearing where due process is followed. At the hearing, parents may be represented by a lawyer, may give evidence, and may cross-examine the school personnel involved. If the parents or guardians of a child disagree with the outcome, they may appeal the decision to the provincial department of education. If they're still dissatisfied, the case may then be taken to the civil court.

> **Canadian Charter of Rights and Freedoms**: 1982 document that enshrined rights and freedoms to serve as the guiding law of the land and that applies to all levels of government.

> **Individualized educational program (IEP)**: a program or a plan for meeting an exceptional learner's educational needs, specifying goals, objectives, services, and procedures for evaluating progress.

Landmark Special Education Decision

Eaton v. Brant County Board of Education (February 15, 1995) Toronto, O.J. No. 315/No. C19214 (Ont. CA)

In a decision long fought for by advocates for the disabled and dreaded by school authorities, The Ontario Court of Appeal held that the Canadian Charter of Rights and Freedoms did indeed create a presumption, and a very strong presumption, in favour of the integration of handicapped persons into the mainstream of the community, and particularly the integration of disabled students into the regular classroom. The Court held that to rebut this presumption, school authorities would bear the onus of proving not only that integration in the regular school was not appropriate in a given circumstance, but also that placement in a segregated setting would be the only appropriate alternative. Further, the Court rewrote the legislative scheme for special education in Ontario, a scheme that sought to provide disabled students with procedural fairness in seeking a reasonable educational program. It held that the legislation must ensure that when a parent, acting on behalf of the disabled student, refuses to consent to a segregated educational placement for the student, school authorities must comply with the wishes of the parent "unless alternatives are proven inadequate."

Source: Reprinted from *Education Law Reporter: Elementary and Secondary Schools*, (6), p. 49.

Figure 6.5 Landmark special education decision

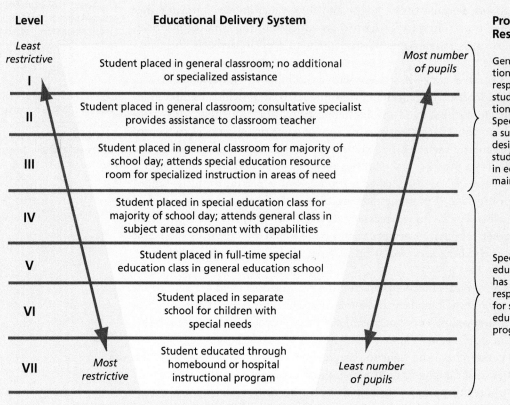

Figure 6.6 Educational service options for students with disabilities

Source: Hardman, Michael L.; Drew, Clifford, J.; Egan, M. Winston, *Human Sexuality: Society, School, and Family,* 7th Edition © 2002. Reprinted by permission of Pearson Education, Inc., Upper Saddle River, NJ.

Least restrictive environment: an educational program that meets a disabled student's special needs in a manner that is identical, insofar as possible, to that provided to students in general education classrooms.

Canadian educators recognize that children with disabilities should be educated in the **least restrictive environment**. In other words, a student must be placed within a general education classroom whenever such inclusion is feasible and appropriate and the child would receive educational benefit. Figure 6.6 shows the educational service options for students with disabilities, from the most inclusive to the most restrictive.

Meeting the Challenge of Inclusion

To help teachers satisfy the requirements of the new inclusive paradigm, school districts across Canada have developed in-service programs designed to acquaint classroom teachers with the unique needs of students with disabilities. In addition, colleges and universities with preservice programs for educators have added courses on teaching students with special educational needs.

The new guidelines require that schools make a significant effort to include *all* children in the classroom. However, *it is not clear how far schools must go to meet this requirement.* For example, should children with severe disabilities be included in general education classrooms if they are unable to complete the academic work? Recent court cases have ruled that such students must be included if there is a potential benefit for the child, if the class would stimulate the child's language development, or if other students could act as appropriate role models for the child. School districts, departments of education, and the Canadian judicial system are presently in an extended process of determining the answers to these and other concerns.

To meet the challenges of inclusion, teachers must have knowledge of various disabilities and the teaching methods and materials appropriate for each. Since teachers with negative attitudes toward students with special needs can convey these feelings to all students in a class and thereby reduce the effectiveness of inclusion (Lewis & Doorlag, 2006), general education teachers must maintain positive attitudes toward students with special needs. An accepting, supportive climate can significantly enhance the self-confidence of students with disabilities.

In addition, Hallahan and Kauffman (2006, pp. 19–20, 22) suggest that all teachers should be prepared to participate in the education of exceptional learners. Teachers should be willing to do the following:

1. Make maximum effort to accommodate individual students' needs.
2. Evaluate academic abilities and disabilities.
3. Refer [students] for evaluation [as appropriate].
4. Participate in eligibility conferences [for special education].
5. Participate in writing individualized educational programs.
6. Communicate with parents or guardians.
7. Participate in due process hearings and negotiations.
8. Collaborate with other professionals in identifying and making maximum use of exceptional students' abilities.

The Debate over Inclusion

While **mainstreaming** refers to the provision of a least restrictive environment, **inclusion** goes beyond mainstreaming to integrate all students with disabilities into general education classes with the active support of special educators and other specialists as well as **assistive technology** and adaptive software. Advocates of inclusion believe that "if students cannot meet traditional academic expectations, then those expectations should be changed. They reject the mainstreaming assumption that settings dictate the type and intensity of services and propose instead the concept of inclusion" (Friend & Bursuck, 2002, p. 4).

Full inclusion goes even further and maintains that "the general education classroom is the most appropriate full-time placement for all students with disabilities—not only those with mild learning and behavior problems, but also those with more severe disabilities" (Lewis & Doorlag, 2006, p. 4). According to the full-inclusion approach, if a child needs support services, these are brought *to the child*; the child does not have to participate in a pull-out program to receive support. Advocates of full inclusion maintain that pull-out programs stigmatize participating students because they are separated from general-education classmates and discourage collaboration between general and special education teachers. Those who oppose full inclusion contend that classroom teachers, who may be burdened with large class sizes and assigned to schools with inadequate support services, often lack the training and instructional materials to meet the needs of all exceptional students. However, while support for full inclusion varies, the trend toward it continues.

Equal Opportunity for Exceptional Learners

Like many groups in our society, exceptional learners have often not received the kind of education that most effectively meets their needs. Approximately 10 percent of the population aged 3 to 21 is classified as exceptional; that is, "they require special education because they are markedly different from most children in one or more of the following ways: They may have . . . learning disabilities, emotional or behavioral disorders, physical

Mainstreaming: providing students with the least restrictive academic environment in which they may comfortably learn the curriculum.

Inclusion: the practice of integrating all students with disabilities into general education classes.

Assistive technology: technological advances (usually computer-based) that help exceptional students learn and communicate.

Full inclusion: the policy and process of including exceptional learners in general education classrooms.

disabilities, disorders of communication, autism, traumatic brain injury, impaired hearing, impaired sight, or special gifts or talents" (Hallahan & Kauffman, 2006, p. 8).

Just as there are no easy answers for how teachers should meet the needs of students from diverse cultural backgrounds, there is no single strategy for teachers to follow to ensure that all exceptional students receive an appropriate education. The key, however, lies in not losing sight of the fact that *the most important characteristics of exceptional children are their abilities*" (Hallahan & Kauffman, 2006, p. 7).

To build on students' strengths, classroom teachers must work cooperatively with special education teachers, and students in special education programs must not be isolated from their peers. In addition, teachers must understand how some people might be perceived as "different" and presumed to be "handicapped" because of their appearance or physical condition. Evidence suggests, for example, that people who are short, obese, or unattractive are often victims of discrimination, as are people with conditions such as cancer, multiple sclerosis, or epilepsy. Significantly, many individuals with clinically diagnosable and classifiable impairments do not self-identify as *handicapped*. The term itself means permanently unable to be treated equally.

Officially labelling students has become a necessity with the passage of the laws that provide education and related services for exceptional students. Classification labels help determine which students qualify for the special services, educational programs, and individualized instruction afforded by law, and they bring to educators' attention many exceptional children and youth whose educational needs could be overlooked, neglected, or inadequately served otherwise. Detrimental aspects include the fact that classification systems are imperfect and have arbitrary cut-off points that sometimes lead to injustices. Labels can evoke negative expectations, which can cause teachers to avoid or underteach exceptional students and cause their peers to isolate or reject them, thereby creating a stigma—sometimes a permanent one. The most serious detriment, however, is that students so labelled are taught to feel inadequate, inferior, and limited in terms of their options for growth.

HOW CAN YOU TEACH ALL LEARNERS IN YOUR INCLUSIVE CLASSROOM?

Teachers have a responsibility to address all students' developmental, individual, and exceptional learning needs. Although addressing the range of student differences in the inclusive classroom is challenging, it can also be very rewarding. While it is beyond the scope of this book to present in-depth instructional strategies to address students' diverse learning needs, attention to four key areas will enable you to create a truly inclusive classroom: collaborative consultation, partnerships with parents, and the use of Universal Design for Learning and Differentiated Instruction and assistive technology for special learners. However, it is important to remember that, whether teaching students with or without special needs, it is critical that the facts and ideas you convey be presented in a clear and understandable manner.

Collaborative Consultation with Other Professionals

Collaborative consultation:
an approach in which a classroom teacher meets with one or more other professionals (such as a special educator, school psychologist, or resource teacher) to focus on the learning needs of one or more students.

One approach to meeting the needs of all students is **collaborative consultation**, in which a classroom teacher meets with one or more other professionals (a special educator, a school psychologist, or a resource teacher, for example) to focus on the learning needs of one or more students. Collaborative consultation often involves shared decision making and co-teaching relationships (Mastropieri & Scruggs, 2010), and participants assume equal responsibility for meeting students' needs. When working with a consultant, general education teachers should "prepare for meetings, be open to the consultant's suggestions, use the consultant's strategies systematically, and document the effectiveness of the ideas [they] try" (Friend & Bursuck, 2002, pp. 95–96).

To meet the educational goals of a student's IEP, regular education teachers are part of an IEP team that includes special educators, other support personnel, and parents. The following special education professionals are among those who consult with and/or collaborate with regular education teachers:

Consulting teacher—a special educator who provides technical assistance such as arranging the physical setting, helping to plan for instruction, or developing approaches for assessing students' learning

Special education resource teacher—a special educator who provides instruction in a resource room for students with disabilities

---

>>> CASE TO CONSIDER | Year of the Four Boys

Jessica,* a very talented teacher with seven years of teaching experience, refers to one of her grade 9 teaching assignments as the Year of the Four Boys. Her school's principal decided that, rather than assign four male students with various physical and mental difficulties to separate classes, she would place all four in the same section. She did, however, restrict the class's size to 24, with 20 of the students categorized as "good."

Boy #1: Quadriplegic as the result of a recent accident, average intelligence, angry, very unhappy, and possibly somewhat embarrassed about his condition. Comes with a full-time personal educational assistant, a large reclining wheelchair, and a laptop computer, which he is just beginning to learn to use.

Comment: No recommendations received as to how to assist this recently paralyzed student.

Boy #2: Brain damaged as the result of oxygen deprivation at birth, smartest student in the class, marvellous sense of humour, spastic body movements. Any loud or unexpected noise causes him to spasm uncontrollably, which can jolt him out of his seat and onto the floor—to the great amusement of his classmates.

Comment: Elementary school recommended keeping all loud or unexpected classroom noises to a minimum.

Boy #3: Suffers from fetal alcohol syndrome (FAS). Has both short-term and long-term memory problems. Work is far below grade level. Often acts out in an inappropriate manner, which causes other students to laugh at him—not with him. Socially promoted for peer group reasons.

Comment: Elementary school recommended giving him all the extra help possible.

Boy #4: Clinically dead for several minutes before being rescued from the bottom of a lake during a recent summer. Serious short-term memory problems. Formerly an energetic and interested student, his behaviour is now less enthused.

Comment: Parents asked his teachers to do everything possible to help him "get back to his normal self."

Jessica's bachelor of education program included only a single three-credit-hour course on how to deal with students with special needs, and none of that course's content offered any specific suggestions for how to deal with the difficulties experienced by the four boys. However, by the end of the school year, she felt she had learned more about how to effectively deal with students with special needs than any number of courses could have taught her.

1. What do you think of the principal's decision to place all four boys in the same class section with 20 "good" students? Why do you think she undertook this action?

2. Do you think the action of the school principal represents good inclusive practice?

3. If you were Jessica, what would be some of the basic elements of the action plan you would construct for dealing with the four boys' situations?

4. Boy #2's situation appears to be the easiest to deal with. List three specific things you, or your school, could immediately put into place to spare him, as much as possible, the spasmodic effects of loud or unexpected noises.

5. What other questions are raised regarding Jessica's and the four boys' situations?

* Jessica teaches in western Canada.

School psychologist—consults with the general education teacher and arranges for the administration of appropriate psychological, educational, and behavioural assessment instruments; may observe a student's behaviour in the classroom

Speech and language specialist—assesses students' communication abilities and works with general education teachers to develop educational programs for students with speech and/or language disorders

Physical therapist—provides physical therapy for students with physical disabilities

Occupational therapist—instructs students with disabilities to prepare them for everyday living and work-related activities

Working with Parents

In addition to working with education professionals to meet the learning needs of all students, effective teachers develop good relationships with parents. Parents of exceptional children can be a source of valuable information about the characteristics, abilities, and needs of their children; they can be helpful in securing necessary services; and they can assist you by reviewing skills at home and praising their children for their learning. Some school districts encourage teachers to contact all of their students' parents or guardians on a regular basis. While this adds one more task to each teacher's workload, boards that have such policies obviously recognize the importance of having a strong relationship with students' homes.

Universal Design for Learning and Differentiated Instruction

Although Universal Design for Learning (UDL) and Differentiated Instruction (DI) are two distinct concepts, teachers can use them in complementary ways in the planning and implementation of programs to reach all learners, and particularly learners with special needs. They both begin with the premise that learning should be student driven rather than program driven and they both embrace individual learner differences. The UDL framework is based on research in the areas of cognitive science, neuroscience, and neuropsychology and focuses on a broad set of principles for curriculum development and instructional design, including flexibility, safety, equitable use, and appropriate attention to the learning environment. While the various provincial curriculum documents determine *what* content will be taught, a DI approach allows teachers to vary *how* the content is taught to a variety of unique learners. Teachers can use a variety of instructional strategies and assessment tools that specifically target the individual needs of students, while also varying student groupings and the physical learning environment. As well, students can be given some choice in the following elements of their learning (Tomlinson, 2004):

- The content (what the students are going to learn)
- The processes (the activities)
- The products (the accomplishment following a learning period)

For more information on UDL and DI, see the following resources:

www.teachspeced.ca

www.edugains.ca/newsite/SpecialEducation/index.html

www.edu.gov.on.ca/eng/document/reports/speced/panel/speced.pdf

Assistive Technology for Special Learners

The ability of teachers to create inclusive classrooms has increased dramatically as a result of many technological advances that now make it easier for exceptional students to learn and communicate. For example, computer-based word processing software and math tutorials can greatly assist students with learning disabilities in acquiring literacy and computer skills. Students with hearing impairments can communicate with other students using telecommunications equipment, and students with physical disabilities can operate computers through voice commands or with a single switch or key. Among the recent developments in assistive technology are the following:

1. Talking word processor
2. Speech synthesizer
3. Touch-screen devices
4. Computer screen image enlarger
5. Teletypewriter (TTY) (connects to telephone and types a spoken message to another TTY)
6. Customized computer keyboards
7. Ultrasonic head controls for computers
8. Voice-recognition software
9. Television closed captioning
10. Word prediction programs
11. Kurzweil reading machine (scans print and reads it aloud)

In addition, assistive technology includes devices to enhance the mobility and everyday activities of people with disabilities (e.g., wheelchairs, lifts, adaptive driving controls, modified keyboards, scooters, laser canes, and feeders).

Modern technology-related special education resources and curriculum materials are available on the Internet. The website of the National Center to Improve Practice

Alsu/Shutterstock

Braille and hearing horns were among the first assistive technologies. How might educators use various types of technology to assist the learning of students with special needs?

Dr. Sheila Bennett

Dr. Sheila Bennett is a professor and former chair in the Department of Teacher Education at Brock University in St. Catharine's, Ontario. Her research interests include inclusion, special education policy, and acquired brain injury. A former classroom and special education teacher and school district resource person, Bennett has been active in the field of special education for many years and has been involved in policy and practical issues in the field. She is co-chair of the Special Education Transformation Document as well as co-author of *Special Education in Ontario Schools*. In her 2009 monograph, Bennett reports that learning environment and the culture of the school setting have "a direct impact on the acceptance of students with exceptionalities" (p. 2). She argues that school administrators play a pivotal role in promoting a culture of inclusion that facilitates success for all students, but particularly for students with exceptionalities. Among the recommendations Bennett makes for educators working to create inclusive learning environments, she suggests:

1. Examine your own beliefs.
2. Work with the school team, including the student.
3. Use a variety of instructional methods, including differentiated instruction and universal design.
4. Extend inclusion to the whole school.

To read Dr. Bennett's monograph in full, visit www.edu.gov. on.ca/eng/literacynumeracy/inspire/research/Bennett.pdf.

in Special Education through Technology, Media, and Materials (www2.edc.org/NCIP) maintains discussion forums for teachers of students with disabilities, and the online library at this site offers information on a variety of resources. The Ontario Ministry of Education document *Learning for All* (2013) also devotes a chapter to assistive technologies. Clearly, the dazzling revolution in electronics will continue to yield new devices to enhance the learning of all students.

How many times have you noticed that certain students always seem to go off on a tangent? These students have trouble staying on topic and remaining focused on classroom content. You know the type—the child who suddenly remarks on the mechanics of airplane propellers when you just taught a lesson on the life cycle of the frog. This behaviour does not go unnoticed by other students in the class, and they observe their teachers to see how we will respond. Often we offer a platitude such as "That's nice, Sam, but can you tell us about frogs?" We used to think that this seeming lack of logic posed a deficit to learning, but can it be an asset? All teachers want their students to succeed, and we want to demonstrate kindness and respect. But I believe we can offer our students something in addition to respect, once we understand the inherent value of differing logic, both in the classroom and in society. In my ongoing work with students, parents, school staffs, and teacher candidates, I try to help educators consider differing logic as an asset.

While all students learn differently, students with exceptionalities tend to top the charts with their own line of logic. The diagnoses are familiar—autism, ADHD, Down syndrome, FAS, and so on. Knowledge of the characteristics, behaviours, and responses may be acquired through teacher education. However, living the experience "in the field" with students who seem to go off topic is an entirely different experience!

Let me tell you about Samuel. While his teacher was explaining geometry, Sam was asking what would happen if he deconstructed his laptop to examine the inner workings; while his peers were reviewing the latest Raptors' basketball stats at recess, Sam was talking incessantly about his video game. If you are thinking that Samuel had a diagnosis of ADHD, you guessed right. Add a learning disability and giftedness to the mix, and you have one very interesting young person. I really enjoyed Sam! We spent a good deal of time talking—he had few friends. What I learned during those chats was to really listen and to follow Sam's line of logic—on his terms. Although we may have started talking about apples, his seemingly sudden switch to movies was actually very logical. The trick was to ask Sam what made him say a certain thing or to inquire what got him thinking in that direction. He could always explain it, and in so doing, his logic raised valuable inquiry-type questions.

My role at the time as administrator in Sam's kindergarten to grade 8 elementary school in Ontario afforded me the opportunity to watch him grow and learn over several years. He had an IEP, and the academic expectations were gradually being met with some success. But by the time Sam had reached grade 7, his behaviours had intensified, his peers and teachers had grown more frustrated, and Sam was being socially ostracized. Teachers, parents, and administration became concerned for his emotional well-being. As Sam talked with me, he confided how tough it was to have no friends at school, and I knew we had to intervene, somehow.

Although the initiative that gradually began to turn things around for Samuel was a team effort involving the special education teacher, the child and youth counsellor from the school board, and me as administrator, I credit Sam's teacher for taking the lead role. She was an advocate for Sam, and it was her positive approach that made all the difference. She was open to allowing other team members into her classroom, and she motivated her entire class to get on board. We all worked together on an intercultural school exchange project. Very simply, our grade 7 class twinned with another class from Japan to exchange stories, photos, and video documentaries about life in Canada versus school life in Japan. It evolved into quite the dynamic, cross-cultural experience! Over a six-week time frame, we allotted several blocks of time per week to focus on this initiative and made sure we used interactive instructional strategies throughout. The focus was on the culture of school belonging, and this lent itself well to themes of bullying prevention and social justice. The process involved student collaboration and a variety of teams, each led by one of the adult educators involved. Of course, the project was never "about Sam"; as far as the class was concerned, it was all about belonging, bullying prevention, and learning about students and school life from another country.

As the video production component of the project got underway, Sam gradually evolved into a lead role on this particular team. It was exciting to watch this unfold! His peers recognized his strengths immediately. He had technological skills already, and his "think-outside-the-box" type of logic was exactly what was needed to propel the videos forward. While his peers on the team were talking about whether their hairstyles looked good in the camera shot, Sam shifted the conversation to things like background lighting and whether or not the kids in Japan would understand why Canadian kids did not wear uniforms. His peers still found Sam frustrating, but they learned to value his logic when he seemed to stray off focus. They weren't just being respectful for the sake of it—they really needed Sam's expertise. Sam, for his part, needed guidance to be able to explain his thinking patiently and succinctly. As for me, I was incredibly proud of everyone involved—teachers, students, and Sam.

Courtesy of Jane Kiyonaga. Used with permission.

SUMMARY

How Do Students' Needs Change as They Develop?

- People move through different stages of cognitive, psychosocial, and moral development throughout their life spans.

- Piaget maintained that children, who reason differently from adults, pass through four stages of cognitive development as they mature. Effective teachers are aware of the characteristics of school-age children's thinking during three of these stages: the preoperational stage, the concrete operations stage, and the formal operations stage.

- According to Erikson's model of psychosocial development, people pass through eight stages of emotional and social development throughout their lives. Each stage is characterized by a "crisis" with a positive and negative pole. Healthy development depends upon a satisfactory, positive resolution of each crisis.

■ Kohlberg believed that moral development, the reasoning people use to decide between right and wrong, evolves through three levels. Evidence suggests that males may base their moral reasoning on rights and rules, and females on altruism and self-sacrifice. Many teachers and schools emphasize character education to "teach" moral reasoning and values.

■ Maslow suggested that human growth and development depends on how well the individual's biological and psychological needs have been met. According to his hierarchy of needs model, people must satisfy their survival and safety needs before addressing "higher" needs such as self-actualization.

■ Teachers must be aware of the developmental stresses and tasks students encounter during childhood and early and late adolescence.

How Do Students Vary in Intelligence?

■ There are conflicting definitions of *intelligence*; they range from "what IQ tests measure" to "goal-directed adaptive behaviour." Some theorists believe intelligence is a single, basic ability, though recent research suggests that there are many forms of intelligence.

■ According to Howard Gardner's theory of multiple intelligences, there are at least eight human intelligences.

How Do Students Vary in Ability and Disability?

■ Some students are "exceptional" because they have abilities or disabilities that distinguish them from other students. Students with physical, cognitive, or emotional disabilities and students who are gifted and talented have unique learning needs.

■ There is a lack of agreement regarding the definition of *learning disability*. Teachers can identify students with learning disabilities by noting difficulties students have acquiring and processing new information. Learning disabilities are the most prevalent disability among students, with attention deficit hyperactivity disorder (ADHD) and attention deficit disorder (ADD) being the most common.

■ There are many forms of giftedness. Among the approaches used to meet the learning needs of gifted students are acceleration, self-directed or independent study, individual education programs, and weekend and summer programs.

What Are Special Education, Mainstreaming, and Inclusion?

■ *Special education* involves a variety of educational services to meet the needs of exceptional students. Provincial and territorial laws, regulations, and policies support models such as the least restrictive environment, individualized educational programs, confidentiality of records, and due process.

■ *Inclusion* integrates all students with disabilities into regular classrooms, with the support of special education services as necessary. *Full inclusion* is the integration of students with disabilities in general education classrooms at all times regardless of the severity of the disability.

How Can You Teach All Learners in Your Inclusive Classroom?

■ Though challenging, teachers have a responsibility to create inclusive classrooms that address the developmental, individual, and exceptional learning needs of all students.

■ Through collaborative consultation—an arrangement whereby the regular classroom teacher collaborates with other education professionals—teachers can meet the needs of exceptional students. Collaborative consultation is based on reciprocity, and all participants assume responsibility for meeting students' needs.

■ By developing effective relationships with parents of exceptional students, teachers acquire valuable information and support.

■ An array of assistive technologies and resources is available to help exceptional students learn and communicate in inclusive classrooms.

APPLICATIONS AND ACTIVITIES

1. Recount an experience you had with an exceptional student or one that involved a person with disabilities. What did you learn from this experience or from your reflection on it that could help you as a teacher?

2. Sensitivity training specialists are fond of activities that sensitize individuals to people with mental or physical limitations. Review the types of disability listed in Table 6.3, select any three of the disabilities, and, in a small group, develop one sensitization activity you could conduct with a class for each of the selections you made.

3. Observe in a classroom that has exceptional students. What steps does the teacher take to meet the needs of these students? Interview the teacher to determine what he or she sees as the challenges and rewards of teaching exceptional students.

4. Observe and interview a student in the age group you wish to teach to conduct a brief case study that focuses on common developmental tasks for that age group and the areas of individual differences highlighted in this chapter. Prepare a written portrait of the student.

5. Investigate sources of information on assistive technologies for students with disabilities or exceptional learners. Identify and explore a specific assistive technology that might be useful for one of the students you have observed in a classroom situation.

Chapter 7
Creating a Community of Learners

contrastwerkstatt/Fotolia

FOCUS QUESTIONS

1. What determines the culture of the classroom?
2. How can you create a positive learning environment?
3. What are the keys to successful classroom management?
4. What teaching methods do effective teachers use?
5. What are some characteristics of effective teaching?

As a teacher I role-model the qualities that I seek to nurture in my students—an open, curious mind and a willingness to explore new ideas. My job is to provide a framework that supports them in building experience of a new environment and provide a foundation for taking new risks. I use the comfort of working with their peers in small groups to move them into a new frame of reference.

—Shirley R. Turner
Secondary-level teacher at Vancouver
Technical School in British Columbia

Recipient of a Prime Minister's Award for
Excellence in Teaching in October 2009

The culture of a classroom is determined by the quality of interactions between students and their teacher. Some teachers create a strict environment, and their students may feel fearful and uncomfortable. Other teachers use humour and a laid-back style to create a friendly environment; their students feel comfortable and have fun while learning.

—THOMAS, teacher education program, first year

Teachers create the learning culture of the classroom by showing passion for the subject and concern for students. Teachers also affect classroom culture through the use of classroom management techniques and classroom setup.

—JAMES, teacher education program, first year

This chapter highlights the importance of organizing the classroom to create a positive learning environment—a cohesive community of learners. For teacher education students, the transition between the study of teaching and actual teaching can be a challenge. You will make that transition smoothly, however, if you understand that to create a cohesive community of learners, "teachers must (1) earn the respect and affection of students; (2) be consistent and, therefore, credible and dependable; (3) assume responsibility for seeing that their students learn; and (4) value and enjoy learning and expect students to do so, too" (Good & Brophy, 2008, p. 77).

WHAT DETERMINES THE CULTURE OF THE CLASSROOM?

As you learned in Chapter 5, one definition of culture is the way of life common to a group of people. In much the same way, each classroom develops its own culture. The culture of a classroom is determined by the manner in which teachers and students participate in common activities.

Classroom activities are influenced by several factors. As a teacher, you will make countless decisions that will shape the physical and social milieus of your classroom. From seating arrangements to classroom guidelines and procedures and the content of the curriculum, you will have a strong influence on the culture that emerges. You will have many methodological choices to make—when to shift from one activity to another, when to use small group discussion rather than direct instruction, and whether to make one requirement more imperative than another, for example.

>>> What Classrooms Look Like

What do Canadian public school classrooms look like? That depends on many variables, including, but not limited to, the following:

- School level (elementary, middle/junior or senior high)
- Age of school (built in the past 10 years, built in the past 30 years, or built more than 30 years ago)
- Location (rural, suburban, urban)
- Size (small, medium, large) and configuration (K–12, P–6, 7–9, 10–12, etc.)

- School leadership
- Socioeconomic background of students
- Content area
- Class size
- Class composition
- Individual teacher experience and philosophy

Classroom Climate

Classroom climate: the atmosphere or quality of life in a classroom, determined by how individuals interact with one another.

One dimension of classroom culture is **classroom climate**—the atmosphere or quality of life in a classroom. The climate of your classroom will be decided by how you interact with your students and "by the manner and degree to which you exercise authority, show warmth and support, encourage competitiveness or cooperation, and allow for independent judgment and choice" (Borich, 2007, p. 167).

Classroom climates are complex and multidimensional; their character is determined by a wide array of variables, many of which are beyond the teacher's control. Nevertheless, our observations of high-performing teachers have confirmed that they take specific steps to create classroom climates that incorporate the following eight characteristics:

1. A productive, task-oriented focus
2. Group cohesiveness
3. Open, warm relationships between teacher and students
4. Cooperative, respectful interactions among students
5. Low levels of tension, anxiety, and conflict
6. Humour
7. High expectations
8. Frequent opportunities for student input regarding classroom activities

The degree to which these dimensions are present within your classroom will be influenced by your style of communication with students. As the following case illustrates, creating a classroom climate characterized by these eight dimensions is

---

⟫⟫ CASE TO CONSIDER | Water and the Classroom Climate

Dari feels uncomfortable as she makes the seemingly endless trip from her desk to the drinking fountain at the back of the room. If she had a choice, she wouldn't make the trip at all. She is well aware that her classmates resent her being allowed to get a drink whenever she wants to, whereas they have to wait until recess or lunch. They know that the medicine she takes every morning makes her thirsty, but they still tease her about being "Teacher's Pet."

"Why can't the others get drinks when they want to?" she wonders. "It wouldn't be any big deal. Besides, Ms. Patterson is always drinking her coffee. She carries that stupid coffee mug around so much that it looks as if it's attached to her body."

"Hey, Ms. Patterson, can I get a drink?" Craig calls out. "It's a really hot day, and I'm thirsty."

"Of course not, Craig. You know my rule about that." Ms. Patterson is obviously annoyed at his question.

Craig persists. "It's not fair. You can drink your coffee whenever you want to."

"I never said life is fair," Ms. Patterson replies. "I'm the teacher, so I have certain privileges. I need to have something to drink because I do most of the talking and my mouth gets dry. Besides, my job is to make sure that you children learn, and I can't do that if you're running to the drinking fountain all the time. It won't kill you to wait until recess to get a drink."

"But we could use a water bottle," Huong suggests.

"No. That won't work. A couple of years ago, I let my students bring water bottles to school, and they used them to squirt one another all the time. When are you people going to learn that no means no?"

"But you let Dari go to the fountain whenever she wants to," Shelby points out.

"Dari has medical problems," Ms. Patterson responds. "Anyway, I know that she'll only get a drink if she really, really needs one. Right, Dari?"

Dari nods self-consciously and then tries to make herself smaller by scrunching low in her seat.

"Yeah, she's special, all right," Guy scoffs. "She's Teacher's Pet."

(Ormrod & McGuire, 2007, p. 111)

1. How would you describe this classroom climate using the eight dimensions?
2. Should Ms. Patterson allow her students to get a drink during class?
3. Is it fair that she drinks coffee in front of her students?
4. How might Ms. Patterson help Dari feel more socially connected to her classmates?

What words might describe the interaction between this teacher and student? What do you think the teacher is saying?

not easy. The moment-to-moment decisions teachers make about how to respond to events can enhance or reduce group cohesiveness and students' motivation to learn.

Although teachers influence the classroom climate by the way they treat students, they also shape it by their instructional decisions. David Johnson and Roger Johnson, two researchers in the area of classroom communication and dynamics, delineate three types of interactions promoted by instructional decisions: cooperative or positive interdependence, competitive or negative interdependence, and individualistic or no interdependence (Johnson & Johnson, 1999). To illustrate, Johnson and Johnson suggest that a group project to measure classroom furniture would promote cooperative interdependence, a race to be the first student to measure the furniture would call for competitive interdependence, and having a student measure the furniture independently would be an example of no interdependence. Johnson and Johnson believe that teachers should use strategies that foster all three forms of interaction, depending on their instructional goals, but that ideally the emphasis should be on furthering cooperative interdependence.

Classroom Dynamics

Interactions between teachers and students are the very core of teaching. The quality of these interactions reveals to students how the teacher feels about them. Teachers who empathize with students, genuinely respect them, and expect them to learn are more likely to develop a classroom climate free of management problems. In classrooms with positive group dynamics, teachers and students work toward a common goal—learning. In classrooms with negative interactions, the energy of teachers and students may be channelled into conflict rather than into learning.

There is no precise formula to guarantee success in the classroom; however, a classroom climate characterized by the following four qualities results in greater student motivation to learn and more positive teacher–student and student–student interactions:

1. Learning activities are well organized, progress smoothly, and are free from distractions or interruptions.

2. The teacher is caring, patient, and supportive, and never ridicules or criticizes students for their efforts to learn.

3. The curriculum is challenging but not so difficult that students become frustrated and decide not to learn.

4. Learning activities are authentic and, to the degree possible, relevant to students' interests and experiences.

Communication Skills Successful teachers possess effective communication skills. They express themselves verbally and nonverbally in a manner that is clear, concise, and interesting. They "are able to communicate clearly and directly to their students without wandering, speaking above students' levels of comprehension, or using speech patterns that impair their presentation's clarity" (Borich, 2007, p. 10). In addition, they are good listeners. Their students feel that not only are they heard, they are understood.

Effective teachers relish the interactive, spontaneous dimensions of classroom discourse. They respond appropriately to events that could derail the plans of less effective teachers—a student's inappropriate behaviour, announcements on the PA system, interruptions by other teachers or parents, arguments between students, or the mood of the class at a given time.

Interactions among Students In addition to engaging in positive, success-oriented interactions with their students, effective teachers foster positive, cooperative interactions among them. As a result, students feel supported by their peers and free to devote their attention to learning. The climate of such a classroom is "mature" and "self-renewing" (Schmuck & Schmuck, 2001). Typically, the classroom climate has evolved through four stages of group development (see Figure 7.1).

During stage 1, students are on their best behaviour. Teachers can use this honeymoon period to their advantage. They can discuss classroom rules and procedures, outline learning goals, and clarify expectations. During stage 2, teachers can encourage student participation and communication while discouraging the formation of cliques.

Groups that have reached stage 2 then move into stage 3, which may last for the remainder of the school year. In stage 3, the group sets clear goals, shares tasks, and agrees on deadlines. A fully evolved group reaches stage 4. In this stage, group members accept responsibility for the quality of life in the group and continually strive to improve it.

In the early 1970s, American educator Jeanne Gibbs developed a research-based community building program called Tribes that is still used in many Canadian schools and even adopted by school districts. The "primary mission of Tribes is to assure the healthy development of every child in the school community so that each has the knowledge, skills and resiliency to be successful in our rapidly changing world" (Gibbs & Ushijima, 2008, p. 480). Gibbs identifies three stages of group development: inclusion, influence, and community. By practising four community agreements—attentive listening, appreciations/no put-downs, right to pass/right to participate, and mutual respect—and by actively building a positive and shared learning environment, a class of students can work together creatively, even when conflicts arise or difficult decisions need to be made.

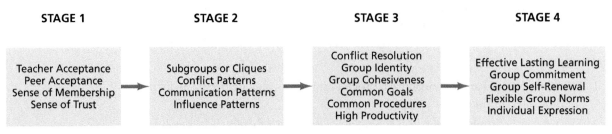

Figure 7.1 Characteristics of groups at four stages of development

HOW CAN YOU CREATE A POSITIVE LEARNING ENVIRONMENT?

A positive classroom climate and positive classroom dynamics are prerequisites for a good learning environment. Creating and maintaining a positive learning environment is a multidimensional challenge. While no single set of strategies will ensure success in all situations, educational researchers have identified teacher behaviours that tend to be associated with high levels of student learning. Effective teachers know how to use these behaviours and for what purposes they are best suited. The following sections address three important dimensions of positive learning environments: the caring classroom, the physical classroom environment, and classroom organization, including procedures for grouping students for instruction and for managing time.

The Caring Classroom

At this point in your preparation to become a teacher, you may feel uncertain of your ability to create a positive classroom climate and to orchestrate the complex dynamics of the classroom so that you and your students become a cohesive, productive, and mutually supportive group. In your quest to achieve these aims, it will help to remember that an authentic spirit of caring is at the heart of an effective learning environment. "[C]aring pedagogy can . . . create or restore self-confidence needed for participating in the positive learning opportunities in the classroom. It can also help form the moral foundation of responsible citizenship, productive community membership and leadership, and lifelong engagement in learning" (italics added) (Paul & Colucci, 2000, p. 45). Canadian educators Kathy Gould Lundy and Larry Swartz (2011) argue that it is essential for teachers to establish inclusive and caring classrooms in order to engage students in critical conversations.

How can you establish a **caring classroom**? First, you can demonstrate caring through your efforts to help all students learn to their fullest potential. You can learn as much as you can about your students' abilities and what motivates them to do their best. You should actually become a student of your students; as one grade 10 student states, an effective teacher "[gets] to know all students well" (Harris Interactive, 2001). You can also support student learning by encouraging and conveying appropriate—neither too high nor too low—expectations.

Caring classroom: a classroom in which the teacher communicates clearly an attitude of caring about students' learning and their overall well-being.

In addition, teachers should recognize that how they speak and listen to students determines the extent to which students believe they are cared about. In a synthesis of research on classroom environments that enhance students' learning, Herbert Walberg and Rebecca Greenberg (1997, p. 46) found that "students learn more when their classes are satisfying, challenging, and friendly and they have a voice in decision making. [When] classes are unfriendly, cliquish, and fragmented, they leave students feeling rejected and therefore impede learning." Table 7.1, based on Walberg and Greenberg's work, presents 15 dimensions of classroom life and how each influences students' learning at the junior and senior high levels.

While students learn best in caring classrooms, Nel Noddings has suggested they must also learn to care for others. Toward this end, she recommends reorganizing the school curriculum around "themes of care" and suggests that "all students should be engaged in a general education that guides them in caring for self, intimate others, global others, plants, animals, the environment, objects and instruments, and ideas" (2002, p. 99). In addition, Noddings asserts that "relations of care and trust should improve (or at least not hurt) achievement, [and] they also might contribute to greater safety, stronger social ties, better citizenship, and greater satisfaction for both teachers and students" (2007, p. 83).

TABLE 7.1 Fifteen Dimensions of the Classroom Environment

Dimension	Percent Positive Influence on Learning	Description
Satisfaction	100 (17)	Students enjoy classroom work and find it satisfying.
Challenge	87 (16)	Students find the work difficult and challenging.
Cohesiveness	86 (17)	Students know one another well and are helpful and friendly toward one another.
Physical Environment	85 (15)	Adequate books, equipment, space, and lighting are available.
Democracy	85 (14)	Students share equally in making decisions that affect the entire class.
Goal Direction	73 (15)	Learning goals are clear.
Competition	67 (9)	Competition among students is minimized.
Formality	65 (17)	Class is informal, with few rules to guide behaviour.
Speed	54 (14)	Students have sufficient time to finish their work.
Diversity	31 (14)	Students' interests differ and are provided for.
Apathy	14 (15)	Students don't care about what the class does.
Favouritism	10 (13)	All students do not enjoy the same privileges; the teacher has favourites.
Cliquishness	8 (13)	Certain students work only with close friends and refuse to interact with others.
Disorganization	6 (17)	Activities are disorganized and confusing rather than well organized and efficient.
Friction	0 (17)	Tension and quarrelling among students characterize the classroom.

Note: Percent indicates the percentage of research studies that reported a positive influence on learning for that dimension; numbers in parentheses indicate number of research studies that investigated that dimension.

Source: Adapted from Herbert J. Walberg and Rebecca C. Greenberg, "Using the Learning Environment Inventory," *Educational Leadership*, May 1997, p. 47.

The Physical Environment of the Classroom

When you become a teacher, the physical environment you work in will probably be similar to that of schools you attended. However, we encourage you, with the help of your students, to make your surroundings as safe, pleasant, and convenient as possible. Fresh air, plants, clean walls, displays of students' work, a comfortable reading

This kindergarten class exhibits some of the characteristics of a caring classroom climate.

Cardinal/Corbis

or resource area, and a few prints or posters can enhance the quality of teacher–student relationships. Seating arrangements and the placement of other classroom furniture also do much to shape the classroom environment. Although seating by rows may be appropriate for whole-group instruction or examinations, other arrangements may be more beneficial for different activities. For example, you can enhance small-group activities by moving desks into small clusters in different parts of the room. Figure 7.2 shows the arrangement of a classroom at an exemplary elementary school. The room is designed to encourage students to learn through discovery at various learning centres.

However you design your classroom, take care to ensure that seating arrangements do not reduce the opportunity of some students to learn. For example, students in some classrooms receive more attention if they are seated in the "action zone"—the middle front-row seats and seats on the middle aisle. Teachers often stand near this area and unknowingly give students seated there more opportunities to speak.

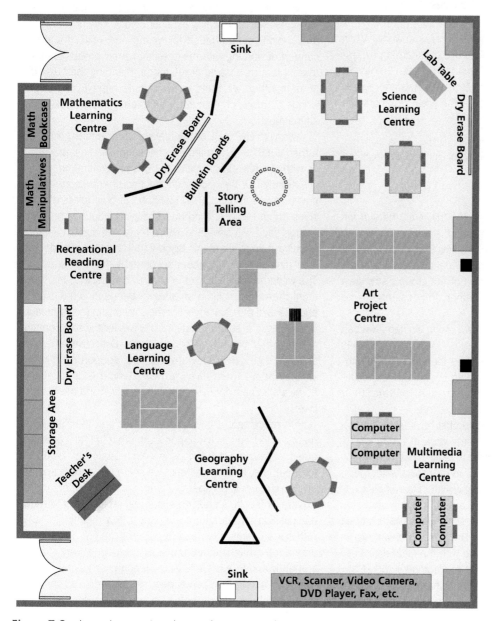

Figure 7.2 Learning centres in an elementary classroom

Some teachers create opportunities to break down the walls of the traditional classroom and move the learning experience outside of the school. Consider teacher Shirley R. Turner, recipient of a 2009 Prime Minister's Award for Excellence in Teaching, who considers the great outdoors her classroom:

> As teachers, our real challenge is to show our passion for learning and share it in a meaningful way with our students.
>
> —Shirley R. Turner

On an unfamiliar trail above the tree line, the summit came into view. We had only one short, steep leg of the path ahead of us to reach the viewpoint below Black Tusk, but, for some of the students, fatigue had overtaken the will to reach the top. I watched intently as two of my group's strongest hikers dropped to the back together; they seemed to be moving as one force.

"C'mon," said one of these two young women, "we can make it together."

That day every student reached the summit. The student's words still resonate years later. For me this is the ultimate reward: seeing my students demonstrate their understanding that learning is a group effort.

I was attracted to British Columbia because of its outstanding natural beauty. During my work at an inner city school in Vancouver I slowly came to realize that many of my students, while surrounded by immense natural wilderness, had never actually experienced the wealth of learning experiences afforded by their own backyard. Although I am a seasoned recreational hiker in my personal life, having climbed Mount Kilimanjaro and kayaked B.C.'s pristine waterways, this was the first time that I played with the idea, dare I say the need, for moving my classroom to the great outdoors.

My love of teaching is rooted in revealing new perspectives to young minds and the charm of watching the

subsequent process of integration. I share my passion for physics and its application all around us in the hope of inspiring potential scientists to play creatively with new ideas. However, before I could share the wilderness with my students, I had to find a valid framework within which to work. This vehicle turned out to be the Duke of Edinburgh Awards Program, which incorporates community service, physical recreation, and life-skill development in a forum that provides a basis for working together in a consultative and collaborative way.

The process of communicating that which I know to be valid, while remaining open to new information, has been a cornerstone to my teaching over the last 20 years. As a teacher I role-model the qualities that I seek to nurture in my students—an open, curious mind and a willingness to explore new ideas. My job is to provide a framework that supports them in building experience of a new environment and provide a foundation for taking new risks. I use the comfort of working with their peers in small groups to move them into a new frame of reference. Planning their expeditions together, we build from a single night in the backwoods to more challenging multiple-day backpacking in alpine meadows.

As with the best of my classroom practices, this has turned out to be a learning experience for all of us, providing us with multiple opportunities to build understanding.

Rarely has the social construction of knowledge had a greater direct impact. There continue to be endless discussions about the best food and dickering about with which groups each will cook and share tents. Wherever it is safe practice, I let my students discover the best way to address their difficulties. I hold them accountable for their success. The wilderness dictates some of its own rules, and I supplement these minimally in an attempt to enhance the experience. One of the challenges for the students in this approach to learning is to shed their digital devices for the sole comfort of each other's company for a few days. Collectively the participants digest their new environment, support each other as they adapt themselves to new standards, and return home with a new appreciation of themselves and their urban lives.

In reaching out beyond themselves and their achievements as individuals to support each other in their collective quest for success, students show each other their potential for greatness. In the classroom we share our understanding of our subject's perspective and create experiences to explore its facets. As teachers, our real challenge is to show our passion for learning and share it in a meaningful way with our students. We need to fully engage our students in education while connecting with them in a way that is authentic and true to ourselves as teachers. Like the leaders from the hiking group, we need to be prepared to walk alongside them, be attentive to their process, willing to

share our experience, and, above all, patient enough to follow their steps with joy in our shared achievement. At the
end of the day we can celebrate our achievements together
as we contemplate a new panorama richer in possibilities
for being shared with the whole group and more poignant
with opportunity.

*Shirley R. Turner is a secondary-level teacher at Van-
couver Technical School in British Columbia. As a recipient
of a Prime Minister's Award for Excellence in Teaching in
October 2009, Ms. Turner was recognized as a champion of
science for students of all ability levels and for her work in
developing outdoor adventures and community service.*

Classroom Organization

A characteristic of positive learning environments is **classroom organization**—the
way teachers and students are grouped for instruction, the way learning tasks are structured, and the way other resources are used. The following sections focus on these
aspects of classroom organization.

Grouping Students by Ability   Two common approaches for grouping students on
the basis of shared characteristics are between-class ability grouping, often called tracking, and within-class ability grouping. Students who attend schools where **between-
class ability grouping** is practised are assigned to classes on the basis of ability or
achievement. This system is not common in Canadian schools. Another form of
between-class ability grouping, especially at the high school level, is based on students'
goals after graduation. For example, many high schools offer honours classes or French
immersion programs.

Research suggests that, for the most part, between-class ability grouping does not
contribute to greater achievement (Good & Brophy, 2008). Although supporters nevertheless claim that teachers are better able to meet the needs of students in homogeneous groupings, most Canadian schools employ heterogeneous grouping that includes
students of varying abilities, including those who are gifted and have other special
needs.

Within-class ability grouping is often used for instruction in reading and
mathematics within a class, where a teacher instructs students in homogeneous
small groups. Within-class grouping is used widely in elementary classrooms. Perhaps you can recall learning to read in a small group with a name such as the Spar-
rows, the Robins, or the Blue Jays. Like tracking, within-class ability grouping can
heighten preexisting differences in achievement between groups of students, especially if teachers give high-achieving groups more attention. Once students are
grouped, they tend not to be regrouped, even when differences in achievement are
reduced.

At best, evidence to support student groupings is mixed. Whether students are
grouped on the basis of ability, curricular interests, or disabling conditions, there is a
danger that some group labels can evoke negative expectations, causing teachers to
underteach certain students and prompting their peers to isolate or reject them. The
most serious consequence, of course, is that students so labelled are taught to feel inadequate, inferior, and limited in their options for growth.

Grouping Students for Cooperative Learning   **Cooperative learning** is an
approach to teaching in which students work in small groups or teams, sharing work
and helping one another complete assignments. Student-team learning, for example, is
a cooperative approach teachers use to increase the basic skills achievement of at-risk
students. In cooperative learning arrangements, students are motivated to learn in

Classroom organization: how
teachers and students in a school are
grouped for instruction and how time is
allocated in classrooms.

Between-class ability grouping:
the practice of grouping students at the
middle and high school levels for instruction on the basis of ability or achievement;
often called *tracking*.

Within-class ability grouping: the
practice of creating small, homogeneous
groups of students within a single classroom for the purpose of instruction, usually in reading or mathematics, at the
elementary level.

Cooperative learning: an approach
to teaching in which students work in
small groups, or teams, sharing the work
and helping one another complete
assignments.

small groups through rewards that are made available to the group as a whole as well as to individual members. Cooperative learning includes the following key elements:

- Small groups (four to six students) work together on learning activities.
- Assignments require that students help one another while working on a group project.
- In competitive arrangements, groups may compete against one another.
- Group members contribute to group goals according to their talents, interests, and abilities.

In addition, cooperative learning is an instructional method that can strengthen students' interpersonal skills. When students from diverse backgrounds and mainstreamed special-needs students all contribute to a common group goal, friendships increase and group members tend to view one another as more equal in status and worth.

Cooperative learning also enables students to learn a variety of roles and responsibilities. Erik Korporaal, a first-year teacher of grades 4 and 5, explains his experience:

> I began by having my students work on simpler, shorter activities in teams of two. For instance, the small groups worked on math problems that they were already familiar with. I did this so that they could focus on working together rather than struggling to understand the problem. Gradually, I increased the difficulty of the tasks as well as the size of the groups. I reinforced positive behaviour and pointed out the types of interactions that led to successful groups. Over time students began to realize the sorts of interactions (e.g., effective communication, listening, delegation of responsibilities, and attention to each member's contributions) that needed to occur in order for their group to succeed. (Oakes & Lipton, 2007, p. 193)

Delivering Instruction   The delivery of instruction is a key element in creating positive learning environments. What the teacher does and what students do have a powerful influence on learning and on the quality of classroom life. A common activity format in elementary schools consists of students doing seatwork on their own or listening to their teachers and participating in whole-class recitations. In addition, students participate in reading groups, games, and discussions; take tests; check work; view films; give reports; help clean up the classroom; and go on field trips.

A teacher must answer the question, "What activity will enable me to accomplish my instructional goals?" Teachers must realize that learning activities should meet students' goals; that is, the activities must be meaningful and authentic for students. **Authentic learning tasks** enable students to see the connections between classroom learning and the world beyond the classroom—both now and in the future.

To understand how authentic learning tasks can motivate students to learn, reflect on your own school experiences. Do you recall memorizing facts only because they would appear on a test? Did you ever wonder why a teacher asked you to complete a learning task? Did you ever feel that a teacher asked you to do busywork?

What kinds of learning tasks motivated you the most? How often were you involved in authentic learning activities such as the following?

- Giving oral reports based on research you conducted
- Writing an editorial for the school or local newspaper
- Representing the pro or con side in a debate
- Conducting an experiment and then writing the results
- Creating a model to illustrate a process, such as photosynthesis, a solar eclipse, or combustion in a gasoline engine
- Completing an art project and then participating in an art exhibit for the community

Authentic learning tasks: learning activities that enable students to see the connections between classroom learning and the world beyond the classroom.

- Tutoring younger children in reading, mathematics, or science
- Developing a website to document an in-class project
- Creating an infomercial using video-editing software and then getting reactions from other classes in your school
- Developing a science WebQuest and then posting it for evaluation

A comprehensive nationwide study of successfully restructured schools reported that "authentic pedagogy" helps students to (1) "construct knowledge" through the use of higher-order thinking, (2) acquire "deep knowledge" (relatively complex understandings of subject matter), (3) engage in "substantive conversations" with teachers and peers, and (4) make connections between substantive knowledge and the world beyond the classroom (Newmann & Associates, 1996; Newmann & Wehlage, 1995).

Structuring the Use of Time How teachers use time affects student learning. **Allocated time** is the time teachers allocate for instruction in various areas of the curriculum. Teachers vary widely in their use of time. Educational researchers Tom Good and Jere Brophy report, for example, that "some students [may receive] as much as four times more instructional time in a given subject than other students in the same grade" (Good & Brophy, 2003, p. 29).

Allocated time: the amount of time teachers allocate for instruction in various areas of the curriculum.

Researchers have shown that **time on task**—the amount of time students are actively engaged in learning activities—is directly related to learning. As anyone who has ever daydreamed while appearing to pay attention can confirm, time on task is difficult to measure. In response to this difficulty, researchers have introduced the concept of **academic learning time**—the amount of time a student spends working on academic tasks with a high level of success (80 percent or higher). Not surprisingly, learning time, like allocated time, varies greatly from classroom to classroom.

Time on task: the amount of time students are actively and directly engaged in learning tasks.

An additional concept that is proving useful in understanding teachers' use of time in the classroom is known as **opportunity to learn (OTL)**. OTL is based on the premise that teachers should use time to provide all students with challenging content through appropriate instruction.

Academic learning time: the amount of time students spend working on academic tasks with a high level of success (80 percent or higher).

Some provincial departments of education have set specific minimum daily guidelines regarding how time should be used in classrooms. For example, the 2007 Nova Scotia Education Department document "Opportunity to Learn: Quantity of Instructional Time" outlines the provincial policy on the quantity of time that should be dedicated to specific programs, including guidelines on the use of instructional time.

Opportunity to learn (OTL): the time during which a teacher provides students with challenging content and appropriate instructional strategies to learn that content.

To increase the time available for active learning, many secondary schools have implemented block or semester scheduling arrangements. **Block scheduling** uses longer blocks of time for each class period, with fewer periods each day. Longer blocks of time allow more in-depth coverage of subject matter and lead to deeper understanding and higher-level applications. Block scheduling also gives teachers more time to present complex concepts and gives students more time to practise applying those concepts to authentic problems. Often, secondary schools operate on a two-week cycle, flipping long and short class periods so that all subject areas benefit from longer blocks of time (Figure 7.3).

Block scheduling: a high school scheduling arrangement that provides longer blocks of time each class period, with fewer periods each day.

WHAT ARE THE KEYS TO SUCCESSFUL CLASSROOM MANAGEMENT?

For most new teachers, **classroom management** is a primary concern. How can you prevent discipline problems from arising and keep students productively engaged in learning activities? Effective classroom management cannot be reduced to a cookbook recipe. However, you can take definite steps to create an effective learning environment in your classroom.

Classroom management: day-to-day teacher control of student behaviour and learning, including discipline.

Week One	Week Two
Warning Bell 8:48 (music)	Warning Bell 8:48 (music)
Period 1 8:55 to 10:10	Period 2 8:55 to 10:10
Home Room 10:10 to 10:15	Home Room 10:10 to 10:15
Period 2 10:20 to 11:35	Period 1 10:20 to 11:35
Lunch 11:35 to 12:25	Lunch 11:35 to 12:25
Period 3 12:25 to 1:40	Period 4 12:25 to 1:40
Period 4 1:45 to 3:00	Period 3 1:45 to 3:00
Dismissal 3:00	Dismissal 3:00

Figure 7.3   Bell schedule

Source: Ajax High School website: www.ddsb.ca/school/ajaxhs/SchoolInformation/bells/Pages/default.aspx

Sound classroom management techniques are based on the guidelines for creating an effective learning environment presented earlier in the chapter: (1) creating a caring classroom; (2) organizing the physical classroom environment; (3) grouping students for instruction; (4) providing authentic learning tasks; and (5) structuring the use of time to maximize students' learning. Positive leadership and preventive planning are thus central to effective classroom management.

In addition, you should remember that classroom management refers to how teachers structure their learning environments to prevent or minimize behavioural problems. Discipline refers to the methods teachers use after students misbehave. Classroom management is prevention-oriented, while discipline is control-oriented. The goal of classroom management is to structure the classroom environment to maximize student attention and minimize disruptive behaviour. Many faculties of education in Canada are moving away from the term *classroom management* in their courses, preferring instead *building effective classrooms*. This shift reflects an emphasis on developing a positive classroom environment rather than "managing" students. Good teachers manage activities, space, and time while giving students more autonomy to manage themselves. Many school districts in Canada are using Stuart Shanker's Self-Regulation framework (2013), which is based on a number of research studies that suggest that self-regulation lays a lifelong foundation for physical, psychological, behavioural, and educational well-being. Children, however, do not naturally know how to self-regulate, but they can be taught to independently plan, monitor, and assess their own learning. For more information on self-regulation in education, see the Education Canada website: www.cea-ace.ca/education-canada/article/self-regulation-calm-alert-and-learning.

The following strategies will help you create a well-managed classroom environment:

- Arrange classroom furniture so that you can easily monitor students' behaviour for signs of inattention and boredom from any point in the room.

- Arrange classroom furniture so that students can move from place to place without disturbing their classmates.

- Keep interesting instructional materials (e.g., a replica of a human skeleton, a model of the solar system, or a large collection of insects) in the classroom to promote curiosity and imagination.

- Allow friends to sit together as long as they are on-task and collaborating in positive ways, and separate students who are having difficulty working together, but only after conflict resolution has been attempted.

- Monitor classroom activity by moving around the room; when students are off-task, move close to them to get them back on track.

Jeffrey Benson, author of the 2014 ASCD book *Hanging In: Strategies for Teaching the Students Who Challenge Us Most*, reminds us that teachers do not control the students, so it is important to be in control of the things you can. As a guest blogger at Education Week Teacher in June 2014, Benson offered several important tips for building a classroom environment that promote trust and respect, including the following:

- In each class, make an effort to have a connection with each student. Greet each by name. Shake their hands. Ask them how the day is going. You build relationships and trust moment by moment.

- Keep your enthusiasm during lessons by focusing on those students who are trying their best. The vast majority of students want school to work for them; invigorate yourself by keeping the majority of attention on them in class.

- Respectfully invite students to join in. When asking questions, preface them by saying, "I want everyone to think about this for 15 seconds, and then I'm asking Fred, Darlene, and Alonso what they think. If you have no response, say "Pass" and I will move on." This is a respectful way to invite more students into a lesson without shaming them by cold calling to prove that they were not paying attention. Never shame students. Instead, provide a heads-up.

- When addressing students not on task, in Ruby Payne's words, use your adult voice: reflective and sincere. Don't lecture, cajole, warn, or dismiss with irritation and frustration.

- Speak to off-task students as individuals, not all at once, not as a united group. Break through their indifference student by student: "I think there is something in this lesson that you in particular will find interesting"; "When you are ready to work, I'll help"; "Thanks for not disrupting the students who were doing the lesson. I really appreciate that, and hope you will work more tomorrow."

- Your class can be an island of respect, with the persistent hope that each individual will find a way to join in. To do so, you have to be in this for the long run. It may take 100 repetitions of your approach to make breakthroughs with some students; most will take fewer repetitions. Your work is building the endlessly welcoming classroom culture that allows each of them to take the step to join in.

- Celebrate your own small successes, student by student.

The Democratic Classroom

Teachers who allow students to participate in making decisions about the physical classroom environment, classroom rules and procedures, modifications to the curriculum, and options for learning activities have fewer discipline problems. Students in **democratic classrooms** have more power and more responsibility than students in conventional classrooms. If students are to live in a democracy, they must learn to manage freedom responsibly; teachers model democracy by giving their students some choices and some control over classroom activities.

Democratic classrooms: a classroom in which the teacher's leadership style encourages students to take more power and responsibility for their learning.

William Glasser, well-known psychiatrist and author of *Quality School* (1998a), *The Quality School Teacher* (1998b), *Choice Theory* (1998c), and (with Karen Dotson) *Choice Theory in the Classroom* (1998), recommends that teachers develop "quality" classrooms based on democratic principles. According to Glasser, many teachers struggle with classroom management because their actions are guided by stimulus–response theory. They try to coerce students through reward or punishment, or what many teachers term logical consequences. Instead, Glasser believes that teachers should establish "quality" environments in the classroom by following choice theory. Choice theory recognizes that human beings make choices that enable them to create "quality worlds" that satisfy four needs: the need to belong, the need for power, the need for freedom, and the need for fun.

From a choice theory perspective, misbehaviour in the classroom arises when students' learning experiences do not enable them to create quality worlds for themselves. Therefore, teachers "must give up bossing and turn to 'leading'" (Glasser, 1997, p. 600). We follow leaders, Glasser says, because we believe they are concerned about our welfare. To persuade students to do quality schoolwork, teachers must establish warm, noncoercive relationships with students; teach students meaningful skills rather than ask them to memorize information; enable them to experience satisfaction and excitement by working in small teams; and move from teacher evaluation to student self-evaluation.

Creating a democratic classroom community is not easy, but the benefits can be significant. Building a democratic classroom community takes time and commitment to the joint goals of both students and teachers and requires a shift from a teacher-centred approach to a student-centred approach, where students have a strong voice in decision making and problem solving.

Preventive Planning

Establishing Rules, Guidelines, and Procedures Successful classroom managers have carefully planned rules, guidelines, and procedures, which they teach early in the year using clear explanations, examples, and practice (Emmer & Evertson, 2009; Evertson & Emmer, 2009; Good & Brophy, 2008). More democratic teachers find teacher-imposed "rules" too heavy-handed and prefer to establish a set of classroom guidelines, co-developed with their students, that lay the foundation for the community's work together during the course of the year. In the Tribes model discussed earlier, the set of community agreements is adopted by everyone and students self- and peer-monitor. Regardless of your approach to establishing these guidelines, they should be clear, concise, reasonable, and few in number. For example, five general guidelines for elementary-age students might include: (1) be polite and helpful; (2) respect other people's property; (3) listen quietly while others are speaking; (4) do not hit, shove, or hurt others; and (5) obey all school rules (Evertson & Emmer, 2009). Guidelines for the secondary level might stipulate the following: (1) bring all needed materials to class; (2) be in your seat and ready to work when the bell rings; (3) respect and be polite to everyone; (4) respect other people's property; (5) listen and stay seated while someone else is speaking; and (6) obey all school rules (Emmer & Evertson, 2009). It is important to apply classroom guidelines consistently and fairly.

Procedures—the routines your students follow as they participate in learning activities—are also essential for smooth classroom functioning and minimizing opportunities for off-task behaviour. How will homework be collected? How will supplies be distributed? How will housekeeping chores be completed? How will attendance be taken? How do students obtain permission to leave the classroom? Part of developing classroom guidelines and procedures is to decide what to do when students do not follow them. Students must be made aware of the consequences for failing to follow rules, and these consequences should follow naturally and logically from the action the student took.

Organizing and Planning for Instruction Organizing instructional time, materials, and activities so that classes run smoothly enables teachers to keep students engaged in learning, thereby reducing the need for redirecting behaviour. Time spent planning authentic learning activities that are appropriate for students' needs, interests, and abilities provides the opportunity to enjoy the professional satisfaction that comes from having a well-managed classroom.

The following examples illustrate how one grade 8 teacher began the school year by carefully organizing and planning for instruction. The teacher across the hall, however, was not as well organized; as a consequence, she is more likely to experience negative behaviours in her classroom as the year progresses.

> Donnell Alexander is waiting at the door for her eighth-graders as students come in the room. She welcomes them individually and says, "Take your seats quickly, please. You'll find your name on the desk. The bell is going to ring in less than a minute and everyone needs to be at his or her desk and quiet when it does. Please log in to the URL on the whiteboard and read through the class website while you're waiting." She is standing at the front of the room, surveying the class as the bell rings. When it stops, she begins, "Good morning, everyone."

> Vicki Williams, who also teaches eighth-graders across the hall from Donnell, is organizing her handouts as the students come in the room. Some take their seats while others mill around, talking in small groups. As the bell rings, she looks up and says over the hum of the students, "Everyone take your seats, please. We'll begin in a couple minutes," and then turns back to finish organizing her materials. (Adapted from Eggen & Kauchak, 2007, p. 380)

Effective Responses to Student Behaviour

When students act inappropriately, effective teachers draw from a repertoire of problem-solving strategies. These strategies are based on their experience and common sense, their knowledge of students and the teaching–learning process, and their knowledge of human psychology. There are many structured approaches to classroom management; some are based on psychological theories of human motivation and behaviour, while others reflect various philosophical views regarding the purposes of education. The first step is to try to understand the root cause of the behaviour. None of these approaches, however, is appropriate for all situations or for all teachers or for all students, and the usefulness of a given method depends, in part, on the teacher's individual personality, leadership style, and ability to analyze the complex dynamics of classroom life. In addition, what works should not be the only criterion for evaluating structured or "packaged" approaches to discipline; what students are taught about their self-worth, acting responsibly, and solving problems is also important (Curwin & Mendler, 1988, 1989).

Severity of Behaviour   Your response to inappropriate student behaviour will depend, in part, on whether an infraction is mild, moderate, or severe and whether it is occurring for the first time or is part of a pattern of ongoing behaviours. For example, a student who throws a wad of paper at another student might receive a warning for the first infraction, while another student who repeatedly throws objects might stay inside during recess to help tidy up the classroom, beginning with the objects thrown. Note that the resulting action is directly tied to the original behaviour. Definitions of the severity of inappropriate behaviours vary from school to school and from province to province. Most importantly, teachers need to consider why the behaviour is happening. In the example above, the student might be bored or seeking attention. There are positive ways to deal with both of these situations that might help redirect the student's focus on his or her work.

Constructive Assertiveness   The effectiveness of your responses to students' incorrect behaviour depends on your ability to use constructive assertiveness (Emmer & Evertson, 2009; Evertson & Emmer, 2009). Constructive assertiveness "lies on a continuum of social response between aggressive, overbearing pushiness and timid, ineffectual, or submissive responses that allow some students to trample on the teacher's and other students' rights. Assertiveness skills allow you to communicate to students that you are serious about teaching and about maintaining a classroom in which everyone's rights are respected" (Emmer & Evertson, 2009; Evertson & Emmer, 2013). Communication based on constructive assertiveness is not hostile, sarcastic, defensive, or vindictive; it is clear, firm, and concise. Constructive assertiveness includes the following three basic elements:

- A direct, clear statement of the problem
- Body language that is unambiguous (e.g., direct eye contact with students, erect posture, and facial expressions that are congruent with the content and tone of corrective statements)
- Firm, unwavering insistence on correct behaviour

Evertson and Emmer (2013) remind teachers that "there are many reasons, but no excuses, for misbehavior" (p. 167). Teachers who use constructive assertiveness always listen to what the student has to say; however, ultimately, disruptive behaviours cannot be tolerated and must be dealt with effectively and consistently in order to maintain a productive and respectful classroom environment.

Assertive discipline: an approach to classroom discipline requiring that teachers establish firm, clear guidelines for student behaviour and follow through with consequences for misbehaviour.

The notion of **assertive discipline**, which requires the teacher to plan positive and negative consequences for predetermined acceptable or unacceptable behaviours (MacNaughton & Johns, 1991), is based on promoting positive reinforcement for compliance. Research on the effectiveness of assertive discipline is mixed. Giving tangible rewards for positive behaviour can lead to a decrease in students' intrinsic motivation (Kohn, 1999). Alfie Kohn (1999), author of the groundbreaking book *Punished by Rewards: The Trouble with Gold Stars, Incentive Plans, A's, Praise, and Other Bribes*, argues that rewarding students only ends up motivating them to seek more rewards rather than being intrinsically motivated and learning through curiosity.

Teacher Problem Solving   When a teacher's efforts to get a student to stop behaving inappropriately are unsuccessful, a problem-solving conference with the student is warranted. A problem-solving conference may give the teacher additional understanding of the situation, thus paving the way for a solution. A conference can also help the teacher and student understand one another's perceptions and begin to build a more positive relationship.

Choice theory: an approach to classroom management developed by psychiatrist William Glasser, based on a belief that students will usually make good choices (i.e., behave in an acceptable manner) if they experience success in the classroom and know that teachers care about them.

The goal of a problem-solving conference is for the student to accept responsibility for his or her behaviour and make a commitment to change it. While there is no "right way" to conduct a problem-solving conference, Glasser's **"choice theory"** lends itself to a conferencing procedure that is flexible and appropriate for most situations.

Students will usually make good choices (such as behaving in an acceptable manner) if they experience success and know that teachers care about them. The following steps are designed to help misbehaving students see that the choices they make may not lead to the results they want.

1. Have the misbehaving student evaluate and take responsibility for his or her actions. Often, a good first step is for the teacher to ask, "What are you doing?" and then, "Is it helping you?"

2. Have the student make a plan for a more acceptable way of behaving. If necessary, the student and the teacher brainstorm solutions. Agreement is reached on how the student will behave in the future and the consequences for failure to follow through.

3. Require the student to make a commitment to follow the plan.

4. Don't accept excuses for failure to follow the plan.

Teacher: Alexis Juurlink, Grade 8 Healthy Living

Action Research is a framework that guides the energies of teachers toward an understanding of why, when, and how students become better learners. This form of inquiry can provide a rich opportunity for reflection on practice and can contribute to ongoing professional development.

One such project was carried out by teacher Alexis Juurlink in her grade 8 Healthy Living class. It started with baseline data collection that identified a problem with some students' disruptive behaviour, including speaking out and moving around the room at inappropriate times, negatively affecting whole-class discussions. Teacher-directed whole-class discussions are an important part of the Healthy Living class for clarifying instructions for assignments, reviewing curriculum material, and providing students with opportunities to share their thoughts. This prompted Alexis to ask, "What are some instructional strategies for decreasing students' disruptive behaviour during whole-class discussions with middle school students?"

A review of current literature was undertaken to examine strategies and methods that Alexis could implement with her class to facilitate more effective whole-class discussions. The literature emphasized the potential value of explicit teaching of social skills, student self-monitoring, and positive reinforcement of behaviour using a school-wide initiative called Positive Effective Behaviour Supports (PEBS).

Alexis crafted three solution strategies:

- Social skills lessons on attentive listening using role play and discussion
- Increasing positive reinforcement through PEBS "Hi-Notes" and verbal praise
- Student self-monitoring of attentive listening during whole-class discussions

It was determined that during solution-skills implementation, data would be collected using the following:

- Student self-monitoring of appropriate behaviour (focus areas included raising hands to speak, listening quietly, focusing on speaker)
- Teacher observation journal
- Tally of disruptive student behaviour by an educational assistant

Alexis concluded that it was unclear which of the solution strategies had the greatest impact on student behaviour and notes that variables such as a new seating arrangement and schedule changes may have influenced the results. However, the data seemed to indicate a decrease in disruptive behaviour following implementation. She plans to disseminate her action research to other teachers in her middle school, particularly those who had indicated similar problems during whole-class discussions.

Alexis Juurlink is a classroom teacher and part-time program support teacher in a small rural school in the Chignecto Central School Board in Nova Scotia.

5. Don't use punishment or react to a misbehaving student in a punitive manner. Instead, point out to the student that there are logical consequences for failure to follow the plan.

6. Don't give up on the student. If necessary, remind the student of his or her commitment to desirable behaviour. Periodically ask how things are going.

Developing Your Own Approach to Classroom Management   No approach to classroom management is effective with all students at all times. How you respond to negative behaviours in your classroom will depend on your personality, value system, and beliefs about children, and will range along a continuum from the "minimum power" of giving students nonverbal cues to the "maximum power" of controlled intervention. Classroom management expert Charles Wolfgang asserts that teachers usually present one of the following three "faces" (or attitudes) to students who misbehave:

1. The relationship-listening "face" involves the use of minimum power. This reflects a view that the student has the capabilities to change his or her own behaviour, and that if the student is misbehaving, it is because of inner emotional turmoil, flooded behaviour, or feelings of inner inadequacy.

2. The confronting-contracting "face" is one of "I am the adult. I know misbehaviour when I see it and will confront the student to stop this behaviour. I will grant the student the power to decide how he or she will change, and encourage and contract with the student to live up to a mutual agreement for behavioural change."

3. The rules-and-consequences "face" is one that communicates an attitude of "This is the rule and behaviour that I want and I will set out assertively to get this action." (Wolfgang, 2001, pp. 4–5)

In your journey toward becoming a professional teacher, you will develop a repertoire of strategies for classroom management; then, when you encounter a discipline problem in the classroom, you can analyze the situation and respond with an effective strategy. The ability to do so will give you confidence, as illustrated by these comments made to the authors by a beginning teacher:

> I went into the classroom with some confidence and left with lots of confidence. I felt good about what was going on. I established a comfortable rapport with the kids and was more relaxed. Each week I grew more confident. When you first go in you are not sure how you'll do. When you know you are doing OK, your confidence improves.

WHAT TEACHING METHODS DO EFFECTIVE TEACHERS USE?

Beliefs about teaching and learning, students, knowledge, and what is worth knowing influence the instructional methods a teacher uses. Variables such as the teacher's style, learners' characteristics, the culture of the school and surrounding community, and the resources available will also influence the methods you use. A model of teaching provides rules of thumb to follow to create a particular kind of learning environment. As the authors of *Models of Teaching* point out, "[m]odels of teaching are really models of learning. As we help students acquire information, ideas, skills, values, ways of thinking, and means of expressing themselves, we are also teaching them how to learn" (Joyce, Weil, & Calhoun, 2009, p. 7). Table 7.2 presents brief descriptions of four widely used models of teaching.

Effective teachers use a repertoire of teaching models and assessment strategies, depending on their situations and the goals and objectives they wish to attain. Your teaching strategies in the classroom will most likely be eclectic—that is, a combination of several models and assessment techniques. As you gain classroom experience and acquire new skills and understanding, your personal model of teaching will evolve, enabling you to respond appropriately to a wider range of teaching situations.

Methods Based on Learning New Behaviours

Many teachers use instructional methods that have emerged from our greater understanding of how people acquire or change their behaviours. **Direct instruction**, for example, is a systematic instructional method that focuses on the transmission of knowledge and skills from the teacher (and the curriculum) to the student. Direct instruction is organized on the basis of observable learning behaviours and the actual products of learning. Generally, direct instruction is most appropriate for step-by-step knowledge acquisition and basic skill development, but is not appropriate for teaching less structured, higher-order skills such as writing, the analysis of social issues, and problem solving.

Extensive research was conducted in the 1970s and 1980s on the effectiveness of direct instruction (Gagné, 1974, 1977; Good & Grouws, 1979; Rosenshine, 1988; Rosenshine & Stevens, 1986). The following eight steps are a synthesis of research on

Direct instruction: a systematic instructional method focusing on the transmission of knowledge and skills from the teacher to the students.

TABLE 7.2 Four Instructional Models

	Goals and Rationale	Methods
Cooperative Learning	Students can be motivated to learn by working cooperatively in small groups if rewards are made available to the group as a whole and to individual members of the group.	• Small groups (four to six students) work together on learning activities. • Assignments require that students help one another while working on a group project. • In competitive arrangements, groups may compete against one another. • Group members contribute to group goals according to their talents, interests, and abilities.
Theory into Practice	Teachers make decisions in three primary areas: content to be taught, how students will learn, and the behaviours the teacher will use in the classroom. The effectiveness of teaching is related to the quality of decisions the teacher makes in these areas.	The teacher follows seven steps in the classroom: • Orients students to material to be learned • Tells students what they will learn and why it is important • Presents new material that consists of knowledge, skills, or processes students are to learn • Models what students are expected to do • Checks for student understanding • Gives students opportunity for practice under the teacher's guidance • Makes assignments that give students opportunity to practise what they have learned on their own
Behaviour Modification	Teachers can shape student learning by using various forms of enforcement. Human behaviour is learned; behaviours that are positively reinforced (rewarded) tend to increase and those that are not reinforced tend to decrease.	• Teacher begins by presenting stimulus in the form of new material. • The behaviour of students is observed by the teacher. • Appropriate behaviours are reinforced by the teacher as quickly as possible.
Nondirective Teaching	Learning can be facilitated if teachers focus on personal development of students and create opportunities for students to increase their self-understanding and self-concepts. The key to effective teaching is the teacher's ability to understand students and to involve them in a teaching–learning partnership.	• Teacher acts as a facilitator of learning. • Teacher creates learning environments that support personal growth and development. • Teacher acts in the role of a counsellor who helps students to understand themselves, clarify their goals, and accept responsibility for their behaviour.

direct instruction and may be used with students ranging in age from elementary to senior high school:

1. Orient students to the lesson by telling them what they will learn.
2. Review previously learned skills and concepts related to the new material.
3. Present new material, using examples and demonstrations.
4. Assess students' understanding by asking questions; correct misunderstandings.
5. Allow students to practise new skills or apply new information.
6. Provide feedback and corrections as students practise.
7. Include newly learned material in homework.
8. Review material periodically.

A direct instruction method called **mastery learning** is based on two assumptions about learning: (1) virtually all students can learn material if given enough time and taught appropriately; and (2) students learn best when they participate in a structured, systematic program of learning that enables them to progress in small, sequenced steps (Bloom, 1981; Carroll, 1963). Mastery learning includes the following:

1. Set objectives and standards for mastery.
2. Teach content directly to students.

Mastery learning: an approach to instruction based on the assumptions that (1) virtually all students can learn material if given enough time and taught appropriately, and (2) learning is enhanced if students can progress in small, sequenced steps.

3. Provide corrective feedback to students on their learning.

4. Provide additional time and help in correcting errors.

5. Follow a cycle of teaching, testing, reteaching, and retesting.

In mastery learning, students take diagnostic tests and are then guided to complete corrective exercises or activities to improve their learning. These may take the form of programmed instruction, workbooks, computer drill and practice, or educational games. After the corrective lessons, students are given another test and are more likely to achieve mastery.

Methods Based on Child Development

As you learned in Chapter 6, children move through stages of cognitive, psychosocial, and moral development. Effective instruction includes methods that are developmentally appropriate, meet students' diverse learning needs, and recognize the importance of learning that occurs in social contexts. For example, one way that students reach higher levels of development is to observe and then imitate their parents, teachers, and peers, who act as models. "Modeling provides students with specific demonstrations of working with the content. . . . The teacher explicitly demonstrates how the students can be successful in the lesson" (Dell'Olio & Donk, 2007, p. 79).

Modelling: the process of "thinking out loud," which teachers use to make students aware of the reasoning involved in learning new material.

Effective teachers use **modelling** by thinking out loud and following three basic steps: (1) demonstrating to students the thinking involved in a task; (2) making students aware of the thinking involved; and (3) focusing students on applying the thinking. In this way, teachers can help students become aware of their learning processes and enhance their ability to learn. "For example, as a teacher demonstrates cutting out a construction paper square to serve as a math manipulative during the next lesson, she might 'think out loud' in class, saying, 'I am cutting this square very carefully because we will be using it today to create fractional shapes. I need the sides of my square to be very neat. My smaller, fraction pieces should be accurate in size'" (Dell'Olio & Donk, 2007, p. 80).

These students are building on prior knowledge and using inquiry to acquire new knowledge. What kinds of learning activities require students to use their cognitive abilities in this way?

Syracuse Newspapers/Li-Hua Lan/The Image Works

Since the mid-1980s, several educational researchers have examined how learners construct understanding of new material. "Constructivist views of learning, therefore, focus on how learners make sense of new information—how they construct meaning based on what they already know" (Parkay, Anctil, & Hass, 2010, p. 168). Teachers with this view focus on students' thinking about the material being learned and, through carefully orchestrated cues, prompts, and questions, help students arrive at a deeper understanding of the material. The common elements of **constructivist teaching** include the following:

Constructivist teaching: a method of teaching based on students' prior knowledge of the topic and the processes they use to *construct* meaning.

- The teacher elicits students' prior knowledge of the material and uses this as the starting point for instruction.

- The teacher not only presents material to students but also responds to students' efforts to learn the material. While teaching, the teacher must learn about students' learning.

- Students not only absorb information but also actively use that information to construct meaning.

- The teacher creates a social milieu within the classroom, a community of learners that allows students to reflect and talk with one another as they construct meaning and solve problems.

Constructivist teachers provide students with support, or **scaffolding**, as they learn new material. By observing the child and listening carefully to what he or she says, the teacher provides encouragement, suggestions, or other assistance to guide the student's learning efforts. The teacher varies the amount of support given on the basis of the student's understanding—if the student understands little, the teacher gives more support; conversely, the teacher gives progressively less support as the student's understanding becomes more evident. Overall, the teacher provides just enough scaffolding to enable the student to "discover" the material on his or her own.

Scaffolding: an approach to teaching based on the student's current level of understanding and ability; the teacher varies the amount of help given (e.g., clues, encouragement, or suggestions) to students based on their moment-to-moment understanding of the material being learned.

The concept of scaffolding is based on the work of L. S. Vygotsky, a well-known Soviet psychologist. Vygotsky (1978, 1986) coined the term *zone of proximal development* to refer to the point at which students need assistance to continue learning. The effective teacher is sensitive to the student's zone of proximal development and ensures that instruction neither exceeds the student's current level of understanding nor underestimates the student's ability.

Methods Based on the Thinking Process

Some instructional methods are derived from the mental processes involved in learning, thinking, remembering, problem solving, and creativity. **Information processing**, for example, is a branch of cognitive science concerned with how people use their long- and short-term memory to access information and solve problems. The computer is often used as an analogy for information processing views of learning:

Information processing: a branch of cognitive science concerned with how individuals use long- and short-term memory to acquire information and solve problems.

> Like the computer, the human mind takes in information, performs operations on it to change its form and content, stores the information, retrieves it when needed, and generates responses to it. Thus, processing involves gathering and representing information, or encoding; holding information, or storage; and getting at the information when needed, or retrieval. The whole system is guided by control processes that determine how and when information will flow through the system. (Woolfolk, 2007, p. 250)

Although several systematic approaches to instruction are based on information processing—teaching students how to memorize, how to think inductively or deductively, how to acquire concepts, or how to use the scientific method, for example—they all focus on how people acquire and use information (see Table 7.3). Psychologists have identified three types of memory stores used in information processing:

1. Sensory memory—information stored briefly until it can be processed by the information-processing system; sensory memory retains information for about one second for vision and two to four seconds for hearing (Leahey & Harris, 2001; Pashler & Carrier, 1996).

2. Working memory—holds information while a person processes it; working memory is the conscious part of our information-processing system.

3. Long-term memory—a permanent store of information; whereas memory is limited to about seven items of information for a few seconds, long-term memory is vast and may remain for a lifetime (Schunk, 2004).

In **inquiry learning** and **discovery learning**, students are given opportunities to inquire into subjects so that they "discover" knowledge for themselves. When teachers ask students to go beyond information in a text to make inferences, draw conclusions, or form generalizations, and when teachers do not answer students' questions, preferring instead to

Inquiry learning: an approach to teaching that gives students opportunities to explore, or *inquire* into, subjects so that they develop their own answers to problem situations.

Discovery learning: an approach to teaching that gives students opportunities to inquire into subjects so that they "discover" knowledge for themselves.

TABLE 7.3 Applying an Understanding of Memory Stores in Your Classroom

Sensory Memory

1. To keep students from losing a sensory memory trace, give them a chance to attend to one stimulus before presenting a second one.

- **Elementary:** A second-grade teacher asks one question at a time and gets an answer before asking a second question.
- **Middle school:** A pre-algebra teacher displays two problems on the overhead and waits until students have copied them before she starts talking.
- **High school:** In a geography lesson, a teacher places a map on the overhead and says, "I'll give you a minute to examine the geography of the countries on this map in the front of the room. Then we'll go on."

Working Memory

2. To avoid overloading students' working memories, conduct lessons with questioning.

- **Elementary:** A first-grade teacher gives students directions for seatwork by presenting them slowly and one at a time. He asks different students to repeat the directions before he has them begin.
- **Middle school:** A teacher in a woodworking class begins by saying, "The hardness and density of wood from the same kind of tree vary, depending on the amount of rainfall the tree has received and how fast it grows." Then, she waits a moment, holds up two pieces of wood, and says, "Look at these wood pieces. What do you notice about the rings on them?"
- **High school:** An Algebra II teacher walks students through the solution to problems by having a different student describe each succeeding step to the solution.

3. Provide frequent practice to develop automaticity and present information in both verbal and visual forms.

- **Elementary:** A first-grade teacher has his students practice their writing by composing two sentences each day about an event of the previous evening.
- **Middle school:** To capitalize on the dual-processing capability of working memory, an eighth-grade history teacher prepares a flowchart of the events that led up to the Revolutionary War. As she questions the students about the topic, she refers to the flowchart for each important point and encourages students to use the chart to organize their note taking.
- **High school:** As a physics teacher discusses the relationship between force and acceleration, he demonstrates by pulling a cart along the desktop with a constant force so the students can see that the cart accelerates.

Long-Term Memory

4. To develop schemas, encourage students to explore relationships between ideas, and between new ideas and prior understanding.

- **Elementary:** During story time, a second-grade teacher asks students to explain how the events in a story contribute to the conclusion.
- **Middle school:** In developing the rules for solving equations by substitution, an algebra teacher asks, "How does this process compare to what we did when we solved equations by addition? What do we do differently? Why?"
- **High school:** To help his students understand cause-and-effect relationships in their study of ancient Greece, a world history teacher asks questions such as: "Why was shipping so important in ancient Greece?" "Why was Troy's location so important, and how does its location relate to the location of today's big cities?" and "Why did Greek city-states exist (instead of larger nation-states)?"

Source: From Paul D. Eggen & Donald P. Kauchak, *Educational Psychology: Windows on Classrooms*, 7e. Published by Merrill, an imprint of Pearson Education. Copyright 2007 by Pearson Education. Reprinted by permission. All rights reserved.

have students develop their own answers, they are using methods based on inquiry and discovery learning. These methods are best suited for teaching concepts, relationships, and theoretical abstractions, and for having students formulate and test hypotheses.

In today's classrooms, when information can be accessed anytime, anywhere via the Internet, teachers can afford to spend more time on higher-order thinking skills that include making inferences and solving problems. Two common approaches to inquiry-based learning are problem-based learning and project-based learning. Problem-based learning experiences are designed to create authentic situations for students, in which they pose a problem to solve and work through the steps, usually in collaboration with others, to find one or more solutions. Problem-based learning is typically multidisciplinary and encourages students with different strengths to work together. Project-based learning is similar, but in this approach, students create a product—a project or presentation based on their learning experience. Often the projects are shared with a wider audience, such as parents or judges at a science fair, which motivates students to create a polished product. A less common approach to inquiry-based or experiential learning is place-based learning, which is also sometimes called service learning. As with project-based learning, place-based learning is also hands-on and student-centred, but the focus is more squarely on real-world relevance. Students engaged in place-based learning might collect stories of local community members while doing a unit on changing family and community traditions in grade 2.

The following example shows how inquiry and discovery learning in a grade 1 classroom fostered a high level of student involvement and thinking.

> The children are gathered around a table on which a candle and jar have been placed. The teacher, Jackie Wiseman, lights the candle and, after it has burned brightly for a minute or two, covers it carefully with the jar. The candle grows dim, flickers, and goes out. Then she produces another candle and a larger jar, and the exercise is repeated. The candle goes out, but more slowly. Jackie produces two more candles and jars of different sizes, and the children light the candles, place the jars over them, and the flames slowly go out. "Now we're going to develop some ideas about what has just happened," she says. "I want you to ask me questions about those candles and jars and what you just observed." (Joyce, Weil, & Calhoun, 2009, p. 3)

Methods Based on Peer-Mediated Instruction

Student peer groups can be a deterrent to academic performance (Sternberg, Dornbusch, & Brown, 1996), but they can also motivate students to excel. Because school learning occurs in a social setting, **peer-mediated instruction** provides teachers with options for increasing students' learning. Cooperative learning, described earlier in the chapter, is an example of peer-mediated instruction. Another example is **group investigation**, in which the teacher's role is to create an environment that allows students to determine what they will study and how. Students are presented with a situation to which they "react and discover basic conflicts among their attitudes, ideas, and modes of perception. On the basis of this information, they identify the problem to be investigated, analyze the roles required to solve it, organize themselves to take these roles, act, report, and evaluate these results" (Thelen, 1960, p. 82).

The teacher's role in group investigation is multifaceted; he or she is an organizer, guide, resource person, counsellor, and evaluator. The method is very effective in increasing student achievement (Sharan & Sharan, 1989/90, pp. 17–21), positive attitudes toward learning, and the cohesiveness of the classroom group. The model also allows students to inquire into problems that interest them and enables each student to make a meaningful, authentic contribution to the group's effort based on his or her experiences, interests, knowledge, and skills.

Peer-mediated instruction: approaches to teaching, such as cooperative learning and group investigation, that utilize the social relationships among students to promote their learning.

Group investigation: an approach to teaching in which the teacher facilitates learning by creating an environment that allows students to determine what they will study and how.

Other common forms of peer-mediated instruction include peer tutoring and cross-age tutoring. In **peer-tutoring** arrangements, students are tutored by other pupils in the same class or the same grade. **Cross-age tutoring** involves, for example, grade 6 students tutoring grade 2 students in reading. Research clearly shows that, with proper orientation and training, cross-age tutoring can greatly benefit both "teacher" and learner (Henriques, 1997; Schneider & Barone, 1997; Utay & Utay, 1997; Zukowski, 1997). Pilot programs pairing students at risk of dropping out of school with younger children and with special-needs students have proved especially successful.

WHAT ARE SOME CHARACTERISTICS OF EFFECTIVE TEACHING?

The outcomes of effective teaching are relatively easy to enumerate: (1) students acquire an understanding of the subject at hand; (2) they can apply what they have learned to new situations; and (3) they have a desire to continue learning. However, if we wish to identify the characteristics of effective teaching, we find ourselves confronted with a more difficult task.

What do effective teachers do when they teach? How do they communicate with students? How do they manage classroom activities? What models of teaching do they use? As the preceding discussions of classroom cultures, learning environments, classroom management, and teaching methods suggest, answers to questions such as these are not easy to formulate. However, one broad, helpful view of the characteristics that underlie all effective teaching is the "Framework for Teaching," developed as part of the Praxis Series: Professional Assessments for Beginning Teachers. According to the Praxis framework, teachers must be proficient in four domains: planning and preparation, structuring classroom environment, instruction, and professional responsibilities. Teachers must be effective in these domains while taking into account individual, developmental, and cultural differences among students and differences among subjects.

SUMMARY

What Determines the Culture of the Classroom?

■ From seating arrangements to classroom rules and procedures to the content and relevance of the curriculum, teachers make many decisions that influence the culture of the classroom.

■ Classroom climate refers to the atmosphere or quality of life in a classroom. The climates established by high-performing teachers are characterized by a productive, task-oriented focus; group cohesiveness; open, warm relationships between teacher and students; cooperative, respectful interactions among students; low levels of tension, anxiety, and conflict; humour; high expectations; and frequent opportunities for student input regarding classroom activities.

How Can You Create a Positive Learning Environment?

■ An important element of a positive learning environment is a caring classroom climate. Teachers show care for students by providing support, structure, and appropriate expectations.

- The physical environment of a classroom—seating arrangements and the placement of other classroom furniture, for example—can make a positive contribution to students' learning.

- Classroom organization (how students are grouped for instruction and how time is used) is an important element of the effective learning environment. Among the patterns for organizing classrooms are grouping students by ability, grouping students for cooperative learning, using activity formats based on authentic learning tasks, and using time to maximize students' learning.

What Are the Keys to Successful Classroom Management?

- The key to successful classroom management is preventing problems before they occur. Teachers who prevent problems foster effective, harmonious interpersonal interactions, understand how their leadership style influences students, and facilitate the development of a cohesive and supportive classroom group.

- Teachers who establish a democratic classroom climate, which allows students to participate in making decisions about rules and procedures, curriculum materials, and learning activities, have fewer discipline problems.

- When management problems occur, effective teachers use a repertoire of problem-solving skills based on experience, common sense, and understanding of the teaching–learning process.

What Teaching Methods Do Effective Teachers Use?

- Although it is difficult to identify all the skills teachers need, research indicates that effective teachers use a repertoire of models of teaching based on students' learning behaviours, child development, the thinking process, and peer mediation.

- Direct instruction and mastery learning are based on the view that learning is the acquisition of new behaviours.

- Modelling, constructivism, and scaffolding are based primarily on an understanding of how students construct meaning as they learn new material.

- Information processing, inquiry learning, and discovery learning are based on our understanding of the cognitive processes involved in learning.

- Peer-mediated instruction, which views learning as taking place in social situations, includes cooperative learning, group investigation, and peer- and cross-age tutoring.

What Are Some Characteristics of Effective Teaching?

- Effective teaching focuses on outcomes—the results of teaching.

- "Framework for Teaching" is a broad view of the characteristics underlying effective teaching. The four domains are as follows:

  1. Planning and preparation
  2. The classroom environment
  3. Instruction
  4. Professional responsibilities

APPLICATIONS AND ACTIVITIES

1. Recall the teachers and classmates you had during your school career. Select one class, and analyze its group processes in terms of the stages of group development discussed in this chapter. What stage of development was reached by the group near the end of the school year? What conditions facilitated or impeded the development of this group?

2. Describe the "ideal" physical classroom environment. How would the seating arrangement facilitate the attainment of your instructional goals and objectives? How would you involve students in arranging the classroom?

3. Describe your leadership style as it relates to classroom management. In which aspects of leadership and classroom management do you feel most and least confident? What might you do, or what skills might you acquire, to strengthen your effectiveness in areas you feel you lack confidence? Develop your ideas into a statement of professional goals.

4. Observe several teachers at the level for which you are preparing to teach, and try to identify the teaching methods they are using as part of their instructional repertoires. Interview one of the teachers to find out why she or he has chosen these particular methods.

5. Prepare a poster depicting a classroom arrangement appropriate for the subject area and grade level for which you are preparing to teach. The poster should indicate the seating arrangement and location of other classroom furniture. In addition, consider how you will establish rules, guidelines, and procedures in your classroom. These guidelines might be related to the following:

- Academic work
- Classroom conduct
- Information to be communicated on your first teaching day
- Information that will need to be communicated later

6. Prepare a flow chart depicting routine activities for a typical day. This chart could include procedures for the following:

- Handling attendance, tardy slips, and excuses
- Distributing materials
- Turning in homework
- Doing seatwork or various in-class assignments
- Forming small groups for cooperative learning activities
- Returning materials and supplies at the end of class

Chapter 8
Developing and Implementing the Curriculum

Flying Colours Ltd/Photodisc/
Getty Images

FOCUS QUESTIONS

1. What is taught in schools?

2. How is a school curriculum developed?

3. What are some current subject-area trends?

> *An educator is entrusted with the most serious work that confronts humankind: the development of curricula that enable new generations to contribute to the growth of human beings and society.*
>
> —William H. Schubert
> *Curriculum: Perspective, Paradigm, and Possibility*

Think back to your experiences as a student at the elementary, middle, junior, and secondary schools you attended. What did you learn? Certainly, the curriculum you experienced included reading, comprehension, writing, spelling, mathematics, science, geography, and history. In addition to these topics, though, did you learn something about cooperation, competition, stress, physical fitness, video games, computers, popularity, and the opposite sex? Or did you learn to love chemistry and hate English grammar?

Why Is Curriculum Development Important to Teachers?

The benefit of developing programs using integrated curriculum is that students will understand more deeply that their skills are transferable. For example, my dream is to be a science and math teacher. This does not mean that students will be free to use run-on sentences in my classroom.

—NADIA, teacher education program, first year

Curriculum goes beyond what we are required to teach by the ministry. When I think about the curriculum, my mind tries to connect different subjects and ideas so that they are woven into a puzzle that stimulates student learning. I want my students to be engaged, to be taking away something valuable from their learning experiences. Curriculum is more than reading, writing, and math. It's exploring, creating, learning.

—LAURA, teacher education program, first year

In today's society, students are bombarded with a multitude of information. It is important that teachers help students develop the necessary knowledge and skills so they can navigate from the "fluff" to the facts. Class time needs to be meaningful and interactive, where students take an active role in their learning. Students should not be silent observers or consumers of information, but rather active producers of knowledge.

—ROSE, teacher education program, first year

WHAT IS TAUGHT IN SCHOOLS?

The countless things you learned in school make up the curriculum that you experienced. Curriculum theorists and researchers have suggested several definitions for **curriculum**, with no one universal meaning. Here are some definitions in current use.

Curriculum: the school experiences, both planned and unplanned, that enhance (and sometimes impede) the education and growth of students.

1. A course of study, derived from the Latin *currere*, meaning "to run a course"

2. Course content, the information or knowledge students are expected to learn

3. Planned learning experiences

4. Intended learning outcomes, the results of instruction as distinguished from the means (activities, materials, etc.) of instruction

5. All the experiences students have while at school

None of the meanings in the list is in any sense the "right" definition. The way we define curriculum depends on our purposes and our situation. If, for example, we were advising a high school student on the courses he or she needed to take in order to prepare for college or university, our operational definition of curriculum would most likely be "a course of study." However, if we were interviewing grade 6 students for their views on the K–6 elementary school they attended, we would probably want to view curriculum as "all the experiences students have while at school." Let us posit an additional definition of curriculum as referring to the experiences, both planned and unplanned, that enhance (and sometimes impede) the education and growth of students.

Kinds of Curricula

Elliot Eisner, a noted educational researcher, said that "schools teach much more—and much less—than they intend to teach. Although much of what is taught is explicit and public, a great deal is not" (2002, p. 87). For this reason, we need to look at the four curricula that all students experience. The more we understand these curricula and how they influence students, the better we will be able to develop effective educational programs.

Explicit Curriculum

Explicit Curriculum The explicit, or overt, curriculum refers to what a school intends to teach students. This curriculum is made up of several components: (1) the goals, aims, and learning objectives the school has for all students; (2) the actual courses that make up each student's course of study; and (3) the specific knowledge, skills, and attitudes that teachers want students to acquire. If we ask a principal to describe the education program at his or her school, our inquiry would be in reference to the explicit curriculum. Similarly, if we ask a teacher to describe what he or she wishes to accomplish with a particular class, we would be given a description of the explicit curriculum.

In short, the **explicit curriculum** represents the publicly announced expectations the school has for its students. These expectations range from learning how to read, write, and compute to learning to appreciate music, art, and cultures other than one's own. In most instances, the explicit curriculum takes the form of written plans or guides for the education of students. Examples of such written documents are course descriptions; curriculum guides that set forth the goals and learning objectives for a school, school district, or province; texts and other commercially prepared learning materials; and teachers' lesson plans. Through the instructional program of a school, then, these curricular materials are brought to life.

> **Explicit curriculum:** the behaviour, attitudes, and knowledge that a school intends to teach students.

Hidden Curriculum

Hidden Curriculum The hidden, or implicit, curriculum refers to the behaviours, attitudes, and knowledge the culture of the school unintentionally teaches students (Parkay, Anctil, & Hass, 2010). What students learn via the **hidden curriculum** can be positive or negative, depending on their day-to-day experiences at school. For example, from teachers who are knowledgeable, well organized, and personable, students are likely to develop positive habits and abilities—cooperating with others, taking responsibility, planning ahead, and forgoing immediate gratification to attain long-range goals. On the other hand, from teachers who are ill prepared, apathetic, or aloof, students are likely to acquire habits and attitudes that are negative and that discourage personal growth and development—a dislike for learning, the ability to deceive or defy adult authority figures, or a tendency to procrastinate.

> **Hidden curriculum:** the behaviours, attitudes, and knowledge the school culture unintentionally teach students.

In the following examples, four students describe the hidden curricula they experienced in school. In examples 1 and 2 (excerpts from letters students wrote to their teachers), the hidden curricula "taught" students to be more confident in their ability to learn. In examples 3 and 4, the hidden curricula undermined the students' confidence and desire to learn.

> Example 1: I was in your Grade 10 English class. I sure felt safe to take a risk in your class. I actually tried hard, knowing I might fail, but felt safe enough to do so. (Paul, Christensen, & Falk, 2000, p. 23)

> Example 2: I was in your Grade 9 class and you praised me for my creative writing. Until that time, I had never thought of myself as a very creative person but your faith in me spurred me on to choose English as my major at the university. (Paul et al., 2000, p. 23)

> Example 3: The teacher just put [material] on the board and if you don't know how, the teacher get angry. I try to get help but when I come after school, they gotta go somewhere and can't help you . . . like when I ask somebody to help me, just because some other kid won't need help, then they think others won't either; some kids are smarter. (Wilson & Corbett, 2001, p. 38)

> Example 4: I was in your 11th grade biology class. I loved science and biology until I took your class. You gave me a great disdain for the subject. Your teaching methods bored the class to tears. We read each chapter out loud at the beginning of the week and spent the rest of the week working quietly on the questions at the end of the

chapter along with the endless dittos you passed out. We never discussed anything and you never taught us anything. We were graded on how well we could come up with the answers you thought were right and heaven forbid if we did not head our paper using the "correct" format. I think the only thing I learned in your class was conformity. (Colucci, 2000, p. 38)

As a result of hidden curricula, students learn more than their teachers imagine. In your role as a teacher, you will not be aware of all that students are learning through the hidden curriculum of your classroom. However, you can increase the likelihood that what it teaches will be positive. By allowing students to help determine the content of the explicit curriculum, by inviting them to help establish classroom rules, and by providing them with challenges appropriate for their stage of development, teachers can ensure that the outcomes of the hidden curriculum are more positive than negative.

Null Curriculum   Discussing a curriculum that cannot be observed directly is like talking about dark matter or black holes—unseen phenomena in the universe whose existence must be inferred because their incredible denseness and gravitational fields do not allow light to escape. In much the same way, we can consider the curricula we do not find in schools; it may be as important as what we do find. Eisner labelled the intellectual processes and content that schools do not teach "the **null curriculum**—the options students are not afforded, the perspectives they may never know about, much less be able to use, the concepts and skills that are not a part of their intellectual repertoire" (2002, pp. 106–107).

For example, the kind of thinking that schools foster among students is largely based on manipulations of words and numbers. Thinking that is imaginative, subjective, and poetic in nature is stressed only incidentally. Students are seldom taught anthropology, sociology, psychology, law, economics, filmmaking, or architecture.

Eisner contends that "certain subject matters have been traditionally taught in schools not because of a careful analysis of the range of other alternatives that could be offered but rather because they have traditionally been taught. We teach what we teach largely out of habit, and in the process neglect areas of study that could prove to be exceedingly useful to students" (2002, p. 103).

Extracurricular/Co-Curricular Programs   The curriculum includes school-sponsored activities—music, drama, special interest clubs, sports, and student council, to name a few—that students may pursue in addition to their studies in academic areas. When such activities are perceived as additions to the academic curriculum, they are termed extracurricular. When these activities are seen as having important educational goals—and not merely as extras added to the academic curriculum—they are termed co-curricular. To reflect the fact that these two labels are commonly used for the same activities, we use the term extracurricular/co-curricular activities.

Though **extracurricular/co-curricular programs** are most extensive at the secondary level, many elementary, middle, and junior high schools also provide students with a broad assortment of extracurricular/co-curricular activities. For those who choose to participate, such activities provide an opportunity to use social and academic skills in many different contexts.

Research shows that the larger a school is, the less likely it is that a student will take part in extracurricular/co-curricular activities. At the same time, those who do participate tend to have a higher self-concept than those who do not (Coladarci & Cobb, 1996). The actual effects of extracurricular/co-curricular activities on students' development, however, are not entirely clear. Although it is known that students who participate in extracurricular/co-curricular activities tend to receive higher grades than

Null curriculum: the intellectual processes and subject content that schools do not teach.

Extracurricular/co-curricular programs: school-sponsored activities students may pursue outside of, or in addition to, academic study.

nonparticipants and are more frequently identified as gifted (Gerber, 1996; Jordan & Nettles, 1999; Modi, Konstantopoulos, & Hedges, 1998), it is not known whether participation influences achievement or achievement influences participation. However, research has shown that participation has a positive influence on the decision to remain in school (Mahoney & Cairns, 1997), educational aspirations (Modi et al., 1998), and the occupation one aspires to and eventually attains (Brown, Kohrs, & Lanzarro, 1991; Holland & Andre, 1987). Furthermore, students tend to identify extracurricular/co-curricular activities as a positive influence on their school careers.

It is also clear that students who might benefit the most from participating in extra-curricular/co-curricular activities—those below the norm in academic achievement and students at risk—tend not to participate. In addition, students from low socioeconomic backgrounds participate less often (Aud, Fox, & KewalRamani, 2010).

Curriculum Content

There is considerable disagreement as to the purpose of schools and where the emphasis of curriculum should be placed. Many Canadians believe that the "basics" of reading, writing, and mathematics plus the development of good work habits should be at the heart of the curriculum. However, there are some who feel that school curricula should also emphasize social and life skills. Many schools have introduced curricula aimed at combating such social problems as violence and racism, including antibullying programs.

When considering what students need to know and be able to do, curriculum developers should evaluate the role of the public school and determine a balance between core curriculum academics and social issues.

HOW IS A SCHOOL CURRICULUM DEVELOPED?

Although there is no easy-to-follow set of procedures for developing curricula, Ralph Tyler provided four fundamental questions that must be answered in developing any plan of instruction. These four questions, known as the **Tyler rationale**, are as follows (Tyler, 1949, p. 1):

1. What educational purposes should the school seek to attain?
2. What educational experiences can be provided that are likely to attain these purposes?
3. How can these educational experiences be effectively organized?
4. How can we determine whether these purposes are being attained?

Tyler rationale: a four-step model for curriculum development in which teachers identify purposes, select learning experiences, organize experiences, and evaluate.

Some educators believe that the Tyler rationale underestimates the complexities of curriculum development because it advocates a straightforward, step-by-step process that is difficult to follow in the "real" classroom. Nevertheless, Tyler's classic work has been used by a great number of school systems to bring some degree of order and focus to the curriculum development process.

The Focus of Curriculum Planning

In discussing curriculum development, it is helpful to clarify the focus of curriculum planning. The target of curriculum planning may be at the macro or the micro level. At the macro level, decisions about the content of the curriculum apply to large groups of students. The national goals for education and provincial-level curriculum guidelines are examples of macro-level curricular decisions. At the micro level, curriculum decisions are made that apply to groups of students in a particular school or classroom. To some extent, all teachers are micro-level curriculum developers—that is, they make numerous decisions about the curricular experiences they provide in their classrooms.

Another dimension of curriculum planning is time orientation—does the planning focus on the present or the future? In addition to national goals and provincial-level curriculum guidelines, semester-long or monthly plans or unit plans are examples of future-oriented curriculum planning. Present-oriented curriculum planning usually occurs at the classroom level and is influenced by the unique needs of specific groups of students. Daily or weekly curriculum decisions and lesson plans are examples of present-oriented curriculum planning.

Student-Centred versus Subject-Centred Curricula

A key concern in curriculum development is whether greater emphasis should be given to the requirements of the subject area or to the needs of students. It is helpful to imagine where a school curriculum might be placed on the following continuum:

Student-Centred ⟵⟶ **Subject-Centred**
Curriculum **Curriculum**

Although no course is entirely subject- or student-centred, curricula vary considerably in the degree to which they emphasize one or the other. A **subject-centred curriculum** places primary emphasis on the logical order of the discipline students are to study. The teacher of such a curriculum is a subject-matter expert and is primarily concerned with helping students understand the facts, laws, and principles of the discipline. Subject-centred curricula are more typical of high school education.

Some teachers develop curricula that reflect greater concern for students and their needs. Though teachers of a **student-centred curriculum** also teach content, they emphasize the growth and development of students. This emphasis is generally more typical of elementary school curricula.

The Integrated Curriculum

Used most frequently with elementary-age students, an **integrated curriculum** draws from several different subject areas and focuses on a theme or concept rather than on a single subject. Early childhood education expert Suzanne Krogh (2000, p. 340) suggests that an integrated approach based on thematic "webs" is a more "natural" way for children to learn:

> [Children] do not naturally learn through isolating specific subjects. These have been determined by adult definition. Children's natural learning is more likely to take place across a theme of interest: building a fort, exploring a sandbox, interacting with the first snow of winter. Teachers can create a good deal of their curriculum by building webs made up of these themes of interest. Done with knowledge and care, a web can be created that incorporates most, or even all, of the required and desired curriculum.

Who Plans the Curriculum?

Various agencies and people outside the school are involved in curriculum planning. Textbook publishers, for example, influence what is taught because many teachers use textbooks as curriculum guides. The Council of Ministers of Education, Canada (CMEC) and the Canadian School Boards Association contribute to curriculum planning by setting national education goals, and individual provincial departments of education develop both broad aims for school curricula and specific minimum competencies for students.

Subject-centred curriculum: a curriculum that places primary emphasis on the logical order of the discipline students are to study. Teachers of such a curriculum are content-area experts and concerned primarily with helping students understand facts, laws, and principles of the discipline.

Student-centred curriculum: curricula that are organized around students' needs and interests.

Integrated curriculum: a school curriculum that draws from two or more subject areas and focuses on a theme or concept rather than on a single subject.

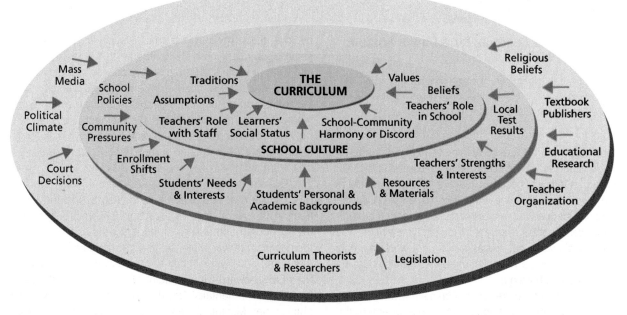

Figure 8.1 Influences on the school curriculum

Within a given school, the curriculum-planning team and classroom teachers plan the curriculum that students actually experience. As a teacher, you will draw from a reservoir of curriculum plans prepared by others, thus playing a vital role in the curriculum-planning process. Whenever you make decisions about what material to include in your teaching, how to sequence content, and how much time to spend teaching certain material, you are planning the curriculum.

What Influences Curricular Decisions?

From the earliest colonial schools to schools of the twenty-first century, curricula have been broadly influenced by a variety of religious, political, and utilitarian agendas. Figure 8.1 illustrates the influence of community pressures, court decisions, students' life situations, testing results, teachers' professional organizations, research results, and other factors. The inner circles of the figure represent factors that have a more direct influence on curriculum development (such as students' needs and school district policies). The outer circle represents factors that are more removed from the school setting or have less obvious effects on the curriculum. Individual schools respond to these influences differently, which further affects their curricula. Let us examine some of these influences in greater detail.

Social Issues and Changing Values Values that affect curriculum planning include prevailing educational theories and teachers' educational philosophies. In addition, curriculum planners respond to social issues and changing values in the wider society. As a result, current social concerns find their way into textbooks, teaching aids, and lesson plans. Curriculum changes are often made in the hope that changing what students learn will help solve social problems or achieve local, province-wide, or national goals.

As Canada's population has grown more culturally diverse, changes in curricula have been made to reflect divergent interests and values. This divergence has led to controversies over curriculum content and to conflicting calls for reform. Additional controversies have arisen over calls for the elimination of all activities or symbols that

A Look into the Learning for a Cause Student Press Initiative

What you choose to do in your classroom can remain in your classroom and end up in the recycle bin or it can become part of the real struggle to improve our lives and the lives of others.

—Michael Ernest Sweet

When I began teaching, the only thing I had in my classroom were walls: the very thing I could have done without. In 2002 I left studies in law to become a teacher because I wanted to make a genuine difference in the lives of people. However, when I first stepped into a classroom as a teacher, I realized that this would not be as easy as I thought. I knew right away that if all I did was what was asked of me, I would not only fall short of making a real difference, I would also become disillusioned and burn out.

The very first time I returned a creative writing assignment to my students I sat and watched in amazement the scene that unfolded. They were anxious to get their papers but not to see my comments or to continue to perfect their work. No, they were anxious to get their numerical grades, to compare them to their peers and then toss the papers into the recycle bin and get the whole thing out of their lives. With all the papers neatly resting in the bin the students returned to their desks and patiently awaited my next assignment. They were not bad students; in fact, they were great kids. This, for them, was the business of school.

I knew there had to be more. I knew this could not be my life as a teacher. It was then that I became obsessed with the question "What could school be?" I knew what it was—a pantheon of busywork—but what could it become? I set out on a journey; it would take five years and a lot of dedication but, in the end, I would come to realize that teaching really is the best career on earth.

As a published writer, I knew there was something fundamentally wrong with children throwing away their creative work. I knew there was something wrong with students only writing one draft, not sharing their ideas and not having an audience. I also knew, as a writer, that what we all want is for someone to read our work and tell us what is good about it. This process can open the floodgates of our imagination and allow us to move forward and excel as writers. It is this authentic appreciation that was missing for my students.

Using print-on-demand technology and companies like our official partner Lulu.com (which were just emerging) and creating assignments relevant to the curriculum, real classroom anthologies of writing concerned with social issues would be produced. I would clear the path for students to receive authentic appreciation for their imaginative creations by getting their work out into the world. Furthermore, I would begin to teach my students that using their passion and imagination might possibly contribute to the resolution of many of our world's most pressing problems. I would show my students that they could learn and make a difference in the world outside our classroom. It would be a defining moment in my teaching career: the moment I decided to make my lessons concern actual world issues—to make my teaching take on a greater purpose and to tear down my classroom walls.

The result was the founding of Learning for a Cause (LFC) in 2004 at Lester B. Pearson High School in Montreal; in the years since its inception, LFC has published five full-length anthologies of student writing. The books' themes include war, violence, racism, prejudice, environment, and poverty, and they have received endorsements from Emmy-award-winning actor Martin Sheen and celebrated environmentalist David Suzuki to world-renowned philosopher Maxine Greene and legendary artists Alex Colville and Robert Bateman. LFC books and students have been featured on CTV and CBC as well as NPR and Vermont Public Radio time and again. They have received reviews in the *Globe and Mail*, the *Montreal Gazette,* and *Canadian Teacher Magazine*. Learning for a Cause won a Quebec Entrepreneurial Award in 2006 and again in 2009. *Down to Earth*, a collection of poetry in response to global warming, recently placed in two categories at the World Indie Book Awards. This is just some of the recognition our student press has been afforded.

I don't share these accolades to impress, but rather to demonstrate that what goes on in a classroom really can connect to, and impact positively on, the world outside—humanity at large. What you choose to do in your classroom can remain in your classroom and end up in the recycle bin or it can become part of the real struggle to improve our lives and the lives of others. What goes on in your classroom can be trapped there as busywork or it can be showcased to the world as a part of a dialogue on creating a better tomorrow. Using student imagination to envision how things "could be" rather than always asking children to regurgitate what "merely is" can make all the difference in your teaching practice. It did for me.

While engaged in writing for authentic audiences, my students still learn the prescribed curriculum—and a lot more. They write in various forms, communicate their learning, edit and proofread and collaborate; they even reach across disciplines and forge connections among issues, peoples, and countries. But what is truly different is that they do it with purpose; they work on real issues in the real world. My students are writing their own story and helping to change minds, awaken ideas, and create a better tomorrow—one book at a time; they are Learning for a Cause.

Michael Ernest Sweet is the founder of the Learning for a Cause student press initiative in Montreal. In 2008, he was appointed to the Canadian Commission for UNESCO in recognition of his contributions to public education. A 2009 recipient of the Prime Minister's Award for Teaching Excellence and an inductee of the National Teachers Hall of Fame, Michael divides his time between Montreal and New York City.

1. How will you shift your students' focus from numerical grades to engaged learning?
2. How might you use digital technologies to engage your students to work on "real issues in the real world"?
3. Consider a real issue in the world today that impacts your students. How might you take a multidisciplinary or integrated approach based on this topic in your curriculum planning?

have their origins in organized religion, including even secularized or commercialized ones such as Halloween and the Easter bunny. Curriculum changes to promote greater social integration or equity among racial or ethnic groups may draw complaints of irrelevancy or reverse discrimination. Traditionalists may object to curriculum changes that reflect feminist views.

As you can imagine, consensus on many curriculum reform issues is never achieved. However, because of their public accountability, schools must consider how to respond to such issues. In the end, the creative and evaluative tasks of choosing and developing curriculum materials are a source of both empowerment and frustration for teachers. Budget constraints, social and legal issues, and provincial and local curriculum mandates often determine curriculum choices.

The Canadian Teachers' Federation believes that education must be provided on an equitable basis to all students through elementary and secondary school programs that do the following:

■ Develop the intellectual, aesthetic, physical, emotional, and ethical capacities of each student.

■ Prepare students to become responsible and productive members of society.

■ Provide opportunities for students to learn about Canadian history, literature, culture, government, and heritage.

■ Enable students to learn about the global community, and about Canada's place within it.

The Canadian School Boards Association issued a statement of national educational goals in 1992. The statement stressed the importance of equal access to quality programs for all school-age children and suggested that school choice should take the form of a range of public school programs designed to address diverse learning needs and interests.

Textbook Publishing   Like curriculum planners, textbook authors and publishers are influenced by trends in education and by social issues. In response to criticism, for example, publishers now tend to avoid bias in terms of gender, religion, class, race, and culture. However, because the goal of business is profit, publishers are most responsive to market trends and customer preferences. They are often reluctant to risk losing sales by including subjects that are controversial or that may be offensive to their bigger customers. They may also modify textbooks to appeal to decision makers in populous provinces, such as Ontario and British Columbia, where province-wide adoptions are possible.

Educators have criticized textbooks for inoffensiveness to the point of blandness, for artificially lowering reading levels (called "dumbing down"), and for using pedagogically questionable gimmicks to hold students' attention. "The quality problem [with textbooks also] encompasses [f]actors such as poor writing, poor content 'coverage,' and failure to engage students in the skills needed to create the knowledge contained in a particular area of study" (Sowell, 1996, p. 158). Although the publishing industry continually responds to such criticisms, you would be wise to follow systematic guidelines in evaluating and selecting textbooks and other curriculum materials.

The Core Curriculum

Core curriculum: a set of fundamental courses or learning experiences that are part of the curriculum for all students at a school.

The school reform movement of the 1980s led to provinces reviewing their curricula, and the result was that many departments of education increased the number of required courses for graduation, or the **core curriculum**. For example, in Saskatchewan, credit requirements were increased in 1987 to 24 from 21. The current Saskatchewan core curriculum principles (revised in 2011 and listed in the following excerpt) include the teaching of basic skills and an expanded range of new knowledge and abilities.

> The two major components of core curriculum are the Required Areas of Study and the Common Essential Learnings. Seven Required Areas of Study form the framework for the curriculum. Six categories of Common Essential Learnings are to be incorporated in an appropriate manner into all courses of study offered in Saskatchewan schools. . . .
>
> To meet community and student needs at the local level, provision is made within the core curriculum to offer Locally Determined Options. In recognition of the diverse needs of students, provision is made through the Adaptive Dimension for teachers to adapt instruction.
>
> Required Areas of Study within the Core Curriculum
>
> ■ Language arts
> ■ Mathematics
> ■ Science
> ■ Social studies
> ■ Health education
> ■ Arts education
> ■ Physical education
>
> Each required area has unique knowledge, skills, and values that are essential for all students at the elementary, middle, and secondary levels. The Required Areas of Study, therefore, are included throughout the school program from the elementary to secondary levels. The Common Essential Learnings within the Core Curriculum are as follows:
>
> ■ Communication
> ■ Numeracy
> ■ Critical and Creative Thinking
> ■ Technological Literacy
> ■ Personal and Social Development
> ■ Independent Learning
>
> (Saskatchewan Education, 2011)

Performance-based education: an educational reform that focuses on developing students' ability to demonstrate mastery of certain desired performances or outcomes.

Outcome-based education: an educational reform that focuses on developing students' ability to demonstrate mastery of certain desired outcomes or performances.

Performance-Based Education

A recent approach to reforming curricula to ensure that all students learn and perform at high levels is known as **performance-based** or **outcome-based education**.

The performance-based approach focuses on assessing students' mastery of a set of rigorous learning goals, expectations, or outcomes. Opponents to performance-based education have expressed concern about the content of the outcomes, who determines them, and how they will be assessed.

The Canadian Curriculum Scene: Web Resources

Most Canadian provinces and territories have similar approaches to their programs of studies. The following regional, provincial, and territorial curriculum websites provide information about core curricula for individual provinces and territories.

Council of Atlantic Ministers of Education and Training
http://camet-camef.ca

Western and Northern Canadian Protocol (WNCP) for Collaboration in Education, K–12
www.edu.gov.mb.ca/k12/cur/process.html

Alberta Ministry of Education
www.education.gov.ab.ca/teachers

British Columbia Department of Education
www.bced.gov.bc.ca/irp/welcome.php

Manitoba Curriculum Development Process
www.edu.gov.mb.ca/k12/cur/process.html

New Brunswick Department of Education
www.gnb.ca/0000/anglophone-e.asp#cd

Newfoundland and Labrador Department of Education
www.ed.gov.nl.ca/edu/k12/curriculum/guides/index.html

Northwest Territories Teachers' Association
www.ece.gov.nt.ca/fr/early-childhood-and-school-services/school-services/curriculum-k-12

Nova Scotia Department of Education
https://sapps.ednet.ns.ca/Cart/index.php?UID=2015090211563564.229.119.98

Ontario Ministry of Education
www.edu.gov.on.ca/eng/curriculum

Prince Edward Island Department of Education and Early Childhood Development
www.gov.pe.ca/eecd/index.php3?number=1025899&lang=E

Québec *Ministere de l'Education* Curriculum Publications
www.learnquebec.ca/en/content/curriculum

Saskatchewan Department of Education Curriculum and Instruction Branch
www.curriculum.gov.sk.ca

Yukon Educational Student Network
www.education.gov.yk.ca/curriculum.html

Future Direction of Canadian Education: A National Influence

In September 1993, the Council of Ministers of Education, Canada (CMEC) endorsed the Victoria Declaration, which outlined a plan for future directions in

Canadian education. The declaration put forth the following beliefs held in common by all education ministers.

> We believe that education is a lifelong learning process. We also believe that the future of our society depends on informed and educated citizens who, while fulfilling their own goals of personal and professional development, contribute to the social, economic, and cultural development of their community and country as a whole. Beyond our borders, Canadian education should reflect the priorities of Canadians while contributing to strengthening Canada's place internationally.

> In April 2008, the Council of Ministers of Education, Canada introduced the Learn Canada 2020 framework. The framework acknowledges that education is a provincial and territorial responsibility, while recognizing that interjurisdictional cooperation can contribute to improving the quality of education in the country. Learn Canada 2020 "recognizes the direct link between a well-educated population and (1) a vibrant knowledge-based economy in the 21st Century, (2) socially progressive, sustainable society, and (3) enhanced personal growth opportunities for all Canadians." (CMEC, 2008)

> The Pan-Canadian Assessment Program (PCAP) builds on CMEC's commitment to determine how well their education systems are meeting the needs of Canadian students and society. PCAP administers cyclical tests of student achievement in science, reading and mathematics and provides this information to ministers of education across Canada, who use this information as a basis for examining the curriculum and other aspects of their school systems.

WHAT ARE SOME CURRENT SUBJECT-AREA TRENDS?

The final section of this chapter examines briefly some of the current trends and issues regarding curricula in elementary, middle, junior high, and high schools. When developing outcomes, provincial departments of education make use of recommended curriculum guidelines from professional associations.

Literacies

The importance of being able to read, write, and communicate orally and through other media cannot be underestimated; these are the tools through which students learn in nearly all other areas of a curriculum. Our definition of literacy in a digital age has shifted from a view of literacy as an entity that we either have or do not have to an understanding that literacy practices are informed by social/cultural contexts. There are multiple pathways to making meaning (Harste, 2003; Street, 1995). We read the world through images, symbols, colours, signs, body language, and in the gaps and margins as well as through printed text. But traditionally, the print text has been privileged in English language arts classrooms. In our digital world, the notion of "text" has broadened to include texts of all kinds, including images, sounds, and even the body.

In 2008, the Language and Literacy Researchers of Canada (LLRC) issued a position statement defining literacy:

> LLRC defines "literacy" broadly, understanding that what it means to be literate is situational, and that individuals generally acquire numerous literacies as they navigate different linguistic spheres. In keeping with this notion, our members promote understanding of literacy acquisition in a range of developmental, socio-cultural, and media contexts.

LLRC promotes language and literacy curricula that engage students in diverse and multiple opportunities to read, write, speak, listen, view, and represent. While the functional aspects of language and literacy are very important, educators also need to ensure that students can develop positive attitudes and values toward language, literacy, and learning. Comprehension, meaning making, and critical inquiry are all essential components of a comprehensive language and literacy program (LLRC, 2008).

A review of the language arts curriculum across the provinces and territories suggests that a critical literacy approach is an effective way to engage learners in critical analyses of texts. The 2007 Ontario Ministry of Education (OME) English curriculum documents define critical literacy as follows:

> The capacity for a particular type of critical thinking that involves looking beyond the literal meaning of texts to observe what is present and what is missing, in order to analyse and evaluate the text's complete meaning and the author's intent. Critical literacy goes beyond conventional critical thinking in focusing on issues related to fairness, equity, and social justice. Critically literate students adopt a critical stance, asking what view of the world the text advances and whether they find this view acceptable. (OME, 2007, p. 110)

Critical literacy involves an analysis and critique of the power relationships among texts, language, social groups, and social practices. It shows us ways of looking at texts of all kinds (print, visual, spoken, multimedia, and performance texts) to examine and challenge the attitudes, values, and beliefs that lie beneath the surface. It empowers teachers and students to participate in a democratic society (a just society regardless of race, culture, class, gender, or sexual orientation) and move literacy beyond text to social action. Literature has the potential to socially transform the reader. Educator Paulo Freire views critical literacy as a vehicle for students and their teachers to learn to "read the world." Freire and Macedo (1987) point out that "Reading the world always precedes reading the word, and reading the word implies continually reading the world" (p. 25).

The "reading wars" of past decades have settled down, and although literacy teachers are sometimes not united as to how reading should be taught, most agree that a blend of phonics instruction and a whole-language approach enhances reading comprehension. Advocates of the **whole-language approach** believe that reading is part of general language development, not an isolated skill that students learn apart from listening, speaking, and writing. Teachers in whole-language classrooms seldom use textbooks; instead, young students write stories and learn to read from their writing, and older students read literature that is closely related to their everyday experiences. A **phonics** emphasis focuses on the sound–symbol relationship in alphabetic writing systems. An eclectic approach to teaching reading is also advocated by the International Reading Association, which states "there is no single method or single combination of methods that can successfully teach all children to read. Therefore, teachers must be familiar with a wide range of methods for teaching reading and a strong knowledge of the children in their care so they can create the appropriate balance of methods needed for each child" (International Reading Association, 1999). As part of a trend to de-escalate the reading wars, then, many schools that emphasized a whole-language approach during the 1990s began to shift to a balanced approach at the start of the new decade.

Theoretically, a balanced literacy approach recognizes that students need to use a variety of strategies to become proficient readers and writers and that literacy activities need to be grounded in contexts that are meaningful and relevant to the students. A balanced literacy program includes the following:

- Modelled Reading (Reading Aloud) and Modelled Writing
- Shared (and interactive) Reading and Shared (and interactive) Writing
- Guided Reading and Guided Writing
- Independent Reading and Independent Writing

Whole-language approach: the practice of teaching language skills (listening, reading, and writing) as part of students' everyday experiences rather than as isolated experiences.

Phonics: a method for teaching reading and writing by correlating sounds with letters or groups of letters.

For more information about balanced literacy, see http://faculty.uoit.ca/hughes/Contexts/BalancedLiteracy.html.

During the past two decades, several new approaches have been incorporated into language arts curricula. Many English language arts teachers have reduced the amount of time spent on grammar, electing instead to teach it as needed within the context of a writing program. English teachers also have generally broadened their view of literature to include more contemporary literature that is relevant to the interests of literacy learners and reflects the cultural and linguistic diversity of Canadian society. Texts are now more broadly defined and reflect a wide variety of genres, modes, and media, new media, new technologies, and nonprint media. In addition, many teachers increasingly using digital tools to explore new ways to teach reading, writing, and media skills.

Although there are no published national standards in Canada, many English language arts teachers belong to provincial or regional affiliates associated with the National Council of Teachers of English (NCTE) and the International Reading Association (IRA) and follow many of the standards established by these organizations. There appears to be consistency in English language arts curriculum documents throughout the country. To keep abreast of trends in literacy education, teachers can access *Language & Literacy*, which is an online journal for educators interested in a broad range of literacy issues encompassing research and teaching in print, oral language, and multimedia, at http://ejournals.library.ualberta.ca/index.php/langandlit.

Mathematics

Although there is no pan-Canadian framework in mathematics curricula, most provinces follow a similar approach to this content area. The current teaching approaches in mathematics embrace a constructivist, learner-centred focus. New math curricula across Canada emphasize problem solving and inquiry. For example, the Common Curriculum Framework for K–12 Mathematics (Western Canadian Protocol for Collaboration in Basic Education, 2000) incorporates the following seven interrelated mathematical processes:

- Communication
- Connections
- Mental mathematics and estimation
- Problem solving
- Reasoning
- Technology
- Visualization

The curriculum development process in Canada has tended to draw on such sources as the National Council of Teachers of Mathematics (NCTM) Curriculum and Evaluation Standards for Mathematics. This American organization has widespread membership in Canada. Since it began working on the Standards 2000 project, a set of pre-K–12 standards released in April 2000, the NCTM has made it clear that basic mathematical skills for the new century should consist of more than computation skills. Standards 2000 emphasizes five mathematical content standards (number and operation; patterns, functions, and algebra; geometry and spatial sense; measurement; and data analysis, statistics, and probability) that students should study with increasing breadth and depth as they move through the grades. In addition, Standards 2000 emphasizes five mathematical processes through which students should acquire and use their mathematical knowledge: problem solving, reasoning and proof, communication, connections, and representation.

Pearson Education

Action Research is a framework that guides the energies of teachers toward a better understanding of why, when, and how students become better learners. This form of inquiry can provide a rich opportunity for reflection on practice and can contribute to ongoing professional development. One such project was carried out by Canadian teacher Lisa Wilson with her grade 8 English language arts classes. It started with baseline data collection that identified 12 students who experienced difficulties in self-selecting books, staying focused on texts, and writing quality journal reflections. This prompted Lisa to ask, "What strategies might help my struggling and striving readers to experience more success in workshop activities?"

A review of current literature was undertaken to examine strategies and methods that Lisa could implement in her silent reading and writing workshops to foster improvement in student performance and enhance the workshop experience. The literature review helped Lisa understand that the problems her students were experiencing were common and aided her in developing strategies. The literature emphasized the importance of providing class time for reading and underlined the value of informal reading conferences, observation of student behaviour, and individual instruction. Further, student accountability may be encouraged through reading logs, reflection journals, and projects.

Lisa wanted to see her students improve and experience success in the following:

- Choosing an appropriate book (interest and reading level)
- Using the big six reading strategies (making connections, questioning, inferring, visualizing, determining importance, and synthesizing)
- Comprehension skills
- Thinking deeply about what has been read

It was determined that students could demonstrate this by providing a well-written journal reflection and being able to discuss their reading during informal reading conferences. One of the key strategies Lisa used was involving the students directly in co-constructing criteria for journal reflections, including format, content, and matters of correctness. She also developed formal instruments to collect data: specifically, informal reading conference forms and observational checklists.

During the implementation of the strategies, Lisa collected data from student reflection journals, informal teacher–student conferences, and observational checklists. The data seemed to suggest the following:

- Students benefited from co-constructing criteria for quality journal reflections.
- The quality of writing improved, and the quantity increased.
- Students were inclined to start reading right away when the teacher began the class by reading silently herself.
- Allowing in-class time for students to read was valuable.

Lisa Wilson is a grade 8 English language arts teacher at Amherst Junior High School in Amherst, Nova Scotia. She is also the literacy mentor in her school. She plans to disseminate the results of her research to her colleagues and fellow literacy mentors in her school district.

What students need is a variety of learning experiences, including **problem-centred learning**, in which students work in small groups on open-ended problems that have many solutions. Rather than simply memorizing facts, working on sets of problems in textbooks, and competing against their classmates, students discover concepts, solve problems similar to those they will encounter in life, and learn to cooperate in small groups.

Technology is increasingly playing a role in mathematics education, especially with more and more school districts adopting a **BYOD (bring your own device)** policy, allowing students to use personal devices (cell phones, tablets, and laptops) for educational purposes. In addition, there is an increasing demand for students to learn

Problem-centred learning: an approach to instruction in which students work in small groups on problems that have many or open-ended solutions.

Bring Your Own Device (BYOD): a policy that allows students to use their personal devices to access an organization's wireless network.

coding (computer programming), with some countries (England and Australia, for example) mandating that all students at every grade should learn to code. This has an impact on mathematics education, as mathematics and coding are a natural fit. Modelling and representing math concepts through code can help enhance understanding.

Science and Technology

Current science curriculum approaches underline the need for students to acquire scientific knowledge, skills, and processes through an inquiry, discovery, or problem-centred method. The teacher's primary role is to guide students in their search for knowledge rather than to act solely as a source of information or right answers.

The first joint development project initiated by the CMEC's 1995 common frameworks for curricula was in the content area of science learning outcomes. This common set of guidelines lays out a framework for scientific literacy in Canada and outlines learning outcomes, which include attitudes, knowledge, and skills for students.

Four foundation statements of science learning guide the development of science curricula across Canada:

- Foundation 1: Science, technology, society, and the environment
- Foundation 2: Skills
- Foundation 3: Knowledge
- Foundation 4: Attitudes

This framework emphasizes a constructivist approach to science learning and encourages learner-centred techniques. The framework is intended to be used as a guide rather than a prescription for science curriculum development and the selection of learning resources.

More recently there has been an emphasis on STEM (Science, Technology, Engineering, and Math) education because of a recognition that in today's increasingly digital world, students need greater scientific and technological literacy than ever before. Rapid changes associated with globalization have had a significant economic, social, and environmental impacts on Canadians. In terms of the environment in

How might these students be meeting science curriculum aims of the Council of Ministers of Education, Canada?

Big Cheese Productions

particular, the need to focus on sustainability and the importance of scientific literacy to help students better understand the world and make informed decisions is reflected in the curricula of all the provinces and territories.

The Organisation for Economic Co-operation and Development's (OECD) Programme for International Student Assessment (PISA) defines **scientific literacy** as "the capacity to use scientific knowledge, to identify questions, and to draw evidence-based conclusions in order to understand and help make decisions about the natural world and the changes made to it through human activity." The recent emphasis on scientific literacy in Canadian curricula reflects the belief that all Canadians, regardless of career path, need to engage with social issues such as global warming, space exploration, genetically modified foods, and medical advancements.

> Scientific literacy: the capacity to use scientific knowledge, to identify questions, and to draw evidence-based conclusions in order to understand and help make decisions that impact human activity and the natural world.

PCAP Science defines scientific literacy as "a student's evolving competencies of understanding the nature of science using science-related attitudes, skills, and knowledge to conduct inquiries, to solve problems, and to reason scientifically in order to understand and make evidence-based decisions about science-related issues" (CMEC, 2013 p. 8). PCAP's Science Assessment Framework (2013) gives an overview of the science-related issues that Canadians should be informed about:

- The usefulness of science to society;
- The negative effects or unintended consequences of science;
- Scientific principles that could enable scientific research or result in the development of new or improved technologies;
- Issues related to science, taking into account personal, community, and environmental factors;
- Social issues; and
- Careers.

The PCAP definition of scientific literacy includes more than information recall. Its use of the term *scientific literacy* rather than *science* highlights the importance that PCAP places on assessing an understanding of the nature of science and the use of science knowledge and skills within societal and environmental contexts.

For more information about scientific literacy in Canadian curricula, please see http://cmec.ca/docs/pcap/pcap2013/PCAP-2013-Science-Assessment-Framework-EN.pdf.

Social Studies

Goals for social studies lack the precision found in other subject areas. Consider, for example, Charles Beard's comment in 1938 that social studies aim at the "creation of rich and many-sided personalities, equipped with practical knowledge and inspired by ideals so that they can make their way and fulfill their mission in a changing society which is part of a world complex" (1938, p. 179). The Alberta Education website (2015) states:

> Social studies provides opportunities for students to develop the attitudes, skills and knowledge that will enable them to become engaged, active, informed and responsible citizens. Recognition and respect for individual and collective identity is essential in a pluralistic and democratic society. Social studies helps students develop their sense of self and community, encouraging them to affirm their place as citizens in an inclusive, democratic society.

Although Canada does not have national guidelines or standards in the social studies curriculum area, common themes can be recognized in the various provinces and territories. For example, the identified vision for the Atlantic Canada social studies curriculum is to "enable and encourage students to examine issues, respond critically and creatively, and make informed decisions as individuals and as citizens of Canada and of an increasingly interdependent world" (Newfoundland & Labrador Department of Education, 2011, p. 1). A recurring theme across Canada is the importance of social studies curriculum in developing citizenship.

Similarly, the Western Canadian Protocol for Collaboration in Basic Education (2000, p. 5) has adopted the following formal definition for social studies:

> Social studies is the study of people in relation to each other and to their world. It is an interdisciplinary subject that draws upon history, geography, economics, law, political science, and other disciplines. Social studies focuses on people's relationships with their social, physical, spiritual, cultural, economic, political, and technological environments. Social studies helps students become active and responsible citizens within their communities, locally, nationally, and globally, in a complex and changing world. Social studies curricula have been expanded in recent years to keep pace with societal trends; specifically, courses or units in culture and diversity and Indigenous studies and women's history have been developed to give voice to those whose stories were previously ignored. Efforts will continue in this area to address such issues as racial, ethnic, cultural, gender, and socio-economic biases and to promote diversity and anti-discrimination in society.

Social studies curricula have also experienced a rapid expansion of information related to the proliferation of the Internet. This development underlines the need to develop media-literate students who can critically interpret and analyze information.

Second-Language Instruction

The majority of Canadian students take school courses in English or French, Canada's two official languages. The federal government funds French and English instruction as second languages. Publicly funded schooling in either language is guaranteed "where numbers warrant" and is decided on a case-by-case basis. In Quebec, only a child whose parent was educated in English can attend an English-language public school (UN Reporting Category: Education, Leisure, and Cultural Activities). Canada has been in the forefront of the French immersion movement.

Many jobs in Canada require French language skills. In its 2013–2018 Roadmap for Canada's Official Languages, the federal government identified education as one of its priorities in the promotion of linguistic duality in Canada. The roadmap sets out objectives that aim to improve the quality of existing second-language instruction and increase participation in second-language programs. In **core French**, the second language is taught in periods that vary in length from school to school. Provinces may recommend a basic core French structure, and school boards may also influence the program. The aims of core French are as follows:

Core French: second language instruction that emphasizes basic communication skills, language knowledge, and appreciation of French culture.

- Basic communication skills
- Language knowledge
- An appreciation of French culture in Canada and beyond (Turnbull, 2000)

Core French concentrates on speaking, reading, listening, and writing in French. The trend in core French instruction is teaching through themes designed to interest students by considering learners' life experiences, intellectual development, and interests. Core French now aims to expose students to more spoken French and allow them to use their skills to communicate in real-life situations. At the start of a core French program, curricula emphasize listening and speaking. Later, emphasis on reading and writing increases. Core French also features learning about francophone culture, with an emphasis on French-speaking Canada.

French immersion subjects such as math, science, and music are taught in French. The language is the medium and not the object of instruction. The goal of immersion is for learners to achieve a level of fluency to function well in a French-speaking community, work in a French-speaking organization, or pursue post-secondary education in French. The Canadian Association of Immersion Teachers (CAIT) works to promote and improve immersion programs in Canada.

The Canadian Association of Second Language Teachers (CASLT) promotes the advancement of second-language opportunities. There are no national standards for second-language teaching in Canada, but CASLT (2003) issued the following statement of beliefs to act as a guide:

- We believe that being able to communicate in a second language contributes to the full development of the human potential.

- We believe that every individual is capable of learning a second language according to his or her needs, interests, and abilities.

- We believe that the opportunity to learn a second language is a fundamental human right.

- We believe that second language learning is an essential component of a formal education.

The Arts

More than any other area, the arts have held an insecure position in school curricula. When faced with budgetary cutbacks or pressure to raise scores on basic skills tests, a cost-conscious public has often considered the elimination of the arts (music, visual art, and dramatic arts). The arts as a means of expression are especially important in the context of current educational reform. Arts education has been positively linked to improved academic achievement, social and emotional development, increased civic engagement, and equitable opportunity for all students (Smith, 2009). Despite a trend in education to reduce class time devoted to the arts, good teachers know how to incorporate learning in, through, and about the arts. Fortunately, there is a trend toward incorporating the arts into the teaching of STEM subjects. The 2015 *Horizon Report* predicts a shift to a focus on STEAM, where the A stands for art+ and will result in a "more balanced curriculum that integrates disciplines such as the arts, design, and humanities into the sciences" (Johnson, Adams Becker, Estrada, & Freeman, 2015, p. 18).

Typically, elementary art and music are limited to one period a week, with instruction given either by regular teachers or by special teachers who travel from school to school. In addition, most elementary students have occasional opportunities to use crayons, watercolour paints, clay, and other art materials as they learn in other subject areas. And, from time to time, many children have the opportunity to participate in dance, puppetry, role play, pantomime, and crafts.

At the middle and junior high levels, instruction in art and music is more structured as well as more voluntary. Students may choose from band, chorus, arts, and crafts. At the high school level, art and music are usually offered as electives.

The National Symposium on Arts Education (NSAE) released policy guidelines for Arts Education in Canadian Schools in 2004. The NSAE recommends that:

- Students engage in the processes of creating, presenting, and responding, giving them a firm foundation in the practices and principles of the individual arts disciplines;

- Students engage in structured arts learning experiences that value intuition and imagination while developing technical and personal skills and a commitment to high standards (learning in the arts);

- Students learn to respond with critical awareness and sensitivity to their own work and the work of others through cumulative experiences in the arts (learning in the arts);

- Students demonstrate, through cumulative experiences in the arts, an understanding of the value of the arts throughout history, as their heritage, in their daily lives, and in the shaping of cultural identities within local and global contexts (learning about the arts);

- The arts be infused throughout the curriculum, building upon a strong curriculum within each arts discipline (learning through the arts);

- Arts education include meaningful interaction among artists, students, and teachers as well as collaborations with arts organizations in the community.

Physical and Health Education

The ultimate aim of physical and health education is to help students develop the knowledge, skills, and attitudes necessary to enable them to lead physically active and healthy lives. At one time, physical education programs consisted largely of highly competitive team sports. Many children, less aggressive and competitive than their peers, did not do well in such programs and experienced a lowered sense of self-esteem. Gradually, instructors began to offer activities designed to meet the needs and abilities of all students, not just the athletically talented. In addition to traditional team sports such as football, baseball, and basketball, and individual sports such as swimming and wrestling, many students in grades K–12 may now participate in a broad array of physical activities, including aerobics, archery, badminton, folk and square dancing, gymnastics, handball, hockey, table tennis, golf, racquetball, curling, skating, volleyball, soccer, and yoga.

Physical and Health Education Canada (PHE Canada) is an organization that advocates for and advances quality programming in this area. It articulates its mission on their website www.phecanada.ca/about-us/vision/mission:

We believe . . .

- that school communities are one of the most influential institutions in the lives of children and youth.

- that being educated in a Health Promoting School that delivers comprehensive, quality physical and health education programs is vital to the optimum growth and development of children and youth.

- that a solid foundation of physical and health education creates the potential for healthy, physically active lives.

- in the importance of leadership development for both students and professionals.

- in the importance of demonstrating leadership and engaging in partnerships and collaborations.

- in the principles of Canadian Sport for Life. (Long-Term Athlete Development)

Although there are no pan-Canadian standards in the area of physical education curricula, most provinces endorse the Quality Daily Education program standards of daily activity for 30 to 60 minutes that emphasizes enjoyment, health, personal fulfillment, and success. The Health and Physical Education curriculum in Ontario has four main sections for each grade:

- **Living Skills:** understanding themselves, communicating and interacting positively with others, and learning to think critically and solve problems
- **Active Living:** active participation, physical fitness, and safety
- **Movement Competence:** skills for moving properly and with confidence
- **Healthy Living:** learning about health, making healthy choices, and understanding the connections to everyday life

Ontario's revised Health and Physical Education curriculum (2015) also includes mental health across the curriculum and sex education, which has been quite controversial and has sparked protests in many school districts across the province.

In 2015, ParticipACTION released its *Report Card on Physical Activity for Children and Youth* to draw attention to the serious problem of physical inactivity among Canadian youth. Canadian children and youth (5- to 17-year-olds) get a D–grade for overall physical activity, with only 9 percent of this part of the population getting the required 60 minutes of heart-pumping activity each day. The report also argues that active play in nature and the outdoors is essential for healthy child development. To access the Report Card, please see www.participac tion.com/wp-content/uploads/2015/03/2015-Report-Card-Highlight-Report-EN-FINAL.pdf.

Other Trends in Education

In addition to subject-specific trends, there are general trends in education in Canada.

Technology in Education   In our increasingly technological society, where students have ubiquitous access to digital devices and the Internet, it is imperative that schools keep pace. There are pockets of innovation, and many school districts are moving to BYOD models. Some provincial services and several school boards offer the provincial curriculum online for distance learning and for course enhancement in small and rural schools. In October 2012, the International Association for K–12 Online Learning (iNACOL) released its *State of the Nation: K–12 Online Learning in Canada* report. The number of K–12 students enrolled in distance education programs in Canada increased from 140 000 in 2009 to 245 252 in 2012. This is a trend that will undoubtedly continue. Technology in education is the focus of Chapter 9 in this text.

Indigenous Education   There has been increased focus on Indigenous education at the elementary, secondary, and post-secondary levels. The federal government in Canada shares responsibility with First Nations communities to provide education to children and youth who live on reserve and attend provincial, federal, or band-operated schools. According to CMEC, "band-operated schools located on reserves educate approximately 60 per cent of the students living on reserves, while 40 per cent go off reserve to schools under provincial authority, usually for secondary school." First Nations children who reside off reserve attend public elementary and secondary schools in their cities, towns, and communities, with the provinces and territories providing the majority of educational services for Indigenous students.

School-to-Work Transitions   Many high schools form partnerships with the private sector and develop school-to-work programs to address current and future needs in industry. In many provinces, **school-to-work programs** and **cooperative education programs** offer students the opportunity to develop employment skills and explore career options. For example, the objectives of cooperative education programs in New Brunswick are as follows:

- To provide students with an opportunity to gain knowledge and work experience in a career area of their choice
- To assist students in developing and expanding employment skills
- To foster positive student expectations and attitudes toward self, others, school, and work
- To develop awareness of better accessibility to students in various occupations
- To encourage cooperation between the business community and the educational system
- To provide employers with a talent pool of trained and prepared potential employees

The program allows students to participate in a regular school program while at the same time developing employment skills through participation in 40–55 hours of in-school instruction and 125–195 hours of nonpaid work experience.

In Nova Scotia, the School-to-Work Transition program is offered in grades 11 and 12 and features an in-school component and a work-experience component. The objective of the program is to facilitate transitions from school to work by providing skills that might increase high school students' likelihood of becoming employed in desirable jobs. It is also designed to help students make better educational and occupational choices and to gain realistic expectations about future occupations.

Implemented in the fall of 2002, the new Ontario high school program reflects a belief in the importance of out-of-class, career-related experiences for students. It requires all school boards to offer cooperative education, work experience, and school-to-work transition programs. In addition, students are required to participate in 40 hours of community involvement that will give them additional experience outside the classroom.

Curricula will likely continue to focus on opportunities that take students outside the traditional walls of the classroom to develop knowledge, confidence, and skills that will help them succeed in the workplace.

SUMMARY

What Is Taught in Schools?

- There are many different definitions for the term *curriculum*. Generally, it refers to the experiences, both planned and unplanned, that either enhance or impede the education and growth of students.
- There are four curricula that all students experience. In addition to learning what teachers intend to teach (the explicit curriculum), students learn from the hidden curriculum, the null curriculum, and extracurricular/co-curricular programs.
- From school policies to national politics, many factors influence what is taught (and not taught) in schools.

How Is a School Curriculum Developed?

■ Curricula are based on the needs and interests of students and reflect a variety of professional, commercial, local, provincial, national, and international pressures.

■ Teachers must be prepared to assume important roles in the curriculum development process, especially in developing student-centred and integrated curricula.

What Are Some Current Subject-Area Trends?

■ Curriculum trends also involve, for example, redefining foreign language study and sex or health education, developing school-to-work programs, providing for active and authentic learning, determining what students will need to know and be able to do in the twenty-first century, and establishing standards in content areas.

APPLICATIONS AND ACTIVITIES

1. Reflect on the 12 000 or so hours that you have spent as a student in K–12 classrooms. What did the hidden curriculum in the classes teach you about yourself?

2. In your opinion, how should teachers and schools respond to censorship issues in curricula and complaints about the content of instructional materials?

3. What is your opinion of the current emphasis on preparing students for the world of work as the chief aim of education? What influences have created this emphasis? What curriculum goals might be sacrificed through a focus on turning out good employees?

4. Large Group Challenge:

   After reading this chapter, your class will assume the role of a school staff that has been given the assignment of working together on an interdisciplinary project with the overarching theme of "If You Love This Planet: Making a Difference Locally and Globally."

   Directions:

   a. Individually, go to "Interdisciplinary Learning in Your Classroom" at www.thirteen.org/edonline/concept2class/interdisciplinary/index.html.

      • Concept to Classroom is an extensive website that presents a series of workshops, including the one above on interdisciplinary learning that includes an introduction by interdisciplinary learning expert Heidi Hayes Jacobs. Go through the workshop lessons to develop an understanding of interdisciplinary learning.

   b. As a class, meet and take on the roles of staff members in a school.

      • The choice of school level will depend on the composition of your education class. For example, if the class is made up of students specializing in elementary, junior high or middle school, and senior high school levels, then assume that you are working in a kindergarten to grade 12 school. If all the students in your class are specializing at the junior high or middle school and senior high levels, then assume that you are working in a grades 7–12 school.

      • Each student in the class will choose a grade level and a content area in which to become an "expert" (e.g., grade 1 math, grade 7 science, grade 11 English language arts [ELA]). In the end, if possible, all content areas taught in your provincial schools should be represented.

   c. Individually, visit the appropriate provincial department of education website for the content area and grade level you have chosen. Explore the information provided to develop an understanding of the various curriculum outcomes set out by the department. For example, ELA content specialists might find that the main strands of focus in the ELA curriculum are reading and writing, speaking and listening, and viewing and representing. You may also find that there are general and specific outcomes for each of these strands at various grade levels.

d. It's time to meet again as a "staff"; everyone now has a basic understanding of the outcomes that need to be met by students in the school at various grade levels and content areas. The staff must explore how students can meet the curriculum outcomes while making a difference locally and globally in the health of the planet.

e. Ultimately, the staff must arrive at a direction and focus for this project, and decide how the interdisciplinary theme will be dealt with at each grade level and in each content area. Possible topics within the theme might include alternative transportation, recycling, reduction of greenhouse emissions, protection of species and ecosystems, and alternative energy sources.

f. The culminating product of this challenge will be a staff presentation on how this interdisciplinary project will look at each grade level and in each content area. Decisions regarding what format the presentation will take and who will be presenting the plan will have to be made by the "staff."

Remember that this task will require brainstorming, cooperation, and consensus building!

5. Find the professional curriculum standards for your subject area(s) online and compare them to the curriculum standards for that subject area in the province where you plan to teach. For example, you might download the National Council for Teachers of Mathematics (NCTM) standards and then compare them with the mathematics curriculum in the province where you plan to teach.

6. Compare and contrast two or more textbooks or curriculum guides that are currently used to teach a unit in a subject area at a grade level you are preparing to teach. Assess the strengths and weaknesses of the unit in each textbook or curriculum guide. Would you use the materials in your classroom? How would you improve them? What other curriculum materials would you incorporate? How would you integrate educational technology? How would you adapt the curriculum for the unit for individual students according to their needs and characteristics?

Chapter 9
The Role of Technology in Education

funkyfrogstock/Fotolia

FOCUS QUESTIONS

1. How is technology transforming teaching and learning?

2. What technologies are available for teaching?

3. How do Canadian teachers use digital technologies and the Internet?

4. What are some digital resources for teaching and learning?

5. What are the challenges of integrating technology into teaching and learning?

The biggest change that I've seen with our staff is the role of the teacher has gone from the person who delivers the instruction to the person who facilitates learning. Students are now empowered to be leaders, to deliver instruction, to problem-solve, and to come up with their own solutions, versus waiting for the teacher.

A superintendent comments on changes after the school district integrated smartphones into grade 5 and 7 classrooms. "Teachers Testing Mobile Methods," *Education Week*, March 18, 2010, p. 26.

Learning how to implement technology into your teaching is not only about connecting with your students but also about preparing your students for the real world, where everything is about using advancing technology for communication.

—PRISCILLA, teacher education program, first year

Technology in the classroom is allowing teachers to connect with students in an entirely innovative way. It is a new medium in which learning can occur, and it is a medium that is often welcomed by students with open arms.

—LINDA, teacher education program, first year

Technology is changing the face of education, allowing students to become the newest innovators. As teachers, we encourage our students to find their passion and become anything they want and dream. In the classroom we are able to give the students the opportunity to explore the world through technology. They can create, design, build, write, sing, record, and much more with the help of technology.

—DEANNA, teacher education program, first year

Today, it is abundantly clear that technology has transformed how, when, and where students can learn. Often referred to as the iGeneration, netgens, millennials, or generation tech, today's students live in a world that is connected to and continually transformed by technology. To them, a network password is more important than a social insurance number.

With few exceptions, students are more "wired" than their teachers. Generations ago, students came to school with notebooks, pencils, and pens; today, they come to school with smartphones, laptops, tablets, and iPods. In addition, they "spend their days immersed in a 'media diet,' devouring entertainment, communication, [and] any form of electronic media. They are master multitaskers, social networkers, electronic communicators, and the first to rush to buy any new technology" (Rosen, 2010, p. 2). A large-scale MediaSmarts (2014) survey indicates that Internet access in Canada is almost ubiquitous, especially for secondary students, with 85 percent of students in grade 11 using smartphones and other portable devices to stay networked. The survey also reveals that three quarters of the students surveyed have a social media profile or blog, which represents a 250 percent increase from 2005. Most students are involved in online gaming, social networking, video and photo sharing, microblogging, media streaming, and accessing information. A noteworthy finding is that sites that enable students to share media they create themselves have gained in popularity, giving them opportunities to be producers rather than just consumers of media (Steeves, 2014).

In a 2012 report to the Ontario Ministry of Education and the Council of Ontario Directors of Education (CODE), called *A Shifting Landscape: Pedagogy, Technology, and the New Terrain of Innovation in a Digital World*, author Pauline Beggs indicates that there has been a shift in the way that school districts in Ontario are approaching the use of technology in school settings. The focus of school boards is on the following:

- Technology that is decidedly more classroom-focused than lab-focused
- Increasingly wireless classrooms that are more "cloud-based" than hard-wired

- Training that places more emphasis on digital literacy and digital citizenship and less emphasis on using hardware and software manuals
- Use of more personal mobile devices with more intuitive user interfaces rather than shared devices with limited access and log-in requirement
- More attention to equitable access and less attention to scheduled access (Beggs, 2012)

HOW IS TECHNOLOGY TRANSFORMING TEACHING AND LEARNING?

For today's students, anywhere, anytime learning is a reality. Their learning options include online instruction, various forms of e-learning, and blended learning—that is, a blending of traditional face-to-face instruction and online learning. Frequently, all or most of their learning materials and resources are available on the Internet, 24 hours a day, seven days a week.

Despite this, Canadian schools have yet to harness technology's full potential for student learning (Fullan & Langworthy, 2014). There are certainly pockets of innovation, but full-scale uptake has not yet occurred. The future holds promise, however, as educators at all levels realize the potential of digital tools of all kinds for learning. A study by The Learning Partnership (2015) offers insights into technology integration in classrooms across Canada. Over 5700 school leaders, teachers, students, and parents/guardians were surveyed and the results indicate resounding support for the use of new technologies in the classroom. Four of the five students surveyed said that they were more interested in classes where new technology is used. The report also suggests that school leaders, teachers, and parents all believe that integrating new technologies enhances teaching and learning (98 percent), improves student achievement (91 percent), and increases student engagement (87 percent).

Educational technology is beginning to transform teaching and learning at many of our nation's schools. Various provincial ministries of education have specific curriculum components related to information and communications technology (ICT), with expected achievements defined for each grade level. Examples of the requirements include the following:

- Nova Scotia's "Exploring Technology" Curriculum
- Manitoba's "Literacy with ICT Across the Curriculum"
- Alberta's "ICT Complete Program of Studies"

Technology enables students to experience events or study phenomena that they cannot witness first-hand. By integrating technology into various learning tasks and across subject areas, teachers can provide students with learning experiences that would have been impossible a few years ago. Most important, careful and purposeful use of educational technology changes the roles of teachers and students and enhances students' higher-order learning and problem-solving skills. As you read the following vignette, consider how the use of educational technology affects the roles of teachers and students.

Classroom teachers use computers to present information to students and to encourage them to expand their understanding of cultural diversity. Further, technology encourages the development of research, writing, and communication skills. In the Queen Charlotte School District, students with visual impairment are provided with tools to assist them in the learning process. For adult learners living in remote locations, technology gives them access to formal learning opportunities not present in their own communities. Although these examples are strikingly different, they are similar in that teachers are using computers as a tool to achieve educational goals and to create particular kinds of learning environments.

Anywhere, Anytime Learning

As mentioned, anywhere, anytime learning is a reality. Increasingly, teachers are blending online and face-to-face instruction. Depending on the purposes of the lesson, the percentage of time spent online and in the face-to-face classroom varies. The following describes a blended learning experience for grade 5 students:

> A group of fifth-graders takes a series of field trips to local water sources where they use handheld computers to gather water samples. When they return to the classroom, they upload their results to a database on the school portal, which aggregates their findings. Then they log onto the project Wiki to document their expedition, allow teachers and administrators to assess their work, read what other classes in the district have found, and share the process with parents and appropriate members of the community.

> At the local university, the scientist in charge of the pollution project studies the aggregated findings and decides the data shows that the source of pollution is not any one factory but runoff from gardens and driveways adjacent to the river. He sends an instant message to the students, teachers, and administrators thanking them. "Gathering this data would have been impossible without your help," he says. "I simply don't have the staff. But I have the evidence I need now to submit a report to the local government so we can stop this pollution from destroying our rivers." The students are excited to be part of an effort to save the beach and rivers they love; they don't want to stop there. They set up a blog to publicize their findings.

> This ultimately leads to a news story, increased local awareness of the pollution problem, a response from the local government, and an eventual reduction in runoff and pollution. The students are galvanized by their success. That they learned a great deal about government, scientific study, and ecosystems is evident from their test scores. And school personnel—even across school boundaries—enjoyed collaborating on the project. (Consortium for School Networking, 2008)

The following are among the advantages that teachers and students realize from such blended learning activities:

- Virtual field trips —Students and their teachers can go anywhere in or out of this world.

- Open discussion—Online discussions allow for reflection, and archived discussions can be evaluated later.

- Accessibility—Students can access learning resources, assignments, and assessment activities from any place that has a computer and an Internet connection.

- Guest lectures—Experts from a global community can participate in classroom activities.

- Vast resources—Almost limitless resources include data banks, publishers' materials, online labs, and virtual worlds.

- Accommodation of learning styles—Online activities allow for audio, video, text, graphics, and interactive animation that appeal to a variety of learning styles.

- Assessment and tracking—Most online interactions can be archived and reviewed at any time by teachers.

Realizing the Full Impact of Technology on Learning

Without a doubt, the World Wide Web; Web 2.0, which enables users to interact through social networking sites, blogs, video-sharing sites, and other host-provided services; mobile learning devices (MLDs); and related telecommunications technologies can transform teaching and learning. However, one of the education questions for the future is "How committed are teachers, administrators, policy-makers, parents and guardians, and the general public to enabling all students to realize the full impact that technology can have on their learning?" As the following comments by the author of *Rewired: Understanding the iGeneration and the Way They Learn* suggest, the future of schools may depend on educators' response to this challenge:

> Although many schools have tried to integrate technology into the curriculum, I feel that they have gone about it the wrong way. These kids are so technologically advanced that simple adaptations to technology and media in the classroom and in school is borrrrring. . . . One twelve-year-old told me: "My teacher thinks she is so cool and with it because she makes these PowerPoints for each lecture with text and graphics that fly in, twist and turn, and display the same information that is in the book and that she lectures about. Maybe when I was 8 that might have been fun and interesting, but it is so yesterday." (Rosen, 2010, p. 16)

Technology and the Challenge to Schools

The Internet and related telecommunications technologies have the potential to transform teaching and learning. However, an issue for education in the twenty-first century is to ensure that committed teachers, administrators, policy-makers, parents, and the general public assist students in realizing the full impact technology can have on their learning. As the following passage suggests, the future of schools may depend on educators' response to this challenge.

> As educators, we need to meet the challenge of increasing student engagement by facilitating learning through digital innovation; however, a number of significant challenges exist. The results of the Learning Partnership's 2014 report, Emerging *Technologies, Evolving Education,* suggest that the most significant barriers to technology integration include (1) lack of effective training and support for educators; (2) lack of educator confidence, comfort, and competence in using technology; (3) IT and infrastructure complications; and (4) lack of allocated time to learn and adopt new methods.

Additionally (and significantly), educators must develop new assessment techniques to evaluate students' learning through the use of advanced telecommunications such as the Internet. The number of correct responses on homework, quizzes, and examinations will no longer suffice to measure educational outcomes.

When you think about your future as a teacher who will be expected to use technology to enhance student learning, you may find that future at once exciting and intimidating, enticing and threatening. You may ask, "Will I be ready to meet the challenge of integrating technologies into my teaching?" In a very real sense, people like you will be expected to develop new ways of using technology in the classrooms of tomorrow.

"One Bite at a Time!"

One Canadian principal of a technology-enriched elementary school, Cheryl Scotland-Moxon, describes how her school staff has embraced technology:

> I have had the opportunity, in my capacity as principal, to experience first-hand all the trials, tribulations, and triumphs information technology creates in a new school. A

Following is a list of educational technologies and instructional strategies that are changing teaching and learning. For each, indicate with an X whether you are "proficient," "somewhat proficient," or "not proficient" with that technology or strategy. Then indicate whether you are "highly committed," "somewhat committed," "opposed," or "neutral" toward using that technology or strategy in your teaching.

After responding to the items, reflect on those to which you are "highly committed" to integrating into your teaching. What steps will you take from this point on to ensure that those technologies and strategies will, in fact, be part of your teaching practice in the future?

Technology or Instructional Strategy	Proficiency Level			Commitment to Using			
	Proficient	Somewhat proficient	Not proficient	Highly committed	Somewhat committed	Opposed	Neutral
1. Social media							
2. Video teleconferencing							
3. Interactive multimedia							
4. Web page authoring							
5. Simulations and gaming							
6. Assistive technologies							
7. Word processing							
8. Desktop publishing							
9. Digital presentations							
10. Spreadsheets/graphing							
11. Databases							
12. Instant messaging							
13. Infographics							
14. Newsgroups							
15. Electronic gradebook							
16. Information retrieval on the Web							
17. Networking with a file server							
18. Scanners							
19. Digital cameras							
20. Podcasts							
21. Blogs, vlogs, or wikis							
22. Learning management systems (e.g., Moodle, Ning)							

saying frequently used at our school is, "You must eat the elephant one bite at a time." In other words, we had to realize that professional development opportunities were scarce, and no amount of complaining about being ill-trained to use the technology was going to make it easier on us.

We realized that everyone had a different comfort zone with using and integrating technology in their teaching. Given the demands of the curriculum, it was not very long before everyone clearly understood that technology is not curriculum. Rather, technology is a wonderful tool with endless possibilities to support the curriculum.

The challenge for teachers is learning from others, having opportunities to share and observe, first-hand, examples of quality technology integration in the curriculum, and time to become "tech-savvy." This takes time, personal motivation on behalf of the teacher to learn, support from the school administrator, support from the School Board, and from colleagues. It also means that we keep in balance our work in technology integration with all the other demands of the classroom. Remember, one bite at a time!

Source: Reprinted with permission from Cheryl Scotland-Moxon.

The following Professional Reflection feature is designed to help you begin the process of planning for your future role. This feature, adapted from the Education Technology Advisory Council (ETAC, 2010, www.doe.mass.edu/boe/sac/edtech/STaR. pdf), provides the Massachusetts School Technology and Readiness (STaR) chart, a comprehensive approach to improving teaching and learning using technology. Its design assumes continual appraisal of the efficacy of technology's contribution to teaching and learning.

WHAT TECHNOLOGIES ARE AVAILABLE FOR TEACHING?

To enhance their classroom instruction, today's teachers can draw from a dazzling array of technological devices. In the early 1980s, the technology available to teachers who wished to use more than the chalkboard was limited to an overhead projector, a 16-mm movie projector, a tape recorder, and, in a few forward-looking school districts, television sets and VCRs. Today's digital tools and technologies offer a plethora of possibilities for teaching and learning beyond traditional materials such as pen and pencil, books, paper, and chalkboards. Teachers and students can use ever-more-powerful computers and mobile devices with cellular capabilities; Smart Boards; camcorders; optical scanners; speech and music synthesizers; laser and three-dimensional (3D) printers; digital cameras; and LCD projection panels. In addition, they can use sophisticated software for web browsing, email, instant messaging, word processing, digital publishing, presentation graphics, spreadsheets, databases and multimedia applications, and ebooks.

Although the array of currently available technology for the classroom is impressive, we can anticipate even more incredible technologies in the future. The 2015 *Horizon Report* identifies six important developments in educational technology for K–12 education: bring your own device (BYOD), makerspaces, 3D printing, adaptive learning technologies, digital badges, and wearable technology. This chapter's Case to Consider feature focuses on the technologies that a high school student might use in the year 2028.

While the term *educational technology* is usually assumed to mean computers in the classroom, many different forms of technology have influenced education.

Educational technology: computers, software, multimedia systems, and advanced telecommunications systems used to enhance the teaching–learning process.

If we broadly define **educational technology** as inventions that enable teachers to reach their goals more effectively, it is clear that, for some time, teachers have been integrating into their classrooms many forms of educational technology, from the humble chalkboard and the overhead projector to televisions and DVD players.

For example, excellent educational television programs are aired by the Canadian Broadcasting Corporation (CBC), by the Public Broadcasting Service (PBS), and by some cable and commercial networks. With the increased availability of video equipment, many schools see students producing their own television documentaries, news programs, oral histories, and dramas. Teachers use closed-circuit television systems to prepare instructional materials for students in the district. In increasing numbers, school districts have **distance learning networks** that use two-way, interactive telecommunications to offer staff development opportunities to teachers, to provide enrichment instruction to students in remote areas, and, in the case of students who live great distances from the nearest school, to offer curriculum to students at home.

Distance learning networks: two-way, interactive telecommunications systems used to deliver instruction to students at various locations.

E-Learning and Virtual Schools

E-learning: education that is delivered via the Internet, satellite broadcast, interactive television, or CD-ROM.

Virtual schools: public schools that offer programs over the Internet.

Canada is a country with wide expanses where small populations are sometimes scattered over great distances. Consequently, there is a growing number of high schools in the nation that are using **e-learning**, or online education, to supplement the school curriculum. **Virtual schools**, in which instruction takes place over the Internet rather than in a traditional classroom, have become increasingly prevalent.

With many hundreds of students now taking multicast video classes in subjects such as pure math, science, physics, Aboriginal studies, and career exploration, distance learning courses have become so popular that, in some cases, administrators have had to limit enrolment.

With the spread of virtual schools, some educators, policy-makers, and researchers have expressed concern about exaggerated claims for online learning. In addition, they are worried about what is lost when students do not meet face to face with their classmates and teachers. The trend toward e-learning and virtual schools will no doubt continue. Meanwhile, several questions must be addressed to ensure that virtual students have quality online learning experiences. These questions are as follows:

- While online learning may be appropriate for high school students, should it be made available to elementary and middle school students? At what stage or age should learners be considered "too young" for e-learning?

- Should online courses be aligned with provincial curricular standards?

- Who should provide for students' technological needs when they take an online course? Who should cover the costs?

- How can we ensure that online teachers are trained effectively to teach via the Internet?

- Should parental approval be required before a child enrols in an online course?

- How can school officials ensure the quality of online courses, especially those offered by teachers in other provinces or countries?

There is an array of technologies available for teacher use in the classroom, as well as guidance on how to plan lessons with students in mind. The International Society for Technology in Education (ISTE) developed the ISTE Standards, formerly known as the National Education Technology Standards (NETS), for teachers (see Figure 9.1).

ISTE's Educational Technology Standards for Teachers

1. **Facilitate and Inspire Student Learning and Creativity**

   Teachers use their knowledge of subject matter, teaching and learning, and technology to facilitate experiences that advance student learning, creativity, and innovation in both face-to-face and virtual environments. Teachers:

   a. promote, support, and model creative and innovative thinking and inventiveness.
   b. engage students in exploring real-world issues and solving authentic problems using digital tools and resources.
   c. promote student reflection using collaborative tools to reveal and clarify students' conceptual understanding and thinking, planning, and creative processes.
   d. model collaborative knowledge construction by engaging in learning with students, colleagues, and others in face-to-face and virtual environments.

2. **Design and Develop Digital-Age Learning Experiences and Assessments**

   Teachers design, develop, and evaluate authentic learning experiences and assessment incorporating contemporary tools and resources to maximize content learning in context and to develop the knowledge, skills, and attitudes identified in the NETS•S. Teachers:

   a. design or adapt relevant learning experiences that incorporate digital tools and resources to promote student learning and creativity.

   b. develop technology-enriched learning environments that enable all students to pursue their individual curiosities and become active participants in setting their own educational goals, managing their own learning, and assessing their own progress.

   c. customize and personalize learning activities to address students' diverse learning styles, working strategies, and abilities using digital tools and resources.

   d. provide students with multiple and varied formative and summative assessment aligned with content and technology standards and use resulting data to inform learning and teaching.

Figure 9.1 National Education Technology Standards (NETS) for teachers, 2008

3. **Model Digital-Age Work and Learning**

Teachers exhibit knowledge, skills, and work processes representative of an innovative professional in a global and digital society. Teachers:

a. demonstrate fluency in technology systems and the transfer of current knowledge to new technologies and situations.
b. collaborate with students, peers, parents, and community members using digital tools and resources to support student success and innovation.
c. communicate relevant information and ideas effectively to students, parents, and peers using a variety of digital-age media and formats.
d. model and facilitate effective use of current and emerging digital tools to locate, analyze, evaluate, and use information resources to support research and learning.

4. **Promote and Model Digital Citizenship and Responsibility**

Teachers understand local and global societal issues and responsibilities in an evolving digital culture and exhibit legal and ethical behavior in their professional practices. Teachers:

a. advocate, model, and teach safe, legal, and ethical use of digital information and technology, including respect for copyright, intellectual property, and the appropriate documentation of sources.

b. address the diverse needs of all learners by using learner-centered strategies providing equitable access to appropriate digital tools and resources.

c. promote and model digital etiquette and responsible social interactions related to the use of technology and information.

d. develop and model cultural understanding and global awareness by engaging with colleagues and students of other cultures using digital-age communication and collaboration tools.

5. **Engage in Professional Growth and Leadership**

Teachers continuously improve their professional practice, model lifelong learning, and exhibit leadership in their school and professional community by promoting and demonstrating the effective use of digital tools and resources. Teachers:

a. participate in local and global learning communities to explore creative applications of technology to improve student learning.

b. exhibit leadership by demonstrating a vision of technology infusion, participating in shared decision making and community building, and developing the leadership and technology skills of others.

c. evaluate and reflect on current research and professional practice on a regular basis to make effective use of existing and emerging digital tools and resources in support of student learning.

d. contribute to the effectiveness, vitality, and self-renewal of the teaching profession and of their school and community.

Figure 9.1 (*continued*)

Computer Technology in the Classroom

Schools are discovering the power of technology to enhance the teaching–learning process. An example of a corporation supporting the use of technology in education is the Samsung Canada Solve for Tomorrow grant program that aims to improve learning in the classroom through innovative uses of technology. In 2014, Samsung Canada committed $1 million in Solve for Tomorrow school technology grants to Canadian public education. The aims of the grants are to raise awareness and interest in STEM subjects and demonstrate how they can positively impact local communities. Samsung worked in collaboration with the Learning Partnership to introduce new technology to 40 schools across Canada.

Other companies, such as SMART, support technology integration in classrooms by rewarding exemplary educators with teaching awards. On the SMART website, teachers can also apply for grants or launch a fundraising campaign to acquire technology for their classrooms.

Industry Canada leads an initiative for the Government of Canada called Computers for Schools (CFS), which refurbishes donated computers and allocates them to schools, libraries, not-for-profit learning organizations, and Aboriginal communities across Canada. Donations are accepted from private individuals, businesses, and government.

Although personal computers may not have transformed all schools so that all students have learning experiences like those described above, information communication technology has had a significant impact on education. Like the dawn of the television era in the 1950s, the widespread availability of personal computers and handheld devices has been heralded as a technological innovation that will change the teaching–learning process.

HOW DO CANADIAN TEACHERS USE DIGITAL TECHNOLOGIES AND THE INTERNET?

Today's teachers can integrate a dazzling array of digital technologies into their teaching, using increasingly powerful online tools to help students learn from the ever expanding sea of information available on the Internet and make their own creative contributions to it. The following sections examine several of the exciting ways that teachers are integrating digital technologies into their teaching.

Online Social Networking

Online social networking refers to an online community of people who share common interests. Participants in online social networking can interact in a variety of ways; chat, email, blogging, voice chat, and discussion groups are among the ways group members communicate. Social networks usually allow a user to create a profile of himself or herself using text, audio, graphics, video, and pictures; then other individuals or groups can access the profile. As a user's circle of "friends" grows, so does a sense of community. Most social networks have security features that permit users to choose who can view their profile or contact them. Several social networking services are available to teachers and students. Facebook, Twitter, and YouTube are only a few examples of those available on the Internet.

Facebook and Twitter According to the Facebook website, "Millions of people use Facebook every day to keep up with friends, upload an unlimited number of photos, share links and videos, and learn more about the people they meet. Facebook's mission is to give people the power to share and make the world more open and connected." And, according to the Twitter website, "Twitter is a real-time information network that connects you to the latest information about what you find interesting. Simply find the public streams you find most compelling and follow the conversations. At the heart of Twitter are small bursts of information called Tweets. Each Tweet is 140 characters in length. . . . Connected to each Tweet is a rich details pane that provides additional information, deeper context and embedded media." Teachers have

Catherine's day starts when the alarm on her tablet goes off at 9:00 a.m. and the tablet projects her schedule for the day, her latest digital messages, and a flow of bite-sized *breaking news* bits (carefully curated from sources specific to her interests) on her bedroom ceiling. Catherine puts on her wearable technology gloves and selects her calendar to begin sifting through her day's schedule. Most of Catherine's courses are accessed through her school's 3D virtual learning platform called the Oasis (a name chosen by the principal in reference to his favourite gaming novel, *Ready Player One* by Ernest Cline). She notices, however, that today's courses are in the only physical classroom in her school—the makerspace lab downtown. Here, her class of 15 is working on independent (but cross-related) projects, creating practical solutions to issues in the school's local community. The project Catherine is working on is connected to the community garden her school helped co-construct with the surrounding community (which is low SES and in need of affordable access to fresh produce). Catherine is programming an automated watering system using a microcomputer (single-board computer) and moisture sensors. Catherine's best friend, Eddy, is developing a sound-based Mandarin to English translation app that will allow the Mandarin-only speakers in the community to easily communicate with the other English-speakers about the garden. Eddy's family comes from China, so this project is personally relevant to him. Knowing how challenging it was for his grandmother to learn English when she first arrived in North America, Eddy wanted to develop a low-cost app that could be used by English language learners effortlessly in socially meaningful settings.

After Catherine puts in some hours at the makerspace lab, she receives a meeting request on her uSmart eyeglasses from her ThinkTank group about their upcoming project for their Young Entrepreneurs class. This class, like all of Catherine's other classes, is subject-integrated and has real-world application, problem solving, and creative approaches embedded into the core content. The group wants to meet in the Oasis thinking-space (a creativity-inspiring space) tonight at 7:00 p.m. to review the success criteria for their project. The group wants to ensure that they will receive all their digital badges for this class within the next two months. The group that manages to receive all its digital badges before the last week of classes in this course will be awarded a trip to Finland to present and network at an EdYouth conference for young entrepreneurs. Catherine's group is developing a wearable technology bracelet that communicates with a programmable kitchen appliance, which doles out food in the correct proportions tailored to one's BMI and his or her projected and actual activity for the day. The group decided to address obesity and heart disease problems with the bracelet by removing the cognitive load associated with decision making and prep in normal weight-loss plans.

When the meeting is finished in the Oasis, Catherine removes her 3D virtual headset and heads into her meditation room, where a guide, through the wireless speakers she programmed using another microcomputer, walks her through a 45-minute mindfulness meditation session. She eventually returns to her room and sets her alarm for 9:00 a.m. again the next morning by speaking to her voice-activated tablet. She also instructs the tablet to turn off all the lights in her house and to close the energy-saving blinds until sunbreak the next morning. Catherine falls asleep easily—fulfilled and connected and excited for the next day of school.

1. How realistic is this scenario for a typical day in the life of a high school student in the year 2028?

2. Technology obviously plays a significant role in Catherine's life. How do you think it shapes the work of Catherine's teachers?

3. Based on this scenario, how will the work life of teachers change between now and the year 2028?

This case study was contributed by Laura Morrison, ICT Instructor at the Faculty of Education, University of Ontario Institute of Technology.

successfully used Facebook and Twitter to facilitate small-group projects, highlight exemplary work, build a sense of community outside the classroom, and showcase student creative expressions.

As a teacher-user of social media, remember that you are in the public eye at all times. Occasionally, there are media reports about teachers being fired or disciplined because of "inappropriate" profiles on Facebook or Instagram—for example, teachers posting personal opinions about students, uploaded pictures of teachers engaged in activities deemed inappropriate, and inappropriate communication between teachers and students. Additionally, some school districts have advised teachers not to "friend" students on social networking sites; teacher–student communication via social networking, districts maintain, is inappropriate.

For example, the Peel District School Board in Ontario issued the following guidelines for teacher use of social networking sites, which is posted on its website:

> Maintaining professional boundaries on social media is critical to sustaining public trust and ensuring relationships with students remain professional. Remember that, on social media, the world is watching.

- All online dialogue and interactions with students should be for educational purposes only.
- Your social media interactions should be professional and reflect the board's character attributes: caring, co-operative, honest, inclusive, respectful and responsible.
- Be mindful of all equity and inclusivity-related board policies and the Ontario Human Rights Code when posting content.
- Your tone should be formal and professional when communicating with students and others via social media.
- Do not send private messages and/or texts to students.
- Never share information with students online that would not be appropriate to share in a classroom, or school/community setting. What is inappropriate in the classroom is also inappropriate on social media.
- Keep your posts positive and do not engage in negative or critical conversations online.
- Retweets, likes and favourites are perceived as endorsements. These interactions should be limited and done with care.

Classroom Example. Mr. Labronski collaborates with three English teachers at three other high schools and uses Twitter to teach creative writing. One of his students tweets the first line of a short story around the network of participating schools and invites contributions to the storyline. Once all Twitter network participants have contributed, students in each class take the tweeted material and develop a coherent, polished short story. In addition to learning about creative writing, students learn to write clear, concise statements because of the 140-character limitation for Twitter.

YouTube   Another website that today's students visit regularly is YouTube. YouTube is an online video clearinghouse where students can watch, upload, and share online videos. Videos range from footage captured with a cell phone to high-end film productions. Users can establish profiles and share favourite videos with their friends. In addition to being a site for watching videos, YouTube is a form of online social networking because it can build a sense of community for users. Teachers are using YouTube in a variety of ways: to access international news coverage, political debates, TED Talks, and diverse opinions; and to enhance classroom lessons with stimulating content. Many schools block access to YouTube because much of the material is inappropriate for educational settings and the videos vary widely in quality. In addition, it can be very time consuming for teachers to preview videos to make sure they are relevant to their educational goals. In lieu of YouTube, many teachers use TeacherTube, which allows them to share video materials with classrooms around the world. Another similar site, SchoolTube, mainly hosts videos produced by students in class with the help of their teachers.

Classroom Example. An English as a second language (ESL) teacher, Ms. Hernandez, uses YouTube to reinforce correct pronunciation and grammar. She gives students the URLs for several YouTube channels that emphasize learning English.

Blogs and Vlogs   A blog (short for Web log) is an online journal constructed by an individual and reacted to by those who visit the blog. A blog usually consists of text, but it can include pictures, links to other websites, and media sources that support the author's views on various topics. Blogging can be interactive because the visitor can offer opinions about the author's statements. A vlog (short for video blog) is very similar, except that the entries are posted as videos rather than text.

Classroom Example. Ms. Casa-Todd uses a professional blog to recap the day's events in her grade 7 classroom. She encourages students and their parents or guardians to join the conversation about activities in her classroom. She finds that blogging is a good way to connect with parents or guardians and to get them involved in their children's education.

Wikis   A wiki is a website created, edited, and maintained by groups of people. A wiki website grows based on user creation and is validated by user reviews. Coming out of the social networking movement, wikis follow the logic that many voices are better than one and allow collaborative work by various authors. A wiki website allows anyone or designated members of a group to create, delete, and/or edit the content on the website. The most famous wiki is Wikipedia, the online encyclopedia created by users all over the world.

Classroom Example. Mrs. Rioas uses a wiki as a build-your-own-story writing assignment. She divides students into groups of five and then asks them to write a shared story on a classroom wiki space. The students have to come up with the topic, develop the storyline, create and edit the work—all in their wiki space. As students work on the wiki, Mrs. Rioas examines different iterations of the story, checks progress, provides feedback, and shares the stories with parents and colleagues.

3D Virtual Reality Worlds   Three-dimensional virtual reality worlds are a dynamic part of online social networking; they can be a powerful learning tool for active, engaged learning with visually rich, hands-on experiences; trial-and-error activities; and virtual participation in events. For example, a teacher might assume the identity of a personal avatar (an online visual image) and take students on a virtual field trip to a museum, an active volcano, a chemistry lab, a spaceship, or other planets and galaxies. Participants are free to navigate, communicate, access resources, and in some cases manipulate the environment as they choose. Dozens of virtual reality worlds are available on the Internet. Among educators, one of the most popular virtual worlds is Second Life (http://secondlife.com).

Classroom Example. Ms. Wang, a history teacher, uses Second Life to help students understand past events and apply their understanding to life today. For example, when studying ancient Greece, she locates an "island" at the Second Life site that resembles ancient Athens. Then she develops roles that students can assume and a problem that confronts them—perhaps conflict with Sparta. Students then clothe their avatars according to their roles and behave as people actually did in ancient Greek society.

Podcasts and Vodcasts   A podcast is a digital media file delivered over the Internet. These files can be played on a computer or mobile device such as a tablet, iPod, or cell phone. A podcast allows for a syndication feed, which delivers digital files to the user automatically once new content is loaded to the site. A podcast can be compared to online radio delivered on the Web, with the recipient able to decide what he or she will hear and when. A vodcast is a video podcast that can be downloaded and viewed from anywhere with a high-speed Internet connection.

Classroom Example. Ms. Pendergrass uses podcasting in her chemistry class. She clips on a small wireless microphone at the beginning of the class period. The microphone is connected to her computer, which is set up to record audio. As she presents content and responds to students' questions, these interactions are recorded in an electronic file. When the session is finished, Ms. Pendergrass opens the audio file, looks for long periods of silence, and edits those out. She then publishes the file to her podcasting site. Students can then download and listen to material she has presented over a week, month, or year.

E-Portfolios   An e-portfolio can serve many different functions; however, it is best known as an assessment tool. An e-portfolio allows students to place work they have completed, or resources they have gathered, in a web-based portfolio. E-portfolios allow teachers and students to track growth and understanding.

Classroom Example. Molly is a high school senior. She began using an e-portfolio during her grade 9 year. Originally, she saw the e-portfolio as a place where she could store her electronic artwork. As she began to publish her work in her portfolio space, however, she expanded the content to include all of her creative academic work. Molly credits her e-portfolio for the scholarship she received to a prestigious university. In her e-portfolio, Molly included her senior project: a photo log of her service-learning activities for the victims of the floods in Alberta. She also included a story she had been working on since her first year of high school, audio files of music she created, and graphics of her artwork. Most impressive, though, are her personal reflections describing her philosophy of life and her professional goals for the future. As she says, "If you want to know who I am, what I can do, and where I can go, look at my e-portfolio."

Mobile Learning   Mobile learning (sometimes termed m-learning) involves the use of mobile technologies to enhance students' learning experiences. Teachers are using smartphones with Internet access like the BlackBerry and the iPhone, the iTouch (an iPhone without the phone), PDAs (personal digital assistants), and Pocket PCs to engage and motivate learners, anytime and anywhere. They realize the potential of mobile learning; they understand that students have ubiquitous access to a vast repertoire of resources and information at their fingertips.

Classroom Example. Mr. Hogendoorn uses cell phones in his beginning French classes at a middle school. His students call in and are recorded as they read aloud French language passages. Mr. Hogendoorn then uploads the recordings to his tablet and listens to them after school hours. He also conducts monthly, mobile-based scavenger hunts for his students. He divides each class into teams of four students and sends them clues in French.

WHAT ARE SOME DIGITAL RESOURCES FOR TEACHING AND LEARNING?

The digital resources available on the Web for teaching and learning are almost endless. Truly, the Web is like a giant wholesale warehouse for consumers and producers alike. With Web 2.0 interactive sites, teachers and students are not just "consumers," they are "producers" as well. Materials in the warehouse enable them to create brand- new products or to develop new ways to use existing products. So much is available that it can be hard to decide which resources to use. Knowing where to look for quality materials is as important as the materials themselves. To make the most out of your time in this warehouse, it is helpful to know about learning objects and open-source materials.

Learning Objects

Learning objects are digital resources that can be reused to support learning. Learning objects are small digital resources that:

- Are self-contained—Each learning object can be used independently.

- Are reusable—A single learning object may be used in multiple contexts for multiple purposes.

- Can be aggregated—Learning objects can be grouped into larger collections of content, including traditional course structures.

- Are tagged with metadata—Every learning object has descriptive information, allowing it to be found easily by a search (Beck, 2010).

The idea behind learning objects is simple. Large chunks of information are broken down into smaller bits of information. For example, a lesson on the Battle of Vimy Ridge might have smaller pieces consisting of a video on the specific duties of Canadian soldiers during the battle, an animated map of the surrounding area, or ideas for activities related to World War I weaponry. These objects are then made available to teachers. Teachers may use the objects sequenced in a manner that fits their instructional objectives. Several online resources are devoted to creating and storing learning objects. Some are discipline-specific, such as the National Science Digital Library funded by the U.S. National Science Foundation. Others are very broad, such as MERLOT (the Multimedia Educational Resource for Learning and Online Teaching) housed at Brock University. Here you'll find classroom materials suitable for a wide range of subjects and grade levels. According to the MERLOT website, there are "tens of thousands of discipline-specific learning materials, learning exercises, and Content Builder web pages," all subjected to a rigorous peer review to ensure the highest quality.

Classroom Example. Ms. Denta has been a substitute teacher at three local high schools during the past year. She is making quite a name for herself as a teacher prepared to teach any subject. Recently, the biology teacher at one of the high schools came down with the flu. The school district called Ms. Denta at 5:00 p.m. and asked her to sub for the teacher. Ms. Denta learned that the teacher was teaching about DNA. To prepare a lesson on DNA, Ms. Denta went to the MERLOT site, as she had done several times during the last few years. At merlot.org, she entered "DNA" in the search box and located an excellent lesson on teaching DNA to high school students. The lesson included animations illustrating the formation of DNA and drag-and-drop animated DNA assessments.

Open-Source Materials

The open-source initiative grew out of the freeware or shareware approach to disseminating software and creating communities of users during the 1990s. Open-source materials are developed by a community of programmers and are distributed for free on the Internet. Users of the materials can, in turn, modify the materials and redistribute them. Although open source is usually associated with software development, the open-source movement is spreading to other areas of education as well, such as the open courseware initiative. The MIT OpenCourseWare project is one such example. MIT has made all of its 1800 courses available for free online. Teachers can examine syllabi, lecture notes, resources, assessments, and teaching materials.

Classroom Example. Mr. Banari is, by all accounts, obsessed with computers. He wants his high school students to become as passionate about computers as he is. He has offered elective computer science and advanced mathematics courses for several years. Usually, a small core of high-ability students take these courses. After visiting the MIT OpenCourseWare site (http://ocw.mit.edu/index.htm), he decided to offer one of the MIT courses, Mathematics for Computer Science, as an elective. Students who signed up for the course knew about MIT's highly ranked programs and were eager to test their abilities at this advanced level.

Digital Resources for Different Subject Areas

As the above classroom examples suggest, the Internet contains a vast amount of free, high-quality learning materials to use in your teaching. The following sections provide a brief sampling of the myriad ways these materials can be used in different subject areas.

The Fine Arts The fine arts—art, music, theatre, and dance—offer numerous opportunities to integrate technology into the fine arts classroom. Teachers have used technology in the fine arts classroom to provide students with opportunities to:

- View famous pieces of art in museums around the world.
- Create and share compilations of art, music, theatre, and dance.
- View legendary performances by various fine artists.
- Experience diverse cultural styles of the fine arts.
- Express themselves artistically.
- Share ideas and thoughts about the fine arts with others.

Classroom Example. In smaller school districts, the opportunity to perform with other musicians can be limited. Technology, however, can be used to overcome the isolation of the artist. For example, Musigy makes it possible for people to perform live music together over the Internet. A performer at one location plugs a guitar, keyboard, microphone, or any other electronic instrument into a computer and connects with other musicians interested in jamming. Teachers have set up global jazz bands, string quartets, and rock-and-roll bands with partner schools around the world. In addition to the audio connection, Musigy includes a video connection that allows performers to view others who are performing at the same time.

Language Arts Language arts—reading, writing, media, oral communication—offers many opportunities for teachers to integrate technology. Language arts teachers have used technology in the classroom to:

- Access great works of literature from special or rare book collections.
- Show students videos of famous speeches.
- Improve student writing by using online writing labs.
- Combat plagiarism by using online plagiarism detection programs.

- Access hard-to-find journals.
- Improve students' word recognition and pronunciation by using animation and audio.
- Increase students' reading comprehension by using audio textbooks or ebooks.

Classroom Example. Grade 1 teacher Diana Battaglia had her students design and create "sillyicious sandwiches" and then had them use digital storytelling to tell the stories behind the creations. Students made important text–self connections, designed commercials for their sandwiches, and created recipes.

Mathematics   Technology has been a part of mathematics for centuries—from the abacus to the supercomputer. Mathematicians have long relied on technology to help solve complex problems.

Similarly, mathematics teachers have integrated technology into their teaching to:

- Help students understand numerical relationships.
- Do math calculations such as addition, subtraction, multiplication, and division;
  - find the square root; and solve trigonometry functions and linear equations.
- Help students estimate and measure.
- Help students deal with the symbolic manipulations needed in algebra and calculus.
- Reduce student anxiety about memorizing complex formulas in geometry and trigonometry.
- Help students understand more complex mathematical concepts and ideas.
- Allow for the application of mathematical solutions to real-world problems.

Classroom Example. Ms. Stone teaches grade 2 and would like to incorporate some computer coding into her mathematics teaching, but does not know how to code herself. Ms. Mahmud, who teaches grade 7, suggests that her students could pair up with Ms. Stone's students and teach them how to code in Scratch (https://scratch.mit.edu) to create geometric patterns. Ms. Stone accepts her offer and suggests that the grade 7 students keep their hands behind their backs and give only verbal instructions so that her grade 2 students can do all the coding themselves. Within 45 minutes her students were successful not only in authoring programs like the one in Figure 9.2 but also in understanding and editing the code to generate different geometric patterns. This helped Ms. Stone cover mathematics curriculum expectations in a new way, where students were in control of the creative process—and she learned how to code in Scratch along with them.

Science   Science teachers from the elementary through high school levels have made extensive use of technology in the classroom. Technology integration has enabled them to:

- Tour the solar system with students.
- Become miniaturized and travel throughout the human body.
- Visit the ocean floor.
- Experience an earthquake.

Many science teachers have their students conduct WebQuests—online inquiry research projects that consist of five parts:

1. An introduction to spark students' interest in the quest
2. A task description explaining the purpose and outcomes of the quest

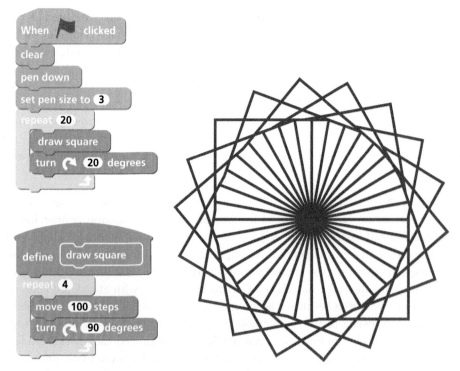

Figure 9.2 Grade 2 students code in Scratch

3. Steps to follow during the quest and resources to be used

4. Evaluation consisting of rubrics and assessment guidelines

5. Conclusion to provide closure

Classroom Example. Students at a rural high school use Second Life to study the human brain in biology class. Students and their teacher will have a virtual meeting with a neurosurgeon from a large urban hospital at a virtual model of the human brain located on a public island in Second Life. At a prearranged time, they meet at the brain stem. After a brief lecture by the doctor and a short question-and-answer session, the doctor leads them to the cerebrum, where she discusses the basic functions of the lobes. Students are able to manipulate the lobes and observe how the lobes react. From the cerebrum, they will visit the cerebellum for a similar experience.

Social Studies Social studies teachers have used technology to explore economics, geography, political science, psychology, and sociology. For example, social studies teachers have used technology to:

■ Allow students to be floor traders on the Wall Street stock market.

■ Enable students to become a leader of state and understand how their political decisions affect the countries they lead.

■ Cope with the poverty, hunger, and political corruption that characterize the lives of people in many developing countries.

■ Examine important primary source documents from different historical periods.

■ Help students experience how crime and violence affect the lives of victims.

Classroom Example. Mrs. Muralia's students have been studying the Israeli–Palestinian conflict for the past week. They have read the textbook, watched a video, listened to historical speeches online, researched articles and current events, and discussed the situation in class. However, it was not until students experienced a video game that allowed them to role-play various characters in this historical conflict that they understood how complex and difficult the situation is. In the video game, students assumed roles of the Israeli prime minister, local Palestinian political leaders, Israeli settlers, Palestinians working in Gaza, or Israeli soldiers. Each student's role called for an action followed by a reaction, followed by another action, and so on. Allowing students to navigate through this complex political landscape in various roles enabled them to begin to think critically and to understand the various points of view that make up the Israeli–Palestinian situation.

Computers and Instruction   Since the early 1980s, the use of computers to enhance instruction has grown steadily. Two of the more common approaches are **computer-assisted instruction (CAI)** (sometimes called computer-*aided* instruction) and computer-managed instruction. Computer-assisted instruction relies on computer programs that provide students with highly structured drill-and-practice exercises or tutorials. Research has shown CAI to be effective with at-risk students and students with disabilities because it accommodates their special needs, and instruction is appropriately paced (Bitter & Pierson, 2005; Bowerman, 2005; Cook & Polgar, 2015; Wiske, Rennebohm Franz, & Breit, 2005). Moreover, CAI can provide students with a positive, supportive environment for learning; students can avoid embarrassment, since their inevitable mistakes while learning are not exposed to peers. Figure 9.3 presents several additional student-centred and technology-centred advantages of CAI. Assistive technologies often include laptops with preloaded software, such as speech recognition, word prediction, and a variety of graphic organizers. Students with hearing impairment can use software that translates speech to text and sign language on screen, while students with visual impairments can use screen reading tools and

> Computer-assisted instruction (CAI): the use of computers to provide students with individualized drill-and-practice exercises or tutorials.

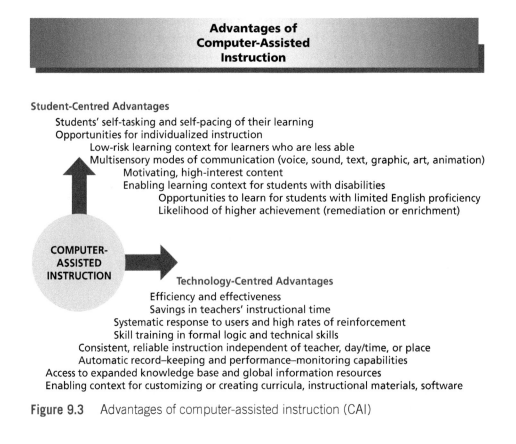

Figure 9.3   Advantages of computer-assisted instruction (CAI)

Braille output technologies to access digital resources. Recent research focusing on the use of iPads with students on the autism spectrum found that the touch-screen technology can provide organizational support and improve students' level of focus (Herbert, 2010). Students living with Autism Spectrum Disorder (ASD) are also experiencing success with assistive tools such as Touch Chat, a digital communication application typically used on a tablet that allows individuals who have difficulty using their voice to communicate. Consider the case of Carter, submitted by his teacher Kerri-Lee Langer:

> Carter is a remarkable young boy with multiple underlying talents and an incredible capacity to communicate his ideas and thoughts to those around him. His eyes light up with the opportunity to participate in special activities, to be engaged in outdoor activities, or to play in the water. Carter loves to demonstrate his ability to complete a puzzle in record time, teach the class the alphabet on the Smart Board, or build a structure as high as he can reach with the Lego blocks. When Carter doesn't get what he wants the first time, he negotiates, debating and presenting his point of view. Carter loves school and enjoys every opportunity to learn. Carter is five years old and is living with autism.
>
> In September when I met Carter and became his teacher he was not speaking any words, displayed little to no visual awareness of those around him, and had limited interaction with his teachers and peers. Carter, like many children with ASD, was living inside his own world—a world that few of us could completely understand. One day his mom came into the classroom to chat and told me that recently doctors had presented to her the idea that her son might have to be sent away for care, words that are heartbreaking to any parent, and unimaginable to this mom. This was the Carter who I was to know at the beginning of my teaching year in my JK/SK/grade 1 classroom: a sweet, adorable child who seemed focused on specific tasks and had great difficulty even wearing new shoes. Carter would soon prove everyone wrong, and with the gentle support of his ASD worker, Anne, and those around him, he began to flourish.
>
> A great deal of Carter's success comes from his nurturing environment at home and at school, but a new-found ability to communicate with those around him has had a tremendous impact on him. Carter is learning to use a program called Touch Chat. This is a digital literacy tool (app) that allows individuals who have difficulty using their own voice to communicate with others via a voice-activated icon touch screen. The Touch Chat screen has generic as well as custom pictures that are programmed to meet individual needs. Carter's Touch Chat is designed specifically for him so that he can communicate with his mom, his teachers, and his peers. Carter is learning to use his device to participate in sharing circle, intentions, work and playtime. By asking questions or stating his requests, his needs can now be met as teachers respond to him through the Touch Chat program, basic sign language, or simple sentences.
>
> Carter has responded very well to this program. He has demonstrated patience to those who are teaching him. I believe that he has reached out to this world of language by making the connection that his future development rests in the ability to allow others to understand his needs. A wonderful moment for me, in Carter's development, was a day when Anne had left the room and Carter wanted to play in the water—a favourite play activity. He found me to get my permission, but I didn't understand his clues. A little frustrated with me, he finally looked up at me with his big brown eyes and said, "Water." It was one of the most precious moments in my teaching career. Carter had made the connection to language and need. He had used his Touch Chat many times with Anne for this activity, but now he had to rely on the power of his own voice, and he did it. Needless to say, Carter got to play in the water!
>
> Carter's vocabulary grows each week, and as his confidence in communicating develops, his ability to engage in all classroom activities also increases and his frustration

decreases. His September diagnosis of working at the level of a 22-month-old has long been forgotten. Carter can recognize his ABCs, count to 10, organize and categorize different materials, and write his name with prompting. All this is done with the determination of one very special little boy. This week Carter surprised us once again. Asking to play using his Touch Chat, he then proceeded to join a group of boys who were building with large wooden blocks. Carter sat down amongst them all and started to construct right along with them. As the boys discussed their design, Carter started to chat away. No real words, but he looked at them and told them with certainty what he thought of the plan. The boys listened and together they created a wonderful structure. Yesterday Carter said "Mom," a word that was added to his Touch Chat several weeks ago so that he could pray for her during our intentions. There was a tear in everyone's eye.

Carter's journey has only just begun, and his ability to communicate using the Touch Chat is the beginning of what I am sure is a lifetime of wonderful opportunities and limitless successes. One determined little boy and one wonderful piece of digital technology and more hugs than can be counted make for a wonderful learning opportunity.

This case study was contributed by Kerri-Lee Langer, a JK/SK/grade 1 teacher in Ontario.

Computer-managed instruction (CMI) relies on programs that evaluate and diagnose students' needs and then, based on that assessment, guide them through the next steps in their learning. CMI records students' progress for teachers to monitor. CAI and CMI can result in reduced teacher–student interactions if the teacher interprets his or her role as primarily that of record keeper or manager. According to the 2015 *Horizon Report*, adaptive learning technologies are software and online platforms that "adjust to individual students' needs as they learn" (p. 42). Adaptive learning technologies are "now capable of learning the way people learn; enabled by machine learning technologies, they can adapt to each student's progress and adjust content in real time or provide customized exercises when they need it" (p. 42). These technologies employ data analytics to provide teachers with information about individual student progress; however, they can be used at the school or district level to evaluate the effectiveness of their programming by making comparisons across classes or schools.

An increasingly popular approach to computer-based instruction is **computer-enhanced instruction (CEI)**. Unlike CAI and CMI, computer-enhanced instruction is less structured and more inquiry-oriented. The following example illustrates how CEI was used in a grade 9 mathematics class to examine a topic of interest to most students: sports data.

Students begin by researching recent news stories about sports, noting how statistics are used. The teacher then guides the class through a model inquiry about athletes' academic and athletic performance in major universities. Students make observations and pose questions about the data and note how the data are used in news articles and various sports-related policies. As they learn to evaluate claims based on statistics, students develop questions about a sports issue that interests them.

Students then apply mathematics to analyze their topic. They learn to use linear equations, correlation and regression analysis, and a variety of visual representations (plots, tables, charts, and graphs) as they apply statistical methods to the analysis of sports issues. They use graphing calculators and spreadsheets to evaluate sports writers' inferences and predictions, as well as to explore different ways of presenting, analyzing, and displaying sports data. Students use word processors, digital images, and *PowerPoint* to record, reflect on, and present their understandings of statistics in sports.

As students delve into the data, they realize that statistics can be accurate or inaccurate, informative, misconstrued, or unclear, depending on how data are processed and

Computer-managed instruction (CMI): the use of computers to evaluate and diagnose students' learning needs and record students' progress for teachers to monitor.

Computer-enhanced instruction (CEI): the use of computers to provide students with inquiry-oriented learning experiences, such as simulations and problem-solving activities.

represented. They learn how to determine whether claims based on data seem reasonable and are supported by contextual information. (Wiske et al., 2005, p. 37)

Unlike in CAI or CMI, in CEI teachers play a critical role in facilitating interactions between computer and student. Teachers must do more than seat students in front of a computer—they must guide students through learning activities that enable them to use technology to arrive at a deeper understanding of the topic at hand.

Some schools are using another inquiry-oriented approach to enhancing instruction with computers—the **microcomputer-based laboratory (MBL)**, sometimes called CBL (computer-based laboratory). Through probes and sensors attached to computers, microcomputer-based laboratories enable students to measure and graph data such as light, sound, temperature, voltage, skin resistance, magnetic field, and heat flow. Students can gather data in the school laboratory or use a battery-operated interface to gather data in the field. For example, Concord Consortium (located at www.concord.org) is a nonprofit research and development organization dedicated to "digital equity" (equal learning opportunities for all students) and to finding new ways to use technology in teaching. It developed MBL curriculum materials that enable students to learn about rainforests using a sensor to gather local data for such variables as humidity, light, dissolved oxygen in rivers and streams, and acid rain. Students then compare local data with those obtained in an actual rainforest. It is clear from this scenario that, as with any meaningful set of instructional objectives and outcomes, teachers engaged in using information communication technology must also engage in a great deal of preparation.

Microcomputer-based laboratory (MBL): the use of computers to gather and then analyze data that students have collected in a school laboratory or in the field.

Home–School Communication Systems

Computer-based **home–school communication systems** such as the Phone Master Notification System are helping busy teachers and parents exchange information. Interfacing a computer program with its

Home–school communication systems: computer-based systems that allow schools to disseminate information to parents and, in turn, enable parents to communicate directly with school personnel.

⟫ How Can Word Prediction Software Enhance the Writing Skills of Students with Disabilities?

"What should I write?" "What words will best express what I want to say?" Although most people find these questions at least somewhat difficult to answer, students with disabilities may confront unique challenges when they write. Some students with learning disabilities may not be able to retain ideas in their memories long enough to express them in writing; others may have difficulty spelling; and students with motor disabilities may be challenged when forming letters with a pen or pencil or making repetitive keystrokes on a word processor.

Students with disabilities that affect their ability to write can be assisted by word prediction software that reduces the number of keystrokes needed to type. When writing with word prediction software, a student types the first letter of a word, and then a numbered list of words beginning with that letter appears on the screen. If the desired word is on the list, the student enters the number and the word is typed automatically. For example, let's say that a student wants to write the word "tonight" to complete the sentence "I will watch television tonight." First, she enters a "t," and a list of common "t" words appears. Since the word "tonight" is not

on this list, she types an "o" and another screen appears. Since "tonight" is on this list, she types a number "3" and the word is entered automatically. Thus, the seven keystrokes needed to write "tonight" were reduced to three.

The following list describes additional features of various word prediction software programs:

- Synthesized speech output

- Prediction methods—Some programs predict on the basis of spelling only, while others consider the words that have come before in the sentence. For example, only nouns are listed after the word "a" or "an."

- List updating—After "learning" a student's vocabulary, some word prediction programs tailor word prediction lists to the student's usage. Some programs update automatically, while others allow the user to decide when to update.

- Prediction window customization

- Keyboard sensitivity adjustment—Keyboard sensitivity can be adjusted to prevent repetition if keys are not quickly released.

computer-based student records can enable teachers to use software to communicate students' progress to parents. Increasingly, schools are using sophisticated home–school communication systems to strengthen their educational programs. Some communication systems even include a "tip line" that uses voice-disguising software to provide students with a safe, anonymous way to provide tips to help reduce school violence. Schools are also using home–school communication systems to disseminate the following kinds of information:

- Absence and tardy parent notification
- Bus schedules
- Club information
- Congratulatory calls
- Invitations to school events
- Lunch menus
- Parent Teacher Association or Parent Teacher Organization information
- Reminders to vote on bond issues
- School cancellations, early dismissals
- Teacher reminders for assignments or activities

WHAT ARE THE CHALLENGES OF INTEGRATING TECHNOLOGY INTO TEACHING AND LEARNING?

Many teachers who began teaching in 1975 were aware of the existence of huge machines—often located on military installations and in university basements and controlled by a few, select geniuses—that used punch cards to process certain types of computation at fairly high speeds. Such teachers had never seen a desktop computer. But by the early 1980s, they were witness to banks of computers in some schools—schools that perhaps had a particularly forward-thinking staff member who assiduously built and maintained a computer lab through scrounging together dollars and ancillary pieces of hardware. Almost certainly, teachers who taught between 1975 and 2016 would have ended their careers taking for granted such things as computerized scheduling and class-by-class attendance tracking, laptops, data projectors, and Smart Boards. Most of those teachers would marvel at how they had ever gotten through the day without access to the personal computing power that would have been unimaginable in their first years in the classroom. The impact of technological change seems vast and impressive; nevertheless, it remains difficult to accurately appraise the effects of information communication technology on teaching and learning.

Despite the challenges of integrating technology in education, most people agree with the premise that digital technologies offer opportunities for innovation that can transform teaching and learning.

In a 2012 Nesta report, *Decoding Learning: The Proof, Promise and Potential of Digital Education*, a group of researchers point out that it is often difficult to determine evidence of positive impact for digital innovations due to limiting factors: (1) evidence is drawn from a huge variety of learning contexts, i.e., "a wide range of teacher experience and learner ability means that too often the impact identified is relatively modest in scale," and (2) findings are focused on how the "technology supports existing teaching and learning practices, rather than transforming those practices" (Luckin, Bligh, Manches, Ainsworth, Crook, & Noss, 2012, p. 8). The authors quite accurately point out that the impact of any given technology depends upon the way it is used, so the focus should be on the pedagogical approach that underlies the technology. Most digital innovations fail for two reasons: they "put technology above teaching and excitement above evidence" (p. 63). In support of this claim, Graham and Richardson (2012) note that "within the current public education schooling experience, there would still appear to be a distinct emphasis on putting the technology well before the pedagogy. It is certainly the trend in the workshops, in the training, and in the purchase of devices and software related to educational technology that we have noted for several years now as educators and researchers within a large, teacher training facility" (p. 7).

Luckin et al. (2012) undertook a review of 1682 studies of technology use in education, and based on their findings, they make a series of recommendations with regard to improving learning with technology. They suggest that adaptive assessment tools offer authentic opportunities, which extend to class data analytics, instant statistics, and the use of digital badges, also identified as a trend in the 2015 *Horizon Report*. The findings also reveal that learning by making is a potentially fruitful approach; this is supported by the 2014 MediaSmarts survey, which found that students were interested in being producers and not just consumers of media. An additional recommendation is that the notion of "practice" needs to be upgraded because practice is "most effective when time is spent on rich, challenging problems accompanied by appropriate feedback rather than misdirected on easy, but ultimately unrewarding, activity" (Luckin et al., 2012, p. 60). Finally, the authors remind us that it is crucial for industry and community partners to work with practitioners and researchers to design and develop digital innovation together, as each entity brings important skills and knowledge to the endeavour.

Apple Classrooms of Tomorrow—Today (ACOT^2)

The Apple Classrooms of Tomorrow—Today (ACOT^2) project is an example of industry and the education sector working collaboratively. To implement the findings of an earlier 10-year ACOT study that began in 1985 and "to help high schools get closer to creating the kind of learning environment [today's] generation of students needs, wants, and expects so they will stay in school" (Apple, Inc., 2008, p. 3), the Apple Classrooms of Tomorrow—Today (ACOT^2) project was launched in 2008. The first phase of the project involved the development of six "essential design principles" for the twenty-first century high school:

- Understanding of twenty-first century skills and outcomes
- Relevant and applied curriculum
- Informative assessment
- A culture of innovation and creativity
- Social and emotional connections with students
- Ubiquitous access to technology

The second phase involved providing participating high schools with online resources based on the six principles. The resources emphasized Web 2.0 sites like YouTube, Second Life, and other social media sites that allow students to produce content, not just consume content. The third phase involved the development of "200 Days for a Lifetime of Success," a grade 9 curriculum to prepare students for success. The curriculum reflects the fact that "students today expect to learn in an environment that mirrors their lives and their futures—one that seamlessly integrates today's digital tools, accommodates a mobile lifestyle, and encourages collaboration and teamwork in physical and virtual spaces" (Apple, Inc., 2008, p. 9).

A Note of Caution

Clearly, educational technology *does* have positive effects on learning and teaching, and indications are that technology will influence all aspects of education even more in the future. However, just as every teaching–learning outcome has an overt or declared curriculum, so does every social setting—including the school—have a covert or hidden curriculum (see Chapter 8). Wise teachers and administrators monitor the hidden curriculum carefully because it is a powerful force that helps shape school climate, and it can exert a strong effect on how students feel about their school, their learning, and themselves. Briefly stated, the "hidden curriculum" embraces the social nuances of the classroom, the school, and the total school-community culture.

Information communication technology, through potent mediums such as the many social networking opportunities available online, can create opportunities that are pursued for harmful purposes, such as the invasion of privacy or cyberbullying. Furthermore, since cell phones can be used to upload images to the Internet in a matter of seconds, teachers must be vigilant with regard to students' use of personal technology in the classroom. In addition, sexting (consensually exchanging nude or sexually explicit images of oneself with a specific person via the Internet) is on the rise. According to the 2014 MediaSmarts survey of Canadian teens, 9 percent of boys and 8 percent of girls sent a sext of themselves and 26 percent of boys and 20 percent of girls had a sext of themselves forwarded to an unwanted recipient. Legal authorities are scrambling to deal with sexting among children and teens under age 18, since the creation and sending of nude photos of people under this age is prohibited through Canada's child pornography laws.

In addition, the privacy of teachers and administrators is at risk in the twenty-first century as never before. For example, during the spring of 2010, a school principal in Nova Scotia was removed temporarily from his position after the school board viewed a school security video of him grabbing a student. Later, the images of the altercation were posted without authorization on a popular Internet video sharing site and "went viral" as hundreds of thousands of people viewed the fracas.

As you contemplate a teaching career, how do you view the use of personal technologies such as cell phones, video sharing sites, and social networking sites in the contexts of student communication, teacher use, and privacy issues?

Broadband Internet Access for All Schools

Internet access is a vital part of a school's capacity to benefit from the vast resources found in cyberspace. Through the Internet, teachers and students can draw from the world's best libraries, museums, and cultural resources.

The technology support available in each school district varies. All elementary schools typically have at least one tech coordinator, sometimes called an Educational Technology Leader (ETL). Although some schools give the ETL teaching release (usually one period), this is often a voluntary position with no release time granted. Larger schools differentiate the role of the ETL so that one person looks after the website and social media (web master) and someone else oversees hardware support (e.g., Apple iOS coordinator). In secondary schools, there is typically at least one tech coordinator, and these positions often come with a one-period release

Joanne Richardson-Landry
Junior High French Teacher, Berwick School
Consultant with the Annapolis Valley Regional School Board,
Berwick, Nova Scotia

When teachers hear the words "technology integration," many automatically begin retracing their lesson plans for hints of Internet use or the presentation of a project via PowerPoint. The average teacher starts fretting that she or he has not used the new portable LCD projector yet and promises her- or himself that it will be put to use during the "next unit." For the busy teacher, allowing students to use technology for research and using PowerPoint and iMovies to present projects has become the norm and is "do-able." The question is, how do we integrate technology so that it is meaningful and effective rather than integrating it because "it's a part of our world"? How does technology fit into our postmodern classrooms, or is the postmodern classroom largely about technology?

The Internet opens up to us a world of varied perspectives and beliefs on virtually every topic imaginable. One can now find out both sides of an issue simultaneously from a variety of sources; therefore, technology has helped move our society into the postmodern era. On the other hand, it can be felt that, although postmodernism focuses on looking at something with more than one lens, there is a pressure that one better be looking at it with the help of technology.

Today's learners seem to have been born with a sense of knowing how to work each new piece of technology as it comes along. This causes educators to panic, because many of us will always be on the outside looking in. Many education systems try to "cure" this by pouring in millions of dollars in technology to make sure all schools are wired. Education departments seem to be more concerned with making sure everyone is wired than with everyone knowing what to do with those wires. In a postmodern society, technology is a cornerstone, yet its use in the classroom must be meaningful and effective. Can we say, as educators, that we are using technology in our classrooms in a meaningful way?

So how does technology fit into our postmodern world? As stated before, it is the cornerstone of the postmodern era.

It allows us to be exposed to countless viewpoints and ideas within a matter of seconds. It gives us choices in how to obtain, store, and present information. It allows our world to become that much smaller but, at the same time, does nothing to close the gap between the "haves" and "have-nots." Does it make a difference in the educational lives of students whether or not their parents own a car? Probably not. Will it make a difference if their parents can afford neither a computer nor access to the Internet? One must also realize that technology is also a well-controlled market and is dictated by corporate moguls such as Bill Gates. We need to be mindful of the fact that, although technology opens up endless possibilities to us, it also dictates our way of life, what we buy, and how we see ourselves.

Technology is here to stay, whether we like it or not. Therefore, it is important that educators are given time and money to explore the capabilities of and links between their classroom and technology. There is wonderful technology to be used in our classrooms, such as WebQuests, podcasts, blogs, and online research, but it takes time for teachers to manipulate these and use them in meaningful ways. "Technology integration" is a popular phrase these days, yet it is important that one integrates it with a purpose and not for the sake of integrating. This is a huge challenge for curriculum developers. Curriculum creators also need to build technology into new textbooks and teacher's guides. Although more and more of this is being done, it is often illustrated as an aside or an added-on activity within the text. This is where technology mentors and consultants play a vital role in educating teachers in finding ways of integrating technology.

It is also important that curriculum developers not become slaves to technology in which everything focuses on the "almighty machine." Because our lives are saturated with technology, it is all the more important to focus on other personal traits that are vital to the healthy functioning of our society, such as cooperation, moral judgment, and empathy. It is the curriculum developer and teacher's ultimate challenge to find a balance between the two.

per day. Many schools rely on central district personnel or computer-savvy teachers for support.

What are the potential repercussions for schools that cannot afford to keep investing in technology?

Access to Technology for All Students

Significant strides have been made toward reducing the **digital divide** between poor and affluent schools. While schools have reduced the number of students per computer, there is evidence of a digital divide if computer use at school and at home is

Digital divide: inequities in access to computer technology that are related to minority-group status, family income, and gender.

Dr. Janette Hughes

Dr. Janette Hughes is Associate Professor and Canada Research Chair, Technology and Pedagogy at the Faculty of Education, University of Ontario Institute of Technology. Her research and teaching interests include critical digital literacies, digital making, adolescent literacies and online identities, writing and digital media, new literacies and conceptualizations of learning, and digital citizenship. Digital literacies encompass all conceptions of engaging in meaning-making, mediated by texts that are read, received, interpreted, produced, and distributed through digital means. She is particularly interested in how digital media enable users to teach, learn, connect, collaborate, communicate, critique, create, and promote social change.

Dr. Hughes's research, which is funded by the Social Sciences and Humanities Research Council and the Ontario Ministry of Research and Innovation, focuses on the relationship between digital media and adolescents' understanding of global issues and how it can be facilitated thorough immersive and performative uses of digital media. She has explored how a production-focused critical digital literacies pedagogy shapes what students learn and how they view themselves and their roles in their community, as well as how public performances of students' digital texts reshape relationships between educational stakeholders and the wider community, both locally and globally. Over the past several years, she has worked with hundreds of elementary and secondary students in classrooms in Ontario using digital tools to explore important societal issues, such as the impact of war on children around the world, the legacy of the residential school system in Canada on Indigenous people, and the role specific media play in adolescents' perceptions of their body image, cyberbullying, and adolescent identities. Using handheld mobile devices to search the Internet for appropriate information and to represent their learning using digital modes for their digital presentations, students engaged in communicative practices that were familiar to them. Connecting to students' digital life-worlds through wikis, video, podcasts, interactive word processing, online postings, and blogging helped teachers to see how critical learning skills were engaged and enhanced by the student participants. More important was the awareness raised within the students' consciousness of how they need to act in ways that can make a difference in their world.

For more information about Dr. Hughes's research, see www.janettehughes.ca.

compared to family income and minority-group status. However, schools can help equalize the disparity in computer use among children from various income categories.

Addressing the digital divide is a priority in school districts across Canada, as educators understand the importance of technologically rich learning opportunities for all students. The need to provide all children and youth in Canada with equal access to digital media, including remote communities, was highlighted in a joint report by UNICEF and the Young and Well Cooperative Research Centre, *Children's Rights in the Digital Age* (2014). Participants from developed countries reported that access to digital media was "necessary to the sense of community, belonging and inclusion that increasingly underpins children's capacity to enact their rights to participation in the contemporary era" (p. 33).

High-Quality, Continuous Training in Technology for Teachers

Using technology to enhance students' learning requires more than investing in the latest hardware or software and connectivity to the Internet. Emailing students, parents, and peers; conducting classroom demonstrations augmented with multimedia; using presentation graphics to address students' varied learning styles; and designing lessons that require students to use the Internet and other digital tools as a resource for inquiry are practices that should be second nature for teachers. Just as new technological skills are needed in the workplace, a high degree of technological literacy is needed in the classroom. Thus, acquiring proficiency in the ever-evolving array of technologies should be an important part of professional development for new and veteran teachers. However, teachers frequently complain of a lack of training in how to use technology to reach their curriculum goals.

In Fullan and Langworthy's 2014 report, *A Rich Seam: How New Pedagogies Find Deep Learning*, the authors share a study from the Innovative Teaching and Learning Research project that investigated how teachers from across seven countries ask their students to use information and communications technologies. The results are not encouraging. Most teachers are still using technology as productivity tools for students—to find information on the Internet, to practise routine skills and procedures, to submit homework, and to write or edit stories, reports, or essays using word processing. Only 3 percent of teachers have their students develop simulations or animations, while only 5 percent have their students use simulations or animations. Another 5 percent have their students work with others from outside class and only 6 percent are creating multimedia presentations. The results of this study indicate that opportunities to learn with and through technology are limited and that actual usage focuses on information consumption and low-level productivity skills (Fullan & Langworthy, 2014, p. 31).

Fortunately, as we approach the end of the second decade of the twenty-first century, teachers and others who have an interest in education are becoming more sophisticated in understanding the strengths and limitations of information communication technology as a tool to promote learning. They know that, like another educational tool—the book—the computer *can* be a powerful, almost unlimited medium for instruction and learning if they carefully reflect on *how* it will further the attainment of their goals and aspirations for their students.

Effective teachers create programs in their classrooms that focus on helping their students become proficient users, thoughtful critics, and creative producers of digital texts and tools of all kinds. To do this, teachers need to ensure that they are participating in ongoing professional development. Teachers attend workshops and conferences—there is no shortage of educational technology offerings across this country and in the United States. School districts also provide technology-related professional development. Perhaps the best kind of informal professional development comes from participating in professional online communities using social media (Hughes & Burke, 2014). Teaching is a creative art, and honing that art cannot be done in the silo of the classroom. Effective educators, regardless of their specific role in education (teacher, administrator, program facilitator, educational assistant, education technology leader), develop strong and supportive professional learning networks.

SUMMARY

How Is Technology Transforming Teaching and Learning?

- Teachers can use technology to achieve educational goals and to create particular kinds of learning environments.

- In many schools and classrooms, technology has already transformed teaching and learning; however, teachers, administrators, policy-makers, and parents must realize that advanced telecommunications will require new approaches to teaching and to assessing students' learning.

What Technologies Are Available for Teaching?

■ Through digital technologies, such as social media and m-learning, teachers are creating learning environments that allow students to become more active in shaping their learning experiences.

■ If *educational technology* is broadly defined as inventions that enable teachers to reach their goals more effectively, then it is clear that, for some time, all teachers have been using various forms of educational "technology."

■ Three common uses of computers in instruction are computer-assisted instruction (CAI), computer-managed instruction (CMI), and computer-enhanced instruction (CEI).

How Do Canadian Teachers Use Digital Technologies and the Internet?

■ Teachers frequently use the Internet to gather information and resources for teaching.

■ Effective teachers engage their students in learning with and through digital technologies.

What Are the Challenges of Integrating Technology into Teaching and Learning?

■ The greatest challenges of integrating technology include (1) lack of effective training and support for educators; (2) lack of educator confidence, comfort, and competence in using technology; (3) IT and infrastructure complications; and (4) lack of allocated time to learn and adopt new methods.

■ Research indicates that technology has a positive impact on students' achievement and attitudes.

■ Enrichment and diversification of teaching and learning opportunities will continue to evolve as information communication technologies become more affordable, more familiar, and easier to use.

What Are Some Digital Resources for Teaching and Learning?

■ There is an endless supply of digital resources available on the Web for teaching and learning.

■ Teachers need to be discerning in their selection of online materials and adapt resources to meet the needs of their students.

APPLICATIONS AND ACTIVITIES

1. In your opinion, what are the most important benefits of technology for education, and what are its most important drawbacks?

2. Write two scenarios: one forecasting how technology will change the teaching profession during the next two decades, and another forecasting the next four decades.

3. With classmates, join or start an online discussion on one or more of the following topics or on another topic from this chapter:

   • Computer simulations and gaming
   • Social media
   • Assistive technologies
   • Adaptive technologies
   • E-learning
   • Interactive multimedia

4. Find out more about professional learning networks. How might you use RSS feeds or online learning networks in your preparation as a teacher? How might you and your students use these forms of educational technology? What knowledge and skills do you need to start or join a professional learning network? Using the Internet, develop a list of resources for both.

5. Survey a local school district to determine the educational technologies used by teachers. How and how often are these technologies used for instruction? What is the availability of computers, mobile devices, and software for student use?

6. Find an online social media site (Facebook group, Pinterest group, blog) frequented by teachers, and enter (or initiate) a discussion on educational technology. What are the teachers' views on integrating technology into the classroom? What digital technologies and tools and instructional activities have they found most effective?

7. Review the brief section in this chapter entitled "A Note of Caution." Do you agree that information on communication technology in schools requires a cautious approach? Ask a number of teachers you know how they feel about social networking sites. Do they use such sites themselves? Do they think limits should be placed on social networking sites in schools? Do teachers believe that such sites contribute to cyberbullying?

8. Prepare a catalogue of interactive multimedia resources and materials that you will use as a teacher. For each entry, include an annotation that briefly describes the resource materials, how you will use them, and where they may be obtained. As with the selection of any curriculum materials, try to find evidence of effectiveness, such as results of field tests, published reviews of educational software, awards, or testimonials from educators. View and report on at least one program you have included in your personal catalogue. Explain in your report how you will integrate this multimedia resource into your curriculum.

PART THREE   THE ART OF TEACHING

Teaching is both a science and an art. Teachers not only need the requisite knowledge of subject matter, learning theories, and teaching strategies, but they also need to understand their students' individual needs to be able to create an effective, rich learning environment. Reflecting on teachers you have learned from over the years, how will you differentiate instruction to meet the needs of all students in your class, and how will you create experiences in your classroom that engage your students in learning?

FOCUS QUESTIONS

1. What are the principles of initial teacher education?

2. What is leadership?

3. What is a profession? What is a professional?

4. How do we describe the teaching profession/professional?

5. How do teachers grow as professionals?

6. To what professional organizations do teachers belong?

7. How do teachers work with educational research?

8. What is teacher leadership?

Leadership is first and foremost about making effective decisions. If the leader makes good decisions, everything else will fall into place. The leader must ensure that the organization objectively evaluates what is known and makes his or her decision on the basis of research, facts and rationality.

—A classroom teacher
From William G. Cunningham and Paula A. Cordeiro,
Educational Leadership: A Bridge to Improved Practice, 2nd Edition
Pearson Education Inc., 2003, p. 2

I have demonstrated leadership by organizing and facilitating Lego Robotics workshops for teachers and other teacher candidates. The workshops revolved around how to program the Lego Robots and how to use Lego Robotics with the Mathematics and Science Curriculum to engage students in new and creative ways.

—**KODY, teacher education program, first year**

I was given the opportunity by the school's principal to implement an informal half-day workshop on a new technology to approximately 40 principals and superintendents. I felt so honoured and excited at the opportunity to share with these individuals who are true professionals in the field of education. I have learned that leadership opportunities are made possible by expanding outside of my comfort zone.

—**JULIE, teacher education program, first year**

During my practicum at a secondary school, I became involved in the school's holiday fundraising campaign. To me, teaching is about making a positive difference in the world; the campaign kept me fresh and gave me a new perspective on teamwork and school spirit. There is no doubt that academics are of great value, but academics alone are not enough to help all of us as learners flourish and reach our full potential.

—**KAITLIN, teacher education program, first year**

During my time at the faculty of education I found lots of opportunities to demonstrate leadership. To model the importance of collaboration, I started an online group to bring my classmates together as an entire graduating class of teachers. It began with the intention to give us a place to share ideas, resources, tips, and tricks, but also to follow each other as we pursue a lifetime career in education.

—**BRENDAN, teacher education program, first year**

The Association of Canadian Deans of Education (ACDE) developed and ratified the **Accord on Initial Teacher Education**, a set of pan-Canadian education initiatives grounded in shared values about teacher education, educational leadership, and educational research.

The Accord lists 12 principles that emphasize the lifelong process of learning, which enhances both the professional growth of individual teachers and the profession of teaching.

Although the Accord's focus is teacher education, the principles provide a vision for the profession of teaching. The Accord on Initial Teacher Education and other accords are located at www.csse-scee.ca/acde/accords.

Accord on Teacher Education: a set of pan-Canadian education initiatives grounded in shared values about teacher education, educational leadership, and educational research.

WHAT ARE THE PRINCIPLES OF INITIAL TEACHER EDUCATION?

ACDE supports the following principles for initial teacher education in Canada. An effective teacher education program does the following:

- Demonstrates the transformative power of learning for individuals and communities
- Envisions the teacher as a professional who observes, discerns, critiques, assesses, and acts accordingly
- Encourages teachers to assume a social and political leadership role
- Cultivates a sense of the teacher as responsive and responsible to learners, schools, colleagues, and communities

- Involves partnerships between the university and schools, interweaving theory, research, and practice and providing opportunities for teacher candidates to collaborate with teachers to develop effective teaching practices

- Promotes diversity, inclusion, understanding, acceptance, and social responsibility in continuing dialogue with local, national, and global communities

- Engages teachers with the politics of identity and difference and prepares them to develop and enact inclusive curricula and pedagogies

- Supports a research disposition and climate that recognizes a range of knowledge and perspectives

- Ensures that beginning teachers understand the development of children and youth (intellectual, physical, emotional, social, creative, spiritual, moral) and the nature of learning

- Ensures that beginning teachers have sound knowledge of subject matter, literacies, ways of knowing, and pedagogical expertise

- Provides opportunities for candidates to investigate their practices

- Supports thoughtful, considered, and deliberate innovation to improve and strengthen the preparation of educators

As you read through this chapter, consider areas of learning that you personally would like to explore more deeply. How might you develop your individual professional growth? How might your individual growth strengthen the profession? How might you participate in leadership activities for positive educational change? How does the Accord on Initial Teacher Education enhance teaching as a profession?

WHAT IS LEADERSHIP?

> It is a "fact" that people seem to know what leadership is and yet often disagree with each other when they talk about it. Most puzzling is that we all seem to think we are right. We all think we know what we are talking about, even when we disagree. And, collectively, we have disagreed on a definition of leadership for over the 100 years of its "modern" lifetime. There are about as many different understandings of what leadership is as there are writers on the topic. (Fairholm & Fairholm, 2009, p. 1)

Leadership: the act of guiding or leading.

This quote by Fairholm and Fairholm (2009) reflects the complexity of **leadership**, leaders, and leading. In simplistic terms, leading is about guiding or influencing. Based on this, a leader is one who guides or influences, and leadership then is the act of guiding or influencing. We believe positions on leadership become complicated when we attempt to describe how or why one might guide or influence a group or organization. The leadership literature spans vast subject disciplines, and in its early stages, research typically focused on the individual as the leader. Over the years, the leadership research has shifted to focus on the followers, the diverse settings where "leading" happens, the cultural contexts of leading, and other complex social, economic, and political facets of leadership, leading, and leaders.

Leadership, Leaders, and Leading

We acknowledge the various positions on leadership, leaders, and leading, and rather than provide a simplistic definition of this complex term, we draw from multiple leadership perspectives. We differentiate the broad ideas around the term *leadership* from other terms such as *management* or *administration*, which are often used interchangeably with it, by attaching the value of change to any and all things "leadership." For the purposes of this chapter, we approach the notion of leadership as one whose underlying value is change as opposed to management or administration, whose underlying values are effectiveness and efficiency, respectively (Gougeon, 2005). Whereas management and administration focus on the mid- and short-term, the focus of leadership is long-term.

Some believe that the key to educational reform is teacher leadership, and that teachers must be given opportunities to evolve as professionals and leaders. This chapter provides an overview of the teaching profession framed within the notion of leadership—that for education to best serve our students, teachers and the teaching profession must "lead" with an eye to the future and for positive change.

WHAT IS A PROFESSION? WHAT IS A PROFESSIONAL?

We have referred to teaching as a **profession** throughout this book; however, if we compare teaching with other professions—law and medicine, for example—perceptions are typically different. Historically, teaching has been labelled a *semi*-profession (Etzioni, 1969), an *emerging* profession (Howsam, Corrigan, Denemark, & Nash, 1976), an *uncertain* profession (Powell, 1980), an *imperilled* profession (Boyer, 1995; Duke, 1984; Freedman, Jackson, & Boles, 1983; Sykes, 1983), an *endangered* profession (Goodlad, 1983), and a *not-quite* profession (Goodlad, 1990).

Although these are outdated perspectives, it is important for beginning teachers to be aware of some of the historical positions regarding the teaching profession. Some of these perceptions may still linger and potentially create obstacles for the profession to fully develop. As beginning teachers, it is important to understand the historical perspectives and events that have shaped teaching so that we can learn from the past and advance the profession.

We use the terms *professional* and *profession* quite frequently, usually without thinking about their meanings. Historically, sociologists have attempted to define professions for a very long time. There have been discussions that not only attempt to explicitly define these terms, but also to debate the extent to which teaching is indeed a profession like medicine or law.

For example, professions have been described as having a systematic body of theory to inform a particular skill, professional authority over a particular area, sanction of the community, a regulative code of ethics, and a culture specific to the profession (Greenwood, 1957).

Arthur Wise (2005) describes a profession as the following:

> A profession is an occupation that seeks to regulate itself by (a) developing a consensus concerning what its practitioners must know and be able to do and (b) developing an accreditation and licensing system to ensure the transmission of that knowledge and skill. An occupation becomes a profession when organizations such as universities, states, and the public accept that system. (p. 318)

Others argue that given today's ever-changing professional and occupational landscape, current attempts at defining professions and previous historical models are no longer relevant. For example, Runte (1995) suggests that continuing the "is teaching a profession?" debate is a needless activity that is misleading and moves the attention away from more important and relevant issues within teaching.

In Canada, the **National Occupational Classification (NOC)** 2011, which describes itself as "the authoritative resource on occupational information in Canada" (www5.hrsdc.gc.ca/NOC/English/NOC/2011/Welcome.aspx), organizes over 40 000 jobs into

Profession: an occupation that requires a high level of expertise, including advanced study in a specialized field, adherence to a code of ethics, and the ability to work without close supervision.

National Occupational Classification (NOC): organizes job titles into occupational group descriptions in Canada.

500 occupational group descriptions within public and private sectors by using a framework of skill type and skill level. Although the NOC's most recent occupation classifications use the terms *profession* or *professional* in a variety of skill areas (e.g., natural and applied sciences and related occupations, health occupations), the common skill level amongst the skill areas differentiating professions/als from nonprofessions/als typically includes a university education. By this definition, then, a **professional** is one who is a qualified member of and engages in a particular profession, and who abides by the regulatory norms established by the profession.

Young, Levin, and Wallin (2014) identified several shared broad characteristics of a profession drawn from the works of Hall (1986), Rich (1984), and Hoy and Miskel (1987). A profession:

1. Has a unique body of knowledge developed through formal education. Members of the profession continue to learn throughout their careers;

2. Provides an essential service respected by society; and

3. Has a high degree of autonomy, has a code of ethics, and is self-regulated.

As you read the next section, reflect upon these typical historical perspectives of professions, and consider how or why the positions confirm or contradict your current understanding of today's teaching profession.

HOW DO WE DESCRIBE THE TEACHING PROFESSION/PROFESSIONAL?

Hargreaves and Lo (2000) describe teaching as a "paradoxical profession" in that public education often faces criticism, government constraints, financial restraints, and issues of respect, yet it is teachers who take on the challenging role of educating a society's children and youth.

> Of all the jobs that are professions or aspire to be so, teaching is the only one that is now charged with the formidable task of creating the human skills and capacities that will enable societies to survive and succeed in the age of information. Even—and especially—in developing countries, it is teachers, more than anybody, who are expected to build learning communities, create the knowledge society and develop the capacities for innovation, flexibility and commitment to change that are essential to economic prosperity in the twenty-first century. (pp. 167–168)

Several sociologists and educators who have studied teaching have identified additional characteristics of occupations that are highly professionalized. Rather than reiterate the futile exercise of finding proof that teaching fits within old sociological frameworks attempting to define "professions," this section will first provide a very brief overview of these more traditional arguments/perspectives about professions, and then it will provide more recent perspectives to reframe the teaching profession.

As you review the descriptions that follow, consider how they apply to teaching and whether what you have learned, experienced, or witnessed supports the characteristics or works that are counter to the traditional notions of a profession.

Specialized Knowledge and Skills

Professionals "possess a high degree of specialized *theoretical knowledge*, along with methods and techniques for applying this knowledge in their day-to-day work . . . [and they] are united by a high degree of in-group solidarity, stemming from their common training and common adherence to certain doctrines and methods" (Abrahamsson, 1971, pp. 11–12).

A profession possesses a specialized body of knowledge that is obtained by its members over a long period of formal education or training (Hall, 1986; Hoy & Miskel, 1987; Rich, 1984). Professionals are granted a certain status because they possess knowledge and skills not normally held by the general public.

In the past, those wanting to become teachers required much less rigorous education, compared to today's teaching requirements. Canadian initial teacher education programs comprise either undergraduate concurrent education programs, post-baccalaureate education programs, or graduate education programs, ranging anywhere from five to six years of post-secondary education.

Within the profession of teaching, however, the knowledge and skill requirements for membership are less precise. In spite of the growing body of **educational research** to guide practice, there is less than unanimous agreement on the knowledge and skills considered necessary to teach. Unfortunately, many beginning teachers place greater value on the classroom practice component of initial teacher education programs, and see the course work as less important. This may be due to the prior assumptions that beginning teachers bring to the profession, and if not addressed in the initial teacher education program, these can serve as barriers to future learning and growth as teachers (Darling-Hammond & Baratz-Snowden, 2007; Feiman-Nemser, 2001). These conceptions or assumptions of teaching may be due to what Lortie (1975) describes as the "apprenticeship of observation," which will be elaborated upon in the following chapter.

In most professions, new members must undergo a prescribed induction period. Physicians, for example, must serve an internship or residency before beginning practice, and most lawyers begin as clerks in law firms. In contrast, teachers do not usually go through a formal induction period before assuming full responsibility for their work. Depending on the school, informal induction activities have occurred for decades; however, formal induction programs are not yet fully developed, consistent, and implemented in all provinces and territories. For example, although Ontario has implemented its New Teacher Induction Program (Ontario Ministry of Education, 2008), not all provinces and territories have such a mandatory induction program.

> **Educational research:** the investigation and study of various topics related to education.

Essential Service Respected by Society

On the one hand, teachers have a monopoly of services. As a rule, only those who are certified members of the profession may teach in public schools. On the other hand, the varied requirements for certification and for teaching in private schools weaken this monopoly. In addition, any claim teachers might have as exclusive providers of a service is further eroded by the past practice of provincial education systems approving temporary, or emergency, certification measures to deal with temporary teacher shortages—a move that establishes teaching as the only profession that allows noncertified individuals to practise.

Perhaps a compelling argument against teachers claiming to be the exclusive providers of a service, however, is the fact that a great deal of teaching occurs in informal, nonschool settings and is done by people who are not teachers. Every day, thousands of people teach various kinds of how-to-do-it skills: how to water-ski, how to make dogs more obedient, how to make pasta from scratch, how to tune a car's engine, and how to meditate, for example.

The level of trust and respect the public extends to teachers as professionals varies greatly. Though all professions have some members who might be described as unprofessional, teaching is especially vulnerable to such charges. The sheer size of the teaching force makes it difficult to maintain consistently high professional standards. Moreover, teaching is subject to a level of public scrutiny and control that other, more established professions have not traditionally tolerated. For example, the teaching profession is one of the only professions that most members of Canadian society have observed and experienced on a daily basis as students for an extended period of time. Teaching is an extremely difficult job, but unfortunately, the student perspective does not usually include the knowledge, skills, planning, and general requirements that underpin the teacher's daily role.

Autonomy, Code of Ethics, and Self-Regulation

Traditionally, professions maintain individual and professional autonomy (Hall, 1986; Hoy & Miskel, 1987; Rich, 1984). In one sense, teachers have considerable autonomy within the guidelines established by local and provincial or territorial authorities. For example, teachers typically have autonomy in how they establish their classroom environment and plan and implement instructional programs within the framework of the provincial or territorial curriculum. Depending on the school, teachers usually work in isolation within their classroom environment with their students. Although the performance of new teachers may be observed and evaluated on a regular basis by supervisors, veteran teachers are observed much less frequently, and they usually enjoy a high degree of autonomy.

There are, however, constraints placed on teachers and their work. Teachers must work within the provincial/territorial statutes, curriculum, and policy, as well as abide by district school board regulations and policies. Moreover, the work of teachers is subject to a higher level of public scrutiny than that found in other professions. Because the public provides "clients" (students) and pays for schools, it has a significant say regarding the work of teachers.

Teachers, like other professionals, have formed a number of vocational associations that are vitally concerned with issues such as admission to the profession, educational standards, examinations and licensing, career development, ethical and performance standards, and professional discipline. Provincial/territorial federations, associations, or unions typically have a code of ethics to which teachers are bound. For example, the Alberta Teachers' Association has a Code of Professional Conduct that specifies standards of professional conduct for teachers in the public school system in Alberta.

In 2015, Saskatchewan introduced *The Registered Teachers Act* to establish the Saskatchewan Professional Teachers Regulatory Board (SPTRB), a teacher regulatory board that is responsible for teacher certification and discipline in Saskatchewan (www. skteacherregulation.ca). Members of the Saskatchewan Teachers' Federation have a Code of Professional Ethics and a Code of Professional Competence that guide teaching behaviours and practices.

Prior to this, the Ontario College of Teachers (OCT) represented the only self-regulating body for teachers in Canada, although, until 2012, the province of British Columbia also had a professional self-regulatory body. The OCT's ethical standards, standards of practice, and professional learning framework describe what it means to be a member of the teaching profession in Ontario (www.oct.ca).

HOW DO TEACHERS GROW AS PROFESSIONALS?

As you will read in the next chapter, Feiman-Nemser (2012) explains that forming a professional identity and building a professional practice support teachers' capacities for further growth. "Becoming" a teacher is a complex and ongoing process and does not stop after the preservice teacher education program. We use the concepts of professional capital (Hargreaves & Fullan, 2012), reflective practice, continuous learning, and involvement in the profession as frameworks to demonstrate how teachers can grow as professionals.

Professional Capital

Drawing from the economic sector's concept of capital, Hargreaves and Fullan (2012) came up with the notion of **professional capital**. Put simply, capital is something that can be described as an asset or wealth that has the potential to create more assets or wealth.

Rather than taking a business capital perspective where education's purpose is seen as serving new markets and is driven and organized around business models of quick returns and low investment, Hargreaves and Fullan (2012) take a professional capital approach.

> Professional capital is about enacting more equal, higher-attaining, more healthy countries in just about every way that counts. This is why successful countries treat their teachers as nation builders, and how they come to yield high returns in prosperity, social cohesion, and social justice. (p. 185)

Professional capital is made up of three components: human capital, social capital, and decisional capital (Hargreaves & Fullan, 2012). Each of these components is briefly described and demonstrates how, through a professional capital framework, not only can teachers develop individually as professionals but the profession and our students can ultimately benefit.

Within the context of teaching, Hargreaves and Fullan (2012) describe human capital as the development of the individual teacher's knowledge and skills required for teaching. This includes knowledge and skill development related to subject content, pedagogy, learners, learning, and social contexts of learners and learning. Human capital also refers to having the passion and moral commitment to serving learners and to continued professional growth. Growing the individual human capital of teachers is not done in isolation, but rather through collaboration with other individuals.

Social capital refers to the collective power of the group, and through trusting and collaborative working relationships with other individual teachers, human capital can be increased. By working deliberately with other teachers to strengthen the school community, individual teachers can be part of a network of learning, communication, and trust. Hargreaves and Fullan (2012) suggest that social capital is more important than human capital because it grows the human capital of individual teachers and for their students.

> Social capital refers to how the quantity and quality of interactions and social relationships among people affects their access to knowledge and information; their senses of expectation, obligation and trust; and how far they are likely to adhere to the same norms or codes of behavior. (Hargreaves & Fullan, 2012, p. 90)

Decisional capital refers to the expertise in making sound decisions about teaching, learners, and learning in complex situations. Hargreaves and Fullan (2012) refer to decisional capital as the essence of professionalism. Professionals attain decisional capital through their experiences, practice, and reflection.

Reflective Practice

Donald Schön (1983, 1987) describes this professional behaviour as **reflection-in-action** and identifies how a teacher might use it to solve a problem in the classroom:

> An artful teacher sees a child's difficulty in learning to read not as a defect in the child but as a defect "of his [or her] own instruction." And because the child's difficulties may be unique, the teacher cannot assume that his [or her] repertoire of explanations will suffice, even though they are "at the tongue's end." The teacher must be ready to invent new methods and must "endeavor to develop in himself [or herself] the ability of discovering them." (1983, p. 66)

Critical reflective practice: the highest level of reflection in which the teacher asks: "How does my teaching positively influence students in their lives beyond the classroom?"

The highest level of reflection, **critical reflective practice**, is the ability of a teacher to go beyond asking such questions as "How could I have made my lesson more interesting? More effective?" to the greater questions of "What is the higher purpose of my teaching, and how can I achieve it?" In other words, "How does my teaching positively influence students in their lives beyond the classroom?"

The professional teacher described by Schön makes careful, sensitive observations of classroom events, reflects on the meaning of those observations, and then decides to act in a certain way. Steven Lacy, an exemplary elementary teacher, describes the reflective decision-making process this way:

> Our effectiveness as teachers is not reflected in the materials and structures of our pedagogy as much as it is in the countless decisions we make every day, decisions that are made in an instant. [D]o I help him with that problem or let him struggle? Do I pursue her question or stick with the lesson? Does this behaviour need to be punished or ignored? Does this composition need to be criticized or praised? (Levey, 1996, pp. 2–3)

Continuous Learning

The professional teacher is dedicated to continuous learning—both about the teaching–learning process and about the subject taught. No longer is it sufficient for career teachers to obtain only a bachelor's degree and a teaching certificate. Teachers are life-long members of learning communities.

Many opportunities are available for teachers to gain new knowledge and skills. Nearly every school district makes provisions for in-service training or staff development. Topics can range from classroom-focused issues, such as authentic assessment, technology-related topics, classroom management, integrated curricula, instructional strategies, or assessment, to school-wide management issues, such as restructuring, shared governance, or school–community partnerships. In upcoming sections of this chapter, other examples of additional continuous learning opportunities through involvement in professional education-related organizations, research activities, and leadership activities are provided.

Involvement in the Profession

Today's teachers recognize that they have the most important role in the educational enterprise and that they have not always been given the power necessary to improve the profession. Therefore, they are taking advantage of the opportunity to examine the decisions that, as professionals, they have the right to make.

Across the country, professional teachers are deeply involved with their colleagues, with professional organizations, with teacher educators, with legislators, with policy-makers, and with others in a push to make teaching more fully a profession. Through their accomplishments, they are demonstrating that they are truly professionals. During the past 25 years, for example, teachers have become more involved in teacher education programs, teacher certification, and professional governance. And, through the efforts of teacher organizations, teachers have also made gains in improving working conditions, salaries, and benefits.

TO WHAT PROFESSIONAL ORGANIZATIONS DO TEACHERS BELONG?

The expanding leadership role of teachers has been supported through the activities of national, provincial, and territorial teacher organizations. These organizations, and the hardworking teachers who run them, support a variety of initiatives to improve teaching and schools. Through their lobbying activities, teacher associations acquaint legislators, policy-makers, and politicians with critical issues in the teaching profession. Many associations have staffs of teachers, researchers, and consultants who produce professional publications, hold conferences, prepare grant proposals, engage in school improvement activities, and promote a positive image of teaching to the public.

The Canadian Teachers' Federation

The **Canadian Teachers' Federation (CTF)** is a national professional organization that speaks and works for teachers nationally. The following is an overview of the CTF's work (www.ctf-fce.ca/en/Pages/About/CTF-Working-for-Teachers.aspx):

Canadian Teachers' Federation (CTF): a national bilingual Canadian organization with 240 000 members from all provinces and territories.

> Founded in 1920, the Canadian Teachers' Federation (CTF) is a national alliance of provincial and territorial teacher organizations that represent nearly 200,000 elementary and secondary school teachers across Canada. CTF is also a member of the international body of teachers, Education International.
>
> CTF speaks out whenever the interests of teachers and students are at stake. We liaise with federal departments and organizations whose work affects education, children and youth; we strive to keep private interests out of public schools; and we work hard to educate governments and citizens about the potential for harm to public interests in international trade agreements.
>
> CTF supports teachers in the collective bargaining process. When Member organizations head into negotiations, we provide information from across the country on teacher salaries, pensions, and the full spectrum of benefits. Our research on education issues like workload, demographics, testing, and funding helps our Member organizations provide stronger representation for teachers. CTF support places teacher negotiators among the most effective and respected in the country.
>
> CTF advances teacher interests by holding seminars and conferences on educational issues. As a national clearinghouse for education research, we provide data collection, analyses, and reporting on trends and issues in education to teacher organizations.
>
> CTF offers teacher opportunities or international exchange and volunteer service to colleagues in developing nations through Project Overseas. Since 1962, Canadian teachers have been volunteering their time and expertise to improve teaching performance and school management in over 50 countries of Africa, Asia, the Caribbean, and the South Pacific. CTF sponsors many other programs of direct support for teachers and teacher organizations in developing countries.
>
> CTF assists all teacher organizations across Canada in difficult times. In Quebec, British Columbia, Ontario and the Northwest Territories, the CTF Defence Fund and the collective solidarity of 200,000 teachers have been mobilized to assist and support teachers in their struggles. Teacher solidarity benefits not only teachers but also students, parents, and public education overall.
>
> CTF gives teachers:
>
> ■ Increased influence with government
> ■ Better salaries and working conditions
> ■ Professional development opportunities
> ■ Service opportunities
> ■ Direct protection in hard times

Teacher Unions and Other Professional Organizations

Teacher unions exist in all provinces and territories, although in some jurisdictions the name used is federation rather than union. While most provinces have a single union that represents all teachers, there are some exceptions. New Brunswick has two affiliated teacher unions with membership determined by language usage (English or French), and Quebec has a similar structure with membership determined by religion. Ontario's structure is the most complex, as there are four separate affiliated unions with membership variously determined by such factors as language, religion, and grade level of instruction.

The teacher federations or unions typically serve as professional teacher organizations that represent, advocate, and protect members within the provincial or territorial jurisdictions. The mission statements and mandates vary and can be accessed at their respective websites. Members pay dues, automatically deducted at source, and the unions negotiate salaries and benefits on behalf of their members. In most jurisdictions, the negotiations are conducted with the provincial or territorial government.

Teacher unions face an interesting dilemma. While they prefer to be viewed as equivalent to professional organizations, such as the provincial bar associations for lawyers or the colleges of physicians for medical practitioners, at times teacher federations act more as trade unions than as purely professional associations. They can, and do, organize strikes, and they can, and do, discipline any of their members who fail to cooperate. In most cases, they are both unions and professional associations.

In addition to provincial teacher unions and the nationally based CTF, numerous other international, national, and provincial organizations represent teachers' professional interests. Many professional associations exist for teachers of specific subject areas, such as mathematics, English, social studies, music, and physical education, as well as for teachers of specific student populations, such as exceptional learners, young children, and students with limited English proficiency.

Canadian Education Association (CEA): a network of educators advancing ideas for greater student and teacher engagement in public education via research and knowledge mobilization.

The **Canadian Education Association** provides an excellent directory of provincial and national organizations, such as Nova Scotia's Association of Science Teachers or the Science Teachers' Association of Ontario. The full directory of organizations can be accessed at http://handbook.cea-ace.ca. By participating in these organizations or simply accessing their Internet-based resources or following their social media feeds, teachers can enhance their learning and their professional networks.

HOW DO TEACHERS WORK WITH EDUCATIONAL RESEARCH?

Today's teachers play an increasingly important role in educational research. By applying evidence from credible research to their daily work, teachers not only continue to develop their own professional growth and practice, but their learners benefit as well. In addition, by informing their practice with educational research, teachers contribute to educational advancements and enhance the professional status of teaching. Teachers should also consider working with colleagues and researchers to identify additional areas to investigate and to participate in research projects.

Increasing numbers of teachers are making important contributions to our understanding of teaching and learning. Prior to the mid-1980s, teachers were the missing "voice" in educational research. However, as teachers and staff developers Holly and McLoughlin (1989, p. 309) noted nearly two decades ago, "We've moved from research on teachers to research with teachers and lately to research by teachers." Since their observation, we have seen the emergence of the **teacher-researcher**, the professional teacher who conducts classroom research to improve his or her practice.

Teacher–researcher: a teacher who regularly conducts classroom research to improve his or her teaching.

Sources of Educational Research

Research findings are reported in numerous educational research journals. As teacher candidates, you have access to your university's online indexes and databases of peer-reviewed journals. As alumni of your university, you may be able to continue accessing your library's resources, usually for a small fee. The research indexes and databases provide users with multiple search functions to locate information on a variety of topics related to teaching and learning. There are other peer-reviewed sources that are accessible to you without a fee.

The **Canadian Society for the Study of Education (CSSE)** is Canada's largest organization of professors, students, researchers, and practitioners in education. The CSSE describes itself as the major national voice for those who create educational knowledge, prepare teachers and educational leaders, and apply research in the schools, classrooms, and institutions of Canada. You can access its peer-reviewed journal, the *Canadian Journal of Education/Revue canadienne de l'éducation*, from its website at www.csse-scee.ca/csse, or you could access the journal directly at http://journals.sfu.ca/cje/index.php/cje-rce.

The CSSE serves as an umbrella organization for national constituent associations spanning a diverse range of topics. You can access the associations' websites at www.csse-scee.ca/associations for additional research information specific to their particular foci:

- Canadian Association for Studies in Indigenous Education (CASIE)
- Canadian Association for Teacher Education (CATE)
- Association of Canadian Deans of Education (ACDE)
- Canadian Association for the Study of Educational Administration (CASEA)
- Canadian Association for the Study of Women and Education (CASWE)
- Canadian Committee of Graduate Students in Education (CCGSE)
- Canadian Association for Curriculum Studies (CACS)
- Canadian Association for Educational Psychology (CAEP)
- Comparative and International Education Society of Canada (CIESC)
- Canadian Association of Foundations of Education (CAFE)
- Canadian Educational Researchers' Association (CERA)

You can also keep up to date on research-informed resources and ideas to inform your practice from many Canadian researchers. With social media, it is easy to follow individual researchers who update their feeds with their educational research areas, educational resources, conferences they attend, and other educational initiatives within their universities. Although there are several social media platform options and many Canadian researchers to follow, we have provided only a few Twitter handles of select education researchers from across the country.

- Alec Couros (@courosa) is a Canadian education researcher and professor of educational technology and learning.
- Theodore Christou (@jipraios) is a researcher, poet, and professor in the history and philosophy of education.
- Allyson Eamer (@Language_Gal) is an education professor and researcher whose area of specialty is sociolinguistics.
- Janette Hughes (@JanetteMHughes) is Canada's Research Chair for Technology and Pedagogy. She does research in critical digital literacies, digital making, civic discourse in classrooms, and young adult fiction.

Canadian Society for the Study of Education (CSSE): Canada's largest organization of professors, students, researchers, and practitioners in education. It serves as a national voice for those who create educational knowledge, prepare teachers and educational leaders, and apply research in the schools, classrooms, and institutions of Canada.

- George Gadanidis (@georgegadanidis) is an education professor and researcher who explores links between math, the arts, and technology.

- Marcea Ingersoll (@MarceaIngersoll) is an education professor and researcher whose areas of interests include new literacies, teacher identity, multimodality, digital spaces, and international teaching.

- Robin Kay (@kayuoit) is a researcher and professor in technology, education, and learning.

- Diana Petrarca (@_DrDi) is an education professor and researcher who explores web-based learning and teacher education. She is currently integrating documentary filmmaking with research on teacher education and teacher development.

In addition to individual education researchers, we have provided a few examples of national and international organizations where teachers can access credible information and resources. You can access their web pages on a regular basis or follow their social media feeds for quick updates.

- The Canadian Education Association provides valuable sources of research for educators on a variety of topics and is accessible at www.cea-ace.ca.

Educational Resources Information Center: a U.S. national information system made up of 16 clearinghouses that disseminate descriptions of exemplary programs, results of research and development efforts, and related information.

- Another source of Internet-based bibliographic records of education literature is the **Education Resources Information Center (ERIC)**. ERIC (http://eric.ed.gov) is a web-based digital library of education research and information sponsored by the Institute of Education Sciences (IES) of the U.S. Department of Education.

- To keep informed about educational technology developments, ensure that you examine the New Media Consortium (NMC) Horizon Reports (www.nmc.org/publications). The reports provide educators with research on, and analyses of, the landscape of emerging technologies for teaching, learning, and creative inquiry from a global perspective, identifying trends and technologies predicted to, drive educational change within a five-year horizon. There are a variety of reports for different educational sectors, including K–12 schools worldwide.

- Edutopia (www.edutopia.org) is a website and online community run by the non-profit George Lucas Educational Foundation. The foundation is devoted to identifying and mobilizing innovative and evidence-based teaching and learning approaches for the K–12 community and provides many resources, ideas, and discussions on a wide range of topics.

- Your Faculty of Education might also provide updates on research and events related to education, such as workshops or speakers.

- By revisiting the chapters in this book, you will note that there are a host of resources and ideas accessible to you as a beginning teacher. Take some time to go back to some of the chapters and bookmark these valuable resources for future use.

Conducting Classroom Action Research

Four decades ago, Robert Schaefer (1967, p. 5) posed the following questions in *The School as the Center of Inquiry*:

> Why should our schools not be staffed, gradually if you will, by scholar-teachers in command of the conceptual tools and methods of inquiry requisite to investigating the learning process as it operates in their own classroom? Why should our schools not nurture the continuing wisdom and power of such scholar-teachers?

Action research: classroom-based study, by teachers, of how to improve their instruction.

Schaefer's vision for teaching has become a reality. Today, thousands of teachers are involved in **action research** to improve their work. Using their classrooms as

"David"—who wishes to remain anonymous—was teaching grades 9 through 11 in an Atlantic Canada high school when one of his students asked for help in getting better grades. The student appeared to be bright and alert, and claimed to study on a regular basis, but only occasionally did she get marks above the B level. Thinking that a solution to the student's difficulties would be relatively simple, David agreed to help, not realizing that he was setting out on an educational journey that would last for the next five years.

He first approached his school counsellor and requested information on how students might improve their study skills. The one relevant document made available by the counsellor contained little in the way of suggestions, so David sought assistance in other areas. What he discovered amazed and discouraged him: nowhere within his school district, at either the middle school or high school levels, was anyone teaching students how to study. Teachers were telling students that they must study, but none of them told students how to do so effectively. At that point, David realized that if anything was to be done, he would have to do it himself.

David decided to start with some action research regarding his own students and their personal study habits. He constructed a questionnaire that students completed anonymously after being told that the tabulated results would be shared with them. After discussing the data with his students, David set out to find a variety of study skill techniques appropriate to the various learning styles common to all classrooms. He had begun reading everything he could find that related in any way to the quest he was on when he made a disheartening discovery in a psychology text: the best study skill a person can have is a good

reading rate. He went back to his classes, gave them a simple page of material to read, timed them, and then calculated their collective reading speeds. With a few exceptions, their reading rates were all at a very low level. David decided that he must teach his students how to read quickly and efficiently if his goal of improving their study skills was to be reached.

In his search for information on speedy but effective reading skills, he went to school counsellors, reading specialists, special educators, conferences of the International Reading Association, and numerous workshops. He quickly learned that no one in his school district was doing anything to improve student reading skills at the secondary level, nor did anyone appear to know how such improvement might be accomplished. Obviously, special attention was given to students with truly serious reading difficulties, but once these students learned to read at a minimally functional level, support was discontinued.

It took five years of reading, discussions with colleagues, and reflection before David was ready to test what he had learned. He chose his grade 9 English class for the first trial because no one would regard teaching students at this level how to study and how to read as being outside the approved curriculum. The students were first presented with a variety pack of study techniques and taught the situations in which each might be most useful. Then, after a careful introduction in which students were informed that they were not required to participate (all did) and that not all of them would necessarily benefit from the process they were to undergo, the reading lessons began: 15 minutes daily over a two-week period. The improvements in student reading rates can be seen in the table below.

Student #	Start Speed	Final Speed	Student #	Start Speed	Final Speed
1	230	310	14	160	455
2	200	225	15	165	475
3	330	500	16	150	315
4	175	290	17	180	270
5	250	410	18	215	330
6	230	490	19	150	210
7	195	370	20	125	180
8	310	505	21	190	260
9	190	460	22	230	350
10	230	520	23	170	210
11	220	375	24	240	380
12	360	780	25	310	540
13	350	610			
				WPM = 220	WPM = 390

Note: These results were acquired by measuring students' comfortable reading rates both before and after the reading rate improvement activities. All results are rounded to the nearest five.

CASE TO CONSIDER   David's Story (continued)

As David's students progressed through the grades, colleagues started to notice that his "graduates" tended to be among their more academically able. His success was garnering interest. Parents started to request that their children be placed in his classes. He received invitations to present at local and provincial conferences. A local university brought David in to share his ideas with preservice teachers. Individual adults with heavy job-related reading requirements came to him for help. David's action research, which led to his becoming an educational leader, forcefully demonstrates the positive effect that a dedicated, professional teacher can have.

1. Why do you think a good reading rate is regarded as the most important study skill?

2. Why do you think "David" wishes to remain anonymous?

3. If David had two grade 9 English classes rather than only the one with whom he tried out his new methodologies, do you believe that he would have been ethically required to give both classes the opportunity to improve their study and reading skills?

4. What generalizations can you make with regard to the data contained in the provided table?

5. Consider the notion of leadership discussed in this chapter. How do David's actions reflect leadership?

6. How has David demonstrated professional capital, reflective practice, continuous learning, and involvement in the profession?

"laboratories," these teacher–researchers are systematically studying the outcomes of their teaching through the application of various research methods. In addition, they are disseminating the results of their research at professional conferences and through various publications.

Simply put, action research is the classroom-based study by teachers, individually or collaboratively, of how to improve instruction. As in the *reflection-in-action* approach described earlier in the chapter, action research begins with a teacher-identified question, issue, or problem: "How can I more effectively motivate a group of students? How do students experience the climate in my classroom? What factors limit parental participation in our school? How can our department (or teacher team) become more collegial? How does computer use in the foreign language classroom affect students' oral communication?" Identification of the question to be investigated via action research is a critical step, as the staff development coordinator at an urban elementary school points out:

> As a member of the school leadership team responsible for staff development, I helped guide the process of designing and carrying out the [action research] projects. One of the major challenges in conducting action research projects for this particular group of teachers was the first step: defining the question or problem to be studied. The delicate part of the facilitator's role for this part of action research is to guide teachers toward questions that accurately represent their real concerns and to help them articulate questions in ways that clarify the important elements. If action research is to be useful and engaging, then questions must focus on significant issues related to the success of students within the classroom. (Mills, 2000, p. 130)

Action research is also "a natural part of teaching. [T]o be a teacher means to observe students and study classroom interactions, to explore a variety of effective ways of teaching and learning, and to build conceptual frameworks that can guide one's work. This is a personal, as well as a professional quest, a journey toward making sense out of and finding satisfaction in one's teaching. It is the work of teacher–researchers" (Burnaford, Fischer, & Hobson, 1996, p. 33).

Action research can be used to study almost any dimension of teaching and learning. At the beginning of the action research cycle, Mills (2000, p. 41) suggests developing an "action plan" consisting of the following steps:

■ Write an area-of-focus statement.

■ Define the variables.

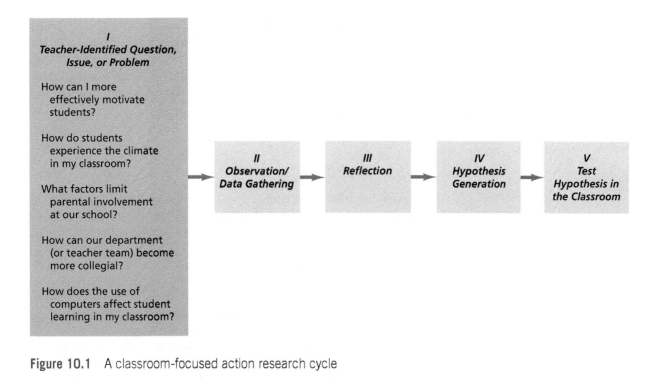

Figure 10.1 A classroom-focused action research cycle

- Develop research questions.
- Describe the intervention or innovation.
- Describe the membership of the action research group.
- Describe negotiations that need to be undertaken.
- Develop a timeline.
- Develop a statement of resources.
- Develop data collection ideas.

Figure 10.1 presents a "taxonomy" of data collection techniques for action research.

Not surprisingly, becoming a teacher–researcher is hard work, given the daily demands of teaching itself. However, more schools are redefining the teacher's role to include action research. These schools realize that action research can provide data on the effectiveness of educational programs, enhance student learning, and energize teachers for professional growth. Four teachers, all members of an action research team, comment on its benefits:

> By far the most rewarding part of working on an action research team was the opportunity to learn and grow with a small group of teacher colleagues. This experience of mutual commitment provided a wonderful staff development experience; by working with these colleagues consistently throughout the year, we were able to explore new ideas and take risks in the classroom with a type of "safety net" in place. For that reason alone, as well as our desire to explore the new questions and challenges raised by our research, we will continue to conduct action research into the effectiveness of our teaching and grading practices. (Mills, 2000, p. 97)

WHAT IS TEACHER LEADERSHIP?

As mentioned at the beginning of this chapter, the underlying value of leadership is change and its focus is long-term. For education to progress in a manner that best serves our students, teachers, and the teaching profession, leadership can no longer be viewed as a solitary effort made by one individual leading the masses into victory. Rather, educational leadership is a shared endeavour, where teachers work with one another, the community, and administrators to effect positive change in the lives of learners. The descriptions and purposes of **teacher leadership** in the literature have shifted over the years, moving from individual orientations to more collective or shared approaches (Lieberman, 2013).

Teacher leadership: a set of skills demonstrated by teachers who do not have formal leadership positions, but who have an influence beyond the classroom, within the school and district school board.

Teacher Leadership for School Improvement

Harris (2005) suggests that teacher leadership has simply become an umbrella phrase for many different things. In her review of the teacher leadership literature, she does, however, highlight several core components extracted from the teacher leadership literature. As you read the summary, consider how you and your colleagues reflect some of these ideas regarding teacher leadership.

> In summary, there are a number of important things to highlight about the definition of teacher leadership. Firstly, teacher leadership is associated with the creation of *collegial norms* among teachers that evidence has shown can contribute to school effectiveness, improvement and development. Second, teacher leadership equates with giving teachers *opportunities to lead*, which research shows has a positive influence upon the quality of relationships and teaching within the school. Third, at its most practical level, teacher leadership means teachers *working as instructional leaders* influencing curriculum, teaching and learning. Finally, teacher leadership is associated with *re-culturing schools*, where leadership is the outcome of the dynamics of interpersonal relationships rather than just individual action. (Harris, 2005, p. 206)

Educational improvement continually and dramatically changes what it means to be a teacher. Teacher leadership carries with it the underlying notion of change within an educational context, which itself is also a broad and complex topic. Teacher leadership has been described in the literature as a key component of school reform, and like the notion of "leadership," the notion of teacher leadership is also complex (Lieberman, 2013).

If the key to successful school development and curriculum improvement is teacher leadership and collaboration, then teachers need opportunities to lead. The following strategies are among the many ways in which teachers can participate in leadership for school improvement:

- Chair or be a member of school committees or projects.
- Take part in school decisions.
- Share ideas with colleagues.
- Implement informal workshops on a new technology or resource.
- Be an associate teacher to teacher candidates.
- Be a mentor to new teachers.
- Improve facilities and technology.
- Work with parents.
- Create partnerships with the community.
- Create partnerships with organizations.
- Participate in research activities with colleges and universities.
- Become a leader in the community.
- Lead efforts to make teachers more visible; communicate positive information.

Teacher Leadership within and beyond the School

Provincially sponsored teacher networks, the professionalization of teaching, shared decision making, and mentor teacher programs are just a few of the strategies that provide unprecedented opportunities for teachers to participate in leadership activities within and beyond the classroom. For example, teachers can take on specific leadership roles, such as curriculum chairs or leads in school or district school board departments and instructional coaches within various curricular areas, including technology.

Teachers can also participate in leadership activities, such as belonging to curriculum development teams or professional groups or associations devoted to growth and development within specific instructional or subject areas. In addition, teachers participate in shared leadership when they contribute to school improvement projects or research activities with colleagues by examining their practices via inquiry-based approaches.

Teacher input into key decisions about teacher preparation, certification, and staff development is important to the teaching profession. Through their involvement with professional certification standards boards and scores of local, provincial, and national education committees, teachers are influencing the character of pre- and in-service education. They serve on curriculum committees, offer workshops and in-service sessions, and act as mentors for teachers new to the profession. Many also teach courses within schools of education on a seconded or part-time basis.

Here is a brief look at the professional activities of Ian McNee, a teacher–leader who continues to work with colleagues both in the public secondary school and college and university systems. His day-to-day activities illustrate the wide-ranging roles of a teacher–leader. In addition to teaching, here are just a few of Ian's leadership activities while serving as liaison and on-site coordinator of a school–college/university partnership.

- Creating twenty-first century learning opportunities for adult learners through the Prior Learning Assessment & Recognition program

- Collaborator on a Managing Information for Student Achievement (MISA) project focused on improving teaching and learning opportunities for college-bound students

- Developing and delivering teaching and learning workshops for newly hired teachers as well as teacher candidates from several Faculty of Education programs

- Delivering staff development training on assessment and evaluation, classroom management, and technology at the point of learning and instruction

- Liaison between several Faculty of Education programs and his home school, acting as both mentor and placement officer for teacher candidates and their associate teachers

- Member of his school's School Improvement Committee with a special emphasis on technology at the point of learning and instruction

- Coaching young athletes at the local, regional, and provincial levels

Helping Teachers Grow as Leaders

This chapter has explored the various ways in which the teaching profession and professionals have been described over the years, as well as the ways in which teaching and teachers have evolved as professionals and leaders. In order to help teacher–leaders continue to learn and grow, research has revealed several conditions that support and enhance teacher leadership development. In her analysis of the teacher leadership literature, Harris (2005) found the following ways in which teacher leadership was fostered. Consider your own experiences, and how these conditions might be reflected in your school communities.

- Teachers require dedicated *time* with colleagues for curricular, instructional, or other school-related discussion, planning, and development activities. The role of the classroom teacher is already busy and complex without additional leadership responsibilities. When teachers participate in leadership activities, they typically do so without additional remuneration. School administrators must consider how to support their teacher–leaders in carrying out their roles in and out of the classroom.

- Teachers need meaningful *professional development opportunities* in a variety of contexts that focus on both teaching- and leadership-related areas. These include activities already mentioned in this chapter, such as leading or participating in work groups, collaborating with colleagues, participating in research activities, and mentoring others.

- Teachers require *structured opportunities* for deliberate collaborations, projects, and research with others. Examples of such opportunities include peer coaching, observation, action research, and reflective practices shared with colleagues.

As beginning teachers, you might also have opportunities to participate in a teacher-leadership role. Moving forward, how might you work collaboratively to participate in activities that enhance your leadership and professional growth?

SUMMARY

What Are the Principles of Initial Teacher Education?

- An effective teacher education program envisions teachers as professionals who are responsive to learners, schools, colleagues, and communities; provides opportunities for teacher candidates to collaborate with practising teachers to develop effective teaching practices; supports a research disposition and climate that recognizes a range of knowledge and perspectives; ensures that beginning teachers understand the development of children and youth (intellectual, physical, emotional, social, creative, spiritual, moral) and the nature of learning; and ensures that beginning teachers have sound knowledge of subject matter, literacies, ways of knowing, and pedagogical expertise.

What Is Leadership?

- The Association of Canadian Deans of Education (ACDE) developed an Accord on Initial Teacher Education that lists 12 principles emphasizing the lifelong process of learning, which enhances both the professional growth of individual teachers and the profession of teaching.

- Leadership is a complex term with multiple perspectives in a variety of disciplines. In its simplest terms, leading is about guiding or influencing with a focus on long-term and positive change.

- The key to educational reform is teacher leadership, and teachers require opportunities to evolve as professionals and leaders.

What Is a Profession? What Is a Professional?

- The idea of what makes a "profession" has been debated in the literature for many years, and many believe that it is an unnecessary and outdated argument because occupational and professional landscapes have changed so much since the conception of "the profession" by sociologists long ago.

- Beginning teachers need to understand the historical perspectives and events that have shaped the teaching profession in order to appreciate and respond to some of the outdated perceptions of professions that may still linger and potentially create obstacles for the profession to fully develop.

- Professions have been historically described as having specialized knowledge and skills and authority over a particular area, providing an essential service respected by society, having a high degree of autonomy and a code of ethics, and being self-regulated.

- The National Occupational Classification, a Canadian resource on occupational information, uses the term *profession* to describe occupations in a variety of skill areas; however, the common skill level shared by occupations deemed as professions is a specialized university education.

- A professional is one who is a qualified member of, and engages in, a particular profession, and who abides by the regulatory norms established by the profession.

How Do We Describe the Teaching Profession/Professional?

- Public education and teachers often face criticism, government constraints, financial restraints, and issues of respect, yet it is teachers who take on the challenging role of educating a society's children and youth.

- Today's teachers require a high degree of specialized knowledge and skills. Canadian initial teacher education programs comprise either undergraduate concurrent education programs, post-baccalaureate education programs, or graduate education programs, ranging anywhere from five to six years of post-secondary education. This is typically followed by an informal and, in some cases, a formal induction program.

- Teachers carry out the essential service of providing formal education within the public school systems. Contradicting the essential service argument of the teaching profession are a variety of factors, including uncertified teaching circumstances and the teaching that occurs in a variety of other contexts, such as continuing education or recreation programs.

- Teaching is subject to a level of public scrutiny and control that other, more established professions have not traditionally tolerated, largely due to the limited "student" perspectives many members of society hold.

- In one sense, teachers have considerable autonomy within the guidelines established by local and provincial or territorial authorities; however, there are also constraints within those same guidelines.

- Teachers have formed a number of vocational associations concerned with issues such as admission to the profession, educational standards, examinations and licensing, career development, ethical and performance standards, and professional discipline.

How Do Teachers Grow as Professionals?

- Professional growth as a teacher is a complex and ongoing process and does not stop after the preservice teacher education program. Professional capital (Hargreaves & Fullan, 2012), reflective practice, continuous learning, and involvement in the profession serve as examples of how teachers can grow as professionals.

- Within the context of teaching, Hargreaves and Fullan (2012) suggest that building profession capital—comprising human, social, and decisional capital—brings about high-yield returns in the profession and in society.

- Teachers also grow through deliberate and critical reflective practice. Donald Schön's (1983, 1987) notions of reflection-in-action (the ability to observe sensitively in classrooms, to reflect on those observations, and to then act accordingly) help teachers frame their professional practice.

- Professional teachers are lifelong members of learning communities, dedicated to continuous learning and active participation in the profession in various contexts related to knowledge and skill development, political involvement, professional governance, and teacher education, to name a few.

To What Professional Organizations Do Teachers Belong?

- Teachers help shape education as a profession through their leadership roles in local, provincial, and national teacher organizations.

- Teachers are members of professional associations for specific subject areas and student populations.

How Do Teachers Work with Educational Research?

- Today's teachers play an increasingly important role in educational research through applying and conducting educational research within their professional practice. By applying evidence from credible research to their daily work, teachers contribute to the profession, their own professional growth, and educational advancements, and their learners benefit as well.

- Many sources of research-informed teaching resources are available on reputable Canadian and international online platforms, including websites, open-access peer-reviewed journals, and social media feeds.

What Is Teacher Leadership?

- Educational leadership is a shared endeavour, where teachers work with one another, the community, and administrators to effect positive change in the lives of learners.

- Teacher leadership is key to school reform, thereby requiring schools to provide teachers with opportunities to work collaboratively with colleagues and participate in leadership activities in order to enhance teaching and learning.

- There are many opportunities for and ways in which teachers can participate in leadership activities and roles within and beyond the school.

- Teachers must be provided with dedicated time with colleagues, structured opportunities for deliberate collaborations, and professional development opportunities in a variety of teaching- and leadership-related areas in order for teacher leadership to grow.

- As teacher candidates or beginning teachers, you might also have opportunities to participate in teacher leadership through sharing new technologies with your associate teacher and staff, hosting informal workshops for other teacher candidates, and working with your faculty in research to enhance education.

APPLICATIONS AND ACTIVITIES

1. Consider the general levels of respect by society for the teaching profession. In your opinion, what accounts for public respect or lack of respect in the teaching profession? What might be the best way to increase respect and trust? Discuss this with another colleague in

the profession and with a friend or family member who is not in the teaching profession. How are the discussions similar? Different? How do you account for the similarities and/or differences?

2. Examine the website and materials of the local teacher union/federation/association within your jurisdiction. What is its mandate? Conduct a search regarding arguments for and against teacher unions/federations/associations. How do the arguments align with your understanding of your local teacher union/federation/association?

3. Locate the code of ethics or other related codes applicable to the teaching profession within your province or territory. How does the code guide teaching behaviour and practices? What are the consequences for any breach of the code within your jurisdiction? How might you use the code as a guide for professional development?

4. Some occupational/career positions are forbidden by law to participate in a strike. It is believed that the loss of their services could result in widespread harm to the social fabric. Consider and discuss with your colleagues which of the following positions (or other occupations/careers) should be deemed essential services and formulate a rationale in support of your perspective. You may want to visit the National Occupational Classification 2011 website (www5.hrsdc.gc.ca/NOC/English/NOC/2011/Welcome.aspx) for additional occupations/careers.

   - Court judges
   - Firefighters
   - Grocery clerks
   - Nurses
   - Physicians
   - Police officers
   - Postal workers
   - Power-line workers
   - Public works and maintenance labourers
   - Snow plow drivers
   - Teachers
   - University faculty

5. Revisit the "How Do Teachers Grow as Professionals?" section in this chapter. How do the actions of reflective practice, continuous learning, and involvement in the profession fit within the notion of professional capital as described by Hargreaves and Fullan?

6. Examine some of the teacher organizations listed in this chapter. What are some of the professional organizations you might join upon graduation? Why? How might you participate in leadership activities within your school or professional organization as a teacher candidate? As a beginning teacher?

Chapter 11
Your First Teaching Position

Credit to come

FOCUS QUESTIONS

1. When do you actually start "becoming" a teacher?

2. How will you become certified or licensed to teach?

3. What is the K–12 teaching landscape for beginning teachers?

4. How will you find your first K–12 teaching job?

5. What are some other career opportunities for teachers?

6. How might you prepare to find your first teaching job?

7. What can you expect as a beginning teacher?

8. How will you continue your professional learning?

> *Learning to teach, especially the kind of teaching reflected in ambitious standards for students and teachers, is a complex, lengthy undertaking. It requires coherent and connected learning opportunities that link initial preparation to new teacher induction and new teacher induction to continuing professional development.*
>
> —Sharon Feiman-Nemser, 2001, p. 1048

What Does It Mean to Become a Teacher?

There are many routes one can take after becoming certified as a teacher. For example, some of my colleagues took positions in the private sector related to teaching others, and there are others with careers in less conventional teaching settings such as the zoo or the Ontario Science Centre. After a few months of teaching, I finally felt like "I am a teacher," but the journey does not end here. Teaching is learning and learning is growing.

—CAMELIA, teacher education program, first year

You make the jump from student to teacher almost overnight, and the pressures are intense. Everything that you have simply observed in your teacher education program is now your responsibility: welcome letters, seating plans, IEPs, report cards—it is all on you. My advice to new teachers is to remind you that nobody starts as the very best teacher that they will be; instead, it is a process of learning and reflecting. I remind myself that becoming a "teacher" is not a destination or final stop.

—MATT, teacher education program, first year

Preservice Education Perspectives

Simon and Jamilla were in the library working on a final group project for their Foundations of Education course. They were both very tired and looking forward to the final practicum of their preservice teacher education program. Simon seemed a little more distracted than usual, and so Jamilla inquired if everything was okay. Simon, hesitant at first, finally admitted that he couldn't focus on the assignment because he had an interview for an occasional teacher position.

"That's wonderful, Simon! I was very nervous for my overseas interview, so I completely understand," said Jamilla. Two months earlier, she secured a job teaching in an international school in the UK for two years. Because Jamilla knew herself well and had realized that supply teaching would not be the best fit with her personality, she had decided to apply for teaching positions overseas so that she would have her own class. She was fortunate that she was able to pick up and teach anywhere, but Simon had young children and was not willing or able to uproot his family and move to a different part of the world.

"I have so much riding on this, J. I'm really nervous and I can't blow it. I don't have time for this stupid assignment," Simon said.

Here we go, thought Jamilla, *the rant about the meaninglessness of coursework*. She braced herself and said, "Simon, I know that you feel lots of our assignments seem meaningless, but have you thought about why we're being asked to consider the implications of some of these historical events on today's schooling in Canada?"

"I really don't care," said Simon dismissively. "I just wanted to learn about how to control my students, how to write a lesson, and how to assess them at the end of the chapter."

These comments made Jamilla feel extremely uncomfortable once again. Her frustration with her classmate was reaching its breaking point. She had been paired with Simon throughout the semester for group assignments, and she had certainly reached her limit. The end of the program was almost upon them, and Simon was still responding to class topics and assignments in the same manner he did when she initially met him at the beginning of the preservice teacher education program. At first she felt that she wanted to help him with interview prep, but she was beginning to change her mind. Jamilla, alongside many of her other classmates, worked really hard throughout the program to understand why and how some of the readings and coursework were relevant to future teaching. At times, she too was frustrated and confused, but the constant cycle of reflection and questioning prompted by her professors helped her to finally begin to make sense of this learning-to-teach process. While she now realized that this program was only the beginning, she believed the courses served as a good foundation and certainly prepared her to continue to learn as a professional. Unfortunately, not everyone in her program agreed with her.

"Listen, Simon," Jamilla began, "you finish prepping for your interview and I'll work on the concept map. I'll pop you a text when it's done so you can access it and provide feedback in our shared folder in the U-drive."

"You're the best, Jamilla," replied Simon. "I've got to go back through those ridiculous course discussion boards to see if I can find some good 'teacher buzzwords' to help me for the interview. Later."

Jamilla watched Simon pack up his laptop and head out of the library. She sighed and continued her work.

Before reading the rest of the chapter:

- Can you relate to either Jamilla or Simon? How?

- Did any of Simon's or Jamilla's comments make you feel uncomfortable? Consider both Jamilla's and Simon's perspectives with respect to the comment(s) that triggered your discomfort.

After reading the chapter:

- How is the *apprenticeship of observation* evident in this vignette?

- What does Jamilla mean by the learning-to-teach process?

- Revisit the comment(s) that may have made you uncomfortable. How might the content of the chapter help you understand these comment(s)?

- Simon and Jamilla attended the same preservice program, were enrolled in the same courses, and had the same assignments. Why do you think Jamilla and Simon have such different perspectives about learning to teach?

- Consider your own personality, circumstances, and needs. Consider the current landscape of teaching in your province, in the rest of Canada, or internationally. What type of teaching position matches your needs? What supports might you access to assist you with your job search locally or abroad?

WHEN DO YOU ACTUALLY START "BECOMING" A TEACHER?

Becoming a teacher does not simply "begin" upon completion of an initial teacher education program. In fact, some educational researchers point out that becoming a teacher actually begins informally, upon entering a school system as young children (Feiman-Nemser, 2012; Lortie, 1975). The *apprenticeship of observation* is a term coined by Dan Lortie to describe how the early and formative experiences as students serve as powerful methods of socializing future teachers (Lortie, 1975). Part of preservice learning, critical to your professional learning and growth, should include deliberate opportunities for reflection on your conceptions of and assumptions about what it means to teach (Darling-Hammond, 2006; Darling-Hammond & Baratz-Snowden, 2007).

Learning to teach is an ongoing and complex process. Sharon Feiman-Nemser (2012) describes learning to teach along a continuum, beginning formally at the preservice level and continuing as a beginning teacher at the induction level. Even as teachers gain years of experience, learning to teach continues via ongoing professional development throughout the course of one's professional career.

Once you graduate from your formal preservice program, what happens next? How does one become qualified to teach in a Canadian public school system? How might one begin the search process for a teaching position? How will your professional learning and development continue? This chapter explores these questions and provides you with some starting resources to help you proceed on your teaching and learning journey.

HOW WILL YOU BECOME CERTIFIED OR LICENSED TO TEACH?

Teaching certificate: a licence to teach issued by a province or territory.

A **teaching certificate** is actually a licence to teach. Canadian provinces and territories typically require a Bachelor of Education degree upon successful completion of a professional teacher education program for teacher certification. Each provincial and territorial requirement will be addressed in the following section.

The Canadian Teachers' Federation (www.ctf-fce.ca/en/Pages/TIC/BecomingaTeacher.aspx) lists additional qualities essential for teaching. These qualities include "a good command of English or French, emotional stability, enthusiasm and a sincere interest in young people. Teachers are also expected to have qualities to enable them to relate well to their students and to establish an environment that is conducive to learning. In addition to advancing literacy skills and preparing students for further academic or vocational studies, teachers should be qualified to promote critical thinking and problem-solving skills in their students, as well as sensitivity to diversity and personal autonomy, and a solid sense of civic responsibility."

Although all jurisdictions, through the power of legislation, have the ultimate authority to change certification requirements in order to comply with the spirit of the **Agreement on Internal Trade/Teaching Profession (AIT)**, some have contractual arrangements that require consultation with, or approval by, the professional teachers' union.

Some jurisdictions recognize subject areas not found in their own K–12 curriculum. For example, religious, heritage, international, and First Nations languages studies are specific to jurisdiction. Certification requirements for each jurisdiction are specified in the subsequent section.

Agreement on Internal Trade/ Teaching Profession (AIT): an intergovernmental trade agreement that requires professions' regulatory bodies to ensure labour mobility in Canada.

Teacher Certification and Classification for Each Province Teacher certification requirements may vary depending upon the certification agency in the province where teachers wish to teach. The Canadian Teachers' Federation (www.ctf-fce.ca) maintains an updated list of information regarding certification requirements for teachers seeking employment in each province.

Table 11.1 shows the certification body or regulation for each province or territory, along with its URL.

TABLE 11.1

Province or Territory	Certification Body or Regulation
Alberta	Certification of Teachers Regulation www.qp.alberta.ca/1266.cfm?page=1999_003.cfm&leg_type=Regs&isbncln=9780779733316
British Columbia	Ministry of Education Teacher Regulation Branch www.bcteacherregulation.ca
Manitoba	Teaching Certificates and Qualifications Regulation https://web2.gov.mb.ca/laws/statutes/ccsm/e010e.php
New Brunswick	New Brunswick Teachers' Association www.nbta.ca
Newfoundland & Labrador	Teacher Certification www.ed.gov.nl.ca/edu/k12/teaching/certification.html
Nova Scotia	Teacher Certification http://certification.ednet.ns.ca
Ontario	Ontario College of Teachers www.oct.ca
Prince Edward Island	Department of Education and Early Childhood Development www.gov.pe.ca/eecd/index.php3?number=1027691&lang=E
Quebec	The *Ministère de l'Èducation, du Loisir et du Sport* (MELS) www.mels.gouv.qc.ca/fileadmin/site_web/documents/reseau/formation_titularisation/ PermisEnseignerHorsQuebec_Juillet2012_a.pdf
Saskatchewan	Teacher Certification www.education.gov.sk.ca/certification
Nunavut	Department of Education www.gov.nu.ca/education/information/nunavut-educators-certification-service
Yukon	Department of Education www.education.gov.yk.ca/employment/teacher_certification.html

Mobility provisions under the AIT entitle a teacher to receive a teaching credential from the receiving province or territory under the following conditions.

All applicants must:

- Hold a valid teaching credential from a Canadian province or territory
- Have completed a professional teacher education program consisting of a minimum of 30 semester credit hours of course work and a practicum for teacher certification
- Provide all documents required by the receiving province or territory
- Satisfy any requirements of the receiving province or territory with respect to "fit and proper person," currency of practice, and language proficiency

Applicants fall into one of three categories.

Category 1   Applicants who have completed a minimum of four years of post-secondary education and hold a degree completed at a university that is a member of the Association of Universities and Colleges of Canada or any other university degree(s) deemed equivalent by the receiving province or territory will be issued a teaching credential in the receiving province or territory based on the following:

An applicant who satisfies the basic requirements of the receiving province or territory will be granted a teaching credential by that receiving province or territory.

OR

An applicant who does not satisfy all requirements of the receiving province or territory will be granted a teaching credential valid for a period of time (to be determined by the receiving province or territory). Said time will be a reasonable period during which the teacher will be required to complete successfully any outstanding academic or professional preparation requirements of the receiving province or territory.

Category 2   Applicants who hold a degree or diploma in vocational, technical, or technological studies equivalent to the requirements of the receiving province or territory will be issued a teaching credential by the receiving province or territory based on the following specifications.

Applicants who satisfy the equivalent standards, including any work experience requirements, of the receiving province or territory will be granted an appropriate teaching credential by the receiving province or territory. In some instances, the teacher may be required to complete successfully any outstanding academic or professional preparation requirements of the receiving province or territory during the validity period of the teaching credential.

Category 3   Applicants who hold a teaching credential based on academic or professional preparation that does not fall into either of the above two categories will be assessed on a case-by-case basis by the receiving province or territory, and may be granted a teaching credential in the receiving province or territory if they meet the necessary equivalent academic and professional preparation requirements. In some instances, the teacher may be required to complete successfully any outstanding academic or professional preparation requirements of the receiving province or territory during the validity period of the teaching credential (Council of Ministers of Education, 1999).

WHAT IS THE K–12 TEACHING LANDSCAPE FOR BEGINNING TEACHERS?

From time to time, teacher demand and supply figures have painted a rather bleak picture for those entering the teaching profession. At other times, finding a job in a preferred location has been relatively easy. Typically, teacher shortages and surpluses occur in response to teacher attrition resulting largely from retirements; however, as noted by the

Ontario College of Teachers (2014) in the most recent *Transition to Teaching Report*, some mid-career teachers in Ontario have also left the profession for a variety of reasons, including government policy changes, funding, and increases or decreases in student enrolment.

With very low unemployment rates for elementary and secondary teachers, the supply of new, additional workers very much depends on the output of graduates from teacher education programs. While there may be different prospects for actual employment gains based on changes in funding, policy, and limited growth in the youth population, the majority of openings are expected to occur as a result of retirement. The ease with which you will find your first teaching position is also related to your area of specialization and to the part of the country you wish to reside in. Although the teacher supply and demand varies depending upon the province and territory, beginning teachers (i.e., recent graduates from initial teacher education programs) typically enter the K–12 teaching profession on a limited-term or occasional contract, and then gradually find full-time jobs.

HOW WILL YOU FIND YOUR FIRST K–12 TEACHING JOB?

Most universities have career services to assist you in your post-graduation job search, but it is a good idea to visit and consult with staff in this department well before your graduation in order to take full advantage of the resources and expertise available to you as a preservice student. When considering demand and supply estimates, remember that jobs are still available in oversupplied areas, but job hunting will be more competitive.

The following resources may also be helpful in guiding your teaching-related job search:

- *Apply to Education* is a recruitment database for teachers, school boards, and hiring principals, connecting teachers with employers. Creating an account is free of charge; however, a $12.00 fee is required to store, encrypt, and send applications to a school board. www.applytoeducation.com

- *Education Canada Network (ECN)* is an e-recruitment network for the education community throughout Canada. If you are a Canadian citizen or permanent resident, you can register and apply to jobs for free; however, there is an annual fee for optional advanced services. www.educationcanada.com

- *Jobs in Education* markets itself as a socially conscious organization that helps those interested in teaching in both K–12 and higher education environments connect with employers. It is a free service for job-seekers to locate education jobs in Canada and abroad. www.jobsineducation.com

- *Workopolis* is Canada's largest online job site, and although it is not entirely devoted to the education community, it does include teaching-related job postings. www.workopolis.com

- Assistance is provided free of charge by the Canada Employment Centres, which are located in all major provincial cities. In Quebec, inquiries should be directed to the nearest Centre Travail. However, not all teaching vacancies are listed.

- The Council of Ministers of Education, Canada website provides the names of the ministries/departments of education for each of Canada's 13 education systems. School board information within each system can be accessed via the department's website. It is, however, considered a breach of professional ethics to apply for a position in an area where the board's relationship with the teachers has been declared unsatisfactory by the teachers' association. www.cmec.ca/en

- Prospective teachers seeking positions in Canadian independent schools could get information from Canadian Accredited Independent Schools, which is the national association that accredits the majority of independent schools. www.cais.ca

If you are seeking a teaching-related job in the United States, you might also find the National Association of Independent Schools—U.S. (www.nais.org) and the Independent Schools Association Network—U.S. (http://isanet.ning.com) to be helpful resources to begin your search.

- If you are considering teaching overseas, the Teachers' Overseas Recruiting Fair (TORF) takes place each year at Queen's University. TORF takes place over three days and gives teachers opportunities to have onsite interviews with international school staff and potentially sign contracts. The information is located on the Queen's TORF website. http://educ.queensu.ca/torf

WHAT ARE SOME OTHER CAREER OPPORTUNITIES FOR TEACHERS?

In addition to teaching in K–12 education environments, qualified teachers could find jobs in other education and education-related fields. There are many jobs that, although removed from the world of the K–12 classroom, would nevertheless enable you to use the skills and knowledge you developed during your preservice teacher education program.

The following outline lists several places other than schools where individuals with teaching backgrounds are often employed. The number of education-related careers is likely to increase in the coming decades.

Industry

- Publishers
- Educational materials and equipment suppliers
- Specialized educational service firms
- Communications industries
- Research and development firms
- Management consulting firms
- Education and training consultants
- Any private industry that requires some type of training specialist, educational programming, or instructional design (web-based or face-to-face) of courses

Government

- Jobs in provincial departments of education
- Community colleges
- Other provincial departments that require training specialists or education program development and implementation

Education-Related Associations

- Research centres and foundations
- Professional associations, such as teachers' associations or teachers' unions
- A list of associations within Canadian education community is located at www. international.gc.ca/education/partners-partenaires.aspx?lang=eng

Community Organizations

- Community action programs—neighbourhood health and legal services centres
- Social service agencies—Boy Scouts, Girl Scouts, YMCAs and YWCAs, boys' and girls' clubs, women's shelters, etc.
- Adult education centres

- Museums
- Zoos
- Provincial parks
- Science centres
- Theatre companies
- Hospitals
- Nonprofit organizations and charities devoted to a wide variety of issues, including but not limited to the environment, animals, addiction and substance abuse, human rights and civil liberties, poverty, and sports, may also benefit from the skills and knowledge that qualified teachers possess. A comprehensive list of Canadian registered charities can be found at www.cra-arc.gc.ca/chrts-gvng/lstngs/menu-eng.html, and lists of Canadian nonprofit organizations categorized by alphabet (A–H and I–Z) can be found at https://charityvillage.com/directories/organizations-a-h.aspx and https://charityvillage.com/directories/organizations-i-z.aspx, respectively.

HOW MIGHT YOU PREPARE TO FIND YOUR FIRST TEACHING JOB?

As indicated by the previous discussion, employment opportunities in teaching can be hard to predict and will vary according to your area of teaching specialty, shifts in enrolment due population dispersal, financial well-being of provinces and school boards, and the thoroughness of your preparation and search for a position. Furthermore, many teachers begin their careers as occasional or supply/substitute teachers, who then might become "limited-term contract" teachers, who then become eligible for a full-time position. Thus, three other factors in the search for a teaching job emerge: persistence, patience, and professionalism.

In the remainder of this section, we consider professionalism as well as useful tips for finding out about teaching vacancies, preparing a résumé and cover letter, preparing for interviews, and selecting a position.

Beginning at the Beginning

Teacher candidates often believe that preparing for the job search begins upon graduation from their preservice teacher education program; however, this is not entirely true. The moment you decide you are going to enter this challenging, complex, and rewarding profession, you are actually beginning to prepare to find your first teaching job. Teacher candidates enrolled in preservice teacher education programs are generally considered affiliate or associate members of the provincial association for the teaching profession in their respective jurisdictions.

And within many jurisdictions, teachers are bound by a professional code of conduct or standards of practice. For example, the Alberta Teachers' Association (www.teachers.ab.ca) has a Code of Professional Conduct that specifies the minimum standards of professional conduct of teachers with respect to pupils, school authorities, colleagues, and the profession. Similarly, in Ontario, the Ontario College of Teachers (www.oct.ca) outlines the vision of professional practice in the *Ethical Standards for the Teaching Profession* as well as the principles that describe the knowledge, skills, and values essential to Ontario's teaching profession in the *Standards of Practice for the Teaching Profession*. In New Brunswick, teachers must also adhere to the Code of Professional Conduct of the New Teachers' Association, a code based on principles related to students, teachers, the profession, and the employer (www.nbta.ca/resources/code_of_ethics/Code_of_

Professional_Conduct.pdf). Violations of the professional codes could potentially lead to a charge of unprofessional conduct and, depending on the severity, consequences ranging from a private reprimand to the suspension of teaching certification.

As an associate or affiliate member, you are also held to the same professional codes as certified teachers, and many preservice programs recognize and address the professional codes or standards for the jurisdiction within which the program resides. Familiarizing yourself with the professional codes specific to your program and jurisdiction could serve as a useful tool for your own personal consideration regarding the ethics and standards of the profession you are expected to uphold. You might also want to reflect on how you enact your professional code toward others, the program, and the profession in general.

Finding Out about Teaching Vacancies

Career service: a department or service within the institution that can help graduates with employment support, including developing a résumé package, preparing for an interview, or searching for job opportunities.

Your college or university probably has a **career service** designed to help graduates find jobs. Well before graduation, you might want to meet with staff in this department for guidance and assistance in not only writing a résumé and cover letter but conducting mock or practice interviews as well. Here are some tips that may be helpful as you begin to organize your formal search for vacancies.

Personal networking will play an important role in landing the right job, and your fellow teacher candidates, faculty members, and the teachers, administrators, and staff at your practicum schools could potentially serve as contacts or leads for future employment. For example, members of your faculty may receive requests from education-related organizations seeking teacher candidates for volunteer or paid opportunities.

- Required application materials may vary depending on the jurisdiction where you hope to teach. In addition to consulting the certification requirements for your province or territory to determine what materials are required for certification (and possibly also for application to K–12 teaching jobs), you should use the resources listed in Table 11.1 to determine what additional materials you might need to submit with your résumé and cover letter. For example, are you required to submit a Canadian Criminal Record Check (CRC) with your application? Do you need to include letters of reference or practicum reports? Do you need to include transcripts? Make detailed lists of the materials you will require for both certification and job applications and create digital or paper folders to keep yourself organized.

- You might also consult your student advisor in the preservice program or career services if you have questions about the documentation required for certification and applications.

- Determine the geographical location(s) where you would like to teach. Depending on your circumstances and the teaching vacancies, you may decide to work overseas, or perhaps you want to teach only within local school boards.

- Using the resources listed in the previous section, create a list of school boards or other organizations and employment services that you will access on a regular basis to formally apply for teaching or teaching-related positions. Bookmark these pages on your computer or mobile device. If possible, subscribe to feeds if available.

- School boards typically base their hiring schedules on need. Based on your preferred geographical area(s), contact the school board or consult the school board website to investigate hiring schedules (if available). Schedule frequent and regular opportunities in your calendar to visit the applicable resources for job postings, as positions may suddenly appear for a limited time period.

- When job postings do become available, have your application materials updated and ready to submit. This means that you need to update your résumé and application materials on a regular basis. After each additional workshop you attend or practicum placement you complete, be sure to immediately add it to your résumé, and keep practicum reports filed. If you are short on time, you might want to create a digital file folder in your email devoted to your application materials and résumé. As you complete workshops or gain new experiences to add to your package, simply store emails in the email folder related to the experiences or send yourself an email about the experience.

Attending Job Fairs

Some provinces have used **job fairs** to advertise and fill teaching positions. Job fairs are designed to bring potential teachers to one location for interviews and information sessions. The procedures used for job fairs vary from province to province. There are usually a number of school boards present and other teacher recruitment organizations; some will have specific job openings, whereas others will give candidates a general idea of possible upcoming positions. A common practice is for job fair organizers to offer and require an online registration for the fair.

Job fairs for beginning teachers usually operate like a marketplace, where each school or school board has its own table or area and candidates visit with the administrators or senior board personnel to talk about positions. Often, candidates are given a specific time to arrive at the fair location. These fairs give beginning teachers the opportunity to network, participate in interview situations, and gain an understanding of the hiring process of various school districts.

Candidates attending job fairs should take along a carefully prepared résumé and a letter of inquiry, and be prepared for an interview. Potential employers may have specific vacancies, and may be prepared to offer a contract that day, especially in specialty areas that are hard to fill, such as technology, music, French, and science.

Job fairs: information sessions that bring teacher candidates and potential employees together to provide information about job openings.

Preparing Your Résumé

A résumé presents a concise summary of an individual's professional experiences, education, and skills. Résumés must be typed and, preferably, no longer than one page (two pages at most). Though there is no right way to prepare a résumé, it should present—in a neat, systematic way—key information that will help an employer determine your suitability for a particular position. Because your résumé will most likely be your first contact with an employer, it must make a good impression. Avoid using heavy or significantly designed or coloured paper for your résumé, as it does not photocopy well.

Ordinarily, a résumé contains the following information:

- Contact information
- Education
- Certificates held
- Experience
- Activities and interests
- Honours and offices held
- Professional memberships
- References

Figure 11.1 is an example of a résumé that you can use as a model. Note that this is only one form of a résumé; there are many others available from a variety of sources. Please refer to the resources listed below for additional examples and guidelines. Other examples can be found at http://resumes-for-teachers.com/samples/elementary-teacher-resume.aspx, but peruse these carefully, noting the differences in quality. It is important to realize that although a résumé is your individual reflection of your life in

Aydin Akbaba

Contact Information
641 Montbeck Crescent
Mississauga, Ontario L5G 1P4
Email: AydinA@AydinA.ca
905-891-1248

Education
Bachelor of Education, Intermediate/Senior – Physics, Mathematics
OCT#000000
Ontario, May 2015
Honours Bachelor of Science (Physics),
University of Ontario Institute of Technology, Oshawa, Ontario, June 2014

Teaching and Related Experience
Grade 7 (Science) Teacher Candidate, October 2014, Fictional Middle School, Toronto District School Board, Toronto, ON
- Observed and assisted associate teacher and other teachers who taught the grade 7 students on rotary
- Preassessed student learning and needs and developed innovative lessons to meet the diverse needs of the students
- Created and implemented lessons for understanding structures and mechanisms (Science and Technology curriculum) and comparing and ordering integers (Mathematics curriculum) using a variety of instructional strategies, including inquiry-based learning, cooperative learning, and activity centres
- Organized after-school tutoring program and developed a unit on using the Web in the classroom
- Attended site-based staff and school community council meetings with a associate teacher

Grade 10 Math, Grade 12 Physics Teacher Candidate, March–April 2015, Fictional Secondary School, Toronto District School Board, Toronto, ON
- Created and taught the trigonometry unit for both MPM2D and MFM2P courses
- Adapted associate teacher's lessons for the grade 12 SPH4U unit on gravitational, electric, and magnetic fields to incorporate two lab inquiries and one computer simulation
- Provided after-school help sessions for math and physics students
- Organized a mini-workshop for Science Department on incorporating technology into lessons
- Assisted associate teacher with supervising the prop club for the school-wide musical production
- Attended site-based staff meetings with an associate teacher

Camp Counsellor and Recreation Director, YWCA Summer Camp May–August, 2014
- Directed summer recreation programs for 140 elementary-aged girls
- Supervised and provided leadership training for 10 camp counsellors

Soccer Referee, Fictional Soccer Club, April–September 2012
- Carried out the rules of the game for the players and coaches of the U12 girls' league
- Applied conflict-resolution strategies to facilitate respectful gameplay and interaction amongst players, parents, and coaches

Volunteer Telephone Counsellor, Child Crisis Hotline, June 2011–June 2013

Physics and Mathematics Tutor, University Learning Centre, September 2011–April 2013

Special Skills
Fluent in written and oral English, French, and Turkish
Skilled classical guitarist

Interests
Running, Soccer, Guitar, Water Skiing

Figure 11.1 Sample résumé

Honours
UOIT Entrance Scholarship
UOIT In-Course Scholarship (awarded to undergraduate students who achieve a minimum 3.7 GPA for the previous year of study) 2012, 2013, 2014
Honours Bachelor of Science with Highest Distinction
Bachelor of Education with Highest Distinction

Professional Memberships
Ontario College of Teachers: #000000
Ontario Association for Mathematics Education
Science Teachers' Association of Ontario

Instructional Technology Skills
Word processing, internet and web, optical scanner, interactive whiteboard, LCD projection panel, audience response systems, physics- and mathematics-related instructional software (open educational resources), and a variety of multimedia-related software

Career Objective
Seeking a position in grades 7–12 related to physics, mathematics, or science.

References
References and credentials file available upon request.

Figure 11.1 (*continued*)

brief, there are some formats that are some more serviceable than others. Make certain that your that information is relevant to the job for which you are applying and that it is accessible at a glance. Remember, you want your résumé to stand out in a tasteful and professional manner, and it should be in a format that members of a hiring committee can read quickly. Since there are many individuals, agencies, and online resources to help you with this important presentation, be sure to look for examples of how to proceed and get someone you trust to critique your documentation before you send it in.

The teacher association or federation or even the subject association for your teaching specialty or jurisdiction will often have useful job search resources. Here are some examples of useful resources specific to teaching and from a variety of teacher organizations:

- BC Teachers' Federation—*Job Search Resources* contains résumé guidelines and interview tips. https://bctf.ca/opportunitiesformembers.aspx?id=5494

- Education Canada Network—*Resource Centre* provides tips for creating cover letters, résumés, and preparing for interviews. http://resource.educationcanada.com

- Elementary Teachers' Federation of Ontario—*Professionalism* contains an excellent section on cover letters, résumés, and interview skills. www.etfo.ca/Resources/ForTeachers/Documents/Professionalism.pdf

- The Ontario Music Educators' Association—*Interview Tips from the OMEA Administrative Advisory Council* provides interview preparation strategies and sample interview questions that could also be applicable to a wide variety of subject areas. www.omea.on.ca/2015/04/interview-tips-from-the-omea-administrative-advisory-council

Writing Letters of Application

As a job seeker, you will be required to write letters of application. A letter of inquiry should accompany your résumé and any additional required documentation as specified by the school district. Some school districts use external organizations for this process. In these situations, you will be required to create an online profile and upload pertinent documentation to support your applications for positions. Be prepared not

Aydin Akbaba
641 Montbeck Crescent
Mississauga, Ontario L5G 1P4

May 5, 2015

Dr. Lawrence Walker
Human Resources Department
Toronto District School Board
555 Fictional Road
Toronto, Ontario M5M 5M5

Dear Mr. Walker:

Please accept the attached application package for a daily occasional teaching position for grades 7–12 (posting #100001) with the Toronto District School Board. This June I will receive my Bachelor of Education degree with Intermediate/Senior qualifications in Physics and Mathematics from UOIT in Oshawa, Ontario.

I have just completed my practicum within your school board at Fictional Secondary School. During that period, I taught both applied and academic grade 10 Mathematics, as well as Grade 12 University Physics. The practica provided me with tremendous learning experiences in working with a diverse student population with varying levels of understanding and skill. My previous middle school practicum at Fictional Middle School also provided me with valuable learning experiences in teaching science and mathematics; however, I was able to also observe and assist in other subject areas with the rotary teachers. I believe that these experiences have prepared me well for the diverse range of daily occasional teacher experiences.

My practica allowed me to apply my course work in learning theory, pedagogy, education law, and individual needs and diversity to the classroom environment under the guidance and mentorship of skilled associate teachers and school staff. I immersed myself in the school community and participated in school co-curricular activities. My UOIT Bachelor of Education program allowed me to enhance my educational technology skills, and I even provided a mini-workshop to help teachers within the science department at Fictional Secondary School integrate technology in meaningful ways into their practice. As a result of my rewarding experiences within your school board, my bilingual skills, and my skills in, and enthusiasm for, working with a wide range of students from grades 7 to 12, I believe I could make a significant contribution to your school board as a daily occasional teacher. I welcome the opportunity to discuss this position in an interview, and I am happy to provide any additional information as needed. I thank you in advance for your consideration.

Sincerely,

Aydin Akbaba

Figure 11.2 Sample letter of application

to receive a reply for each letter of inquiry you send out. Many school districts are unable to respond to all inquiries.

Letter of application: a letter written in application for a specific teaching vacancy in a school district.

A **letter of application** (often called a cover letter) indicates your interest in a particular position and outlines your qualifications for that job. As most districts have several vacancies at any given time, it is important that the first sentence of your letter refer to the specific position for which you are applying. The body of the letter should then highlight why you would be an excellent choice to fill that position. Inform the reader that your credentials file will be sent on request or will be forwarded by your placement office. Close the letter by expressing your availability for an interview (see Figure 11.2).

Participating in a Job Interview

The interview is one of the most important steps in your search for an appropriate position. School personnel may ask a wide range of questions, both structured and open-ended,

What questions might be asked in an interview for a teaching position? What questions should you prepare about the teaching position?

regarding topics such as curriculum, planning, assessment, instructional strategies, professionalism, classroom management, and special education, to name a few. Consult the resources listed in the preceding section for more examples of potential interview questions.

Depending on the nature of the teaching position and district, typically, you might be interviewed by two or three school personnel, such as school administrators, department leads, or classroom teachers. The interview enables the district or school to obtain more specific information regarding your probable success as an employee, and it gives you an opportunity to ask questions about what it is like to teach in the district. By asking questions, you can demonstrate your interest in working in the district. Increasingly, just as is the case with model résumés, an Internet search will yield suggestions for interview questions that might be asked, and even suggestions of questions you might choose to ask when the lead interviewer looks at you, smiles, and says, "Your turn." At some point in the interview process, you may be given an opportunity to present brief highlights from your professional portfolio. Or, if you have created Internet or electronic versions of your portfolio, you could give the hiring official(s) the URL or a copy via a USB flash drive.

Accepting an Offer

Imagine that you are notified that a school district would like to hire you. Your job search efforts have paid off! In the competition for positions, you have been successful. However, accepting your first teaching position is a major personal and professional step. Before signing a contract with a district, you should carefully consider job-related questions such as the following:

- In regard to my abilities and education, am I suited to this position?

- Would I like to work with this school's students, administrative staff, and teachers?

- Is the salary I am being offered sufficient?

- Will this position likely be permanent?
- Would I like to live in or near this community?
- Would the cost of living in this community enable me to live comfortably?
- Are opportunities for continuing education readily available?

If you accept the offer, you will need to return a signed contract to the district, along with a short letter confirming your acceptance. As a professional courtesy, you should notify other districts to which you have applied that you have accepted a position elsewhere.

WHAT CAN YOU EXPECT AS A BEGINNING TEACHER?

As mentioned previously, as a beginning teacher your first position will depend on the type of contract (i.e., short-term, long-term, full-time) you secure. If, for example, your first teaching job is a daily occasional position, then your preparation will be different from a first-time teacher beginning a three-month teaching position in a grade 7 classroom.

Regardless of the teaching position you secure, it is still very important to prepare, seek professional supports, and look after yourself to prevent early career burnout. This section provides some suggestions to help you begin preparing for your first teaching job. As discussed earlier, teacher supply and demand comes in waves, and in the current economic and education climates, teachers seeking entry into a school board typically need to first work on a part-time or limited-term contract. There are exceptions based on current shortages or needs of particular specialty areas; however, more than likely, beginning teachers will enter the profession via daily, short-term, and limited long-term contracts prior to taking on a full-time teaching position with a school board. The remainder of the chapter briefly addresses the importance of teacher induction and then focuses primarily on beginning teachers entering the daily occasional teaching role.

Beginning Teacher Induction

Teacher induction is often framed as a transition from preservice preparation to practice, from student of teaching to teacher of students. As these phrases imply, induction brings a shift in role orientation and an epistemological move from knowing about teaching through formal study to knowing how to teach by confronting the day-to-day challenges. Becoming a teacher involves forming a professional identity and constructing a professional practice. Both aspects of learning to teach must unfold in ways that strengthen the beginning teacher's capacity for further growth. (Feiman-Nemser, 2012, p. 120)

Teacher induction programs that provide mentorship and support for beginning teachers have had positive results, including increased teacher retention and student achievement (Kutsyuruba, Godden, & Tregunna, 2014). As we noted at the beginning of the chapter, learning to teach is a complex and ongoing process, and this means that induction is another part of the learning-to-teach process (Feiman-Nemser, 2012). Key tasks of learning to teach in the induction phase include learning the contexts of teaching (students, curriculum, community), designing responsive curriculum and instruction, creating a learning community in the classroom, enacting a beginning repertoire, and developing a professional identity (Feiman-Nemser, 2012).

In a review of Canadian induction programs, Kutsyuruba, Godden, and Tregunna (2014) found great variation in the types of support available for new and beginning teachers across the country. For example, induction or mentorship programs were either mandated and offered by the provincial/territorial government, offered through the teacher association or union or in a hybrid manner between multiple bodies, or offered at the school district level. You are strongly encouraged to learn about the types of supports that are available to you as a beginning teacher within your jurisdiction and to consider how you might seek the supports that address your needs.

Daily Occasional Teaching (Supply or Substitute Teaching)

As previously mentioned, depending on your geographical location and the needs of the jurisdiction where you hope to work, you may more than likely begin your career as a daily occasional teacher (also referred to as a supply or substitute teacher).

The 2014 *Transition to Teaching Report* found that beginning teachers in Ontario remain in the daily supply teacher role for multiple years, and that the number of years has increased over the last decade. For example, one in six teachers remains in the supply teacher role even after five years after graduation from a preservice program (OCT, 2014).

Some beginning teachers appreciate beginning their careers as daily supply teachers, which enables them to ease into the profession and gain experience without the large amount of preparation that is often involved in that challenging first year of teaching. Supply teaching also provides new teachers with opportunities to network with a wide variety of teachers and school administrators, experience a variety of schools and grade levels, and practise various instructional and classroom management strategies with a diverse group of students while maintaining a relatively flexible schedule.

On the other hand, some beginning teachers do not like the inconsistency and unpredictability of supply teaching. If you work for a large school district, you might be travelling to a new school each day, requiring you to quickly learn school policies, procedures, and routines. Depending on the school community, you might feel supported by other staff members or you may feel isolated in the classroom. Depending on the circumstances of the classroom teacher's absence, you may need to adapt quickly and be prepared for a brief or partial set of lesson plans.

The following tips and resources serve as useful guides for beginning occasional teachers:

■ Beginning supply teachers new to a school district often have opportunities to attend workshops for orienting new teachers to the position and school district. Take full advantage of such orientation sessions, and if these sessions are not offered, search the district's website for any staff resources and policies regarding daily occasional work. Become familiar with the policies in general, and if you require additional information, ensure that you have a contact name for someone in the human resources department who can answer your questions.

■ The teacher associations or federations for the jurisdiction often have resources to support occasional teachers. Although the following examples are from Ontario teaching organizations, they still serve as excellent resources for occasional teachers outside this jurisdiction to consider prior to entering the role.

  ■ The Elementary Teachers' Federation of Ontario has created a website specifically for occasional teachers seeking resources on the occasional teacher role, resources by subject, or classroom supports. http://etfo-ots.ca
  ■ The Ontario Secondary School Teachers' Federation's *Survival Skills for Occasional Teachers* provides practical tips to help beginning teachers transition to the occasional teacher role. www.osstf.on.ca/en-CA/resource-centre/educators-resources/survival-skills-for-occasional-teachers

- The Ontario English Catholic Teachers Association's *Daily Occasional Teacher Survival Guide*, written by occasional and classroom teachers, provides helpful tips specific to the occasional teaching role and includes examples of scenarios as well as tips to prepare for those last-minute calls to the school. www.oecta.on.ca

⟫⟫⟫ VOICES FROM THE FIELD | Navigating the New Teacher Landscape

Caitlin Dougherty
Elementary Teacher, Durham District School Board

Dear New Teacher:

So, you're close to finishing or have just finished your final few days in the faculty of education. Congratulations—what an accomplishment! Now, what's the next step? Having been a teacher candidate only a few years ago, I believe this is the time that the patience, perseverance, organization, and professionalism you practised as a teacher candidate will really come into play.

The summer after I graduated from the B.Ed. program at UOIT, I applied to more than 100 Primary/Junior (K–6) positions. Every time a new job was posted, I revised my cover letter and résumé, and if possible, drove to the school to hand in my application in person. I decided that in order to set myself apart from all the other candidates, I needed to make my application stand out somehow. I chose to design a business card to attach to the front of my application. But it couldn't just be any old business card; it needed to pop— and the result was a vibrant blue business card with crisp white print. I received several positive comments about my cards, and how they made my application really stand out from the rest. I often left my application at the office, but a few times I had the opportunity to speak briefly with the principal or vice-principal. It was my first experience interviewing, and I made sure to make an impression at every opportunity. This is something to also remember as you enter schools during your practicum.

Over time, I became more and more confident, and although I hadn't received one response to an application, I felt exhilarated and confident walking through the doors of a new school, thinking that one day, all my hard work would pay off. While I was applying to long-term occasional positions, I knew that my first experience in the classroom would likely be as a daily occasional (supply or substitute) teacher, so I began to focus my attention on achieving an interview with the school board. I updated my application and reapplied as often as possible.

Finally, in late July, I received the call I had been waiting for—I had an interview for the daily occasional teacher list! This was by far the biggest moment in my life to date. In order to prepare for my interview, I focused on everything I had learned as a teacher candidate, including lesson planning, assessment, classroom management, and much more.

I reviewed some of the lesson and unit plans I had created during my field placements, reflected on my experiences in the classroom, and thought about how I could speak to my skills and abilities as a teacher using real examples when possible. My interviewers made the whole process so comfortable, and before I knew it, we were shaking hands and saying goodbye. Not long after that interview, I received the phone call I had been anticipating. My interview had been successful, and I was a shiny, brand-new daily occasional teacher; I was on top of the world.

My first day on the job came with a whirlwind of emotions: I was excited, nervous, and anxious, but I was also proud of what I had accomplished and confident in my ability as a teacher. Before leaving each school at the end of the day, I made sure to leave a detailed note for the homeroom teacher, reporting how the day had gone, and I left my business card in case he or she would like to have me back in his or her classroom in the future. It wasn't long before I was offered an extended occasional position, where I worked as a teacher librarian. The following summer, I received my first long-term occasional (LTO) position teaching grade 2 for 11 weeks. All of those emotions I felt on my first day as a daily occasional teacher came rushing back, but this time even more intensely than ever.

The school principal assigned me a mentor to help me along the way, and I couldn't imagine having been as successful without her support and guidance. She helped me gain more confidence in my abilities as a teacher and taught me how to balance making learning engaging, meaningful, and fun with managing classroom behaviour. She and I have remained good friends, and I owe much of my success in that first LTO experience to her support and assistance. Afterward, I went back to daily occasional for a while, but desperately missed the daily interactions with my own class. I continued to be patient and persevere, and a few months later I received my second LTO position, this time in a grade 1 class, which lasted until the end of the year. This was when I realized that teaching K–3 students, particularly grade 1 French Immersion, was my passion. I found my niche, and I was excited to continue to grow and learn as a teacher.

At the end of that school year, I was offered a full-time position teaching grade 1 French Immersion. All of my hard work and dedication finally paid off, and my hopes and dreams had come to fruition. Just as my first days as a daily and long-term occasional teacher were filled with a variety of emotions, my first day in my very own grade 1 class was incredible beyond words. One difference, however, was that the feelings of excitement, accomplishment, and success pushed all feelings of nervousness aside; today was the day that I had worked so hard to achieve, and I was going to revel in it.

My first year as a permanent teacher was an incredible learning experience, building on the foundations provided by my faculty of education experiences as well as the invaluable experiences as an occasional teacher. I am currently preparing for my second year teaching grade 1, and I can't wait to build on my learning experiences from last year and improve for the coming year. The path from my year in the preservice teacher education program to my position as a grade 1 French Immersion teacher took patience, persistence, organization,

confidence, and professionalism. It is essential to be open to new learning and perspectives different from your own, to be flexible and professional, to make connections, and to show initiative. Although the process of securing full-time employment as a teacher can take time, it's all worth it in the end. There is no growth in teaching without learning; therefore, use every teaching experience as a learning opportunity, cherish those first teaching moments, and don't let your emotions discourage you; let them motivate and encourage you. I wish you all the best as you embark on your new journey as a teacher—the best is yet to come!

Courtesy of Caitlin Dougherty, Elementary Teacher,
Durham District School Board. Used with permission.

HOW WILL YOU CONTINUE YOUR PROFESSIONAL LEARNING?

Preparing, inducting, and developing teachers who are deeply concerned about students, well grounded in their subjects, and excited about learning is critical to the improvement of K–12 education.

—Feiman-Nemser, 2001, p. 1050

As noted earlier, new teacher induction or mentorship opportunities may or may not be readily available to you as a beginning teacher, depending on where you teach as well as the type of position you secure. Unfortunately, daily supply teachers typically do not have as many opportunities for the types of induction or mentorship activities as do their beginning teacher counterparts who have longer and limited-term contracts. In their *Supply Teachers in New Brunswick Report 2012* (www.nbta.ca/misc/SupplyTsSurvey2012.pdf), the New Brunswick Teacher Association (NBTA) found that daily supply teachers appreciated and desired opportunities for professional development. One of the recommendations emerging from the report was to provide supply teachers with improved access to opportunities for professional learning.

Similarly in Ontario, while some daily supply teachers reported engaging in teacher inquiry, collaborative teaching with colleagues, collaborative learning opportunities, engaging with subject or specialist associations, and participating in school self-evaluation, the opportunities were considerably lower for daily supply teachers than for beginning teachers who had secured long-term occasional or regular teaching positions (OCT, 2014). Interestingly, 67 percent of daily supply teachers who were in their first two years of teaching enrolled in Additional Qualifications courses to further enhance their knowledge and skills in various teaching-related topics or subject areas. If you are unable to take a formal professional development type of course, there are still numerous ways for you to continue your professional learning as a beginning teacher, but this will require you to intentionally commit to being a reflective teacher. Zeichner and Liston (2013) identified five key features integral for reflective teaching. After reading the following excerpt from their book *Reflective Teaching: An Introduction* (2nd edition), consider how you embody reflective teaching.

A reflective teacher:

1. Examines, frames, and attempts to solve the dilemmas of classroom practice;

2. Is aware of and questions the assumptions and values he or she brings to teaching;

3. Is attentive to the institutional and cultural contexts in which he or she teaches;

4. Takes part in curriculum development and is involved in school change efforts; and

5. Takes responsibility for his or her professional development. (Zeichner & Liston, 2013, pp. 6–7).

We will briefly consider these five key features of reflective teachers as described by Zeichner and Liston (2013) by providing you with questions to contemplate about your own professional teaching.

1. Reflective teachers examine, frame, and attempt to solve the dilemmas of classroom practice.

   Donald Schön (1987) describes reflection-in-action and reflection-on-action as ways in which teachers and other professionals learn from their experiences and further develop as practitioners. This requires practitioners to intentionally consider or frame situations that may not always have clear solutions as problems to consider. Reflecting upon the problematic situations and reframing the problem to see or think about it differently also requires deliberate action.

   Consider the context of your teaching:
   - Are there some areas of your practice that you do on autopilot without deliberate attention? (Zeichner & Liston, 2013)
   - How do you actively pay attention to the dilemmas of classroom practice?
   - How will you learn more about questions and dilemmas you experience as a practitioner?

2. Reflective teachers are aware of and question the assumptions and values they bring to teaching.

   As we discussed at the beginning of the chapter, teachers' previous experiences as students play a very large role in how they approach their own practice. Unfortunately, prior assumptions about teaching, if ignored, may pose challenges for teachers' growth as professionals.

   Consider some of your own practices and ideas about teaching and learning:
   - How do you describe teaching and learning? From where did you draw to respond to this question?
   - When you are in a classroom, do you consider why you are doing what you are doing? Why? Why not? How might thinking about this help you as a teacher?
   - What or whose perspective(s) do you consider when you attempt to frame and reframe a practice problem?

3. Reflective teachers are attentive to the institutional and cultural contexts in which they teach.

   Consider the contexts of where you teach:
   - How do you consider the school, school board, or school community contexts in decision-making processes within your own practice?
   - If you are not aware of the institutional and cultural contexts within your teaching environment(s), how might you learn more about the people who live within the community?
   - How will you learn about your students' strengths and build upon those strengths?

4. Reflective teachers take part in curriculum development and are involved in school change efforts.

We realize that, depending on the nature of your teaching position, you may not have regular opportunities to develop curriculum and participate in school change endeavours. However, you may still be able to gain access to information specific to your local context if this information is framed within curricular topics and school change initiatives in your jurisdiction.

Consider your school or provincial/territorial area:

- How might you learn more about areas of foci for your particular jurisdiction?
- What key initiatives are currently being implemented, and how might you learn more about these initiatives?
- How might the resources listed earlier in the chapter help you in learning more about curricular and school developments?
- If you do have access to participating in curriculum development or school change efforts, what questions or insights might you contribute to your community? How do you prepare for participating in collaborative initiatives within your school community? How might you learn from your students, their families, your colleagues, school administrators, and other members of the school community?

5. Reflective teachers take responsibility for their professional development.

Your preservice teacher education program only provided a foundation upon which you must build as you progress through your teaching career. After graduation, regardless of your teaching position, the only person who is responsible for your continued growth as a teacher and learner is you. This is applicable to all teachers, even if you are still waiting to secure your first teaching position.

Consider your own professional development needs:

- As a professional, why is it important to continue learning about teaching and learning? Do you think you will ever reach a point where you have learned everything you need to learn about teaching and learning? Why? Why not?
- How do you know what areas you would like to learn more about? How might you go about learning more?
- If you are working consistently within a school or school district, how might you reach out within the school or larger district community to further develop your professional growth?
- Are there professional staff development opportunities for beginning teachers at the school or district level?
- Are there opportunities for you to participate in collaborative processes or discussions regarding instruction, curriculum, or classroom management topics?
- Are there any social media opportunities for you to participate via digital spaces in conversations about teaching and learning?
- How might you learn about free online books or journals related to teaching and learning?
- Are there fellow graduates from your preservice program with whom you might be able to continue professional conversations?

Connected Learning

A plethora of resources for beginning teachers exists in a variety of digital spaces, making it easier for today's educators to access resources, pose questions, and have discussions with other educators via mobile devices. Social networks, collaborative and synchronous digital meeting spaces, Massive Open Online Courses (MOOCs), recorded webinars, livestreaming of presentations, and even web-based conferences are just a few examples of how digital technologies can connect you to other educators, educational resources, and discussions to continue your own learning-to-teach process.

It is impossible to include all of the wide variety of Canadian and international digital listings that encourage teacher professional learning; however, the following examples of Twitter feeds and webinars represent a few starting points for beginning teachers.

Get Connected

> *The power of Twitter is not Twitter itself; it's the connections it facilitates. Those connections can break the sense of professional isolation that many teachers feel within the walls of their own schools while reinvigorating their lesson plans by exposing them to a daily global idea exchange.*
>
> —Max Cooke, Director of Communications for the Canadian Education Association

Twitter is an online social network where you can read and post messages within a 140-character space. You can follow colleagues you know or other professional teacher organizations to keep connected to areas of interest.

Here are some great web-based resources with Twitter feeds:

- *Edutopia: What Works in Education* provides tips, strategies, research, videos, and opportunities to learn about a variety of teaching and learning topics. www.edutopia.org/ **@edutopia**

- *TED Ed* is "a library of short, captivating videos that engage inquisitive learners all over the world." http://ed.ted.com/ @TED_ED

- The Association for Supervision and Curriculum Development (ASCD) is a global community dedicated to excellence in teaching, learning, and leading. ASCD Webinars provide links to activities, archived webinars, and opportunities to connect with other educators www.ascd.org/professional-development/webinars/ascd-webinar-archive.aspx @ASCD

What are some formal and informal forms of continued learning in which you will participate as a teacher? How might you use social media to stay connected to professional communities?

Pavel L Photo and Video/Shutterstock

Lydia Stewart-Goodison

Dr. Diana Petrarca is Associate Professor and founding member of the Faculty of Education at the University of Ontario Institute of Technology. She is currently the Bachelor of Education program director and teaches courses in foundational methods, learning tools, and leadership. In 2013, Dr. Petrarca was awarded the UOIT Teaching Excellence Award for tenured and tenure-track faculty.

As a teacher educator and researcher, Dr. Petrarca has worked with many preservice teacher education students who are excited and passionate about teaching. One thing she has noticed over the years is that these future teachers quickly find themselves surprised and overwhelmed by the demands and workload of the program and profession. She believes that this reflects what other teacher education researchers have found in their work: that many individuals enter preservice teacher education programs with the notion that learning is a simple transfer of information (Feiman-Nemser & Buchmann, 1989) and that "teaching is an enormously difficult job that looks easy" (Labaree, 2000, p. 228).

The deeply entrenched and personal assumptions about teaching and learning that future teachers bring to preservice teacher education programs pose potential challenges to their learning and development as teachers if these assumptions and beliefs about teaching and learning are not addressed (Darling-Hammond & Baratz-Snowden, 2007). This reflects Dan Lortie's (1975) notion of the "apprenticeship of observation," meaning that after many years of schooling, the student experience of participating in and observing schools and teaching from a student perspective largely shapes the conceptions of what it means to teach.

Dr. Petrarca is currently working on a SSHRC-funded research project, *The (Un) Making of the Teacher*, that explores a small group of teacher candidates' (i.e., preservice teacher education program students) conceptions of what it means to "teach" as they progress through a one-year preservice teacher education program. The title of the research emerged when someone, upon learning that Dr. Petrarca is a teacher educator, suggested that she "makes" teachers. Dr. Petrarca considered the comment and replied quickly with, "No, I actually try to 'unmake' teachers by helping beginning teachers challenge their deeply ingrained notions and assumptions about teaching and learning so that they can reframe their ideas as they move forward in their educator journey."

Her "data" consists of videotaped individual and small-group participant interviews, videotaped observations, and video diaries created by the teacher candidate participants. Two key conceptions of teaching and learning that the teacher candidates identified as changing quite drastically very early in the program were the complexity of the role of the teacher and the labour-intensiveness of planning lessons for their students. All participants admitted that while they entered the preservice teacher education program believing that a teacher's work is challenging and labour-intensive, they were quite surprised at the depth and breadth of the work. For example, all the participants felt overwhelmed by the extent to which, as future teachers, they needed to understand learners, the learning process, curriculum, pedagogy, cultural contexts, educational law, and a whole host of other knowledge and skills, and then apply this learning to create safe learning environments where students can have optimal learning experiences.

Educating children and youth is a remarkable responsibility and requires a vast array of skills and knowledge, but unfortunately, at times, the media and films devalue or misrepresent this multifaceted and sometimes challenging role. Through the final product or output of this research, a documentary film, Dr. Petrarca hopes to shed some sorely needed light on the "unmaking" process whereby her participants document their journey and challenge their underlying assumptions about teaching and learning for everyone to see.

SUMMARY

When Do You Actually Start "Becoming" a Teacher?

- Learning to teach is an ongoing and complex process. As you formally begin a preservice teacher education program, you should deliberately examine your own assumptions about teaching and learning and consider how they may pose challenges to your learning.

How Will You Become Certified or Licensed to Teach?

- Mobility provisions under the Agreement on Internal Trade/Teaching Profession entitle a teacher to receive a teaching credential from the receiving province or territory under certain conditions. Teacher certification requirements may vary depending upon the certification agency in the province or territory where teachers wish to teach.

What Is the K–12 Teaching Landscape for Beginning Teachers?

- Teacher demand and supply in content areas and geographic regions influences finding a teaching position.

- Graduates from initial teacher education programs typically enter the K–12 teaching profession on a limited-term or daily occasional contract, and then gradually find full-time jobs.

- In addition to teaching in K–12 education environments, qualified teachers could find jobs in other education and education-related fields.

How Might You Prepare to Find Your First Teaching Job?

- Three important factors in searching for a teaching job are persistence, patience, and professionalism.

- Many beginning teachers begin their careers in limited-term or daily supply teaching positions.

- Be sure to use the tips and resources provided in this chapter to help you learn about teaching vacancies.

- A résumé is a concise summary of an individual's experiences, education, and skills. A letter of inquiry is used to find out if a school district has any teaching vacancies, and a letter of application (or cover letter) indicates an individual's interest in and qualifications for a teaching position.

What Are Some Other Career Opportunities for Teachers?

- In addition to teaching in K–12 education environments, qualified teachers can find jobs in other education and education-related fields, for example in the industry sector, government, research centres, and nonprofit and community organizations.

What Can You Expect as a Beginning Teacher?

- Beginning teachers benefit from induction programs where they are provided with supports and mentoring as they enter the profession.

- Most new teachers begin their careers as occasional teachers (also known as supply teachers or substitute teachers), and depending on the jurisdiction, there may be supports specifically for the occasional teacher role.

How Will You Continue Your Professional Learning?

- New teacher induction or mentorship opportunities may or may not be readily available to you as an occasional teacher. There are still numerous ways for you to continue your professional learning as a beginning teacher, but these require that you intentionally commit to being a reflective teacher.

- Resources for beginning teachers exist in a variety of digital spaces, making it easier to access resources, pose questions, and have discussions with other educators via mobile devices.

APPLICATIONS AND ACTIVITIES

1. Record in your journal the steps you need to take to obtain your teaching certification. Include due dates for tasks, and schedule them in your calendar so that you don't miss important steps and/or deadlines.

2. Peruse some of the interview resources listed in this chapter, and take some time to reflect on your responses. In addition, brainstorm questions you might ask potential employers.

3. Consider the school district or jurisdiction where you would like to find your first teaching position. Go to the district's website and find out information about the size, facilities, mission statement, school philosophy, special programs, type of populations it serves, and professional development opportunities for teachers.

4. Develop and practise a "one-minute sell" stating who you are and what skill sets and experience set you apart from other beginning teachers.

5. Draft a preliminary professional résumé. (Review the section in this chapter titled "Preparing Your Résumé" and the résumé prepared by Aydin Akbaba in Figure 11.1.)

   In your résumé, under "Personal Data," provide a current address and a permanent address. Under "Education," specify an anticipated graduation date. Under "Experience," include work experience that indicates your ability to work with people. Begin with your most recent experiences and present information in reverse chronological order. When you have finished your preliminary résumé, exchange with a classmate and critique each other's work.

6. Reflect on your assumptions about teaching and learning at the outset of your preservice teacher education program. How have they changed (or not)? Why have they changed (or not changed)?

Chapter 12
Education Issues for the Twenty-First Century

Andresr/Shutterstock

FOCUS QUESTIONS

1. What knowledge and skills will prepare students for a global information age?

2. How can schools and teachers provide an outstanding education for all learners?

3. How can community-based partnerships address social problems that hinder students' learning?

4. How will the charter school movement affect equity and excellence in education?

5. What does the future hold for your province or territory?

6. What can teachers and schools learn from international education?

7. What is our vision for the future of education?

At the turn of the century and into the new century, more and more educators are working in a world of intensifying and rapid change. . . . New technologies, greater cultural diversity, the skills called for in a changing economy, restructured approaches to administration and management, and a more sophisticated knowledge-base about teaching and learning, are all pulling students and their teachers in new directions.

—Mission Statement excerpt,
International Centre for Educational Change,
Ontario Institute for Studies in Education,
University of Toronto

>>> **READERS' VOICES** | What Is the Future of Education?

The future of education should revolve around creating strong, inclusive, collaborative classroom experiences for students and teachers. Education needs to be relevant to the world around students; they need to be engaged in the digital spaces and through the technologies they are consuming. Educators need to understand that it is okay for the students to teach them from time to time, as in many cases students are the experts.

—BRENDAN, teacher education program, first year

I envision education systems that are centred on problem-based learning, allowing students to be creative and free thinkers. Rather than using rigid textbook problems that have little real-world application, I envision students focusing on the pertinent issues of today—environment, economy, technology, and diversity.

—SABRINA, teacher education program, first year

Though no one has an educational crystal ball that can give a totally accurate glimpse of how the profession of teaching will evolve during the twenty-first century, powerful forces are shaping schools and teaching. Moreover, thousands of teachers are collaborating and playing key leadership roles in shaping that future. The conditions under which teachers will work in this century will provide a dramatic contrast to those that many teachers experienced throughout much of the previous century. Isolation, lack of autonomy and self-governance, and few chances for professional growth are being replaced by collaboration, empowerment, stronger professionalism, and opportunities to provide leadership for educational change.

WHAT KNOWLEDGE AND SKILLS WILL PREPARE STUDENTS FOR A GLOBAL INFORMATION AGE?

What knowledge and skills will students need to succeed in a global information age? Teachers in every generation have asked this question. Sixteen years into this century, the answer is confounded by conflicting theories, expectations, and values. One thing everyone agrees on, however, is that increasing cultural diversity in Canada and other countries and increasing global economic interdependence will call for strong communication and cooperation skills. People will need to be able to live together well and use environmental resources wisely. To equip students to do this, teachers will need to ensure that all students develop knowledge, skills, attitudes, and values in key areas. This will involve engaging students as partners in their own learning through an emphasis on inquiry-based learning. It also means that teachers will need to harness the capacity of digital technologies to engage students and to improve academic achievement. For their part, school districts will need to continue to provide support for educators in preparing students for a rapidly changing, technology-driven, globalized world.

Literacy in Language, Mathematics, and Science

To solve the problems of the future, students will need to be able to write and speak clearly and succinctly. To access critical information from enormous data banks, they will need to be able to read complex material with a high degree of comprehension. Moreover, the continued development of user-friendly technologies, such as voice-activated software, will not reduce the need for high-level language arts literacy. In addition to strong skills in reading and writing, students will need to be able to apply mathematical and scientific concepts to solve new problems. For example, they will need to be able to analyze unfamiliar situations, pose appropriate questions, use trial-and-error methods to gather and evaluate relevant data, and summarize results.

New Technology Skills

Students of the future will also need to attain high levels of skill in digital technologies. They will need to be able to access, understand, and manipulate digital information as both consumers and producers. To teach students skills in accessing the vast stores of information that proliferate their lives, our nation's schools will become more technologically rich, and teachers more technologically sophisticated. In such an environment, students will not only learn to use computers as tools to access information, but they will also use them to communicate globally and to generate creative solutions to real-world problems.

Problem Solving, Critical Thinking, and Creativity

Students of the future will need to be able to think rather than to remember. Although the information that students learn in schools may become outdated, the thinking processes they acquire will not. These processes focus on the ability to find, obtain, and use information resources for solving problems or taking advantage of opportunities. Students will need to learn how to cope with change, how to anticipate alternative

What knowledge and skills for the twenty-first century does this learning activity support? What else will students need to know and be able to do in the future?

Christopher Futcher/E+/Getty Images

future developments, how to think critically, and how to analyze and synthesize large amounts of complex data.

Forecasts about the future share one common factor—they place a priority on creative thinking to solve problems. The acquisition of structured bodies of knowledge, while important, is not sufficient preparation for the future. Students must learn to think creatively. Students who are stretched to develop their creativity today will become the adults who solve tomorrow's problems.

Can creative thinking be taught? William J. J. Gordon (1968, 1971a, 1971b, 1975), who has devoted his career to the study of creativity, believes it can. Gordon developed synectics, a teaching method based on the thinking process, which is designed to "teach" creativity through the use of metaphor and analogy. **Synectics** is based on the assumptions that (1) creativity is important; (2) creativity is not mysterious; (3) in all fields, creative invention draws from the same underlying intellectual processes; and (4) the creativity of individuals and groups is similar (Joyce, Weil, & Calhoun, 2004). In his 2006 TED Talk, "Do Schools Kill Creativity?," creativity expert Sir Ken Robinson argues that we need to create an education system that nurtures rather than undermines creativity.

Synectics: a method for "teaching" creativity through the use of metaphors and analogies.

Social Awareness, Communication Skills, and Team Building

In an increasingly connected world, students must be able to communicate with people from diverse cultures. The ability to create a better world in the future, then, will surely depend on our willingness to celebrate our rich diversity through the kind of communication that leads to understanding, friendly social relations, and the building of cohesive teams.

An important lesson for students is that poverty, discrimination, violence, crime, and unequal opportunities, wherever they occur, affect us all. To solve these and other social problems, students will need to become socially aware, politically active, and skilled in conflict resolution strategies.

Global Awareness and Conservation Skills

Tomorrow's students will need to recognize the interconnectedness they share with all countries and with all people. Our survival may depend on being able to participate intelligently in a global economy and respond intelligently to global threats to security, health, environmental quality, and other factors affecting the quality of human life. The curriculum of the future must emphasize cultural diversity in order to honour Canada's changing population. Respect for the views and values held by others, an orientation toward international cooperation for resolving global issues, and practical knowledge of and skills in, for example, the conservation of natural energy resources are issues that will continue to challenge students in the future.

Physical and Mental Health and Wellness Education

With ever-rising health care costs, an increasing incidence of mental illness, the spread of pandemic and epidemic diseases such as Ebola and SARS, higher risks of cancer, and longer life spans, it is imperative that students acquire appropriate knowledge, skills, and attitudes in the area of health education. To live healthy lives, then, students of tomorrow will need consumer education in order to select from among an increasingly complex array of health care services. In addition, they will need to be able to make informed choices among alternatives for the prevention or treatment of problems relating to substance abuse, nutrition, fitness, and mental health. Sex education, still a matter for debate in some communities, seems more critical today than at any time in the past.

Ethics and Global Citizenship

The school culture and the curriculum reflect both national and community values. The traditional practice of using values-clarification activities in the classroom, however, has been criticized by some for promoting relativism at the expense of family values or religious doctrines. Yet as we witness the effects of violence in schools, racial intolerance, sexual exploitation of children, drunk driving, white-collar crime, false advertising, unethical business practices, excessive litigation, and so on, many citizens are calling for schools to pay more attention to issues of public morality and ethical behaviour. In response to harassment and intimidation that can lead to violence in the hallways, for example, many Canadian schools have implemented safe school policies and procedures (see Chapter 5). Good citizenship goes beyond the local context of the school community, however, and school districts across Canada are teaching our students about global awareness, Internet safety, and global and digital citizenship. Students need to be respectful and considerate in their interactions with others, both online and offline.

Aesthetic Awareness

Another challenge for teachers and schools is to encourage creativity and greater appreciation for the arts. Many observers of Canadian education contend that emotional, spiritual, aesthetic, and reflective, or meditative, dimensions of life receive less emphasis than analytical thinking and practical life skills. Although literature and drama are standard fare in curricula, for example, most students know little about music, painting, and sculpture. Public school students are rarely taught art history or principles of design or other criteria for evaluating creative works. As a result, students may lack the concepts and experiences that lead to an appreciation of beauty and the development of aesthetic judgment.

Lifelong Self-Directed Learning

The key educational priority that should guide teachers of the future is to cultivate within each student the ability, and the desire, to continue self-directed learning throughout his or her life.

It has often been said that one of the primary purposes of schooling is for students to learn how to learn. In a world characterized by rapid social, technological, economic, and political changes, all persons must take responsibility for their own learning. Career changes will be the norm, and continuing education over a lifetime will be necessary.

HOW CAN SCHOOLS AND TEACHERS PROVIDE AN OUTSTANDING EDUCATION FOR ALL LEARNERS?

Although we don't know exactly how teaching will change during this century, we do know that teachers will continue to have a professional and moral obligation to reach all learners, many of whom will be from environments that provide little support for education.

Although the family will continue to remain a prominent part of our culture, evidence indicates that many children live in families that are under acute stress. Contemporary family arrangements are more fluid than ever before. There are a larger number of single parent, same-sex, and blended families, and more parents are cohabitating rather than getting married.

Equity for All Students

A dominant political force in the twenty-first century will be continued demands for equity in all sectors of Canadian life, particularly education. For example, the legalities of school funding laws will be challenged where inequities are perceived, and tax reform measures will be adopted to promote equitable school funding. Classroom teachers will continue to be held accountable for treating all students equitably.

In Chapter 5, you learned about the importance of preparing instructional materials and strategies to meet the learning needs of students from diverse cultural, ethnic, and linguistic backgrounds. In Chapter 6, you learned how to create an inclusive classroom to meet the needs of all students, regardless of their developmental levels, intelligences, abilities, or disabilities. In addition, you should create a learning environment in which high-achieving and low-achieving students are treated the same way. Thomas Good and Jere Brophy (2008) reviewed the research in this area and found that several teacher behaviours revealed an unequal treatment of students. The behaviours identified include waiting less time for low-achieving students to answer questions, interacting with them less frequently, giving them less feedback, calling on them less often, seating them farther way, failing to accept and use their ideas, smiling at them less often, making less eye contact, praising them less, demanding less, grading their tests differently, and rewarding inappropriate behaviours.

Effective teachers establish respectful relationships with *all* students; they listen to them, they give frequent feedback and opportunities to ask questions, and they demand higher-level performance. In their assessment of students' learning, they give special attention to the questions they ask of students. Research indicates that most questions teachers ask are **lower-order questions** (those that assess students' abilities to recall specific information). Effective teachers, however, also ask **higher-order questions**, which demand more critical thinking and answers to questions such as "Why?" and "What if?" In addition, to reach all learners and prepare them for the future, effective teachers provide students with active, authentic learning experiences.

Lower-order questions: questions that require students to recall specific information.

Higher-order questions: questions that require the ability to engage in complex modes of thought (e.g., synthesis, analysis, and evaluation).

Active, Authentic Learning

Since the 1970s, educational researchers have increased our understanding of the learning process. Though learning theorists and researchers disagree about a definition for *learning*, most agree that **learning** "occurs when experience causes a relatively permanent change in an individual's knowledge or behavior" (Woolfolk, 2007, p. 244). Research into multiple intelligences and universal design has broadened our understanding of this definition of learning. In addition, research in the fields of neurophysiology, neuropsychology, and cognitive science will continue to expand our knowledge of how people think and learn.

Our growing understanding of learning indicates that all students learn best when they are actively involved in authentic activities that connect with the "real world." Small-group activities, cooperative learning arrangements, field trips, experiments, and integrated curricula are among the instructional methods you should incorporate into your professional repertoire.

Learning: changes in behaviour the individual makes in response to environmental stimuli; the acquisition and organization of knowledge and skills.

HOW CAN COMMUNITY-BASED PARTNERSHIPS ADDRESS SOCIAL PROBLEMS THAT HINDER STUDENTS' LEARNING?

Earlier in the book, we examined social problems that affect schools and that place students at risk of dropping out: poverty, family stress, substance abuse, violence and crime, teen pregnancy, STDs, and suicide (see Chapter 5). We also looked at intervention programs that schools have developed to ensure the optimum behavioural, social, and academic adjustment of at-risk children and adolescents to their school experiences: peer counselling, full-service schools, school-based inter-professional case management, compensatory education, and alternative schools and curricula. Here, we describe innovative, community-based partnerships that some schools have developed recently to prevent social problems from hindering students' learning.

The range of school–community partnerships found in today's schools is extensive. For example, the Toronto District School Board, Canada's largest school district, partners with a vast number of community organizations to offer employment services, settlement services, language services, and skills development to families of students in their system. All school districts partner with local and provincial social service agencies, which make significant contributions to students' education.

The Community as a Resource for Schools

To assist schools in addressing the social problems that impact students, many communities are acting in the spirit of a recommendation made by Ernest Boyer: "Perhaps the time has come to organize, in every community, not just a *school* board, but a *children's* board. The goal would be to integrate children's services and build, in every community, a friendly, supportive environment for children" (Boyer, 1995, p. 169). Partnerships between communities and schools form when individuals, civic organizations, or businesses select a school, or are selected by a school, to work together for the good of students. The ultimate goals of such projects are to provide students with better school experiences and to assist students at risk.

Civic Organizations To develop additional sources of funding, many local school districts have established partnerships with community groups interested in improving educational opportunities. Some groups, such as the Lions Club or Girls Inc., have actively supported a variety of school projects. Others adopt or sponsor schools and enrich their educational programs by providing funding, resources, or services.

Volunteer Mentor Programs Mentorship is a trend in community-based partnerships today, especially with students at risk. Parents, business leaders, professionals, and peers volunteer to work with students in neighbourhood schools. Goals might include dropout prevention, high achievement, improved self-esteem, and healthy decision making. Troubleshooting on lifestyle issues often plays a role, especially in communities plagued by drug dealing, gang rivalry, casual violence, and crime. Mentors from organizations such as Big Brothers and Big Sisters of Canada also model success for participating children and adolescents.

Corporate–Education Partnerships Business involvement in schools has taken many forms, including, for example, contributions of funds or materials needed by a school, release time for employees to visit classrooms, adopt-a-school programs, cash grants for pilot projects and teacher development, educational use of corporate facilities and expertise, employee participation, and student scholarship programs. Extending beyond advocacy, private sector efforts include job initiatives for disadvantaged youths, in-service programs for teachers, management training for school administrators, minority education and faculty development, and even construction of school buildings.

Involvement of the business community with education is not without its critics. Maude Barlow, in her book *Class Warfare: The Assault on Canadian Schools* (1994, pp. 1–8), points out, in strong language, that the effort of transnational corporations to infiltrate Canadian schools is a serious problem that must be addressed. She writes about the United States, where Burger King operates fully accredited high schools, as does its main competitor, McDonald's, and writes also of New Zealand, where "students are writing exams brought to them by Reebok and Coca Cola . . . [with] the corporate logos on each exam" (Barlow, 1994, p. 7). Chief executive officers of 99 Canadian corporations surveyed by the *Financial Post* "said they should be, and very soon would be, in the schools (Barlow, 1994, p. 7). More recently, Canadian filmmaker Jill Sharpe visited school districts in Canada and the United States to explore how corporate investments impact schools, curricula, and students, and produced the 2007 documentary *Corporations in the Classroom*.

Schools as Resources for Communities

The view that schools should serve as multipurpose resources *for* the community is a shift from the more traditional perspective of schools needing community support to meet the needs of students affected by social problems. By focusing not only on the development of children and youth, but on their families as well, schools ultimately enhance the ability of students to learn. As Ernest Boyer (1995, p. 168) puts it, "No arbitrary line can be drawn between the school and life outside. Every [school] should take the lead in organizing a *referral service*—a community safety net for children that links students and their families to support agencies in the region—to clinics, family support and counseling centers, and religious institutions."

Beyond the School Day   Many schools and school districts are serving their communities by providing educational and recreational programs before and after the traditional school day and during the summers. Increasingly, educational policy-makers recognize that the traditional school year of approximately 190 days is not the best arrangement to meet students' learning needs. Several school districts across Canada have considered alternatives to the traditional schedule of classes from September to June, with July and August off for summer vacation.

Proposals for year-round schools and educationally oriented weekend and after-school programs address the educational and developmental needs of students impacted by social problems. Proponents of year-round schooling argue that many students forget some of what they have learned the previous school year when they are away from school for two months. This so-called "summer achievement gap" correlates to socioeconomic status, with a greater gap created for more disadvantaged students. Research suggests, however, that there is only a limited impact and that gaps between advantaged and disadvantaged students continue to grow despite the length of time between holidays (Brown, 2009). To find out more about a study by the Toronto District School Board on year-round schooling, see www.tdsb.on.ca/Portals/research/docs/reports/RT_YRSchoolingRevSept09.pdf.

While only about 100 schools across Canada have adopted a year-round schedule, modified schedules and the creation of programs that extend beyond the traditional school day can address the needs of parents and the requirements of the work world. Every day, thousands of elementary-age "latchkey" children arrive home to an empty house. After-school educational and recreational programs are designed to (1) provide children with supervision at times when they might become involved in antisocial activities, (2) provide enrichment experiences to widen children's perspectives and increase their socialization, and (3) improve the academic achievement of children not achieving at their potential during regular school hours (Fashola, 1999). A study conducted at the University of Toronto showed that children who participated in after-school programs over the course of several years completed their homework more often, achieved higher grades, and were less likely to drop out of school. They also had improved social skills and more positive attitudes about school (Mishna, 2013).

Social Services   In response to the increasing number of at-risk and violence-prone children and youth, many schools are also providing an array of social services to students, their families, and their communities. Investing money in special programming for this population to prevent future problems is more cost effective than dealing with the fall-out later (incarceration/detention, school dropouts, gang violence, mental health, and addiction issues).

The Canadian Youth in Challenging Contexts (CYCC) Network was established in 2011 to improve the mental health and well-being of children and youth in challenging contexts. The work of the CYCC Network primarily focuses on knowledge mobilization and seeks to link evidence-informed practice to what service providers are learning and to local community knowledge. In their 2013 *Youth Engagement* report, the authors indicate that engaging in an activity "outside the self" in a "meaningful and sustained" way leads to more positive mental health as well as healthier connections with peers and supportive adults (p. 6). This in turn decreases risky behaviour such as substance use and risky sexual activity and increases participation in more positive activities that build community. The report also suggests that giving students a voice is a powerful way to engage them in community activities.

Community programs that promote youth engagement are becoming more popular across the country. For example, RE-create Outreach Art Studio in Hamilton, Ontario, runs an art program for at-risk youth. In June 2015, the organization held an exhibit that featured art that communicated a story about the relationship between Hamilton's homeless and marginalized youth and the public spaces they inhabit. The project gave local youth a voice to make recommendations about how these spaces might be made more accommodating. Programs like these promote civic engagement while building community.

In Chapter 5, we looked at how some schools provide educational, medical, social, and/or human services, and how the school-based inter-professional case management model uses case managers to deliver services to at-risk students and their families. Although many believe that schools should not provide such services, an increase in the number of at-risk students suggests that the trend is likely to continue, with more schools requiring a coordinating organization that brings together the array of community agencies working with children and youth in order to coordinate efforts, increase support, and monitor progress. More social initiatives, such as parent support, groups, infant nurseries, and programs for students with special needs, are likely to form a more prominent part of future Canadian schooling.

HOW WILL THE CHARTER SCHOOL MOVEMENT AFFECT EQUITY AND EXCELLENCE IN EDUCATION?

Charter schools: independent schools, often founded by teachers, that are given a charter to operate by a school district or province, with the provision that students must demonstrate mastery of predetermined outcomes.

One of the most interesting experiments in Canadian education during the past decade has been the development of **charter schools**. While there are only 13 such schools in Canada, all in Alberta, these schools present a new direction in educational reform.

Charter schools offer a modern and flexible approach to the complex teaching environment of today. While held fully accountable to a publicly elected government body, they control their own budget, staffing, programs, and services to better meet the needs of their students.

Charter schools are independent, innovative, outcome-based public schools. The charter school concept allows a group of teachers, parents, or others who share similar interests and views about education to organize and operate a school. Charters can be granted by a local school district or by the province. In effect, charter schools offer a model for restructuring that gives greater autonomy to individual schools and promotes school choice by increasing the range of options available to parents and students within the public school system. Proponents of charter schools argue that public schools, which are regulated by provincial governments, do not have the required flexibility to meet the needs of all students (Lawton & Brown, 2012).

To open a charter school, an original charter (or agreement) is signed by the school's founders and a sponsor (usually the local school board). The charter is a specific document that outlines the school's special purpose(s) and the rules that govern its operation (Lawton & Brown, 2009). The charter also specifies the learning outcomes that students will master before they continue their studies. Charter schools, which usually operate in the manner of autonomous school districts (a feature that distinguishes them from the alternative schools operated by many school districts), are public schools and must teach all students. If admission requests for a charter school exceed the number of available openings, students are selected by a draw.

Because charter schools are designed to promote the development of new teaching strategies that can be used at other public schools, they can prove to be an effective tool for promoting educational reform and the professionalization of teaching in the future. Moreover, charter schools give teachers unprecedented leadership opportunities and the ability to respond quickly to students' needs.

The United States and For-Profit Schools

Other than a short-lived experiment in Nova Scotia with Public–Private Partnership (P–3) schools, there are no **for-profit schools** in Canada. However, in the United States—which often provides us with a hint of future educational directions—one of the most controversial educational issues for the twenty-first century is the practice of turning the operation of public schools over to private, for-profit companies. Advocates of the **privatization movement** believe that privately operated schools are more efficient; they reduce costs and maximize "production"—that is, student achievement. Opponents are concerned that profit, rather than increasing student achievement, is the real driving force behind for-profit schools. Critics are also concerned that school districts may not be vigilant enough in monitoring the performance of private education companies.

Like Maude Barlow, Canadian essayist and novelist John Ralston Saul is very concerned about the possible privatization of our schools. In his article "In Defence of Public Education" (Saul, 2002, p. 12) he states: "Our country has been built, from the very beginnings of its democratic system 150 years ago, upon a happy linkage between democracy and public education." He makes the additional comment that "if society and its leaders are not willing to fund the [educational] system, then we collectively, and they specifically, must all take responsibility for the decline of our own children and the children of our fellow citizens" (Saul, 2002, p. 12). Whether Canadian schools will succumb to the private sector's desire to become more deeply involved in education as a business initiative is an unsettled issue.

For-profit schools: schools that are operated, for profit, by private educational corporations.

Privatization movement: moving an organization or institution from public (government) ownership to private ownership.

WHAT CAN TEACHERS AND SCHOOLS LEARN FROM INTERNATIONAL EDUCATION?

The world has truly become smaller and more interconnected as telecommunications, cyberspace, and travel by jet bring diverse people and countries together. As we continue to move closer together, it is clear that education is crucial to the well-being of every country and to the world as a whole. Governments around the world are working together to develop programs and innovations that have the potential to be scaled and replicated. There is much to be learned from the efforts of other countries that are dealing with remarkably similar issues. For example, European Schoolnet was formed by 31 Ministries of Education across Europe. The knowledge-building network was established to enable educators in Europe to share experiences and problems and to learn from each other. One of their main objectives is to "identify evidence, scalable and transferable practice and emerging priorities in education in Europe" (www.eun.org). In Canada, Michael Fullan (2014), an expert in whole-system education reform, is a partner in a global initiative called New Pedagogies for Deep Learning, which also involves teachers, schools, school districts, and education experts from Spain, the United States, Denmark, Australia, Singapore, Portugal, England, and Ireland. As a result of the universal challenges that confront educators, we are entering an era of increasing cross-national exchanges that focus on sharing resources, ideas, and expertise for the improvement of education worldwide.

Comparative Education

Comparative education: the comparative study of educational practices in different countries.

As the nations of the world continue to become more interdependent, educational policies and practices will be influenced increasingly by **comparative education**—the study of educational practices in other countries. Comparative education studies show how school systems in other countries work and how Canadian students compare with students in other countries on certain measures of schooling and achievement. In addition, research in comparative education enables professionals to share information about successful innovations internationally. Teachers can collaborate on global education projects and test change models that other countries have used to help match educational and societal needs and goals.

Canada is part of the Organisation for Economic Co-operation and Development (OECD), whose mission is to promote policies in a variety of sectors, including education, with the aim of improving the economic and social well-being of people worldwide. OECD's Program for International Student Assessment (PISA) ranks countries based on scores in reading, mathematics, and science testing. Canadian students regularly rank highly in international assessments. In 2009, in reading, Canada ranked fifth behind China, Korea, Finland, and Singapore; in mathematics, Canada ranked eighth; in science, Canada ranked seventh. In a 2010 McKinsey report, Ontario was selected as one of the 20 school systems around the world "that have achieved significant, sustained, and widespread gains in student outcomes on international and national assessments from 1980 onwards" (Mourshed, Chijioke, & Barber, 2010).

Lessons from Other Countries

Canadian educators can learn a great deal from their colleagues around the world regarding what works and what doesn't work in other countries. When considering the possibility of adopting practices from other countries, however, it is important to remember that educational practices reflect the surrounding culture. When one country tries to adopt a method used elsewhere, a lack of support from the larger society may doom the new practice to failure. In addition, it is important to recognize that the successes of another country's educational system may require sacrifices that are unacceptable to our way of life. Nevertheless, there are many practices around the world that Canadian educators and policy-makers might consider.

Support for Teachers and Teaching   In many other countries, teachers and the profession of teaching receive a level of societal support that surpasses that experienced by teachers in Canada. For example, teachers in many countries are accorded greater respect than their Canadian counterparts. In addition, most Canadian teachers have about one hour or less per day for planning, and the average teacher works an average of 50–55 hours per week. Although teachers are often criticized in the media for making too much money and having their summers off, Canadian teachers actually work between 10 and 20 hours per week outside of regular school hours and earn salaries below the OECD average (OECD, 2014). Class sizes also tend to be higher across Canada than in many other OECD countries, where the trend has been to reduce sizes to an OECD average of 24 students in an elementary class.

Internationally, high teacher attrition rates have led many countries to invest more resources in beginning-teacher support programs in order to provide novice teachers with positive experiences. In Canada, mentoring and induction support for beginning teachers occurs in a variety of ways, including provincially and locally. In some areas, provincial teacher associations or federations oversee these programs (Kutsyuruba et al., 2014). For example, the Ontario Ministry of Education implemented a New Teacher Induction Program (NTIP) in 2010. NTIP offers the following supports:

1. Orientation for all new teachers to the school and school board

2. Mentoring for new teachers by experienced teachers

3. Professional development and training in areas such as safe schools, classroom management, effective communication, and instructional strategies

In British Columbia, a New Teacher Mentoring Project was established in 2012 by the BC Teachers' Federation, in partnership with the University of British Columbia and the BC School Superintendents' Association. The goals of the NTMP are as follows:

■   To provide a coherent, research-based, and sustainable system of support for teachers in their early years throughout the province

■   To be responsive to the diversity and distinctiveness of district cultures and practices in all regions of B.C.

■   To ensure that mentorship is nonevaluative and nonremedial, and that participation is voluntary

■   To demonstrate joint commitment from the participating district administration and teacher union

■   To reach out to educators in rural areas of B.C.

■   To provide professional learning through inquiry and critical reflection on practice

Parental Involvement   The powerful influence of parental involvement on students' achievement is well documented (Banda, Coleman, & Matuszny, 2007; Olsen & Fuller, 2010). Japan probably leads the world when it comes to parental involvement in education. Japanese mothers frequently go to great lengths to ensure that their children get the most out of the school's curriculum. The *kyoiku mama* (literally, education mother) will tutor her child, wait for hours in lines to register her child for periodic national exams, prepare healthy snacks for the child to eat while studying, forgo television so that her child can study in quiet, and ensure that her child arrives on time for calligraphy, piano, swimming, or martial arts lessons. Though few Canadian parents might wish to assume the role of the *kyoiku* parent, it seems clear that Canadian students would benefit from greater parental involvement.

Dr. Marianne Larsen

Dr. Marianne Larsen is Associate Professor at the Faculty of Education, University of Western Ontario. She has a long-standing commitment to and passion for teaching and research in comparative and international education. One of her current areas of research is international service learning (ISL). Over the past few years, she has conducted a number of case studies about the complex ways that experiences such as ISL shape university students, including preservice teachers, as global citizens. Her recent work in this area focuses on the impact of ISL on host communities and envisioning more mutually beneficial ways to engage host communities in planning and facilitating ISL programs, especially in Global South settings. Dr. Larsen is the editor of *International Service* *Learning: Engaging Host Communities* (2016), which involved researchers and host community members from Southern and Western Africa and Central and North America who collaborated in sharing their research and their experiences working with ISL programs. Her interest in ISL is part of a broader interest in the overall processes and effects of the internationalization of higher education. She has been researching how internationalization policies are taken up on the ground as well as the role of higher-education leaders in advancing internationalization agendas. Dr. Larsen also has an interest in history, theory, and methodology in the field of Comparative and International Education. She has researched and written about the state of comparative education in Canadian universities, historically and in the contemporary moment; historical research in the field; and new ways of conceptualizing the research that takes place in comparative and international education. Her current research on global citizenship builds on her previous related research and teaching. A few years ago, she developed a curriculum resource book for elementary school teachers, in partnership with the Thames Valley District School Board and the NGO Free the Children, entitled *ACT! Active Citizens Today: Global Citizenship for Local Schools*. You can download the teaching kit, which is widely used by social studies teachers across Canada, at www.tvdsb.on.ca/act.

Pressure to Excel

There have been many calls to make Canadian schooling more rigorous; a longer school calendar, longer school days, more homework, and harder examinations, for example, have all been proposed. These changes, it is assumed, would increase student achievement and find favour with the majority of the public that wants greater academic rigour. More often than not, Japan, Korea, and other Asian countries are held up as models for the direction Canadian education might emulate. But should Canadian schools be patterned after schools in these countries? Several people who have studied and experienced Asian schools are beginning to think not. If parents want their children to achieve at the level of Asian students, which is often only a few percentage points higher on standardized examinations, they must understand the sacrifices made by Asian students and their parents. Most students in Japan, for example, attend a private school or see a tutor in addition to regular school hours. This places financial pressure on many families who cannot afford to pay for additional schooling but feel it is necessary for their children to compete for entrance into top schools. A recent report from the Japanese Cabinet Office revealed that there was a sharp increase in suicides for children aged 18 and under during two periods of the year—the two periods that coincide with the end of school breaks and the beginning of school terms. To combat the issue, a campaign targeting parents and teachers is attempting to promote extra vigilance during these susceptible periods.

Lessons from Finland

While Asian countries (Singapore, Hong Kong, South Korea, Japan, and Taiwan) still rank highest in mathematics and sciences according to the OECD's PISA tests, Finland continues to outrank other European countries, Canada, the United States, and Australia. Finland's education system has become a model for the rest of the world. Systemic reform, which began in the 1970s and continues today, is yielding consistently high results across schools, regardless of a family's socioeconomic status or a student's ability. An OECD report, *Finland: Slow and Steady Reform for Consistently High Results*, attributes the country's success in educating all of its children to a publicly funded, equitable school system that focuses on teaching excellence and a philosophy of collective school responsibility for students who are struggling.

All schools in Finland share a national core curriculum, but it is not as prescriptive as Canadian curricula. All teachers in Finland, regardless of whether they teach elementary or secondary school, are required to obtain a master's degree prior to receiving a teaching qualification. This required fifth year focuses on theory and practice and is paid for by the state. Interestingly, there are no mandated standardized tests in Finland, aside from one exam at the end of high school, and teachers in Finland spend fewer hours at school each day and less time in the classroom than their North American counterparts. Homework is kept to a minimum and compulsory schooling does not begin until age seven.

Researchers who have studied the educational practices in Finland note that the quality of teachers and teaching is the foundation of Finland's success. Linda Darling-Hammond (2010) examined the teacher preparation programs in Finland and observes:

> Teachers' preparation includes both extensive course work on how to teach—with a strong emphasis on using research based on state-of-the-art practice—and at least a full year of clinical experience in a school associated with the university. These model schools are intended to develop and model innovative practices, as well as to foster research on learning and teaching.
>
> Within these model schools, student teachers participate in problem-solving groups, a common feature in Finnish schools. The problem-solving groups engage in a cycle of planning, action, and reflection/evaluation that is reinforced throughout the teacher education program and is, in fact, a model for what teachers will plan for their own students, who are expected to use similar kinds of research and inquiry in their own studies. Indeed, the entire system is intended to improve through continual reflection, evaluation, and problem-solving, at the level of the classroom, school, municipality, and nation. (pp. 25–26)

Probably the most admirable principle of the Finnish system is the steadfast determination that teachers and schools have to ensure that all students have the same opportunities to succeed.

WHAT IS OUR VISION FOR THE FUTURE OF EDUCATION?

Imagine that it is the year 2025, and we are visiting Westside Elementary School in a medium-size city. All the teachers at Westside are fully certified and have salaries that are on par with those of other professionals with comparable education and training. About half of the 55 teachers at Westside have also earned advanced professional certification. These teachers are known as lead teachers and may earn as much as $100 000 per year. Westside has no principal; the school is run by an executive committee of five lead teachers elected by all teachers at the school. One of these lead teachers is elected to serve as committee chair for a two-year period. In addition, the school has several student interns and educational assistants who are assigned to lead teachers as part of their graduate-level teacher-preparation program. Finally, teachers are assisted by a diagnostician; a technology specialist; a computer specialist; a video specialist; a social worker; a school psychologist; four counsellors; special remediation teachers in reading, writing, mathematics, and oral communication; bilingual and English as a second language teachers; and special-needs teachers.

What vision of the school of the future does this photograph suggest? What might you add to the image to achieve a broader perspective on tomorrow's teachers and learners?

michaeljung/Shutterstock

Westside Elementary operates many programs that illustrate the close ties the school has developed with parents, community agencies, and businesses. The school houses a daycare centre that provides after-school employment for several students from the nearby high school. On weekends and on Monday, Wednesday, and Friday evenings, the school is used for adult education and for various community group activities. Executives from three local businesses spend one day a month at the school visiting with classes and telling students about their work. Students from a nearby college participate in a tutoring program at Westside, and the college has several on-campus summer enrichment programs for Westside students.

Westside has a school-based health clinic that offers health care services and a counselling centre that provides individual and family counselling. In addition, from time to time, Westside teachers and students participate in service-learning activities in the community. At the present time, for example, the grade 5 classes are helping the city develop a community garden in an empty space near the school.

All the facilities at Westside—classrooms, the library, the multimedia learning centre, the gymnasium, the cafeteria, and private offices for teachers—have been designed to create a teaching–learning environment free of all health and safety hazards. The cafeteria, for example, serves meals based on findings from nutrition research about the best foods and methods of cooking. The school is carpeted, and classrooms are soundproofed and well lit. Throughout, the walls are painted in soft pastels tastefully accented with potted plants, paintings, wall hangings, and large murals depicting life in different cultures.

The dress, language, and behaviours of teachers, students, and support personnel at Westside reflect a rich array of cultural backgrounds. In the cafeteria, for example, it is impossible not to hear several languages being spoken and to see at least a few students and teachers wearing non-Western clothing. From the displays of students' work on bulletin boards in hallways and in classrooms to the international menu offered in the cafeteria, there is ample evidence that Westside is truly a culturally diverse and inclusive school and that gender, race, sexual orientation, and class biases have been eliminated.

Each teacher at Westside is a member of a teaching team and spends at least part of his or her teaching time working with other members of the team. Furthermore, teachers determine their schedules, and every effort is made to assign teachers according to their particular teaching expertise. Students attend Westside by choice for its excellent teachers;

its curricular emphasis on problem solving, human relations, creative thinking, and critical thinking; and its programs for helping at-risk students achieve academic success.

Instruction at Westside is supplemented by the latest technologies. In this bring your own device (BYOD) environment, students can use their own smartphones or tablets, or they can access the mobile devices available in each classroom. There are no desks in rows; students either sit in pods around multi-touch tables or use the flexible seating at the various learning centres around the room. Teachers use blended learning, or a "flipped classroom" approach, that requires students to view videos or access content prior to class so that in-class time can be spent on hands-on activities, projects, and class discussions. To better engage their students, teachers gamify elements of their classrooms through the use of simulations or digital badges. Some teachers gamify assessment by replacing letter grades with "experience points" and encouraging their students to "level up." Keeping parents connected to their children's learning via mobile apps is also helping to improve student achievement.

Every classroom has a multimedia suite that, in addition to everyday use, is used frequently during satellite video conferences with business executives, artists, scientists, scholars, and students at schools in other provinces and countries. Westside Elementary's technological capabilities permit students to move their education beyond the classroom walls as they determine much of how, when, where, and what they learn.

Tomorrow's Teacher

Teaching and the conditions under which teachers work may change in some fundamental and positive ways during the next two decades. Teaching will become increasingly professionalized, for example, through such changes as more lengthy and rigorous preservice teacher education programs, salary increases that put teaching on par with other professions requiring similar education, greater teacher autonomy, and an expanded role for teachers in educational policy-making. There will be more teachers who are African, Arabic, and Asian Canadian, along with members of other ethnic and racial groups. There will be greater recognition for high-performing teachers and schools through such mechanisms as master teacher programs and career ladders. Tomorrow's teachers will achieve new and higher levels of specialization. The traditional teaching job will be divided into parts. Some of the new jobs appear on the following list:

- Learning diagnostician
- Researcher for software programs
- Courseware writer
- Curriculum designer
- Mental health diagnostician
- Evaluator of learning performances
- Evaluator of social skills
- Small-group learning facilitator
- Large-group learning facilitator
- Media-instruction producer
- Home-based instruction designer
- Home-based instruction monitor

Though we cannot claim to have handed you an educational crystal ball so that you can ready yourself for the future, we hope you have gained both knowledge and inspiration from our observations in this chapter. Certainly, visions of the future, such as the one of Westside Elementary, will not become a reality without a lot of dedication and hard work. The creation of schools like Westside will require commitment and vision on the part of professional teachers like you.

What Does the Future Hold for Your Province or Territory?

Predict the future of education in your province or territory in terms of the following list of innovations and trends. Rate each development according to whether it already exists in your province or when you think it will become common practice in the schools—within the next 5 or the next 15 years. If you don't know the status of a particular development in your province, find out. Add at least one new item representing a trend in your province that does not appear on the list. When you have finished rating the items, share your results with your classmates. What reasons or evidence will you give for your predictions?

Innovation/Trend	Now	Within 5 years	Within 15 years	Not Likely
1. Alternative, authentic assessment of students' learning	___	___	___	___
2. Cross-age tutoring/mentoring	___	___	___	___
3. Peer counselling/peer coaching	___	___	___	___
4. Faculty teams/team teaching	___	___	___	___
5. Business–school partnerships	___	___	___	___
6. Community–school teaming	___	___	___	___
7. School-based clinics/counselling centres	___	___	___	___
8. Organized after-school programs	___	___	___	___
9. Year-round schools	___	___	___	___
10. School development	___	___	___	___
11. Equity in school funding	___	___	___	___
12. Open enrolment/school choice	___	___	___	___
13. Smartphones in the classroom	___	___	___	___
14. Student computer networking	___	___	___	___
15. Video teleconferencing	___	___	___	___
16. Interactive multimedia	___	___	___	___
17. Multimedia distance learning	___	___	___	___
18. Sex education	___	___	___	___
19. Mental health education	___	___	___	___
20. Character education curricula	___	___	___	___
21. Globalism/diversity education	___	___	___	___
22. Aesthetics orientation	___	___	___	___
23. Alcohol and drug intervention	___	___	___	___
24. Reduction of gender bias	___	___	___	___
25. Reduction of discrimination based on race, sexual orientation, class	___	___	___	___
26. Inclusion of students who have special needs	___	___	___	___
27. Teacher empowerment	___	___	___	___
28. Constructivist teaching approaches	___	___	___	___
29. Charter schools	___	___	___	___
30. Corporate–education partnerships	___	___	___	___
31. For-profit schools	___	___	___	___
32. Makerspace_____	___	___	___	___
33. _____	___	___	___	___

Education in 2025?

It is not unrealistic to imagine that teachers in schools during the year 2025 will be well-paid, self-governing professionals who have developed specialized areas of expertise. This vision becomes more possible with each teacher who makes a commitment to its realization. However, the constancy of change is a reality with which all teachers must learn to contend. As American educator Dr. J. R. Harris writes in the following essay, change can be a very positive thing, but the teaching profession is not without its constancies.

Heraclitus is credited with observing approximately 2500 years ago that nothing endures but change; this remark is repeated nowadays to the point of cliché. Change being a constant is good news for educators. Why? In most North American jurisdictions, young persons surrender approximately 12 000 hours to some sort of formal schooling. Most students are conscious during these hours, and for most young people, these hours are tendered during what is arguably the most dynamic time of their lives. Consequently, it is fervently hoped that educators guide, orchestrate, and assist with enormous change during each student's time in their care. If describable (measurable) change does not occur each school year for each and every student, then student needs are not being met, which implies that schools operate in a state of educational deficiency.

Change itself, however, can promote both advancements and a feeling that we can never catch up; the advent of information technology serves as an example of both of these conditions. It is astonishing to think that in 1970 personal computers did not exist. Computers were primitive and cumbersome, and one dared not "fold, staple, or mutilate" in any way the data cards used to feed information to computers. Less than half a century later, it is estimated that over 1 billion personal computers are in use, some of them so small that they require a small stylus for use, the average person's fingers being too large to be effective. As their size has decreased, computers have developed inversely and exponentially in terms of storage capacity. Nevertheless, there are constraints to advances in the realm of information technology, including:

■ The cost of staying "up to date,"

■ Having technology sufficient for and appropriate to the needs of all learners,

■ The explosion of available information with no certain way of ensuring the quality of that information,

■ Time management,

■ The increasing ease with which learners can plagiarize, and

■ The protection of individual privacy, to name but a few.

The reality and inevitability of upheaval in curriculum for schools seems to bear out the view that the only constant is change.

■ Ongoing change in the teaching of mathematics and language arts appears to be an enduring norm.

■ Many jurisdictions have many more mathematics courses at the secondary level than was the case in the 1960s when students took algebra and geometry.

■ The aims and methodologies of teaching language arts go through regular cycles. How many decades has it been since it was standard pedagogical practice for English teachers standing "in front" of a room full of students to refer to the "subject," "predicate," or "subordinate clause" of a sentence?

■ In the 1960s and 1970s, courses with names such as (or similar to) Personal Development and Relationships, Career and Life Management, and Computer Technology *did not exist.*

- How many people in 1960 imagined that a day would come when students living in remote, rural communities could earn their high school certificate though the delivery of curriculum via technology-based virtual learning environments?

Schools continue to evolve to reflect societal pressures with respect to priorities in curriculum, equity issues, human rights, and personal safety. A few examples follow:

- Second language immersion
- Lack of program availability resulting in litigation
- The multilingual/multiethnic classroom
- First Nations curriculum
- The inclusive classroom
- School board positions in which someone's job description includes words such as "human rights" and/or "cross cultural understanding"
- Substance abuse education programs
- The school's "lockdown practice" becoming as prevalent as the fire drill

In the twenty-first century, it is demanded that education budgets be stretched further and further. The size of most school systems administered by school boards has increased dramatically, and the busing of students to and from school now governs school daily schedules so that buses can perform more than one run for different populations. Consequently, sometimes students in one school start classes at 8:00 a.m., with students being dismissed at 2:00 p.m., while in a neighbouring school, teaching starts at 9:10 with dismissal occurring at 3:30. Economy thus dictates that busing has a direct and powerful effect on most schools' scheduling, curriculum, teaching, learning, and extracurriculars.

There have always been those who enjoy portraying the teaching profession as an easy job with a short working day enjoyed by overpaid teachers with numerous holidays and long lazy summers beckoning them toward their natural state of sloth. While this stereotype has never been true, the teaching profession and teachers are adapting to reflect the times:

- In many jurisdictions, teacher education programs require prospective teachers to complete a two-year program after their first baccalaureate degree.
- Increasingly, teachers are accountable to register for, participate in, and file with their school board their completion of a certain number of in-service/professional development experiences during a stipulated time frame.
- It is expected that teachers function adeptly in classrooms composed of increasingly diverse student populations.
- Increasingly, the idea of year-long schooling is moving from theoretical concept to legislated probability.

Having made these observations, though, it is important to note that some things really do remain the same. Students still need:

- Teachers who try to understand them;
- Teachers who are concerned with the entire learner (not just the course syllabus);
- Teachers who strive to provide their students with a rich and meaningful delivery and mediation of curriculum;
- Teachers who are concerned for the well-being, emotional health, and safety of their students;
- Teachers who offer encouragement;

- Teachers who provide students with appropriate curricular and co-curricular challenges;

- Teachers who provide students with frequent and fair assessment and evaluation;

- Teachers who teach appropriately to the assessments they set for students; and

- Teachers who establish a caring and respectful learning environment for *all* students.

About 600 years after Heraclitus, Marcus Aurelius uttered a statement linking the ever-changing universe to individual thought. If teachers make available the pedagogical conditions listed above, then (to paraphrase Marcus Aurelius) there is reason to hope for our students; regardless of the persistence of change in education, the lives of learners will be what their thoughts make them.

Source: Essay by J. R. Harris, 2007; original material prepared for this text.

SUMMARY

What Knowledge and Skills Will Prepare Students for a Global Information Age?

- Conflicting theories, expectations, and values make it difficult to answer what students need to know and be able to do in the future; however, increasing cultural diversity and global economic interdependence call for communication and cooperation skills and wise use of environmental resources.

How Can Schools and Teachers Provide an Outstanding Education for All Learners?

- To reach all learners, teachers must understand how some families are under acute stress, how crime and violence impact students' lives, and how to develop curricula for equity and diversity as well as instructional repertoires that develop the potential of students from varied backgrounds.

- In addition to preparing instructional materials and strategies for students from diverse backgrounds, teachers treat students equitably when they treat high- and low-achieving students the same way. Research has identified several teacher behaviours that reflect inequitable treatment of low-achieving students: waiting less time for them to answer questions, interacting with them less frequently, giving them less feedback, calling on them less often, seating them farther away, failing to accept and use their ideas, smiling at them less often, making less eye contact, praising them less, demanding less from them, grading their tests differently, and rewarding inappropriate behaviours.

- Effective teachers establish positive relationships with all students by listening to them, giving frequent feedback and opportunities to ask questions and engage in inquiry-based learning, and demanding higher-level performance by asking higher-order questions that require more critical thinking.

How Can Community-Based Partnerships Address Social Problems That Hinder Students' Learning?

- Communities help schools address social problems that hinder students' learning by providing various kinds of support.

- Civic organizations raise money for schools, sponsor teams, recognize student achievement, award scholarships, sponsor volunteer mentor programs, and provide other resources and services to enrich students' learning.

- Corporate–education partnerships provide schools with resources, release time for employees to visit schools, scholarships, job initiatives for disadvantaged youth, in-service programs for teachers, and management training for school administrators.

How Will the Charter School Movement Affect Equity and Excellence in Education?

- Charter schools—independent, innovative, outcome-based schools—were developed in response to perceived inadequacies in the public schools. A charter is obtained from a local school district or a provincial/territorial government.

What Can Teachers and Schools Learn from International Education?

- The challenges and opportunities for teachers in the twenty-first century are remarkably similar worldwide, and teachers in different countries can learn much from one another. Comparative education, the study of educational practices in other countries, enables educators to collaborate internationally.

- A study conducted by the Organisation for Economic Co-operation and Development (OECD) indicates that Canadian schools are among the best in the world.

- Many other countries provide greater support for teachers and the teaching profession, have greater parental involvement, and take more steps to nurture beginning teachers.

What Is Our Vision for the Future of Education?

- Teaching and the conditions under which teachers work may change in some fundamental and positive ways during the next two decades.

- Globalization, technological innovation, cultural diversity, and other factors will determine what teaching might be like by the year 2025.

APPLICATIONS AND ACTIVITIES

1. Select one of the following areas and create an infographic that forecasts changes that will occur during the next two decades: education, energy, environment, food, the economy, governance, family structure, demographics, global relations, media, and technology. On what current data are your forecasts based? How might these changes affect teaching and learning?

2. Think about two children you know and project them into the future, 20 years from now. What skills are they likely to need? Which talents should help them? How can schools better promote the development of these skills and talents?

3. Environmental Conservation: If students are to live in a world where all living things exist in a sustainable environmental balance, they must be made aware of how such a state can be achieved. In a small group, select a grade level and one of the following subject areas: English language arts, mathematics, social studies. Determine three things that you as a teacher could do, within the grade level and subject area you selected, to encourage your students' participation in attaining such a condition. Be prepared to present your recommendations to the class.

4. Values (Character) Education: There is a general belief among parents and other members of the public that schools should inculcate in students good moral values. Many teachers, however, are uncomfortable with the idea of teaching a values-based curriculum. Instead, they prefer to teach about values, presenting all sides of an issue and then letting students make their individual decisions as to the position they adopt. In a small-group situation, examine the values listed below. Determine which ones, if any, should be directly taught to students at the junior high level. Be prepared to make a report for the class.

   - Stealing is always wrong.
   - Democracy is the best possible system of government.
   - Moderate drinking of alcohol is acceptable for those of legal age.
   - Prejudice against others is never acceptable.

5. Investigate the websites for the Organisation for Economic Co-operation and Development (OECD) and the Canadian Teachers' Federation (CTF) and gather information on educational systems in other countries. In what areas of the curriculum, and at what levels, is the achievement of Canadian students at, or above, the international average? What conclusions about the strengths and weaknesses of Canadian schools can you draw from your analysis of these data?

6. Interview the principal at a nearby school and ask him or her to describe what the school will be like in 10 years. Then interview several teachers at the school. Compare the forecasts of the principal with those of the teachers. What might account for any differences you find?

7. Search for examples of school–community partnership arrangements in the local school district. Find out if these partnerships are progressing and propose a new one based on your specific knowledge of the community.

PART FOUR YOUR TEACHING FUTURE

Teachers are lifelong learners. How will you continue to learn and grow as you gain experience as a teacher? Imagine what teaching will look like in 20 years, and consider how you will adapt to the evolving role of the teacher in a digital age.

_____

_____

_____

_____

_____

_____

_____

_____

_____

_____

_____

_____

_____

_____

_____

_____

_____

_____

_____

_____

_____

_____

_____

_____

_____

_____

_____

_____

_____

_____

_____

_____

_____

_____

_____

Glossary

A

Academic learning time (p. 187): the amount of time students spend working on academic tasks with a high level of success (80 percent or higher).

Accord on Teacher Education (p. 261): a set of pan-Canadian education initiatives grounded in shared values about teacher education, educational leadership, and educational research.

Action research (p. 272): classroom-based study, by teachers, of how to improve their instruction.

Aesthetics (p. 55): the branch of axiology concerned with values related to beauty and art.

Aims of education (p. 116): what a society believes the broad, general purposes of education should be—for example, socialization, achievement, personal growth, and social improvement.

Agreement on Internal Trade/Teaching Profession (AIT) (p. 285): an intergovernmental trade agreement that requires professions' regulatory bodies to ensure labour mobility in Canada.

Allocated time (p. 187): the amount of time teachers allocate for instruction in various areas of the curriculum.

American tradition (p. 63): an approach to education that the frontier experience of the United States modified to make it more practical than the British model upon which it was originally based.

Anti-racist education (p. 127): a movement that focuses on examining the power imbalances between racialized people and nonracialized/white people.

Assertive discipline (p. 192): an approach to classroom discipline requiring that teachers establish firm, clear guidelines for student behaviour and follow through with consequences for misbehaviour.

Assistive technology (p. 167): technological advances (usually computer-based) that help exceptional students learn and communicate.

Attention deficit disorder (ADD) (p. 161): a learning disability characterized by difficulty in concentrating on learning.

Attention deficit hyperactivity disorder (ADHD) (p. 161): a learning disability characterized by difficulty in remaining still so that one can concentrate on learning.

Authentic learning tasks (p. 186): learning activities that enable students to see the connections between classroom learning and the world beyond the classroom.

Axiology (p. 55): the study of values, including the identification of criteria for determining what is valuable.

B

Behaviourism (p. 60): a philosophical orientation based on behaviouristic psychology that maintains that environmental factors shape people's behaviour.

Benefit packages (p. 8): various negotiated nonsalary compensation provided to teachers in addition to their negotiated salaries.

Between-class ability grouping (p. 185): the practice of grouping students at the middle and high school levels for instruction on the basis of ability or achievement; often called *tracking*.

Block scheduling (p. 187): a high school scheduling arrangement that provides longer blocks of time each class period, with fewer periods each day.

Bring your own device (BYOD) (p. 217): a policy that allows students to use their personal devices to access an organization's wireless network.

British North America Act (BNA Act) (pp. 71, 86): the act that established Canada as a nation and laid the framework for public institutions such as schools.

C

Canadian Charter of Rights and Freedoms (p. 165): 1982 document that enshrined rights and freedoms to serve as the guiding law of the land and that applies to all levels of government.

Canadian Education Association (CEA) (p. 270): a network of educators advancing ideas for greater student and teacher engagement in public education via research and knowledge mobilization.

Canadian Parents for French (p. 94): nationwide volunteer organization to promote teaching of French in schools, especially French immersion programs.

Canadian School Boards Association (CSBA) (p. 89): national voice of school boards in Canada comprised of 10 provincial school board associations.

Canadian Society for the Study of Education (CSSE) (p. 271): Canada's largest organization of professors, students, researchers, and practitioners in education. It serves as a national voice for those who create educational knowledge, prepare teachers and educational leaders, and apply research in the schools, classrooms, and institutions of Canada.

Canadian Teachers' Federation (CTF) (p. 269): national bilingual Canadian organization with 240 000 members from all provinces and territories.

Career service (p. 290): a department or service within the institution that can help graduates with employment support, including developing a résumé package, preparing for an interview, or searching for job opportunities.

Caring classroom (p. 181): a classroom in which the teacher communicates clearly an attitude of caring about students' learning and their overall well-being.

CEGEP (p. 75): *collège d'enseignement général et professional*, a Quebec junior college that students can attend for one or two years of study.

Character education (p. 150): an approach to education that emphasizes the teaching of values, moral reasoning, and the development of "good" character.

Charter schools (p. 316): independent schools, often founded by teachers, that are given a charter to operate by a school district or province, with the provision that students must demonstrate mastery of predetermined outcomes.

Child abuse (p. 107): any kind of harm that causes injury to a child, including physical, sexual, and emotional abuse, and neglect.

Child Abuse Registry (p. 135): record kept of individuals who have abused children.

Choice theory (p. 193): an approach to classroom management, developed by psychiatrist William Glasser, based on a belief that students will usually make good choices (i.e., behave in an acceptable manner) if they experience success in the classroom and know that teachers care about them.

Cisgender (p. 129): when one's biological sex matches his or her gender identity and expression.

Classroom climate (p. 178): the atmosphere or quality of life in a classroom, determined by how individuals interact with one another.

Classroom culture (p. 123): the "way of life" characteristic of a classroom group; determined by the social dimensions of the group and the physical characteristics of the setting.

Classroom management (p. 187): day-to-day teacher control of student behaviour and learning, including discipline.

Classroom organization (p. 185): how teachers and students in a school are grouped for instruction and how time is allocated in classrooms.

Code of ethics (p. 97): a set of guidelines that defines appropriate behaviour for professionals.

Cognitive development (p. 147): the process of acquiring the intellectual ability to learn from interaction with one's environment.

Cognitive science (p. 61): the study of the learning process that focuses on how individuals manipulate symbols and process information.

Collaborative consultation (p. 168): an approach in which a classroom teacher meets with one or more other professionals (such as a special educator, school psychologist, or resource teacher) to focus on the learning needs of one or more students.

Collective bargaining (p. 101): a process followed by employers and employees in negotiating salaries, hours, and working conditions; in most provinces, school boards must negotiate contracts with teacher organizations.

Comparative education (p. 317): the comparative study of educational practices in different countries.

Computer-assisted instruction (CAI) (p. 246): the use of computers to provide individualized drill-and-practice exercises or tutorials to students.

Computer-enhanced instruction (CEI) (p. 248): the use of computers to provide students with inquiry-oriented learning experiences, such as simulations and problem-solving activities.

Computer-managed instruction (CMI) (p. 248): the use of computers to evaluate and diagnose students' learning needs and record students' progress for teachers to monitor.

Concrete operations stage (p. 147): the stage of cognitive development (seven to 11 years of age) proposed by Jean Piaget in which the individual develops the ability to use logical thought to solve concrete problems.

Constitution Act, 1982 (p. 86): historic act amending Canada's Constitution, most notably by setting out the *Charter of Rights and Freedoms* and by providing methods to further amend the Constitution without the British Parliament.

Common or Case Law (p. 103): law developed by courts and judges based on the interpretation of provincial and federal laws, and then recorded and published for use in successive cases.

Constructivism (p. 61): a psychological orientation that views learning as an active process in which learners *construct* understanding of the material they learn—in contrast to the view that teachers transmit academic content to students in small segments.

Constructivist teaching (p. 197): a method of teaching based on students' prior knowledge of the topic and the processes they use to *construct* meaning.

Cooperative education programs (p. 224): programs designed to develop employability skills and help students explore career options by offering both an in-school and a work experience component.

Cooperative learning (p. 185): an approach to teaching in which students work in small groups, or teams, sharing the work and helping one another complete assignments.

Core curriculum (p. 212): a set of fundamental courses or learning experiences that are part of the curriculum for all students at a school.

Core French (p. 220): second language instruction that emphasizes basic communication skills, language knowledge, and appreciation of French culture.

Corporal punishment (p. 106): physical punishment applied to a student by a school employee as a disciplinary measure.

Council of Ministers of Education, Canada (p. 89): established in 1967, acts as a forum for provincial and territorial ministers of education to meet and discuss matters of mutual interest.

Criminal record (p. 135): record kept of individuals convicted of criminal offences.

Critical multiculturalism (p. 127): an approach that focuses on examining the impact of structural racism in schools and encourages educators and students to work toward social change.

Critical pedagogy (p. 59): educational theory and teaching and learning practices designed to raise students' critical awareness regarding oppressive social conditions.

Critical reflective practice (p. 268): the highest level of reflection in which the teacher asks: "How does my teaching positively influence students in their lives beyond the classroom?"

Cross-age tutoring (p. 200): a tutoring arrangement in which older students tutor younger students; evidence indicates that cross-age tutoring has positive effects on the attitudes and achievement of tutee and tutor.

Cultural identity (p. 125): an overall sense of oneself, derived from the extent of one's participation in various subcultures within the national macro-culture.

Culture (p. 123): the way of life common to a group of people; includes knowledge deemed important, shared meanings, norms, values, attitudes, ideals, and view of the world.

Curriculum (p. 204): the school experiences, both planned and unplanned, that enhance (and sometimes impede) the education and growth of students.

Cyberbullying (p. 10): the use of digital technology devices such as cell phones and the Internet to harass, threaten, or intimidate others.

D

Dame-schools (p. 63): colonial schools, usually held in the homes of widows or housewives, for teaching children basic reading, writing, and mathematical skills.

Democratic classrooms (p. 189): a classroom in which the teacher's leadership style encourages students to take more power and responsibility for their learning.

Departmentalization (p. 123): an organizational arrangement for schools in which students move from classroom to classroom for instruction in different subject areas.

Deputy minister of education (p. 89): appointed civil servant whose position is directly below the minister of education; responsible for the day-to-day management of the department of education.

Digital divide (p. 254): inequities in access to computer technology that are related to minority-group status, family income, and gender.

Direct instruction (p. 195): a systematic instructional method focusing on the transmission of knowledge and skills from the teacher to the students.

Discovery learning (p. 199): an approach to teaching that gives students opportunities to inquire into subjects so that they "discover" knowledge for themselves.

Distance learning networks (p. 234): two-way, interactive telecommunications systems used to deliver instruction to students at various locations.

Diversity (p. 123): differences among people in regard to gender, race, ethnicity, culture, and socioeconomic status.

Due process (p. 100): a set of specific guidelines that must be followed to protect individuals from arbitrary, capricious treatment by those in authority.

Duty of care (p. 103): special obligation of teachers to prevent reasonably foreseeable harm to those under their supervision. Duties often clarified through regulations, school board bylaws, policy statements, and job descriptions.

E

E-learning (p. 234): education that is delivered via the Internet, satellite broadcast, interactive television, or CD-ROM.

Education act (p. 89): provincial statute that creates an education system and provides for its management and funding.

Educational philosophy (p. 51): a set of ideas and beliefs about education that guide the professional behaviour of educators.

Educational Resources Information Center (ERIC) (p. 272): a U.S. national information system made up of 16 clearinghouses that disseminate descriptions of exemplary programs, results of research and development efforts, and related information.

Educational research (p. 265): the investigation and study of various topics related to education.

Educational technology (p. 234): computers, software, multimedia systems, and advanced telecommunications systems used to enhance the teaching–learning process.

Emotional intelligence (p. 117): a level of awareness and understanding of one's emotions that allows the person to achieve personal growth and self-actualization.

English as a second language (ESL) (p. 79): English language training for individuals whose first language is not English.

English tradition (p. 63): a model of education based on church control, class, and separate schools for boys and girls.

Epistemology (p. 54): a branch of philosophy concerned with the nature of knowledge and what it means to know something.

Essentialism (p. 57): formulated in part as a response to progressivism, this philosophical orientation holds that a core of common knowledge about the real world should be transmitted to students in a systematic, disciplined way.

Ethical dilemmas (p. 100): problem situations in which an ethical response is difficult to determine; that is, no single response can be called "right" or "wrong."

Ethics (p. 55): a branch of philosophy concerned with principles of conduct and determining what is good and evil, and right and wrong, in human behaviour.

Ethnic group (p. 124): individuals within a larger culture who share a racial or cultural identity and a set of beliefs, values, and attitudes and who consider themselves members of a distinct group or subculture.

Exceptional learners (p. 158): students whose growth and development deviate from the norm to the extent that their educational needs can be met more effectively through a modification of regular school programs.

Existentialism (p. 58): a philosophical orientation that emphasizes the individual's experiences and maintains that each individual must determine his or her own meaning of existence.

Explicit curriculum (p. 205): the behaviour, attitudes, and knowledge that a school intends to teach students.

Extracurricular/co-curricular programs (p. 206): school-sponsored activities students may pursue outside of, or in addition to, academic study.

F

Field experiences (p. 34): opportunities for teachers-in-training to experience first-hand the world of the teacher, by observing, tutoring, and instructing small groups.

First Nations, Métis, and Inuit (p. 88): three unique groups of Aboriginal peoples recognized by the Canadian Constitution.

Formal operations stage (p. 147): the stage of cognitive development (11 to 15 years of age) proposed by Jean Piaget, in which cognitive abilities reach their highest level of development.

For-profit schools (p. 317): schools that are operated, for profit, by private educational corporations.

French tradition (p. 63): based on church-controlled schools with classes often taught by members of the clergy.

Full inclusion (p. 167): the policy and process of including exceptional learners in general education classrooms.

G

Gender (p. 124): the socially constructed roles we enact based on our sex.

Gender bias (p. 130): subtle bias or discrimination on the basis of gender; reduces the likelihood that the target of the bias will develop to the full extent of his or her capabilities.

Gender expression (p. 129): the ways that we present our gender through dress, demeanour, and actions and how these are interpreted based on gender norms.

Gender-fair classroom (p. 130): education that is free of bias or discrimination on the basis of gender.

Gender fluid (p. 129): a gender that varies over time or includes a mix of both male and female.

Gender identity (p. 128): the way we define how we align (or don't align) with what we see as options for gender.

Gifted and talented (p. 162): exceptional learners who demonstrate high intelligence, high creativity, high achievement, or special talent(s).

Grievance (p. 101): a formal complaint filed by an employee against his or her employer or supervisor.

Group investigation (p. 199): an approach to teaching in which the teacher facilitates learning by creating an environment that allows students to determine what they will study and how.

H

Hidden curriculum (p. 205): the behaviours, attitudes, and knowledge the school culture unintentionally teaches students.

Hierarchy of needs (p. 152): a set of seven needs, from the basic needs for survival and safety to the need for self-actualization, that motivate human behaviour.

Higher-order questions (p. 311): questions that require the ability to engage in complex modes of thought (e.g., synthesis, analysis, and evaluation).

Home–school communication systems (p. 249): computer-based systems that allow schools to disseminate information to parents and, in turn, enable parents to communicate directly with school personnel.

Home-schooling (p. 80): the practice of parents taking on the role of teacher and educating their children at home.

Humanism (p. 60): a philosophy based on the belief that individuals control their own destinies through the application of their intelligence and learning.

Humanistic psychology (p. 59): an orientation to human behaviour that emphasizes personal freedom, choice, awareness, and personal responsibility.

I

Inclusion (p. 167): the practice of integrating all students with disabilities into general education classes.

Independent schools (p. 79): also known as private schools, which charge a tuition fee.

Indian Residential Schools Settlement Agreement (p. 87): the largest class-action settlement in Canadian history as a result of a lawsuit put forth by former residential school students against the federal government and churches, resulting in compensation and the mandated establishment of the Truth and Reconciliation Commission of Canada (TRC).

Indigenous people (p. 88): peoples (First Nations, Métis, and Inuit) who were the first inhabitants of Canada.

Individualized educational program (IEP) (p. 165): a program or a plan for meeting an exceptional learner's educational needs, specifying goals, objectives, services, and procedures for evaluating progress.

Information processing (p. 198): a branch of cognitive science concerned with how individuals use long- and short-term memory to acquire information and solve problems.

Inquiry learning (p. 199): an approach to teaching that gives students opportunities to explore, or *inquire* into, subjects so that they develop their own answers to problem situations.

In-service workshops (p. 42): on-site professional development programs in which teachers meet to learn new techniques, develop curricular materials, share ideas, or solve problems.

Institution (p. 119): any organization a society establishes to maintain, and improve, its way of life.

Integrated curriculum (p. 208): a school curriculum that draws from two or more subject areas and focuses on a theme or concept rather than on a single subject.

Intelligence (p. 155): the ability to learn; the cognitive capacity for thinking.

Interactive teaching (p. 16): teaching characterized by face-to-face interactions between teachers and students; in contrast to preactive teaching.

J

Job analysis (p. 30): a procedure for determining the knowledge and skills needed for a job.

Job fairs (p. 291): information sessions that bring teacher candidates and potential employees together to provide information about job openings.

K

Knowledge base (p. 25): the body of knowledge that represents what teachers need to know and be able to do.

L

Latchkey children (p. 134): children who, because of family circumstances, must spend part of each day unsupervised by a parent or guardian.

Leadership (p. 262): the act of guiding or leading.

Learning (p. 311): changes in behaviour the individual makes in response to environmental stimuli; the acquisition and organization of knowledge and skills.

Learning disability (LD) (p. 160): a limitation in one's ability to take in, organize, remember, and express information.

Least restrictive environment (p. 166): an educational program that meets a disabled student's special needs in a manner that is identical, insofar as possible, to that provided to students in general education classrooms.

Letter of application (p. 294): a letter written in application for a specific teaching vacancy in a school district.

Liability (p. 107): responsibility for damages or harm.

Logic (p. 56): a branch of philosophy concerned with the processes of reasoning and the identification of rules that will enable thinkers to reach valid conclusions.

Lower-order questions (p. 311): questions that require students to recall specific information.

M

Mainstreaming (p. 167): providing students with the least restrictive academic environment in which they may comfortably learn the curriculum.

Mastery learning (p. 196): an approach to instruction based on the assumptions that (1) virtually all students can learn material if given enough time and taught appropriately and (2) learning is enhanced if students can progress in small, sequenced steps.

Metaphysics (p. 54): a branch of philosophy concerned with the nature of reality.

Microcomputer-based laboratory (MBL) (p. 249): the use of computers to gather and then analyze data that students have collected in a school laboratory or in the field.

Microteaching (p. 35): a brief, single-concept lesson taught by a teacher education student to a small group of students; usually designed to give the education student an opportunity to practise a specific teaching skill.

Minister of education (p. 89): elected cabinet minister with the formal responsibility for the provincial department of education and its staff.

Ministry or department of education (p. 89): the provincial or territorial government ministry responsible for all aspects of education.

Modelling (p. 196): the process of "thinking out loud," which teachers use to make students aware of the reasoning involved in learning new material.

Modes of teaching (p. 18): different aspects of the teaching function—for example, teaching as a way of being, as a creative endeavour, as a live performance, and so on.

Montessori method (p. 80): a method of teaching, developed by Maria Montessori, based on a prescribed set of materials and physical exercises to develop children's knowledge and skills.

Moral reasoning (p. 147): the reasoning process people follow to decide what is right or wrong.

Multiple intelligences (p. 157): a perspective on intellectual ability, proposed by Howard Gardner, suggesting that there are at least seven types of human intelligence.

N

National Occupational Classification (NOC) (p. 263): organizes job titles into occupational group descriptions in Canada.

Negligence (p. 103): failure to exercise reasonable, prudent care in providing for the safety of others.

Normal schools (p. 63): schools that focused on the preparation of teachers.

Null curriculum (p. 206): the intellectual processes and subject content that schools do not teach.

O

Observations (p. 34): field experiences wherein a teacher education student observes a specific aspect of classroom life, such as the students, the teacher, the interactions between the two, the structure of the lesson, or the setting.

Open-space schools (p. 122): schools that have large instructional areas with movable walls and furniture that can be rearranged easily.

Opportunity to learn (OTL) (p. 187): the time during which a teacher provides students with challenging content and appropriate instructional strategies to learn that content.

Outcome-based education (pp. 29, 212): an educational reform that focuses on developing students' ability to demonstrate mastery of certain desired outcomes or performances.

Outcome-based or Performance-based teacher education (p. 29): an approach to teacher education emphasizing outcomes (what teachers should be able to do, think, and feel) rather than the courses they should take.

P

Pan-Canadian Education Indicators Program (PCEIP) (p. 134): a joint venture of Statistics Canada and the Council of Ministers of Education.

Parent Involvement Committee (PIC) (p. 94): an advisory body for Ontario school boards that provides advice, information, and support to help schools increase parental involvement in their child(ren)'s education.

Parochial schools (p. 63): schools founded on religious beliefs.

Pedagogical content knowledge (p. 25): the knowledge accomplished teachers possess regarding how to present subject matter to students through the use of analogies, metaphors, experiments, demonstrations, illustrations, and other instructional strategies.

Peer counselling (p. 139): an arrangement whereby students, monitored by a school counsellor or teacher, counsel one another in such areas as low achievement, interpersonal problems, substance abuse, and career planning.

Peer-mediated instruction (p. 199): approaches to teaching, such as cooperative learning and group investigation, that utilize the social relationships among students to promote their learning.

Peer-tutoring (p. 200): an arrangement whereby students tutor other students in the same classroom or at the same grade level.

Perennialism (p. 56): a philosophical orientation that emphasizes the ideas contained in the great books and maintains that the true purpose of education is the discovery of the universal, or perennial, truths of life.

Performance-based education (p. 212): an educational reform that focuses on developing students' ability to demonstrate mastery of certain desired performances or outcomes.

Performance-based teacher education (p. 29): an approach to teacher education emphasizing performance (what teachers should be able to do, think, and feel) rather than the courses they should take.

Personal development view (p. 29): the belief that teachers become more effective by increasing their self-knowledge and developing themselves as persons.

Petites écoles (p. 63): early schools within the French tradition that provided a rudimentary education.

Phonics (p. 215): a method for teaching reading and writing by correlating sounds with letters or groups of letters.

Practicum (p. 35): a short field-based experience during which teacher education students spend time observing and assisting in classrooms.

Praxis (p. 59): practical application or exercise of an art, science, skill, or branch of learning.

Preoperational stage (p. 147): the stage of cognitive development (two to seven years of age) proposed by Jean Piaget in which the individual begins to use language and symbols to think of objects and people outside of the immediate environment.

Privatization movement (p. 317): moving an organization or institution from public (government) ownership to private ownership.

Problem-centred learning (p. 217): an approach to instruction in which students work in small groups on problems that have many or open-ended solutions.

Profession (p. 263): an occupation that requires a high level of expertise, including advanced study in a specialized field, adherence to a code of ethics, and the ability to work without close supervision.

Professional (p. 264): one who is a qualified member of, and engages in, a particular profession, and who abides by the regulatory norms established by the profession.

Professional capital (p. 267): a term coined by Hargreaves and Fullan (2012) to describe the combination of human capital, social capital, and decisional capital.

Professional portfolio (p. 39): a collection of various kinds of evidence (e.g., projects, written work, and video demonstrations of skills) documenting the achievement and performance of individuals in an area of professional practice.

Progressivism (p. 57): a philosophical orientation based on the belief that life is evolving in a positive direction, that people may be trusted to act in their own best interests, and that education should focus on the needs and interests of students.

Prosocial values (p. 116): values such as honesty, patriotism, fairness, and civility that promote the well-being of a society.

Psychosocial crisis (p. 148): a life crisis at one of eight different stages of growth and development. According to psychologist Erik Erikson, individuals must resolve each crisis to reach the next stage.

Psychosocial development (p. 147): the progression of an individual through various stages of psychological and social development.

R

Race (p. 124): a concept of human variation used to distinguish people on the basis of biological traits and characteristics.

Reflection (p. 42): the process of thinking carefully and deliberately about the outcomes of one's teaching.

Reflection-in-action (p. 267): the process of engaging in serious, reflective thought about improving one's professional practice while engaged in that practice.

Reflective teaching log (p. 37): a journal of classroom observations in which the teacher education student systematically analyzes specific episodes of teaching.

Research-based competencies (p. 29): specific behaviours that educational research has identified as characteristic of effective teachers.

Residential schools (p. 87): government-funded, church-run schools established to eliminate parental involvement in the intellectual, cultural, and spiritual development of Aboriginal children, dating back to the 1870s. The last of the over 130 residential schools closed in 1996.

Rotary instruction (p. 122): the system whereby homeroom teachers provide basic instruction in subjects such as mathematics and language arts and subject specialists teach the rest.

S

Scaffolding (p. 197): an approach to teaching based on the student's current level of understanding and ability; the teacher varies the amount of help given (e.g., clues, encouragement, or suggestions) to students based on their moment-to-moment understanding of the material being learned.

School advisory councils (p. 94): councils mandated at school levels to allow and encourage parents and community members to become involved in school-level decision making; also referred to as parent advisory councils or committees.

School boards (p. 91): the primary governing body of a local school district.

School culture (p. 122): the collective "way of life" characteristic of a school; a set of beliefs, values, traditions, and ways of thinking and behaving that distinguish it from other schools.

School improvement research (p. 132): research studies that identify the characteristics of schools that improve over time.

School-to-work programs (p. 224): educational programs, often developed collaboratively by schools and industry, that emphasize the transfer of knowledge and skills learned at school to the job setting.

School-within-a-school (p. 140): an alternative school (within a regular school) designed to meet the needs of students at risk.

School year (p. 75): the required number of days required for students to attend school.

Scientific literacy (p. 219): the capacity to use scientific knowledge, to identify questions and to draw evidence-based conclusions in order to understand and help make decisions that impact human activity and the natural world.

Scottish tradition (p. 64): offered both elementary and secondary education to boys and girls in combined classes regardless of their social class.

Self-assessment (p. 42): the process of measuring one's growth in regard to the knowledge, skills, and attitudes possessed by professional teachers.

Self-contained classroom (p. 122): an organizational structure for schools in which one teacher instructs a group of students (typically, 20 to 30) in a single classroom.

Self-regulation (p. 117): the ability to stay calmly focused and alert.

Separate schools (p. 63): publicly funded schools based on religion or language.

Service learning (p. 117): a teaching and learning approach that includes community service and reflection to promote civic responsibility.

Sex (p. 128): the biological makeup of a person's reproductive anatomy.

Sex role socialization (p. 129): socially expected behaviour patterns conveyed to individuals on the basis of gender.

Sex role stereotyping (p. 129): beliefs that subtly encourage males and females to conform to certain behavioural norms regardless of abilities and interests.

Social reconstructionism (p. 58): a philosophical orientation based on the belief that social problems can be solved by changing, or *reconstructing*, society.

Special education (p. 164): a teaching specialty for meeting the special educational needs of exceptional learners.

Stages of development (p. 147): predictable stages through which individuals pass as they progress through life.

Standard of care (p. 104): level of care expected of school personnel; level of care to be that of careful or prudent parents in the care of their own children.

Student-centred curriculum (p. 208): curricula that are organized around students' needs and interests.

Student diversity (p. 3): differences among students in regard to gender, race, ethnicity, culture, and socioeconomic status.

Student-mobility rates (p. 10): the proportion of students within a school or district who move during an academic year.

Student variability (p. 3): differences among students in regard to their developmental needs, interests, abilities, and disabilities.

Students at risk (p. 133): students whose living conditions and backgrounds place them at risk for dropping out of school.

Students with disabilities (p. 159): students who need special education services because they possess one or more of the following disabilities: learning disabilities, speech or language impairments, mental retardation, serious emotional disturbance, hearing impairments, orthopedic impairments, visual impairments, or other health impairments.

Subject-centred curriculum (p. 208): a curriculum that places primary emphasis on the logical order of the discipline students are to study. Teachers of such a curriculum are content-area experts and concerned primarily with helping students understand facts, laws, and principles of the discipline.

Substitute teaching (p. 38): temporary teachers who replace regular teachers absent due to illness, family responsibilities, personal reasons, or professional workshops and conferences.

Successful school (p. 131): schools characterized by a high degree of student learning, results that surpass those expected from comparable schools, and steady improvement rather than decline.

Superintendent or director of education (p. 92): the chief administrator of a school district.

Supply or daily occasional teaching (p. 38): temporary teachers who replace regular teachers absent due to illness, family responsibilities, personal reasons, or professional workshops and conferences.

Synectics (p. 309): a method for "teaching" creativity through the use of metaphors and analogies.

T

Teacher centres (p. 42): centres where teachers provide other teachers with instructional materials and new methods, and where teachers can exchange ideas.

Teacher–researcher (p. 270): a teacher who regularly conducts classroom research to improve his or her teaching.

Teacher–student ratios (p. 10): a ratio that expresses the number of students taught by a teacher.

Teacher leadership (p. 276): a set of skills demonstrated by teachers who do not have formal leadership positions, but who have an influence beyond the classroom, within the school and district school board.

Teaching certificate (p. 284): a licence to teach issued by a province or territory.

Teaching simulations (p. 35): an activity in which teacher education students participate in role plays designed to create situations comparable to those actually encountered by teachers.

Time on task (p. 187): the amount of time students are actively and directly engaged in learning tasks.

Tort liability (p. 104): conditions that would permit the filing of legal charges against a professional for breach of duty and/or behaving in a negligent manner.

Transgender (p. 129): people who identify with or express a gender identity that differs from the one that corresponds to that person's sex at birth.

Tyler rationale (p. 207): a four-step model for curriculum development in which teachers identify purposes, select learning experiences, organize experiences, and evaluate.

V

Vicarious liability (p. 107): responsibility of an employer for damage caused by an employee, even though the employer may not have done anything wrong.

Virtual schools (pp. 80, 234): public schools that offer programs over the Internet.

W

Whole-language approach (p. 215): the practice of teaching language skills (listening, reading, and writing) as part of students' everyday experiences rather than as isolated experiences.

Within-class ability grouping (p. 185): the practice of creating small, homogeneous groups of students within a single classroom for the purpose of instruction, usually in reading or mathematics, at the elementary level.

Y

Youth Criminal Justice Act **(p. 103):** act replacing the *Young Offenders' Act* to ensure criminal justice for youth; emphasizes rehabilitation and reintegration of youth.

References

Abrahamsson, B. (1971). *Military professionalization and political power*. Stockholm: Allmanna Forlagret.

Acheson, K. A., and Gall, M. D. (1997). *Techniques in the clinical supervision of teachers: Preservice and inservice applications*, 4th ed. New York: Longman.

Alberta. Alberta Education. (2005). The heart of the matter: Character and citizenship education in Alberta schools. Retrieved January 4, 2015, from http://education.alberta.ca/media/547951/heartmatter.pdf.

Apple, Inc. (2008). *Apple classrooms of tomorrow—today: Learning in the 21st century*. Cupertino, CA: Author.

Aristotle. (1941). Politics (Book VIII). In R. McKeon (Ed.), *The basic works of Aristotle*. New York: Random House.

Armstrong, A., and Casement, C. (2000). *The child and the machine: How computers put our children's education at risk*. Beltsville, MD: Robins Lane Press.

Armstrong, H. D. (Ed.). (2004). *Praxis of school administration and teacher leadership*. Calgary Detselig Enterprises.

Armstrong, P. A. (2008). *What teachers expect in reform: Making their voices heard*. Lanham, MD: Rowman & Littlefield Education.

Artz, S. (1999). *Sex, power, and the violent school girl*. New York: Teachers College Press.

Association of Canadian Deans of Education (ACDE). (2006). General accord. Vancouver Author.

Aud, S., Fox, M., and KewalRamani, A. (2010). *Status and trends in the education of racial and ethnic groups* (NCES 2010–015). U.S. Department of Education, National Center for Education Statistics. Washington, DC: U.S. Government Printing Office.

Ballantine, J. H. (1997). *The sociology of education: A systematic analysis*, 4th ed. Upper Saddle River, NJ: Prentice Hall.

Banda, D., Coleman, T., and Matuszny, R. (2007). A progressive plan for building collaborative relationships with parents. *Teaching Exceptional Children*, 39(4), 24–31.

Banks, J. A. (1997). *Teaching strategies for ethnic studies*, 6th ed. Boston: Allyn and Bacon.

Banks, J. A. (1999). *An introduction to multicultural education*, 2nd ed. Boston: Allyn and Bacon.

Barlow, M. (with Robertson, H.) (1994). *Class warfare: The assault on Canada's schools*. Toronto: Key Porter.

Barman, J., McCaskill, D., and Hebert, Y. (1986). *Indian education in Canada. Volume 1: The legacy*. Vancouver: University of British Columbia Press.

Beard, C. (1938). *The nature of the social sciences*. New York: Charles Scribner.

Beck, R. J. (2010). What are learning objects? Retrieved from http://www4.uwm.edu/cie/learning_objects.cfm?gid=56.

Becker, H. J. (1999). *Internet use by teachers: Conditions of professional use and teacher-directed student use*. The University of California, Irvine, and the University of Minnesota: Center for Research on Information Technology and Organizations.

Beggs, P. (2012). *A Shifting landscape: Pedagogy, technology, and the new terrain of innovation in a digital world*. Toronto: Curriculum Services Canada.

Belsey, B. (2009). An introduction to bullying for educators. Retrieved from www.bullying.org/htm/main.cfm?content=1116.

Bennett, C. I. (1999). *Comprehensive multicultural education: Theory and practice*, 4th ed. Boston: Allyn and Bacon.

Bennett, S. (2009). Including students with exceptionalities. (Research Monograph #16 in the series *What Works? Research into Practice*, published by the Ontario Ministry of Education, Literacy and Numeracy Secretariat). Retrieved from www.edu.gov.on.ca/eng/literacynumeracy/inspire/research/Bennett.pdf.

Bennett, W. J., and Gelernter, D. (2001, March 14). Improving education with technology. *Education Week* on the Web. Retrieved October 18, 2007, from www.edweek.org/ew/ewstory/cfm?slug=16online20.

Benson, J. (2014). *Hanging in: Strategies for teaching the students who challenge us most*. Alexandria, VA: ASCD.

Berliner, D. C., and Biddle, B. J. (1995). *The manufactured crisis: Myths, fraud, and the attack on America's public schools*. Reading, MA: Addison Wesley.

Bernstein, B. B. (1996). *Pedagogy, symbolic control, and identity: Theory, research, critique* (critical perspectives on literacy and education). New York: Taylor and Francis.

Besner, H. F., and Spungin, C. I. (1995). *Gay and lesbian students: Understanding their needs*. Washington, DC: Taylor and Francis.

Bezeau, L. M. (2007). *Educational administration for Canadian teachers*. Retrieved February, 2010, from www.unb.ca/education/bezeau/eact/eacttoc.html.

Bitter, G. G., and Pierson, M. E. (2005). *Using technology in the classroom*, 6th ed. Boston: Allyn and Bacon.

Bloom, B. S. (1981). *All our children learning: A primer for parents, teachers, and other educators*. New York: McGraw-Hill.

Bolgatz, J. (2005). *Talking race in the classroom*. New York: Teachers College Press.

Bolman, L. G., and Deal, T. E. (2002). *Reframing the path to school leadership: A guide for teachers and principals*. Thousand Oaks, CA: Corwin Press.

Booth, A., and Dunn, J. F. (Eds.). (1996). *Family–school links: How do they affect educational outcomes?* Mahwah, NJ: Lawrence Erlbaum Associates.

Borich, G. D. (2000). *Effective teaching methods*, 4th ed. Upper Saddle River, NJ: Merrill.

Borich, G. D. (2007). *Effective teaching methods: Research-based practice*. Upper Saddle River, NJ: Pearson Education.

Bowerman, M. (2005). Technology for all: Successful strategies for meeting the needs of diverse learners. *Technological Horizons in Education (T.H.E.) Journal, 32*(10), 20, 22, 24.

Boyer, E. (1995). *The basic school: A community for learning*. Princeton, NJ: The Carnegie Foundation for the Advancement of Teaching.

Bracey, G. W. (1993). "Now then, Mr. Kohlberg, about moral development in women . . ." In G. Hass and F. W. Parkay (Eds.), *Curriculum planning: A new approach*, 6th ed. (pp. 165–166). Boston: Allyn and Bacon.

Brameld, T. (1956). *Toward a reconstructed philosophy*. New York: Holt, Rinehart and Winston.

Brameld, T. (1959). Imperatives for a reconstructed philosophy of education. *School and Society, 87*, 246–267.

Brien, K. (2002, January). School discipline and the law: Perspective of high school vice-principals. Paper presented for the University of Calgary Online Conference "Linking Educational Research and Practice." Retrieved October 24, 2003, from www.ucalgary.ca/~lrussell/brien.html.

British Columbia Teachers' Federation. (2007). Code of ethics. In *Members' guide to the BCTF 2003–2004*. Retrieved August 10, 2007, from http://bctf.ca/ProfessionalResponsibility.aspx?id=4292&printPage=true.

Bronfenbrenner, U. (1979). *The ecology of human development: Experiments by nature and design*. Boston: Harvard University Press.

Brown, A. F., and Zuker, M. A. (2007). *Education law*, 4th ed. Toronto: Thomson Carswell.

Brown, F. B., Kohrs, D., and Lanzarro, C. (1991). The academic costs and consequences of extra-curricular participation in high school. Paper presented at the Annual Meeting of the Educational Research Association.

Brown, R. (2009). Is there a case for year-round schooling? *Organizational Development, 4*(3). Retrieved from www.tdsb.on.ca/Portals/research/docs/reports/RT_YRSchooling RevSept09.pdf.

Bruner, J. S. (1960). *The process of education*. New York: Random House.

Bryce, P. H. (1922). *The story of a national crime: An appeal for justice to the Indians of Canada*. Ottawa: James Hope and Sons.

Bucky, P. A. (1992). *The private Albert Einstein*. Kansas City: Andrews and McMeel.

Burden, P. R., and Byrd, D. M. (1999). *Methods for effective teaching*, 2nd ed. Boston: Allyn and Bacon.

Burnaford, G., Fischer, J., and Hobson, D. (1996). *Teachers doing research: Practical possibilities*. Mahwah, NJ: Lawrence Erlbaum Associates.

Burstall, K. (1993, Spring). The quality teacher. *Aviso*. Nova Scotia Teachers Union.

Buzzell, J. B. (1996). *School and family partnerships: Case studies for regular and special educators.* Albany, NY: Delmar Publishers.

Calder Stegemann, K. J., and Roberts, W. L. (2015). Students at risk in the classroom (Teacher Education Series). Toronto Pearson Canada.

Caldwell, B. (2005). School-based management. *Education policy series*, International Academy of Education. France: International Institute for Educational Planning (IIEP).

Caldwell, B. & Spinks, J. (2007). Raising the Stakes: From Improvement to transformation in the reform of schools. London: Routledge.

Campbell, D. M., Melenyzer, B., Nettles, D., and Wyman, R. (2003). *How to develop a professional portfolio: A manual for teachers*, 3rd ed. Boston: Allyn and Bacon.

Canadian Association for Health, Physical Education, Recreation and Dance (CAHPERD). (2006, August). Awards news. Retrieved July 24, 2007, from www.cahperd.ca/eng/story_detail.cfm?id=225.

Canadian Association for Health, Physical Education, Recreation and Dance (CAHPERD). (2006). Quality daily physical education. Retrieved August 20, 2007, from www.cahperd.ca/eng/physicaleducation/about_qdpe.cfm.

Canadian Association of Second Language Teachers. (2003). Beliefs. Retrieved November 3, 2003, from www.caslt.org/Info/mission.htm#beliefs.

Canadian Council on Learning. (2010). Access and barriers to educational services for Canadian children with disabilities. Retrieved March 17, 2015, from www.ccl-cca.ca/pdfs/OtherReports/201009KohenUppalKhanVisentinExeSum_EN.pdf.

Canadian Education Association (CEA). (2007). *Public education in Canada: Facts, trends and attitudes.* Toronto: CEA. Retrieved from www.cea-ace.ca/sites/default/files/cea-2007-public-education-in-canada.pdf.

Canadian Education Research Information System (CERIS). (n.d.). Introduction to Canadian education. Retrieved August 10, 2007, from www.cea-ace.ca/res.cfm?subsection=rep.

Canadian Institute of Child Health. (2000). *The health of Canada's children: A CICH profile*, 3rd ed. Ottawa: Canadian Institute of Child Health.

Canadian Mental Health Association. (2015). Suicide and youth. Retrieved June 13, 2015, from http://toronto.cmha.ca/mental_health/youth-and-suicide/#.Vbjw8DBVhBd.

Canadian Teachers' Federation. (2000). Assessment and evaluation. Retrieved November 15, 2003, from www.ctf-fce.ca/en/issues/assessment/testing-policy.html.

Canadian Teachers' Federation. (2003). What is CTF? Retrieved November 1, 2003, from www.ctf-fce.ca/en/default.htm.

Canadian Teachers' Federation. (2006). Make a difference: Be the change. Retrieved July 9, 2010, from www.ctf-fce.ca/TIC/Default.axpx?SID=625892.

Canadian Teachers' Federation. (2008). Cyberbullying in schools: National poll shows Canadians' growing awareness. Retrieved July 9, 2010, from www.ctf-fce.ca/Newsroom/news.aspx?NewsID=-873341035.

Canadian Youth in Challenging Contexts Network. (2013). Youth engagement: Empowering youth voices to improve services, programs, and policy. Retrieved from http://cyccnetwork.org/en/engagement.

Cantor, L. (1989). Assertive discipline—more than names on the board and marbles in a jar. *Phi Delta Kappan*, 71(1), 57–61.

Cappon, P. (2011). Exploring the 'Boy Crisis' in education. Canadian Council on Learning. Retrieved April 30, 2015, from www.ccl-cca.ca/pdfs/OtherReports/Genderereport20110113.pdf.

Carmichael, L. B. (1981). *McDonogh 15: The making of a school*. New York: Avon Books.

Carroll, J. (1963). A model of school learning. *Teachers College Record*, 64, 723–733.

Cawelti, G. (1999). *Portraits of six benchmark schools: Diverse approaches to improving student achievement.* Arlington, VA: Educational Research Service.

Center for Research on Effective Schooling for Disadvantaged Students. (1992). Helping students who fall behind, Report No. 22. Baltimore, MD: The Johns Hopkins University.

Center for the Study and Prevention of Violence, University of Colorado at Boulder. (1998). Response to the Columbine school incident. Retrieved April 21, 1999, from www.colorado.edu/cspv.

Centers for Disease Control and Prevention. (1998). Youth risk behavior surveillance—United States, 1997. Atlanta, GA: Centers for Disease Control and Prevention.

Cheeks, E. H., Flippo, R. F., and Lindsey, J. D. (1997). *Reading for success in elementary schools*. Madison, WI: Brown and Benchmark.

Children's Mental Health Ontario. (2013). Building a better school environment for youth with mental health and addiction issues. Retrieved May 2, 2015, from www.kidsmen talhealth.ca/documents/res-building-a-better-school-environment-for-youth-with-men tal-health-and-addiction-issuesv2.pdf.

Clandinin, J. (2013). Personal practical knowledge: A study of teachers' classroom images. In C. J. Craig, P. C. Meijer, and Broeckmans, J. (Eds.), *From teacher thinking to teachers and teaching: The evolution of a research community* (pp. 67–95). Bingley, UK: Emerald Group Publishing Ltd.

CMEC (2008). *Education in Canada*. Toronto: Author.

Coladarci, T., and Cobb, C. D. (1996). Extracurricular participation, school size, and achievement and self-esteem among high school students: A national look. *Journal of Research in Rural Education, 12*(2), 92–103.

Collins, A., and Halverson, R. (2009). *Thinking education in the age of technology*. New York: Teachers College Press.

Colucci, K. (2000). Negative pedagogy. In J. L. Paul, and K. Colucci (Eds.), *Stories out of school: Memories and reflections on care and cruelty in the classroom* (pp. 27–44). Stamford, CT: Ablex.

Committee for Economic Development. (1994). *Putting learning first: Governing and managing schools for high achievement*. New York: Research and Policy Committee, Committee for Economic Development.

Cook, A., and Polgar, J. (2015). *Assistive Technologies: Principles and practice*, 4th ed. St. Louis: Elsevier.

Council of Ministers of Education. (1995, February). Pan-Canadian protocol for collaboration on school curriculum. Retrieved November 3, 2003, from www.cmec.ca/protocol-eng. htm.

Council of Ministers of Education. (1999, September). AGREEMENT-IN-PRINCIPLE: Labour mobility chapter of the Agreement on Internal Trade/Teaching Profession. Retrieved August 27, 2007, from www.cmec.ca/else/agreement.en.stm.

Council of Ministers of Education, Canada (CMEC). (n.d.). Education in Canada: An overview. Retrieved from www.cmec.ca/299/Education-in-Canada-An-Overview.

Council of Ministers of Education, Canada (CMEC). (2013). Science assessment framework. Pan-Canadian Assessment Program (PCAP).

Counts, G. (1932). *Dare the school build a new social order?* New York: The John Day Company.

Crocker, R. K., and Dibbon, D. C. (2008). *Teacher education in Canada*. Kelowna, BC: Society for the Advancement of Excellence in Education (SAEE).

Crowther, F., Kaagan, S. S., Ferguson, M., and Hann, L. (2002). *Developing teacher leaders: How teacher leadership enhances school success*. Thousand Oaks, CA: Corwin Press.

Curwin, R., and Mendler, A. (1988, October). Packaged discipline programs: Let the buyer beware. *Educational Leadership, 46*(6), 68–71.

Curwin, R., and Mendler, A. (1989, March). We repeat, let the buyer beware: A response to Canter. *Educational Leadership, 46*(6), 83.

Dafna, K. (2010). *Access and barriers to educational services for Canadian children with disabilities*. Ottawa: Canadian Council on Learning.

Darling-Hammond, L. (2006). Constructing 21st-century teacher education. *Journal of Teacher Education, 57*(3), 300–314. doi: 10.1177/0022487105285962.

Darling-Hammond, L. (2010). *The flat world and education*. New York: Teachers College Press.

Darling-Hammond, L., and Baratz-Snowden, J. (2007). A good teacher in every classroom: Preparing the highly qualified teachers our children deserve. *Educational Horizons, 85*(2), 111–132.

Davis, G. A., and Rimm, S. B. (1998). *Education of the gifted and talented*, 4th ed. Boston: Allyn and Bacon.

Deal, T. E., and Peterson, K. D. (1999). *Shaping school culture: The heart of leadership*. San Francisco: Jossey–Bass Publishers.

Deal, T. E., and Peterson, K. D. (2009). *Shaping school culture: Pitfalls, paradox, and promises*, 2nd ed. San Francisco: Jossey–Bass Publishers.

Dede, C. (2005). Planning for neomillenial learning styles: Implications for investments in technology and faculty. In D. Oblinger and J. Oblinger (Eds.), *Educating the net generation*. Boulder, CO: EDUCAUSE.

Dehue, F., Bolman, C., and Vollink, T. (2009). Cyberbullying: Youngsters' experiences and parental perception. *CyberPsychology & Behavior*, 11, 217–223. doi:10.1089/cpb.2007.0008.

Dell'Olio, J. M., and Donk, T. (2007). *Models of teaching: Connecting student learning with standards*. Thousand Oaks, CA: Sage.

Department of Education, Newfoundland and Labrador. (2011). Social Studies Curriculum Guide.

Department of Justice Canada. (1982). *Canadian Charter of Rights and Freedoms*. Enacted as Schedule B to the Canada Act 1982 (U.K.), 1982, c. 11, which came into force on April 17, 1982. Retrieved October 3, 2003, from http://laws.justice.gc.ca/en/Charter.

Dickinson, G. M. (2001). Teacher, trust, and the law: The matter of sexual misconduct. *Orbit*, 32(2), 15–19.

Dobbins, K. (2005). Getting ready for the net generation. *EDUCAUSE Review*, 40(5), 8–9.

Dollase, R. H. (1992). *Voices of beginning teachers: Visions and realities*. New York: Teachers College Press.

Dryfoos, J. (1998). *Safe passage: Making it through adolescence in a risky society*. New York: Oxford University Press.

Duke, D. L. (1984). *Teaching: The imperiled profession*. Albany, NY: State University of New York Press.

Dykgraaf, C. L., and Kane, S. (1998, October). For-profit charter schools: What the public needs to know. *Educational Leadership*, 56(2), 51–53.

Eby, J. (1996). *Reflective planning, teaching, and evaluation: K–12*, 2nd ed. Upper Saddle River, NJ: Merrill, 14.

Economist. (1999, January 16). A contract on schools: Why handing education over to companies can make sense.

education@canada. (n.d.). International gateway to education in Canada. Retrieved August 10, 2007, from www.educationcanada.cmec.ca/EN/home.php.

Education Technology Advisory Council (ETAC). (2010). Massachusetts School Technology and Readiness Chart (STaR Chart). Retrieved from www.doe.mass.edu/boe/sac/edtech/STaR.pdf.

Education Week on the Web. (1999, July 29). Issue paper: Privatization of public education.

Eggen, P., and Kauchak, D. (2007). *Educational psychology: Windows on classrooms*, 7th ed. Upper Saddle River, NJ: Pearson Education.

Eisner, E. W. (1998). *The kind of schools we need: Personal essays*. Portsmouth, NH: Heinemann.

Eisner, E. W. (2002). *The educational imagination: On the design and evaluation of school programs*, 3rd ed. New York: Macmillan College.

Eisner, E. W. (2006). The satisfactions of teaching: How we teach is ultimately a reflection of why we teach. *Educational Leadership*, 44–46.

Elam, S. M., Rose, L. C., and Gallup, A. M. (1996, September). The 28th Annual Phi Delta Kappan Gallup Poll of the public's attitudes toward the public schools. *Phi Delta Kappan*, 41–59.

Ellis, L., Robb, B., and Burke, D. (2005). Sexual orientation in United States and Canadian college students. *Archives of Sexual Behavior*, 34(5), 569–581.

Emerson, R., Fretz, R., and Shaw, L. (Eds.). (1995). *Writing ethnographic fieldnotes*. Chicago: University of Chicago Press.

Emmer, E. T., and Evertson, C. M. (2009). *Classroom management for middle and high school teachers*, 8th ed. Boston: Pearson Education.

Epstein, J. L. (1992). School and family partnerships. In M. C. Alkin (Ed.), *Encyclopedia of Educational Research*, 6th ed. New York: MacMillan.

ERIC Clearinghouse. (1993). *Value search: Parent involvement in the educational process*. Eugene, OR: ERIC Clearinghouse on Educational Management.

Erikson, E. H. (1997). *The life cycle completed: Extended version with new chapters on the ninth stage of development by Joan M. Erikson*. New York: W.W. Norton.

Erickson, H. I. (2008). *Stirring the head, heart, and soul: Redefining curriculum, instruction, and concept-based learning*. Thousand Oaks, CA: Corwin Press.

Etzioni, A. (Ed.). (1969). *The semi-professions and their organization: Teachers, nurses, social workers.* New York: The Free Press.

Evans, L. (2013). Diversity in Canada: An overview. Canadian immigrant. Retrieved October 22, 2015, from http://canadianimmigrant.ca/guides/moving-to-canada/diversity-in-canada-an-overview.

Evertson, C. M., and Emmer, E. T. (2013). *Classroom management for elementary teachers,* 9th ed. Boston: Pearson.

Fairholm, R. M., and Fairholm, G. W. (2009). *Understanding leadership perspectives.* New York: Springer Science and Business Media.

Fashola, O. (1999). Review of day and after-school programs and their effectiveness. John Hopkins University: Centre for Education Study for Research on the Education of Children Placed at Risk.

Feiman-Nemser, S. (2001). From preparation to practice: Designing a continuum to strengthen and sustain teaching. *Teachers College Record,* 103(6), 1013–1055.

Feiman-Nemser, S. (2012). *Teachers as learners.* Cambridge, MA: Harvard Education Press.

Feiman-Nemser, S., and Buchmann, M. (1989). Describing teacher education: A framework and illustrative findings from a longitudinal study of six students. *Elementary School Journal,* 89(3), 365–377.

Feldhusen, J. F. (1997). Educating teachers for work with talented youth. In N. Colangelo and G. A. Davis (Eds.), *Handbook of gifted education.* Boston: Allyn and Bacon.

Ferris, S. (2008). A teacher's voice: Lost and found in paradox. *Curriculum in Context,* 35(1), 16–17.

Fleming, T. (1997, November). Provincial initiatives to restructure Canadian school governance in the 1990s. *Canadian Journal of Education Administration and Policy,* 11. Retrieved May 26, 2003, from www.umanitoba.ca/publications/cjeap/articles/thomasfleming.html.

First Nations Studies Program at University of British Columbia [UBC]. (2009). The residential school system. Retrieved from http://indigenousfoundations.arts.ubc.ca/home/government-policy/the-residential-school-system.html.

Freedman, S., Jackson, J., and Boles, K. (1983). Teaching: An imperiled profession. In L. Shulman and G. Sykes (Eds.), *Handbook of teaching and policy.* New York: Longman.

Freire, P. (1972). *Pedagogy of the oppressed.* Harmondsworth: Penguin.

Freire, P. (2007). *Pedagogy of the oppressed.* New York: Continuum.

Freire, P., and Macedo, D. (1987). *Literacy: Reading the word and the world.* London: Taylor and Francis.

Friend, M., and Bursuck, W. D. (2002). *Including students with special needs: A practical guide for classroom teachers.* Boston: Allyn and Bacon.

Fullan, M., and Langworthy, M. (2014). *A rich seam: How new pedagogies find deep learning.* London: Pearson.

Furger, R. (1999, September). Are wired schools failing our kids? PC World. Retrieved October 18, 2007, from www.pcworld.com/printable/article/id,11950/printable.html.

Gadanidis, G., and Hughes, J. (2011). Performing big math ideas across the grades. *Teaching Children Mathematics,* 17(8), 486–496.

Gagné, R. M. (1974). *Essentials of learning for instruction.* Hinsdale, IL: Dryden.

Gagné, R. M. (1977). *The conditions of learning,* 3rd ed. New York: Holt, Rinehart and Winston.

Galway, G., Sheppard, B., Brown, J., and Wiens, J. (2013, September). The impact of centralization on local school district governance in Canada. *Canadian Journal of Educational Administration and Policy,* 145, 1–34.

Gandara, P., and Fish, J. (1994, Spring). Year-round schooling as an avenue to major structural reform. *Educational Evaluation and Policy Analysis,* 16(1), 67–85.

Garbarino, J. (1999). *Lost boys: Why our sons turn violent and how we can save them.* New York: Free Press.

Gardner, H. (1983). *Frames of mind.* New York: Basic Books.

Gardner, H. (1995, November). Reflections on multiple intelligences: Myths and messages. *Phi Delta Kappan,* 200–203, 206–209.

Gardner, H. (1997). Multiple intelligences as a partner in school improvement. *Educational Leadership,* 20–21.

Gardner, H. (1999). *The disciplined mind: What all students should understand*. New York: Simon and Schuster.

Gaskell, J. (1995). *Secondary schools in Canada: The national report of the exemplary schools project*. Toronto: Canadian Education Association.

Gehrke, N. (1988, Summer). Toward a definition of mentoring. *Theory into Practice*, 190–194.

George Lucas Educational Foundation. (2004, February 9). From hula to high tech. Retrieved from www.glef.org/php/article.php?id=Art_1126&key=137.

George Lucas Educational Foundation. (2008, February 9). Visual acuity: From consumers to critics and creators. Retrieved July 9, 2010, from www.edutopia.org/media-literacy-skills.

George, P. (1995). *The Japanese secondary school: A closer look*. Columbus, OH: National Middle School Association; and Reston, VA: National Association of Secondary School Principals.

Gerber, S. B. (1996). Extracurricular activities and academic achievement. *Journal of Research and Development in Education*, 30(1), 42–50.

Gerstner, L. V., Semerad, R. D., Doyle, D. P., and Johnston, W. B. (1994). *Reinventing education: Entrepreneurship in America's public schools*. New York: Dutton.

Ghosh, R. (2001). *Redefining multicultural education*, 2nd ed. Toronto: Nelson Thomas Learning. (1996, 1st ed. Toronto: Harcourt Brace & Co.).

Ghosh, R., and Galczynski, M. (2014). *Redefining multicultural education*, 3rd ed. Toronto: Canadian Scholars' Press Inc.

Gibbs, J., and Ushijima, T. (2008). *Engaging all by creating high school learning communities*. Windsor, CA: Center Source Systems.

Gilligan, C. (1993*). In a different voice: Psychological theory and women's development*, 2nd ed. Cambridge, MA: Harvard University Press.

Giroux, H. A. (1999). Schools for sale: Public education, corporate culture, and the citizen-consumer. *The Educational Forum*, 63(2), 140–149.

Glasser, W. R. (1997, April). A new look at school failure and school success. *Phi Delta Kappan*, 596–602.

Glasser, W. R. (1998a). *Quality school*, 3rd ed. New York: Harper Perennial.

Glasser, W. R. (1998b). *The quality school teacher: Specific suggestions for teachers who are trying to implement the lead-management ideas of the quality school*. New York: Harper Perennial.

Glasser, W. R. (1998c). *Choice theory: A new psychology of personal freedom*. New York: HarperCollins.

Glasser, W. R., and Dotson, K. L. (1998). *Choice theory in the classroom*. New York: Harper Perennial.

Glickman, C., Gordon, S. P., and Ross-Gordon, J. M. (2001). *SuperVision and instructional leadership*, 5th ed. Boston: Allyn and Bacon.

Glickman, C., Gordon, S. P., and Ross-Gordon, J. M. (2004). *SuperVision and instructional leadership*, 6th ed. Boston: Allyn and Bacon.

Global News. (2014). Wage comparison: How B.C. teachers compare to others in Canada. Retrieved September 1, 2014, from GlobalNews. http://globalnews.ca/news/1346218/wage-comparison-how-b-c-teachers-salaries-rank-across-canada.

Goldhammer, R., Anderson, R. H., and Krajewski, R. J. (1993). *Clinical supervision: Special methods for the supervision of teachers*, 3rd ed. Fort Worth, TX: Harcourt Brace Jovanovich.

Goleman, D. (1997). *Emotional intelligence*. New York: Bantam Books.

Goleman, D. (1998). *Working with emotional intelligence*. New York: Bantam Books.

Gonzales, L. D. (2004). *Sustaining school leadership: Beyond the boundaries of an enabling school culture*. Landham, MD: University Press of America.

Good, T. L., and Brophy, J. E. (2008). *Looking in classrooms*, 10th ed. Boston: Pearson Education.

Goodlad, J. (1983, Spring). Teaching: An endangered profession. *Teachers College Record*, 575–578.

Goodlad, J. (1990). *Teachers for our nation's schools*. San Francisco: Jossey-Bass Publishers.

Gordon, D. T. (Ed.). (2003). *Better teaching and learning in the digital classroom*. Cambridge, MA: Harvard Education Press.

Gordon, W. J. J. (1968). *Making it strange, Books 1 and 2*. Evanston, IL: Harper and Row.

Gordon, W. J. J. (1971a). *Invent-o-rama*. Cambridge, MA: Porpoise Books.

Gordon, W. J. J. (1971b). *What color is sleep?* Cambridge, MA: Porpoise Books.

Gordon, W. J. J. (1975). *Strange and familiar, Book 1*. Cambridge, MA: Porpoise Books.

Gougeon, T. (2005). *Lecture: A modest proposal for a leadership typology* [Class notes]. Retrieved from University of Calgary EDER 798.01 Leadership in Higher Education Blackboard site.

Government expenditure on education as % of GDP (%). (2016). Retrieved from http://data. worldbank.org/indicator/SE.XPD.TOTL.GD.ZS.

Graham, R., and Richardson, W. (2012). Leveling the playing field: Assistive technology, special education, and a Canadian perspective. *American International Journal of Contemporary Research*, 2(1), 6–15.

Grant, G., and Murray, E. (1999). Using video cases to promote reflection among preservice teachers: A qualitative inquiry. Paper presented at the annual meeting of the American Educational Research Association, New York.

Grant, P. G., Richard, K. J., and Parkay, F. W. (1996, April). Using video cases to promote reflection among preservice teachers: A qualitative inquiry. Paper presented at the Annual Meeting of the American Educational Research Association, New York.

Greene, M. (1995). What counts as philosophy of education? In W. Kohli (Ed.), *Critical conversations in philosophy of education*. New York: Routledge.

Greenwood, E. (1957). Attributes of a profession. *Social Work*, 2(3), 45–55.

Hall, R. (1986). Professionalization and bureaucratization. *American Sociological Review*, 33(1), 92–93.

Hallahan, D. P., and Kauffman, J. M. (2000). *Exceptional children: Introduction to special education*, 8th ed. Boston: Allyn and Bacon.

Hallahan, D. P., and Kauffman, J. M. (2006). *Exceptional learners: Introduction to special education*, 8th ed. Boston: Allyn and Bacon.

Hankins, K. H. (1998). Cacophony to symphony: Memoirs in teacher research. *Harvard Educational Review*, 68(1), 80–95.

Hansen, D. (1995). *The call to teach*. New York: Teachers College Press.

Hanvey, L. (2001, November). Children and youth with special needs. Ottawa: Canadian Council on Social Development. Retrieved August 30, 2007, from www.ccsd.ca/pubs/2001/specialneeds/specialneeds.pdf.

Hardman, M. L., Drew, C. J., and Egan, M. W. (2002). *Human exceptionality: School, community and family*, 7th ed. Boston: Allyn and Bacon.

Hargreaves, A., and Fullan, M. (2012). *Professional capital*. New York: Teachers College Press.

Hargreaves, A., and Lo, L. (2000). The paradoxical profession: Teaching at the turn of the century. *Prospects: Quarterly Review of Comparative Education*, 30(2), 167–180.

Harris, A. (2005). Teacher leadership: More than just a feel-good factor? *Leadership and Policy in Schools*, 4(3), 201–219.

Harris, A., and Muijs, D. (2004). *Improving school through teacher leadership*. Berkshire, UK: Open University Press.

Harris Interactive, Inc. (2001). *The MetLife survey of the American teacher: Key elements of quality schools*. New York: Author.

Harste, J. (2003). What do we mean by literacy now? *Voices from the Middle*, 10(3), 8–12.

Hauser, M., and Rauch, S. (2002). *New teacher! An exciting and scary time*. 2002 job search handbook for educators. Columbus, OH: American Association for Employment in Education.

Health Canada. (2013). Summary of Results of Youth Smoking Survey 2012–2013. Retrieved March 25, 2015, from www.hc-sc.gc.ca/hc-ps/tobac-tabac/research-recherche/stat/_survey-sondage_2012-2013/result-eng.php.

Heath, S. B. (1983). *Ways with words*. Cambridge, UK: Cambridge University Press.

Henkin, R. (2012). Confronting bullying: It really can get better. *English Journal*, 101(6), 110–113.

Henriques, M. E. (1997, May). Increasing literacy among kindergartners through cross-age training. *Young Children*, 42–47.

Henry, E., Huntley, J., McKamey, C., and Harper, L. (1995). *To be a teacher: Voices from the classroom*. Thousand Oaks, CA: Corwin Press.

Henry, M. (1993). *School cultures: Universes of meaning in private schools*. Norwood, NJ: Ablex.

Henry, M. E. (1996). *Parent–school collaboration: Feminist organizational structures and school leadership*. Albany, NY: State University of New York Press.

Herbert, M. (2010, November). The iPad–Breaking new ground in special education. District Administration: Solutions for School District Management. Retrieved from www.districtadministration.com.

Hinduja, S., and Patchin, J. W. (2009). Cyberbullying: An exploratory analysis of factors related to offending and victimization. *Deviant Behavior*, 29, 129–156. doi:10.1080/01639620701457816.

Hoh, P. S. (2008). Cognitive characteristics of the gifted. In J. A. Plucker and C. M. Callahan (Eds.), *Critical issues and practices in gifted education: What the research says* (pp. 57–83). Waco, TX: Prufrock Press.

Holland, A., and Andre, T. (1987, Winter). Participation in extracurricular activities in secondary schools. *Review of Educational Research*, 437–466.

Holly, M. L., and McLoughlin, C. (Eds.). (1989). *Perspectives on teacher professional development*. New York: Falmer Press.

Holt-Reynolds, D. (1999). Good readers, good teachers? Subject matter expertise as a challenge in learning to teach. *Harvard Educational Review*, 69(1), 29–50.

Howsam, R. B., Corrigan, D. C., Denemark, G. W., and Nash, R. J. (1976). *Educating a profession*. Washington, DC: American Association of Colleges for Teacher Education.

Hoy, W. K., and Miskel, C. G. (1987). *Educational administration*, 3rd ed. New York: Random House.

HP Home: HP Canada Awards $336,000 in Technology. Retrieved July 24, 2007, from www.hp.ca/corporate/features/featurestory.php?fileId=57420.

Hughes, J. (2007). Mentoring at different stages of a teacher's career. Retrieved from http://faculty.uoit.ca/hughes/Teaching/mentoring.html.

Hughes, J., and Burke, A. (2014). *The digital principal*. Toronto: Pembroke Publishers.

Hunter, M. (1994). *Enhancing teaching*. New York: Macmillan.

Hurwitz, S. (1999, April). New York, New York: Can Rudy Crew hang tough on vouchers and pull off a turnaround in the nation's biggest school system? *The American School Board Journal*, 36–40.

Idol, L. (1998). Optional extended year program, *Feedback*, Publ. No. 97.20. Austin Independent School District, TX, Office of Program Evaluation.

Igoa, C. (1995). *The inner world of the immigrant child*. New York: Lawrence Erlbaum Associates, Publishers.

Ingersol, R, and Strong, M. (2012). What the research tells us about the impact of induction and mentoring programs for beginning teachers. *Review of Educational Research*, 81(2), 201–203.

Inoue, A. (1996, October 10). Creating schools with special characteristics. Paper presented at the eighth Washington State University College of Education/Nishinomiya Education Board Education Seminar. Washington State University, Pullman.

International Reading Association. (1999, April). *Using multiple methods of beginning reading instruction*. Newark, DE: International Reading Association.

International Society for Technology in Education. (2008). National educational technology standards (NETS) for teachers 2008. Retrieved from www.iste.org/standards/ISTE-standards/standards-for-teachers.

Jackson, P. (1965). The way teaching is. *NEA Journal*, 54, 10–14.

Jamieson, B. (2006, September). State of the teaching profession 2006. *Professionally Speaking*. Ontario College of Teachers Press.

Jeary, J. (2001). *Character education*. Calgary Board of Education.

Johnson, D. W., and Johnson, R. T. (1999). *Learning together and alone: Cooperative, competitive, and individualistic learning*, 5th ed. Boston: Allyn and Bacon.

Johnson, J., and Immerwahr, J. (1994). *First things first: What Americans expect from the public schools, a report from Public Agenda*. New York: Public Agenda.

Johnson, L., Adams Becker, S., Estrada, V., and Freeman, A. (2015). *NMC Horizon Report: 2015 K–12 Edition*. Austin, TX: The New Media Consortium.

Johnson, M. J., and Brown, L. (1998). Collegial support teams. In D. J. McIntyre, and D. M. Byrd (Eds.), *Strategies for career-long teacher education: Teacher education yearbook VI*. Thousand Oaks, CA: Corwin Press.

Jonassen, D. (2000). *Computers as mindtools for schools: Engaging critical thinking*, 2nd ed. Columbus, Ohio: Merrill.

Jonassen, D. H., Peck, K. L., and Wilson, B. G. (1999). *Learning with technology: A constructivist perspective*. Upper Saddle River, NJ: Merrill.

Jones, J. (1994). Integrated learning systems for diverse learners. *Media and Methods*, 31(3).

Jordan, W. J., and Nettles, S. M. (1999). *How students invest their time out of school: Effects on school engagement, perceptions of life chances, and achievement*. Baltimore, MD: Center for Research on the Education of Students Placed at Risk.

Joyce, B., Weil, M., and Calhoun, E. (2004). *Models of teaching*, 7th ed. Boston: Allyn and Bacon.

Joyce, B., Weil, M., and Calhoun, E. (2009). *Models of teaching*, 8th ed. Boston: Allyn and Bacon.

Karsenti, T., and Colin, S. (2013). Why are new teachers leaving the profession? Results of a Canada-wide survey. *Scientific & Academic Publishing*, 3(3), 141–149. Retrieved June 27, 2015, from http://article.sapub.org/10.5923.j.edu.20130303.01.html.

KIDLINK. (2002). Kidproj in KidSpace. KIDLINK Society. Retrieved August 30, 2007, from www.kidlink.org/KIDPROJ/projects.html.

Kirkpatrick, H., and Cuban, L. (1998). Computers make kids smarter—right? *TECHNOS Quarterly*, 7(2), 26–31.

Koh, C. (2015). *Understanding and facilitating learning for the Net Generation and twenty-first-century learners through motivation, leadership and curriculum design*. Amsterdam: Springer.

Kohlberg, H. (2010). The cognitive-developmental approach to moral education. In F. W. Parkay, E. J. Anctil, and G. Hass (Eds.), *Curriculum leadership: Readings for developing quality educational programs*, 9th ed. (pp. 147–159). Upper Saddle River, NJ: Allyn and Bacon/Pearson.

Kohn, A. (1999). *Punished by rewards: The trouble with gold stars, incentive plans, A's, praise, and other bribes*. New York: Mariner Books.

Kottler, J. A., and Zehm, S. J. (1993). *On being a teacher: The human dimension*. Thousand Oaks, CA: Sage Publications.

Krogh, S. L. (2000). Weaving the web. In F. W. Parkay and G. Hass (Eds.), *Curriculum planning: A contemporary approach*, 7th ed. (pp. 338–341). Boston: Allyn and Bacon.

Kulik, J. A. (2004). Meta-analytic studies of acceleration. In N. Colangelo, S. G. Assouline, and M. U. M. Gross (Eds.), *A nation deceived: How schools hold back America's brightest students (pp. 13–22)*. Iowa: The Connie Belin and Jacqueline N. Blank International Centre for Gifted Education and Talent Development.

Kutsyuruba, B., Godden, L., and Tregunna, L. (2014). Curbing early-career teacher attrition: A pan-Canadian document analysis of teacher induction and mentorship programs. *Canadian Journal of Educational Administration and Policy*, 161, 1–42.

Labaree, D. F. (2000). On the nature of teaching and teacher education: Difficult practices that look easy. *Journal of Teacher Education*, 51(3), 228–233.

Language and Literacy Researchers of Canada. (2008). Position statement. Retrieved December 5, 2015, from www.csse-scee.ca/docs/cacs/llrc/LLRCPositionStatement.pdf.

Lawton, S., and Brown, D. (2009). Effective charter schools and charter school systems. *Planning and Changing*, 40. Retrieved from www.thecanadianencyclopedia.ca/en/article/charter-schools.

Lawton, S., and Brown, D. (2012). Charter schools. *Historica Canada*. Retrieved from www.thecanadianencyclopedia.ca/en/article/charter-schools.

Leahey, T., and Harris, R. (2001). *Learning and cognition*, 5th ed. Upper Saddle River, NJ: Merrill/Prentice Hall.

Learning Disabilities Association of Canada. (2002, January). Official definition of learning disabilities. Retrieved March 15, 2015, from www.ldac-taac.ca/Defined/defined_new-e.asp.

Leatherdale, S. T., and Ahmed, R. (2011). Screen-based sedentary behaviours among a nationally representative sample of youth: Are Canadian kids couch potatoes? *Chronic Diseases and Injuries in Canada*, 31(4). Retrieved from www.phac-aspc.gc.ca/publicat/hpcdp-pspmc/31-4/ar-01-eng.php.

Levey, S. (1996). *Starting from scratch: One classroom builds its own curriculum*. Portsmouth, NH: Heinemann.

Levin, D., and Arafeh, S. (2002). *The digital disconnect: The widening gap between Internet-savvy students and their schools*. Washington, DC: The Pew Internet and American Life Project.

Lewis, A. (1992). Helping young urban parents educate themselves and their children. *ERIC/CUE Digest*, 85.

Lewis, R. B., and Doorlag, D. H. (2006). *Teaching special students in general education classrooms*, 7th ed. Upper Saddle River, NJ: Merrill.

Lieberman, A. (1990). Foreword. In S. Mei-ling Yee (Ed.), *Careers in the classroom: When teaching is more than a job*. New York: Teachers College Press.

Lieberman, A. (2013). Teacher leadership: An introduction. *The New Educator*, 9(3), 169–172.

Lieberman, A., and Friedrich, L. (2010). Teacher leadership: Developing the conditions for learning, support, and sustainability. In A. Hargreaves, A. Lieberman, M. Fullan, and

D. Hopkins (Eds.), *Second international handbook of educational change* (pp. 647–667). Dordrecht: Springer Netherlands.

Lieberman, A., and Miller, L. (2004). *Teacher leadership*. San Francisco: Jossey–Bass Publishers.

Littky, D. (2004). *The big picture: Education is everyone's business*. Alexandria, VA: Association for Supervision and Curriculum Development.

Lortie, D. C. (1975). *Schoolteacher: A sociological study*. Chicago: University of Chicago Press.

Luckin, R., Bligh, B., Manches, A., Ainsworth, S., Crook, C., and Noss, R. (2012). *Decoding learning: The proof, promise and potential of digital education*. London, UK: Nesta.

Lundy, K., and Swartz, L. (2011). *Creating caring classrooms*. Toronto: Pembroke Publishers.

MacKay, A. W., and Sutherland, L. I. (1992). *Teachers and the law: A practical guide for educators*. Toronto: Emond Montgomery Publications.

MacKay, A. W., Sutherland, L., and Pochini, K. (2013). *Teachers and the law: Diverse roles and new challenges*, 3rd ed. Toronto: Emond Montgomery Publications.

MacKinnon, G. (2006). Contentious issues in science education: Building critical thinking patterns through two-dimensional concept mapping. *Journal of Educational Multimedia and Hypermedia*, 15(4), 433–445. Chesapeake, VA: AACE.

MacKinnon, G., and Vibert, C. (2004). Webcasting: Modeling distance collaboration in corporate settings. *Journal of Instruction Delivery Systems*, 18(1), 19–22.

MacKinnon, G. R., and Vibert, C. (2002). Judging the constructive impacts of communication technologies: A business education study. *Education and Information Technology*, 7(2), 127–135.

MacLeod, J. (1995). *Ain't no makin' it: Aspirations and attainment in a low-income neighborhood*. Boulder, CO: Westview Press.

MacNaughton, R. H., and Johns, F. A. (1991, September). Developing a successful schoolwide discipline program. *NASSP Bulletin*, 47–57.

Maddux, R., and Johnson, L. (2006). *Type II uses of technology in education: Projects, case studies and software applications*. Binghampton: Haworth.

Mahoney, J., and Cairns, R. B. (1997). Do extracurricular activities protect against early school dropout? *Developmental Psychology*, 33(2), 241–253.

Marshall, K. (2003, May). Recovering from HSPS (hyperactive superficial principal syndrome): A progress report. *Phi Delta Kappan*, 701–709.

Martinez, M. E. (2006). What is metacognition? *Phi Delta Kappan*, 87(9), 696–699.

Martino, W. (2008). *Boys' underachievement: Which boys are we talking about?* (Research Monograph #12 in the series *What Works? Research into Practice*, published by the Ontario Ministry of Education, Literacy and Numeracy Secretariat). Retrieved from www.edu.gov.on.ca/eng/literacynumeracy/inspire/research/Martino.pdf.

Maslow, A. (1987). *Motivation and personality*, 3rd ed. Boston: Addison-Wesley Publishing.

Maslow, A. (1998). *Toward a psychology of being*, 3rd ed. New York: Wiley & Sons.

Mastropieri, M. A., and Scruggs, T. E. (2010). *The inclusive classroom: Strategies for effective instruction*, 4th ed. Upper Saddle River, NJ: Merrill/Pearson.

May, S. (1999). *Critical multiculturalism: Rethinking multicultural and antiracist education*. London, UK: Falmer Press.

McBeath, A. (2002, April). Untitled. *Educational Leadership*, 15.

McCain, T., and Jukes, I. (2001). *Windows on the future: Education in the age of technology*. Thousand Oaks, CA: Corwin Press.

McCoubrey, S., and Sitch, G. (2001). Instructor's guide: Teaching students' rights to pre-service and beginning teachers. *Education and Law Journal*, 11.

McCourt, F. (2005). *Teacher man: A memoir*. New York: Simon and Schuster.

McHugh, J. (2005, October). Synching up with the iKid: Connecting to the twenty-first-century student. *Edutopia Magazine*.

McKenna, M., and Willms, J. D. (1998, September). Expanding parental involvement in Canadian schools. Policy brief. Atlantic Centre for Policy Research, University of New Brunswick, 3–4.

McLeod, S. (2011). Are we irrelevant to the digital, global world in which we now live? *University Council for Educational Administration*, 52(2), 1–28.

McLeskey, J., Rosenberg, M. S., and Westling, D. L. (2010). *Inclusion: Effective practices for all students.* Upper Saddle River, NJ: Pearson.

Mehlinger, H. D. (1996, February). School reform in the Information Age. *Phi Delta Kappan,* 400–407.

Mental Health Canada. (2015). Crisis Intervention: ADHD. Retrieved April 28, 2015, from www.mentalhealthcanada.com/ConditionsandDisordersDetail.asp?lang%20=e&category=60.

Merideth, E. M. (2000). *Leadership strategies for teachers.* Arlington Heights, IL: SkyLight Professional Development.

Miller, B., Moon, J., Elko, S., and Spencer, D. B. (2000). *Teacher leadership in mathematics and science: Casebook and facilitator's guide.* Portsmouth, NH: Heinemann.

Mills, G. E. (2000). *Action research: A guide for the teacher researcher.* Upper Saddle River, NJ: Merrill/Prentice Hall.

Mishna, F., Cook, C., Gadalla, T. Daciuk, J., and Solomon, S. (2010). Cyber bullying behaviors among middle and high school students. *American Journal of Orthopsychiatry,* 80(3), 362–374.

Mishna, F. (2013). After the bell: Canadian students in after-school programs gain higher grades, improved social skills. Retrieved from www.rbc.com/newsroom/news/2013/20130822-after-school.html.

Modi, M., Konstantopoulos, S., and Hedges, L. V. (1998). Predictors of academic giftedness among U.S. high school students: Evidence from a nationally representative multivariate analysis. Paper presented at the Annual Meeting of the American Educational Research Association, San Diego. ERIC Document No. ED422-356.

Molino, F. (1999). My students, my children. In M. K. Rand and S. Shelton-Colangelo (Eds.), *Voices of student teachers: Cases from the field* (pp. 55–56). Upper Saddle River, NJ: Merrill.

Montgomerie, T., King, C., and Dropko, K. (1994). A needs assessment and a design for a distance education system: The Rural Advanced Community of Learners (RACOL). Retrieved August 21, 2007, from www.racol.ualberta.ca/documents/documents/RACOLfinal.doc.

Morris, V. C., and Pai, Y. (1994). *Philosophy and the American school: An introduction to the philosophy of education.* Lanham, MD: University Press of America.

Morris, V. G., Taylor, S. I., and Wilson, J. T. (2000). Using children's stories to promote peace in classrooms. *Early Childhood Education Journal,* 28(1), 41–50.

Morton, C. (1996, February). The modern land of Laputa: Where computers are used in education. *Phi Delta Kappan,* 416–419.

Mourshed, M., Chijioke, C., and Barber, M. (2010). *How the world's most improved school systems keep getting better.* London: McKinsey & Company.

Murnane, R. J., and Levy, F. (1996). *Teaching the new basic skills: Principles for educating children to thrive in a changing economy.* New York: Free Press.

Murphy, J. (1999, April). Reconnecting teaching and school administration: A call for a unified profession. Paper presented at the Annual Meeting of the American Educational Research Association, Montreal.

Murphy, J. (2005). *Connecting teacher leadership and school improvement.* Thousand Oaks, CA: Corwin Press.

National Center for Education Statistics. (2008, February 28). Fast facts. Retrieved from http://nces.ed.gov/fastfacts/display.asp?id=372.

National Council for the Social Studies. (1994). *Expectations of excellence: Curriculum standards for the social studies.* Washington, DC: National Council for the Social Studies.

National Education Association. (2003). *Meeting the Challenges of Recruitment and Retention.* Washington, DC: NEA Press. Retrieved October 18, 2007, from www.nea.org/teacher shortage/images/rrg-full.pdf.

National School Safety Center. (2007). *Working together to create safe schools.* California: Westlake Village.

Nelson, J. L., Carlson, K., and Palonsky, S. B. (2000). *Critical issues in education: A dialectic approach,* 4th ed. New York: McGraw-Hill.

Newmann, F. M., and Associates (Eds.). (1996). *Authentic achievement: Restructuring schools for intellectual quality.* San Francisco: Jossey–Bass Publishers.

Newmann, F. M., and Wehlage, G. G. (1995). *Successful school restructuring: A report to the public and educators by the Center on Organization and Restructuring of Schools.* Madison, WI: University of Wisconsin, Center on Organization and Restructuring of Schools.

Nieto, S. (2003). *What keeps teachers going?* New York: Teachers College Press.

Noddings, N. (2002). *Educating moral people: A caring alternative to character education.* New York: Teachers College Press.

Noddings, N. (2007). *When school reform goes wrong.* New York: Teachers College Press.

Noll, J. W. (Ed.). (1999). *Taking sides: Clashing views on controversial educational issues,* 10th ed. Guilford, CT: McGraw-Hill.

Norris, C. (1994). Computing and the classroom: Teaching the at-risk student. *Computing Teacher,* 21(5), 12, 14.

North Central Regional Educational Laboratory. (1993). Policy briefs, report 1, 1993. Elmhurst, IL: NCREL.

Northwest Regional Educational Laboratory. (1999). *Arts education: Basic to learning.* Portland: Northwest Regional Educational Laboratory.

Nova Scotia Department of Education. (2001). *Nova Scotia teacher certification handbook.* Halifax: Nova Scotia Department of Education.

Nova Scotia Department of Education. (2012). *Nova Scotia Public Education Teacher Supply and Demand: 2012 Update Report.* Halifax: Nova Scotia Department of Education.

Nova Scotia Education and Culture. (1999). *Foundation for the Atlantic Canada social studies curriculum.* Halifax: Atlantic Provinces Education Foundation.

Oakes, J., and Lipton, M. (2007). *Teaching to change the world,* 3rd ed. Boston: McGraw-Hill.

OECD. (2014), *Education at a Glance 2014: OECD Indicators,* OECD Publishing. http://dx.doi.org/10.1787/eag-2014-en

Olsen, G., and Fuller, M. L. (2010). *Home and school relations: Teachers and parents working together,* 4th ed. Upper Saddle Rivier, NJ: Pearson Education.

Ontario College of Teachers. (2014). *Transition to teaching report.* Toronto: Ontario College of Teachers.

Ontario Education Services Corporation. (2014). Good governance: A guide for trustees, school boards, directors of education and communities. Retrieved September 15, 2015, from http://cge.ontarioschooltrustees.org/files/en_good-governance.pdf.

Ontario Human Rights Commission. (2001, December). *Report of the Ontario Human Rights Commission.* Toronto: Queen's Printer for Ontario, 2006.

Ontario Ministry of Education. (2005). *Education for all: The report of the expert panel on literacy and numeracy instruction for students with special education needs, kindergarten to Grade 6.* Retrieved March 5, 2015, from www.edu.gov.on.ca/eng/document/reports/speced/panel/speced.pdf.

Ontario Ministry of Education. (2005). *Many roots, many voices: Supporting English language learners in every classroom.* Toronto: Queen's Printer for Ontario.

Ontario Ministry of Education. (2007). *The Ontario Curriculum, English.* Toronto: Queen's Printer for Ontario.

Ontario Ministry of Education. (2008). *Finding common ground: Character development in Ontario schools, K–12.* Toronto: Queen's Printer for Ontario. Retrieved February 14, 2015, from http://www.edu.gov.on.ca/eng/document/reports/literacy/booklet2008.pdf.

Ontario Ministry of Education. (2008). *NTIP: Induction Elements Manual.*

Ontario Ministry of Education. (2009). *Realizing the promise of diversity: Ontario's equity and inclusive education strategy.* Toronto: Queen's Printer for Ontario. Retrieved April 30, 2015, from www.edu.gov.on.ca/eng/policyfunding/equity.pdf.

Ontario Ministry of Education. (2013). *Learning for all: A guide to effective assessment and instruction for all students, kindergarten to grade 12.* Toronto: Queen's Printer for Ontario: Author.

Ontario Ministry of Education. (2015). Parent involvement committees. Retrieved from www.edu.gov.on.ca/eng/parents/PIC.html.

Ontario School Trustees. (2014). Good governance: A guide for trustees, school boards, directors of education and communities. Retrieved from http://cge.ontarioschooltrustees.org/files/en_good-governance.pdf.

Oppenheimer, T. (1997, July). The computer delusion. *The Atlantic Monthly,* 45–62.

Ormrod, J. E. (2006). *Essentials of educational psychology.* Upper Saddle River, NJ: Merrill/Pearson Education.

Ormrod, J. E., and McGuire, D. J. (2007). *Case studies: Applying educational psychology*. Upper Saddle River, NJ: Pearson Education.

Osterman, K. F. (2000). Students' need for belonging in the school community. *Review of Educational Research, 70*(3), 323–367.

Ottawa-Carlton District School Board (Board Procedure PR.585.CUR), June, 2000.

Ottawa Citizen. (2007, March 30). Canada's top 20 jobs.

Ozmon, H. W., and Craver, S. M. (1999). *Philosophical foundations of education*, 6th ed. Upper Saddle River, NJ: Merrill.

Pajak, E. (1999). *Approaches to clinical supervision: Alternatives for improving instruction*. Norwood, MA: Christopher-Gordon.

Pansegrau, M. (1997, Fall). Public education governance undergoes facelift as change sweeps nation's school boards. *Spectrum*. Retrieved October 3, 2003, from www.cdnsba.org/energyinnovators/articles.html.

Parkay, F. W., Anctil, E., and Hass, G. (2010). *Curriculum leadership: Readings for developing quality educational programs*, 9th ed. Upper Saddle River, NJ: Allyn and Bacon/Pearson.

Parkay, F. W., and Oaks, M. M. (1998, April 15). Promoting the professional development of teachers: What the U.S. can learn from other countries. Paper presented at the Annual Meeting of the American Educational Research Association, San Diego.

Pashler, H., and Carrier, M. (1996). Structures, processes, and the flow of information. In E. Bjork and R. Bjork (Eds.), *Memory* (pp. 3–29). San Diego, CA: Academic Press.

Paul, J. L., Christensen, L., and Falk, G. (2000). Accessing the intimate spaces of life in the classroom through letters to former teachers: A protocol for uncovering hidden stories. In J. L. Paul and T. J. Smith (Eds.), *Stories out of school: Memories and reflections on care and cruelty in the classroom* (pp. 15–26). Stamford, CT: Ablex.

Piirto, J. (1999). *Talented children and adults: Their development and education*. Upper Saddle River, NJ: Merrill.

Pitton, D. E. (1998). *Stories of student teaching: A case approach to the student teaching experience*. Upper Saddle River, NJ: Merrill.

Portelli, J., and Solomon, R. P. (2001). *A wolf in sheep's clothing: The erosion of democracy in education*. Calgary: Detselig Enterprises, 136.

Posner, G. J. (2003). *Field experience: A guide to reflective teaching*, 6th ed. Boston: Pearson Education.

Powell, A. G. (1980). *The uncertain profession*. Cambridge, MA: Harvard University Press.

Power, E. J. (1982). *Philosophy of education: Studies in philosophies, schooling, and educational policies*. Englewood Cliffs, NJ: Prentice Hall.

PREVNet. (2015). Bullying. The facts. Retrieved March 21, 2015, from www.prevnet.ca/research/bullying-statistics/bullying-the-facts.

Public Safety Canada. (2010). A statistical snapshot of youth at risk and youth offending in Canada. National Crime Prevention Centre. Retrieved May 22, 2015, from www.publicsafety.gc.ca/cnt/rsrcs/pblctns/ststclsnpsht-yth/ssyr-eng.pdf.

Rallis, S. F. (1990). Professional teachers and restructured schools: Leadership challenges. In B. Mitchell and L. L. Cunningham (Eds.), *Educational leadership and changing contexts of families, communities, and schools* (89th NSSE yearbook). Chicago: University of Chicago Press.

Ravitz, J. L., Becker, H. J., and Wong, Y. T. (2000, July). Survey report: Constructivist-compatible beliefs and practices among U.S. teachers. The University of California, Irvine, and the University of Minnesota: Center for Research on Information Technology and Organizations.

RCM Research Corporation. (1998). *Time: Critical issues in educational change*. Portsmouth, NH: RCM Research Corporation.

Renzulli, J. S. (1998). The three-ring conception of giftedness. In S. M. Baum, S. M. Reis, and L. R. Maxfield (Eds.), *Nurturing the gifts and talents of primary grade students*. Mansfield Center, CT: Creative Learning Press.

Rich, J. M. (1984). *Professional ethics in education*. Springfield, IL: Charles C. Thomas.

Richardson, V. (Ed.). (2001). *Handbook of research on teaching*, 4th ed. Washington, DC: American Educational Research Association.

Rideout, V., Foehr, U., and Roberts, D. (2010). *Generation M2: Media in the lives of 8- to 18-year-olds*. Menlo Park, CA: Kaiser Family Foundation Study.

Ripple, R. E., and Rockcastle, V. E. (Eds.). (1964). *Piaget rediscovered: A report of the conference on cognitive studies and curriculum development.* Ithaca, NY: Cornell University, School of Education.

Robinson, A. (2008). Teacher characteristics. In J. A. Plucker and C. M. Callahan (Eds.), *Critical issues and practices in gifted education: What the research says* (pp. 669–680). Waco, TX: Prufrock Press.

Robinson, K. (2006). Do schools kill creativity? TED talk, www.ted.com/talks/ken_robinson_says_schools_kill_creativity?language=en.

Roehr Institute. (2000). *Count us in: A demographic overview of childhood and disability in Canada.* Toronto: Roehr Institute.

Rogers, B. (2002). *Teacher leadership and behaviour management.* London; Thousand Oaks, CA: Sage Publications.

Rogers, C. (1961). *On becoming a person.* Boston: Houghton Mifflin.

Rogers, C. (1982). *Freedom to learn in the eighties.* Columbus, OH: Merrill.

Rogers, K. (1991). *The relationship of grouping practices to the education of the gifted and talented learner.* Storrs, CT: University of Connecticut, National Research Center on the Gifted and Talented.

Rogon, K. (1993). Grouping the gifted and talented. *Roper Review, 16,* 8–12.

Rosen, L. (2010). *Rewired: Understanding the iGeneration and the way they learn.* New York: Palgrave.

Rosenshine, B. (1988). Explicit teaching. In D. Berliner and B. Rosenshine (Eds.), *Talks to teachers.* New York: Random House.

Rosenshine, B. (1995). Advances in research on instruction. *The Journal of Educational Research, 88*(5), 262–268.

Rosenshine, B., Meister, C., and Chapman, S. (1996). Teaching students to generate questions: A review of the intervention studies. *Review of Educational Research, 66*(2), 181–221.

Rosenshine, B., and Stevens, R. (1986). Teaching functions. In M. C. Wittrock (Ed.), *Handbook of research on teaching,* 3rd ed. New York: Macmillan.

Runte, R. (1995). Is teaching a profession? In G. Taylor and R. Runte (Eds.), *Thinking about teaching: An introduction* (pp. 288–299). Toronto: Harcourt Brace.

Salas, K., Tenorio, R., Walters, S., and Weiss, D. (2004). *The new teacher book: Finding purpose, balance, and hope during your first years in the classroom.* Milwaukee, WI: Rethinking Schools.

Sallie Mae Corporation. (1995). *A report from the 1994 Sallie Mae symposium on quality education.* Washington, DC: Sallie Mae Corporation.

Salovey, P., and Sluyter, D. J. (Eds.). (1997). *Emotional development and emotional intelligence: Educational implications.* New York: Basic Books.

Sandholtz, J. J., Ringstaff, C., and Dwyer, D. C. (1997). *Teaching with technology: Creating student-centered classrooms.* New York: Teachers College Press.

Saskatchewan Education. (2011). Renewed core curriculum. Retrieved October 22, 2015, from www.publications.gov.sk.ca/deplist.cfm?d=11&c=2437.

Saskatchewan School Trustees Association. (1997). Canadian educational governance update. Retrieved June 12, 2003, from www.ssta.sk.ca/research/governance/csbacan.htm.

Saul, J. R. (2002). In defence of public education. *Horizons, 1*(1), 8–14. Ottawa: Canadian Teachers' Federation.

Scales, P. C. (2001). The public image of adolescents. *Society, 38*(4), 64–70.

Scardamalia, M., and Bereiter, C. (1994). Computer support for knowledge-building communities. *Journal of Learning Sciences, 3*(3), 265–283.

Scardamalia, M., and Bereiter, C. (2003). Knowledge building environments: Extending the limits of the possible in education and knowledge work. In A. Distefano, K. E. Rudestam, and R. Silverman (Eds.), *Encyclopedia of distributed learning* (pp. 269–272). Thousand Oaks, CA: Sage.

Scardamalia, M., and Bereiter, C. (2015). Education in an open informational world. In R. A. Scott and S. M. Kosslyn (Eds), *Emerging trends in the social and behavioral sciences: An interdisciplinary, searchable, and linkable resource.* Hoboken, NJ: John Wiley & Sons.

Schaefer, R. (1967). *The school as the center of inquiry.* New York: Harper and Row.

Schmuck, R. A., and Schmuck, P. A. (2001). *Group processes in the classroom,* 8th ed. Boston: McGraw-Hill.

Schneider, R. B., and Barone, D. (1997, Spring). Cross-age tutoring. *Childhood Education,* 136–143.

Schön, D. (1983). *The reflective practitioner: How professionals think in action.* New York: Basic Books.

Schön, D. (1987). *Educating the reflective practitioner: Toward a new design for teaching and learning in the professions.* San Francisco: Jossey–Bass Publishers.

Schön, D. (1991). *The reflective turn: Case studies in and on educational practice.* New York: Teachers College Press.

Schunk, D. (2004). *Learning theories: An educational perspective,* 4th ed. Upper Saddle River, NJ: Merrill/ Prentice Hall.

Schwartz, J. E., and Beichner, R. J. (1999). *Essentials of educational technology.* Boston: Allyn and Bacon.

Schwebel, A. J., Coslett, H. B., Bradt, J., and Friedman, R. (1996). *The student teacher's handbook,* 3rd ed. Mahwah, NJ: Lawrence Erlbaum Associates.

Search Institute. (2010). How many assets do young people have? Minneapolis: Author. Retrieved October 12, 2015, from www.search-institute.org/content/40-developmental-assets-adolescents-ages-12-18.

Shanker, S. (2013). *Calm, alert and learning: Classroom strategies for self-regulation.* Toronto: Pearson Education Canada.

Sharan, Y., and Sharan, S. (1989/1990, December/January). Group investigation expands cooperative learning. *Educational Leadership,* 17–21.

Shenk, D. (1998). *Data smog: Surviving the information age.* New York: HarperEdge.

Shulman, L. (1987). Knowledge and teaching: Foundations of the new reform. *Harvard Educational Review,* 57(1), 1–22.

Sigalit, U., and Van Lehn, K. (1995). STEPS: A simulated, tutorable physics student. *Journal of Artificial Intelligence in Education,* 6(4), 405–437.

Singer, A. (1994, December). Reflections on multiculturalism. *Phi Delta Kappan,* 284–288.

Skinner, B. F. (1972). Utopia through the control of human behavior. In J. M. Rich (Ed.), *Readings in the philosophy of education.* Belmont, CA: Wadsworth.

Slavin, R. E. (2000). *Educational psychology: Theory and practice,* 7th ed. Boston: Allyn and Bacon.

Smith, D. D. (2007). *Introduction to special education: Making a difference,* 6th ed. Upper Saddle River, NJ: Pearson.

Smith, F. (2009). Why arts education is crucial, and who's doing it best. Edutopia. Retrieved from www.edutopia.org/arts-music-curriculum-child-development.

Smith, K. B., and Meier, K. K. (1995). *The case against school choice: Politics, markets, and fools.* Armonk, NY: M. E. Sharpe.

Smolkin, R. (1999, February 27–28). The reading debate rages. Moscow-Pullman *Daily News,* 1A, 10A.

Smyth, W. (1995). *Clinical supervision: Collaborative learning about teaching.* New York: State Mutual Book and Periodical Service.

Snyder, J. F. (1999). The alternative of substitute teaching. In *Job search handbook for educators* (p. 38). Evanston, IL: American Association for Employment in Education.

Snyder, K. J., and Anderson, R. H. (Eds.). (1996). *Clinical supervision: Coaching for higher performance.* Lanham, MD: Scarecrow Press.

Sowell, E. J. (1996). *Curriculum: An integrative introduction.* Boston: Allyn and Bacon.

Spring, J. (1998). *Conflict of interests: The politics of American education,* 3rd ed. Boston: McGraw-Hill.

Spring, J. (1999). *American education,* 8th ed. New York: McGraw-Hill.

Spring, J. (2008). *The American school: From the Puritans to no child left behind,* 7th ed. Boston: McGraw-Hill.

Sricharatchanya, P. (1996, November 5). Education reforms are also crucial. *Bangkok Post,* 15.

Stanley, G. F. (1936). *The birth of western Canada: A history of the Riel rebellions.* Reprint (1992) University of Toronto Press.

Statistics Canada. (2001a). *A profile of disability in Canada.* Catalogue No. 89-577-XIE. Ottawa: Housing, Family and Social Statistics Division. Retrieved August 30, 2007, from www.statcan.ca/english/freepub/89-577-XIE/89-577-XIE2001001.pdf.

Statistics Canada. (2001b). *Canada's ethnocultural portrait: The changing mosaic.* Retrieved October 11, 2003, from www12.statcan.ca/english/census01/Products/Analytic/companion/etoimm/canada.cfm.

Statistics Canada. (2001c). Sprott, J. B., Doob, A. N., and Jenkins, J. M. *Problem behaviour and delinquency in children and youth.* Catalogue number 85-002-XPE Vol. 21, No 4. Retrieved August 18, 2007, from www.statcan.ca/english/freepub/85-002-XIE/0040185-002-XIE.pdf.

Statistics Canada. (2002a). Bushnik, T., Barr-Telford, L., and Bussière, P. *In and out of high school: Results from the first cycle of the youth in transition Survey.* Catalogue # 81-593-MIE_No. 014.

Statistics Canada. (2011). Immigration and ethnocultural diversity in Canada. Retrieved October 21, 2015, from www12.statcan.gc.ca/nhs-enm/2011/as-sa/99-010-x/99-010-x2011001-eng.cfm.

St. Michel, T. (1995). *Effective substitute teachers: Myth, mayhem, or magic?* Thousand Oaks, CA: Corwin Press.

Stanford, B. H. (1992). Gender equity in the classroom. In D. A. Byrnes and G. Kiger (Eds.), *Common bonds: Anti-bias teaching in a diverse society.* Wheaton, MD: Association for Childhood Education International.

Steeves, V. (2014). *Young Canadians in a wired world, phase III: Trends and recommendations.* Ottawa: MediaSmarts.

Sternberg, R. J. (1996, March). Myths, countermyths, and truths about intelligence. *Educational Researcher,* 11–16.

Sternberg, R. J. (2002). Beyond g: The theory of successful intelligence. In R. J. Sternberg and E. L. Grigorenko (Eds.), *The general actor of intelligence: How general is it?* (pp. 447–479). Mahwah, NJ: Lawrence Erlbaum.

Steinberg, L., Dornbusch, S., and Brown, B. (1996). *Beyond the classroom: Why school reform has failed and what parents need to do.* New York: Simon and Schuster.

Stoll, C. (1996). *Silicon snake oil: Second thoughts on the information highway.* New York: Anchor.

Stoll, C. (1999). *High-tech heretic: Why computers don't belong in the classroom and other reflections by a computer contrarian.* New York: Doubleday.

Stone, R., and Cuper, P. H. (2006). *Best practices for teacher leadership: What award-winning teachers do for their professional learning communities.* Thousand Oaks, CA: Corwin Press.

Street, B. (1995). *Social Literacies: Critical approaches to literacy in development, ethnography and education.* New York: Routledge.

Swearer, S. M., Espelage, D. L., Vaillancourt, T., and Hymel, S. (2010). What can be done about school bullying? Linking research to educational practice. *Educational Researcher,* 39(1), 38–47.

Sykes, G. (1983). Contradictions, ironies, and promises unfulfilled: A contemporary account of the status of teaching. *Phi Delta Kappan,* 65(2), 87–93.

Tannock, R. (2007). The educational implications of attention deficit hyperactivity disorder. (Research Monograph #3 in the series *What Works? Research into Practice,* published by the Ontario Ministry of Education, Literacy and Numeracy Secretariat). Retrieved from www.edu.gov.on.ca/eng/literacynumeracy/inspire/research/Tannock.pdf.

Tapscott, D. (1999, July 6). Kids, technology and the schools. Computerworld.

Teacher supply and demand: Facts and statistics on education funding and teaching in Alberta. (n.d.). Retrieved August 27, 2007, from www.education.gov.ab.ca/FactsStats/PWC/supply.pdf.

Terman, L. M., Baldwin, B. T., and Bronson, E. (1925). Mental and physical traits of a thousand gifted children. In L. M. Terman (Ed.), *Genetic studies of genius,* Vol. 1. Stanford, CA: Stanford University Press.

Terman, L. M., and Oden, M. H. (1947). The gifted child grows up. In L. M. Terman (Ed.), *Genetic studies of genius,* Vol. 4. Stanford, CA: Stanford University Press.

Terman, L. M., and Oden, M. H. (1959). The gifted group in mid-life. In L. M. Terman (Ed.), *Genetic studies of genius,* Vol. 5. Stanford, CA: Stanford University Press.

Thelen, H. A. (1960). *Education and the human quest.* New York: Harper and Row.

The Teacher Educator. (2011). Voices in education: Traditional or alternative teacher education (Featured Article). *The Teacher Educator,* 46(3), 177–181. doi: 10.1080/08878730.2011.583191.

Third, A., Bellerose, D., Dawkins, U., Keltie, E., & Pihl, K. (2014). Children's rights in the digital age. Young and Well Cooperative Research Centre, Melbourne.

Tombari, M. L., and Borich, G. D. (1999). *Authentic assessment in the classroom: Applications and practice.* Upper Saddle River, NJ: Merrill.

Tomlinson, C. A. (2004). *La classe différenciée.* Montreal: Chenelière/McGraw-Hill.

Trent, B., and Chisholm, J. S. (2012). "Everything . . . affects everything": Promoting critical perspectives toward bullying with thirteen reasons why. *English Journal,* 101(6), 75–80.

Trotter, A. (1998, October 1). A question of effectiveness. *Education Week: Technology Counts 1998,* 18, 6–9.

Truth and Reconciliation Commission of Canada. (2012). *Truth and Reconciliation Commission of Canada interim report*. Winnipeg, Canada: Author. Retrieved from www.myrobust.com/websites/trcinstitution/File/Interim%20report%20English%20electronic.pdf.

Truth and Reconciliation Commission of Canada. (2015). *Honouring the truth, reconciling for the future: Summary of the final report of the Truth and Reconciliation Commission of Canada*. Winnipeg, Canada: Author. Retrieved from www.trc.ca/websites/trcinstitution/File/2015/Honouring_the_Truth_Reconciling_for_the_Future_July_23_2015.pdf.

Turnbull, M. (2000). Introduction: What is core French? Core French FAQ. Retrieved October 11, 2003, from www.cpfnb.com/core_FAQ/CoreFAQ.html.

Tyler, R. (1949). *Basic principles of curriculum and instruction*. Chicago: University of Chicago Press.

Uchida, D., Cetron, M., and McKenzie, F. (1996). *Preparing students for the 21st century*. Arlington, VA: American Association of School Administrators.

UK Government News Release. (2014, February 4). Year of Code and £500,000 fund to inspire future tech experts launched. Retrieved from www.gov.uk/government/news/year-of-code-and-500000-fund-to-inspire-future-tech-experts-launched.

UNICEF Innocenti Research Centre. (2012). Measuring child poverty: New league tables of child poverty in the world's rich countries. Innocenti Report Card 10, UNICEF Innocenti Research Centre, Florence.

United Nations Educational, Scientific and Cultural Organization (UNESCO). (2008). *Inclusive education: The way of the future*. UNESCO International Conference on Education, November 25–28. Geneva: Author.

Utay, C., and Utay, J. (1997). Peer-assisted learning: The effects of cooperative learning and cross-age peer tutoring with word processing on writing skills of students with learning disabilities. *Journal of Computing in Childhood Education*, 8(2/3), 165–185.

Vaughn, S., Bos, C. S., and Schumm, J. S. (1997). *Teaching mainstreamed, diverse, and at-risk students in the general education classroom*. Boston: Allyn and Bacon.

Vreeman, R., and Carroll, A. (2007). A systematic review of school-based interventions to prevent bullying. *Archives of Pediatrics and Adolescent Medicine*, 161, 78–88.

Vygotsky, L. S. (1978). *Mind in society: The development of higher mental process*. Cambridge, MA: Harvard University Press.

Vygotsky, L. S. (1986). *Thought and language*. Cambridge, MA: MIT Press.

Wagner, K. (1998). Choice in public education. Policy Watch. Vancouver: Society for the Advancement of Excellence in Public Education. Retrieved October 24, 2002, from www.geocities.com/Athens/5909/choices.html.

Walberg, H. J., and Greenberg, R. C. (1997, May). Using the learning environment inventory. *Educational Leadership*, 45–47.

Wallace, R. M. (2004, Summer). A framework for understanding teaching with the internet. *American Educational Research Journal*, 41(2), 447–488.

Walsh, M. (1999, May). Two reports offer bright outlook for education industry. *Education Week*, 18(36), 5.

Walters, L. S. (1999, January/February). What makes a good school violence prevention program? *Harvard Education Letter*.

Washington, W. (1998). Optional extended year program feedback. Austin Independent School District, TX, Department of Accountability, Student Services, and Research.

Wasserman, S. (1994, April). Using cases to study teaching. *Phi Delta Kappan*, 602–611.

Webb, L. D., Metha, A., and Jordan, K. F. (1999). *Foundations of American education*, 3rd ed. Englewood Cliffs, NJ: Prentice Hall.

Wechsler, D. (1958). *The measurement and appraisal of adult intelligence*, 4th ed. Baltimore, MD: Williams and Wilkins.

Western Canadian Protocol for Collaboration in Basic Education. (2000). Retrieved October 20, 2003, from www.wcp.ca.

Whitacker, T. (2012). *What great teachers do differently*. Larchmont, NY: Eye on Education Press.

Williams, J. (1999, April 18). Urban schools' obstacles hindering technology. *Milwaukee Journal Sentinel*.

Wilson, B. L., and Corbett, H. D. (2001). *Listening to urban kids: School reform and the teachers they want*. Albany: State University of New York Press.

Wirt, F. M., and Kirst, M. W. (1997). *The political dynamics of American education*. Berkeley, CA: McCutchan.

Wise, A. E. (2005). Establishing teaching as a profession: The essential role of professional accreditation. *Journal of Teacher Education, 56*(4), 318–331.

Wiske, M. S., Rennebohm F., K., and Breit, L. (2005). *Teaching for understanding with technology*. San Francisco: Jossey–Bass Publishers.

Wohlstetter, P. (1995, September). Getting school-based management right: What works and what doesn't. *Phi Delta Kappan*, 22–24, 26.

Wohlstetter, P., and Anderson, L. (1994, February). What can U.S. charter schools learn from England's grant-maintained schools? *Phi Delta Kappan*, 486–491.

Wolfgang, C. H. (2001). *Solving discipline problems: Methods and models for today's teachers*, 5th ed. Boston: Allyn and Bacon.

Woolfolk, A. E. (2007). *Educational psychology*, 10th ed. Boston: Allyn and Bacon.

Wray, H. (1999). *Japanese and American education: Attitudes and practices*. Oxford, UK: Bergin and Garvey Publishers.

Yamamoto, K., Davis, O. L., Jr., Dylak, S., Whittaker, J., Marsh, C., and van der Westhuizen, P. C. (1996, Spring). Across six nations: Stressful events in the lives of children. *Child Psychiatry and Human Development*, 139–150.

Young, L., Levin, B., and Wallin, D. (2014). *Understanding Canadian schools: An introduction to educational administration*, 5th ed. Retrieved from http://home.cc.umanitoba.ca/~wallind/understandingcanadianschools5.html.

Zeichner, K., and Liston, D. (2013). *Reflective teaching: An introduction*, 2nd ed. Hoboken, NJ: Taylor and Francis.

Zepeda, R., Mayers, R. S., and Benson, B. N. (2002). *The call to teacher leadership*. West Larchmont, NY: Eye on Education, 71–91.

Zukowski, V. (1997, Fall). Teeter-totters and tandem bikes: A glimpse into the world of cross-age tutors. *Teaching and Change, 5*(1), 71–91.

Name Index

A

Abrahamson, B., 264
Adams Becker, S., 221
Ahmed, R., 12
Ainsworth, S., 251
Alberta Education, 219
Anctil, E. J., 149t, 197, 205
Andre, T., 207
Apple, Inc., 251
Armstrong, P. A., 132
Aud, S., 207

B

Baldwin, B. T., 159
Ballantine, J. H., 122
Banks, J. A., 118, 124, 128
Baratz-Snowden, J., 265, 303
Barber, M., 316
Barlow, M., 313
Barman, J., 72
Barone, D., 200
Beard, C., 219
Becker, H. J., 52f
Beggs, P., 229
Belsey, B., 135
Bennett, S., 158, 159
Benson, J., 189
Bereiter, C., 28
Bernstein, B. B., 119
Bezeau, L. M., 86, 87, 91, 94
Bitter, G. G., 246
Bligh, B., 251
Bloom, B. S., 195
Boles, K., 263
Bolgatz, J., 127
Borich, G. D., 178, 180
Bowerman, M., 246
Boyer, E., 263, 313
Bracey, G. W., 150
Bradt, J., 36
Brameld, T., 58, 59
Breit, L., 246
Brien, K., 103
Bronson, E., 159
Brophy, J. E., 177, 185, 190, 311
Brown, B., 199
Brown, D., 315
Brown, F. B., 207
Brown, J., 91, 92
Brown, R., 315
Buchmann, M., 303
Bucky, P. A., 4
Burke, A., 255

C

Burnaford, G., 274
Bursuck, W. D., 167

Cairns, R. B., 207
Calder Stegemann, K. J., 132
Caldwell, B., 95
Calhoun, E., 195, 199, 309
Campbell, D. M., 40
Canadian Association of Second Language
     Teachers (CASLT), 221
Canadian Council on Learning, 129, 159
Canadian Education Association (CEA), 92, 270
Canadian Society for the Study of Education (CSSE), 271
Canadian Teachers' Federation (CTF), 9, 10, 269, 284
Canadian Youth in Challenging Contexts (CYCC), 314
Cappon, P., 129
Carlson, K., 55
Carrier, M., 198
Carroll, A., 135
Carroll, J., 195
Chijioke, C., 316
Chisholm, J. S., 135
Clandinin, J., 25
Cobb, C. D., 206
Coladarci, T., 206
Colin, S., 4
Collins, A., 28
Colucci, K., 181, 206
Consortium for School Networking, 230
Cook, A., 246
Cordeiro, P. A., 260
Corrigan, D. C., 263
Coslett, H. B., 36
Council of Ministers of Education, Canada (CMEC), 87, 89,
     90, 90f, 91, 214, 219, 286
Craver, S. M., 49, 58
Crook, C., 251
Cunningham, W. G., 260
Curwin, R., 191

D

Dafna, K., 159
Darling-Hammond, L., 265, 284, 319
Deal, T. E., 118, 122
Dehue, F., 135
Dell'Olio, J. M., 196
Denemark, D. W., 263
Dollase, R. H., 41
Donk, T., 196
Doorlag, D. H., 167
Dornbusch, S., 199
Drew, C. J., 166f
Duke, D. L., 263

E

Eby, J. W., 17f
Education Canada, 188
Education Law Reporter: Elementary and Secondary Schools, 165f
Education Technology Advisory Council (ETAC), 233
Education Week, 227
Egan, M. W., 166f
Eggen, P. D., 191, 198t
Eisner, E. W., 4, 15, 25, 204, 206
Emmer, E. T., 190, 192
2009 Equity and Inclusive Education survey, 135
Erickson, H. I., 23
Erikson, E. H., 149
Erikson, J. M., 149
Espelage, D. L., 135
Estrada, V., 221
Etzioni, A., 263
Evans, L., 123
Evertson, C. M., 190, 192

F

Fairholm, G. W., 262
Fairholm, M. R., 262
Fashola, O., 314
Feiman-Nemser, S., 265, 266, 282, 284, 296, 299, 303
Ferris, S., 3
First Nations Studies Program at UBC, 87
Fischer, J., 274
Foehr, U., 12
Fox, M., 207
Freedman, S., 263
Freeman, A., 221
Freire, P., 59, 118, 215
Friedman, R., 36
Friend, M., 167
Fullan, M., 229, 255, 266, 267, 316

G

Gadanidis, G., 30
Gagné, R. M., 194
Galczynski, M., 125
Galway, G., 91, 92
Gardner, H., 156, 158
George Lucas Educational Foundation, 12
Gerber, S. B., 207
Ghosh, R., 125
Gibbs, J., 180
Gilligan, C., 150
Glasser, W. R., 189, 190, 193
Global News, 8
Godden, L., 296
Goleman, D., 117
Good, T. L., 177, 185, 190, 194, 311
Goodlad, J., 263
Gordon, W. J. J., 309
Gougeon, T., 263
Graham, R., 251
Grant, P. G., 35
Greenberg, R. C., 181, 182t

Greenwood, E., 263
Grouws, D. A., 194

H

Hall, R., 264, 265, 266
Hallahan, D. P., 162, 167, 168
Halverson, R., 28
Hankins, K. H., 22
Hansen, D., 18
Hansen, D. T., 50
Hardman, M. L., 166f
Hargreaves, A., 264, 266, 267
Harper, L., 24, 41
Harris, A., 276, 277
Harris, J. R., 323
Harris, R., 198
Harris Interactive, Inc., 3, 181
Harste, J., 214
Hass, G., 149t, 197, 205
Health Canada, 134
Heath, S. B., 119
Hebert, Y., 72
Hedges, L. V., 207
Henkin, R., 135
Henriques, M. E., 200
Henry , E., 24, 41, 119, 128
Herbert, M., 247
Hinduja, S., 135, 136
Hobson, D., 274
Hoh, P. S., 163
Holland, A., 207
Holly, M. L., 270
Howsam, R. B., 263
Hoy, W. K., 264, 265, 266
Hughes, J., 30, 41, 255
Huntley, J., 24, 41
Hymel, S., 135

I

Ingersol, R., 41
International Reading Association (IRA), 215
International Society for Technology in Education (ISTE), 235f–236f
2010 International Youth Survey, 134

J

Jackson, J., 263
Jamieson, B., 4
Johns, F. A., 192
Johnson, D. W., 179
Johnson, L., 28, 221
Johnson, R. T., 179
Jonassen, D., 28
Jordan, K. F., 80, 207
Joyce, B., 195, 199, 309

K

Karsenti, T., 4
Kauchak, D. P., 191, 198t

Kauffman, J. M., 162, 167, 168
KewalRamani, A., 207
Koh, C., 27
Kohlberg, H., 150
Kohn, A., 192
Kohrs, D., 207
Konstantopoulos, S., 207
Kottler, J. A., 29
Krogh, S. L., 208
Kulik, J. A., 163
Kutsyuruba, B., 296, 317

L

Labaree, D. F., 303
Language and Literacy Researchers of Canada
 (LLRC), 214, 215
Langworthy, M., 229, 255
Lanzarro, C., 207
Lawton, S., 315
Leahey, T., 198
Learning Disabilities Association of Canada, 161
Learning Partnership, The, 229, 231
Leatherdale, S. T., 12
Levey, S., 268
Levin, B., 87, 91, 100, 102, 264
Lewis, R. B., 167
Lieberman, A., 276
Lipton, M., 6, 186, 187, 190
Liston, D., 299, 300
Lo, L., 264
Lortie, D. C., 265, 284, 303
Luckin, R., 251
Lundy, K., 181

M

Macedo, D., 215
MacKay, A. W., 103, 104, 106, 107
MacLeod, J., 119
MacNaughton, R. H., 192
Maddux, R., 28
Mahoney, J., 207
Manches, A., 251
Martinez, M. E., 15
Martino, W., 129, 130
Maslow, A. H., 60, 152, 152f
Mastropieri, M. A., 164, 168
May, S., 127
McCaskill, D., 72
McCourt, F., 9
McGuire, D. J., 178
McHugh, J., 12
McKamey, C., 24, 41
McLeod, S., 14
McLeskey, J., 164
McLoughlin, C., 270
MediaSmarts, 228, 251
Melenyzer, B., 40
Mendler, A., 191
Metha, A., 80
Mills, G. E., 274, 275

Ministry of Education, 94
Mishna, F., 314
Miskel, C. G., 264, 265, 266
Modi, M., 207
Morris, V. C., 54
Morris, V. G., 135
Mourshed, M., 316

N

Nash, R. J., 263
National Occupational Classification (NOC), 263
National Symposium on Arts Education (NSAE), 221
Nelson, J. L., 55
Nettles, D., 40, 207
New Brunswick Teachers' Association (NBTA), 299
Newfoundland and Labrador Department of Education, 220
Newmann, F. M., 187
Newmann, F. M. & Associates, 187
Nieto, S., 15
Noddings, N., 181
Noss, R., 251
Nova Scotia Department of Education, 8

O

Oakes, J., 6, 186, 187, 190
Oden, M. H., 159
Ontario College of Teachers (OCT), 266, 287
Ontario Ministry of Education (OME), 126, 164, 215,
 223, 265
Ormrod, J. E., 15, 178
Osterman, K. F., 135
Ottawa Citizen, 4
Ozmon, H. A., 49, 58

P

Pai, Y., 54
Palonsky, S. B., 55
Parkay, F. W., 35, 197, 205
Pashler, H., 198
Patchin, J. W., 135, 136
Paul, J. L., 181
PCAP's Science Assessment Framework, 219
Peterson, K. D., 118, 122
Pierson, M. E., 246
Pitton, D. E., 37
Pochini, K., 103, 104, 106, 107
Polgar, J., 246
Portelli, J., 30
Posner, G. J., 37
Powell, A. G., 263
Power, E. J., 60
Project SUMIT (Schools Using Multiple Intelligence
 Theory), 157f

R

Ravitz, J. L., 52f
Rawson Wheeler, Patricia J., 31
Reflective Teaching: An Introduction (Zeichner & Liston), 299
Rennebohm, F. K., 246

Renzulli, J. S., 162
Rezai-Rashti, G., 130
Rich, J. M., 264, 265, 266
Richard, K. J., 35
Richardson, W., 251
Rideout, V., 12
Ripple, R. E., 148
Roberts, D., 12
Roberts, W. L., 132
Robinson, A., 163
Rockcastle, V. E., 148
Rogers, C., 60
Rosen, L., 231
Rosenberg, M. S., 164
Rosenshine, B., 194
Runte, R., 263

S

Salovey, P., 157
Saskatchewan School Trustees Association, 92
Saul, J. R., 315
Scales, P. C., 153
Scardamalia, M., 28
Schaefer, R., 272
Schmuck, P. A., 180
Schmuck, R. A., 180
Schneider, R. B., 200
Schön, D., 267, 300
Schubert, W. H., 203
Schunk, D., 198
Schwebel, A. J., 36
Scotland-Moxon, C., 231
Scruggs, T. E., 164, 168
Search Institute, 153
Shanker, S., 117, 188
Sharan, S., 199
Sharan, Y., 199
Sheppard, B., 91, 92
Shulman, L., 30
Skinner, B. F., 60
Slavin, R. E., 157, 159
Sluyter, D. J., 157
Smith, D. D., 159
Smith, F., 221
Snyder, J. F., 39f
Solomon, R. P., 30
Spring, J., 118
St. Michel, T., 39
Stanldy, G. F., 70f
Statistics Canada, 123, 159
Sternberg, L., 199
Sternberg, R. J., 156
Stevens, R., 194
Street, B., 214
Strong, M., 41
Supply Teachers in New Brunswick Report 2012, 299
Sutherland, L., 103, 104, 106, 107
Swartz, L., 181
Swearer, S. M., 135
Sykes, G., 263

T

Tannock, R., 161
Taylor, S. I., 135
Terman, L. M., 159
Thelen, H. A., 199
Tomlinson, C. A., 170
Toronto District School Board, 312
Tregunna, L., 296
Trent, B., 135
Truth and Reconciliation Commission of Canada (TRC), 88
Turnbull, M., 220
Tyler, R., 207

U

UK Government News Release, 28
UNESCO, 126
UNICEF, 254
UNICEF Innocenti Research Centre, 121, 134
University of Toronto, 307
Ushijima, T., 180
Utay, C., 199
Utay, J., 199

V

Vaillancourt, T., 135
Vreeman, R., 135
Vygotsky, L. S., 197

W

Walberg, H. J., 181, 182t
Wallin, D., 87, 91, 100, 102, 264
Wasserman, S., 35
Webb, L. D., 80
Wechsler, D., 155
Wehlage, G. G., 187
Weil, M., 195, 199, 309
Western Canadian Protocol for Collaboration in Basic Education, 216, 220
Westling, D. L., 164
Whitacker, T., 4, 15
Wiens, J., 91, 92
Wilson, J. T., 135
Wise, A. E., 263
Wiske, M. S., 246
Wolfgang, C. H., 193
Wong, Y. T., 52f
Woolfolk, A. E., 123, 311
Wyman, R., 40

Y

Yamamoto, K., 153
Young, L., 87, 91, 100, 102, 264
Young and Well Cooperative Research Centre, 254

Z

Zehm, S. J., 29
Zeichner, K., 299, 300
Zukowski, V., 200

Subject Index

Canadian Society for the Study of Education (CSSE), 271
Canadian Sport for Life principles, 222
Canadian Teacher Magazine, 210
Canadian Teachers' Federation (CTF), 7, 9, 10, 84, 89, 211, 269, 270, 284, 285
Canadian Youth in Challenging Contexts (CYCC), 314
Cappon, Dr. Paul, 129
career service, 290
caring classroom, 181–182
  students' care for others in, 181
Carmichael, Cheryl, 121
cell phones, 13
Centre Travail, 287
challenges for teachers, 9
character education, 150
  components of, 150
charter schools, 314–315
  creation of, 314
  definition of, 314–315
  to promote new teaching strategies, 315
Child, Youth, and Family Services Act (Newfoundland and Labrador), 94
child abuse, 107
  guidelines for reporting, 107
  indicators for, 107, 108t–109t
Child Abuse Registry, 135
childhood,
  latchkey stress in, 153
  psychosocial school-age stage of development, 153
  stresses in, 153
Childhood and Society (Erikson), 149
child pornography, 252
Children's Mental Health Ontario, 138
Children's Rights in the Digital Age, 254
choice theory, 190, 193
Choice Theory (Glasser & Dotson), 189
Choice Theory in the Classroom (Glasser), 189
Christou, Theodore, 271
cisgender, 129
Clandinin, J., 25
classroom,
  academic learning time, 187
  action research in, 272–275
  allocated time, 187
  assistants, 35–36
  authentic pedagogy for positive, 186–186
  block scheduling, 187, 188f
  choice theory of misbehaviour in, 190
  climate, 178–179
  communication skills in, 180
  computer technology in, 236–237
  creating inclusive, 128
  culture, 177–181
  democratic, 189–190
  dimensions of life in, 181
  dimensions of the environment in, 182t
  dynamics, 179–180
  ethical dilemmas in, 100
  gender-fair, 130–131
  management in, 9–10
  multimedia in, 321

opportunity to learn (OTL), 187
organization of to create a positive learning environment, 177–179
outdoors, 184–185
physical and social milieu of, 177–178
physical environment, 182–183
progressively oriented, 58
qualities in for student motivation and positive interactions, 179–180
quality environments in, 189–190
self-contained, 122
strategies for creating moral communities in, 150, 151f
student interactions in, 180
teacher–student interactions in, 123
technology in fine arts, 243
technology in language arts, 243–244
technology in science, 244–245
technology in social studies, 245–246
time on task, 187
time structures in, 187
values-clarification activities in, 310
violence in, 9–10
classroom climate, 178–180
  creating a positive, 181–182
  stages of group development for, 180, 180f
  teachers' influence on, 179
  variables in, 178–179
classroom culture, 123
classroom dynamics, 179–180
  for student motivation and positive interactions, 179–180
classroom management, 187–189
  based on effective learning environments, 188
  to minimize behavioural problems, 188
  planned rules, guidelines, and procedures, 190–191
  structured approaches to inappropriate student behaviour, 191
  trust and respect promotion, 189
classroom observations, 34
  field experiences, 34
  focused and purposeful, 34
  methods for, 34
classroom organization, 185–187
  between-class ability grouping, 185
  cooperative learning student grouping, 185–186
  within-class ability grouping, 185
Class Warfare: The Assault on Canadian Schools (Barlow & Robertson), 313
Cline, Ernest, 238
code of ethics, 97, 266
  provincial and territorial, 98–100
codes of conduct, 266
coding (computer programming), 28
cognitive development, theory of, 147–148
  concrete operations stage, 147
  formal operations stage, 147
  information processing approach to learning, 197
  preoperational stage, 147
  social environment interaction with, 148
cognitive science, 61, 311
collaborative consultation, 168–169
  individualized educational plans (IEPs) and, 169

with parents, 170
  special education and regular education teachers, 169–170
collective bargaining, 101
collège d'enseignement général et professional (CEGEP), 75
collegiality, 31
Collins, A., 28
Colville, Alex, 210
common (case) law (school authority), 103
Common School Act (1816, Ontario), 68
Common School Act (1820, Ontario), 68
Common School Act (1865, British Columbia), 70
Common School Act (1871, New Brunswick), 66
communication, 23
  technology, 27–28, 28
community support, 12, 313
comparative and international education, 318
Comparative and International Education Society of Canada (CIESC), 271
comparative education, 316
compensatory education, 312
computer-assisted instruction (CAI), 246, 246f
computer-enhanced instruction (CEI), 248
  teachers' critical role in, 249
computer-managed instruction (CMI), 246, 248
Computers for Schools (CFS), 237
computer technology as educational mindtool, 28
Concord Consortium, 249
Confederation, 71
Constitution Act, 1982 (prev. *British North America Act (BNA Act) of 1867*), 70, 71, 93
  education for First Nations peoples under, 72
  governance of schools and, 86
  limitations of, 86
constitutional law (school authority), 102–103
constructive assertiveness, 192
  elements of, 192
constructivism, 59, 61
  teaching methods based on, 197
Constructivist-Compatible Beliefs and Practices Among U.S. Teachers (Ravitz, Becker, & Wong), 52f
constructivist perspective on education, 52
constructivist teaching, 197
Cooke, Max, 302
cooperative education programs, 224
cooperative learning, 185–186, 195t
  elements of, 186
  peer-mediated instruction and, 199
  role learning and responsibilities in, 186
  students' interpersonal skills and, 186
cooperative work, 23
Cordeiro, Paula A., 260
core curriculum, 212
core French, 220–221
  aims, 220
  teaching trends in, 220–221
corporal punishment, 106–107
corporate–education partnerships, 312–313
Corporations in the Classroom (documentary), 313
Council of Atlantic Ministers of Education and Training, 213
Council of Ministers of Education, Canada (CMEC), 77, 84, 89, 90, 134, 208, 213, 214, 218, 223, 287

Council of Ontario Directors of Education (CODE), 228
Council on African-Canadian Education, Nova Scotia, 94
Counts, George, 59
Couros, Alec, 271
Craver, Samuel M., 49
creative endeavour mode (of teaching), 18
creativity in classroom, 5
  for the future, 308–309
criminal record checks, 135, 290
critical literacy, 215
  for the future, 308
critical multiculturalism, 127
Critical Multiculturalism: Rethinking Multicultural and Antiracist Education (May), 127
critical pedagogy, 59
  praxis in, 59
critical reflective practice, 268
critical thinking, 5
Cronbach, Lee, 25
cross-age tutoring, 200
cultural identity, 125
culturally literate, 57
cultural mosaic, 127
cultural voices, 127–128
culture,
  common dimensions of, 124
  definition of, 123–124, 177
  dimensions of, 124
  language and, 125, 125f
  regional, 124
Cunningham, William G., 260
curricula (school), 54
  between 1918 and 1939, 74
  arts, 221–222
  Canadian School Boards Association (CSBA) and planning, 208
  components of core, 212
  content, 207
  Council of Ministers of Education, Canada (CMEC) and planning, 208
  culturally diverse, 125, 209, 211
  definitions of, 204
  development, 78
  diversity in future, 309
  Eurocentric focus, 125
  existentialism and, 58
  explicit type, 205
  extracurricular/co-curricular programs type, 206–207
  gender-specific roles, 129
  great books of the Western world, 57
  hidden type, 205–206, 252
  for inclusive education, 126
  influences on, 209, 209f
  integrated, 208
  language arts and new approaches, 216
  macro-level target of planning, 207–208
  mathematics, 216–217
  metaphysics and, 54
  micro-level target of planning, 207–208
  null type, 206
  perennialism in, 57

curricula (*continued*)

physical and health education, 222–223

planners, 208–209

promotion of equity and diversity in, 127–128

provincial and territorial, 71, 89

questions in development of, 207

science and technology, 218–219

second language instruction, 220–221

social issues and changing values influence on, 209, 211

social studies, 219–220

stereotypes and, 129

student-centred, 61

student-centred *vs.* subject-centred, 208

textbook authors and publishers' influence on, 211–212

time orientation in planning, 208

Tyler rationale in development of, 207

types, 204–207

Curriculum: Perspective, Paradigm, and Possibility (Schubert), 203

Curriculum Readings for Developing Educational Programs (Anctil & Hass), 149*t*

cyberbullying, 10, 78, 137

educational technology and, 252

long-term effects of, 135

suicide and, 137

technology advancements and, 135–136

D

daily occasional (supply or substitute) teaching, 38–39, 289, 297

advantages and disadvantages of, 39*f*

professional development opportunities for, 299

qualifications for, 38–39

resources for, 297–298

tips for, 297

Daily Occasional Teacher Survival Guide, 298

Dare the School Build a New Social Order? (Counts), 59

Darling-Hammond, Linda, 319

Dawson, Sir John William, 66, 71

daycare facilities, 78

Deal, Terrence, 118

Decoding Learning: The Proof, Promise and Potential of Digital Education, 250–251

dedication mode (of teaching), 19

democratic classroom, 189–190

benefits of, 190

guidelines for, 190

instruction organizing and planning, 191

procedures for, 190

departmentalization, 123

Department of Indian Affairs (DIA), 73

deputy minister of education, 89

desire to serve, 6

developmental stages of students, 24

developmental stresses, 153

in adolescence, 153

in childhood, 153

Dewey, John, 22, 57, 74, 115

diabetes, 105

dialectics, 56

differentiation, 7

digital cameras, 13, 233

digital divide, 253–254

digital media, 254

digital resources,

fine arts, 243

language arts, 243–244

learning objects, 242

mathematics, 244

open source materials, 242–243

social studies, 245–246

for teachers, 241–243

direct instruction, 194

effectiveness of, 194

mastery learning method of, 195

director of education, 92

disabilities,

autism, 160*t*

deaf-blindness, 160*t*

generalized definitions for, 159

hearing impairments, 160*t*

intellectual impairments, 160*t*

labelling cautions, 159

learning disability (LD), 160–162

orthopedic impairments, 160*t*

serious emotional disturbance (SED), 160*t*

specific learning, 160*t*

speech or language impairments, 160*t*

types of, 160*t*

visual impairments, 160*t*

disability *vs.* handicap, 158–159

discipline,

approaches, 191

assertive, 192

strategies, 191

discovery learning, 198–199

distance education programs, 223

distance learning networks, 234

diversity, 24

challenge of, 11

computer use for understanding of cultural, 229

cultural, 8–9

dimensions of, 126

ethnic, 8–9

instructional materials for, 128

job opportunities for teachers, 8–9

in schools, 38, 123–124

divorce rate, 134

Dobson, Warren, 16

Dotson, Karen, 189

Dougherty, Caitlin, 298

Douglas, Thomas, 69

Down's syndrome, 172

Down to Earth, 210

dropping out rate (students), 133

drug-education programs, 78

due process, 100–101

individualized educational plans (IEPs) and, 165

Durham District School Board (DDSB), 139

duty of care, 103–104

E

Eamer, Allyson, 271
Early Development Instrument (EDI), 139
Eaton v. Brant County Board of Education (1995), 165*f*
Education Act (Ontario), 131
education act (public schools act), 89
educational environment challenges, 11
educational improvement, 276
educational leadership, 261
   complexities of, 262
   underlying value of change in, 263
Educational Leadership, 4, 182*t*
Educational Leadership: A Bridge to Improved Practice
   (Cunningham & Cordeiro), 260
educational philosophy, 50–53
   aesthetics area of, 54
   axiology area of, 55
   constructivist perspective, 52*f*
   critical pedagogy, 59
   epistemology area of, 54–55
   ethics area of, 55
   learning beliefs, 52
   logic area of, 56
   metaphysics area of, 54
   personal, 51
   teaching beliefs about knowledge, 53
   teaching beliefs about students, 52–53
   teaching beliefs about what should be taught, 53–54
   transmission perspective, 52*f*
Educational Psychology: Windows on Classrooms
   (Eggen & Kauchak), 198*t*
educational research, 261, 265
   action research, 272–275
   national constituent associations for, 271
   teacher-researcher, 270–271
educational technology, 229, 234
   abundance of, 252
   affects on roles of teachers and students, 229
   challenges of integrating, 250–251
   cyberbullying and, 252
   digital divide and, 253–254
   invasion of privacy and, 252
   is here to stay, 253
   recommendations for improving learning using, 251
Educational Technology Leader (ETL), 252–253
educational television programs, 234
education budgets, 324
Education Canada, 188
Education Canada Network (ECN) e-recruitment
   network, 287, 293
*Education for All: The Report of the Expert Panel on Literacy
   and Numeracy Instruction for Students with Special Education
   Needs, Kindergarten to Grade 6* (Ontario Ministry
   of Education), 164
education programs for teachers, 24
Education Quality and Accountability Office,
   Ontario, 94
Education Resources Information Center (ERIC), 272
Education Technology Advisory Council (ETAC), 233
Education Week, 227

Edutopia: What Works in Education, 302
Edutopia website, 272
effective assessment practices, 32
effective classroom management, 31
effective teaching skills, 31
   creating learning environment for all, 311
Egale Canada Human Rights Trust, 131
Egan, Kieran, 62
Einstein, Albert, 4, 57
Eisner, Eliot, 4, 204, 206
e-learning, 229, 234
elementary education,
   characteristics, 74
Elementary Teachers' Federation of Ontario, 293, 297
email, 14
Emerging Technologies, Evolving Education, 231
emotional intelligence, 117
empathy, 31
empowerment mode (of teaching), 18–19
English as a second language (ESL) programs, 79, 123, 125,
   125*f*, 239
English language learners (ELLs), 126
English tradition (educational philosophy), 63
   Church of England, 63
   dame-schools, 63
   public schools, 63
   Puritans and, 63
   Society for the Propagation of the Gospel in Foreign Parts
     (SPG), 63, 66, 67
epistemology, 54–55
   authority-based knowledge, 54
   divine revelation based knowledge, 55
   experience-based knowledge, 55
   intuition-based knowledge, 55
   reason and logic based knowledge, 55
e-portfolios, 241
2009 Equity and Inclusive Education survey
   (Ontario), 135
equity in education, 311
Erikson, Erik, 147, 148, 149, 153
essentialism, 56, 56*f*, 57
   critics of, 57
ethical dilemmas in classroom, 55, 100
ethical standards for teachers, 97–98, 99
Ethical Standards for the Teaching Profession, 289
Ethical Visions of Education (Hansen), 50
ethics, 55
   public morality and ethical behaviour, 310
ethnic group, 124
ethnic minorities, 123
European Schoolnet, 316
evaluation trends, 77
exceptional learners, 158–159
   equal opportunities for, 167–168
   labelling and, 168
   teachers' participation in education of, 167
existentialism, 56, 56*f*, 58
explicit curriculum, 205
Exploring the "Boy Crisis" in Education (Cappon), 129
extended families, 134
extracurricular/co-curricular programs, 206–207

Massachusetts Institute of Technology (MIT) OpenCourseWare project, 243
Massachusetts School Technology and Readiness (STaR) chart, 233
massive open online courses (MOOCs), 44, 301
Master's degrees in education, 33
mastery learning, 195
  diagnostic tests for, 196
  learning assumptions for, 196
  steps in, 195–196
mathematics, 13
  curricula, 216–217
  technology for teaching, 244
May, Stephen, 127
McCall, Kelly, 6, 7
McCaskill, D., 72
McCourt, Frank, 9
McGill University, 66, 71
McKinsey report (2010), 316
McNee, Ian, 277
Measuring Child Poverty (UNICEF), 121, 134
media diet, 228
MediaSmarts, 228, 251, 252
Meilleur, Jean-Baptiste, 65
melting pot, 127
Melville, Herman, 57
memory,
  in information processing, 198, 198t
  long-term, 198, 198t
  sensory, 198, 198t
  short-term, 197, 198t
  working, 198, 198t
Mental Health Canada, 159
mental health of children and youth, 77–78
  statistics, 137–138
mentoring, 41–42
  for beginner teachers, 317
  community-based partnerships for, 312
  importance of for teacher preparation, 41–42
  of student teachers, 43–44
metaphysics, 54
Métis peoples, 69, 88
Metrical Scale of Intelligence, 155–156
microcomputer-based laboratory (MBL), 249
microteaching, 35
  steps in, 35
millennials, 228
minister of education, 89
ministry (department) of education, 89
Mishna, Faye, 10
mobile learning devices (MLDs), 231
mobile learning (m-learning), 241
Moby-Dick (Melville), 57
modelling, 196
  basic steps in, 196
Models of Teaching (Joyce, Weil, & Calhoun), 194
Montessori, Maria, 79
Montessori method, 80
Montessori schools, 79–80
Montreal Gazette, 210
moral reasoning, stages of, 147, 149–150, 149t
  conditions for internalizing moral principles, 150

criticism of, 150
  full formal reasoning, 150
motivation, 32
Multicultural Act (1988), 127
multicultural education, 127
multiculturalism, 124
Multimedia Educational Resource for Learning and Online Teaching (MERLOT), 242
multiple intelligences, 156–158, 157f, 311

N

National Association of Independent Schools, 288
National Center to Improve Practice (NCIP) in Special Education through Technology, Media, and Materials, 171–172
National Council of Teachers of English (NCTE), 216
National Council of Teachers of Mathematics (NCTM) Curriculum and Evaluation Standards for Mathematics, 216
2011 National Household Survey, 123
National Indian Brotherhood (NIB), 73
National Issues in Education Poll (2008), 10
national macro-culture, 124
National Occupational Classification (NOC), 263–264
National Research Center on the Gifted and Talented, University of Connecticut, 162
National Symposium on Arts Education (NSAE), 221
nature of being, 54
negligence in schools, 103–104
  before and after school hours, 105
  bullying, 106
  in classroom, 105
  duty of care, 103–104
  emergency situations, 105
  off school property, 106
  in playground areas, 105
  special classrooms and laboratories, 105
  sports activities, 105–106
  standard of care, 104
  tort liability law, 104–105
  violence and risk assessment, 106
netgens, 228
neurophysiology, 311
neuropsychology, 311
New Brunswick,
  school system in prior to 1875, 66
New Brunswick Department of Education, 213
New Brunswick Teachers' Association (NBTA), 98, 299
  Code of Professional Conduct, 289
New England Planters, 66
Newfoundland and Labrador,
  school system in prior to 1875, 67
Newfoundland and Labrador Department of Education, 213
Newfoundland and Labrador Teachers' Association, 99
New France schools, 62, 63, 65
New Media Consortium, 272
New Pedagogies for Deep Learning global initiative, 316
New Teacher Induction Program (NTIP, Ontario), 265, 317
New Teacher Mentoring Project (NTMP, British Columbia), 317
Noddings, Nick, 181
nondirective teaching model, 195t
North-West Territories Act (1875), 70
Northwest Territories Teachers' Association, 99, 213

Saskatchewan Department of Education Curriculum and Instruction Branch, 213
Saskatchewan Professional Teachers Regulatory Board (SPTRB), 93, 266
Saskatchewan Teachers' Federation, 100
    Code of Professional Ethics and Code of Professional Competence, 266
satisfaction (from teaching),
    subject passion, 4
    teacher–learning process passion, 4
    teaching life passion, 4
Saul, John Ralston, 315
scaffolding, 197
Scardamalia, M., 28
Schaefer, Robert, 272
Schön, Donald, 267, 268, 300
School Act (1843, Ontario), 69
school advisory councils, 94
school-as-family, 118
School as the Center of Inquiry (Schaefer), 272
school-based management, 95
school boards, 91–92
    budgeting, 95–96
    as corporations, 91
    functions, 91
    organization of, 92
    powers and duties of, 91
    responsibilities of, 91, 92
    restructuring of, 92
school community, 121
school-community partnerships, 312
school culture, 122
school district policies, 103
    community programs after school day, 314
school effectiveness, 131–132
    basic skill emphasis characteristic in, 132
    collegiality characteristic in, 132
    frequent, systematic evaluation characteristic in, 132
    high expectation characteristic in, 132
    orderly environment characteristic in, 132
    sense of community characteristic in, 132
    sense of purpose characteristic in, 132
    strong leadership characteristic in, 132
school funding formulas, 75–77
    capital funding, 76
    local, 77
    maintenance, 76
    operating, 76
    provincial and territorial, 89
school hours, 7
school improvement research, 132
School of Education Teaching Specialties, Acadia University, 27
school reform movement (1980s), 212
schools,
    community environments and, 119, 121
    community programs after school day, 314
    crime and violence in, 134–135
    cultures of, 121, 122
    departmentalization in, 123
    distinguishing characteristics of, 118–119

    elementary, 122
    evolution of, 323
    formal practices of, 122–123
    for-profit, 322
    full-service, 312
    impact of technology on, 231
    improvement research, 132
    middle, 122–123
    open-space, 122
    partnerships with educational community groups, 312
    physical environments of, 122
    pressure on students to excel in, 318
    private, 119
    public, 119
    as reflection of society, 119
    research into effectiveness of, 132
    rural, 119
    satisfying requirements of inclusion in, 166–167
    secondary, 122–123
    as social institutions, 119–120
    social problems and impact on, 133–134, 312
    suburban, 119
    successful, 131–132
    urban, 119
    virtual environments of, 122
schools of thought for teaching, 56–57, 56*f*
    essentialism, 56, 56*f*, 57
    existentialism, 56, 56*f*, 58
    perennialism, 56–57, 56*f*
    progressivism, 56, 56*f*, 57–58
    social reconstructivism, 56, 56*f*, 58–59
school-to-work programs, 223–224
school-within-a-school, 140
school year, 75
Schubert, William H., 203
Science, Technology, Engineering, and Math (STEM) education, 218–219
    shift to focus on Science, Technology, Engineering, Arts, and Math (STEAM) education, 221
Science, Technology, Engineering, Arts, and Math (STEAM) education, 221
scientific literacy, 219
    definition of, 219
Scotland-Moxon, Cheryl, 233
Scottish migration (to Canada), 64
Scottish tradition (educational philosophy), 64
secondary education,
    characteristics, 75
second-language instruction, 78–79, 220–221
    core French, 220–221
seizures, 105
self-actualization, 152, 152*f*
self-assessment (for professional growth), 42
self-care, 31
self-confidence, 77
self-contained classroom, 122
self-esteem, 77, 155
self-knowledge, 23, 62
self-regulation, 117, 188
sense of humour, 31
service learning, 117

sex, 128
sex role socialization, 129
sex role stereotyping, 129
sexting, 10, 252
sexual orientation, 131
  harassment and, 131
Shakespeare, William, 57
Shanker, Stuart, 117, 188
Sharpe, Jill, 313
Sheen, Martin, 210
*Shifting Landscape, A: Pedagogy, Technology, and the New
  Terrain of Innovation in a Digital World* (Beggs), 228
Shulman, L., 30
Simon, Theodore, 155
Simon Fraser University, 62
single-parent families, 134, 311
Skinner, B. F., 60
Sluyter, David, 157
SMART, 237
Smart Boards, 233
smartphones, 228
social class,
  schools and, 118
social environment challenges, 11
socialization,
  of future teachers, 284
socialization (aim of education), 116–117
  service learning in, 117
social media, 10
  cyberbullying and, 135
  Facebook, 13, 27, 238
  iTunes, 13
  MySpace, 13
  Twitter, 13, 27, 238, 302
  YouTube, 239
social networking sites, 231
social problems, 11
  impact on schools of, 133–134
  peer counselling programs for, 139
  resources for, 11
  school intervention programs for, 138
  Uniting Our Nations intervention program for, 139
social reconstructivism, 56, 56f, 58–59
  premises for, 58
  progressivism and, 59
Social Sciences and Humanities Research Council
  (SSHRC), 87, 254
social services, 314
social stratification,
  schools and, 118
social web movement, 14
Socrates, 56
Socratic method of teaching, 56
special education, 164
  assistive technology for, 171–172
  changes in laws for, 164–165
  equal opportunities for students needing, 168
Special Education Resource Teacher (SERT), 156
special-needs students, 158–159
speech and music synthesizers, 233
speech recognition software, 246

speech synthesizer, 171
Spring, Joel, 118
stages of development, 147
  childhood to adulthood transition, 153
  cognitive, 147–148
  effective teaching methods based on, 196–197
  exceptional learners, 158–159
  hierarchy of needs model, 152, 152f
  intellectual capabilities in, 154–155
  intelligence and multiple intelligences, 156–158
  moral, 147, 149–150, 149t
  psychosocial, 147, 148–149, 148t
standard of care, 104
Standards of Practice for the Teaching Profession, 289
Standards 2000 project, 216
Stanford-Binet Intelligence Scale, 162
State of the Nation: K–12 Online Learning in Canada report, 223
Station v. Travelers Insurance Co. (1974), 104
Statistics Canada, 9, 87, 123, 131, 134, 159
step-parent families, 134
stimulus–response model of behaviour, 60
*Story of a National Crime, The: An Appeal for Justice to the
  Indians of Canada* (Bryce), 73
Strachan, Dr. John, 69
student-centred curriculum, 208
student characteristics,
  aptitudes, 24
  learning styles, 24
  readiness to learn new material, 24
  stages of development, 24
  talents, 24
student discipline, 74
student diversity, 3
student inappropriate behaviours, 191
  approaches to depend upon severity of, 191
  choice theory for, 192
  confronting-contracting face for, 194
  constructive assertiveness to, 192
  problem-solving conference for, 192
  problem-solving strategies for, 191
  relationship-listening face for, 193
  rules-and-consequences face for, 194
student interaction, 5
student-mobility rates, 10
student needs, 7
student(s),
  aptitudes, 24
  developmental stages, 24
  learning styles, 24
  negative views of, 53
  as net generation, 27, 28
  readiness to learn new material, 24
  talents, 24
students at risk, 133
  factors for, 133
  family stress factor in, 133–134
students with disabilities,
  computer-assisted instruction (CAI) for, 246, 246f
  educational service options for, 166f
  generalized definitions for disabilities, 159
  least restrictive environment for, 166

self-regulation of, 266
status of, 103–104
theory into practice instruction model for, 195t
use of technology, 236–237
workload of, 14–15
teacher salaries, 33
Teachers' Overseas Recruiting Fair (TORF), 288
teacher–student ratios, 10
teacher unions, 269–270
teaching,
action research as natural part of, 274
altruistic mode, 19
as an essential service, 265–266
Canadian laws and, 101
as a career, 4
characteristics of good, 15, 16
as creative endeavour, 18
critical assessments of new technology, 27
decisional capital, 267
diverse learning needs reason for, 3
empowerment in, 18–19
essential qualities for, 284–285
as ethical enterprise, 97–98
for excellence, 19
five modes of, 18
human capital in, 267
influences, 5–6
interactive, 16
knowledge base for, 25
as a paradoxical profession, 264
practical benefits of, 7
privileges of working with children reason for, 3–4
as a profession, 2, 263–264
promotion of students' learning reason for, 2–3
reasons for, 6
reflective action in, 17–18, 17f
rights and responsibilities balance in, 100–101
service through, 6
social capital in, 267
subject matter view of, 30
undesirable aspects of, 9
unique qualities of youth reason for, 3
teaching certificate, 284
categories of applicants for, 286
teaching portfolio, 39–40
contents, 40
teaching salaries, 7–8
teaching simulations, 35
computer-based, 35
technical and vocational training, 73–74
Technical Education Act (1919), 73
technology, 11, 78
challenges of, 12
critical assessments of new, 27–28
educational, 229, 234
educational trends, 223
impact of on schools, 231
keeping up to date with, 26
knowledge of integrating into teaching, 25–26
nature of learning and advancements in, 28
new skills for the future, 308
as problem-solving process, 27–28

school boards' approach to, 228–229
students use of, 12–14
support, 253
teachers and, 12–13
teaching strategies and, 14
wearable, 233
technology-based virtual learning environments, 324
TED Ed, 302
teenage parenthood, 133, 134, 136
teletypewriter (TTY), 171
Terman, Lewis, 156, 159
texting, 12, 14, 135
Thames Valley District School Board, 318
theory into practice instruction model, 1i95t
ThinkTank group, 238
Thorndike, Edward Lee, 74
three-dimensional (3D) printers, 233
three-dimensional (3D) virtual learning platform, 240
three-dimensional (3D) virtual reality worlds, 240
three R's, 71
time on task, 187
tokenism, 128
Toronto District School Board (TDSB), 140, 312
Toronto school shootings (2007), 10, 135
tort liability law, 104–105
touch-screen devices, 171
Toward a Psychology of Being (Maslow), 152f
transgender, 129
transition bilingual education program, 125f
Transition to Teaching Report, 287, 297
transmission perspective on education, 52
Treaty of Utrecht, 72
Tribes community building program, 180
Truth and Reconciliation Commission of
        Canada (TRC), 87–88
    Interim Report (2012), 88
    mandate, 87–88
    objectives of, 88
    recommendations, 88
Turner, Shirley R., 176, 184, 185
Tyler, Ralph, 207
Tyler rationale, 207

U

unemployment, 133
United Nations Childrens Fund (UNICEF), 121
Uniting Our Nations, 139
universal design, 311
Universal Design for Learning (UDL) and Differentiated
        Instruction (DI), 164, 168
    framework, 170
University of British Columbia, 74, 317
University of Ontario Institute of Technology, 93, 303
University of Ottawa Institute of Technology, 254
University of Toronto, 33
University of Western Ontario, 318
(Un) Making of the Teacher, The (Petrarca), 303
Urban Network to Improve Teacher Education (UNITE), 30
urban schools challenges, 11
U.S. Department of Education, 272
Use of Resources in Education (Dewey), 115